ARIZONA
PLACE NAMES

WILL C. BARNES

ARIZONA
PLACE NAMES

Introduction by Bernard L. Fontana

The University of Arizona Press
TUCSON

Third printing 1997
Copyright © 1988
The Arizona Board of Regents

THE UNIVERSITY OF ARIZONA PRESS

All Rights Reserved
Manufactured in the United States of America

∞ This book is printed on acid-free, archival-quality paper.

99 98 97   5 4 3

Library of Congress Cataloging-in-Publication Data
Barnes, Will C. (Will Croft), 1858–1936.
   Arizona place names.
   Bibliography: p.
   1. Names, Geographical—Arizona—Dictionaries.
2. Arizona—History, Local.   I. Title.
F809.B27 1988   917.91′003′21   87-35835
ISBN 0-8165-1074-1

British Library Cataloguing-in-Publication Data
A catalogue record for this book is available from the British Library.

INTRODUCTION

An Arizona Classic

My personal copy of Will Barnes's *Arizona Place Names* — the original, 1935 edition — is dirty and a few of its fast-brittling pages are torn. Not only that, but the back cover has broken away at the spine and the front cover is about to do the same thing.

This reissue comes none too soon. The old copy couldn't take too many more Arizona miles rattling around in a glove compartment with maps, flashlight, screwdriver, crescent wrench, bottle opener, corkscrew, pencils, matchbooks, unidentified keys, loose screws, tire gauge, and other assorted necessities. Neither could it stand much more page turning, however gently one may touch the aging paper. The first-edition "Barnes" has earned its retirement and will come to rest alphabetically in my library between Volume I of Bartlett's *Personal Narrative of Explorations and Incidents . . .* and George Barker's printed essay on the social functions of *Pachuco* as that Spanish argot used to be spoken in Tucson.

Readers unfamiliar until now with Barnes's original *Arizona Place Names* are about to make a new friend. He doesn't overwhelm us with scholarly erudition, fussing unduly, for example, over the etymology of names derived from any of Arizona's eighteen Indian languages, nine of which are mutually unintelligible. He talks to us instead. He tells us that Yuma County's S.H. Mountains were called that by miners because of their resemblance to "the edifice in the rear of most country dwellings." And who but Barnes would quote Charles Poston's doggerel to let us know that "Pima" comes from the Piman Indian expression for "I don't know"? To wit:

> You ask a Pima how to go,
> Or something that he does not know,
> He's sure to answer you 'pima'-ch.' ['I don't know.']
> If favors asked he says 'pia'ch.' ['No.']

With this book we come away with a sense of *place*, perhaps, even more than we do of names. To understand why, we need to know something about the author.

Barnes, all 5'4" of him, got to Arizona in 1880 as a first-class private in the U.S. Army when he was 22 years old. He did a stint as a post telegrapher at Fort Apache, a time when he won a Medal of Honor for gallantry and, so far as one can now judge, for not getting killed or wounded on hazardous duty during a brief uprising among Western Apaches. He even became a *de facto* foster parent to two Apache children whose father, Apache scout Dead Shot, was executed for mutiny and desertion in the wake of the uprising. And while he was at Fort Apache, he made the acquaintance of peripatetic anthropologists and writers Frank Hamilton Cushing and Adolph F. A. Bandelier, not to mention soldier-ethnologist-writer John Gregory Bourke.

1

In 1882 Barnes and fellow solider Victor Gomez bought cattle and began to moonlight in the livestock business, one that became Barnes's full-time job after his early honorable discharge in 1883 because of an eye problem. He owned and operated the Esperanza Cattle Company in northern Arizona until the turn of the century. In the interim, he served as an appointee to the Arizona Livestock Sanitary Board; he was elected Republican commissioner for Apache County (1892); and he was elected in 1894 to serve in the 18th Arizona Territorial Legislature where he led a successful drive to create Navajo County by splitting Apache County into halves. In 1897 he married Edith Talbot, daughter of a prominent Phoenix merchant who later became mayor of Phoenix.

Barnes left Arizona for northeastern New Mexico and another ranch in 1900. He sold out in 1906 and a few months later became the Albuquerque-based inspector of grazing in the national forests. From Albuquerque, he was transferred to Washington, D.C., where he remained in the U.S. Forest Service until completing twenty-one years of service.

It was almost natural that he became the first person to compile a book of Arizona place names. His Forest Service work helped him become an expert in the use of maps. Precise location of ranches, grazing lands, and other locales was a requisite for his position. And Barnes had a special proclivity for record keeping, making note of the books he had read and on his travels, including mileage and amounts of money spent, and writing down stories of people he had met and anecdotes collected along the way. He also became a great indexer, getting the Forest Service files in his Washington office in easy-to-retrieve form. In 1930, he wrote to his editor at Doubleday Doran: "Making indexes is my meat. I've made dozens of them. . . . Previously, the Forest Service had none. Now, due to my fussing, they are always used" (Abbott 1979:241).

Even more than his work in the Forest Service, however, it was Barnes's appointment in 1920 to the U.S. Board on Geographic Names that launched him on the Arizona project. The board's job was to decide on disputed names, to standardize others, and to approve new ones. This body, a unit of the U.S. Geological Survey in the Department of the Interior, comprised sixteen voting members from various federal agencies. It was Barnes's high-level position in the Forest Service that earned him one of the positions, and it was an appointment he relished. His concern for place names had surfaced at least as early as 1895 when he had led the charge to create Arizona's Navajo County, not only insisting that it be called by that name rather than "Colorado County" as others had proposed, but that Navajo be spelled such rather than "Navaho." He succeeded on both counts (Abbott 1979: 243–44).

Late in 1927, Barnes left the Forest Service to become paid secretary of the U.S. Board on Geographic Names. He held that post for the next two and a half years until his retirement in mid-1930 at the age of 72. And he used much of that time working on his Arizona book, taking full advantage of the next-door map collections of the Library of Congress and carrying on voluminous correspondence with people knowledgeable about Arizona's past. He put the information on some 4,500 file cards, using the U.S. Geographic Board's format. After he and his wife moved to Phoenix in 1930, the work continued and the cards multiplied until the time came to convert them to typescript. By 1934, his manuscript was ready to be printed. He first sent it to the University of Oklahoma for publication, but the University of Arizona intervened to get the job done. The present volume, first issued several months before his death in 1936, is the result (Abbott 1979: 244–45, 251).

Barnes's Arizona and New Mexico life, more than a quarter-century of it, was spent on the ground. He was on horseback and on foot. He was a soldier, cattleman, and rural politician. His friends were the literate and illiterate: soldiers, cowboys, miners, writers, forest rangers, scientists, politicians, merchants, laborers, ordinary folk, and extraordinary citizens. He had personally visited or seen a great many of the places listed in his book. He knew countless "old-timers" who could — and did — share their firsthand knowledge or their reminiscences of how or why this place or that got its particular name. *Arizona Place Names* is sprinkled with citations from letters written to Barnes by innumerable early-day Arizonans: Fred Croxen, Carl Hayden, Mrs. George F. Kitt, Harry Martin, J. W. Girdner, John Rockfellow, Edward L. Doheny, Henry Boice, D. M. Riordan, and many more whose names are familiar to enthusiasts of our state's history.

The place name entries were written by a person who knew and loved the land, its past, and its people. Enthusiasm shines through on every page, an ardor conveyed by a writer whose works appeared in such popular journals of his day as the *Saturday Evening Post, Harper's Weekly, McClure's Magazine, Overland Monthly, Out West, Atlantic Monthly,* and *Arizona Highways.* He also wrote for *Scientific American, Cosmopolitan, Argonaut, American Forestry, Breeder's Gazette,* and *Arizona Historical Review.* His published reminiscences, *Apaches and Longhorns* (Los Angeles: Ward Ritchie Press, 1941), one of the best books yet written about late nineteenth- and early twentieth-century Arizona, was reprinted in facsimile by the University of Arizona Press in 1982.

There are those who will question the reason for reissuing a book published more than a half century ago. Sharp-eyed readers will challenge some of the entries, as they always shall in works of this kind. Barnes could not know in the 1930s, for example, that William A. Douglass (1979) of the University of Nevada at Reno would later question the long-held notion that "Arizona" is derived from the Piman Indian words meaning "place of the little spring," *ali shonak.* Douglass, a scholar of Basque language, culture, and history, has had the temerity to suggest that "Arizona" is derived from the Basque words *aritz ona*, which mean "good oak." True enough, when "Arizona" first appeared on maps after a silver strike occurred at a site of this name in 1736, Basques were involved and the place is one where oak trees do, in fact, grow. It is, however, also the site of a little spring in what was once Piman territory.

A few entries are possibly even more questionable, such as Barnes's giving credence to the assertion that "Avra Valley" is "said to be a Papago word meaning 'Big Plain,'" when, perhaps, he should have known *avra* is simply a variant spelling for the Spanish *abra*, one of whose common meanings is "valley." A state with a Picacho Peak ("Pointed Peak," as if there could be any other kind), after all, is entitled to its Avra Valley ("Valley Valley").

So are there many names new to Arizona since 1935 which do not appear: Sierra Vista, Green Valley, Sun City, Rio Rico, Oro Valley, South Tucson, La Paz County, Bullhead City, Lake Havasu City, and the Tohono O'odham Nation, to name a few. Nor is there a Why, whose name Barnes would have loved. And other places will no longer be recognized by their old descriptions. Barnes's Scottsdale, for example, was a "village east of Phoenix," and no modern writer would refer to the Navajo Indians as "one of our largest so-called 'Blanket tribes.'"

Such shortcomings, if they are that, need to be laid aside in the realization that Will C. Barnes's *Arizona Place Names* is itself an important piece of history and a rollicking fine contribution to Arizona's literature. In her 1960 revision and expansion of Barnes's book, Byrd Granger expressed it well when she wrote, "Place names are like quick-silver: They refuse to be still." And while she noted that "ultimately there must be another and still another revision of place names," she recognized that "Will Barnes had done a job unique in tone and content" (Granger 1960: V, VII).

Sidney Pattison, an English professor whose review of the first edition appeared in the April 1935 issue of the *Arizona Historical Review*, made the case for Barnes: "We are grateful to him for opening so rich a field for the enjoyment of all who have any love of frontier flavor, imagination touched by humor, and a salty raciness possessed by all too few."

Readers will agree.

BERNARD L. FONTANA

FURTHER READING

Abbott, Mary
    1979   "A million dollars worth of fun." Will Barnes' *Arizona Place Names. Journal of Arizona History*, Vol. 20, no. 2 (Summer), pp. 239–54. Tucson, Arizona Historical Society.

Douglass, William A.
    1979   On the naming of Arizona. *Names*, Vol. 27, no. 4 (December), pp. 217–34. Potsdam, New York, American Name Society.

Fontana, Bernard L.
    1960   Arizona place names. *Arizona Highways*, Vol. 36, no. 3 (March), pp. 2–5. Phoenix, Arizona Highway Department.

Granger, Byrd H.
　1960　Will C. Barnes' *Arizona Place Names*. Revised and enlarged
　　　　edition. Tucson, The University of Arizona Press. [A portion of
　　　　this book, *Grand Canyon place names*, was published sepa-
　　　　rately the same year.]
　1983　*Arizona's names: X marks the spot*. [Tucson?], Falconer Pub-
　　　　lishing Company.
Scheips, Paul. J.
　1960　Will Croft Barnes, soldier and citizen of Arizona. *Arizona and
　　　　the West*, Vol. 2, no. 3 (Autumn), pp. 205–11. Tucson, The Uni-
　　　　versity of Arizona Press.
　1981　Will Croft Barnes: a westerner of parts. *Great Western Series*,
　　　　no. 15. Washington, D.C., Potomoc Corral. The Westerners. [An
　　　　abbreviated version was published in 1982 in *Apaches and Long-
　　　　horns: the reminiscences of Will C. Barnes*, pp. ix–xx. Tucson,
　　　　The University of Arizona Press.]
Wallace, Andrew
　1960　A chronological list of the works of Will C. Barnes. *Arizona and
　　　　the West*, Vol. 2, no. 3 (Autumn), pp. 211–12, Tucson, The Uni-
　　　　versity of Arizona Press.
　1960　A dedication to the memory of Will Croft Barnes, 1858–1936.
　　　　Arizona and the West, Vol. 2, no. 3 (Autumn), pp. 203–4. Tucson,
　　　　The University of Arizona Press.

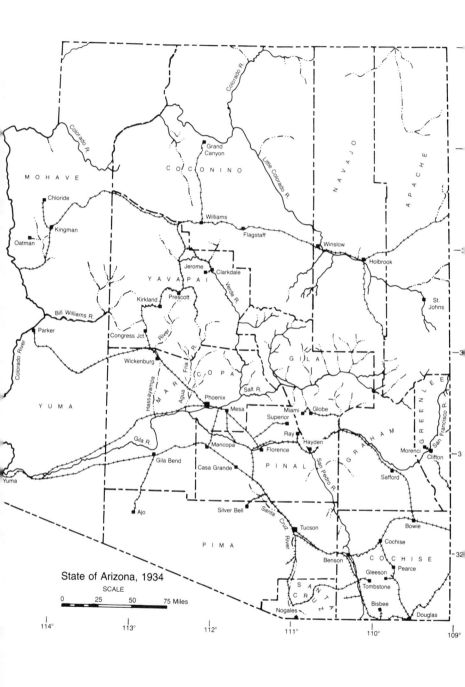

State of Arizona, 1934

SCALE

0   25   50   75 Miles

ABBREVIATIONS

A. G. W.	A. G. Wells, President of the Santa Fe R. R.
A. T. & S. F. R. R.	Atchison, Topeka & Santa Fe Rail Road.
E. P. & S. W. R. R.	El Paso & South Western Rail Road.
G. L. O.	General Land Office, Washington, D. C.
Ind. Res.	Indian Reservation.
Lat.	Latitude.
Long.	Longitude.
N. F.	National Forest.
N. M.	National Monument.
N. P.	National Park.
P. M.	Postmaster.
P. O.	Post Office.
q. v.	which see.
R.	Range.
Sec.	Section.
sic.	written thus—so spelled. Used to indicate unusual spelling by the original writer.
Sp.	Spanish.
S. P. R. R.	Southern Pacific Rail Road.
T.	Township.
U. S. G. B.	United States Geographic Board, Washington, D. C.
U. S. G. S.	United States Geological Survey, Washington, D. C.
U. S. N. F.	United States National Forest.
U. S. F. S.	United States Forest Service.

The name of the postmaster is for the *first* one appointed unless otherwise stated.

ARIZONA PLACE NAMES

BY

WILL C. BARNES*

Abbie Waterman Peak   Pima Co.   Roskruge Map, 1893.

In T. 12 S., Rs. 8 & 9 E. Hornaday, *Camp Fires on Desert and Lava,* writes:

"North of Robles well-in-the-desert rose . . . . . . the Roskruge range, Sam Hughes butte, and the Abbie Waterman mountains. Beyond Abbie's real estate holdings were the Silver Bell mines." *Arizona Gazetteer* of 1881 says: "The Abbie Waterman is a silver mine of great promise which is being vigorously prospected by its owners." A note in the Arizona Pioneers Historical Society Library of Tucson says the camp was first called "Silver Hill." Old timers say that the peak was named for Abbie Waterman, wife of Governor Waterman of California. They claim that she was the first white woman to climb the peak.

This is an error. The identity of Abbie Waterman is well established through George Roskruge and others who knew her and her husband. She was the wife of J. C. Waterman who came to Arizona from Missouri and lived at Oracle for several years.

The peak was named for Abbie Waterman, but the range was named Waterman mountains q. v. for Gov. Waterman who was not related to her.

Abra   Yavapai Co.   Railroad Maps.

Sp. "a fissure, a gorge." Station on Ash Fork-Phoenix branch of A. T. & S. F. R. R. 29 miles south of Ash Fork. Is near a deep canyon, hence name given it by engineers.

Acacia   Cochise Co.

Station on E. P. & S. W. R. R. About 4 miles from Douglas. Origin unknown.

Acme   Mohave Co.

Station on A. T. & S. F. R. R., established about 1881. "Just another name," A. G. W. Later changed to Topock, q. v. P. O. established April 15, 1902, John R. Livingston, P. M.

Adair   Navajo Co.

About 2½ miles west of Showlow on Fools Hollow. Mormon settlement established 1878. Called Fools Hollow because "nobody but a fool would try to make a living there."

After Wesley Adair, member of Company C, Mormon Battalion. He lived here for a time then moved to Showlow. His son, Aaron, lived on the place for some years after that. P. O. established as Adair Dec. 4, 1899, Jesse J. Brady, P.M. See Fools Hollow and Bagnall.

---

*Former Assistant Forester and Chief of Grazing, U. S. Forest Service; Former Secretary U. S. Geographic Board.

Adair Wash   Navajo Co.   Map, Sitgreaves N. F., 1924.

Small wash in northeast corner sec. 12, T. 9 N., R. 21 E. West of Showlow settlement. Flows north into Showlow creek about 2 miles below Showlow. After Wesley Adair and his family who settled here about 1878.

Adamana   Apache Co.

Station on A. T. & S. F. R. R. 25 miles east of Holbrook. On north bank of Rio Puerco. Established about 1890 as a point from which tourists could visit the Petrified Forest to the south.

Every writer visiting this forest has undertaken to weave a romance about the name "Adamana." Several have claimed that it was from an early settler Adam and his wife Anna. Lillian Whiting, in *The Land of Enchantment*, claimed the name was of geological origin from the word "adamant" referring to the diamond-like hardness of the petrifactions. Others have written equally fanciful stories about the name. The fact is that in the early days, 1879-1890, two partners, Jim Cart and Adam Hanna, grazed several thousand sheep on range about the Petrified Forest. Their ranch was south of the Puerco opposite present railroad station of Carrizo.

Driving back from the sheep camp at the forest one December night in 1885 Mrs. Cart and two small children were caught in a blizzard. Abandoning the team they took shelter under an overhanging bluff where they were found frozen to death almost in sight of home.

Hanna married a young woman in Holbrook whose name, unfortunately for the romancers, was Maggie, not Anna.

The name was coined by a Santa Fe official, just who has been long ago forgotten, out of the old Scotsman's two names, "Adam Hanna." Hanna died years ago and is buried in the little *campo santo* at Holbrook.

Adams Mesa   Maricopa Co.   Map, Tonto N. F., 1927.

In T. 3 N., R. 7 E. Prominent mesa about 5 miles east of Fort McDowell. Elevation 2,515 feet. "After Jeff Adams, cattleman and for several years sheriff of Maricopa county, who had a ranch near this mesa."

Adams River

See Virgin river.

Adamsville   Pinal Co.   Smith Map, 1879; Eckhoff, 1880.

Village dating from about 1866, on north side of Gila river, 3 or 4 miles west of Florence. Located 1866 by and named for Charles Adams.

One of the first settlements in Pinal county. In 1871 name changed to Sanford for Captain George B. Sanford. 1st U. S. Cavalry, then stationed at Fort McDowell. Later Adamsville was restored. Farish says the first modern flour mill in Arizona was erected here 1868. Hinton, 1873, says: "At Adamsville there are two stores and a mill. It is 4 miles to the Ruggles ranch."

According to McClintock and other writers this was rather a wild and woolly place in the early Seventies. Nick Bichard moved his steam flouring mill from the Pima village, known as Casa Blanca, to Adamsville, 1869. McClintock says: "Known to few is the fact that a resident of Adamsville in 1869 and a clerk for Nick Bichard was John P. Young, the San Francisco journalist, early editor of the San Francisco Chronicle." P. O. established 1871, William Dupont, P. M. See also Whites Mill.

Adams Well   Yuma Co.   G. L. O. Map, 1921.

At lower end Castle Dome mountains. Well, dug by Samuel Adams about 1860. According to Fish, Adams was a character of those days. He ran for district judge at first Territorial election and was defeated. In 1866 ran on an independent ticket for Delegate to Congress. Was defeated by Coles Bashford. Adams' great hobby was the improvement of the Colorado river, which gave him the title of "Steamboat Adams."

Adonde   Yuma Co.   Smith Map, 1879; G. L. O., 1923.

Sp. "where." Early day stage station about 35 miles east of Yuma. Here were several deep wells. When the railroad came along new wells were put down 2 or 3 miles to the east and the new station was called Wellton, q. v.

According to the Yuma Sentinel, Jan. 12, 1879, the place was called Adonde by the railroad company for but a few months. Station was opened Jan. 9, 1879.

Agassiz Peak   Coconino Co.   G. L. O. Map, 1921.

Elevation 12,340 feet. In T. 23 N., R. 7 E. Three miles south of Humphreys Peak. Named by Gen. W. J. Palmer in his "Report on Surveys of 1867-68." After Louis Agassiz, celebrated Swiss scientist.

Agassiz   Coconino Co.   G. L. O. Map, 1909.

Station A. T. & S. F. R. R. about 3 miles west of Flagstaff. After nearby peak. Since superceded by Milton, q. v.

Agathla Needle   Apache Co.   U. S. G. S. Map, 1923.

Elevation 6,825 feet. On some maps marked "Peak." Father Haile says: "A Navajo word Ag-ha-la, meaning 'much wool.' A rock or place where deer, sheep and antelope rub themselves. In other words a scratching place for animals in the spring while they are shedding." On Navajo Ind. Res., in Monument valley, east side Moonlight creek.

"It is a spire or volcanic neck which rises 1,125 feet above Monument valley. The most impressive of all volcanic necks in the Navajo country." Gregory.

Father Haile's spelling is doubtless correct, although on all maps and in Gregory it is Agathla.

Agua Azul   Coconino Co.

Sp. "blue water." This was Padre Garces' name for the Indians he found in Cataract or Havasu canyon. The water that comes from the large spring in the canyon has a decidedly blue tinge which undoubtedly suggested the name. See Havasu.

Agua Caliente   Maricopa Co.   Smith Map, 1921; U. S. G. S., 1923.

Sp., "hot water." Village and hot springs about 3 miles north of Gila river. Noted for their curative values in certain diseases. Garces visited them 1775. Coues says: "The spring is situated almost exactly on lat. 53 in T. 5 S., R. 10 W., about 1½ miles from King Woolsey's ranch." In 1748 Kino visited and named the spring "Santa Maria del Agua Caliente." He talked of locating a mission there. King Woolsey owned and lived at the springs for several years. Poston writes in *Apache Land:*

"Agua Caliente, in Spanish called,
A spring that heals e'en them who crawled."

J. Ross Browne about 1863 in *The Apache Country* writes: "While encamped at Grinnel's station Poston, White, and myself rode about 6 miles to the ranch of Martin and Woolsey near the Agua Caliente. We had a glorious bath in the springs which are about a mile and a half from the ranch." The White referred to was Ammi White. P. O. established Mar. 12, 1867, Patrick Mc-Kannon, P. M. See Hyder Station.

Agua Dulce Mountains   Pima Co.   G. L. O. Map, 1921;
                                                 U. S. G. S., 1923.

Sp., "sweet water." Desert water hole in extreme southwest corner of county near Mexican line.

Agua Fria   Maricopa Co.   Scott Map, Maricopa County, 1929.

Stage station of the Eighties. East side Agua Fria near Calderwood Butte. In T. 5 N., R. 1 E. The well known Capt. Calderwood ran this station and dispensed hospitality to all comers. It was the point from which supplies for the Relief mine were sent. See Calderwood Peak.

Agua Fria River   Yavapai Co.   G. L. O. Map, 1921;
                                                 Prescott N. F., 1927.

Sp., "cold water." Rises west side Mingus mountain. Flows south, lost in desert near Beardsley station on A. T. & S. F. R. R. Early name; origin unknown.

Agua Fria Valley Post Office   Yavapai Co.   G. L. O. Map, 1892.

Name of the post office at head of Agua Fria valley. In T. 13 N., R. 2 E. About 12 miles due east of Prescott. Old station and P. O. on the Black Canyon road. Darrel Duppa ran this station for several years. See his name for history. *Tucson Citizen*, Mar. 30, 1872, states that Duppa was attacked here by Apaches and badly wounded Mar. 24, 1872. James M. Barney, Phoenix, says the Bowers Bros., had a flour mill here as early as 1869. P. O. established under above full name May 2, 1875, Dennis Marr, P. M.

Agua Sal Creek   Apache Co.   G. L. O. Map, 1921.

Sp., "salt water." On Navajo Ind. Res. Rises in T. 7 N., R. 8 W., near Canyon del Muerto. Flows northwest, joins Chinle creek, in T. 11 N., R. 10 W., east of Carson mesa. "The water is very alkaline." Gregory.

Agua Verde Mountains and Creek

See Tanque Verde.

Aguila Mountains   Pima and Yuma Cos.   U. S. G. S. Map, 1923.

Sp. "eagle." In Ts. 9, 10 S., Rs. 10, 11 W. On county line. There is also an Eagle Tank here. Mountains probably took the name from it.

Aguila   Maricopa Co.   U. S. G. S. Map, 1923.

Station A. T. & S. F. R. R., in T. 7 N., R. 9 W., north end Harqua Hala mountains, 27 miles west of Wickenburg. After nearby mountains. P. O. established Mar. 30, 1910, Frank Spurger, P. M.

Aguirre Peak   Pima Co.   U. S. G. S. Map, 1923.

Southern end Baboquivari mountains, near Mexican line in T. 21 S., R. 7 E. After Epifanio Aguirre, killed by Apaches near this peak. "Epifanio Aguirre was a well known government freighter and contractor of early days. Born in Chihuahua, Mexico; educated in eastern part of U. S. Married Mary Bernard at Westport, Mo. Came west and settled in Chihuahua. Jan. 16, 1870, he and a party were attacked by Apaches near Sasabe, Arizona, and all killed excepting his brother Conrado, who escaped. Aguirre's wife went back to Westport. In 1874 she returned and taught school at Tucson for many years."

Aguirres Lake

See Buenos Aires.

Ah-ah-pook Creek   Mohave Co.   G. L. O. Map, 1892.

Mohave name, origin or meaning unknown. Rises near Cygnus peak. Flows south into Spencer creek east side of Aquarius range.

Ajax Hill   Cochise Co.   Judge Map, 1916

Elevation 5,315 feet. In sec. 22, T. 22 E., R. 21 S. 4 miles southwest of Tombstone. Said to have received the name from an old prospector known as Ajax.

Ajo   Pima Co.   G. L. O. Map, 1921; U. S. G. S., 1923.

Sp. "garlic." Elevation 1,850 feet. Railroad station and copper mine, at southern end of Tucson, Cornelia and Gila Bend R. R. Station established 1916. One of the oldest mines in State, worked continuously from 1855. First shipments of ore to San Francisco in 1856. Emory called it Ajo in 1854.

"The Ajo company was formed in San Francisco in 1854, with Major General Robert Allen, U. S. A., president; E. E. Dunbar, secretary-manager. First ore packed to Yuma on mule back at a cost of $105 a ton." Poston. Named after the Ajo mountains. Wild garlic grows all over the hills in good seasons.

"Dr. McDougal found two very interesting plants. One was the Ajo lily, from which the mountain range and valley are named. The root we found, tasted very like an onion set." Hornaday. In 1926, residents of Ajo tried to change the name to Greenway in honor of Major John C. Greenway, of the Rough Riders, who developed the mine, built the railroad to it and did much for the town. The change was not approved by the U. S. Geographic Board, because of its rule against supplanting old, well established names by new ones. P. O. established Aug. 29, 1900, John M. Hoover, P. M.

Ajo Mountains   Pima Co.   U. S. G. S. Map, 1923.

They form the southwest boundary of the Papago Ind. Res. Near lat. 32°, long. 112° 40'.

Akaba, Mount   Coconino Co.   Map, Tusayan N. F., 1927.

Grand Canyon N. P. In sec. 8, T. 34 N., R. 3 W. On south side of canyon at Matkatamiba canyon. So named by U. S. Geological Survey, from name of a local Indian family.

Alamo   Maricopa Co.

Sp. "white poplar." Stream here is lined with cottonwoods, commonly known as alamos. It was the first station, 15 miles south of Phoenix, on old stage line to Maricopa Wells. Viall Ransom was owner and keeper according to *Arizona Gazetteer* of 1881.

Alamo   Yuma Co.   U. S. G. S. Map, 1923.

On Bill Williams Fork, north side Buckskin mountains, in T. 11 N., R. 13 W. P. O. established under name "Alimo" March 30, 1911. Changed to Alamo later. Vincent M. Devine, P. M.

Alamo Spring   Apache Co.   U. S. G. S. Map, 1923.

In T. 7 N., R. 11 W. On Navajo Ind. Res. Sp., as above.

Alder Canyon   Coconino Co.   Map, Sitgreaves N. F., 1924.

Heads in Alder lake, near Tonto rim. Enters east side West Chevelon at sec. 20, T. 14 N., R. 14 E. So called because area around lake was covered with alder trees.

Alder Creek   Maricopa Co.   Map, Tonto N. F., 1927.

East side Verde river, rises in sec. 2, T. 6 N., R. 8 E. Flows southwest, enters Verde at Maverick mountain. So called for dense growth of alders along it.

Alder Lake   Coconino Co.   Map, Sitgreaves N. F., 1924.

Wet weather lake near "Crook road" in sec. 34, T. 12 N., R. 13 E. The U. S. troops that fought with Apaches the battle of Big Dry Wash, July 17, 1882, camped here after the fight for a couple of days to shoe horses and mules, take care of their wounded, etc. As late as 1894 the author saw many trees about this and Deer lake, where the soldiers had carved their names, regiments and dates in the soft bark. In 1916, however, he was unable to find a single tree on which a name could be discovered.

Aldona   Pima Co.

Station, E. P. & S. W. R. R. About 5 miles east of Tucson. After Al. Donau (Alfred S. Donau) cattleman, merchant, and real estate dealer of Tucson who came to Arizona in 1883. Was a member of Territorial Legislature 1899.

Aldrich   Cochise Co.   G. L. O. Map, 1909.

In T. 12 S., R. 26 E. Station on S. P. R. R. In Railroad pass about 12 miles east of Willcox. "A switch 4 miles east of Raso, formerly Railroad pass. It is between Raso and Luzena. I cannot learn for whom it was so named, or for what." Letter, W. T. Brinley, S. P. Agent.

Alexandra (sic)   Yavapai Co.   Smith Map, 1879; G. L. O., 1892.

Named after T. M. Alexander, who with Col. Bigelow laid out the townsite at Peck mine. Known later as Alexander. On Turkey creek about 6 miles north of Crown King. Alexander was the owner of the Black Warrior mine. P. O. established Aug. 6, 1878, Joseph S. Drew, P. M.

Algert   Coconino Co.

On Navajo Ind. Res. After Charles H. Algert, early Indian trader. Now called Blue canyon q.v.

Algodon   Graham Co   U. S. G. S. Map, 1923; Crook N. F., 1931.

Sp. "cotton." Six miles due south of Safford. First called Lebanon. Small hamlet in T. 8 S., R. 26 E. P. O. established June 13, 1915, Effie Lee, P. M.

Alhambra   Maricopa Co.   U. S. G. S. Map, 1923.

In T. 2 N., R. 2 E. On Ash Fork-Phoenix branch A. T. & S. F. R. R. About 5 miles north of Phoenix. "Josiah Harbert, who owned the land on which the town was located, came from Alhambra, Calif., which he also named. He called this place for the California town." Letter A. E. Hinton. P. O. established July 13, 1893, Arthur E. Hinton, P. M.

Alicia   Maricopa Co.   U. S. G. S. Map, 1923.

In T. 4 E., R. 2 S. Spanish for Alice. Station on Arizona-Eastern R. R. 12 miles north of Maricopa. Named for Alice Masten, daughter of N. K. Masten, first president Maricopa and Phoenix R. R.

Aliso Creek   Gila Co.   Map, Crook N. F., 1926.

Sp. "alder tree." Rises east of Globe in T. I N., R. 16 E. Flows southeast, enters San Carlos river near Rice school. There are large groves of alders along the stream.

Aliso Spring   Santa Cruz Co.   Map, Coronado N. F., 1927.

Sp. "alder tree." In sec. 21, T. 21 S., R. 12 E. In Tumacacori mountains. Hinton says: "The Aliza (sic) Pass, with its welcome spring near the top."

Allah   Maricopa Co.   R. R. Maps.

Station on Hassayampa river, on Ash Fork-Phoenix branch A. T. & S. F. R. R., 4 miles south of Wickenburg. In early days this location with its great groves of cottonwoods, was called "The Garden of Allah." From this came the name Allah. Favorite early day picnic grounds for Phoenix Sunday schools, etc. P. O. established Nov. 16, 1917, Frances E. Sanger, P. M.

Allan Lake   Coconino Co.   U. S. G. S. Map, 1923.

In sec. 28, T. 17 N., R. 9 E. About 6 miles south of Mormon lake. After "Broncho Jim" Allan, pioneer horseman of this vicinity.

Allantown   Apache Co.   U. S. G. S. Map, 1923.

In T. 22 N., R. 30 E. On A. T. & S. F. R. R. near New Mexico line. "After Allan Johnson of the early A. & P. R. R. Construction dept." A. G. W. Johnson and his brother settled near this place in the Eighties and ran cattle for several years.

Allen City or Allen's Camp   Navajo Co.

Settlement on Little Colorado river about 3 miles above Joseph City. Located by Wm. C. Allen, Mar., 1876. First name suggested was Ramah City. Changed to St. Joseph Jan. 21, 1878, after the Mormon prophet Joseph Smith. See McClintock *Mormon Settlement.* First P. O. here called Allen City. Opened Aug. 25, 1876, John McLaws, P. M.

Allen   Pima Co.

Settlement Papago Ind. Res. near Cubabi. Named for J. B. Allen, at one time Adjt. Gen'l. of Arizona, and a member of the Territorial Legislature. Farish says: "He furnished a wagon loaded with arms and ammunition for the Camp Grant Massacre expedition in 1871." He had a store and station at old Maricopa Wells. P. O. established July 5, 1882, J. B. Allen, P. M. See Quitojoa City.

Alma   Maricopa Co.   U. S. G. S. Mesa Sheet.

Settlement about a mile west of Mesa, in sec. 21, T. 1 N., R. 5 E. Originally called Stringtown; now part of Mesa. Henry and William N. Standage, former a member of the Mormon Battalion, were the first settlers, in Jan., 1880. Alma was one of the Mormon Prophets and a High Priest.

Alma   Pinal Co.   G. L. O. Map, 1883-1892.

Sp., "a soul, a spirit." P. O. and settlement on San Pedro river 6 miles above old Camp Grant. In T. 7 S., R. 16 E. P. O. established May 12, 1891, Frank M. Doll, P. M.

Alma Mesa   Greenlee Co.   Map, Crook N. F., 1926

Sp. "Tableland of the Spirit." Prominent mesa lying partly in Arizona, partly in New Mexico. In T. 1 N., R. 32 E.

"Alma, New Mexico, was named by Morris E. Coates after the town of Alma, Colorado, from which he came. Coates established the first store at Alma. Mexican hamlet here was then called 'Los Vallos.' " Letter, Ben F. Nabours, Forest Ranger.

Alpha   Maricopa Co.

P. O. established May 1, 1894, Tennie Cameron, P. M. Small settlement on Gila river near Agua Caliente. Origin unknown.

Alpine   Apache Co.   Map, Apache N. F., 1927

At head of San Francisco river, in sec. 12, T. 5 N., R. 30 E. Elevation 8,000 feet. In Sept., 1880, the author was with Troop E, 6th Cavalry, Capt. Adam Kramer, scouting through here. Indians under Victorio had gone through this valley ahead of the troops and killed several men and women who were buried by the soldiers as they were found. It was then known as Bush valley, after Anderson Bush, first settler, who was not a Mormon. Called Frisco by the Mormons later because near headwaters of Frisco river. About 1882 name was changed to Alpine because of its altitude. P. O. established Jan. 7, 1885, William G. Black, P. M. Jacob Hamblin, early Mormon missionary and pioneer is buried here. He died Aug. 31, 1886.

Alsap Butte   Coconino Co.

Grand Canyon N. P. On west wall of Canyon, about 3 miles southeast of Point Imperial, near lat. 36° 15′, long. 111° 57′ at northeast corner of Park. Named for John T. Alsap, born in Kentucky, 1832; died Phoenix, Arizona, 1886. Settled near Phoenix, 1869. Lawyer, county and district attorney, probate judge of Maricopa county, and "Father of that county." Farish. Named by Frank Bond in 1930. Decision U. S. G. B.

Altamont   Maricopa Co.

In Buckeye valley. P. O. established July 16, 1895, Harriet Toothaker, P. M. Origin unknown.

Altar Valley   Pima Co.   G. L. O. Map, 1921

"A well known highway led up from Mexico through this valley in early days." "Altar in Sonora was named by Father Kino because near it was a little mountain which he thought resembled an altar." Letter, Dr. Frank Lockwood. In R. 9 E. East side Baboquivari range. See First Chance.

Alto   Santa Cruz Co.   Map, Coronado N. F., 1927

Sp. "high." P. O. and early mining camp, on Baca grant No. 3, in T. 21 S., R. 14 E. P. O. established June 6, 1912, Minnie A. Bond, P. M.

Alvarez Mountains   Pima Co.   G. L. O. Map, 1921.

In T. 19 S., R. 4 E. Papago Ind. Res. Origin unknown.

Amado   Santa Cruz Co.   G. L. O. Map, 1921, Amado; Coronado N. F., 1927, Amadoville.

In sec. 7, T. 20 S., R. 13 E. Station on Tucson-Nogales branch S. P. R. R. 37 miles south of Tucson in Santa Cruz valley. Named for prominent Spanish pioneer family that lived here and ran many cattle on the range. Railroad station opened about 1910. P. O. established as Amadoville June 17, 1919, Manuel H. Amado, P. M. Changed to Amado Feb. 27, 1920.

Amboy   Mohave Co.

Point at mouth Bill Williams river, on Colorado river, where according to Farish, Col. Poston in Feb., 1865, urged the War department to establish a military post. Origin unknown.

Ambush Water Pocket   Mohave Co.

"Near here the two Howlands, and Dunn, of Powell's first party were ambushed and killed by Indians, 1869." Dellenbaugh. On north side of Shivwits plateau, near lat. 36°, long. 113° 30'. Local authorities say this was often called "Pen Pockets" because they corralled or penned wild horses here. A "water pocket" seems to have been the local name for what is now called "tanks," or "water holes."

American Flag   Mohave Co.   Smith Map, 1879.

Early day silver mining camp. West side Hualpai mountains, near lat. 35°. Hinton locates it 35 miles southeast of Mineral Park. "The camp was named for its first big mine, the 'American Flag.'"

American Flag   Santa Cruz Co. Hamilton Map, 1886; G. L. O., 1892.

Mining camp and ranch, established in early part of Eighties. See Oracle for history. P. O. established Dec. 28, 1880, Peter H. Loss, P. M.

American Peak   Santa Cruz Co.   Map, Coronado N. F., 1927.

Elevation, 5,241 feet. In T. 23 S., R. 16 E. At head of Alum gulch east side Patagonia mountains. "Undoubtedly named after the American mine near here, of the early Sixties."

American Ranch   Yavapai Co.

Early day stage station on road Ehrenburg to Prescott. "Owned by J. H. Lee, who ran a store and station here. Indians attacked the station killing Lee. A man then leased the place, took a sack of flour, placed strychnine in it, left the store open and the sack handy for all comers. Some soldiers under Dan Leary, the scout, came along and found twenty-four dead Indians and fourteen more very sick in a nearby Indian camp. The affair raised an awful fuss among the Indian lovers of the east." Orick Jackson.

"About the middle of September, 1875, we arrived at American ranch some 10 miles from Whipple." Mrs. Summerhayes.

Amity   Apache Co.   Map, Apache N. F., 1926.

According to McClintock, this was one of the two "wards" of the original Round valley settlement. Founded 1882. The other ward was Omer. Located in sec. 7, T. 8 N., R. 28 E. In 1888 the two were consolidated and called Union, later Eager after the two Eager brothers. See Eager and Round valley.

Amole Peak   Pima Co.   U. S. G. S. Map, 1923.

Sp. "soap root." In T. 13 S., R. 12 E. In Tucson mountains. Old timers say there was a heavy growth of yucca, "amole," on this mountain, hence the name.

Amole Station   Pima Co.

Station on S. P. R. R. 33 miles east of Tucson. Amole or soap weed is very plentiful here.

Anderson Canyon   Coconino Co.   U. S. G. S. Map, 1921.

In T. 8 N., R. 10 E. Heads north of Mount Geronimo. Runs northeast, enters Canyon Diablo in T. 20 N., R. 12 E. about 4 miles above railroad station of that name. "The canyon and spring at its head were named after Jim Anderson of Flagstaff. Anderson Gap and Anderson Mesa were also named for him." Letter, Al. Beasley, Flagstaff.

Andrews Spring   Coconino Co.   Map, Tusayan N. F., 1927.

In T. 21 N., R. 1 E. At head of Hell's canyon south side Bill Williams mountain. "Named for T. Andrews, who took up a claim near this spring in 1903. It was also known as Twin springs because there are two of them. Real Twin springs is however, in the next township." Letter, Ed. Miller, Forest Supervisor.

Andrus Canyon   Mohave Co.   U. S. G. S. Map, 1923.

Rises east of Shivwits plateau at Ivanpah spring. Runs southeast into Colorado river, near lat. 36° 5', long. 113° 20'. "The topography hardly justifies calling it a canyon. Generally referred to as 'the draw at Andrus spring.' After Capt. James Andrus who, 1866, led the party that killed the Indians who murdered Dr. Whitmore and Robert McIntire near Pipe springs." Letter, O. H. Olson, Cedar City.

Andrus Spring   Mohave Co.   U. S. G. S. Map; G. L. O. Maps, 1921
as Upper and Lower Andrus Springs.

In Andrus canyon, east side of Shivwits plateau, north side of Colorado river. "After Capt. James Andrus, pioneer stockman. He was an early settler at St. George, Utah, and developed this 'seep' for stockwatering purposes. He died several years ago." Letter O. H. Olsen, Forest Ranger.

Angel Point   Yuma Co.   G. L. O. Map, 1921.

Turning point on eastern boundary Colorado River Ind. Res. at Tyson's wash. Origin unknown.

Angell   Coconino Co.   G. L. O. Map, 1921.

On A. T. & S. F. R. R., 22 miles east of Flagstaff. "After the first assistant superintendent Atlantic and Pacific R. R. G. W. Angell." A.G.W.

Angora   Gila Co.   G. L. O. Map, 1923.

In T. 11½ N., R. 10 E. About 8 miles north of Payson. Named by John F. Holder, who ran Angora goats near here for many years. P. O. established June 25, 1900, John F. Holder, P. M.

Animas Mountain   Pima Co.   U. S. G. S. Map, 1923.

West side Baboquivari valley, Papago Ind. Res.

Anita   Coconino Co.   Map, Tusayan N. F., 1927.

In southeast corner T. 29 N., R. 1 E. Station Grand Canyon branch A. T. & S. F. R. R. 45 miles north of Williams. Named for the "Anita" mine q.v. U. S. F. S. Ranger station here. P. O. established Aug. 17, 1914, Grace E. Lockridge, P. M.

Anita Mines   Coconino Co.   G. L. O. Map, 1909.

In T. 22 N., R. 2 E. About 6 miles west of Anita station. There is a short branch railroad from the mine to Grand Canyon main line. Mines owned by Ferd Nellis of Williams and named after one of his family. Buckey O'Neill was for a time interested in the mine with Nellis.

Antares   Mohave Co.   U. S. G. S. Map, 1923.

Town and railroad station on A. T. & S. F. R. R. about 6 miles west of Hackberry. Origin unknown.

Antelope Hill   Yuma Co.   G. L. O. Map, 1921.

In T. 8 S., R. 17 W. An early day stage station on old Yuma-Tucson road. South side Gila river. Hinton's *Hand Book* calls it Antelope peak. About 50 miles east of Yuma. "It is a singular mass of volcanic rock whose northern side rises bold and sheer to its ragged top." Hinton. J. Ross Browne, wrote January, 1864: "It was called Antelope Peak station. It was in charge of two soldiers who had hay for supplying government teams." Poston speaks of the many antelope near this station which was undoubtedly the origin of the name. In *Apache Land* he writes:

> "We next pass peak of Antelope,
> Where road with river had to cope;
> Where once, in happy days gone by,
> The harmless antelope could fly
> To quench their thirst with Gila drink."

Antelope Hill   Pinal Co.   G. L. O. Map, 1921.

Elevation 4,540 feet. In T. 7 S., R. 2 E. About 6 miles west of Feldman. There is another Antelope peak due west of, and near Casa Grande.

Antelope Peak   Pinal Co.   G. L. O. Map, 1921; U. S. G. S., 1923.

In T. 7 S., R. 2 E. Near western line Pinal Co. In Table Top mountains.

Antelope Peak, Valley and Creek   Yavapai Co.   Smith Map, 1879;
G. L. O. Map, 1921.

Elevation 5,786 feet. In Weaver mining district, southwest corner Yavapai county, east of Congress. "I killed three antelope and we gave the peak this name, Antelope." Peeples Diary, 1863. The creek rises at the peak.

Antelope Spring   Cochise Co.   U. S. G. S. Map, 1925.

In T. 20 S. R. 24 E. About 15 miles southeast of Tombstone. Noted watering place in old Indian and cattle days. Springs were camping place of soldiers guarding men at heliograph station which Gen. Miles established in his Geronimo campaign, 1886.

Antelope Spring   Coconino Co.   Beale Map, 1858; Eckhoff, 1880.

Spring at which Beale camped about 4 miles south of San Francisco spring. Farish quotes Banta "It was what we know now as Old Town Spring."

Beale says "We jumped a herd of antelope here and the Indian hunters killed one. This gave it the name Antelope."

Antelope Spring   Navajo Co.

See Jaditquo or Jadito.

Antelope Valley   Mohave Co.   U. S. G. S. Map, 1923.

On north side Colorado river, east of Uinkaret plateau. "The newcomers found many antelope in this valley."

Antelope Valley   Yavapai Co.   G. L. O. Map, 1892.

Early day post office and stage station on Kirkland creek. Not the Antelope valley where Peeples' party killed the antelope. It seems to have been only the name for the station and post office. P. O. established Oct. 1875, Charles G. Genung, P. M. According to P. O. records the Stanton office was closed when that of Antelope valley was established.

Anvil Mountain   Yuma Co.   U. S. G. S. Map, 1923.

South end Eagle Tail mountains. "At a distance it resembles a huge blacksmith's anvil."

Anvil Rock—Station   Yavapai Co.   G. L. O. Map, 1921.

Descriptive name for a huge rock, a landmark for the region, in T. 19 N., R. 8 W. Just north of Luis Maria Baca Land Grant. *Arizona Gazetteer*, 1881, states: "There is a stage station near this rock by the same name. About 68 miles northwest of Prescott. C. P. Wilder, owner and station keeper."

A 1 (A One) Mountain   Coconino Co.   Map, Coconino N. F., 1928.

In sec. 2, T. 21 N., R. 6 E. Solitary peak named after Arizona Cattle Co. of Flagstaff which ran the A 1 (A One) brand of cattle in the early Nineties. Capt. Bulwinkle, former Chief of the Insurance Fire Patrol of Chicago, was its manager at one time. His wild rides on blooded race horses from Flagstaff to the headquarter ranch near this mountain, in Fort valley, were the talk of the ranges. Nine miles in about as many minutes was his aim. He was killed by his horse falling on him on a dark night in 1896. On some maps as Crater hill.

Apache   Cochise Co.   Post Route Map, 1929.

On E. P. & S. W. R. R. north of Douglas. "To remember the old days of the Apache raids." A monument erected to commemorate the surrender of Geronimo and his band in 1886 to the military forces was dedicated here April 29, 1934. The surrender was a few miles off in Skeleton canyon. P. O. established May 22, 1908, John W. Richart, P. M.

Apache Butte   Navajo Co.   U. S. G. S. Map, 1923.

In T. 18 N., R. 18 E. About 4 miles south of Little Colorado river. So named by the author. In 1883 some Mexican sheep herders with whom we were having trouble corralled the author and J. W. Benham on this butte and came very near wiping them out. Help came at the critical moment.

Apache Cave   Maricopa Co.   Map, Tonto N. F., 1927.

Celebrated cave in sec. 10, T. 3 N., R. 10 E. Sometimes called Skull Cave. On north side Salt river above Horse Mesa dam. In 1872, troops under Major Brown U. S. A. practically wiped out a band of Apaches who took refuge here. Troops could not charge the cave but fired volley after volley against its sloping roof which is still splashed with lead from the bullets. The deflected bullets did deadly work. For many years there were skulls, human bones, old shoes, clothing, cartridge shells and such plunder, lying about the cave.

Apache County

In the extreme northeast corner of State; created from Yavapai county, 1879. County seat, St. Johns.

Apache, Fort   Apache Co.   Smith Map, 1879, Camp Apache; Eckhoff, 1880, Fort Apache.

"Post first established May 16, 1870 as Camp Ord, after Gen. E. O. C. Ord, by Col. John Green and several troops of the 1st U. S. Cavalry. August 1, 1870 it was called Camp Mogollon. Changed to Camp Thomas in Sept., 1870; Camp Apache, Feb. 2, 1871; and Fort Apache, April 5, 1879." Heitman. Post located at Forks of White river on White Mountain or Fort Apache Ind. Res. Shows for first time on any known map as Camp Apache; Colton's map, 1873. In 1924 post was abandoned, and turned over to Indian service for Indian school purposes. Frank Staples, P. M. Aug. 13, 1879. "The wire for the telegraph line from Camp Apache to Camp Thomas on the Gila was packed by fifty big pack mules from Camp Verde to Apache over the Mogollon mountains in November, 1874." John G. Bourke in *New Mexico Historical Review*, Jan., 1934.

Apache Indians

A people, the majority of whom live on two reservations in east-central Arizona. Numbered about 5,000 in 1920.

"The name is probably from Apache, meaning enemy. Is also the Zuni name for the Navajo who were designated *Apaches de Nabaju* by the early Spaniards in New Mexico." Hodge.

These Apaches are divided into a number of local groups: Aravaipas; Coyoteros or White mountains; Chiricahuas, removed by the government in 1886 and now at Ft. Sill, Okla.; Tontos; Warm Spring; San Carlos, or Pinals. There are also the Apache-Mohaves and the Apache-Yumas. The Jicarillo-Apaches and the Mescalero-Apaches are on reservations in New Mexico.

The Apaches call themselves "N'de" or "Inde" meaning "the people." They are of the Athapascan family. Each group speaks a different language although there is some lingual similarity. See Aravaipa.

Apache Indian Reservation

See Fort Apache Ind. Res.

Apache Junction   Pinal Co.   Scott Map, Maricopa Co.

On Apache Trail to Roosevelt, just inside Pinal county at junction with Superior highway. Group of gasoline and eating stations, with an interesting menagerie of local wild animals.

Apache Lake   Maricopa Co.

Formed by the Horse Mesa dam built by Salt River Valley Water Users Assn. to conserve water coming through turbines at Roosevelt dam. Waters reach almost to the Roosevelt dam.

Apache Leap   Pinal Co.   Map, Crook N. F., 1929.

In southeast corner sec. 36, T. 1 S., R. 12 E. Steep escarpment just above Superior. Here a number of Apaches are said to have leaped to their deaths when pursued by soldiers in the Seventies.

There is, however, no historical basis for this story. On Queen Creek canyon.

Apache Maid Mountain   Coconino Co.   Map, Coconino N. F., 1928.

Head of Wet Beaver creek, in T. 15 N., R. 8 E. "About 1873 the troops in a fight with Indians at this point killed an Apache woman. Her living baby was taken to Fort Verde by the troops who gave the mountain this name." Letter R. W. Wingfield, Camp Verde.

Forest Ranger Oscar L. McClure writes: "The first settlers came through this region with troops moving from Santa Fe to Camp Verde. From the Mahan mountain they sent a scout ahead who was to start a big smoke for them to follow when he found a good trail. When the smoke first raised a young Apache girl saw it and came to the fire. She had been lost for several days and was nearly starved. She stayed with the party and was eventually adopted by one of them." McClure says this story was told him by a member of the party named Gash, who vouched for its truth.

Apache-Mohave

Branch of the Apache family. They have a separate language and have nearly always lived away from the main Apache reservation. They are of Yuman stock possibly formed in part from captives from the Mohave and Yavapai tribes. According to Hodge the name Yavapai means "sun people" or "people of the sun." Their range was along and west of the upper Verde river.

Apache Mountains   Gila Co.   G. L. O. Map, 1921.

In Ts. 2, 3 N., Rs. 15, 15½ E. Short range extending from Rockinstraw (sic) mountain north to and beyond Apache peaks, into the San Carlos Ind. Res. Called "Sierra Apache" on Crook N. F. map. See Apache peaks.

Apache National Forest   Apache and Greenlee Cos.

Created by Presidential Proclamation, 1898, as Black Mesa Forest Reserve, after the nearby Black mesa. Renamed 1907 as the Apache National Forest. A large part lies in Cattron county, New Mexico. Area in Arizona, 1931, 707,989 acres. Supervisor's Headquarters, Springerville.

Apaches—Ojos Calientes, or **Warm Spring Apaches**

"So called from their former residence at Ojo Caliente or Warm Springs, in southwestern New Mexico. An Apache tribe of New Mexico who originally were probably Chiricahua Apaches in the main and possibly the Gilenos of Benavides in 1630. Victorio and Nana were among their most noteworthy leaders in recent times." Hodge. Bourke, *On the Border*, says: "Loco and Victorio prominent chiefs of the Warm Springs band over in New Mexico had been camped at old Fort Craig, New Mexico, ever since September, 1869, waiting for a reserve to be established where they and their children could live in peace." This reservation was established by President Grant in April, 1868. In August, 1877, President Hayes restored the land to the public domain because valuable minerals had been discovered on the reservation. Victorio and his people were removed to Fort Apache soon after this.

He is said to have told General Crook, at Fort Apache, "My fathers lived and died at Ojo Caliente. We want to live and die there. Send us back and we will always be friends. Keep us here and we will die fighting like brave men."

Victorio and his people "died fighting like brave men." But the war they carried on for five or more years took the lives of several hundred innocent men, women, and children, and easily cost the United States government several million dollars.

General Sherman, in his report for 1881 says: "I do not know the reasons for the Interior Department insisting on the removal of these Indians to Arizona. They must have been very cogent to justify its cost to the settlers and the government. Victorio's capture is not very probable, but his killing however cruel it may be, will be done in time." The record is one we Americans should not be proud of.

Apache Pass   Cochise Co.   Smith Map, 1879; Eckhoff, 1880.

Narrow defile between Dos Cabezas, and Chiricahua mountains. In early days this pass was used generally by travellers through southern Arizona. Apaches were very active and many white people were killed here. P. O. established Dec. 11, 1866, George Hand, P. M. P. O. name changed to Fort Bowie June 22, 1880. Sidney R. DeLong was P. M. following Hand, May 25, 1870. See Fort Bowie.

Apache Peak   Cochise Co.   Map, Coronado N. F., 1927.

Elevation 7,884 feet. In T. 19 S., R. 19 E. West slope of Whetstones.

Apache Peak   Pinal Co.   U. S. G. S. Map, 1923; Coronado N. F., 1927.

Elevation 6,456 feet. In sec. 19, T. 10 S., R. 16 E. In Santa Catalina mountains south of Oracle.

Apache Peaks   Gila Co.

Four or five closely grouped peaks south of Salt river and east of Pinal creek. Principal peak located in lat. 33° 31′ 35″ N., long. 110° 43′ 48″ W. Not Apache mountains. Decision U. S. G. B.

Apache Point   Coconino Co.

In Grand Canyon N. P. In lat. 36° 12′ 30″ N., long. 112° 29′ W. On left rim of canyon across river southwest of Powell plateau. Named for Indian tribe. Decision U. S. G. B.

Apache Springs   Navajo Co.

Springs at head of Forestdale creek, Fort Apache Ind. Res. Named by Mormon settlers who located here, 1879; were removed by the military, 1880.

Apache Terraces   Coconino Co.

In Grand Canyon N. P. In lat. 36° long. 112° 28′. On left canyon wall below Apache Point. Well defined, terraced bench area. Named for Apache tribes.

Apache Trail   Maricopa and Gila Cos.

Name "invented" by railroad officials on completion of Bowie to Globe branch of S. P. R. R. Came into use about 1919 when Prof. Abner Drury of Berkeley, Calif., was commissioned by the S. P. R. R. to reconstruct the established nomenclature of points on Roosevelt dam highway.

For publicity purposes the name "Apache Trail" was extended to cover the road to Globe, 40 miles beyond the dam.

For conversational purposes the stage drivers in early days

invented weird tales for their passengers. "Mormon Flat" was the scene of the massacre of a party of Mormons, "Tortilla Flat" was where early Mexican travellers stopped to cook tortillas, etc., etc. Fairy tales, all.

Worst of all, established historic names which the pioneers of Arizona desired perpetuated were ruthlessly changed into meaningless Spanish words. For over half a century this trail was known generally, as the "Tonto Trail," because it led direct from Tonto basin to the Salt River valley.

In Nov. 1888, the author brought a band of saddle horses through the basin to the valley via this Tonto Trail. Where the Salt enters the granite gorge now blocked by the Roosevelt dam, were two trails down the river. One took his choice.

From Tonto creek north of the present dam, one trail led over the southern flank of the Four Peaks, kept on top of Salt River canyon for about 20 miles, then dropped into it at Horse Mesa, crossed the river, climbed out on south side and followed up Pranty creek, where Old Man Pranty had his cabin, to the back bone at its head. There one followed along the watershed east of Superstition mountains to the open desert near Goldfields.

Or, if one came down the Salt river he turned from that stream a little below the present settlement of Livingston, climbed out along Campaign creek around Windy Hill, and picked up the Tonto Trail near head of Le Barge creek. Both trails were passable but very rough. The settlers used them only in emergencies, taking the trail over Reno Pass when time permitted.

The Apaches used these trails to reach and raid their long time enemies, the Pimas and Maricopas.

Apache—Yuma or Yulkepai

One of the divisions of the Apache nation. "Until 1904 there lived with the Apaches of Arizona a number of Indians of Yuman stock, particularly Mohave—Apaches or Yavapai, but these are now mostly established at old Camp McDowell." Hodge.

Farish says: "The word Yuma probably means 'spotted belly sparrows.'" He fails to say where he got the idea.

Apacheria

Appears on John Senex's map of 1710 and most early Spanish maps as an area in the eastern part of central Arizona running into New Mexico west of Rio Grande. Also marked "Apacheland" on some early American maps. Coues describes it as "The indefinite area or region in Arizona and New Mexico in which Apaches roamed."

Father Kino in his diary, according to Bolton, says: "Apacheria which lies to the north and northeast of us and extends northwest to the very large Colorado river or Rio del Norte above the 35th, 36th, and 37th parallel and beyond. By way of this same Apacheria we shall be able to enter to deal with New Mexico and its newest provinces."

Apiary Well   Maricopa Co.   U. S. G. S. Map, 1923.

On north bank Gila river, north end Painted Rock mountains. In T. 4 S., R. 8 W. Origin unknown.

Apex   Coconino Co.   U. S. G. S. Map, 1923.

Highest point and station on Grand Canyon branch A. T. & S. F. R. R. In sec. 34, T. 30 N., R. 2 E. "The apex of the line, hence the name." A. G. W.

Apostoles, Rio de los

"So Kino is said to have called the Gila." Coues. See Gila river.

Aquarius Plateau, Range, and **Cliffs**   Mohave Co.
G. L. O. Map, 1921; U. S. G. S., 1923.

East side Yavapai county near county line. In Ts. 11, 12 N. "The slopes were full of leaping torrents and clear lakes so Whipple gave it the name of Aquarius in 1854." Dellenbaugh. Wheeler says: "From the numerous streams flowing from it we called it the Aquarius range."

Arastra Gulch (sic)   Gila Co.   Map, Tonto N. F., 1926.

"In upper Tonto basin, about three miles southwest of Payson. So called because there were a number of arrastras operating here in early years. Most of the early miners came from California and used the word gulch commonly. This gulch has in recent years been called Single Standard Gulch for a mine located there a few years ago." Letter, Forest Ranger, Croxen.

An arrastra was a primitive, home-made grinding machine, or mill. In a circular pit filled with ore a large granite rock was dragged round and round by a mule. The abrasion gradually wore the ore down to dust. It was a slow process and only rich ores were worked. See Arrastra.

Aravaipa   Graham Co.   G. L. O. Map, 1921;
Crook N. F., 1927.

In sec. 36, T. 5 S., R. 19 E. P. O. and ranch. Cattle headquarters for Hon. Bert Dunlap for years. First called Dunlap. P. O. established under Aravaipa, April 18, 1892, because of another Dunlap post office. Neil P. McCullum P. M. See Aravaipa Apaches for origin of name; see also Fort Breckenridge. Aravaipa, decision, U. S. G. B.

Arcadia Vista   Maricopa Co.

Settlement along east base Camelback mountain, about 12 miles northeast of Phoenix. "Just a name given by the first settlers who came out onto the desert for health and sunshine. It is now quite a place."

Aripine   Navajo Co.   Post Route Map, 1929.

P. O. and ranch about 15 miles southeast of Heber. "It is in the pines and has such good fresh air. It is known also as the Sundown Ranch." Letter, P. M. According to John Murray it was first called "Joppa," q.v. P. O. established Aug. 25, 1922, Grace M. Turley, P. M.

Archi

See Santa Rosa.

Arivaca   Pima Co.   G. L. O. Map, 1921; U. S. G. S., 1923.

In T. 21 S., R. 10 E. Old ranch, town and mining headquarters on Aravaipa creek. "A Piman word and former Piman village west of Tubac dating from prior to 1833. Abandoned during Piman revolt, 1751." Hodge.

Reduction works of the Cerro Colorado or Heintzelman mine were located here, 1880. Dan Ming in *Scientific and Mining Press* says: "There was an Arivaipa mine in the Santa Ritas in 1857. The Spanish spelled it 'Aribac.' " Bancroft says: "Aribac or Arivaca appears on a doubtful map of 1733 as a Pueblo." P. O. established April 10, 1878, Noah W. Bernard, P. M.

Arivaca Creek   Pima Co.   U. S. G. S. Map, 1923.

In T. 23 S., R. 11 E. Dry wash. Rises near Ruby. Flows northwest through Altar valley into Santa Cruz river in T. 10 N., R. 9 E.

Arivaca Grant   Pima Co.   G. L. O. Map, 1883.

In T. 21 S., Rs. 9, 10 E. Spanish Land Grant 6 miles north of Oro Blanco. Owners claimed 26,508 acres. Court of Private Land Claims rejected entire claim as fraudulent.

Aravaipa Apaches

Apache tribe whose home was in Aravaipa canyon, a tributary of the San Pedro river. According to Hodge, "The name is from the Pima, meaning 'girls.' Possibly applied to these people for some unmanly act."

These were the Apaches killed in the Camp Grant Massacre, 1871. In 1872 the remnant was moved to San Carlos Agency. Hodge spells the name "Ari-vai-pa," which was approved by the U. S. G. B. but later changed to "Ara-vai-pa." Lumholtz says: "This word may come from the Papago 'Alivaipia,' a small spring or water hole."

Aravaipa Creek   Graham Co.

Stream rising in T. 9 S., R. 22 E., near Eureka spring. Flows southwest into San Pedro river, in Pinal county, in T. 7 S., R. 16 E. See Aravaipa. Also First Chance.

Arivaipa (sic), **Fort**   Pinal Co.

"First name of Fort Breckenridge." Heitman. About 60 miles northwest of Tucson on San Pedro river. Established May 8, 1860.

Arizmo   Cochise Co.

Colony from Missouri located here. Coined the word from the two abbreviations Ariz. and Mo. P. O. established Sept. 19, 1903, Lewis A. Gregory, P. M.

Arizola   Pima Co.

Station and farming community on S. P. R. R. 26 miles east of Maricopa, established about 1892. Was the headquarters of James Addison Reavis who claimed the best part of Maricopa and Pinal counties on an alleged Spanish grant. Called himself "Baron of the Colorados." Lived here in almost royal state. Landed eventually in the federal penitentiary. McClintock's account is well worth reading. See also Reavis. April 2, 1931, George Mauk, U. S. Marshall for Arizona, writes: "Arizola was established in 1892 by a man named Thomas from Carthage, Mo. His daughter's name was Ola. He coined the word from part of Arizona and her name. I was the first R. R. Agent there in spring of 1894." P. O. established April 29, 1892, Julia A. Fishback, P. M.

Arizona

"This name is taken from an Indian pueblo at the 'little spring' from Ari-small and son-a spring or fountain." Taylor.

"An Aztec word, Arizuma, signifying 'silver bearing.' " Sylvester Mowry.

"Meaning 'Arid zone or desert.' " Gannett.

"At a point 85 miles southwest of Tucson, is a place in Sonora called Banera, some 8 miles west of Sasabe. Three hundred years ago many Indians lived on a creek here now called Sucalito, but the Indians call it 'Aleh-zone' meaning 'young spring.' " McFarland.

In 1854 New Mexico memorialized Congress for the creation of the Territory of Arizona. These names were suggested: Pimeria, Gadsonia, and Arizona. The latter was adopted as the most euphonious. Arizona then was part of New Mexico in Dona Ana county. This bill died but was re-introduced in Congress in 1859. Reported out in December, 1860, as an "Act to organize the Territory of Augumo" (sic). No reason given for the change in name." Farish.

McClintock says: "There is no doubt that Arizona was named after some springs near Banera 8 miles south of the border and about 85 miles below Tucson. These springs are called 'Aleh-zon' by the Papago, meaning 'small spring.' They also apply the name to a small nearby mountain and a ranch."

This origin is now accepted by all modern historians. The word Arizona seems to have first been used in printed or written form by Padre Ortega, sometime prior to 1754. He speaks of " 'The Real of Arizona,' meaning the country or province by that name."

Lieut. Hardy, English Navy, used the word in a book he published in 1827. He spoke therein of "the Arizona Mine." Bancroft says: "Anza used this name as early as 1774 when he speaks of a 'Mission of Arizona.' " In 1829 Ward published a book in London on Mexico in which he spoke of a place called "Arizona."

Arizona—Territory and State

Arizona was declared a Confederate Territory by Jefferson Davis and a proclamation issued August 1, 1861, by Lieut. Col. John R. Baylor, C. S. A., declared it under Confederate rule. This describes Arizona as "All lands in the Territory lying south of latitude 34°."

Congress later passed an Act creating the Territory of Arizona, approved by President Lincoln Feb. 24, 1863. The Act designated the entire western part of the then Territory of New Mexico as the new Territory. The newly appointed officers of Arizona Territory took possession December 29, 1863, at Navajo springs, in the present Apache county about 3 miles south of the A. T. & S. F. railroad station of Navajo springs a few miles from the western line of New Mexico. Here they believed themselves well inside the new area. First Legislature was organized at Prescott, September 26, 1864. Arizona became a state Feb. 14, 1912. Known as the "Valentine state."

Arizona and Swansea R. R.   Yuma Co.   U. S. G. S. Map, 1923.

Short line built in 1910 from Bouse station, Parker branch A. T. & S. F. R. R. to the Swansea mine, south of Bill Williams Fork.

Arizona City   Yavapai Co.   G. L. O. Map, 1908.

Small mining camp on Big Bug creek, about 5 miles north of Mayer.

Arizona City   Yuma Co.

According to P. O. records, Yuma was first called Arizona City. Population, 1871 about 1,200. A weekly paper, *The Arizona Free*

Press, was published here. P. O. named Arizona City, established Oct. 28, 1869, James M. Barney, P. M. The first district court convened here Oct. 28, 1878. See Yuma.

Arizona County

Created 1860 by an Act of Legislature of New Mexico, of which the present state was then a part. Act reads: "All that part of the Territory of New Mexico situated west of a line running due north and south from northern to southern boundary line of Dona Ana county, through a point one mile distant easterly from what is called the Overland Stage Mail Station, to the Apache Caves, shall be and hereby is, created into a county to be called and known as the county of Arizona." Northern line was apparently the Gila river. Tubac was the county seat; population 2,697. An Act of July 8, 1861, changed the county seat to Tucson.

Arizona Plateau

See Plateau of Arizona.

Arizona Seal

See Seal mountain.

Arizonan or **Arizonian**

Words much discussed for some years. Majority of writers and papers now use "Arizonan" as being more satisfactory and euphonious.

Arkill (sic)   Cochise Co.   R. R. Maps.

Station Globe-Bowie division Arizona-Eastern R. R., 14 miles north of Bowie station. After Seth T. Arkills, of the R. R. construction department, 1895.

Arlington, Town and **Valley**   Maricopa Co.   U. S. G. S. Map, 1923.

Town in T. 1 S., R. 5 W. In Arlington valley. Early settlement on Buckeye canal. P. O. established Nov. 23, 1899, Moses E. Clanton, P. M. Valley extends northeast from Gila Bend mountains.

Armer   Gila Co.   Map, Tonto N. F., 1927.

In sec. 1, T. 4 N., R. 13 E. Settlement and post office. After a family of pioneer cattlemen. P. O. established March 2, 1884, Mrs. Lucinda Armer, P. M.

Armer Gulch   Gila Co.   Map, Tonto N. F., 1926.

Heads at Armer mountain, flows south into Roosevelt lake, in T. 4 N., R. 13 E. After Armer family.

Armer Mountain   Gila Co.   Map, Tonto N. F., 1926.

In southern part of T. 6 N., R. 12 E. In Sierra Ancha mountains about 10 miles north of east end of Roosevelt lake. Named for Armers.

Armistead Creek   Mohave Co.

Somewhere west of Truxton springs. "We named it Armistead creek after Major Armistead, U. S. Army. A running stream of pure and excellent water, near Saavedra springs." Beale's Report, July 4, 1859. Armistead was with Beale's party. Location of stream not known.

Arnett Creek   Pinal Co.   G. L. O. Map, 1909.

Stream rising at Apache Leap, flowing northwest, joins Queen creek at Superior, southwest of Picket Post mountain. After a family by this name that had a ranch on Queen creek about 1885.

Arntz   Navajo Co.   Santa Fe Maps

Station 8 miles east of Holbrook, on A. T. & S. F. R. R. "For W. P. Arntz, trainmaster Albuquerque Division, later Chief Clerk at San Francisco, Calif." A. G. W.

Arrastra Creek   Yavapai Co.   Map, Prescott N. F., 1927.

Sp. "to drag along." Often spelled Arastra. So called from the presence of these primitive grinding machines for reducing gold ores. In T. 11 N., R. 1 W. Rises east side Longfellow ridge flows southeast into Turkey creek. See Arastra.

Arrowhead Terrace   Coconino Co.

In Grand Canyon N. P. Spur descending southwest towards Colorado river. Between Stone creek and Galloway canyon. So designated because of its form; like an arrowhead. Named by Frank Bond.

Arroya de la Tenaja   Yuma Co.

See La Paz.

Artesa Mountains   Pima Co.   Bryan Map, 1920; U. S. G. S., 1923.

West side Baboquivari valley, Papago Ind. Res. In lat. 30° 30', long. 112°. Origin or meaning unknown.

Artesia   Graham Co.   U. S. G. S. Map, 1923.

Settlement in Gila valley, east side Pinaleno mountains. In T. 9 S., R. 26 E. First artesian water in Gila valley found here. P. O. established Jan. 31, 1912, Aldo A. Allred, P. M.

Artillery Peak   Mohave Co.   U. S. G. S. Map, 1923.

East end Rawhide mountains, in T. 12 N., R. 13 W. North side Bill Williams river. "Following down the Bill Williams Fork we passed the mouth of the Santa Maria. On the right a volcanic cone was named Artillery Peak." Whipple's Report, 1854. Marcou, his geologist, says: "Whipple so named it. It is in the southern end of the Cerbat range; is pointed and has blackish sides."

Ash Creek   Gila Co.   Smith Map, 1879; San Carlos Ind. Res., 1917.

On San Carlos Ind. Res. Rises south side Natanes plateau; flows northwest, enters San Carlos river in T. 21 E., R. 1 N. At certain places along this stream there were fine groves of ash trees.

Ash Creek   Graham Co.   U. S. G. S. Map, 1923.

Rises lower end Mescal mountains. Flows northwest into Gila about 3 miles above Winkelman. "Because of the many ash trees along its course."

Ash Spring   Greenlee Co.

About 30 miles east of Pima. For the ash trees at the spring. Favorite watering and camping place of early days. Scene of killings by Indians, supposed to be the Apache Kid, of Horatio Merrill and his 14-year-old daughter, Dec. 3, 1895.

Ashdale   Maricopa Co.   Map, Tonto N. F., 1928.

In sec. 6, T. 7 N., R. 5 E. Forest Ranger station and ranch on Cave creek. "So called because of the fine ash trees along the creek."

Ash Flat   Graham Co.   U. S. G. S. Map, 1923.

Large open valley in southeast corner, San Carlos Ind. Res. Northeast of Gila mountains. Bonita creek flows across it.

Ash Fork   Yavapai Co.   G. L. O. Map, 1921.

Elevation 5,128 feet. Station and division point on A. T. & S. F. R. R. For many years stages for Prescott started from here. In Jan., 1892, the Prescott-Phoenix branch began building south from Ash Fork. Named by F. W. Smith, Gen'l. Supt. of old Atlantic and Pacific R. R. in 1882, because of ash trees on the town site. P. O. established April 2, 1883, Henry W. Kline, P. M.

Ashurst   Graham Co.   G. L. O. Map, 1921.

On southern side Gila river, on Arizona-Eastern R. R., one mile west of Cork station. After U. S. Senator Henry F. Ashurst. McClintock says: "first called Redlands." P. O. established Jan. 8, 1919.

Ashurst Lake   Coconino Co.   Map, Coconino N. F., 1928.

In T. 19 N., R. 9 E. Northeast of Mormon lake. After William Ashurst, pioneer cattleman, father of Senator Ashurst. In 1900 Mr. Ashurst was prospecting in the Grand Canyon above Bright Angel creek. Accidentally caught under a dislodged boulder he was unable to release himself and died of exhaustion. When found he had written his last messages in a small note book which lay by his side. He was buried on the rim on the Canyon above.

Assumption, Rio de la

See Gila river.

Atascosa Mountain   Santa Cruz Co.   Smith Map, 1879; Map, Coronado N. F., 1931.

Sp. "atasco," a barrier, an obstruction. In southwest Santa Cruz county, at south end of Tumacacori mountains, in T. 23 S., R. 11 E. "To the west of the Santa Cruz valley at Tubac, the Atascoso range, brown, bald and bare, looked down on the old town; a rugged specimen of Arizona range." Hinton.

Athos   Mohave Co.   Santa Fe folders.

Station on A. T. & S. F. R. R. 18 miles west of Kingman. "First called Signal. In 1912 name was changed to Tungsten. In 1913 was named Athos for no particular reason except to save telegraphing. It was short and quickly written." Letter, S. W. Simpson, Supt.

Atlantic and Pacific Land Grant

Federal grant to Atlantic and Pacific R. R. covering every alternate section of land 30 miles wide on each side of the track. Added to this, was another strip 10 miles wide on each side known as "lieu lands," to replace lands already in private ownership within the original grant, such as patented homesteads, military reservations, Spanish grants, etc. This made a strip of land 80 miles wide, the track its center, every alternate unclaimed section of which belongs to the railroad. Extends entirely across the State. Some of this land has been sold to lumbermen, stockmen, and settlers, but the greater part is still in the hands of the railroad.

Grant covered originally over ten million acres.

Aubrey Peak and **Landing**   Mohave Co.   G. L. O. Map, 1921.

Peak in T. 12 N., R. 15 W. Landing is at mouth of Bill Williams Fork. Important early day landing place for Colorado river steamers, 250 miles above Yuma. Named for Francois Xavier Aubrey, known as the "Skimmer of the Plains." In 1850 he rode horseback from Santa Fe, New Mexico to Independence, Mo. on a wager of $1,000 that he could do it in eight days. He finished in three hours less than that time, killing several horses on the ride. He repeated the ride later in even less time." By one account, Aubrey was killed by Indians in southwestern Colorado, August 13, 1871. Historians agree however that he was killed at Santa Fe in a personal encounter with Major Weightman. P. O. so named established Oct. 2, 1866, Henry F. Lightner, P. M.

Aubrey Spring   Coconino Co.   G. L. O. Map, 1921.

Hualpai Ind. Res. Under upper rim of Grand Canyon, in approximately T. 28 N., R. 8 W. After Francois X. Aubrey. See Aubrey Landing.

Aubrey, Valley and **Cliffs**   Coconino Co.   G. L. O. Map, 1921.

Valley lies along main A. T. & S. F. R. R. A favorite stock grazing area. Cliffs are on east side of Colorado river near Hualpai Ind. Res. Extend south about 40 miles from Grand Canyon. See Audrey and Aubrey.

Audrey   Yavapai Co.   Smith Map, 1879, Audrey; G. L. O., 1921, and U. S. G. S., 1923, spelled Audley.

Station on A. T. & S. F. R. R. 11 miles west of Seligman. At head of Aubrey valley and should be spelled that way. After F. X. Aubrey. See Aubrey Landing. "It was originally Aubrey, but there was another station on the Santa Fe by this name of much earlier use, so it was changed to Audrey." A. G. W.

Aultman   Yavapai Co.   U. S. G. S. Map, 1923; Prescott N. F., 1928.

In T. 14 N., R. 4 E. Early settlement and P. O. on Verde river. "After a family by this name which once lived here. P. O. discontinued in 1915. There is now nothing but a service station and small store." Letter, R. W. Wingfield, P. M., Camp Verde. "Mr. Boyer, an old timer, says Aultman was the name of the old post office at the Conger mill. It was named after a man named Aultman who lived there. He says the name has always been used for the Middle Verde P. O. whenever they have had one." Letter, Forest Supervisor Grubb, Prescott. P..O. established June 10, 1896, John H. Lee, P. M.

Avondale   Maricopa Co.

In T. 1 N., R. 1 W. Station on Buckeye branch Arizona-Eastern R. R., 20 miles west of Phoenix. "Avondale was the name given the town site laid out by the R. R. one mile west of Coldwater. P. O. and station were established there. But, when the station was abandoned the P. O. was moved back to the Coldwater location, but the postal authorities retained the name Avondale." Letter, E. B. Pentland, P. M. See Coldwater.

Avra Valley   Pima Co.   U. S. G. S. Map, 1923.

East of Silver Bell. "Said to be a Papago word meaning 'Big Plain.' " Letter, P. M., Rillito. "A vast flood basin into which many arroyos run down from the surrounding mountains to lose themselves therein." Hornaday.

"On April 6, 1934, the name Avra was brought to our attention by the U. S. G. S. which pointed out that many maps gave two names for the same valley. Avra for the northern fraction and Altar for the southern. The Board thereupon decided the question as follows. Avra valley in Arizona for the northern section which drains north; its waters ultimately reaching the Gila river. Altar valley is the valley of the Rio Altar in Mexico draining southwest; its waters ultimately reaching the Gulf of California." Letter Secretary U. S. G. B. July 13, 1934.

This indicates there are two separate valleys, one in Mexico sloping to the southwest from close to the American line; the other draining to the north in Arizona.

Awatobi (sic)   Navajo Co.   Gregory Map, 1916; G. L. O., 1921.

Village and canyon about 6 miles east of Keam's Canyon. "One of the old Hopi Pueblos. Word is Hopi and means 'High place of the Bow,' referring to the Bow People Clan. One of the original villages of Tusayan; visited by Tobar and Cardenas in 1540; Espejo in 1583; Onate in 1598. Seat of Franciscan Mission of San Bernardino in 1629 under Father Porras who was poisoned by the Hopi in 1633. Pueblo was attacked and burned in Nov. 1700, by men from the neighboring pueblos who disliked the inhabitants because of their friendly feeling for the Spanish. The walls of the old Spanish church are still standing." Hodge.

The Spanish called it "Agua-tuy-ba." Dr. Walter Hough says in his book *The Hopi:* "Here may be traced the walls of the Mission of San Bernardino de Awatobi, a large church built out of blocks of mud mixed with straw. When I visited the site in 1892, there was nothing but a great mound of drifting sand to mark the spot where the ancient city was said to be buried." In 1898 the city was dug from the sands by Dr. Fewkes. It lies at the southern end of the Jadito Mesa. Originally the canyon it is in was called Coal Canyon, because of a small coal mine there. Arizona officials asked to have it changed to Awatobi, which was done. Decision U.S.G.B.; Awatubi.

Ayer Peak   Coconino Co.

Mountain at right of Hance canyon in Grand Canyon. Called Ayer peak for Mrs. Ed. E. Ayer of Flagstaff and Chicago, the first white woman to descend the canyon at this point." Mr. Ayer came to Flagstaff in 1881 and started the Ayer Lumber Co. He was a pioneer of Arizona, serving in the California Volunteer Regiment in 1860. President of the Field Columbian Museum at Chicago for many years." James.

Azansosi Mesa   Navajo Co.   Gregory Map, 1913.

Mesa about 10 miles from the Utah line; northwest of Kayenta P. O. Navajo Ind. Res. According to Father Haile, this is the Navajo name for Mrs. John Wetherell, wife of the discoverer of the Mesa Verde ruins. Mesa so called by Gregory. Sept. 30, 1933, Mrs. Wetherill writes: "Name should be spelled, As-thon-So-sie, meaning 'slender woman.' "

Aztec   Cochise Co.

P. O. established July 21, 1887, William W. Smith, P. M. Name changed to Wilgus, Feb. 21, 1891. See Wilgus.

Aztec   Santa Cruz Co.   Eckhoff Map, 1880.

Location of the old Aztec mill of early years. On the Sonoita river 8 or 10 miles below Camp Crittenden. P. O. established Dec. 6, 1878, Christian Foster, P. M.

Aztec   Yuma Co.   U. S. G. S. Map, 1923.

Station on S. P. R. R. established 1881. Eighty miles east of Yuma. P. O. established Sept. 12, 1889, Charles A. Dallen, P. M.

Aztec Hills   Yuma Co.   U. S. G. S. Map, 1923.

In T. 7 S., R. 12 W. 3 miles south of Aztec station, S. P. R. R.

Aztec Pass   Yavapai Co.   U. S. G. S. Map, Prescott sheet, 1892;
G. L. O., 1921.

Ten miles west of Juniper P. O. near lat. 34° 54′, long. 112° 58′. In Santa Maria mountains east of Baca grant, west side Williamson valley, which Wheeler called "Val de Chino." "From a fancy founded on the evident antiquity of the ruins, we have given the name Aztec Pass, to this place." Wheeler, Jan. 23, 1853.

Aztec Peak   Gila Co.   Map, Tonto N. F., 1927.

In sec. 5 T. 5 N., R. 14 E. Aztec is a common name all over the southwest. Bud Armer says his father called it "Lookout Peak" because they used it as a lookout in hunting cattle and horses. He did not know how or when the name Aztec originated. See Armer.

Aztlan

Name of a proposed town at junction of Verde and Salt rivers to which, Oct. 24, 1864, the first Territorial Legislature tried to move the capital from Prescott. See La Paz and Walnut Grove.

There was also a mining camp by this name located about 6 miles south of Prescott where in 1866 a rather primitive quartz mill was erected to handle ores from Peck mine.

"The name is generally accepted to cover the region from which came the Aztecs or the native races in Mexico at the time of the Spanish conquest." Said by some writers to have been in Jalisco or Michoacan on the west coast of Mexico.

The French student and writer, Biart, says: "It was the original country of the Aztecs."

Aztlan was the name of the first Masonic lodge in Arizona. Opened in the upper rooms of the old log capital at Prescott, July 25, 1866.

Azul, Rio de

See Bill Williams river.

Baba Canora

See Babocomari.

Babbitts   Coconino Co.   G. L. O. Map, 1892.

In T. 20 N., R. 8 E. Station Central Arizona R. R. south of Flagstaff. "We had to have some stations on this road so we named them for local people. After the Babbitt Bros. who had a large store at Flagstaff." Letter, M. J. Riordan, Flagstaff.

Babocomari Land Grant   Cochise and Santa Cruz Cos.
G. L. O. Map, 1921.

Mexican land grant owned, 1880-1886, by Dr. E. B. Perrin, W. C. Land, I. N. Towne, and others. Occupied as headquarters for their cattle interests. According to Hodge this is a Papago word, meaning unknown.

The full name is San Ignacio del Babacomari (sic). Grant made originally to Ignacio and Eulalia Elias, Dec. 25, 1832. The U. S. Land Court approved to Dr. E. B. Perrin 34,707 acres of the total claimed.

Babocomari River   Santa Cruz Co.   G. L. O. Map, 1921.

Rises in Babocomari Land Grant eastern edge Canelo Hills; flows northeast, enters San Pedro river at Fairbanks in T. 20 S., R. 21 E. Cremony, in 1850 writes: "A pretty little stream which the Mexican hunters referred to as Baba Canora entered the San Pedro about 25 miles above where we camped. Near a ruined hacienda were the remains of an orchard of fruit trees. The wild horses which the Mexicans were hunting were all over this valley."

Baboquivari Mountains   Pima Co.   U. S. G. S. Map, 1923.

East side Papago Ind. Res. in R. 7 E. Extends from Mexican border north to Quinlan mountain. East side Altar valley. Franciscan Fathers say it is a Papago word meaning "narrow in the middle." Lumholtz adds: "When viewed from the valley there is a well developed waist about the middle of the mountain." Papago name is "Vav ki valik."

Harold Bell Wright in *Long Ago Told* calls it "Behoo-ku-vu-legi," drawn in in the middle. Papago legends say the mountain was once shaped like an hour glass but a tremendous upheaval came and the top slid off leaving only the lower part of the hour glass effect remaining. The international boundary commission of 1891-1896, calls these the Pozo Verde mountains, after the nearby water holes. "Because the holes were always surrounded by tall green rushes and other aquatic shrubbery."

Emory, 1854, says the name means "Water on the mountains" from a Papago word " 'Babu'-water, and 'qui'-mountains or rock." Decision U. S. G. B.

Baboquivari Peak   Pima Co.   G. L. O. Map, 1921.

In Baboquivari mountains. Elevation 7,740 feet. In T. 19 S., R. 7 E. Papago Ind. Res. Hinton, 1876, wrote: "The sharp peak of the Baboquivari is in sight all day, a well defined, eagle-headed peak." Name in Papago means, "with its bill or beak in the air." Descriptive name.

Baca Float Grant   Yavapai Co.

See Luis Maria Baca Grant.

Bacobi   Navajo Co.   G. L. O. Map, 1923.

One of the modern Hopi villages lying a few miles north of Oraibi. In T. 16 E., R. 29 N. See Hotevila.

Badger and Soap Creeks   Coconino Co.

Two small streams entering Colorado river about 10 miles due west of Lee's Ferry on north side. Rise under Vermillion cliffs.

"Jacob Hamblin killed a badger on one of these creeks. It was carried to another creek and put on the fire to boil. In the morning, instead of stew, the alkalai in the water and the fat from the badger had resulted in a kettle of soap. Hence the name." Fish Ms.

Badgers Well   Pima Co.

Waterhole in Papago Ind. Res. In Comobabi mountains. Origin not known.

Bagdad   Yavapai Co.   G. L. O. Map, 1912.

On Burro creek western side of county. Origin unknown. P. O. established Feb. 26, 1910, Henry A. Geisendorfer, P. M.

Bagley   Navajo Co.

First name for Taylor on Showlow creek. Was also called Walker. "Daniel Bagley was an early settler on the site of Taylor." Fish Ms.

Bagnall   Navajo Co.   Map, Sitgreaves N. F., 1924.

On Bagnall Hollow about 5 miles north of Showlow. In sec. 21, T. 10 N., R. 21 E. Originally settled by George Bagnall, shoemaker who followed his trade here, about 1881-1885. His boots were all local product, leather tanned at Snowflake, etc. When Bagnall left here about 1886, Aaron (Rone) Adair and his brothers moved into the Hollow above Bagnall's old place and the location then became Adair.

Bagnall Hollow   Navajo Co.   Map, Sitgreaves N. F., 1924.

Dry wash near Fort Apache Ind. Res. in T. 10 N., R. 21 E. Runs northeast into Showlow creek in sec. 11, T. 10 N., R. 21 E., 3 miles below Showlow settlement. See Bagnall.

Baker Butte   Coconino Co.   G. L. O. Map, 1883; Rand-McNally, 1883; Elliott, 1884, Backer. U. S. G. S., 1923, Baker.

Elevation 8,120 feet. In T. 12 N., R. 9 E. On rim of basin. Capt. John G. Bourke, Crook's Aide, told the author about 1882, this was named by Crook for an army surgeon named Baecker and should be spelled that way. There is, however, no record of such an officer. Smith map, 1879, has it Backer's Butte, which perhaps is the correct word. There is a story in the upper basin to the effect that the butte was named for a man named Baker who once owned and worked a mine on this butte and had several half breed Indian sons. Rather doubtful.

Baker Mountain   Gila Co.   G. L. O. Map, 1921; Tonto N. F., 1927.

In Ts. 5, 6 N., R. 14 E. South side Reynolds creek, Sierra Ancha range, south of Center mountain. "In 1885 John H. Baker planted potatoes at this mountain and packed them to Silver King some 40 miles away. Has since been known as Baker Mountain." Letter, Rex King, Forest Supervisor, Safford. Sometimes called Lookout mountain. Also Fray Marcos mountain.

Baker Peaks   Yuma Co.   U. S. G. S. Map, 1923.

In T. 9 S., R. 17 W., south of S. P. R. R. Two small buttes standing close together. North peak is 1,416 feet, South peak, 1,409 feet in elevation. "After a man named Baker who drove stage between Blue Water and Tucson. Murdered by Mexicans in Dec. 1871." Letter, Mrs. J. B. Martin, Salome.

Bald Hill   Yavapai Co.   Map, Prescott N. F., 1927.

In T. 18 N., R. 1 W. Bald isolated butte north side Verde river. There is another Bald hill near Prescott q. v.

Bald Hill   Yavapai Co.

An isolated mountain in sec. 17, T. 14 N., R. 1 W. About 5½ miles northeast of Prescott N. F. See Glassford mountain.

Bald Knob   Cochise Co.   Map, Coronado N. F., 1927.

In T. 22 S., R. 28 E., in Sulphur Springs valley, 12 miles north of Douglas. An outstanding "bald" mountain.

Bald Mountain   Yavapai Co.   G. L. O. Map, 1921.

In Black hills about 2 miles southwest of Squaw peak. Descriptive name.

Baldy Mountain   Apache Co.   U. S. G. S. Map, 1923.

See Thomas peak.

Baldy Mountain   Greenlee Co.   G. L. O. Map, 1921.

Elevation 6,415 feet. In T. 3 S., R. 32 E. Crook N. F. About 12 miles northeast of Clifton. Summit is bare, or bald.

Ballard Mountain   Cochise Co.   G. L. O. Map, 1921.

In Escambrosa ridge, 4 miles west of Bisbee. "Ballard was the first mine operator at Bisbee." Letter, M. C. Egnell, Bisbee.

Ballenger   Navajo Co.

Settlement on Little Colorado river, located by, and named for, Jesse O. Ballenger in March, 1876.

"Ballenger was the leader of one of the four companies of Mormons who came early in 1876, to establish settlements in Northern Arizona. Ballenger's company located 4 miles southwest of Sunset Crossing east side Little Colorado river, east of present Winslow. Later it was called Brigham City." q. v. Mormon settlement.

Balls of Silver   Santa Cruz Co.

See Bolas de Plata.

Bangs Mountain   Mohave Co.   U. S. G. S. Map, 1923.

Elevation 7,500 feet. East side Virgin mountains. In extreme northwest corner of State. Clarence King named it for James E. Bangs, clerk with his party.

"After several days below St. George, Utah, we made a long, hard ride and climb. Camped at the base of what is now called Mount Bangs, the highest peak of the Virgin Mountains." Dellenbaugh.

Bangharts   Yavapai Co.   Eckhoff Map, 1880.

Stage station, on road between Ash Fork and Prescott, where stages stopped for meals. The presence of Banghart's attractive daughters made this place very popular. Located 1866, and owned by George Banghart. Now called Del Rio, on A. T. & S. F. R. R. Said to be the location of the Postle ranch where the first Territorial capital was located. First called Chino, later Banghart's with George W. Banghart P. M. Nov. 13, 1885. Gov. Safford visited Banghart's in 1873 and mentions the visit in his report for that year. Banghart died at Del Rio in July, 1895.

Bannon   Apache Co.   G. L. O. Map, 1920.

Apache N. F. In T. 10 N., R. 25 E. Small settlement and P. O. After James Bannon, early settler and cattleman. Elizabeth S. Marble, P. M., March 19, 1920.

Banta Point   Coconino Co.

In Grand Canyon N. P. on west wall of canyon, near northeast corner of park. In lat. 36° 13', long. 111° 55'. Named for A. F. Banta by Will C. Barnes. Banta, a pioneer of pioneers, was chief scout for General Crook, at Fort Whipple, 1865-1871. "Born in Indiana, 1846. Under name of Charles A. Franklin, went to Arizona 1863; member of 12th Legislature; chief guide, Wheeler expedition, 1873; district attorney, 1879-80; Probate Judge Apache Co., 1881-82; postmaster, deputy sheriff, and Deputy U. S. Marshall, etc." Farish.

Banta's name, up to about 1882, was Charles A. Franklin.

When the author first met him at Fort Apache in 1880, he was known as Charles Franklin and was U. S. Census Agent. Later he changed his name to A. F. Banta. A brother, Henry Banta, died at Flagstaff about 1892. Banta was elected to the Twelfth Territorial Legislature Jan. 1883, as C. A. Franklin. He again changed his name about 1888 when he entered the banking business in St. Johns.

In his personally written history Banta says: "In 1870 my name was Charles Elbert Franklin." But in his story "The Message to Garcia" he calls himself "Charley Franklin Banta." Later in an article in *Pick and Drill*, July 3, 1897, he calls himself "Albert Franklin Banta." See Springerville.

Barbencita Butte   Coconino Co.

In Grand Canyon N. P. Just above mouth of Nankoweap creek, near lat. 36° 18′, long. 111° 53′. Named by Frank Bond for Barbencita, a friendly chief of the Navajos, who in 1871 aided the second Powell expedition through the canyon. Decision U. S. G. B.

Barbershop Canyon   Coconino Co.   Map, Coconino N. F., 1928.

Heads about 3 miles east of Generals springs in sec. 9, T. 12 N., R. 11 E. Runs north into East Clear creek, in north end of T. 13 N., R. 11 E.

"On the east slope of Dick Hart Ridge, at a spring, there was a sheep shearing plant. One of the men was a good barber and shaved the men and cut their hair. So they called it Barbershop Spring and Canyon." Letter, E. R. Smith, Forest Ranger.

Bargeman Wash and Well   Navajo Co.   Gregory Map, 1916.

In T. 23 N., R. 16 E. North of Winslow. Wash flows into Cone creek south of Tolani lakes. After Joe Bargeman, local stockman, who about 1888, came here, dug a well and located a herd of cattle, much to the disgust of the Navajos who claimed the range as theirs.

Barkerville   Pinal Co.

P. O. and store about 32 miles southeast of Florence. In Round valley on old stage road, Tucson to Florence. After the Barker family who had an early day cattle ranch here. P. O. established about 1885, Mrs. Ruth B. Barker, P. M.

Bar M. Canyon   Coconino Co.   Map, Coconino N. F., 1927.

Short canyon, north of Rock Top mountain. In T. 17 N., R. 8 E. "Matt Burch ran cattle here in the Bar M brand for many years. Named after his outfit." Letter, Bud Ming, Ray.

Barnes Peak   Gila Co.   Map, Crook N. F., 1926.

Elevation 5,028 feet. In sec. 31, T. 2 N., R. 14 E. So called by Dr. F. L. Ransome, U. S. G. S. "after a prospector by this name who had a mine at this peak in the Silver King district." Ransome discovered an unusual geological formation near the Barnes mine which he called "Barnes Conglomerate." Hinton. Ransome U. S. G. S. No. 12, 1903.

Barney Spring   Coconino Co.   Map, Coconino N. F., 1927.

In sec. 31, T. 19 N., R. 6 E. "Jim Barney ran stock west of Oak Creek in early days. The Barney pasture and this spring where he lived were named after him." Letter, Ed Miller, Forest Supervisor.

Barnhart Canyon   Gila Co.   Map, Tonto N. F., 1926.

In upper Tonto basin, east side Mazatzal range. Empties into Rye creek in sec. 18, T. 9 N., R. 9 E. "Named for Barnhart, a settler who located a ranch at the mouth of the canyon in Rye creek." Fred Croxen, Forest Ranger.

Barr   Pinal Co.   R. R. Maps.

Spur, Phoenix & Eastern R. R., 3 miles east of Florence.

Fort Barrett   Maricopa Co.

Small fortification at White's Mill, Pima Village, on Gila river. Erected by California troops in April, 1862. Named by Gen. Carlton for Lieut. James Barrett, Co. A, California Volunteers, killed in fight with Confederate troops at Picacho. q. v.

Heitman's List says: "It was established May 31, 1862, and abandoned July 23, 1862.

"At the Pima Villages was a small post named Fort Barrett, after the first Union officer killed in the Arizona campaign. It was in reality only an earth work thrown around a trading post." McClintock.

Barriers, The   Mohave Co.

Some rapids in the Colorado river described by J. Ross Browne in 1866, as about half way between Yuma and La Paz. Rhodes who had a ranch in Santa Cruz county near Tubac also had a ranch at these rapids in 1866. He was drowned near it while crossing the river. See Rhodes.

Basalt Creek   Coconino Co.

Grand Canyon N. P. Intermittent stream rising in lat. 36° 08', long. 111° 53'. Flows southeast into Colorado river. Skirts southwest base of "Basalt cliffs." Geological descriptive name. Named by Frank Bond.

Basin   Mohave Co.

"The place was a regular basin in the mountains." Letter, P. M., Hackberry. P. O. established March 17, 1904. Eugene D. Chandler, P. M.

Bass   Coconino Co.   G. L. O. Map, 1921.

In T. 30 N., R. 2 E. Coconino plateau Grand Canyon N. P. Station on Grand Canyon R. R. After W. W. Bass, early settler, explorer, guide for this entire region. Born Shelbyville, Ind., 1849. Locator of Mystic spring in the canyon.

According to George Wharton James, Captain Burro, a Havasupai Indian, led Bass to this spring which he, Ross, previously could not discover. For this, Bass gave him a sack of flour and half a beef. Bass built a good trail to the spring. The author camped there with him for several days in Dec., 1888. Bass died at Wickenburg, Jan. 18, 1933, at the age of 84. His ashes were scattered in the Grand Canyon.

Bass Point   Coconino Co.

See Havasupai Point.

Bassett Peak   Graham Co.   U. S. G. S. Map, 1923.

In T. 10 S., R. 20 E., at lower end of Galiuro mountains in Crook N. F. "After Bob Bassett, early day cattleman who ran cattle near this peak." Letter, H. T. Firth, Safford.

Batamote Mountains and Well   Pima Co.   G. L. O. Map, 1921.

In T. 11 S., Rs. 4-5 W., mountain east of Childs Station. Bata-mote Well is at its foot. Papago for arrow weed. Lumholtz says: "Tom Childs lives at Batamote." See Childs Station.

Batesville   Pinal Co.   G. L. O. Map, 1893.

On Gila river about 12 miles above Riverside. After J. T. Bates of Bates, Newman and Co., mining men of 1893. An advertise-ment in the *Tucson Enterprise,* July 27, 1893, tells of the fine future of the town. "Invest your surplus cash in Batesville lots and reap a rich reward." Batesville is not listed in 1933 among Arizona towns, large or small.

Bates Well   Pima Co.   U. S. G. S. Map, 1923.

Also called Growler Well. In Papago, Tjuni-kaat, "where there is sahuaro fruit." About 20 miles north of Quitovaquito at southern end Growler mountains. In T. 14 S., R. 6 W.

Hornaday says: "The Mexicans call it 'El Veit,' but for what or whom, I don't know. It is commonly called the Growler Well after the nearby mountains."

Battle Flat   Yavapai Co.   Map, Prescott N. F., 1927.

In T. 11 N., R. 1 W. North side Tuscumbia creek. "Small open area a few miles east of Walnut Creek, in the Bradshaw mountains, where in May, 1861, five or six men had a fight with Indians." Farish.

"The fight was in May, 1864, with a band of Indians. Fred Henry, Samuel Herron, and several others were in it." Banta. "Named for a battle by Steward Hall, Frank Binkely, De Mor-gan Scott, Samuel Herron and Fred Henry who were camped there. They were attacked by Apaches and had a three days fight in June, 1864. Several of the men were wounded but help finally came and the Apaches withdrew." Fish Ms.

Battleship Mountain   Mohave Co.   G. L. O. Map, 1921.

In T. 20 N., R. 20 W. "Northeast of Goldroad at north end of Ute mountains. About 12 miles east of Colorado river. De-scriptive name. It resembles a huge battleship." Letter, P. M., Kingman.

Battleship Peak   Yuma Co.   G. L. O. Map, 1921.

In T. 9 N., R. 15 W. About 8 miles south of Swansea. "A very descriptive name. The peak looks like some great battleship of modern times." Letter, P. M., Swansea.

Bawtry   Cochise Co.   R. R. Guides.

Station on S. P. R. R. about 19 miles east of Bowie. Origin and meaning unknown.

Bayard   Yavapai Co.   G. L. O. Map, 1892.

Mining camp on Humbug creek near Wasson peak. Named after James A. Bayard, Secretary of Territory, 1887. P. O. established, May 25, 1888. William B. Long, P. M.

Beal   Mohave Co.   Santa Fe Folders.

First railroad station on eastern side Colorado river, east of the Needles on A. T. & S. F. R R. "Beal was trainmaster for this division in the early days of the Atlantic & Pacific R. R. The station was named after him and not for the explorer." A. G. W.

Beale Camp   Mohave Co.

This was at Beale's springs near Kingman. Fish says it was a military camp up to about 1876. "Camp Beale Springs was established as an Indian Agency in Jan., 1873. It was a post office on the Beale's Springs Ind. Res." Farish. On Heitman's List, it is called "Camp Beale's Springs, 43 miles east of Fort Mohave, on the Big Sandy. Established, May 25, 1871. Abandoned April 6, 1874." See Beale spring.

Beale Spring   Mohave Co.   Smith Map, 1879; G. L. O., 1892.

A few miles northwest of Kingman. Named for Lieut. E. F. Beale, the explorer. Beale was a graduate midshipman and lieutenant in U. S. Navy during the Mexican war. At its close, Beale resigned from the Navy, and became an explorer. Most widely known was his *Survey for a wagon road from Fort Smith, Ark., to the Colorado river, 1858-59.* Died in 1893. Named many places in northern Arizona. His brother George was one of his party in these years.

"Beale's Spring did not differ from the other ranches except that possibly it was even more desolate. A German lived there who must have had a knowledge of cookery, for we bought a peach pie which we ate with relish. I remember we paid him a big silver dollar for it." *Vanished Arizona,* September, 1874.

Hinton says: "Beale's Spring is an abandoned military post." P. O. established by this name March 17, 1873, Benjamin H. Spear, P. M. See Camp Beale.

Bean   Cochise Co.

Station near present town of Teviston. P. O. established under the name Bean, Sept. 28, 1881, Henry A. Smith, P. M. Shortly after this, the name was changed to Teviston, q. v. Origin unknown.

Bear   Yavapai Co.   Santa Fe Folders.

Station on Drake and Clarkdale branch, A. T. & S. F. R. R., 32 miles southeast of Ash Fork. "While building the road a bear was shot here." A. G. W.

Bear Creek   Gila Co.   G. L. O. Map, 1921.

On San Carlos Ind. Res. Tributary of San Carlos river from north, in T. 19 E. Rs. 1, 2 N.

Bear Headland   Coconino Co.

In Grand Canyon N. P. In lat. 36° 18', long. 112° 36'. "On west side upper reach of Coconino Plateau, with an outline strongly resembling the head of a bear." Named by Frank Bond.

Bear Hills   Yuma Co.   G. L. O. Map, 1921.

East of Haystack peak, west side of Ranegras plains.

Bear Mountain   Greenlee Co.   U. S. G. S. Map, 1923.

Northwest corner, T. 2 N., R. 30 E. On Mogollon Rim, Crook N. F.

Bear Springs   Cochise Co.   Smith Map, 1879.

"Ojos de los Osos." At southern end Whetstone range, about 35 miles from Tucson.

Here, May 5, 1871, Lieut. Howard B. Cushing, 3rd. U. S. Cavalry, was mortally wounded in a fight with ambushed Apaches under Cochise. Cushing, who came to Arizona in 1869, was one of the famous Cushing brothers. One blew up the Rebel Ram "Albermarle"; another was killed at Gettysburg; still another enlisted in the Navy during the Civil War and died in the service. Fish, very gracefully, calls Cushing "The Custer of Arizona."

Bear Spring   Coconino Co.

Spring at which Beale camped near the San Francisco mountains in July, 1859. Beale says: "It was about 4 miles west of where we met the two men on camels." This was about 20 miles west of the Cosnino cave. Undoubtedly the present day Elden spring, about 4 miles northeast of Flagstaff.

Bear Springs   Navajo Co.

So called, because on the roundup about 1885, a bear was killed here by roping him. At one of the heads of Dacker wash, in T. 11 N., R. 17 E., about 10 miles east of Phoenix Park.

Ranch located about 1886, by one James Stott, a boy from Massachusetts, who started a horse ranch here known as the "Circle Dot" ranch. Because of his alleged affiliations with questionable horse dealers, he was taken from his cabin here in August, 1887, by a vigilance committee and hanged, with two other men, near where the Holbrook-Pleasant Valley trail crossed the Verde road.

Bear Valley Mountains

See Pajarita.

Bear Wallow Creek   Greenlee Co.   U. S. G. S. Map, 1923;
Apache N. F., 1926.

Rises in Blue range, in T. 3 N., Rs. 28, 29 E. flows northwest into Black river at Greenlee county line. "In 1884 when Pete Slaughter drove his cattle into this valley bears were very numerous. Their 'wallows' were everywhere along the creek, where the animals came to fight flies." Letter, Arthur Slaughter, Springerville.

Beardsley   Maricopa Co.   G. L. O. Map, 1921.

Station and P. O. on A. T. & S. F. R. R. 24 miles northwest of Phoenix, in T. 1 W., R. 4 N. After Will H. Beardsley of New York and Phoenix, who started an irrigation project here in 1888.

Beauchamp Peak   Apache Co.

On White Mountain Ind. Res. Named by Woolsey for J. W. Beauchamp, one of his party killed on this mountain by Apaches, in July, 1864. Woolsey with one hundred volunteers left Prescott March 29, 1864. His report to Gov. Goodwin, July 24, 1864, states:

"Mr. J. W. Beauchamp left camp to go to the top of this high, round mountain. He was waylaid and shot by six Indians who left him for dead. He was alive when we arrived but died before reaching camp. His body was buried at the foot of the mountain, which we named Beauchamp Peak. The San Carlos River headed on the northeast side of the peak."

The San Carlos heads in the Natanes mountains near Natanes peak and it was probably this peak Woolsey was describing.

Beauford, Clay

See Mt. Buford.

Beautiful Valley   Apache Co.   G. L. O. Map, 1920.

Valley about 15 miles long, in Ts. 2, 3 N., R. 10 W. On Navajo Ind. Res. north of Ganado mesa. "So called by the first persons who entered this valley."

Beaver Creek   Yavapai Co.   U. S. G. S. Map, 1923.

Formed by Dry, and Wet Beaver creeks at Montezuma Castle, in T. 14 N., R. 5 E. Flows southwest, enters Verde river at Camp Verde. Early settlers found many beavers in this stream.

Beaver Dam   Mohave Co.

"Settlement on Beaver Dam creek. The people asked for a post office but the department would not accept this name. So they compromised on Littlefield, q. v. The Church records speak of the damage done to the pioneers' dams and ditches by beavers. The Mormons claim this was the first Anglo-Saxon settlement in the original Arizona, 1863. There is still a town called Beaver Dam but no P. O. It is 3 miles east of the Nevada line." Letter, Walter Cannon, P. M., St. George, Utah.

Beaver Dam Creek   Mohave Co.   Smith Map, 1879; G. L. O., 1921.

Rises in Lincoln county, Nevada, on east side of Mormon mountains. Enters Mohave county, Arizona, near long. 114°; flows southeast, enters Virgin river at Littlefield. Some historians assume that this Beaver Dam creek was the Virgin river. The old maps, however, show it as a separate stream entering the Virgin from the west, at St. Thomas.

Beaver Dam Mountains   Mohave Co.   U. S. G. S. Map, 1920.

Extend from junction Beaver Dam creek and Virgin river, northeast into Washington county, Utah.

Beaver Falls   Coconino Co.

Waterfall in Supai canyon 2 miles below Mooney falls. So called by G. Wharton James for the many beavers in the stream.

Beaver Ranch   Navajo Co.

Early name for the Reidhead crossing of Showlow. When Reidhead first located here in the early Eighties, they caught several beavers along the stream.

Becker Lake   Apache Co.

Artificial lake or reservoir in secs. 19, 28, 30, T. 9 N., R. 29 E. Built by Becker brothers of Springerville in 1893 to impound water to irrigate land in Round valley.

Bedrock Canyon   Coconino Co.

In Grand Canyon N. P. lat. 36° 19½', long. 112° 27½', drains into Colorado river west of Feroz Terrace, west slope of Powell plateau. Named by Frank Bond.

Begashibito Canyon   Navajo Co.   Gregory Map, 1916.

Canyon and stream rising east of White mesa, near Navajo county line, runs south into Klethla valley. Haile says: "A Navajo word meaning 'cattle water.' "

Bek-i-hatso Lake   Apache Co.   U. S. G. S. Map, 1923.

On Navajo Ind. Res. Near lat. 36°, long. 109° 40'. On head of west branch Chinle creek. Navajo word meaning "big lake." Haile.

Belgravia   Pinal Co.   G. L. O. Map, 1921.

Mine and village in Mescal mountains near Kelvin. "Mill site for Arizona Hercules mine. Named by Mr. Adams, of the Hercules, for a suburb of Johannesburg, South Africa, where he once lived. Place now abandoned, buildings gone, nothing left. About one mile from Kelvin." Letter, G. H. Steger, P. M., Ray. P. O. established April 15, 1918. Fred. O. Locke, P. M.

Bell Butte   Maricopa Co.   Map, Maricopa Co., 1928.

Outstanding bell-shaped butte, near the "Double buttes" about 2 miles southwest of Tempe. So called from its shape.

Bell Butte   Pinal Co.   G. L. O. Map, 1921.

About 12 miles west of Kelvin, north side Gila river. In T. 3 S., R. 12 E. At Silver Bell mine. So called for the mine.

Bell's Canyon   Yavapai Co.   Smith Map, 1879

Small stream flowing into Kirkland creek, about 10 miles southwest of Prescott at upper end Peeples valley. Two prospectors, Bell and Sage, were killed here by Indians in 1864. On Nov. 10, 1866, Mr. Leihy, U. S. Supt. of Indian Affairs, and a Mr. Evarts, his clerk, were murdered in this canyon, either by Mexicans or Apaches. Leihy was Poston's successor as Commissioner of Indian Affairs, and on his way to Prescott. The canyon was named for Bell.

Bell Rock   Yavapai Co.   Map, Coconino N. F., 1927.

Butte in sec. 6, T. 16 N., R. 6 E. "It is said to resemble a bell. Name given it by old man James who settled here in 1876." Letter, Ed. Miller, Flagstaff.

Bellemont   Coconino Co.   G. L. O. Map, 1921.

On A. T. & S. F. R. R. Sawmill and lumbering center. "A coined word in honor of Miss Bella Smith, daughter of F. W. Smith, Gen'l. Supt. A. & P. R. R., in construction days." A. G. W. P. O. established March 2, 1887, Frank W. Payne, P. M.

Bellevue   Gila Co.   G. L. O. Map, 1921; Crook N. F., 1926.

Named by Whelen brothers for its fine view. In T. 15 S., R. 14 E. About 8 miles south of Globe. P. O. established July 30, 1906, Edward P. Whelen, P. M.

Benedict, Mount   Santa Cruz Co.   U. S. G. S. Map, 1903; G. L. O., 1921, Benedict.

About 4 miles northeast of Nogales, in sec. 28, T. 23 S., R. 14 E., on Santa Cruz river. Originally a ranch or small mining camp which has disappeared. "Named for an old prospector of local fame. First called Gold Hill because gold was found on its slopes." A. S. Wingo, Forest Ranger. "Smith's map, 1879 shows it Benedictine." Hinton, 1879.

Ben Nevis Mountain   Pima Co.   G. L. O. Map, 1892; U. S. G. S., 1923.

Papago Ind. Res., in Quijotoa mountains. Near lat. 32° 10'. Originally named Quijotoa. Papago word meaning "Carrying-basket mountain." A Scotsman, Alexander McKay, discovered a rich out-crop on this mountain and renamed it Ben Nevis for his homeland.

Another story is that S. A. Manlen gave it this name to honor McKay. Was the center of several lively mining booms.

Benson   Cochise Co.   R. R. Folders.

Elevation 3,575 feet. Town on S. P. R. R. about 48 miles east of Tucson, in T. 17 S., R. 20 E. Benson was an important early shipping point for mines to the south.

"Named by the S. P. R. R. for a peddler who made frequent trips through this place in early days." Letter, L. D. Redfield, Benson. There are several stories about this name, none being well authenticated.

An old list of stage stations, 1880, shows this as "Benson City, William Ohnesorgan owner and keeper of the station, 50 miles east of Tucson."

Capt. Gerald Russell, 3rd. U. S. Cavalry, with eighteen men, had a fight with Cochise and one hundred fifty Indians near here in March, 1871. But for timely arrival of help he and his men would all have been killed. Azul, famous Apache chief, was killed in this fight.

P. O. established July 26, 1880, John Russ, P. M.

Benton   Greenlee Co.   G. L. O. Map, 1908.

"Small settlement at junction Blue and Little Blue rivers, some 50 miles north of Clifton. Named for an early resident who hunted and trapped in this region for many years. Killed by Apaches in the early Eighties." Letter, W. W. Pace, Safford. P. O. established Oct. 10, 1903, Max A. Balke, P. M.

Berados Station   Navajo Co.

Stage station and store at Puerco crossing, 2 miles east of Holbrook. Farish and McClintock spell it as above. E. C. Bunch gives it: "Berrando." The author's recollection is that the person for whom it was named spelled it "Berado." On maps of 1873 as Berado. His full name was Berado Fraiyes, or Fraides, but he only used his given name, Berado.

On Smith map, it is Berado's store; on Eckhoff, Berado's Post Office.

An important point on the old Santa Fe—Prescott Star Mail Route in 1880, when Fort Apache and the Mormon settlements on Silver creek began to get mail from the east over the A. T. & S. F. R. R. The old adobe buildings used by Berado were still there in 1882. See Horsehead Crossing.

Bernardino (sic)   Cochise Co.   G. L. O. Map, 1921.

Station on E. P. & S. W. R. R. about 20 miles northeast of Douglas. Sometimes spelled Bernardina. Original name was San Bernardino. After John Slaughter's famous ranch by this name.

Berry   Mohave Co.   Maps, A. T. & S. F. R. R.

Station on A. T. & S. F. R. R. About 9 miles north of Kingman. "I am unable to say for whom or what this station was named." G. W. Simpson, R. R. Supt.

Betata-kin Ruin   Navajo Co.   Gregory Map, 1916.

North of Marsh Pass, Navajo Ind. Res. Navajo word, which Haile spells Bitatakin, "houses in the rock shelves" or "side hill house."

Bibo   Apache Co.   U. S. G. S. Map, 1923.

Flag station and trading post on A. T. & S. F. R. R. on Puerco river, southwest corner T. 19 N., R. 25 E. After Sol Bibo who had a trading post here 1880-1890.

Bicard's Store   Pinal Co.   Eckhoff Map, 1880.

Station on old Florence stage road about 20 miles east of Maricopa Wells. Bicard Bros. ran three flour mills: one here; another at Adamsville, q.v.; the third at Phoenix, which was burned Sept. 2, 1871.

In the *Tucson Citizen*, Nov. 8, 1873, they advertised: "Flour, cornmeal, pinola, semitella, graham flour and bran from our own mill at Sanford." Signed, Nick Bicard, San Francisco; William Bicard, Sanford, Arizona Territory.

Bidahochi   Navajo Co.   Gregory Map, 1916; G. L. O., 1921.

Spring and trading post in T. 23 N., R. 21 E., Julius Wetzler, trader, 1888-1892. Navajo word meaning "red rock slide," from a rock slide on mountain back of store.

Big Canyon   Navajo Co.   Map, Ft. Apache Ind. Res., 1928.

Stream rising at Big mountain; flows southwest into Cedar creek in sec. 19, T. 7 N., R. 22 E. Named after Big mountain.

Big Creek   Graham Co.   Map, Crook N. F., 1926.

Rises south slope Mount Graham, flows southwest into Grant creek, Fort Grant Military reservation. One of the main sources of water for Fort Grant.

Big Mountain   Navajo Co.   U. S. G. S. Map, 1923;
                                      Map, Ft. Apache Ind. Res., 1928.

In T. 8 N., R. 22 E., 10 miles west of Cooley mountain. So called because it is a very large "fat" mountain solitary and alone.

Big Bonito Creek   Apache and Navajo Cos.

See Bonito creek.

Big Bug   Yavapai Co.   Smith Map, 1879.

In T. 12 N., R. 1 E. Mining camp on Big Bug creek about 15 miles southeast of Prescott. Named after the creek. According to local records the camp was first called Red Rock. Changed to Big Bug Mar. 29, 1881. P. O. established Aug. 22, 1895, Margaret E. Wheeler, P. M.

Big Bug Mesa and Creek   Yavapai Co.   U. S. G. S. Map, 1923.

In T. 12 N., R. 1 W., about 12 miles southeast of Prescott. Banta writes it was so named by John Marion in 1863. According to Orick Jackson, and others, when the first prospectors came to this creek it was covered with large water bugs, probably "skippers," so they named it Big Bug creek, and the name stuck.

Big Chino Valley

See Chino valley.

Big Dry Fork   Coconino and Navajo Cos.

On Sitgreave's map, 1851, also Smith's, 1879, as Big Dry Fork. It is undoubtedly the present East Clear creek, which enters Little Colorado river from south, 3 miles east of Winslow. Sitgreaves in his list of camps, says it is "8 miles from Chevelon Fork" which is exactly the distance. Sitgreaves camped at this wash, Oct. 3, 1852, and speaks of the "deep, rocky canyon, utterly impassable. Had to cross it at its junction with the Little Colorado river." See Big Dry wash and Clear creek.

Big Dry Wash   Coconino Co.

Scene of the last fight between U. S. troops and Apaches in Arizona. Lieut. Col. A. W. Evans, 3rd Cavalry Commanding Officer, called it the "Battle of the Big Dry Wash," in his official report. It was really on East Clear creek, in T. 13 N., R. 11 E.

"The fight was July 17, 1882, 3 to 6 P. M. Lieut. Col. A. W. Evans commanding. Indians were White Mountain Apaches under Na-ti-a-tish. We found only twenty-two dead bodies. I counted them myself the next day for the official record." Letter General Thomas Cruse, May 18, 1929.

Forest officers have located the battlefield on East Clear creek west of where General Springs canyon enters that creek at northwest corner T. 13 N., R. 11 E. in Coconino N. F. Name Big Dry wash is found on only one map, Eckhoff's of 1880, which was doubtless the army officer's source for the name. Sitgreaves in 1851, called the present day Clear creek, "Big Dry Fork." q. v.

Bigelow Mountain   Pima Co.   Map, Coronado N. F., 1927.

In T. 12 S., R. 16 E. In Catalina mountains northeast of Tucson. "Named for Lieut. John Bigelow, Jr., 10th U. S. Cavalry, retired, who scouted through the Santa Ritas in the early Seventies, looking for hostile Apaches. Son of John Bigelow, Ambassador to France, 1864-1867, and brother of Poultney Bigelow, the writer." Letter, Forest Supervisor, Fred Winn.

Big Fields   Pima Co.   U. S. G. S. Map, 1923.

Papago Ind. Res. Papago village near lat. 32°, long. 112°. There was once a large Papago farming area here, hence the name.

Big Canyon

See First Hollow.

Big Horn Mountains and Peak   Maricopa Co.   Smith Map, 1879; G. L. O., 1921.

Mountains about 60 miles northwest of Phoenix, near Yuma county line, southeast of Harqua Hala mountains. Noted as such by Bartlett in 1852. Peak is at the lower end of the range, in T. 3 N., R. 8 W. The Big Horn was a very common animal in this region in the Eighteenth Century. See Tucsonimo.

"At the point of the Big Horn mountains, where Carson shot a big mountain sheep." Journal, Capt. A. R. Johnston, with Kearny's expedition, Nov. 17, 1846. This was another Big Horn range. See Painted Rock.

Big Horn Springs   Mohave Co.

"We found at a white feldspar cliff, a fine spring sheltered by alamos, willows, and an acacia which bore a new variety of mistletoe. Some Big Horn mountain sheep were frightened away at our approach." Whipple.

Big Horn Well   Maricopa Co.   U. S. G. S. Map, 1923.

In T. 2 N., R. 8 W. In Harquahala plains. Early day watering place. South of Big Horn peak, and so called for it.

Big Jonnie Gulch   Pinal Co.   Globe, Quad., 1903.

In Pinal mountains. Flows southwest into Pinal creek, about 6 miles northwest of Globe. So called after the "Big Jonnie Gold mine." This was one of the integral parts of the Old Dominion mine, some 6 miles northeast of Globe. After a miner known all over the region as "Big Jonnie." Letter, Dan. Williamson, Globe.

Big Lake   Apache Co.   Map, Apache N. F., 1926.

In T. 6 N., R. 28 E. Large natural lake on east slope of Mount Thomas (Baldy) which in early days had no visible outlet. In recent years it has been tapped by an irrigation ditch. In early days herds of wild game, deer, elk, and others stood belly deep in the water to escape the deer flies which hovered over them in swarms. The author has seen cattle and game animals in the late Eighties, standing in the lake in almost solid herds to avoid the winged pests. They would hardly stir out of their tracks so absorbed were they in protecting themselves.

Big Sandy River and Dry Wash   Mohave Co.   G. L. O. Map, 1921.

In T. 11 N., R. 12 W. Stream rising in Cottonwood cliffs, in eastern part of county, to form Bill Williams river. Wheeler says: "It was so named by Joseph R. Walker."

Big Springs   Coconino Co.   Map, Kaibab N. F., 1926.

U. S. Forest Ranger Station, Kaibab N. F. in northwest corner, T. 37 N., R. 1 W. Some very large springs rise here from which comes the name. They drain into Nail canyon.

Billie Creek   Navajo Co.   Map, Sitgreaves N. F., 1928.

Stream rising in northwest corner T. 8 N., R. 24 E. At edge Fort Apache Ind. Res. Flows into Showlow creek at Lakeside reservoir. After Billie Scorse, an eccentric Englishman who lived on this stream for many years. Brother of Harry Scorse, Holbrook sheepman.

Billings   Apache Co.   G. L. O. Map, 1892.

In T. 19 N., R. 25 E. Station on A. T. & S. F. R. R., named for an engineer with first Atlantic & Pacific construction party. On Rio Puerco of the West. A. E. Henning of Plano, Ill., established the Billings Cattle Co. here about 1883.

Bill Williams Mountain   Coconino Co.   All Maps.

Elevation 9,264 feet, about 6 miles southeast of Williams on A. T. & S. F. R. R. According to James, the Havasupai Indians call this Hue-ga-woo-la or Bear mountain. Named for Bill Williams, famous scout, guide, and hunter, but when or by whom, not established. Appears on most early maps and mentioned by all early explorers.

October 23, 1852, Capt. Sitgreaves speaks of the Bill Williams river, or fork. He shows it and the mountain on his map.

December 28, 1853, Whipple writes: "Southwest we saw Bill Williams Mountain where the stream of the same name is said to rise."

Coues writes: "Old Bill Williams was the noted character of unsavory repute with whom Fremont had his disastrous experiences in the San Juan mountains in 1848."

Mike Burns says the Apache-Mohaves called the mountain "Jock-ha-weha" meaning "covered with cedar." Farish.

Ives camped at the foot of this mountain Apr. 30, 1857, and called it by this name. Who named it Bill Williams mountain will probably never be known.

Bill Williams River, or Fork   Yuma Co.   All Maps.

In T. 11 N., R. 12 E. Stream formed by the junction of Big Sandy and Santa Maria rivers. Flows west into Colorado river. Named after Bill Williams. Coues says: "It was first named Rio de San Andres by Oñate because he was there on St. Andrews day, Nov. 30, 1605." Whipple was the first person to explore it from top to bottom. The claim is made that the name Bill Williams was given it in 1840 by Joseph Walker. Sitgreaves called it that in 1851; it shows on his map of that date, as well as the mountain, marked "sometimes called Williams Fork, it is so called by the trappers." Coues says: "Garces is not to be credited with the actual discovery of this stream. It had been located and named long before." Hodge thinks Walker gave it this name in 1840.

Wheeler says: "Bill Williams Fork at the junction of the Big Colorado is 25 feet wide and 2 feet deep, a clear sparkling stream." On its upper reaches he found beavers, mountain sheep and all kinds of game. In another place Coues says: "it was called and mapped as Rio Azul by Sidelmaier in 1744," a name which Coues thinks "was sadly misapplied."

Coues continues: "The precise date of the application of this name Bill Williams Fork has escaped me, but it scarcely antedated the Pacific R. R. survey. I am under the impression that it originated with Joseph R. Walker in about 1840. Sitgreaves mentions it in 1851."

Bancroft says: "Williams Fork, formerly the Santa Maria." Beale speaks of it in his diary October 18, 1857 as "Bill Williams Fork." "Williams," river decision U. S. G. B.

Biltabito   In New Mexico   Gregory Map, 1916.

Spring and Indian settlement Navajo Ind. Res. Navajo word meaning "spring under a rock." There is a well known Indian trading post here. The place is just over the line in New Mexico in San Juan county. For many years believed to be in Arizona.

Bingham Peak   Greenlee Co.   Map, Crook N. F., 1926.

In sec. 13, T. 1 N., R. 29 E. Named for Lieut. Theodore A. Bingham, engineer officer of the department in the early Eighties who made several scouting expeditions through this region with troops from Fort Apache.

Binghamton   Pima Co.

Mormon settlement near Fort Lowell on the Rillito east of Tucson. McClintock mentions it. A post office for a short period. Named for Nephi Bingham, its founder.

Bisbee   Cochise Co.   All Maps.

Elevation, 5,400 feet. Important copper mining camp in Mule gulch, a narrow canyon of the Mule mountains about 30 miles south of Tombstone. The Copper Queen and other great copper mines are here.

"The town was started in 1877, after discovery of the mines by Jack Dunn, a local prospector. It is claimed by some that George Warren was the first discoverer of the mine here. The camp was named in honor of Judge DeWitt Bisbee, one of the early stockholders and a brother-in-law of the Williams brothers, for many years managers of operations in these mines." Letter, Wm. A. Greene. P. O. established Sept. 7, 1880, Horace C. Stillman, P. M.

Bisbee Junction

See Osborne Junction.

Biscuit Peak   Graham Co.   U. S. G. S. Map, 1923;
                                            Crook N. F., 1927.

In T. 8 S., R. 9 E. In Galiuro mountains. The origin of this name is unknown.

Bishop Knoll   Gila Co.   Map, Tonto N. F., 1926.

In upper Tonto basin. In sec. 2, T. 9 N., R. 10 E. About 2 miles northwest of Gisela, on Tonto creek. "So called for the Bishop who presided over the destinies of the town of Gisela when it was a Mormon settlement." Letter, Forest Ranger Croxen.

Bishop Springs   Coconino Co.

After S. A. Bishop, of Beale's party who came to Beale's camp at the San Francisco mountains, Apr. 19, 1859, with the camel train and mail from Los Angeles.
"Thus far they are the best springs of the road. I have named them Bishop's Springs." Beale.

Bissel Point   Grand Canyon N. P.

See Comanche Point.

Bitsihuitsoe Butte   Apache Co.   Gregory Map, 1916.

Navajo word, "At the knoll." Haile. Near Yale Point, Navajo Ind. Res., west side Chinle creek.

Bitter Springs   Coconino Co.   G. L. O. Map, 1921.

Spring on old road to Lee Ferry, about 18 miles south of the ferry. On Navajo Ind. Res. west side Echo cliffs.
"The waters of the spring have a very bitter taste."

Bitter Spring   Mohave Co.   Ives Map, 1858.

Spring located by Beale on his map of 1858. East side Cerbat range, near Kingman. Was apparently just across this range, east from what he called Saavedra spring.

Bitter Well   Pinal Co.   G. L. O. Map, 1921; U. S. G. S., 1923.

In T. 9 S., R. 2 E. Water hole on Papago Ind. Res. "The water has a very bitter taste."

Black Bill Park   Coconino Co.   Map, Coconino N. F., 1928.

In T. 22 N., R. 8 E. An open park in the forest. After an old timer known locally as "Black Bill." Three miles northeast of Elden mountain. "Black Bill West" (H. Conard) took up 160 acres of land in what is now called "Black Bill Park" through which he supposed a projected railroad to the Grand Canyon, would pass. The road was never built and he abandoned the land. Died at the Pioneers Home in Prescott about 1926." Letter, Harold S. Colton, Flagstaff.

Black Butte   Maricopa Co.   U. S. G. S. Map, 1923.

A western end of Vulture mountains, in T. 6 N., R. 7 W. "Simply a big black butte."

Black Butte   Pinal Co.   Signal Quad., 1924.

Elevation, 1,782 feet. On Gila River Ind. Res. at lower end Sacaton mountains. Isolated peak of dark volcanic rock.

Black Canyon   Navajo Co.   U. S. G. S. Map, 1923.

Heads at the "Rim," about 8 miles south of Heber, in T. 11 N., R. 16 E. Runs northwest, enters Chevelon canyon at northwest corner T. 16 N., R. 17 E. Except from melting snows or summer rains canyon is always dry. Well water is found at moderate depths at Heber. From the open valley below, the canyon shows a dark line which gives it the name.

Black Canyon   Yavapai Co.   Smith Map, 1879; Eckhoff, 1880; G. L. O., 1921.

On the old stage road, Prescott to Phoenix, about 35 miles east of Prescott. The actual Black canyon was about 10 miles long and was on Bumble Bee. At Gilette it opened out onto the flat country near the junction of New river and Agua Fria. "Black Canyon hill" was a "one way" grade. Drivers waited for each other at certain turn-outs, they blew a horn as a warning of their coming.

Black Canyon Range   Mohave Co.   Hinton Map, 1878; G. L. O., 1921.

Range in northwest corner of State, extending from Boulder canyon southerly along the "Black canyon of the Colorado," hence its name. From T. 20 S., Rs. 65, 66 E. to T. 25 S. R. 21 W. Named so by Lieut. Mallory. The Black range immediately south is really an extension of this range.

Black Creek   Apache Co.   Gregory Map, 1916; U. S. G. S., 1923.

Intermittent stream rising in Chuska mountains, on Navajo Ind. Res. near State line above Fort Defiance. Flows southwest, enters Puerco river at Houck Station on A. T. & S. F. R. R.

Black Diamond Peak and Station   Cochise Co.. Map Coronado N. F., 1927.

In T. 18 S., R. 24 E. "Early day stage station in Dragoon mountains. Named for a mine carrying a black mineral which the miners called 'Black Diamond.'" Letter of E. G. Mettler, Forest Ranger. P. O. established Feb. 12, 1902, W. H. Schofield, P. M.

Black Draw   Cochise Co.   G. L. O. Map, 1921.

Dry wash heading west side Guadalupe mountains. Runs southeast, enters Old Mexico at San Bernardino in T. 24 S., R. 30 E.

Black Falls   Coconino Co.   U. S. G. S. Map, 1923.

In T. 26 N., R. 10 E. On Little Colorado river about 40 miles northeast of Flagstaff. Named for falls in the river which here runs over several "bars" of black lava.

Black Gap, Station and Pass   Maricopa Co.   U. S. G. S. Map, 1923.

Station established 1916, on Tucson, Cornelia and Gila Bend R. R. about 12 miles southwest of Gila Bend. "Station is in a pass between the two parts of the Saucida mountains, known as Black Gap, from the color of the rock."

Black Hills   Graham and Greenlee Cos.   G. L. O. Map, 1921.

On line of these counties. Short range called Pelencillo on U. S. G. S. map, 1923.

Black Hills   Pinal Co.   U. S. G. S. Map, 1923.

Short range on west side of Gila river in Ts. 7, 8 S., R. 16 E.

Black Hills Yavapai Co. G. L. O. Map, 1921.

In Ts. 12, 13, 14 N. The Jerome mine and camp is in this range. So named by Whipple "because of their dark forbidding appearance."

Black Knob Cochise Co. U. S. G. S. Map, 1923.

Elevation, 5,824 feet. In T. 23 S., R. 25 E. Isolated butte north side E. P. & S. W. R. R. 12 miles northwest of Douglas.

Black Knob Coconino Co. U. S. G. S. Map, 1923.

On Navajo Ind. Res., east side Little Colorado river, near long. 111° 30'. An isolated, black, volcanic cone.

Black Lake Apache Co. Gregory's Map, 1916; G. L. O., 1921.

In T. 4 N., R. 6 E. Few miles west of New Mexico state line. Simpson creek drains into it. Has no known outlet. "So called because when Simpson's party first saw it from the mountains to the east, the water looked dark, almost black." See Simpson creek.

Black Mesa Maricopa and Yavapai Cos. G. L. O. Map, 1921.

In Ts. 8, 9 N., R. 4 E. On east side of New river in both counties. On Tonto N. F. map, this range is called Cook Mesa after William (Billy) Cook prominent cattleman of this region.

Black Mesa Navajo and Apache Cos. G. L. O. Map, 1921.

Long, well marked mesa, 2,200 feet high, extending northwest to southeast from Marsh pass to Yale point, Navajo Ind. Res. "At a distance it is very dark-colored, almost black." Not to be mistaken for the Black mesa in Fort Apache Ind. Res. So named by Gregory. See Mesa la Vaca.

Black Mesa Coconino, Navajo and Yavapai Cos.
  Smith Map, 1879; G. L. O., 1920, Mogollon Mesa.

Known as "The Rim of the Basin." So called by early settlers and others because very dark in color. Extends east from Camp Verde to intersect the road from Holbrook to Ft. Apache. A survey of the Fort Apache Ind. Res. in 1879 established the Black mesa as its northern boundary. This mesa is known also as "The Rim," or "The Mogollon Rim."

Black Mesa Yavapai Co. Map, Tonto N. F., 1927.

In Ts. 9, 9½ N., R. 2 E. Large dark-colored mesa in forks of Agua Fria river and Bumble Bee creek. Bumble Bee canyon was generally called "Black canyon." q.v. "Just another Black canyon." Letter, Joe Hand, Forest Ranger.

Black Mesa Yavapai Co. G. L. O. Map, 1921

Sp. "Sierra Prieta." East side Chino valley. "So called by Whipple in 1853, because it was dark or black with Juniper trees." McClintock.

Black Mesa Yuma Co. U. S. G. S. Map, 1923.

In T. 3 N., R. 17 W. Isolated black butte at south end Plumosa mountains.

Black Mesquite Spring Gila Co. Smith Map, 1879.

West side Pinto creek about 5 miles from Salt river. On north slope Pinal mountains. "We made our way to Mesquite springs where the ranch of Archie McIntosh has since been erected. He belonged up in the Hudson Bay country; was totally unacquainted with Arizona, but a wonderful man in any country. McIntosh was one of Crook's most trusted scouts." Bourke.

Black Mountain   Coconino Co.   Map, Coconino N. F., 1928.

In T. 18 N., R. 3 E Large mesa east side Sycamore canyon named after George Black, at one time owner and manager of the Coconino Cattle Co." Letter, E. G. Miller, Flagstaff.

Black Mountain   Pinal Co.   G. L. O .Map, 1921

Elevation 5,563 feet. In T. 7 S., R. 13 E. About 5 miles northwest of Mammoth.

Black Mountain   Yavapai Co.   Map, Prescott N. F., 1927

In T. 11 N., R. 3 W. North of Walnut Grove. "A name, nothing more."

Black Peak   Pima Co.   G. L. O. Map, 1921.

In T. 22 S., R. 10 E. At county line, south of Arivaca.

Black Peak   Yuma Co.   G. L. O. Map, 1921.

Elevation, 1,656 feet. In T. 9 N., R. 19 W. Turning point on east boundary Colorado River Ind. Res. About 4 miles southeast of Parker.

Black Point   Pinal Co.   U. S. G. S. Map, 1923.

In T. 1 S., R. 10 E. Short mesa on Queen creek, west of Esthwaite on Magma—Arizona R. R.

Black Range   Mohave Co.   G. L. O. Map, 1921.

In T. 18 N., R. 20 W. Early day mining camp southeast of Mohave City.

Black Range   Mohave Co.   U. S. G. S. Map, 1923.

Often called Black mountains. An extension to the south of Black Canyon range from T. 23 N., R. 20 W. So called by Ives who writes:

"The range east of the Mohave Valley we call the Black Mountains. . . . . . Where the river breaks through the chain there is doubtless a stupendous canyon." Ives' *Report,* 1858.

Coues writes: "The earliest name for this range I know is the Black Range of Ives' *Report.* In my time (1865) it was called the Sacramento Range from the name of the valley to the east. Garces calls it Sierra de Santiago or St. James Range."

The Sacramento range does not appear on any map. Mallory, however, called the southern end of this range Blue ridge.

P. O. established as Blue ridge April 20, 1917, Pansy W. Keyes, P. M. See Blue ridge.

Black River   Apache Co.

Rises northwest corner T. 6 N., R. 28 E., in White mountains on eastern slope Baldy mountain. Flows east, south, and west around base of Baldy, through Apache N. F. and Ind. Res. Joins White river to form Salt river about 15 miles west of Ft. Apache, near lat. 33° 48', long. 110° 10'. Emory, Oct. 26, 1846, calls this the "Prieto" (Sp. "Black or Dark"), which is the earliest reference found to this stream and its name.

Black Rock Spring   Navajo Co.

See Smith spring.

Black Rock Spring   Mohave Co.   U. S. G. S. Map, 1923.

On west slope Grand Wash cliffs, in T. 25 N., R. 13 W. "There is a large very black rock near this spring."

Blacktail Canyon   Coconino Co.

Grand Canyon N. P. lat. 36° 15', long. 112° 28', drains into Colorado river on right (north) bank. "Intermittent arroyo rising well up on the Powell plateau, between Tobar and DeVaca Terraces." So named by Frank Bond.

Black Tank

See Wagathile Tank.

Black Warrior   Gila Co.   Map, Crook N. F., 1926.

Named for mine located by Silas Tidwell. In T. 1 N., R. 15 E., 4 miles northwest of Globe. P. O. established Aug. 26, 1899, David A. Abrams, P. M.

Blackwater   Pinal Co.   U. S. G. S. Map, 1923.

Indian village on Gila River Ind. Res. in T. 4 S., R. 7 E. Papago name is "Oo-Kut," "Standing Tree." The Pima "Calendar sticks" speak as early as 1871-72 of a Pima Indian known as "Old Man Blackwater" but who he was or how he got the name no one can say. P. O. established April 18, 1907, Samuel Pinckley, P. M.

Blaisdell   Yuma Co.   G. L. O. Map, 1921.

Station on S. P. R. R., 6 miles east of Yuma. After a Yuma valley pioneer Hiram W. Blaisdell, chief engineer of the Mohawk Canal Company who built the Araby canal in 1888. P. O. established March 23, 1896, John McIves, P. M.

Blalack   Yuma Co.   Map, S. P. R. R.

"Blalack is the name of a local land owner here. The store however is called 'Gila Center.' " Letter P. M., Blalack. P. O. and R. R. station on S. P. R. R. south side Gila river about 10 miles east of Yuma. P. O. established April 22, 1927. Mrs. Alice M. Moyer, P. M.

Blanchard   Yavapai Co.

P. O. established Aug. 17, 1903, Anne M. Williams, P. M. See Iron King.

Blanchard Crossing   Navajo Co.   Smith Map, 1879; Eckhoff, 1880.

Rock crossing on Little Colorado river, 8 miles east of Winslow. Blanchard was one of the firm of Breed and Blanchard who had a store here 1878 to 1883. Was Santa Fe Star route stage station. The route crossed the river here going southwest through Chavez Pass. Blanchard and a man named Joe Barrett were found dead in the store in December, 1881. A posse followed the trail of the murderers, capturing two men, one known as "Thick lipped Joe," Joe Waters, the other William Campbell. At St. Johns they were taken from jail and hanged by "unknown parties." This place also known as Sunset Crossing because the "Star Mail" route to Prescott crossed the river here going west through Sunset pass. See Sunset, also Breed Crossing.

Blind Indian Creek   Yavapai Co.   Map, Prescott N. F., 1927.

Rises in T. 11 N., R. I W., flows southwest into Arrastra creek.

"Charles B. Genung once told me that the first prospectors on this creek found an old blind Indian camped there. So they gave it this name." Letter, L. J. Putsch, Forest Ranger.

Bloody Basin　　Yavapai Co.　　Map, Prescott N. F., 1927.

Large, very rough so-called "basin." In extreme southeast corner of Yavapai county, on west side Verde river, east of Turrett Peak. In Ts. 9, 10, 11 N., Rs. 5, 6 E. "Said to have been so called because of the many battles with Indians that took place in this region."

Bloody Tanks　　Gila Co.　　U. S. G. S. Globe Quad., 1902.

Wash rising in southeast corner of T. 14 E., R. 1 N. Flows northeast into Miami Flat, near Black Warrior mine, in sec. 20, T. 15 E., R. 1 N. Bloody Tanks are at head of this wash. So named from a fight here in winter of 1863-64 between whites and Maricopa Indians on one side, and Apaches on the other. King Woolsey was captain.

Encounter was also known as the "Pinole Treaty" because Woolsey offered the Apaches a feast of pinole (Apache corn) before the fight as a token of friendship. It has often been stated that Woolsey put strychnine in the food.

Bancroft alludes to it as "an outrageous massacre, the Indians being coaxed to the feast and nearly all slaughtered by Woolsey's party." Peeples, who was present, denies this.

McClintock says: "The spot was about 9 miles across the hills from Globe, near the present site of Miami." McClintock's story of this affair is undoubtedly as nearly correct as it can be made.

"Pinole is the heart of Indian corn baked, ground and mixed with brown sugar. When dissolved in water it affords a delicious beverage. It quenches thirst and is very nutritious." Emory's Report, 1846.

J. Ross Browne also gives an interesting account of the affair.

Bloxton　　Santa Cruz Co.　　Roskruge Map, 1893; List S. P. R. R. Stations.

Station on Benson-Nogales branch of S. P. R. R. About 17 miles northeast of Nogales, on the Sanford ranch. Sanford ran about 13,000 sheep here in 1881, much to the disgust of his cattlemen neighbors.

"Bloxton was named after Bob Bloxton, son-in-law of D. A. Sanford. It was about 4 miles west of Patagonia." *Arizona Yesterdays*.

Blue　　Greenlee Co.　　U. S. G. S. Map, 1923; Apache N. F., 1926.

In T. 3 N., R. 31 E. P. O. and settlement on Blue river, 3 miles west of State line. Named after Blue river. P. O. established Nov. 3, 1898, Max A. Balke, P. M. First called Whittum, q.v.

Blue Bell　　Yavapai Co.　　Map, Prescott N. F., 1927.

On Turkey creek in T. 11½ N., R. 1 E. Station Prescott and Middelton branch, A. T. & S. F. R. R. 35 miles southeast of Prescott. After Blue Bell mine about one mile west of station.

Blue Canyon　　Coconino Co.　　G. L. O. Map, 1921; U. S. G. S., 1923.

In T. 14 N., R. 32 E. Trading post, Moenkopi wash, Navajo Ind. Res. "One of the best known and most characteristic features of this region." Gregory. The formation is a decided blue. First called Algert. See also Dot-Klish.

Blue House   Gila Co.   U. S. G. S. Map, 1923.

Mountain, San Carlos Ind. Res. On east side Salt River Draw. Near lat. 33° 58′, long. 110° 35′. Not known how or when this name originated.

Blue Jay Peak   Graham Co.   Map, Crook N. F., 1931.

In sec. 7, T. 8 S., R. 23 E. The most easterly of the two peaks north of Taylor pass, on crest of Graham mountains.

Blue Mountain   Cochise Co.   G. L. O. Map, 1909-1921.

In T. 16 S., R. 31 E. About 6 miles north of Paradise. In the distance peak has a blue tinge.

Blue Mountain   Coconino Co.   U. S. G. S. Map, 1923.

In T. 26 N., R. 9 W. Eastern line Hualpai reservation. At Yampai divide. "Looking at it from the valley this mountain always has a deep blue shade."

Blue Mountain

See Sierra Azul.

Blue Point   Maricopa Co.   Map, Tonto N. F., 1927.

Notable point or steep bank with blue clay face, north side Salt river at end Tonto Sheep trail. Two_miles below Stewart Mountain dam, in T. 2 N., R. 8. Sheep bridge is short distance below.

Blue Range   Greenlee Co.   U. S. G. S. Map, 1923.

Short range of which Rose peak is southern end. West side Blue river. Takes name from river.

Blue Ridge   Coconino Co.   G. L. O. Map, 1921.

Coconino N. F. in T. 14 N., Rs. 10, 11 E. Table-land east of Long valley, between Jack's canyon and Clear creek. Is heavily timbered and from below has deep blue color. Locally called Blue ridge.

Blue Ridge Mountains   Mohave Co.

Southern part of what Ives called "Black mountains," near Colorado river in northwest corner of county. Lieut. Mallory, according to Hinton called this southern end of range, the Blue Ridge mountains. The northern end he called Black Canyon range. Both are on early maps. See Black mountains.

Blue Ridge Peak   Navajo Co.   Map, Apache N. F., 1926.

In sec. 4, T. 9 N., R. 23 E. An outstanding peak surmounted by a government fire lookout tower. Ridge is called locally Blue ridge from its color when seen from the open country along the Colorado river to the north.

Blue River   Greenlee Co.   Map, Crook and Apache N. Fs.

Rises Cattron county, N. M. in upper part of T. 6 S., R. 21 W. Flows southwest into Arizona through Apache and Crook N. Fs., enters San Francisco river near Gatlin Ranger Station. Spanish called the range at the head of this river "Sierra Azul," "blue mountains," hence the name.

Blue River   Gila Co.   Map, San Carlos Ind. Res., 1917.

Stream rising in northeast corner of T. 3 N., R. 20 E. Flows southwest into San Carlos river about 6 miles above Rice, in T. 1 N., R. 19 E. Just a name.

Blue Water   Pima Co.   Hinton Map, 1878; Smith, 1879

Stage station old overland route about 45 miles northwest of Tucson. Fish says it was owned by Sam Wise in 1867. Origin unknown. War Dept. records quote Capt. Shinn, 3rd. U. S. Artillery, Report, June 2, 1862: "The well here is 69 feet deep with two and a half feet of water standing in it. It will furnish fully 4,000 gallons a day. There is good grama and galleta grass near."

Bodoway Mesa

See Broadway mesa.

Boggs Ranch   Yavapai Co.   Smith Map, 1879; Bradshaw
                                          Quad., 1903.

Stage station on Big Bug creek. Theo. W. Boggs located the ranch in early 60's; lived there for many years.

Bolada   Yavapai Co.   Post Route Map, 1929.

P. O. and mining camp, 6 miles south of Venezia. "Three families living here coined the word from the first two letters of each name, Bones-Lane-Dandera, Bo-la-da." Letter, W. H. Ryan, P. M. Bolada. P. O. established Feb. 25, 1921, Alice Bones, P. M.

Bolas de Plata

Sp. "Balls of Silver." Fabulous stories were told in the early part of 1700's concerning values of mines in Arizona and northern Sonora. Hinton quotes Henry Howe to the effect that he, Howe, had seen a copy of a "royal decree of Philip the Fifth, dated May 28, 1741, which speaks of certain 'Bolas: planchas y otras piezas de plata,' (balls, plates and other pieces of silver) weighing in all about 4,000 pounds. It mentions one particular mass of pure silver weighing 2,700 pounds."

Other writers also mention such valuable finds. Still others have written of like deposits which they have called "Planchas de Plata" (silver plates). There is considerable doubt as to the alleged values. Those early Spaniards were prone to write overly enthusiastic accounts of their discoveries in this new land.

Bon   Pinal Co.   R. R. Maps.

Station S. P. R. R. about 10 miles east of Maricopa. "This station was named after Chief Dispatcher H. G. Bonorden." Letter, Paul Shoup.

Bonellis Crossing   Mohave Co.

Early Mormon settlement on Colorado river near mouth of Virgin river. Later called Stones Ferry, q. v. After Daniel Bonelli who came from the Muddy and settled on the Colorado about 6 miles from the Virgin.

"Bonelli's Ferry consisted of a flat boat which a man pulls across the river with a line. For two persons and a wagon the charge is ten dollars; 50 cents for each additional person. The river can be forded here but is very dangerous." Elliott.

Boneyard, The   Apache Co.   Map, Apache N. F., 1926.

In sec. 27, T. 6 N., R. 29 E. In fall of 1880 two men brought some cattle from Texas and located them in these high mountains. Heavy snows caused the death of them all. Their bleaching bones marked the spot for years.

Bonita   Graham Co.   Rieckers Map, 1880; U. S. G. S., 1923.

Sp. "pretty." In T. 10 S., R. 23 E. P. O. and ranch of early days 5 or 6 miles southwest of Fort Grant. So named by Miles L. Wood, after Sierra Bonita mountains, name often given the Graham range. This place was a "dead fall" hangout where soldiers from Fort Grant went for recreation and excitement— and generally found it. Was just outside the military reservation. P. O. established Feb. 25, 1884, Ed. Hooker, P. M.

Bonita Creek   Graham Co.   Smith Map, 1879.

Rising near head Ash Flat, San Carlos Ind. Res. Near lat. 33° 20′, long. 110°. Flows southeast, enters Gila river in T. 6 S., R. 28 E. Dry wash for most of its course. Called Gila Bonita on G. L. O. map, 1921.

Bonito Creek   Apache Co.

Small stream rising on southwest slope Baldy mountain flowing southwest; enters Black river in T. 3 N., R. 23 E., 5 miles west of Poker mountain. On G. L. O. map, shows as formed by Little Bonito and Hurricane creeks in T. 24 E., R. 4 N. On Apache Ind. Res. map of 1928 this creek is called Big Bonito. q.v.

Boot Peak   Yuma Co.   G. L. O. Map, 1892.

Descriptive name. Resembles a huge top boot. About 10 miles north of Yuma east side Colorado river. Dr. Newberry of Ives' party says: "So named by Ives in 1858."

Boot Lake   Coconino Co.

See Lake Borne.

Boquillas   Cochise Co.   Map. Coronado N. F., 1926.

Sp. "little mouth, small opening in an irrigation ditch." Station Bisbee-Tucson branch S. P. R. R. 60 miles southeast of Tucson. After nearby Land Grant by this name.

Boquillas Grant   Cochise Co.   G. L. O. Map, 1921.

Sp. San Juan de Boquillas y Nogales. Small Mexican grant lying on both sides San Pedro river of which Fairbanks is about the center. Grant sold in 1853 to Ignacio Elias Gonzales and Nepomuceno Felix, for the sum of $240. The U. S. Land Court granted 17,355 acres and rejected 29,721 of the 47,076 acres claimed. Title vested in George Hearst and Janet G. Howard. Now used as a cattle ranch by Haggin and Tevis of California.

Borne (Lake)   Coconino Co.   G. L. O. Maps. 1882. 1912. 1921.

In T. 19 N., R. 10 E. Coconino N. F. about one mile southeast of Ashurst lake. "Origin of name not known. Is now called Boot lake because of its peculiar shape." Letter, Forest Supervisor Ed. Miller.

Bosque   Maricopa Co.   U. S. G. S. Map, 1923.

Sp., "forest, grove." Station S. P. R. R. There was a heavy growth of Ironwood and Mesquite here. About 35 miles west of Maricopa. "Station established 1895 when the Phoenix Wood and Coal Co. began cutting wood on the desert near here and shipping it to Phoenix. The author was a member of the firm. The wood cutters were arrested by the U. S. Marshal "for cutting timber on government land" and some 5,000 cords of wood lying near this switch were seized by the Federal government.

Matter finally adjusted, the wood released, and after that the Government was paid 25 cents an acre for "cutting timber on public lands."

Botkin   Yavapai Co.   G. L. O. Map, 1909.

In T. 16 N., R. 1 E. Station on United Verde and Pacific R. R., in Verde valley. "Named after a section foreman, Robert Botkin, in charge of the track here for several years. Switch long since abandoned." Letter, H. F. Hughes, Auditor, Jerome.

Bottom City   Maricopa Co.

See Lehi.

Boulder Canyon Dam   Mohave Co.

On Colorado river below mouth of Boulder wash, between Arizona and Nevada. Location of government dam to control the Colorado river and furnish water and power for Arizona and southern California. Generally called "the Hoover Dam" after former President Hoover.

Boulder Creek and Mining Camp   Yavapai Co.
U. S. G. S. Map, 1923.

In approximately T. 15 N., R. 10 W. On Burro creek near western line of Yavapai county.

Boundary Commission

See Emory. See Tinajas Altas.

Boundary Cone   Mohave Co.   G. L. O. Map, 1921.

In sec. 33, T. 19 N., R. 20 W. in Oatman district, east side Ute mountains. So marked and named on Ives' map, 1858. His report has a picture of it. Peak from which all government surveys in northern Arizona were started. "A plug of white Rhyolite." Ransome.

Bourke Point   Coconino Co.

Grand Canyon N. P., near northeast corner lat. 36° 17', long. 111° 56'. Two miles east of Point Imperial. Named for Capt. John G. Bourke, aid-de-camp to General Crook; writer, soldier, historian, author of several books on Arizona. Bourke first came to Arizona in 1869. Name suggested by the author.

Bouse, Town and Wash   Yuma Co.   G. L. O. Map, 1921.

On Parker branch A. T. & S. F. R. R. at junction Arizona-Swansea R. R. "Named for Tom Bouse, trader and storekeeper here of early days. Town was first called Brayton, q.v. Bouse Wash rises at southern end of Ranegas plain, flows northeast, enters Colorado River Ind. Res. near lat. 34°, near A. T. & S. F. R. R. Sometimes called Lotus valley or Riego valley." Letter, C. A. Walter. P. O. established Jan. 22, 1907, Wm. E. Enos, P. M.

Bouse Hills   Yavapai Co.   G. L. O. Map, 1921.

East side Arizona-Swansea R. R. After Tom Bouse.

Bowers Ranch   Yavapai Co   Smith Map, 1879; Eckhoff, 1880.

On Agua Fria, 20 miles southeast of Prescott. After Nathan Bowers, early resident of Prescott, member of the first Territorial Live Stock Sanitary Board, 1887. Ranch first located by King Woolsey and called Woolsey ranch. "At the Bowers' ranch on the Agua Fria, one sits down to supper in a room which once formed part of a prehistoric dwelling." Bourke.

Bowie   Cochise Co.   G. L. O. Map, 1892-1921.

In sec. 4, T. 13 S., R. 28 E.   Station, S. P. R. R., at junction Globe branch line. First called Tres Cebollas, Sp. "three onions." Also called Teviston for Capt. Tevis, q.v., and also Bean. Bowie was named of course for the old fort not far away. P. O. established March 18, 1911, Henry Heurich, P. M.

Bowie, Fort   Cochise Co.   Map, Coronado N. F., 1931.

In T. 15 S., R. 28 E. Fort Bowie, or Camp Bowie, located in Apache pass, north end Chiricahua mountains. One of the earliest military posts in Arizona. Located about 14 miles southeast of Bowie R. R. station. Named for Col. George W. Bowie, Fifth California Infantry Volunteers. Many Indian fights took place here and it was one of the most dangerous and dreaded parts of the stage road. When the railroad was built in 1881 it lost its importance.

"Fort Bowie with its grewsome graveyard filled with such inscriptions as 'Killed by Apaches'; 'Met his death at the hands of Apaches'; and again 'Tortured to death by Apaches.' One visit to that graveyard was guaranteed to furnish the most callous with nightmares for a month." Bourke.

In 1872 Gen. Crook placed the Chiricahua-Apaches on a reservation west of the fort, where they remained until 1876, when John P. Clum moved them to San Carlos.

See McClintock's *History of Arizona* for full history of this post. Heitman's List says it was established July 28, 1862.

Bowie Peak   Cochise Co.   Map, Coronado N. F., 1931.

In T. 15 S., R. 29 E. Directly east of old fort. General Miles mentions this peak in his *Personal Recollections.* He states it was a heliograph station close to Fort Bowie during his Geronimo campaign. Miles writes: "It was the most important of all the stations in the number of messages handled."

Bowley   Pima Co.

Stage station 35 miles from Tucson on the road to Quijotoa. Bowley was a noted cook and station keeper of early days. On a list of stage stations published in 1883.

Bowyer Peak   Yuma Co.   G. L. O. Map, 1921.

Elevation 2,125 feet. West side Dome Rock mountain. "After the nearby Bowyer mine. Close to eastern line Colorado Ind. Res. In R. 5 N. Mine owned by Joe Bowyer for whom the peak was named." Letter, O. G. Keiser.

Boyles   Greenlee Co.   G. L. O. Map, 1923.

Ranch on Blue river a few miles above junction with San Francisco river. About 40 miles north of Clifton. Named for Abe and Dick Boyles, local cattlemen.

Boysag Point   Mohave Co.

On north rim Grand Canyon, 2½ miles north of Havasu creek. So named from an Indian word for "bridge," because the point can only be reached by a small artificial bridge. Decision U. S. G. B.

Bradford Well   Yuma Co.   U. S. G. S. Map, 1923.

Desert well, 9 miles south of Vicksburg. "Cattle camp and desert watering place owned by Thomas W. Bales." *Routes to the Desert.*

Bradley Point   Coconino Co.

In Grand Canyon N. P., on lower north wall of canyon about 2 miles northeast of Suspension bridge, near lat 36° 6′, long. 112° 3′. Named for G. Y. Bradley, member of Powell's first party, 1869, through the Grand Canyon. Named by Frank Bond.

Bradshaw City   Yavapai Co.   Smith Map, 1879.

Mining camp east side Bradshaw mountains, in Tiger mining district. After William D. Bradshaw for whom mountains were named. Lieut. Lyle of Wheeler's Expedition visited this place Oct., 1871. He says: "It is reached by a very steep, rough trail and contains about one dozen log houses and a store." P. O. established July 1, 1874, Noah C. Sheckells, P. M. See Bradshaw's Ferry, Mountains.

Bradshaw Ferry   Yuma Co.   Smith Map, 1879; Eckhoff, 1880.

Called Olive City at first. Shows as Bradshaw's Ferry on some maps. Bradshaw was authorized by the legislature to charge for ferriage:

Wagon and two horses	$4.00
Carriage and one horse	3.00
Saddle horse	1.00
Footman	.50
Live cattle and horses	.50 per head.
Sheep	.25 per head.

Bradshaw Mountains   Yavapai Co.   Smith Map, 1879; G. L. O., 1921.

South of Prescott. After William D. Bradshaw, an early miner here. "He ran for Delegate to Congress in July, 1864, as a Democrat, against Charles D. Poston, Republican, who defeated him." McClintock.

"Bradshaw committed suicide at La Paz in 1864 and is buried there. He operated a ferry at La Paz for some time." Letter, C. B. Genung. On Hamilton's map, they show as "Bradshaw or Silver mountains." Hinton says: "There were three Bradshaw brothers, Wm., Ben, and Ike. They came to Arizona in 1863."

Brady Butte   Yavapai Co.   Map, Prescott N. F., 1927.

In sec. 19, T. 12 N., R. 1 W. On west side Tuscumbia creek. "After Francis Brady who worked a mine here about 1881." Letter, Forest Ranger, Stewart.

Brady Peak   Coconino Co.

Grand Canyon N. P. On west wall, near northeast corner of Park, in lat. 36° 15′, long. 111° 58′. Named for Peter R. Brady, Arizona pioneer, born Georgetown, D. C., 1825; graduate U. S. Naval Academy, 1844; resigned 1846; Lieut. Texas Rangers in Mexican War. Came to Tucson in 1854, Special Agent U. S. Court of Private Land Claims in the Peralta-Reavis Land fraud case; State Senator in several legislatures, the last in 1898. Died in Tucson, 1902. Named by Frank Bond.

Branaman   Pinal Co.   R. R. Maps.

Station Phoenix & Eastern R. R. 7 miles east of Ray Junction. Origin unknown.

Brandenburg Mountain   Pinal Co.   Map, Crook N. F., 1926.

In sec. 27, T. 6 S., R. 17 E., on north side Aravaipa creek. "Named for J. C. Brandenburg who settled on the Aravaipa in the early Eighties and raised vegetables and fruit, hauling them to Mammoth for sale." Letter, Bud Ming, Ray.

Brannock   Cochise Co.   G. L. O. Map, 1892.

In T. 16 S., R. 29 E. P. O. and ranch in Dos Cabezas region. Located at forks of Piney and Bonita creeks, west slope Chiricahua mountains. Headquarters for the well known Riggs' brothers cattle and mining interests. Name for Riggs' given name but the postal authorities first spelled it Brannick. About 55 miles northeast of Tombstone. P. O. established Aug. 16, 1887, Brannock Riggs, P. M. The first settler was Louis Prue, in Dec., 1878.

Brayton   Yuma Co.

First name of Bouse, q.v. Was the store for Harqua Hala mine. Owned by Brayton Commercial Co. Brayton was the middle name of John Brayton Martin of the company. "This was the first name of Bouse, the name being changed in Jan., 1907. The old timers wanted it named after Thomas Bouse, one of the first settlers. So we agreed." Letter, Mrs. John B. Martin, Arcadia, Calif. Brayton P. O. established May 19, 1906, William E. Enos, P. M.

Breckenridge, Fort   Pinal Co.   Smith Map, 1877, 1879.

Just below junction Aravaipa and San Pedro rivers. Garrisoned in 1856. Later called Camp Grant. Abandoned Oct., 1866 by General Orders 39, Dept. Calif. "Fort Breckenridge was located at junction of San Pedro and Nevissa rivers, but abandoned shortly because of its unhealthfulness." McFarland, *History Arizona*. On page 208, however, he writes: "In July, 1861, the only federal troops in the territory abandoned Forts Breckenridge and Buchanan. The two forts were later reduced to ashes."

McClintock says: "It was re-established by Lieut. Col. E. E. Eyre in 1862 and re-christened Camp Sanford in honor of the governor of California. There was much malaria caused by drinking stagnant water from the river where there were many lagoons from a succession of beaver dams. The camp was moved to Fort Grant, 1873."

"This post was first called Aravaipa and established May 8, 1860. So named for the then Vice President of the United States." Heitman's List.

Breckenridge Spring   Coconino Co.

"This spring lies between Kendrick and Sitgreaves mountains. I have named it for Mr. Breckenridge of my party." Beale's Report, 1857.

Breeds Crossing   Navajo Co.   Smith Map, 1879, Blanchard.

Known also as Sunset Crossing, q.v. Rock ford on Little Colorado about 8 miles east of present Winslow. About 1880 when A. T. & S. F. R. R. was being built along here J. H. Breed and Wm. Blanchard had a general store at this ford, which was the only safe crossing on the river. Mail stages for Prescott always used this crossing. Breed was first Treasurer of Navajo county.

"Mr. George Beale found an excellent rock ford, the only rock bottom yet discovered on this river. The whole train crossed in safety." Beale's Report, April 7, 1858.

Breon   Mohave Co.

Store and station not on any map. East of and not far from Mohave City. Named after Paul Breon, P. M. at Mohave City in 1877 who had a store there. P. O. established at Breon April 6, 1883, Allen H. Grant, P. M.

Bridle Creek   Yavapai Co.   U. S. G. S. Map, 1923.

Western part of county near county line. Rises T. 15 N., R. 9 W. Flows south into Santa Maria river. Origin unknown.

Bridwell, Welford Chapman

See Mt. Buford.

Briggs   Yavapai Co.   G. L. O. Map, 1892.

Mining camp on Hassayampa river west side Bradshaws, near southern line of county. P. O. established Dec. 30, 1890. Emery W. Fisher, P. M.

Brigham City   Navajo Co.   Eckhoff Map, 1880;
McClintock Map in *Mormon Settlement*.

Small hamlet west side Little Colorado 2 miles north of Winslow. Started by a colony of Mormons under Jesse Ballenger in 1876. First called Ballenger. In Sept., 1878, changed to Brigham City, "in honor of the first President of the Church." The Mormons built an excellent stone fort here which was torn down and had entirely disappeared by 1884-85. There was once a small pottery factory here which turned out a very fair grade of crocks, bowls and other such articles.

In January, 1879, place had a population of 277. There was a water power grist mill here, built in 1878 which was later hauled up to Woodruff but never rebuilt. The old machinery lay in a heap near Woodruff for many years. Brigham City was abandoned about 1888 by all but one or two families. Brigham City was a mail station on the historic Star route mail line between Santa Fe and Prescott. Stage line swung by Brigham City, and went on west through the Sunset pass. The grist mill mentioned was donated by the Mormon Church authorities in Utah "to the settlements on the Little Colorado river in Arizona. The Church sent it by teams to Lee Ferry and the Arizona settlers sent there for it and hauled it to Brigham City where it was set up and began turning out flour May 23, 1878." Fish Ms. P. O. established April 10, 1878, James T. Woods, P. M.

Bright Angel Creek   Coconino Co.

Rising near southern boundary Kaibab N. F., flows south through Grand Canyon N. P. Enters Colorado river nearly opposite El Tovar.

"Its waters were very clear. The name was applied by the Major on his first trip to offset the name 'Dirty Devil,' applied to a stream farther up." Dellenbaugh.

"The little affluent we have discovered here is a clear, beautiful creek or river. We have named one stream away above in honor of the great chief of the 'Bad Angels' and as this is in beautiful contrast we conclude to name it 'Bright Angel.' " Powell, Aug. 16, 1869.

Broadway (sic) Mesa   (Bodaway)   Coconino Co.
G. L. O. Map, 1921.

Navajo Ind. Res. west side Echo cliffs, along Marble canyon, west of Hamblin creek. Piute word of unknown meaning.

On Gregory's map, 1916, as Bodaway mesa, which is doubtless the correct spelling and name.

Broncho Creek   Cochise Co.   Smith Map, 1879.

Rises in Dragoon mountains; flows southwest into San Pedro river near Old Presidio of San Pedro.

Broncho Mine

See Brucknow mine.

Bronco Mountain   Coconino Co.   G. L. O. Map, 1921.

In T. 17 N., R. 8 E. Coconino N. F. Near head of Beaver creek. "At one time there was a large number of wild or bronco horses running here."

Brookbank Canyon   Navajo Co.   Map, Sitgreaves N. F., 1924.

Dry wash west of Heber heading in T. 11½ N., R. 15½ E. Enters Pearce wash in sec. 8, T. 14 N., R. 17 E. After J. W. Brookbank who located here in 1884. He later lived at Holbrook.

Brookline   Cochise Co.   G. L. O. Map, 1909, 1921.

Station Calabasas and Fairbank branch railroad. At eastern corner Babocomari Grant.

"A small stream comes into the San Pedro from the west. Town is located at the point where the S. P. line crosses the stream or brook. Hence Brookline." Letter, A. L. Henley, P. M.

Brooklyn   Pima Co.   G. L. O. Map, 1892.

Early day mining camp near Quijotoa in T. 15 S., R. 2 E. "The mine was called the Brooklyn. The owner came from Brooklyn, N. Y." This was one of several townsites laid out on slope of Quijotoa mountain. See New Virginia, Virginia and Logan City.

Brooklyn Peak   Yavapai Co.   Map, Tonto N. F., 1927.

In sec. 4, T. 9 N., R. 4 E. On Prescott N. F. North side of Squaw peak. After nearby Brooklyn mine.

Brownell Mountain and Settlement   Pima Co.

U. S. G. S. Map, 1923.

Store and settlement Papago Ind. Res. near lat. 32° 20', long. 112° 10'. According to P. A. Schilling of Ray, the Papago name for this mountain is "Ta-vo-num," meaning "a small hat."

"Mr. Brownell, the store keeper at Brownell, in the Quijotoa range, was a Civil War veteran and miner who discovered this copper mine at the foot of the mountain. Mine and settlement named for him." Letter, Col. J. J. Munsey, Sells.

P. O. established April 3, 1903, Frank Brownell, P. M.

Bruce Canyon   Santa Cruz Co.   G. L. O. Map, 1921.

Canyon between the Huachuca mountains and Canello hills. Rises west side Huachuca military reservation, runs north into Babocomari creek on grant of that name. Part of it is called Sycamore canyon. After Charles M. Bruce. See Mount Bruce for history.

Bruce, Mount   Santa Cruz Co.   U. S. G. S. Map, 1923.

In T. 20 S., R. 18 E. Northeast end Mustang mountains. After Charles M. Bruce, nearby cattleman, secretary of Arizona Territory May 8, 1893, and later Assistant Commissioner of General Land Office at Washington, D. C. under President Wilson.

On top of this peak is a bronze tablet placed there by resolution of the Pima County Supervisors, Louis Bodecker, James Lamb, and Ed Land, which reads: "erected in honor of Charles M. Bruce,. . . . .," etc.

Brucknow Mine and Ranch   Cochise Co.

Shows on Hinton's map, 1886, as Bronkow. On Smith's map, 1879, as Broncho. About 3 or 4 miles east of Charleston. Undoubtedly meant for Brucknow.

"The old Brucknow house a mile east of the San Pedro river was built in 1858 by Frederick Brucknow, graduate University of Westphalia, scholar and scientist, who, exiled from Germany, drifted into these solitudes. He began to dig a mine near his place when an Indian arrow toppled him over. It was at this spot that Schieffelin made his famous remark about 'finding his tombstone.' " Burns. Not mapped by this name.

Brush Mountain   Gila Co.   G. L. O. Map, 1923.

In T. 8 N., R. 17 E. Fort Apache Ind. Res. West side Salt River draw. "The cover of the mountain is mostly dense brush, oak, manzanita, etc."

Bryce, Town and Peak   Graham Co.   G. L. O. Map, 1921; Crook N. F., 1926, Bryce.

In T. 6 S., R. 25 E. Town on north bank Gila river opposite peak in sec. 3, T. 5 S., R. 26 E. After Ebenezer Bryce, Sr., who founded a Mormon settlement here in 1883. P. O. established Aug. 6, 1884, Nephi Packer, P. M. Spelled Brice on some maps.

Buchan   Maricopa Co.   S. P. R. R. Folders

Station S. P. R. R. 24 miles east of Gila Bend. "Origin unknown." Paul Shoup.

Fort Buchanan   Santa Cruz Co.   Pumpelly Map, 1860; G. L. O., 1921.

On Sonoita river, near present Patagonia. Named for President Buchanan, 1856. Pumpelly visited this fort in 1860 and writes: "Continuing our journey we reached Fort Buchanan. A few adobe houses scattered over considerable area and without even a stockade around it. It was some 22 miles northeast of Tubac on the Sonoita."

Heitman's Register says it was first called Camp Moore. Heitman records a fight in that vicinity between Apache Indians and Co. D, 1st Dragoons, Aug. 26, 1860. Post abandoned by U. S. troops July 23, 1861, due to the Civil War and the approach of a body of Confederates. The Confederates destroyed the post soon after this date. The California Column reoccupied it but abandoned it shortly. In 1865 but six men were stationed here.

"Buchanan was abandoned and then rebuilt in 1868 and renamed Fort Crittenden in honor of Gen. Thomas L. Crittenden of Kentucky. It was on the Sonoita." Cady. Cady was a soldier in this post and afterwards lived near it for many years.

Farish says: "In the autumn of 1857 a detachment of the First Dragoons arrived in the Santa Cruz valley and established Fort Buchanan. The officers were Col. Blake, Major Stein (sic), and Capt. Ewell."

Its abandonment in 1861 is probably what Poston meant when he wrote:

"Old Fort Buchanan of rueful name
Forever linked to nation's shame."

May, 1929, the State Highway Commission erected a sign on the site of this post which reads: "Near this place, Camp Moore was first established in November, 1858, by Major Enoch Steen, 1st. U. S. Dragoons, with companies B, C. D, and K of that regiment. It was then in the territory of New Mexico. Name changed to Ft. Buchanan in honor of President Buchanan, in May, 1852. It was destroyed by U. S. forces July 23, 1863."

Buck Mountain   Mohave Co.   U. S. G. S. Map, 1923.

North of Chemehuevi mountains. In T. 16 N., R. 18 W. An isolated group between Blick mountain on west and north, and Franconia to south.

Buck Peak   Yuma Co.   U. S. G. S. Map, 1923.

At northern end Cabeza Prieta range, near long. 114°. Close to Mexican line, almost directly south of Mohawk station. "In the early days a great many Big Horns were seen about this peak." Letter, J. D. Wirt, P. M., Mohawk.

Buckeye   Maricopa Co.

Elevation 886 feet. In T. 1 S., R. 3 W. Farming settlement on Buckeye canal. About 3 miles from north bank of Gila, 30 miles southwest of Phoenix. On Arizona, Eastern R. R. Originally called Sidney, but changed to Buckeye by C. M. Clanton, "because most of the early settlers came from Ohio." Buckey O'Neill was once interested in this canal but it was not named for him although sometimes it is said to have been. P. O. established March 10, 1888, Miss Cora J. Clanton, P. M.

Buckeye Hills   Maricopa Co.   U. S. G. S. Map, 1923.

In Ts. 1, 2 S., Rs. 3, 4 W. On south bank, Gila river. After the town of Buckeye.

Buckhorn Basin and Creek   Gila Co.

Stream heading east side Four peaks. Flows into Roosevelt lake. Near its head is a basin in which an early hunter found the heads of two bucks with their horns locked in death. This gave it the name. "Crook was made the target of every sort of malignant assault. Only an example need be given; the so-called Buckhorn Basin Massacre.

"Most circumstantial and detailed accounts were printed of the killing, by a raiding party of Apaches, of a small band of miners who fought to the death. This story was closely investigated by Major William Rafferty, 6th Cavalry, who found no murder, no cave, no miners. Nothing but a Buckhorn Basin." Bourke.

Buckskin Mountains   Coconino Co.   Smith Map, 1879;
                                              Eckhoff, 1880.

Known also as the Kaibab plateau, on north side Grand Canyon. So called because formerly the Navajo and other Indians and the white settlers, obtained their supply of buckskin from the large number of Mule deer found in these mountains. Is now within the Kaibab N. F. and the Grand Canyon, N. P. There is also a Buckskin mountain in Yuma county.

Buckskin Mountains   Yuma Co.   G. L. O. Map, 1909;
                                          U. S. G. S., 1923.

Short range extending east and west about 10 miles south of and parallel to Bill Williams river. In T. 10.

Buckskin Wash   Navajo Co.   Map, Sitgreaves N. F., 1924.

Dry wash, heading in T. 11½ N., R. 16 E. Runs northwest into Black canyon at Heber. After well known settler and cattleman. Lehi Howard, who built a cabin on this wash in the early Eighties. He always dressed in buckskins. A tall, picturesque man. Always known as "Old Buckskin."

Buell   Pima Co.

Station, S. P. R. R. about 29 miles east of Tucson.

Buell Park   Apache Co.   Gregory Map, 1916.

In T. 2 N., R. 6 W. On Navajo Ind. Res. About 12 miles north of Fort Defiance. Named for Major Buell, U. S. A., who commanded a small post here in Kit Carson's time. There is a fine Yellow Pine forest here.

Buena   Cochise Co.   G. L. O. Map, 1921.

In T. 20 S., R. 21 E. Town on S. P. branch line from Lewis springs to Fort Huachuca. East of Huachuca military reservation. Sp., "good." "Just a name for an unimportant switch." P. O. established Oct. 25, 1913, John H. Downer, P. M.

Buena Vista Land Grant   Santa Cruz Co.   G. L. O. Map, 1921, Maria Santissima del Carmen Grant.

Original grant of Oct. 24, 1831, was to Doña Josefa Morales. Title approved to Maish and Driscoll by the Land Grant Court for only 7,592 acres of the 18,648 claimed. Known officially as Maria Santissima del Carmen Grant. On Mexican border directly east of Nogales.

Buena Vista Peak   Cochise Co.   G. L. O. Map, 1921.

Elevation 8,826 feet. In southern end of T. 17, S., R. 30 E. East side Chiricahua range, Coronado N. F. Southwest of Paradise. "From this peak a beautiful view of the valley can be had. Hence the name given it by officers of the U. S. G. S. party."

Buena Vista   Pima Co.   G. L. O. Map, 1909.

In T. 22 S., R. 8 E. Settlement about 3 miles north of Sasabe. Sp., "good view."

Bueno   Yavapai Co.   G. L. O. Map, 1892.

Village on upper Turkey creek, east side Bradshaw mountains. About 15 miles southeast of Prescott. After the well known "Bully Bueno" mine located here, 1872. P. O. established June 27, 1881, Marion A. Vickroy, P. M.

Buenos Aires   Pima Co.   U. S. G. S. Map, 1923.

Indian settlement in T. 21 S., R. 8 E. "There is no town, only a ranch. Many years ago a U. S. customs inspector was stationed here. It is sometimes called Aguirres' lake because a Mexican, Pedro Aguirre, dug a well and built an artificial lake here for irrigation purposes." Letter P. M., Arivaca. P. O. established Feb. 6, 1892, Mrs. Beatrice Aguirre, P. M.

Buford Hill (sic)   Graham Co.   Map, Crook N. F., 1926.

In sec. 7, T. 7 N., R. 21 E. About 6 miles east of Klondyke. After Clay Beauford, former Indian agent at San Carlos, who located a ranch in Aravaipa canyon which he called "Spring Gardens." Here on retirement, he lived for many years. See Mount Buford.

Buford Mountain (Mount Beauford)   Maricopa Co.
                    Smith Map, 1879; G. L. O., 1892, Bufford.

In sec. 1, T. 7 N., R. 5 E.   Near head of Cave creek, 4 miles east of Ashdale Ranger Station.   Tonto N. F.   "Is not named on Tonto map of 1927.   On the old Tonto base map is called 'Humboldt mountain' but is known to old timers as Mount Buford.   It is about 4 miles north of Kentuck mountain."   Letter, Joe Hand, Forest Ranger.   This mountain was undoubtedly named for Clay Beauford who in 1863 at fifteen was in Pickett's division of the Confederate army.   As Sergeant, 5th. U. S. cavalry, he came to Arizona in 1870.   Chief of Scouts and Captain San Carlos Indian Police 1874-1880; member Thirteenth Territorial Legislature from Graham Co., 1885.   In Jan., 1879, he legally changed his name to Welford Chapman Bridwell, his correct name.   Died in Los Angeles in 1929.   See *Arizona Historical Review*, October, 1930, for his remarkable career.   See Humboldt mountain.

Bullard Peak   Greenlee Co.

Elevation 7,862 feet.   In T. 1 S., R. 32 E.   Crook N. F.   Few miles west of New Mexico line east of Blue river.   "In November 1870 at Silver City, N. M., citizens followed a raiding party of Apaches who had stolen most of the horses in the town.   John Bullard was captain.   They followed the trail into the region between Dry Creek and the Frisco river; struck the Indians and wiped them out.   Almost at the last shot an Apache fired point blank at Bullard who fell mortally wounded.   His body was brought to Silver City for burial."   Twitchell.   Decision U. S. G. B.

Bullard Peak   Yavapai Co.   U. S. G. S. Map, 1923.

In T. 8 N., R. 10 W.   There is also a peak by this name in Greenlee county.   See Bullard wash.

Bullard Wash   Yavapai Co.

Rises in Date Creek mountains west of Congress; flows generally northwest; enters Santa Maria river at Alamo Camp, in Yuma county, in T. 11 N., R. 13 W.

"An old prospector named Bullard has worked a mine about 5 miles south of Bullard Peak for many years.   The Wash and Peak were both named for him."   Letter, P. M., Congress Junction.

Bulldog Mine   Maricopa Co.   Scott Map, Maricopa Co., 1929.

In T. 2 N., R. 8 E.   Well known mine east of Mesa.   One of the general group owned by George U. Young, known collectively as "Goldfield."   About 3 miles west of road to Roosevelt dam.

Bullrush Wash   Mohave Co.   U. S. G. S. Map, 1923.

In Antelope valley, north side Colorado river.   Enters Kanab creek in T. 39 N., R. 3 W.   "There was once a large cienega or swamp on this wash filled with 'cat-tails' or bullrushes."   Letter, Forest Ranger Sapp.

Bulls Head Peak   Mohave Co.   G. L. O. Map, 1921.

West side Black range in T. 21 N., R. 20 W.   Descriptive name.

Bumble Bee   Yavapai Co.   Map, Prescott N. F., 1927.

In T. 10 N., R. 2 E.   P. O., creek, mine, about 6 miles east of Crown King.

"Uncle Tom Saunders told me that in 1863 he and some other prospectors found a bumble bee's nest full of honey in the cliffs along the creek.   Several of the party were badly stung so they named it Bumble Bee Creek." Letter, L. J. Putsch, Forest Ranger. Station was at times called Snider's Station after the man who owned it for some years. List of Arizona Stage Stations, 1880, shows it as "Bumble Bee—James Bobo, keeper and postmaster." Creek rises near Cordes in T. 11 N., R. 2 E. P. O. established 1879, William D. Powell, P. M.

Bunkerville   Mohave Co.   G. L. O. Map, 1923.

Named for Edward Bunker, member of Mormon Battalion. On south side Virgin river about 45 miles southeast of St. George, Utah. It was in that part of Mohave county returned to Nevada by Congress. Bunker is said to have died at St. David on the San Pedro.

Burch Mesa   Gila Co.   Map, Tonto N. F., 1926.

In sec. 36, T. 11 N., R. 9 E. Located about 2 miles northwest of Payson. "Named for William Burch of Burch and McDonald who first settled in Big Green Valley." Letter, Forest Ranger, Fred Croxen.

Burch Peak   Mohave Co.   G. L. O. Map, 1921.

In T. 17 N., R. 15 W., Hualpai mountains. "Named for an old prospector named Burch who had several mining claims on south side of this peak in 1873." Letter, P. M., Yucca.

Burger Well   Maricopa Co.   U. S. G. S. Map, 1923.

In T. 1 N., R. 8 W., in Centennial wash, south Saddle mountain. "Well was dug by John Burger. Was on the old stage road to Agua Caliente and a water station in early days." Letter, H. C. Gable, Arlington.

Burkes   Yuma Co.   Smith Map, 1879.

In T. 10 W., R. 5 S. Well known station on Yuma-Tucson road, south side Gila river, opposite Agua Caliente, 108 miles east of Yuma Station. Was run by and named for William H. Burke who was the first P. M. at Sentinel.

G. R. Whistler, station keeper at Burkes, was murdered by Ventura Núñez, July 7, 1874. Núñez was captured in Sonora, brought back and hanged near this station. See Nunez Station.

Poston was here in 1864. He calls it Burks Ford. Billy Fourr of Dragoon was the first owner. He writes, in Jan., 1933: "I sold the Burks (sic.) Station to J. R. Whistler."

"Burkes Station was opened Dec. 5, 1877, to keep the Military Telegraph line in repair between Stanwix and Gila Bend. Abandoned Nov. 30, 1880, because of S. P. R. R. arrival." Letter, Chief of Weather Bureau, May, 1933.

Burkes Tanks   Coconino Co.

On Little Colorado river about 13 miles southwest Grand Falls. Named by Erastus Snow, Oct. 25, 1878, for Hubert Burke, one of his party.

Burns   Pinal Co.

Station P. and E. R. R. about 4 miles below Winkelman. "Named for a man named Burns who had a farm and small bunch of cattle here in 1898. Sold them to Dan Carroll." Letter, Bud Ming, Ray

Burnt Well   Maricopa Co.   U. S. G. S. Map, 1923.

In T. 2 N., R. 9 W. Watering place in Harqua Hala plains. "A fire ran over this region many years ago cleaning out the grass and brush, hence the name." Letter, H. C. Grable, Arlington.

Burnt Ranch   Yavapai Co.

About 7 miles northeast of Prescott. There was a battle with Apaches at this ranch in 1865. Two men were killed. The Indians then burned it, after which it was known as the "Burnt Ranch."

Burro Creek   Mohave Co.   G. L. O. Map, 1921; U. S. G. S., 1923.

Rises in Baca Grant No. 5 in Yavapai county. Flows southwest, enters Big Sandy river in T. 14 N., R. 13 W.

Burro Spring   Navajo Co.   U. S. G. S. Map, 1923.

In T. 27 N., R. 15 E. On Hopi Ind. Res. Favorite camping place on road to Hopi villages. "At Burro springs, which makes the Oraibi road feasible for travelers, tanks have been sunk in the rock. A cover of poles protects the supply not only from stock but too rapid evaporation." Gregory.

Bush Valley   Apache Co.

See Alpine.

Butler Pass   Yuma Co.   G. L. O. Map, 1921.

In T. 8 N., R. 15 W. North side Cunningham wash. After Sam Butler, pioneer miner. One of the Butler Brothers. See Butler well.

Butler Valley   Yuma Co.   U. S. G. S. Map, 1923.

North side Harcuvar mountains. "Named after Sam Butler, who lived here in 1888. Two brothers named Butler owned the Clara mine here." Letter, Alma Beeler, P. M., Bouse. See Clara.

Butler   Yuma Co.   G. L. O. Map, 1921; U. S. G. S., 1923.

In T. 8 N., R. 14 W. Well in Cunningham wash. "Named after Sam Butler. Twelve miles southeast of Swansea. See Butler Valley." Letter Mrs. J. B. Martin, Salome.

Butler Mountains   Yuma Co.   U. S. G. S. Map, 1933.

Small, isolated range 6 miles west of Tinajas Altas mountains close to Mexican border. Named by E. D. Wilson after Dr. G. M. Butler, Dean College of Mines, Univ. of Ariz., Tucson.

Butte   Pinal Co.

Mining camp. P. O. established Apr. 17, 1883, Maurice B. Fleishman, P. M. P. O. records in Washington show such an office but do not locate it other than in Pinal county.

Butte City

See Haydens Ferry.

Butte Spur   Pinal Co.   R. R. Map.

Loading spur on railroad south side Gila river near "The Buttes." About 25 miles east of Florence.

Butterfield Southern Overland Mail Co.

Vishner in *Pony Express* writes, "It was established early in 1858 from St. Louis to San Francisco, 2,759 miles. Started as a semi-weekly but was soon made six days a week."

Farish says: "The government paid a million dollars a year for this daily service, on a 20-day schedule. In 1861, due to the war, Congress authorized the company to change their route from Arizona to the central route via South Pass, Colorado and Salt Lake." The first Butterfield stage via Arizona from the east arrived at Los Angeles Oct. 7, 1858.

Butterfly Mountain   Maricopa Co.   G. L. O. Map, 1921.

Elevation 4,163 feet. In Estrella mountains west side Gila river, Gila River Ind. Res. "Origin probably from Spanish word mariposa, a butterfly." See Maricopa Indians.

Buzzard Roost Mesa   Gila Co.   Map, Tonto N. F., 1927.

In T. 8 N., R. 12 E. Near head of Spring creek about 10 miles southwest of Youngs. In early days there was a buzzard roost here where these birds gathered in large numbers.

Bylas   Graham Co.   Map, Crook N. F., 1927;
G. L. O. Map, 1909, Bilas.

P. O. and settlement south side Gila river, 6 miles northwest of Geronimo. "So called after an Apache chief by this name." Letter, L. O. Townsend, P. M.

Bylas lies at the eastern edge San Carlos lake. Thos. E. Reed, P. M., Sept. 13, 1917.

Cababi   Pima Co.   G. L. O. Map, 1892, 1921.

In T. 15 S., R. 4 E. Papago village and mountain. Means "Hidden springs" in Papago, according to Loomis. Called Cababi on some maps, Cubabi on others. Cababi is approved spelling. P. O. established March 12, 1883, under name Cubabi, Robert N. Choate, P. M.

Cabeza Prieta   Yuma Co.   G. L. O. Map, 1921.

Sp., "black head" or "dark head." Small peak southeast of Yuma, west of Mohawk valley. Near line of Mexico.

Cactus   Maricopa Co.

In T. 3 N., R. 3 E. P. O. and settlement in Phoenix mountains, about 12 miles north of Phoenix. P. O. established May 4, 1918, William C. Hyatt, P. M. "Just a name for a little settlement. There was plenty of cacti around."

Cactus   Maricopa Co.   R. R. Maps.

Spur, Phoenix and Eastern R. R., 8 miles east of Phoenix. On Salt river opposite Tempe. "The desert here is covered with many kinds of cacti."

Cactus Mountain   Yavapai Co.   Map, Coconino N. F., 1928.

In sec. 9, T. 12 N., R. 6 E. Solitary peak north side of West Clear creek. "The mountain has but little timber and is covered with cactus of several varieties. Hence the early settlers gave it this name." Letter, W. J. Brown, Forest Ranger.

Cactus Pass   Mohave Co.   Hinton Map, 1878; Smith, 1879.

Pass through Cottonwood range on Hardyville-Prescott road, west of Cross mountain. Wheeler was here January 30, 1855, and says: "From the peculiar vegetation, we give it the name of Cactus Pass. We can look easterly through it and see the bulk of Cross mountain and the Aquarius range. The pass is a deep gorge in a high range of granite mountains."

Calabasa Mountains (sic)　　　Apache Co.　　　Mallory Map, 1876;
Smith, 1879.

"Calabaza," Sp. "pumpkin" or "gourd." Range, at boundary between Arizona and Colorado extreme northeast corner of State. Origin unknown.

Calabasas (sic)　　　Santa Cruz Co.　　　Smith Map, 1879; G. L. O., 1921.

Settlement made here about 1763. Was a "visita" of the Jesuits. Town started and named 1865 by Calabasas Land and Mining Co. Ten miles northwest of Nogales, on railroad. P. O. established Oct. 8, 1866, under spelling "Calabazas." P. O. records show it was changed to Calabasas Dec. 19, 1882.

Calderwood Peak　　　Maricopa Co.　　　U. S. G. S. Map, 1923.

In T. 5 N., R. 1 E. Lies between Agua Fria and New river. After Capt. M. H. Calderwood, Speaker Ninth Legislature, 1877: Sergeant at Arms, Eighteenth Legislature, 1895. Was stationed at Tubac 1865 and at Camp Mason, 1866, as Captain California Volunteers. Died, Phoenix, May 15, 1913. For twenty-five years ran the stage station at crossing of Agua Fria river on Black Canyon road. Station was some 6 miles from present town of Marinette. Called Agua Fria station, on the old maps. P. O. opened Jan. 6, 1892, under name Calderwood, Amer. D. McGinnis, P. M.

Calhoun, Camp　　　Imperial Co., Calif.

"This camp which later became Fort Yuma was established in fall of 1849 by Lieut. Cave J. Coutts in command of the Boundary Survey escort, under Whipple." Farish.
Undoubtedly named after John C. Calhoun, the statesman. See Fort Yuma.

Call's Landing

See Callville.

Callville　　　Pah-Ute Co.　　　Smith Map, 1879.

Directly east of Las Vegas, Nev. Established Dec. 17, 1864, by Anson Call of the Mormon church. On Colorado river at head of navigation. Hinton says it was 402 miles from Yuma and 16 miles west of Virgin river. Also known as Call's Landing. On west side of river in what is now Nevada, then called Arizona. That part of Arizona was annexed to Nevada, 1867. Before this annexation a P. O. was established Jan. 25, 1867, Henry F. Dibble, P. M.
An early effort of the Mormon church to establish itself in northern Arizona. Call came, "as an agent in trust of the Church." Church authorities planned to bring their immigrants into the country via steamer up the Gulf of California and the Colorado river; Callville being presumed to be the head of navigation.
There was much jealousy between the Mormon settlers and Mr. Hardy who had established a ferry not far from Call's place. Call started a town which did not prosper. The *Deseret News* of June, 1869, tells of its abandonment.

Calumet　　　Cochise Co.

Station E. P. & S. W. R. R., 2 miles from Douglas. Named after the mine at Bisbee.

Calva   Graham Co.   G. L. O. Map, 1921.

San Carlos Ind. Res. Station on Arizona-Eastern R. R. about 15 miles east of San Carlos. Will be covered by waters of San Carlos reservoir. Road has been rebuilt on a higher grade above flow line.

"Station first called Dewey but was washed out by a big flood. When rebuilt name was changed to Calva, after a local Apache sub-chief, who lived here and had a small farm on the river." Letter, S. T. Arkills, Globe.

Camelback   Maricopa Co.   U. S. G. S. Map, 1923.

Elevation 2,700 feet. Part of Phoenix mountains. Lies north of Arizona canal about 10 miles north of Phoenix. Has a striking resemblance to a kneeling camel.

Cameron   Coconino Co.   G. L. O. Map, 1924.

Town and P. O. west side Little Colorado river at government bridge in T. 9 E., R. 29 N. After U. S. Senator Ralph H. Cameron. P. O. established Sept. 12, 1924, Stanton K. Bovim, P. M.

Cameron   Pinal Co.   R. R. Maps.

Townsite 14 miles east of Casa Grande station, S. P. R. R. Laid out, 1924, by Amos Hess. Named for U. S. Senator Ralph H. Cameron.

Cameron, Camp   Santa Cruz Co.   Rand McNally Map, 1877; G. L. O., 1883.

Early military post on Santa Cruz about 15 miles northeast of Tubac. Was named after Simon Cameron, Secretary of War under President Lincoln. Was an uncle of the Cameron Bros., well known cattle raisers near here, 1882-90.

Heitman List says: "established Oct. 1, 1866; abandoned Mar. 7, 1867." See Camp Connor.

Cameron Pass   Santa Cruz Co.   G. L. O. Map, 1909.

In T. 22 S., R. 18 E. Pass through Canelo hills. After the Cameron Bros. who for years ran cattle on the San Rafael Grant.

Cameron Trail   Coconino Co.

Named for U. S. Senator Ralph H. Cameron. First name given present Bright Angel Trail. Cameron had several copper mines in the canyon to reach which he built this trail. He sold the trail to Coconino county and the name was changed to Bright Angel.

Camino del Diablo   Yuma Co.

Sp., "Road of the Devil." Desert road from Sonora to Gila river near Yuma.

"At the Tule Desert along the International Boundary the trail becomes the famous Camino del Diablo or Devil's Road. It probably derives its name from the fact that between 3,000 and 4,000 wayfarers are said to have died on it from hunger, thirst, and fatigue. It is said to be the most terrible trail in all the southwestern region." Hornaday.

Camino del Obispo   Apache and Navajo Cos.   Sitgreaves Map, 1851.

Sp., "Road of the Bishop." So named from the journey taken by Bishop Lamy from Santa Fe to the Zuni—Hopi villages. See *Death comes for the Archbishop*, Cather.

Camp   A Military Post or Camp

Will be found under its name; e.g. Camp Thomas under T. Town or P. O. called Camp Thomas should be under Camp.

Campaign Creek   Pinal Co.   Map, Crook N. F., 1926.

Rises northeast corner Pinal county; flows northeast across corner Maricopa county, into Gila county; enters Pinto creek from west about 2 miles from Roosevelt lake.

According to local authorities U. S. troops made this stream their headquarters during Crook's Indian campaigns, 1873.

Campbell   Mohave Co.

In T. 22 N., R. 18 W. About 12 miles northwest of Kingman. "Campbell was named for the superintendent of a mine near Cerbat in the late Eighties. Tubman Ayres, the postmaster, was a well known character of those early days." Letter, J. R. Livingston. P. O. established Feb. 19, 1896, Tubman L. Ayres, P. M.

Campbells Blue   Apache Co.   U. S. G. S. Map, 1923

In T. 5 N., R. 29 E. Flows southeast, enters Blue river in sec. 6, T. 4 N., R. 21 W. just over line into New Mexico. After William Campbell, cattleman and sheriff, Apache county, 1888, who ranged cattle along this stream.

Camp Creek   Maricopa Co.   G. L. O. Map, 1921; Tonto N. F., 1926.

In sec. 19, T. 7 N., R. 5 E. Rises at Maverick butte, near Ashdale Ranger station, flows southeast into Verde river at Needle rock in T. 5 N., R. 7 E. Summer resort camping place for Phoenix people.

Camp Grant Wash   Pinal Co.   U. S. G. S. Map, 1924.

In T. 9 S., R. 14 E. Wash flows northwest into Gila river about 2 miles above Feldman. Old Camp Grant was located at mouth of this wash. See Grant.

Camp Harry J. Jones

See Harry J. Jones.

Camp Verde Post Office   Yavapai Co.

Established Sept. 23, 1874, as Camp Verde, William S. Head, P. M. Head was then Post Trader at the fort. See also Verde.

Camp Wood Mountain   Yavapai Co.   Map, Prescott N. F., 1927.

Isolated peak, southeast corner Baca Float No. 5. Early day stage station of Camp Wood was located at this peak, which took its name from the camp. See Wood.

Cane Beds, and Spring   Mohave Co.   U. S. G. S. Map, 1923.

In T. 41 N., R. 6 E. West of Kaibab Ind. Res. Well known Mormon settlement 1866-75. "When settlers first came here they found beds of wild cane growing in the district. Some can still be found, hence the name." Letter, Annie W. Wilkinson, P.M. P. O. established June 15, 1917, Cora H. Cox, P. M.

Cane Canyon   Coconino Co.   Map, Kaibab N. F., 1926.

In T. 36 N., R. 3 E. Canyon and stream rising near Bright Angel highway. Runs northeast into Colorado river, in sec. 30, T. 38 N., R. 6 E. Heads in some springs around which are beds of so-called cane or reeds.

Canelo (sic)   Santa Cruz Co.   G. L. O. Map, 1921;
                                                    U. S. G. S., 1923.

In T. 21 S., R. 18 E. "Canela," Sp., "cinnamon." South of Babocomari grant. When this small range was in Mexico, prior to the Gadsden purchase, they were known as the 'Canela hills' because from the south they have a light brown color, similar to the spice named. "I moved here in 1904 and asked for a P. O. to be called 'Canille.' This spelling was mine, there being no known spelling of the name and none of the few settlers knew how, or why, these hills were so spelled. Name was approved and P. O. established. Later the Forest Service set aside a Ranger Station site here, as Canela." Letter, Robert A. Rodgers, ex-Forest Ranger. Canela was later changed, officially to Canelo. Either is correct Spanish for this name. P. O. established as Canille Aug. 22, 1904, Robert A. Rodgers, P. M. Canelo, decision U. S. G. B., 1903.

Canelo Hills   Santa Cruz Co.   U. S. G. S. Map, 1923.

In Ts. 21, 22, S., Rs. 16, 17 E. East side Sonoita creek, northeast of Patagonia. Sp. "canela," cinnamon. "The Mexicans describe a bluish roan cow by the word canelo." Letter, Forest Ranger Scholefield.

Cane Springs Wash   Santa Cruz Co.   U. S. G. S. Map, 1923.

Rises eastern slope Hualpai mountains, runs east into Big Sandy in T. 18 N., R. 13 W.

Canoa   Pima Co.

"Crossing the Santa Cruz, we passed the Canoa, a stockade house used as an inn. A place destined to see in the following year, an awful massacre. Fourteen miles more brought us to the old Spanish military post of Tubac." Pumpelly, 1860.

Shows as a settlement on all maps. East side Santa Cruz river, about 25 miles above Calabasas, on Canoa Land Grant. q.v.

Canoa Land Grant   Santa Cruz Co.   G. L. O. Map, 1879.

In Santa Cruz valley, above Calabasas. "In the presidio of Tubac, granted in 1821 to Tomas and Ygnacio Ortez. Confirmed by Mexican government 1849, and again by U. S. Surveyor General, 1880. Title vested in Maish & Driscoll of Tucson, for 17,208 acres of the 47,000 acres claimed." Spanish name was "San Ignacio de la Canoa."

"Name canoa, means in Spanish a canoe, in some instances, in others a water trough. Old timers say there was here at one time an old watering trough hewn from a huge cottonwood tree, which gave the ranch the name."

Canyon de Chelly   Apache Co.

Small creek rising in Tunicha mountains almost exactly on Arizona-New Mexico boundary line. Navajo word "Tschegi" or "de, sche-ay-e," "among the cliffs," "ghosts or evil spirits." Hodge. Not in any dictionary but so interpreted by Indians. Most of the year this is a dry wash. Heads at Sonsella buttes near State line. Flows northwest, joins Canyon del Muerto in T. 5 N., R. 9 W., to form Chinle creek.

"The orthography of Canyon de Chelly (pronounced "de Shay") was obtained from Señor Donaciano Vigil, Secretary of the Province of New Spain, who states that it is a word of

Indian origin, probably a corruption by the Spanish of the Navajo term or word, 'Tse-yi'; the Rock canyon." Gregory. Kit Carson's command had a fight here with Navajos in Jan., 1864.

Canyon del Oro   Pima Co.   Eckhoff Map, 1880, Gold Canyon.

Gold creek canyon. Canyon and stream heading in Catalinas, north of Tucson. Joins Santa Cruz river a few miles above Tucson. "The old road from Tucson to old Camp Grant at the mouth of the Aravaipa on the San Pedro, ran through this canyon. Several men were killed here in May, 1870, by Apaches." Farish.

"Tradition says gold was found in abundance in this canyon in early days." Bourke. P. O. established Mar. 28, 1881, Jose D. Camaco, P. M.

Canyon   Yavapai Co.   U. S. G. S. Map, 1923.

In T. 9 N., R. 2 E. On Agua Fria river. Early day stage station and P. O. in Black canyon. Also called Goddards, after Charles V. Goddard. P. O. established here as Canyon May 19, 1894, Charles V. Goddard, P. M. See Goddards.

Canyon Creek   Gila Co.   U. S. G. S. Map, 1923.

Apache Ind. Res. Rises under the Rim, 3 miles above the old Ramer ranch, near Fort Apache Ind. Res. Flows southeast into reservation; joins Salt river in Gila county, 10 miles southeast of Sombrero butte in T. 5 N., R. 16 E. "So called because its upper part runs in a very deep canyon."

Canyon Bonita   Apache Co.   Gregory Map, 1916.

Sp., "Pretty" creek about 5 miles long; rises in Quartzite canyon, flows southwest into Black creek. Fort Defiance is located on this stream from which the fields about it are irrigated. Ives called it "Canyon Bonito," in 1857; "The walls are abrupt, with brilliant and varied colors. Toward the south they form what has been most appropriately called 'Canyon Bonito.'" Ives. Gregory refers to it sometimes as "Canyon Bonito" at others as "Bonito creek."

Canyon Chelly, Fort   Apache Co.

According to Heitman's list, an early post in the Navajo country on Canyon Chelly.

Canyon del Muerto   Apache Co.   U. S. G. S. Map, 1923.

Sp. "canyon of the dead." Part of Spruce brook. According to Powell's Fourth Report, this was named by James Stevenson in August, 1882, from the fact that while exploring the ruins of the "Casa Blanca" his party found several human skeletons in one of the rooms.

Canyon Diablo   Coconino Co.   Smith Map, 1879; G. L. O., 1921.

Sp. "devil's canyon." Heads in southwest corner, T. 17 N., R. 10 E. At northeast side of Hutch mountain. P. O. and R. R. Station on A. T. & S. F. R. R. 26 miles west of Winslow. Canyon is 256 feet deep at railroad bridge. Enters Little Colorado river 6 miles northwest of Leupp. Is generally dry excepting in rainy season or when snow in the mountains is melting.

"Dec. 13, 1853: We were surprised to find at our feet a chasm probably 100 feet deep and 300 across. Descent was impossible. We followed the right bank to its junction with the Colorado

Chiquito and camped. . . . . The canyon has been named Canyon Diablo." Wheeler. Beale crossed it on Apr. 11, 1857, he writes: "It is appropriately named, being a deep chasm with perpendicular rock sides. It might be easily bridged."

When the A. & P. R. R. came to this canyon in Nov., 1881, work was held up for some time by lack of bridge materials. E. E. Ayer had a huge shipment of material for his proposed saw mill at Flagstaff. He built a road across the canyon and hired ox teams to haul the stuff. His mill was soon furnishing sawed ties for the railroad. P. O. established Nov. 15, 1886, Chas. H. Algert, P. M.

Canyon Lake   Maricopa Co.

Name of lake or reservoir formed by building the dam at Mormon Flat about 47 miles from Phoenix, q.v.

Canyon Lodge   Coconino Co.   G. L. O. Map, 1921.

Summer resort on Oak Creek canyon above Cornville. P. O. established Nov. 20, 1924, Earl M. Cundiff, P. M.

Canyon Padre   Coconino Co.   U. S. G. S. Map, 1923.

Heads in T. 19 N., R. 10 E., 5 miles northeast of Mormon lake. Runs northeast, enters Canyon Diablo near railroad station of that name. Origin or meaning unknown.

Cape

See under last name, e.g. Cape Royal, see Royal.

Capitals of Arizona

The capital of Arizona has been moved several times. The bill creating the Territory in Feb., 1863, named Tucson as the capital. When finally passed the name had been eliminated and no location made. The Goodwin party reached what was first known as Fort Whipple, later Camp Clark, still later Postle's Ranch, in the Little Chino valley in Jan., 1864, and the first capital was undoubtedly established there.

About April 1, 1864, it was moved to Prescott. Oct. 24, 1864, the First Territorial Legislature undertook to remove the capital from Prescott to Walnut Grove in Yavapai county. Bill however failed to pass. By Act of the Fourth Legislature Nov. 1, 1867, it was moved to Tucson. Prescott again became the capital in January, 1877, but a bill was passed on Jan. 28, 1889, to move it to Phoenix. The Legislature adjourned on Jan. 29, to meet at Phoenix Feb. 7, 1889.

Capitan Mountain   Gila Co.   Map, Crook N. F., 1926.

Sp. "captain." In southwest corner T. 2 S., R. 16 E. San Carlos Ind. Res. In Mescal mountains.

Capitano Creek   Gila Co.   G. L. O. Map, 1892.

Sp. "creek of the captain." In southwest corner San Carlos Apache Ind. Res. North side Mescal mountains. Flows into Gila river about 35 miles below San Carlos.

Capitol Butte   Yavapai Co.   Map, Coconino N. F., 1928.

In sec. 2, T. 17 N., R. 5 E. "Nobody seems to know where this butte got the name, 'Capitol.' People at Sedona say it was once called 'Judge Otey's Tombstone' because the Judge frequently remarked he would like to be buried at what is now known as Capitol Butte." Letter, Ed. Miller, Forest Supervisor.

Captains, The   Apache Co.   G. L. O. Map, 1921.

Two prominent buttes in forks of Canyon de Chelly and Monument canyon, Navajo Ind. Res. "These points stand out in the valley like huge sentinels. The Mexicans gave them the name of El Capitanos." Gregory.

Cardenas Creek   Coconino Co.

Grand Canyon N. P. rising near Cardenas butte, on south wall of Canyon. Flows north into Colorado river. Decision U. S. G. B.

Carl Pleasant Dam

See Lake Pleasant.

Carleton, Lake   Coconino Co.   Map, Military Division, New
                                             Mexico, 1864; G. L. O., 1866.

About 20 miles southeast of Bill Williams mountain. There is no lake in this vicinity except the well known Mormon lake which must be the one referred to as Carleton. There is no record of this lake anywhere else. Gen. Carleton who commanded U. S. troops in New Mexico, 1862, was probably never in this immediate region although he was in Tucson with the California Volunteers May 2, 1862. Parts of his command, however, were all over northern Arizona and could have named the lake for him.

An old "Military Map of New Mexico" of 1864 in Historical Society files at Tucson shows a "camp on Lake Carleton" at this exact spot i.e. Mormon Lake. Such a camp is not listed in any known register of military camps of those days.

Carnero Lake   Apache Co.   Map, Apache N. F., 1926.

Sp., "mutton." In sec. 6, T. 8 N , R. 27 E., on Carnero creek. Well known sheep-watering place.

Carpenter   Graham Co.

P. O. established Mar. 30, 1904, Roda H. Carpenter, P. M. Ranch P. O. for the Carpenter family. In Gila valley near Boyles.

Carr Peak   Cochise Co.   Map, Coronado N. F., 1927.

Elevation 9,214 feet; sec. 15, T. 23 S., R. 20 E. After Col. E. A. Carr, 6th. U. S. Cavalry, who campaigned against Apaches in this region in early Eighties.

Carr Lake   Coconino Co.   Map, Sitgreave's N. F., 1924.

In sec. 4, T. 11½ N., R. 13 E. Originally called Lake No. 2. Renamed by cowboys of the Waters Cattle Co., about 1886, for the General Manager of that company, E. R. Carr.

Carrigan Camp   Yuma Co.

See Osborne well.

Carrigan Peak   Yuma Co.   G. L. O. Map, 1921.

Elevation 2,400 feet. Near town of Swansea. "After an old prospector by this name." Letter, Alma Beeler, P. M., Bouse.

Carrington Spring   Mohave Co.

"Near Harry Edwards mountain Mr. Carrington reported a fine running spring a few miles east of 'Saavedra Spring' which was at the northern end of the Cerbat Range on the western slope. I have called the spring after its discoverer, Carrington's Spring." Beale. See Saavedra.

Carrizo   Navajo and Gila Cos.   U. S. G. S. Map, 1923;
                                             Fort Apache Ind. Res., 1928.

In T. 5 S., R. 19 E.   Creek rising under Rim at northwest corner Fort Apache Ind. Res. Flows southeast into Salt river about 30 miles west Fort Apache.

Carrizo   Navajo Co.   U. S. G. S. Map, 1923.

Sp. "cat-tails or rush."   Station A. T. & S. F. R. R., 14 miles east of Holbrook, on Rio Puerco. When the railroad was built there was quite a swamp here in which cat-tails grew.

Carrizo   Apache Co.   U. S. G. S. Map, 1923.

T. 14 N., R. 6 W.   Indian village and Mission school, Navajo Ind. Res., northeast corner State. "There is a fine spring of excellent water here which is piped into the school and residences." Gregory.

Carrizo   Apache Co.   Gregory Map, 1916; U. S. G. S., 1923.

Mountain, Navajo Ind. Res., northeast corner State. "Carrizo Mountain like Navajo Mountain rises as a solitary mass to a height of 9,420 feet." Gregory.

Carrizo   Apache Co.   U. S. G. S. Map, 1923.

Dry wash rising at State line east of St. Johns. Flows southwest, entering Little Colorado river about 6 miles north of St. Johns in T. 14 N., R. 27 E.

Carrizo Wash   Navajo Co.   Smith Map, 1879.

Dry wash east of Lithodendron creek, rises on Navajo Ind. Res. enters Puerco river between railroad stations of Carrizo and Adamana. Gregory says: "It was so named by Whipple."

Carson Mesa   Apache Co.   Gregory Map, 1916; G. L. O., 1921.

West side Chinle creek, Navajo Ind. Res. After Col. C. Carson who, 1863, conducted an expedition against Navajo Indians all over this region.

Carson Plains   Pima and Yuma Cos.

"The Southern Arizona Desert was once called Carson Plains for Kit Carson." Letter, F. W. Hodge.

Casaba   Maricopa Co.   U. S. G. S. Map, 1923.

In T. 2 S., R. 5 E. On Chandler branch Arizona-Eastern R. R. Town and P. O. "After the casaba melon which is raised around here."

Casa Blanca   Pinal Co.   Smith Map, 1879; Eckhoff, 1880.

In secs. 35, 36, T. 3 S., R. 4 E. Trading post near the so-called "Pima villages." On south side Gila, a few miles west of Maricopa wells. About 6 miles south of "Snaketown."

Ross Browne says: "Ammi White's Trading Post and flour mill, was near the Casa Blanca." Ammi M. White was Pima Indian agent before 1864. He built a flour mill here before that year, which was destroyed, according to the Pima "Calendar Stick," by the great flood of Sept., 1868. White's was probably the first flour mill in the Territory. It was a water-power mill. See First Flour Mill.

Origin of the name Casa Blanca is doubtful. After careful study of the matter, the author feels that the Pimas and Mexicans would speak very naturally of "Ammi White's house," as a prominent one in the region in that time. By translation and natural use it soon became "Casa Blanca," i.e. "White's House"; a very easy way for the name to become fixed permanently and its origin forgotten. See also Casa Blanca, Santa Cruz Co. and the Pima villages; also Madero canyon.

Casa Blanca Creek   Santa Cruz Co.   Roskruge Map, 1893; Coronado N. F., 1927.

In T. 21 S., R. 16 E. Stream rising near Josephine creek, flowing southeast into Sonoita creek about 2 miles above Crittenden. See Whitehouse for origin. U. S. G. S. sheet shows this as Josephine creek, undoubtedly an error.

Casa Blanca   Santa Cruz Co.   G. L. O. Map, 1892.

In T. 21 S., R. 16 E. Station on railroad, Calabasas to Fort Huachuca. On Sonoita creek at junction with Casa Blanca creek from which the station took its name.

"When Fort Crittenden was occupied there was an adobe house at mouth of this canyon built by Theodore Welish which was white washed and plastered. It has long since disappeared but the house gave the canyon and postoffice its name." Letter, R. A. Rodgers, Nogales. P. O. established Apr. 27, 1882, Thomas Hughes, P. M.

According to reports, this canyon was also called Madera canyon (Sp., "lumber") because the first saw mill in Arizona was located near here. There is another Casa Blanca in Pinal county near Florence. See also Santan for possible origin of name.

Casa Grande   Pinal Co.   G. L. O. Map, 1892.

Elevation 1,395 feet. T. 6 E., R. 6 S. Station on S. P. R. R., 21 miles east of Maricopa. After the old ruin near by. P. O. established Sept. 10, 1880, Jerry Troyer, P. M.

Casa Grande Mountain   Pinal Co.   G. L. O. Map, 1921.

Elevation 2,323 feet, in T. 7 S., R. 6 E. Small isolated butte on south side S. P. R. R. For the near-by ruin.

Casa Grande Ruins   Pinal Co.

Sp., "large or grand house." In T. 5 S., R. 8 E., about 5 miles southwest of Florence. "One of the best preserved ancient ruins in the southwest. De Niza first speaks of it in 1539. Casteneda mentions it in 1540 although it is unlikely he ever really saw it. Father Kino visited it in November, 1694. Early explorers found it in ruins and apparently hundreds of years old. Surrounded by many miles of old irrigation ditches it was evidently once the center of a dense population. June 22, 1892, it was made a National Park but on August 3, 1918, was changed to a National Monument.

Emory visited these ruins Nov. 10, 1846. He writes: "A large pile which seemed the work of human hands was seen to the left. It was the remains of a three-story mud house pierced for doors and windows. The walls were 4 feet thick and formed by layers of mud about 2 feet thick. It was no doubt built by the same race that once so thickly peopled the region." Col. Poston was here, 1863. He writes poetically, and sarcastically:

"The Casa Grande stands alone
One league from road to old Tucson
No other nation neath the sun
Would let this ruin, to ruin run."

Papago name for these ruins is Vah-ah-Kei, "Dragon Fly."

Cascabel   Cochise Co.   G. L. O. Map, 1921

In T. 13 S., R. 19 E. Sp., "bell or rattle." On San Pedro river. "The rattle of a rattle snake. So named by A. Herron who located the town. In clearing the land he found many rattlers." Letter, Edith A. Macia, P. M. P. O. established June 13, 1916, Alex. Herron, P. M.

Cashion   Maricopa Co.   G. L. O. Map, 1921.

In T. 1 N., R. 1 E. Agricultural settlement and P. O. about 12 miles west of Phoenix, on Buckeye branch, Arizona-Eastern R. R. After Angus Cashion, prominent farmer and stockman of vicinity. P. O. established Nov. 27, 1911, Fred L. Bush, P. M.

Casimoro Peak   Graham Co.   G. L. O. Map, 1921; Crook N. F., 1926.

In sec. 36, T. 5 S., R. 26 E. In Gila range about 8 miles northeast of Safford. 'Now generally known as Webber peak. After John Webber, an early settler in the Gila valley. Nobody knows the name 'Casimiro.' " Letter, Rex King, Forest Supervisor. See Webber Peak.

Casner Mountain   Coconino Co.   Map, Coconino N. F., 1928.

In T. 18 N., Rs. 3, 4 E., east side Sycamore canyon. After G. R. Casner, who grazed sheep in this vicinity in early days.

Cassadero Mountain

See Cazadero.

Cassadora

Named after a sub-chief of the San Carlos Apache tribe who with a small band lived in the Gila valley now covered by the waters of the Coolidge Dam.

In 1873 several whites were killed by Apaches in the vicinity of his camp. The deed was laid to them. Cassadora claimed the killing was done by "bad Indians" and that none of his people were responsible. But the citizens refused to believe his story and demanded arrests. Troops were ordered out with instructions to hunt the murderers down and to "take no prisoners."

Cassadora and all his band, fearing death, immediately took to the hills. A troop of cavalry under Captain J. M. Hamilton found their trail. The Indians, men, women, and children, were on foot. Hamilton was within a short distance of their camp. In the evening an Apache squaw came to the cavalry camp. She asked to see the commander. She told him the Indians he was following wanted to surrender.

Hamilton sent her back with the information that his orders were to take no prisoners and none of the Apaches would be allowed to surrender. The woman went back to her camp with this terrible ultimatum. Next morning the entire band, holding their hands in the air as a token of peace, appeared outside Hamilton's camp. With Cassadora at their head the Indians asked for mercy. He told Hamilton "We were afraid because some bad Indians had killed white men, so we ran away. That was wrong. We cannot fight for we have no arms or ammunition. Our food is gone; we are suffering from hunger; our moccasins are worn out, you can see our tracks on the rocks where our feet have left blood. We do not want to die but if we must, we prefer to die by the bullets from your soldiers' guns than from hunger. So we have come to your camp asking for peace." His pathetic story made a strong appeal to Captain Hamilton's humanity. He swore he would rather lose his place in the army than kill these Indians in cold blood. He gave them food and protection while he sent to headquarters for orders.

The order to "take no prisoners" was promptly rescinded. Cassadora and his band surrendered to Hamilton on February 18, 1874, and were escorted by the troopers back to the homes they had left so suddenly.

Castle Butte   Coconino Co.   G. L. O. Map. 1921.

In R. 12 E., on Hopi Ind. Res., about 6 miles northeast of Tuba City. Resembles a huge castle.

Castle Butte   Navajo Co.   Gregory Map, 1916; G. L. O., 1921.

In T. 22 N., R. 19 E. Prominent butte looking like a castle about 25 miles north of Joseph City. Descriptive name. P. O. established Sept. 25, 1919, Irene E. Robinson, P. M.

Castle Creek   Yavapai Co.   G. L. O. Map, 1921.

Stream rising in T. 9 N., R. 2 W. in Wickenburg mountains. Flows southeast, enters Agua Fria river in approximately T. 6 N., R. 1 E. For many miles it flows through a picturesque canyon having castellated rock walls. The old Wickenburg stage road followed its bed for several miles. Castle Hot springs are in this canyon. q.v.

Castle Dome   Yuma Co.   G. L. O. Map. 1921.

Small mining hamlet located about 1862 on Castle Dome range about 50 miles northeast of Yuma. "The Castle Dome mines were discovered in 1863; supposed to be immensely rich, but were abandoned when the ore turned out to be chiefly lead. Large quantities of lead were subsequently shipped to San Francisco and from 1869-70 the mines were profitably worked." Bancroft.

P. O. established Dec. 17, 1875, William P. Miller, P. M.

Castle Dome County

One of the four counties on Mowry's original map of 1860. Later called Yuma county. q.v.

Castle Dome Landing   Yuma Co.   G. L. O. Map, 1921.

In T. 5 S., R. 21 W. Steamboat landing on Colorado river about 45 miles above Yuma. Shipping point for Castle Dome mining district. *Arizona Gazetteer* for 1881 says the smelter for the Castle Dome Mining Co. was located here. P. O. established Aug. 6, 1878, Andrew H. Cargill, P. M.

Castle Dome Mountains   Yuma Co.   Smith Map, 1879, G. L. O., 1921.

Range extending from northwest to southeast, 30 miles east of Colorado river, northeast of Yuma. In shape resembles a huge castle. Said to have been named "Cabeza de Gigante" (Giant's Head) by de Niza in 1744.

Castle Dome Mountain   Maricopa Co.   Map, Tonto N. F., 1931.

Elevation 5,316 feet. About 8 miles due east Fish Creek station. Near southeast corner sec. 11, T. 2 N., R. 11 E. From its dome-like formation.

Castle Hot Springs   Yavapai Co.   G. L. O. Map, 1921.

In T. 7 N., R. 1 W., group of large springs, some hot, some cold, with medicinal value. On Castle creek in Hieroglyphic mountains. About 25 miles from A. T. & S. F. R. R. In early days when the Wickenburg, Vulture and Phoenix stage stopped here for meals passengers were furnished with towels and invited to swim in the natural rock pool below the station. Later it became a well known winter health-resort.

Said to have been named in 1867 by Col. Chas. Craig, U. S. Army, commanding Whipple Barracks, who had a fight with Apaches in this canyon. The castle-like cliffs suggested the name. Springs discovered by a prospector named George Munroe. In 1878 Munroe sold the location to Uncle Tom Holland who lived there for many years. P. O. called Hot springs, q.v.

Castle Peak   Gila Co.   G. L. O. Map, 1921; Tonto N. F., 1927.

In T. 7 N., R. 15 E. Descriptive name.

Castle Peak   Mohave Co.   U. S. G. S. Map, 1923.

On Shivwits plateau near lat. 36° 10′, long. 113° 30′, north side of Colorado river. Descriptive name.

Cat Mountain   Pima Co.   U. S. G. S. Map, 1923.

In T. 14 S., R. 13 E. 6 miles southwest of Tucson. Origin unknown.

Catalina   Pinal Co.

Small settlement. P. O. established Jan. 4, 1881, John T. Young, P. M. P. O. records do not locate it.

Catalina Mountains   Pima Co.

See Santa Catalinas.

Catalpa   Gila Co.   G. L. O. Map, 1892.

In T. 4 N., R. 13 E. Town and P. O. about 3 miles southeast of Armer.

"The first settler was George Danforth who located here in 1876. In 1877 Robinson brought the first band of sheep into this region. Place so called for the many catalpa trees on Robinson's land where the first P. O. was established, 1880. Robinson had his main sheep camp at foot of Four Peaks on east side of range." Hinton.

Robinson seems also to have planted fruit trees as well as catalpas, for the Globe *Silver Belt* of June. 22, 1889, extends thanks to him "for a box of magnificent peaches grown on his ranch on Salt River."

There is a letter in the Pioneers' Library at Tucson written by Charles M. Mullen of Tempe in which is described very fully the death of Robinson at the hands of Apaches in 1877 because he set a spring gun at his ranch and killed an Indian. Story seems not justified for Robinson was alive and in Globe several years after this was said to have happened.

Neither this place, nor the "Grove of Robinson" q.v. appears on any maps of today. It was evidently on what is now called Medler wash. On Smith map, 1879, and Eckhoff, 1880, this is called "The Grove of Robinson."

Cataract, Canyon and Creek   Coconino Co.   U. S. G. S. Map, 1923;
G. C. N. P., 1927.

Heads at Williams, flows northwest into Grand Canyon. Named for a series of beautiful waterfalls in the stream. They begin 10 or 15 miles from the Grand Canyon. The creek heads in several springs, waters of which are heavily charged with lime. See Elliott's *History of Arizona*.

Garces, 1776, called it "Rio de San Antonio." Ives, 1858, called it "Cataract" and also "Cascade Creek." The Canyon begins about 20 miles northeast of Williams, runs northwest and enters Grand Canyon in Tusayan N. F. near line between Rs. 4, 5 W. Lower end of canyon for some 10 or 12 miles is called Supai or Havasupai canyon. In Havasu Ind. Res.

Indians live in this canyon part of year and produce fine crops of peaches, alfalfa, etc. They first secured trees and seed from John D. Lee who hid away in this canyon for several years after the Mountain Meadow Massacre. "Havasu" means blue. The water has that color. See Coanini creek and Havasu canyon. On some maps as Havasu creek. Havasu, decision U. S. G. B.

Cathedral Rock   Pima Co.   Roskruge Map, 1893;
Coronado N. F., 1927.

In T. 12 S., R. 15 E. A huge bulk on top of the Catalinas, which caused the early Spanish to call the mountain, "La Iglesia," "The Church." From a distance this rock looks exactly like some huge Tudor church. See Santa Catalinas.

Catoctin   Yavapai Co.   G. L. O. Map, 1921.

Early day mining camp and P. O. on upper Hassayampa creek, near Senator mine. After the Catoctin Gold mine. P. O. established Dec. 29, 1902, Henry N. Tharsing, P. M.

Catholic Peak   Gila Co.   G. L. O. Map, 1921; Tonto N. F., 1921.

In T. 8 N., R. 15 E. Near line Apache Ind. Res. about 15 miles west of Ellison's ranch. "The peak resembles a crude cross." Letter, Walter J. Pinson, Forest Ranger.

Cave Creek   Cochise Co.   Map, Coronado N. F., 1927.

Rises east slope Chiricahua mountains, flows northeast into Sulphur Springs valley. Near head of this creek is a large natural cave from which stream gets its name.

Cave Creek   Maricopa Co.   Smith Map, 1879; G. L. O., 1921.

In T. 6 N., R. 4 E. Stock-raising center and P. O. on creek of same name. Stream rises approximately in T. 8 N., R. 5 E., in Lime Creek mountains, flows southeast. "Origin of name doubtful. There are two or three good sized caves used by Indians for many years near Cave Creek P. O. Old timers tell of a man named Cave who once lived on headwaters of creek, from which came the name. Take your choice." Letter, Joe Hand, Forest Ranger.

Hand is about right. The Phoenix papers of early Eighties often mention a visiting miner, Ed. Caves, who lived on Cave Creek for many years. Was generally known as "Old Rackensack" for the famous Rackensack mine he discovered and worked in Cave Creek District. P. O. established April 28, 1890, William Gillingham, P. M.

Cavot   Cochise Co.

Station on S. P. R. R. about 27 miles east of Bowie station. Origin unknown.

Cazadero, Mountain and Spring   Gila Co.

In T. 19 E., R. 2 N., San Carlos Apache Ind. Res. North side San Carlos river, southern slope Natanes plateau. Mountain spelled Cassadora. The spring, Cassadare on G. L. O. map, 1921. On U. S. G. S. map, 1923, mountain is Cassadero. Proper spelling unquestionably is Cazadero. Sp. "hunting grounds."

"Casadora was a Pinal-Apache chief who lived on the San Carlos reservation 1879-80, went to Washington with Clum and a party of Apaches in 1876." Charles T. Connell, in Phoenix *Republic* Apr. 16, 1930. Spring and mountain named undoubtedly for this chief.

Cazador (sic)   Cochise Co.

Sp., "hunter, sportsman." Station on E. P. & S. W. R. R., 15 miles northwest of Douglas. Old timers say this was named after Casadora, the Apache chief.

Cebaletta (sic) Mountain   Pima Co.

Sp., "a tender young onion." This seems to be the narrow ridge or range connecting Santa Ritas with Rincon range. Shows only on Roskruge map, 1893, on which it extends from Fuller's Pass, on the north to Mount Ochoa in the south. Not on any other map. Origin unknown.

Cedar   Mohave Co.   G. L. O. Map, 1921; U. S. G. S., 1923.

In T. 16 N., R. 15 W. P. O. and ranch, south of Deluge wash lower end Hualpai range. About 15 miles west of Wickieup. "There is considerable scrub cedar around here." P. O. established Sept. 24, 1895, Ira M. George, P. M. Called Cedarville on G. L. O. map, 1892.

Cedar Creek   Gila Co.   G. L. O. Map, 1921; Ft. Apache Ind. Res.

Rises west slope Deer Spring mountain, flows southwest into Carrizo creek near Salt river. "It is heavily timbered with cedar."

Cedar Mountain   Coconino Co.   U. S. G. S. Map, 1923; Tusayan N. F., 1927.

Elevation 7,057 feet. In T. 31 N., R. 6 E. Grand Canyon N. P., east side Grand Canyon, at northeast corner Tusayan N. F. "A cedar-covered peak."

Center Mountain   Gila Co.   Map, Tonto N. F., 1926.

In secs. 16, 21, 22, T. 6 N., R. 14 E. According to Bud Armer "was first called Baker's Horse mountain after Old Man Baker who had a horse ranch near here many years ago."

Cedar Mountain   Yavapai Co.   U. S. G. S. Map, 1928.

In T. 13 N., R. 6 E., on north side Clear creek in Verde valley, Coconino N. F.

Cedar Springs   Graham Co.   G. L. O. Map, 1892.

Headquarters ranch, in the Eighties, for Norton & Stewart Cattle Co., west side Pinaleno range, about 16 miles from Fort Grant on road to Camp Thomas. On Oct. 2, 1882, Geronimo and his band leaving San Carlos for Mexico attacked a wagon train belonging to M. Samaniego of Tucson, in sight of the stone cabin at the ranch in which were Mrs. Mowlds and two men. Indians did not disturb them and they saw the entire fight through the port holes. Mrs. Mowlds' husband was killed by the Indians under her eyes as he was returning to the station.

Apaches destroyed wagon loads of merchandise for San Carlos. They would tear open the bales of goods and ride away with long streamers of calico hanging from their saddle horns. They scattered flour and sugar on the ground and had a good time generally. During the killing four or five troops of 6th Cavalry arrived and had a pitched battle with them which lasted until night when the Indians, men, women, and children, escaped. They killed their dogs and every white horse so they could not be seen or heard while leaving. So far as results were concerned the fight was a draw.

For several days before this break on Oct. 2, 1882, Gen. Sherman, then Chief of the Army, had been at San Carlos agency looking into the Indian situation. On the evening of Sept. 30 he sent a long official wire to the Secretary of War. He closed with something like the following: "In my judgment these Apaches are now well satisfied; are peaceable; and I feel sure we shall have no further trouble with them." He left for Grant next day.

The author sat in the telegraph office at Fort Apache and heard this message sent. Sherman and his party with a small escort missed the Chiricahuas by the narrowest of margins. The military authorities at Whipple and Grant spent some mighty anxious hours until he was reported safe into Grant. A bit of unwritten history.

P. O. established Sept. 27, 1887, Barney E. Norton, P. M.

Cedar Springs   Navajo Co.   G. L. O. Map, 1930.

In T. 24 N., R. 19 E., about 2 miles outside south line of Navajo Ind. Res. "Original Cedar station was abandoned and office moved 5 miles north to 'Tees-too.' Known to the Navajos as Dine-be-Too, 'Indians water.' It is in heavy cedar country. Orville Hathorne originally started a store here." Letter, J. W. Richards, Joseph City. P. O. established Apr. 1, 1910, Charles Hubbell, P. M. Name changed to Tees Too, Dec., 1930. q.v.

Cedarville   Mohave Co.

See Cedar.

Cement Well   Yuma Co.

In sec. 22, T. 2 N., R. 5 W. Belongs to the Flower Pot Cattle Co. "A watering place on a desert road. The well sides were cemented up." *Routes to the Desert.*

Cementosa Tank   Yuma Co.   U. S. G. S. Map, 1923.

Sp., "cement-like." Water hole northwest end Littlehorn mountains. "These are large natural tanks near Alamo Spring. Rock is the so-called conglomerate, very like cement in its water-holding possibilities." *Routes to the Desert.*

Cemetery Hills   Yuma Co.

See Cemetery ridge.

Cemetery Ridge   Yuma Co.   U. S. G. S. Map, 1923.

Southwest Eagle Tail mountains, near lat. 113° 30' about 6 miles west Maricopa line. Some maps have it "Cemetery Hill." "According to local reports several prospectors were killed here in the Seventies and their bodies buried on the hill or ridge." Letter, Fred Notbush.

Center Mountain   Gila Co.   Map, Tonto N. F., 1927.

In T. 6 N., R. 14 E. "It lies between McFadden Horse mountain and Baker mountain. Hence has always been called Center mountain." Letter, T. T. Swift, Forest Supervisor. G. L. O. map, 1921, shows two mountains, Lookout and Baker.

Centennial Wash   Yuma and Maricopa Cos.   U. S. G. S. Map, 1923.

Rises south side Harcuvar mountains, runs southeast, enters Gila river in Arlington valley, in T. 2 S., R. 5 W. Named from Centennial Wells station on old Ehrenburg stage line, established 1876, Centennial year. Henry Wickenburg is said to have dug the well and opened the station.

Central   Graham Co.   U. S. G. S. Map, 1923.

In T. 6 S., R. 25 E. On Gila about 2 miles below Thatcher. Town and P. O. Arizona-Eastern R. R. Settled about 1883. Named from Central canal. First settlers were Orson and Joseph Cluff, 1882. They had been driven from Forestdale on Apache Ind. Res. P. O. established Jan. 11, 1886, William Asay, P. M.

Cerbat   Mohave Co.   G. L. O. Map, 1921; Hamilton, 1886.

Sp., "A popgun, blow gun." In T. 22 N., R. 18 W. Town, mining camp, on Kingman branch A. T. & S. F. R. R., and range of mountains. In Cerbat range, one mile south of Mineral. Cerbat was county seat, 1874.

"Cerbat, 35 miles from Hardyville, contains about 100 inhabitants." Hinton. "A wide valley divided the Black mountains from a high, snow-capped range called the 'Cerbat Range' by Whipple." Ives. Whipple speaks of the Big Horn or Cerbat range as located near junction of Big Sandy river with Santa Maria range. This could not have been the present range by that name. It was probably what is shown as Aquarius cliffs on G. L. O. map, 1921. Whipple says that Cerbat is Coco-Maricopa name for Big Horn sheep.

"June 9, 1776. I went three leagues and a half northeast to a Sierra that I named Sierra Morena." Garces. Coues says: "Sierra Morena is of course the Cerbat range already indicated as first so called by Whipple in 1854. It means 'blackish' or 'swarthy.'" P. O. established Dec. 23, 1872, William Cory, P. M.

Cerro Colorado   Pima Co.   Eckhoff Map, 1880; G. L. O., 1892.

In T. 20 S., R. 10 E. Sp., "Red Hill." At foot of Atascosa range. Mines on east side Altar valley. Pumpelly says: "The Heintzelman mine was also known as the 'Cerro Colorado.'" Prof. Pumpelly, a geologist and mining expert, was superintendent of the Salero group of mines, 1860-1862. His book *Across America and Asia* is an interesting account of conditions in southern Arizona in those days. Smith map shows both names. P. O. established Apr. 17, 1879, William S. Read, P. M.

Cerro del Temporal

See Windy point.

Cerro Gordo   Apache Co.   U. S. G. S. Map, 1923.

Mountain near north boundary Fort Apache Ind. Res. in T. 9 N., R. 25 E. Sp. "Cerro," hill or peak; "Gordo," big, fat; i.e. Big hill.

Cerro Montoso (sic) (Montuoso)   Apache Co.   G. L. O. Map, 1921.

In T. 27 E., R. 8 N., about 8 miles due north of Greer. Sp., "Cerro," a hill, the back bone of an animal. "Montuoso," hilly, mountainous. Probably a descriptive name meaning the back-bone of a mountain.

Chaistla Butte   Navajo Co.   Gregory Map. 1916; U. S. G. S., 1923.

Elevation 6,000 feet. In northeast corner of county, short distance north of Kayenta P. O., Navajo Ind. Res. "Navajo for 'beaver pocket.'" Haile. Hodge thinks this is a Hopi word meaning elk. He says it is the Hopi name for the Elk Clan.

Chalender   Coconino Co.   G. L. O. Map, 1921.

On A. T. & S. F. R. R. Lumber and saw mill town. "For George F. Chalender, Supt. of Motive Power, A. & P. R. R." A. G. W. P. O. established May 2, 1883, Harry L. Harris, P. M.

Chambers   Apache Co.   U. S. G. S. Map, 1923.

In T. 21 N., R. 27 E. Flag station A. T. & S. F. R. R. "After Edward Chambers, Vice President, Santa Fe R. R." A. G. W. Charles Chambers ran a trading post at this point for years before the railroad came. He was here as late as 1888. It was generally supposed this station was named for him. Frank L. Hathorne was first P. M., June 27, 1907. Name changed to Halloysite, q.v. Changed back to Chambers June 1, 1930.

Chamiso (sic)   Pima Co.

Station on S. P. R. R. about 45 miles east of Tucson. Sp., half burned wood. "About 1890 a large pile of mesquite cord wood caught fire and burned here." Note: The word Chamiza (sic) according to stockmen's usage means certain kinds of edible brush or shrubs.

Chandler   Maricopa Co.   G. L. O. Map, 1921.

In T. 1 S., R. 5 E., in secs. 27, 28, 33, 34. Elevation 1,210 feet. Station and P. O. S. P. R. R. about 7 miles south of Mesa. Named for A. J. Chandler who built the first canal system on the desert from Mesa. First Ter. Vet. Surgeon, Arizona Livestock Sanitary Board, appointed August, 1887. Home of the San Marcos hotel. P. O. established Apr. 11, 1912, Ernest E. Morrison, P. M.

Chaol Canyon   Coconino Co.   Gregory Map, 1916.

Navajo Ind. Res. Stream heading near White Mesa at lat. 36° 30', long. 111°, flows northwest into Navajo creek. Navajo word meaning pinyon. "Gregory wanted to call this Dortch for a local man but as he was a living person the U. S. G. B. refused to approve the name."

Chapparal (sic)   Yavapai Co.   G. L. O. Map, 1921.

P. O. and mining camp after mine by this name about 1873. In T. 13 N., R. 1 E., near McCabe mine. "Named for the mine here which was located in a dense growth of chaparral on the mountain side." Sp., "chaparral," brush, a live oak forest or thicket. Stockman's word signifying a dense brush thicket.
P. O. established May 24, 1894, Harmon B. Hanna, P. M.

Charleston   Cochise Co.   Eckhoff Map, 1880.

Town on San Pedro river about 6 miles south of Fairbank. For lack of water at Tombstone the stamp mill of the Tombstone Mine and Milling Co. was located here.

"There was a bridge over the river so the ore teams would not be delayed by flood. Alfred Henry Lewis called the place 'Red Dog' in his writings. Named for the city in South Carolina by early miners." Letter, A. C. Henry, Tombstone.

"The tall cottonwoods that shaded the village, still stand by the San Pedro. Beneath them are only a few crumbling adobe walls." *Tombstone.* First called Millville, q.v. P. O. established Apr. 17, 1879, Charles D. Handy, P. M.

Charmingdale   Yavapai Co.

Mining camp named after a man by the unusual name of Charmingdale Rogers. "He built the first public school in Prescott and taught children for more than a year." Farish. *Arizona Gazetteer,* 1881, states it was about 30 miles north of Prescott on the road to Mineral Park. P. O. established Jan. 30, 1879, Samuel C. Rogers, P. M.

Chase Creek   Greenlee Co.   Map, Crook N. F., 1928.

First railroad in Arizona was built up Chase creek between Clifton and Metcalf. The first locomotive ever operated in Arizona was over this 20-inch gauge line in 1880. After Chase, an early prospector. Creek rises in sec. 5, T. 2 S., R. 29 E., above the town of Granville; flows southeast, enters San Francisco river at Clifton.

Chaves (sic) Pass and Station   Coconino Co.   Smith Map, 1879; Coconino N. F., 1927.

In T. 16 N., R. 12 E. Pass and stopping place on old Santa Fe-Prescott star route mail line. Named for Col. J. Francisco Chavez, who commanded troops that came to Arizona as escort to first Gubernatorial party arriving in Arizona December, 1863. Hinton calls this Jarvis Pass, which he says is "about 14 miles from Sunset Pass." Often called Jarvis as late as 1886. A corruption of its original name. See Capt. King's story *Sunset Pass.*

Chediski Mountain   Navajo Co.

In T. 9 N., R. 15½ E. Rises to a height of about 1,000 feet. In northeast part Fort Apache Ind. Res. Apache name meaning "long white rock." Decision U. S. G. B.

Cheene Peak   Pinal Co.

In T. 4 S., R. 8 E. On Gila River Ind. Res. about 6 miles northwest Florence. Now known as Walker Butte, q.v. According to George T. Adams, P. M. "the name should be spelled as it is pronounced, i.e. 'Chee-nee,' a Pima Indian word meaning a Bird's mouth or beak. The peak is very sharp resembling somewhat a bird's beak."

Chemehuevi Indians

"A Shoshone tribe, an off-shoot of the Paiuti. They occupied east side of Colorado river from Bill Williams Fork to the Needles, also some country west of river in California, in Chemehuevi valley. They have a language quite distinct from their neighbors'." Hodge. Locally, the Cocopas are classed with the Chemehuevi.

Chemehuevi Valley and Mountain   Mohave Co.

U. S. G. S. Map, 1923.

East side Colorado river below A. T. & S. F. R. R. "After the Indians who, according to Garces, occupied the valley, 1775." Hodge. Ives says: "Whipple named this valley after the Indians in 1853. It lies at mouth of Bill Williams Fork extending north to the Needles which, on its northern end, and Mount Whipple on its southern side, designate the points where river enters and leaves Chemehuevi valley." See Mount Whipple.

Cherokee   Mohave Co.   G. L. O. Map. 1921.

In T. 24 N., R. 11 W. Station on A. T. & S. F. R. R. about 6 miles southwest Peach springs. "Just another name." A. G. W.

Cherry   Yavapai Co.   Map, Prescott N. F., 1927.

In sec. 16, T. 14 N., R. 3 E. Early town on Cherry creek. P. O. established Dec. 22, 1893, Tessie L. DeKuhn, P. M. A later and separate office from that of 1884.

Cherry Creek   Gila Co.   Map, Tonto, N. F., 1927.

Rises' under Rim, about 10 miles north of Young P. O., flows south through Pleasant valley, enters Salt river in south part of T. 4 N., R. 14 E. There were many wild cherry trees along its course in early days.

Cherry creek   Yavapai Co.   G. L. O. Map, 1921; Prescott N. F., 1927.

In sec. 3, T. 14½ N., R. 4 E. Station on Prescott-Middletown branch A. T. & S. F. R. R., 21 miles east of Prescott. "The town and creek was named for wild cherry trees which grew along the creek in great profusion." Letter, Frank Grubb, Forest Supervisor. Hinton called it "Wild Cherry creek, a running stream. Water, grass, and wood abundant." P. O. established Mar. 13, 1884, Cecilia de Kuhn, P. M.

Cherums Peak   Mohave Co.   Smith Map, 1879; Eckhoff, 1880.

In T. 23 N., R. 17 W. In Cerbat range, 12 miles north of Kingman. "This range- the Cerbat- culminates in a peak about 7,000 feet elevation, called Cherums from an Indian chief whom I knew in 1881, a venerable old whiskey soaker. Also called Serum; Sherum, or Srum." Coues. Bourke says he was a Hualpai chief.

Cheto   Apache Co.   G. L. O. Map, 1921.

"On the main A. T. & S. F. R. R. about 20 miles west of New Mexico line. First called Sanders, for C. W. Sanders, office Engineer, A. T. & S. F. R. R. Changed to Cheto because of another Sanders station on Santa Fe." A. G. W. In the early days was a well known Navajo trading post run by a man named Art Sanders. In spite of Mr. Wells' statement, local people all believe it was named for him, just as Houck, McCarty, Chambers, and several other places along here were named for early settlers and Indian traders.

Chevellon Butte   Coconino Co.   U. S. G. S. Map, 1923; Sitgreaves N. F., 1926.

In T. 15 N., R. 14 E. Solitary butte or mesa, elevation 6,935 feet. Its level top is covered with prehistoric ruins. After stream to the east. Sometimes spelled "Shevellons." Sitgreaves spelled it Chevlons.

Chevelon Creek, Chevelon Fork of Little Colorado, East Chevelon
Navajo and Coconino Cos.

In sec. 9, T. 11½ N., R. 14 E. Stream in Coconino county formed by junction Woods and Willow Springs canyons. Flows northeast through rough canyon into Little Colorado river at Hardy, on A. T. & S. F. R. R. After an early trapper and scout of this region. "Known among the trappers as Chevelon Fork from one of that name who died upon its banks from eating some poisonous root." Sitgreaves.

"Here we found a curious stream flowing into the Colorado Chiquito from the south, about 25 yards wide and 6 or 8 feet deep. We found otter and beaver signs every foot of the way. Ascending a few miles, found a deep canyon which was a sheer precipice several hundred feet high. At the bottom was a fine stream." Beale.

The author located a cattle ranch at its mouth, 1883, and lived there for several years. There were otter in the stream then. Butte and stream are both shown on Sitgreaves map, 1852. He spells it Chevelons in the text, but Chevlons on his map in both places. Chevelon is decision U. S. G. B. About 1879 Mormons from Sunset and Brigham City came into upper end of this canyon to make a settlement. They graded an excellent wagon road into the canyon at the Forks, which was called "Mormon Crossing." Located a number of homesteads and called it "The Valley of Agalon." "Where Joshua fought with the five Kings of the Amorites and broke them and chased them."

There were about ten cabins here in 1883, each having a "claim notice" written on a smooth board nailed on the door. Lot Smith once told the author they hoped to make a permanent settlement but the creek was not sufficient for irrigation purposes, so they gave it up. See West Chevelon.

Chiavria Point   Coconino Co.

In Grand Canyon N. P. on west wall in northeast section of Park, near lat. 36° 10', long. 111° 54'. "Named for Juan Chiavria, noted Maricopa chief and settlers' friend during Apache troubles. He and other Indians were with King Woolsey at the celebrated Pinole Treaty or Massacre at Bloody Tanks." Named by Frank Bond. Decision U. S. G. B.

Chic-hil-ti-calli (Red House)   Graham Co.

The best authorities feel this is the old ruin mentioned by several early Spanish explorers, especially Casteneda, Jaramillo and Coronado. These all speak both of Casa Grande and this place. Casteneda describes it as "made of colored or reddish earth." And again, "the building was made of red earth." Later writers have confused the two buildings and locations and assumed they were the Casa Grande Ruins, near Florence. Hodge feels however, that this is not the case. He thinks that "Red House" is the ancient Gila valley ruin, 2 miles southeast of Safford, near Pueblo Viejo. His main argument for this is, "because the ruin lies about 500 yards from a beautiful bank of red clay, that packs hard and makes a fine finish."

Chikapanagi Mesa   Coconino Co.

Grand Canyon N. P. lat. 36° 21', long. 112° 38'. Low table land area on left bank of Colorado river below "Ole" and "Matkatamiba" canyons and "Chikapanagi Point."

"Named by me for a Hava Supai Indian boy who was with me in the Canyon. The name is Supai for 'Bat.' The boy's face reminded the Indians of a bat, hence the name." James. Decision U. S. G. B.

Chilchinbito Spring   Navajo Co.   Gregory Map, 1916; G. L. O., 1921.

Father Haile says "It is a Navajo word and means Sumac Spring." In Hopi Ind. Res. at extreme northeast corner of reservation, under Black mesa.

Childs   Pima Co.   U. S. G. S. Map, 1923.

P. O. and station Tucson-Cornelia and Gila Bend R. R., in T. 11 S., R. 6 W. Station established, 1916. "Named for Tom Childs of Decker and Childs who operated and owned a ranch here." Letter, Supt. S. P. R. R., Tucson. Childs also had a mine near Ajo about 1884. *Arizona Sentinel* of Sept. 7, 1872, speaks of "Tom Childs of the firm of Decker and Childs of Pima Co." Barney says this same Tom Childs was night watchman and village zanjero at Phoenix, 1876.

Childs   Yavapai Co.

Transformer plant Arizona Power Co. "After a man named Childs who ran a ranch on the Verde river, at the mouth of Fossil creek." Letter, Landon Y. Woodmansee, Oct. 17, 1912.

Childs Mountain   Pima Co.   U. S. G. S. Map, 1923.

In T. 11 S., Rs. 6, 7 W. "Named for Tom Childs, an old time cattleman who ran cattle here in early days." Letter, Supt. S. P. R. R., Tucson.

Chilito   Gila Co.   G. L. O. Map, 1921; Crook N. F., 1926.

Sp., "Little peppers." In sec. 27, T. 4 S., R. 15 E. "Mining camp and Post office at Tornado peak. Headquarters, London-Arizona Mining Co., 3 miles west of Christmas. So named by Mexican miners." Letter, O. E. Clendenin. P. O. established June 11, 1913, George B. Chittenden, P. M.

Chiminea Mountain   Santa Cruz Co.   Map, Coronado N. F., 1927.

Sp., "chimney or shelf." In T. 22 S., R. 11 E. About 2 miles north of Ruby P. O. Descriptive name.

Chimopovy (sic)   Navajo Co.   G. L. O. Map, 1892.

P. O. and trading post Hopi Ind. Res. Hopi village about 15 or 20 miles west of Walpi. Name not in Hodges *Hand Book*. "This word has been changed through many years use. On P. O. lists and government records it is Chim-oo-povy, meaning a tall jointed grass or reed." Letter, F. H. McBride. P. O. established June 24, 1926, Mrs. Marietta Eubank, P. M. On Post route map, 1929, is spelled Shi-mo-pavy. See Shon-go-povi.

China Peak   Cochise Co.   Map, Coronado N. F., 1927.

Elevation 7,125 feet. In T. 16 S., R. 23 E., west of Cochise peak in Dragoons. "China peak derived its name from a mine near this peak which was worked and financed by California Chinamen for several years. So it came to be known by this name." Letter, J. A. Rockfellow, Cochise.

Chin-le (Chin lee)   Apache Co.   U. S. G. S. Map, 1923.

In T. 5 N., R. 10 W. Well known trading post, in Navajo Ind. Res., on Chinlee creek. " 'Chinle,' Navajo name for a place where water emerges from a canyon's mouth." Gregory.
P. O. established Jan. 15, 1903, Charles L. Day, P. M.

Chin-le Creek   Apache Co.   Gregory Map, 1916.

On Navajo Ind. Res. "The main Chin-le, from its head 6 miles northwest of Ganado, is about 100 miles long. Flows generally northwest, crosses into Utah near long. 109° 40'. Enters San Juan about 60 miles above that point. Tyende creek is its chief western tributary." Gregory.

Chinlini Canyon   Apache Co.   Gregory Map, 1916.

On Navajo Ind. Res. west side Carrizo mountains, in northwest corner of county. "Where the waters run out." Haile. The word in Navajo is spelled "I-chi-ni-li." Anglicized to Chin-li.

Chino   Yavapai Co.   G. L. O. Map, 1921.

Station A. T. & S. F. R. R., 4 miles west Seligman. At head Big Chino valley. See Chino valley.

Chino Creek   Yavapai and Coconino Cos.   Map, Prescott N. F., 1927.

Rises northwest of Mount Floyd southeast end Aubrey cliffs in T. 26 N., R. 6 W., runs through Chino valley entering Verde river in approximately T. 17 N., R. 1 W. See Chino.

Chino Valley P. O.   Yavapai Co.   Map, Prescott N. F., 1927.

In sec. 10, T. 16 N., R. 2 W., Chino valley, about 6 miles south of Del Rio. P. O. established Oct. 6, 1879, Benj. J. Wade, P. M. Closed in 1882. Nov. 13, 1883, reopened, Geo. W. Banghart, P. M. Banghart later moved to Del Rio or Bangharts, few miles above. This P. O. was opened again as Chino valley Apr. 11, 1923, Mrs. Sidney T. Fritsche, P. M. For some years it was called Jerome Junction. q.v.

Chino Valley   Yavapai Co.   G. L. O. Map, 1921, Big Chino Valley.

About 35 miles northwest of Prescott in open country between Prescott and Tusayan N. Fs. Originally called Big Chino valley. Named by Whipple, 1853, who called it "Val de Chino." "Chino," he writes, "is said to be the local Mexican name for grama grass, which grows luxuriantly in this valley."

Chlarson's Canyon

See Frye.

Cholla   Cochise Co.

Station S. P. R. R. about 20 miles east of Willcox. Located in a great stretch of cholla cactus.

Cholla Mountain   Maricopa Co.   G. L. O. Map, 1921.

In T. 6 N., R. 1 E., about 2 miles southeast of Castle Hot springs. So called for cholla cactus found all over the mountain.

Chiricahua   Cochise Co.

In T. 21 S., R. 21 E. Station E. P. & S. W. R. R., east side Chiricahua range, 3 miles from Douglas. After Chiricahua Indians who once ranged over this region. P. O. established Sept. 14, 1907, Henrietta Powell, P. M.

Chiricahua Apaches

"An important division of the Apache. So called for their former home in mountains under that name in southeastern Arizona. Their own name is 'Aia ha.' The most warlike of the Arizona Indians. Their noted leaders were Cochise, Mangus, Juh, and Geronimo." Hodge. They were all removed to Florida, 1886. Hodge says the name Chiricahua means "A great mountain."

Chiricahua Buttes   Gila Co.   Map, San Carlos Ind. Res., 1917.

Peak southeast corner of T. 3 N., R. 21 E., about 4 miles south of Black river. After a band of Chiricahua-Apaches who lived here.

Chiricahua National Monument   Cochise Co.

Map, Coronado N. F., 1927.

In T. 29½ E., R. 16 S. Set aside 1924 to preserve interesting rock formations here.

Chiricahua Peak   Cochise Co.   Map, Coronado N. F., 1927.

In T. 18 S., R. 30 E., Chiricahua mountains. "This peak is part of what is locally known as Snowshed. Formerly called Round mountain; also Turkey mountain. Name changed by government 1904." Letter, J. C. Hancock, Paradise. See Snowshed peak.

Chiu Chuschu   Pinal Co.   G. L. O. Map, 1921; U. S. G. S., 1923.

In T. 8 S., R. 5 E., Papago village. Papago Ind. Res., north end Silver Reef mountains. "Name sometimes spelled Chiu-chiuschiu. Is at head of Santa Rosa valley. Often called 'Chu Chew.' Papago word meaning 'many caves in mountains.' Mountain nearby is full of caves, hence the name. It is a very old village." Letter, W. C. Shako.

Chloride   Mohave Co.   U. S. G. S. Map, 1923.

In Cerbat mountains, northern end branch railroad from Kingman. From character of local ores.

Station Chloride branch A. T. & S. F. R. R. 27 miles north of Kingman. "Chloride Flat, 6 miles north of Mineral Park, had two smelting furnaces several years ago. There are several gold mines in this vicinity and some indications of cinnabar." Hinton. P. O. established Mar. 27, 1873, Robert H. Choate, P. M. Smith map, 1879, calls it Chloride City.

Chocolate Mountains   Yuma Co.   U. S. G. S. Map, 1923.

In Ts. 2, 3, 4 S., Rs. 20, 21 W. north of Colorado river. From color of hills.

Christmas   Gila Co.   G. L. O. Map, 1921.

P. O. and mining camp at end Winkelman branch, Arizona-Eastern R. R. In Dripping Springs mountains in T. 4 S., R. 16 E., 22 miles northeast Winkelman.

"Dennis O'Brien and Bill Tweed located copper claims in Dripping Springs mountains about 1878. In 1882 Dr. James Douglas located claims adjoining. All were found to be within San Carlos Apache Ind. Res. and prospectors were forced to leave. In 1900 someone at Washington became interested and eventually reservation lines were changed. This decree was signed a few days before Christmas, 1902. A wire was sent to George Crittenden and his partner N. H. Mellor which reached them at their camp on Christmas Eve. They acted promptly; reaching the Gila at midnight they waited for daylight, forded the stream, and made their locations. 'I guess we jumped the claims of O'Brien, Tweed, and Dr. Douglas all right,' says Mellor, 'but it was Christmas day in the morning so we filled our stockings and named the place Christmas in honor of the day.'" *Arizona Republic*, Phoenix, Dec. 24, 1930.

In recent years the little P. O. here is swamped with Christmas letters and cards sent under cover from all parts of the

United States to be mailed out from the office bearing official stamp "Christmas." P. O. established June 17, 1905, William Swingle, P. M.

Christopher Creek   Gila Co.   Map, Tonto N. F., 1926.

About 27 miles northeast of Payson. Heads at large spring under Mogollon rim; empties into Tonto creek from east. Named for a Frenchman, Isador Christopher, first settler on this creek. "In the Apache raid July, 1882, Indians came to this ranch. Christopher was away and they burned his two log houses. U. S. troops came up while fire still burned. Christopher had killed a bear the day before, skinned and hung it in one of the cabins. Soldiers supposed the remains to be those of Christopher killed and burned by Apaches." Letter, F. W. Croxen. Local settlers afterwards claimed that the soldiers buried the remains with due solemnity as those of a human. Those old timers loved to joke about the army people.

Christopher Mountain   Gila Co.   Map, Tonto N. F., 1926.

In T. 11 N., Rs. 12, 13 E. Named for Isador Christopher. See Christopher creek.

Christvale

See Crystoval.

Chromo Butte   Gila Co.   U. S. G. S. Map, 1923.

Turning point boundary line San Carlos Ind. Res. in sec. 20, T. 2 N., R. 16 E., about 10 miles northeast of Globe. The author thought this should have been Chrome from the mineral. Poston however calls it Chromo Butte and Hinton lists a Chromo mine near here so name is probably correct.

Chrysolite   Gila Co.   G. L. O. Map, 1921; Crook N. F., 1926.

In sec. 35, T. 5 N., R. 17 E. Asbestos mining camp. Word chrysolite covers several brilliant stones, notably olivine and peridot, classed as gems, which are found in this mine. Hence the name. P. O. established June 27, 1916, Nels A. Nelson, P. M.

Chrystoval   Yuma Co.   G. L. O. Map, 1892.

Station S. P. R. R. in early days. About 40 miles east of Yuma. Took the place of stage station at this point known as "Spanish Ranch." Named for the man, Chrystoval, who ran the ranch. The R. R. later shortened it to Stoval. q.v. On some maps called Christvale. P. O. established Sept. 23, 1888, Oscar F. Thornton, P. M.

Chuar Creek   Coconino Co.

Grand Canyon N. P. Rises near lat. 36° 13', long. 111° 53', northwest Gunther's Castle, flows southwest into Lava creek. "After one of Powell's Kaibab Indians, 'Chuar-oo-um-peak,' young Kaibab chief, usually called Frank by settlers and Chuar by his own people. He was a remarkably good man." Dellenbaugh. Decision, U. S. G. B.

Chu Chew

See Chiu-Chuschu.

Chuck Box Lake   Navajo Co.   G. L. O. Map, 1923.

In northeast corner Fort Apache Ind. Res. "About 1887 or 1888, Frank Wallace, range foreman of Waters Cattle Co., took their chuck wagon to this lake on the roundup. Road was so rough that they had to unload and pack out leaving the heavy chuck box behind." Letter, A. F. Potter, Los Angeles, Calif.

Chupan Mountain   Pima Co.   U. S. G. S. Map, 1923.

North end and east side Mesquite mountains, Papago Ind. Res. Near lat. 32°, long. 112° 30′, about 25 miles west of Sells.

Church Rock   Navajo Co.   U. S. G. S. Map, 1923.

Navajo Ind. Res. East side Navajo county, south of Tyende creek in lat. 36° 45′, long. 110°. Descriptive name, resembles a large church.

Chuska Mountains   Apache Co.   Gregory Map, 1916; G. L. O., 1921.

In Ts. 7, 8, 9 N., R. 6 W. Navajo word meaning "White spruce." There is a fine body of spruce here that extends into New Mexico. Father Haile spells it "Chush-gai." On Navajo Ind. Res. along State line.

Cibecue   Navajo Co.   U. S. G. S. Map, 1923.

Indian camp, farm, and creek. There is now a branch Indian school here.

August 30, 1881, Capt. E. C. Hentig, 6th. U. S. Cavalry, with six enlisted men of Gen. Carr's command, were killed here in a fight with Apaches. Nock-aye-de-Klinney, Apache Medicine Man, was killed by the troops.

Hurley, interpreter at Apache, shortly after the fight, told the author that when Gen. Carr asked an Apache scout what they called the place, he replied, "She-be-Ku," meaning "My house"; (she, "my," becue, "house"). Carr accepted this as a name for the place. Later the author secured substantially the same story from another Apache.

Three White Mountain Apaches, Dandy Jim, Dead Shot, and Skippy, enlisted Indian Scouts who turned against troops at the fight, were tried for mutiny by military Court Martial at Fort Grant and hanged there, Mar. 3, 1882. Two others were sent to Alcatraz prison for life. Dead Shot's squaw hanged herself at San Carlos on the day of execution.

Creek rises in northwest corner of Fort Apache Ind. Res. flows south into Salt river about 10 miles west of junction White and Black rivers which form Salt. P. O. established here for Indian School, Mar. 18, 1910, Agnes W. Chambers, P. M.

Cibola   Apache Co.

"Name given by Fray Marcos of Niza, to cluster of villages occupied by Zuni tribe, 1539. He heard the word in Sonora and it may have been a corruption of 'Shiuona,' Zuni name for the range held by that tribe." *Century Dictionary.*

Hodge says: "A name given any buffalo-hunting Indians by the Mexican-Spanish." The word was given the buffalo by early Spanish adventurers. The "Seven cities of Cibola" were the famous cities of which Coronado went in search, 1540-41. See Seven Pueblos.

Cibola   Yuma Co.   G. L. O. Map, 1921.

In T. 1 S., R. 24 W. Town and valley on Colorado river some 50 miles above Yuma. After Spanish name for the Hopi villages. P. O. established Feb. 28, 1903, Louis W. Bishop, P. M.

Cienega, The   Pima Co.   Smith Map, 1879; Eckhoff, 1880.

Sp., "A marsh, a swamp." The word was used by the Mexicans in early days to designate any wet grassy meadow where hay was cut. Word really means "hundred springs," "cien," hundred; "agua," water or springs. It was generally pronounced "Sinicky" or "Senicky" by the uninformed. Old stage station about 15 miles southeast Tucson. This was "Shot Gun" Smith's well-known stage station about 3 miles from present railroad station of Pantano. In 1868 Smith was attacked here by Apaches. He killed a number and the rest withdrew.

"The cienega now called Pantano by the railroad people." Bourke. John O. Dunbar, well-known editor, has an advertisement in Jan., 1880, in Tucson papers to the effect that his hotel here was open for business. It was a lovely spot in those days, full of birds, and a grassy meadow with grand old Cottonwood trees around the house. After a week in Tucson in February, 1880, it seemed like a Garden of Eden to the author. There were flocks of glorious red- and yellow-shouldered black birds, golden finches, and other brilliant birds in the meadow. Ed. Vail says that in 1880 this cienega was a succession of lovely meadows right on top of the ground. In ten or fifteen years it had become a deep wash; too many cows. See Pantano, Cienega Railroad station.

Cienega   Yavapai Co.   Map, Prescott N. F., 1925.

In T. 13 N., R. 2 E. Ranch and stopping place on road from Verde to Prescott. On head of Cienega creek. P. O. established Apr. 25, 1877, George W. Hance, P. M. He owned the place at that time.

Cienega   Pima Co.

On E. P. & S. W. R. R., about 25 miles east Tucson. Named after old Cienega stage station of early days which was near here. Elliott's map, 1844, calls it "Punta de Agua," Point of Water. Bourke uses this same name here. See Pantano.

Cienega Creek   Graham Co.   U. S. G. S. Map, 1923.

Small stream eastern part San Carlos Ind. Res. Enters Eagle creek about 6 miles south of Double Circle ranch.

Cienega creek   Santa Cruz and Pinal Cos.   U. S. G. S. Map, 1928.

Rises in Canelo hills, Santa Cruz county, runs northeast, enters Pantano wash in T. 17 S., R. 18 E., about 4 miles east of Pantano.

Cienega Amarilla   Apache Co.   Smith Map, 1879.

Sp., "Yellow Meadows." "On Cienega creek, about 15 miles southeast of Springerville, on the old wagon road to Rio Grande at Fort Craig." Hinton. Was so called because the salt grass on the meadow turned yellow very early in the fall and remained that color until spring. Was a favorite camping place for freighters and travellers to the Rio Grande. About 1885 it was owned or claimed by the well known Ike Clanton who had a gang of men around him of dubious character. See Saint Michaels.

Cimarron Mountains   Pima Co.   U. S. G. S. Map, 1923.

In Ts. 11, 12 S., Rs. 2, 3 E. Sp., "wild, an outlaw." Mexicans call mountain sheep "cimarron."

Mountain sheep must have been very plentiful in this region for Father Kino says: "Four leagues west of the Casa Grande they (Manje and his party) reached the *rancheria* of Tusonimo, where there was a mound of mountain goat horns like a hill, this goat being their common food. Manje estimated 100,000 horns in the pile." Kino's Memoirs. See Sheridan hills. On G. L. O. map, 1921, it is a single peak in T. 11 S., R. 2 E. See Tusonimo.

Cinch Hook Butte   Coconino Co.   Map, Coconino N. F., 1928.

In sec. 6, T. 12 N., R. 9 E., on the Rim north of Pine. "This rock forms a perfect 'cinch hook' and was so named by settlers as early as 1880." Letter, P. I. Stewart, Forest Ranger.

Cinnibar   Yuma Co.   G. L. O. Map, 1921.

Old mining camp west slope Dome Rock mountains. "At first they thought they had a quicksilver or cinnibar mine here. It failed to develop."

City Creek   Gila Co.   Eckhoff Map, 1880; Tonto N. F., 1926.

Stream and canyon draining north and west side of North peak of Mazatzals, emptying into East Verde, in sec. 17, T. 10 N., R. 9 E.

"There was in the late Seventies a Mormon settlement called Mazatzal city on the Verde where this creek joins it. They abandoned it and moved to Pine about 1882. Creek was called City Creek by these settlers." Letter, Fred Croxen, Forest Ranger. See Mazatzal City.

Clack   Mohave Co.

"P. O. located in Cerbat mountains at Oro Plata mine. My brothers and I were mining here. Was named for our family. About 3 miles south of Mineral Park. We served about 75 miners with mail." Letter, G. H. Clack, Kingman, 1933.

P. O. established July 26, 1898, John W. Babson, P. M.

Clanton, Hills and Well   Yuma Co.   U. S. G. S. Map, 1923.

East side of county near Maricopa line. After "Old Man Clanton," well known among pioneer mining men. He later moved to Tombstone where he and his family became somewhat noted characters. See Tombstone.

Clara Peak   Yuma Co.

In T. 4 S., R. 21 W., about 5 miles east Colorado river. See Klara.

Clara Well   Yuma Co.   G. L. O. Map, 1921.

Elevation 1,500 feet. On Bouse wash. "For many years Butler brothers hauled water from this well to their mine. The Clara also hauled water from it as it was the only well in the region. Was known locally as 'Clara' well, after the mine." Letter, J. E. Matteson. See Butler Well, also Klara.

Clark—Camp Clark   Yavapai Co.

In Little Chino valley. Established 1864. After John A. Clark, Surveyor General, New Mexico, one of first officials to report on mines in this region. "This camp was first called Fort Whipple, according to Banta." Farish.

"Camp Clark is claimed to have been the first capital of Arizona. After three or four months it was moved to Prescott. The *Arizona Miner* was issued first at this place March 9, 1864, publisher, Tisdale Hand." *Report of Governor of Arizona,* 1897.

Clark Peak   Graham Co.   Map, Crook N. F., 1931.

In sec. 15, T. 8 S. R. 23 E. In Graham mountains east of Taylor Pass. Located in, and named for Clark mining district.

Clark Valley   Coconino Co.   Map, Coconino Co., 1928.

In T. 20 N., R. 8 E., part of valley now covered by Lake Mary. After John Clark, one of first settlers here.

Clarksdale   Yavapai Co.   U. S. G. S. Map, 1923.

In T. 16 N., R. 3 E. Same location as Bear. In Verde valley. Location of Senator Clark's United Verde smelters. After Senator Clark.

Clarkston   Pima Co.

Village a mile east of Ajo and a suburb of that town.

Clay Park   Yavapai Co.   Map, Coconino N. F., 1927.

In southeast corner T. 18 N., R. 7 E. About 5 miles southeast Wilson mountain. "After Ben Clay, who located here in early Eighties. Was first called Jack's ranch." Letter, Ed. Miller, Forest Supervisor. See Jacks canyon.

Claypool   Gila Co   U. S. G. S. Map, 1923.

In T. 1 N., R. 15 E. Small mining camp about 4 miles northwest of Globe on Miami branch railroad. Named for Senator W. D. Claypool. P. O. established July 21, 1917, Frank E. Hall, P. M.

Clay Springs   Navajo Co.   U. S. G. S. Map, 1923.

In sec. 11, T. 11 N., R. 19 E. P. O. and ranch on a "wet weather seep" or spring, that comes from a clay bank. Few miles northeast of Pinedale. P. O. established Mar. 12, 1917, Dora Peterson, P. M.

Clear Creek   Coconino and Navajo Cos.   U. S. G. S. Map, 1923; Coconino N. F., 1928.

In T. 12 N., R. 10 E. Rises in Long valley, flows northeast into Little Colorado at Hobson station A. T. & S. F. R. R. Its upper end is called East Clear creek to differentiate it from Clear creek on Verde slope which heads very near East Clear creek. Sitgreaves, 1851, called this "The Big Dry Fork." The "Battle of the Big Dry wash" took place on this stream on its east side a few miles below Generals springs. See Big Dry Fork. Smith map, 1879 and Hamilton, 1866, call it "Big Dry Fork."

Clear Creek   Coconino and Yavapai Cos.   Map, Coconino N. F., 1928.

Rises in T. 13 N., R. 9 E. on north side of Bakers butte, flows north and west, enters Verde river in T. 13 N., R. 5 E., about 5 miles below Camp Verde. Now called West Clear creek to distinguish it from the Clear creek flowing into Little Colorado river.

Clearwater   Yavapai Co.   G. L. O. Map, 1892.

In T. 18 N., R. 3 W. Station old Arizona and Prescott R. R., in Big Chino valley. P. O. established June 9, 1887, David W. Clearwater, P. M. Station named for Clearwater family.

Cleator (sic)   Yavapai Co.   Map, Prescott N. F., 1929.

In sec. 2, T. 10 N., R. 1 E. P. O. and station Prescott and Middelton branch A. T. & S. F. R. R. 44 miles southeast of Prescott. "Named for James P. Cleater who owned the townsite. The railroad wrongly spells the name Cleator." Letter, James P. Cleater, P. M. It was first called Turkey q.v. P. O. established Feb. 14, 1913, James P. Cleater, P. M.

Clemenceau   Yavapai Co.   U. S. G. S. Map, 1923.

P. O. and station in Verde valley on Clarksdale branch A. T. & S. F. R. R. After the French statesman. Originally called Verde but changed in Jan., 1920, to avoid confusion with Camp Verde. "This place originally known as Verde, was located in 1917. There being so many Verdes, it seemed wise to choose a new name. Mr. George Tener, Vice President of the company, agreed to calling it 'Clemenceau' for the great Frenchman." Letter, Hon. James S. Douglas.

"Clemenceau evidently appreciated the honor for in his will he left a vase to the town which he described as 'designed by Chaplet in a light lilac color which will be found on the shelf above the mirror in my study! The vase will be placed in a suitable case in the High school of the town." Letter, The Mayor of Clemenceau. Decision U. S. G. B.

Clement Powell Butte   Coconino Co.

Grand Canyon N. P. on west bank Bright Angel creek, near lat. 36° 9', long. 112° 5', about 3 miles north of Suspension bridge. Named for Clement Powell, Asst. Photographer, Second Powell Expedition, 1871-72, through the Grand Canyon. Full name given because there were three Powells in the two expeditions; "J. W.," "Wm. H.," and "Clement." Decision U. S. G. B.

Clifton   Greenlee Co.   G. L. O. Map, 1921.

In T. 4 S., R. 30 E., elevation 3,464 feet. County seat on San Francisco river, mouth of Chase creek. Settled about 1873 by miners who developed rich copper deposits here. On E. P. & S. W. R. R. (Old Ariz. & N. M. narrow gauge). One of oldest and richest copper camps in Southwest.

"The town was started in a basin surrounded by high cliffs hence Clifton." Letter, W. A. Smith.

A. F. Banta says: "In 1864, Henry Clifton, Recorder of the Hassayampa district, and four other prospectors . . . . discovered copper mines on the San Francisco and he was honored in the naming of the locality."

Hinton's Handbook shows a Clifton Gold mine recorded in the Big Bug district in 1878 which gives some color to Banta's statement.

Charles M. Shannon, whose uncle founded the district, says his uncle often told how they first camped here "under the huge cliffs," which suggested the name Clifftown. Doubtless correct. P. O. established Mar. 8, 1875, Charles Lezinsky, P. M.

Cliffs   Coconino Co.   G. L. O. Map, 1921.

Station A. T. & S. F. R. R., 5 miles east Flagstaff near Walnut Canyon cliff dwellings. Named by Santa Fe survey engineers because of nearby cliff dwellings.

Cline   Gila Co.   G. L. O. Map, 1892; U. S. G. S., 1923.

Town and creek upper end Roosevelt lake. Creek flows into Tonto creek in T. 5 N., R. 10 E. Named for Christian Cline, early cattleman. Cline family still ranges cattle here. P. O. established Nov. 25, 1891, Mrs. Ella E. Webb, P. M.

Clip   Yuma Co.   G. L. O. Map, 1882.

Old station and landing place on Colorado river about 15 miles above Norton. Origin unknown. Was a rich silver mine, 1886. P. O. established Feb. 6, 1884, Anthony G. Hubbard, P. M.

Clostermeyer Lake   Coconino Co.   Map, Coconino N. F., 1927.

In sec. 27, T. 25 N., R. 6 E. For William Clostermeyer, pioneer cattleman who enlarged the lake, 1886, by building a dam.

Clothos Temple   Yuma Co.

See Klothos Temple.

Cluff Cienega   Apache Co.   U. S. G. S. Map, 1887.

In sec. 30, T. 8 N., R. 24 E. Apache Ind. Res. at McNary. After Bishop Benjamin Cluff who, 1879-80 cut hay here under contract for Fort Apache. The last elk known to have been killed by hunters in the White mountains was shot on this cienega, 1882, by army packers who camped here to obtain *Aparejo* grass. Spelled Clough on some early maps. P. O. records show that the Bishop spelled his name Cluff when P. M. at Central, Graham Co., in 1887.

Cluff Peak   Graham Co.   Map, Crook N. F., 1926.

In sec. 35, T. 6 S., R. 21 E. After Benjamin Cluff. See Cluff Cienega.

Coal Canyon

See Awatubi.

Coanini Creek   Coconino Co.

Powell says: "This is the most important stream from the south. It heads near San Francisco mountains and joins the Colorado at great depths." From Powell's location when he wrote this must be present Cataract or Havasupai creek.

Cobre Grande Peak   Graham Co.   U. S. G. S. Map, 1923.

Sp. "big copper." On Crook N. F. in T. 5 S., R. 20 E.

Cochibo   Pima Co.   U. S. G. S. Map, 1923.

In T. 17 S., R. 3 W., Papago Ind. Res. Indian village about 40 miles west of Sells east side Ajo range. "Kochi," a pig; "bo," a pond. Pigs were found near this pond, hence the name." Father Oblasser.

Cochise   Cochise Co.

Station S. P. R. R. at junction Arizona Eastern R. R. to Douglas. After Cochise, Apache chief. P. O. established July 21, 1887, Silas H. Gould, P. M.

Cochise Butte   Coconino Co.

Grand Canyon N. P. near northeast corner of Park and lat. 36° 13' N., long. 111° 53' W. Named for Apache chief, Cochise. Decision U. S. G. B.

Cochise County

In southeastern corner State. Created out of Pima county, 1881. Tombstone was county seat for many years; now at Bisbee. Located on Continental divide. After Cochise; Cocheis; or Cheis, Apache chief. According to best posted authorities this Apache's real name was "Cheis," Apache word meaning "wood." Capt. Bourke frequently wrote it this way. Official and legal name is Cochise.

Cochise Head   Cochise Co.   Map, Coronado N. F., 1927.

Peak elevation 8,100 feet, northern part Chiricahua mountains in T. 16 S., R. 30 E.

Cochise Peak   Cochise Co.   Map, Coronado N. F., 1927.

In Dragoon mountains. Elevation 6,500 feet. Eight miles west of Pearce. For the Apache chief Cochise.

Cochise Stronghold   Cochise Co.   Map, Coronado N. F., 1927.

In T. 17 S., R. 23 E. On eastern side Dragoon mountains. On Stronghold canyon. So called because Cochise used this basin as a hiding place. Forest Ranger station is located here. Gen. Miles had a heliograph station near here in 1886 during the Geronimo campaign.

"While watering his horses in Cochise Stronghold Capt. Gerald Russell, K Troop, 3rd. U. S. Cavalry, was assailed by Cochise and his band. At the first shot poor Bob Whitney, his guide, was killed. He was an unusually handsome fellow of great courage and long service against the Apaches." Bourke. See Horse Shoe canyon. This stronghold was near the center of the original Chiricahua Ind. Res. established by agreement between Gen. O. O. Howard and Cochise, Oct. 12, 1872. Agency headquarters were at Sulphur springs. Abandoned 1876 when Indians were moved to San Carlos Ind. Res.

According to Indian Agent Jeffords and John A. Rockfellow, "Cochise died here and was buried at the mouth of the canyon overlooking Sulphur Springs valley. After burial the Apaches rode their ponies back and forth over the area about the grave, completely obliterating it."

Tucson Star, June 13, 1874: "Cochise died June 8, 1874. He was about 70 years of age."

Upper end of Stronghold is now an auto park and public camp ground named by the U. S. Forest Service, "Cochise Memorial Park."

Cochran   Pinal Co.

On Arizona-Eastern R. R. about 15 miles east of Florence. On the Gila river. Named for John S. Cochran, first P. M., Jan. 13, 1905.

Cocklebur   Pinal Co.   U. S. G. S. Map, 1923.

In T. 7 S., R. 4 E. Papago village in Papago Ind. Res. "Because of the heavy crop of cockleburs the Papagos had in their fields one summer."

Cocks Comb   Coconino Co.   Map, Kaibab N. F., 1926.

Range running north and south between North and South canyons in Kaibab N. F. Narrow, sharp, pointed ridge resembling a rooster's comb.

Coconino County

Northern part of State, east of Yavapai county. Created, 1893, out of Yavapai county. So called from Havasupai Indian word meaning "little water." Flagstaff, county seat.

Said to be the largest county in U. S. Name suggested by D. M. Riordan of Flagstaff. In the original bill it was called "Frisco" after the peak near Flagstaff; then, "Tusayan." Riordan, however, insisted on an Indian name.

Bartlett says: "The Cosninos I presume to be the same as

the Coch-ni-ch-nos whom Mr. Antoine Leroux met in his late journey down the Colorado." Hodge believes these were the Havasupai or Supais. He says the name means "people of the green water, or willow people."

Coconino   Coconino Co.   G. L. O. Map, 1921.

Station, Grand Canyon branch, A. T. & S. F. R. R. 8 miles from Grand Canyon.

Coconino National Forest   Coconino Co.

On Jan. 2, 1908, this Forest was established from parts of three areas: San Francisco Mountains Forest Reserve, established Aug. 17, 1898; Black Mesa Forest Reserve, established Aug. 17, 1898; and the Grand Canyon Forest Reserve, established Feb. 20, 1893. June 28, 1910, the western part was created into the Tusayan N. F. Area of Coconino N. F. in 1931, 1,915,850 acres. Supervisor headquarters, Flagstaff.

Coconino Plateau   Coconino Co.

Tusayan N. F. A broad geological plateau on south side of Grand Canyon, in T. 31 N., Rs. 1, 2, 3 E.

"A name given by C. Hart Merriam, 1892, to the belt of higher country, extending from the vicinity of Bass' camp on the Canyon, southeasterly to Coconino Point overlooking the Little Colorado river." Letter, H. H. Robinson U. S. G. S., Washington, D. C. Afterwards covered by the more extensive name "Plateau of Arizona."

Coconino Point   Coconino Co.   U. S. G. S. Map, 1923.

In T. 29 N., R. 9 E. In Tusayan N. F. An outstanding headland on the rim of the Grand Canyon.

Cocopah Indian Reservation   Yuma Co.   G. L. O. Map, 1921.

Small Indian reservation on Colorado river about 10 miles below Yuma. " 'Cocopa,' Papago word meaning 'those who live on the river.' " Lumholtz.

Cocoraque Butte   Pima Co.   G. L. O. Map, 1921.

In T. 14 S., R. 10 E. On east side Roskruge mountains. Hodge writes he would spell it "Co-co-ra-qui"; says it is an Indian word but does not know its meaning or origin.

Coffer Creek   Coconino Co.   Map, Coconino N. F., 1928.

In T. 18 N., R. 3 E. Stream rising east side Black mountains. Flows southeast into Oak creek in sec. 34, T. 16 N., R. 4 E. "Tradition says a man named Coffer lived here many years ago."

Cold Spring Wash   Mohave Co.   U. S. G. S. Map, 1923.

Rises near Diamond butte, runs south, enters Colorado river in T. 31 N., R. 9 W.

Coldwater   Maricopa Co.

On Agua Fria river, in T. 1 N., R. 1 W. "Coldwater claims the distinction of being one of the very earliest stage stations in this region. It was run by 'Uncle Billy Moore' (W. G. Moore) who still lives here although very feeble. The first well dug here carried very clear, cold water, hence the name." Letter, E. B. Pentland, Coldwater. See Avondale.

P. O. established as Coldwater, July 2, 1896, Mary V. Jones, P. M.

Coledon   Maricopa Co.   G. L. O. Map, 1909.

Station S. P. R. R. about 4 miles east of Gila Bend. "Was originally called Cole, after a R. R. engineer named Cole, but was changed about 1926. Coledon seemed a better word to telegraph." Letter, Supt. S. P. R. R., Tucson.

Coleman Lake   Coconino Co.   U. S. G. S. Map, 1923.

In T. 21 N., R. 2 E. In Tusayan N. F. southeast of Bill Williams mountain. "So named for an old homesteader known to every one as 'Dad Coleman.' He built the dam which makes the lake." Letter, H. L. Benham, Williams. On Smith map, 1879, it is shown as Collins ranch, elevation 5,526 feet. On Eckhoff map it shows as McCollum ranch, 5,526 feet elevation.

Colfred   Yuma Co.   G. L. O. Maps, 1909, 1921.

In T. 8 S., R. 16 W. "Station S. P. R. R. About 50 miles east of Yuma. A coined word. Named for Col. Fred Crocker, Treasurer, S. P. R. R. in 1881." Letter, Paul Shoup.

College Peak   Cochise Co.

Station or spur on E. P. & S. W. R. R., about 14 miles from Douglas. "Station named after nearby College Peak." Letter, Supt., S. P. R. R. See College peaks.

College Peaks   Cochise Co.   Map, Coronado N. F., 1925;
Hinton, 1886; G. L. O., 1892, 1921.

Two peaks south of E. P. & S. W. R. R. In T. 23 S., R. 29 E., upper end Perilla mountains. North peak no elevation; South, 6,385 feet. "Prior to 1901 known locally as Saddle mountain, also 'The Nipples.' Origin not known." Carl B. Scholefield, Forest Ranger.

"I have never been able to learn the origin of College Peak. The H. G. Howe map of 1889 gave it that name. William Sutley tells me that in the early Eighties he knew it as Silver Creek Peak." Letter, John A. Rockfellow, 1931. One writer says: "Some college boys camped at the foot of one of these peaks. One of them fell over a cliff and was killed." This must have been before 1892 for the name College shows on G. L. O. map of that year.

Collins Ranch   Coconino Co.

See Coleman lake.

Collins Well   Coconino Co.

See Kerlins.

Colmorico Caves   Coconino Co.

"July 18, 1859, at San Francisco spring. We started and traveled to Colmorico caves. We found an abundance of water in the rocks in the vicinity. We found a deep, rocky canyon which was filled with water. . . . In it we saw mountain trout." Beale. This must have been the caves which in Apr., 1857, Beale called Cosnino. q.v. There is nothing in his history to explain this name or reason for the change.

Colorado Bridge   Apache Co.

Shows on Elliott's map, 1866, near present St. Johns. Undoubtedly location of first bridge built across Colorado river in this vicinity. Date of bridge building by Jose Seavedra (sic) and father said to be Dec., 1872. which is confusing. The map certainly would not show the bridge unless one was there. It is also unlikely that there was a bridge before Seavedra built his.

Colorado Camp   Mohave Co.

On Colorado river, near mouth Bill Williams river. "On Colorado Ind. Res. 40 miles north of La Paz. Established Nov. 25, 1868. Abandoned 1871." Hammersley Army Register.

According to McClintock this was a sub-post of Fort Yuma on the Mohave reservation.

Colorado Chiquito River

See Little Colorado.

Colorado City   Yuma Co.

P. O. established under this name, now called Yuma, March 17, 1858, John B. Dow, P. M. He served a short time. Lansford W. Hastings was appointed in his place. Was then in Doña Ana county, New Mexico, and his commission was issued and dated that way. See Yuma.

Colorado Crossing   Mohave Co.

See Pierce Ferry.

Colorado River   Coconino, Mohave, and Yuma Cos.

Originally this river was described as "formed by the Green and Grand rivers in southeastern Utah in northwest part of San Juan county." For over one hundred years it was so defined by all explorers, geographers and historians. In 1890 a decision of the U. S. G. B. defined this river as "The great river of the Plateau region flowing into the Gulf of California."

On Mar. 24, 1921, owing to a desire for state publicity, the Colorado Legislature changed the name Grand to Colorado. This stream was described by this law as follows: "Rising in T. 6 N., R. 75 W. in Grand county, Colorado, near Lulu pass on the east slope of Mount Richthofen."

On July 25, 1921, Congress, against the advice of the U. S. G. B., passed an act approving this change by the Colorado State Legislature. Grand River was thus completely wiped off the map. The whole thing was a case of political re-christening and an unfortunate geographic precedent. Present Colorado river should therefore, be defined as follows: "Rising in Grand county, Colorado, near La Poudre Pass, on east slope of Mount Richthofen, flows southwest through Colorado, Utah, Arizona and Mexico, forming part of the east boundary of Nevada and California. It includes the stream in Grand county, Colorado formerly known as the North Fork of Grand river. Empties into Gulf of California."

Coues writes: "This stream has been variously designated as 'The Firebrand' or 'Rio del Tizon' by Melchoir Diaz in 1540; because the Indians carried firebrands or torches to warm their hands." (More likely it was to enable them to start fires.) Alarcon in 1540 called it the "Rio de Buenaguia," "River of Good Guidance or Safe Conduct."

Oñate in 1604 called it the "Rio Grande de la Buena Esperanza," River of Good Hope. At its mouth in Mexico Oñate called it "Puerto de la Conversion de San Pablo."

In 1776, Garces called it "Rio de los Martyrs," "River of Martyrs." Coues says: "This was prophetic for in 1781 at or near the mouth of the Gila, Garces and three other priests were murdered by Yuma Indians." George Wharton James says: "The Hualpai Indians called it 'Hackatai.'"

The name Colorado is from the Spanish meaning "Red." At times of flood this name is well suited. According to Lummis, it was also mapped as the Rio Colorado del Norte, and the Rio Colorado del Occidente. Our early American pioneers also called it the "Red River of the West"; and the "Red River of California." Garces says the local Indians called it "Javill" or "Hah-weal."

Lummis says that what we now call the "Little Colorado" (Colorado Chiquito) was first called Rio Colorado by Oñate in 1604.

"As a matter of fact, when the Little Colorado is at full flood it is an extremely colorful stream from the reddish soil through which it flows. Just when the name Colorado was first applied to the lower river is not known." Dellenbaugh.

Colorado River Ind. Res.   Yuma Co.   Eckhoff Map, 1880;
G. L. O., 1892; U. S. G. S., 1923.

On Colorado river about 50 miles above Yuma. Extends from La Paz to a few miles above Parker. One of the oldest Indian Reservations in Arizona. Established by President Grant, 1873. Lies partly in California. Col. Poston was first Supt. of Indian Affairs in Arizona. In 1864 he lived at La Paz. See Poston.

Colossal Cave   Pima Co.   Coronado N. F., 1927.

A large natural cave on Posta Quemada canyon, 8 miles off Tucson-Douglas highway and 19 miles east of Tucson. On south slope of Wrong mountain in Rincon range. Owned by the State. First discovered by a man named Ross, 1879.

An S. P. R. R. train was robbed in 1884 and the robbers trailed to this cave. One man was found dead. The others escaped. On Christmas, 1902, some Tucson people found some old Wells-Fargo sacks which proved to be part of the 1884 hold-up upon identification in San Francisco. The robbery of Army Paymaster Wham, that same year, has been erroneously confused with this cave.

Colter   Apache Co.

In T. 6 N., R. 29 E. Town named after James G. H. Colter, father of State Senator Fred Colter. Settled by the elder Colter, 1872. On Little Colorado river, 4 miles above Springerville.

"Colter arrived at this place in 1872 from Eau Claire, Wis. He brought with him a reaper and mower, his idea being to raise barley for Fort Apache. Barley was eight or nine dollars a hundred at that time." Farish. See Nutrioso.

Colter Butte   Coconino Co.

Grand Canyon N. P. On west wall of Canyon, about 4 miles southeast of Point Imperial, at northeast corner of Park. Named for James G. H. Colter. Farish says Mr. Colter was born in Nova Scotia, 1844. He was a farmer; freighter; stockraiser; Apache Indian and desperado fighter. Decision U. S. G. B. See Colter.

Colter Creek   Apache Co.   Map, Apache N. F., 1926.

Rising west of Gobbler peak in sec. 29, T. 7 N., R. 30 E. Flows north into Nutrioso creek about 2 miles below Nutrioso town. After the family of cattlemen and pioneers who lived on this creek for many years.

Columbia   Yavapai Co.   G. L. O. Map, 1909.

Village in T. 8 N., R. 1 W. On Humbug creek west of Tip Top mine and town. After a mine by that name in this vicinity. P. O. established Sept. 25, 1894, M. Joseph Nolan, P. M.

Columbine   Graham Co.   Map, Crook N. F., 1926.

Forest Ranger station and settlement on west slope of Mount Graham. "The columbine flower was found here on the meadows, hence the name."

Columbus   Pima Co.

See Sahuarita.

Comate   Pima Co.   Bryan Map, 1920; U. S. G. S., 1923.

Papago Ind. Res. Papago village in lat. 31° 25', long. 112° 20'. See Los Comates.

Comanche Point   Coconino Co.   G. L. O. Map, 1921; Tusayan
    N. F., 1927; Grand Canyon, 1927.

On Grand Canyon rim near lat. 36° 5', long. 111° 48'. After tribe of Plains Indians. James calls it Bissel Point, probably after Mr. Bissel, an early official of the A. T. & S. F. R. R. Comanche is decision U. S. G. B.

Comb Ridge   Apache Co.   U. S. G. S. Map, 1923.

Navajo Ind. Res. in extreme northwest corner Apache county at Colorado state line. "It is a long, narrow ridge with many exceedingly sharp narrow points like a comb." Gregory.

Comet   Pinal Co.   U. S. G. S. Florence Quad., 1902.

In sec. 1, T. 2 S., R. 11 E. Peak about 20 miles northeast of Florence, in Crook N. F. "After the Comet mine near the peak." See Cornet.

Commerce   Apache Co.

Washington records show a P. O. was established by such a name Mar. 17, 1887, William B. Gardner, P. M. Gardner failed to file bond and office was not opened. No information in records as to location.

Commission Creek, and Settlement   Pima Co.

F. Brerton the French mining engineer who examined Mowry's Patagonia mine, 1861. mentions this creek. "Its waters never dry up," he writes, "and are sufficient to run several mills. It is about a mile from the mine." Undoubtedly he meant the Patagonia mine. The U. S. Boundary Commission camped on this creek when they made the boundary survey through here about 1858-59.

Comobabi Mountains   Pima Co.   G. L. O. Map, 1892, 1921;
    Lumholtz, 1912.

Papago word meaning "where the kom tree grows." "Kom," a tree with red berries. Sp. "Comaro." On Papago Ind. Res. Mountains and Indian settlement near lat. 32°, long. 112°.

"Two Papago villages, 50 miles west of Tucson, occupying two commanding ridges with a sandy wash between. Here we found about thirty very decent houses and a handmade tank of dark brown water full of wigglers." Hornaday.

Concho   Apache Co.   G. L. O. Map, 1921.

Sp., "a shell." In T. 12 N., R. 26 E. Mexican hamlet about 16 miles west of St. Johns, on Concho creek.

So named by the first settlers from resemblance of the little valley to a shell. The first settlers, Mexicans, came here from the Rio Grande in New Mexico, 1865.

In 1879 some Mormons under B. H. Wilhelm moved into the upper end of valley and located about a mile from Concho. Sept. 20, 1880, a church was organized and the place named Erastus after Erastus Snow, then President of the Snowflake Conference. Later at a church meeting held at St. Johns in Dec. 1895, they abandoned this name and accepted Concho for both places. P. O. established as Concho Mar. 21, 1890, Leandro Ortega, P. M.

The children of the Concho schools for several years have received a Christmas treat of candy provided by a fund left by Mrs. Stanton, a former teacher at Concho, 1892-1899. The fund was to be placed at interest and interest used to buy the candy. Mrs. Stanton was also a teacher at the little town of Gisela which she named.

Concho   Apache Co.   U. S. G. S. Map, 1923.

Creek rising in foothills above Vernon flowing southeast enters Little Colorado at Hunt in T. 14 N., R. 26 E. After the settlement.

Congress   Yavapai Co.   G. L. O. Map, 1921.

In T. 10 N., R. 6 W. Station, Ash Fork-Phoenix branch A. T. & S. F. R. R. Station and shipping point for Congress gold mine. Mine named by Dennis May, its locator. At east end Date Creek mountains. "Diamond Joe" Reynolds owned this mine and did much development work on it. He died at the mine in Mar., 1891. P. O. established Jan. 19, 1895, Eliphalet B. Gage, P. M.

Conley Points   Gila Co.   Map, Tonto N. F., 1926.

In upper Tonto basin. Several small peaks on west side East Verde, just below crossing of Payson-Pine highway. "Named for Conley family who settled near these points in early Eighties. Sometimes called 'Indian Delias Place' for an Indian squaw who once filed a homestead claim on this same flat." Letter, F. W. Croxen, Forest Ranger.

Connel Gulch   Yavapai Co.   G. L. O. Map, 1921.

Heads near Camp Wood in sec. 3, T. 16 N., R. 6 W., runs south into Sycamore creek in T. 14½ N., R. 6 W., about 8 miles northwest of Hillside. "After George Connel who came to this region, 1873. He had a ranch and ran cattle in the Pitchfork brand for several years on upper Walnut creek. He located a homestead in the Gulch which took his name. Old residents agree that Connel Gulch flows west and is known as Boulder creek where it joins Burro creek." Letter, Frank Grubb, Prescott. These streams are not yet fully defined or located. U. S. G. S. map, 1923, calls this Cottonwood creek. Cottonwood however is another creek heading near Connel Gulch, joining it farther down.

Connor, Camp   Santa Cruz Co.

According to Heitman's List this was an early post 15 miles northeast of Tubac. G. L. O. map, 1888, shows a Camp Cameron on this same location. Connor was undoubtedly a misprint for the correct name, "Cameron."

Con Quien   Pima Co.

Sometimes called Coon canyon. Papago village at eastern end of Ajo mountains, near lat. 32°, long. 112° 30'. After Jose Maria Ochoa, Head Chief and Captain of Papagos, 1870-1885. He was called "Con Quien" by whites and Indians. He so signed himself to deeds in May, 1880, which attempted to convey to Robert F. Hunter title to two or three million acres of Papago land. The name Coon canyon undoubtedly was an error in transcribing the name Con Quien. See history of Con Quien in decision U. S. Supreme Court U. S., 1926. Pueblo of Santa Rosa vs. A. B. Fall, Sec'y. of the Interior. Sp., "Con Quien," meaning "with whom." Was a favorite game of cards of early days in Arizona often played by Indians.

Constellation   Yavapai Co.   U. S. G. S. Map, 1923.

P. O. and mining camp about 12 miles northeast of Castle Hot springs in Wickenburg mountains. After a mine by this name located here. P. O. established Apr. 29, 1901, Wm. F. Roberts, P. M.

Contention   Cochise Co.   Eckhoff Map, 1880; Hamilton, 1886, Contention; G. L. O., 1892, Contention City.

P. O. and milling town on San Pedro river about 10 miles northwest of Tombstone. Town established, 1879. Station on E. P. & S. W. R. R., 16 miles from Benson. Mill was located on the river to secure water. After the Contention mine, one of the great producers at Tombstone. "So called because of a quarrel between Dick Gird and Williams and Oliver. They divided the claims and Gird called his the 'Contention.'" P. O. established Apr. 6, 1880, John McDermott, P. M.

Continental   Pima Co.   Map, Coronado N. F., 1925.

In T. 18 S., R. 14 E. Station Calabasas branch S. P. R. R. The Continental Rubber Co. about 1914 had here a large plantation of Gayule, a rubber-producing shrub. Rubber experiment failed. Named for this company. Station is on Canoa Land Grant. P. O. established July 11, 1917, Stanley F. Morse, P. M.

Continental, Mountain   Maricopa Co.   Map, Tonto N. F., 1927.

In T. 6 N., R. 5 E., about 5 miles northeast of Cave creek P. O. "An ordinary slate mountain. So called after the Continental mine which was worked near it for several years." Letter, Joe Hand, Forest Ranger.

Cook, Mesa   Maricopa and Yavapai Cos.

See Black mesa.

Cooley   Apache Co.   U. S. G. S. Map, 1923.

Apache Ind. Res. at southern end Apache R. R. After Corydon E. Cooley, Gen. Crook's scout who lived for many years a few miles west on road to Fort Apache. Originally known as Cluff Cienega, q.v. Name changed to McNary about 1924 for commercial reasons. After James G. McNary, one of the owners. P. O. established as Cooley, Jan. 17, 1919, James C. Webster, P. M. Changed to McNary in 1925.

Cooley, Mountain   Navajo Co.

Fort Apache Ind. Res. About 3 miles south of Pinetop. After Corydon E. Cooley who lived near the mountain for many years. He was Gen. Crook's favorite scout. Married "Mollie" the daugh-

ter of Pedro, well-known White Mountain chief.
"One of the white men at Camp Apache, Sept., 1872, was Corydon E. Cooley, who had married a woman of the Sierra Blanca
band and had acquired a very decided influence over them.
Cooley's efforts were always in the direction of bringing about a
better understanding between the two races." Bourke.
Official War Department records show that "Corydon E. Cooley,
was First Lieut. First New Mexico Cavalry. Appointed Reg.
Quartermaster Aug. 19, 1861. Discharged by expiration term of
service on April 27, 1863." Cooley died March 19, 1915.

Cooleys Ranch   Navajo Co.

In T. 8½ N., R. 23 E. On Fort Apache Ind. Res. About one
mile west of Kinney mountain. Early home of C. E. Cooley,
about 24 miles from Fort Apache on the Holbrook road, at
what was known as "The Forks of the Road" because here the
road to Horsehead Crossing (Holbrook) and Springerville,
forked. See Cooley mountain and Showlow.

Coolidge   Pinal Co.   R. R. Maps.
Elevation 1,400 feet. In T. 8 S., R. 8 E. Station, 19 miles from
Picacho, on Phoenix and Wellton branch S. P. R. R. After President Calvin Coolidge. "Town established 1926, in the center of
the area to be irrigated by waters impounded by the Coolidge
dam." P. O. established June 14, 1926, Mrs. Dora H. Nutt, P. M.

Coolidge Dam   Gila Co.

Location at Box canyon about 4 miles below town and P. O.
of San Carlos. P. O. established May 7, 1928, under above name,
Wilford C. Rupkey, P. M.
Dam is of unusual construction, the Dome plan being new in
this kind of structure. Reservoir area involved submergence of
old town of San Carlos, established 1872 as military post. Notable
for locale of Geronimo; Apache Kid; Naches and other Apache
chieftains. Removal involved 20 miles S. P. R. R. track. Cost of
removal $2,400,000, of which the Government paid $1,000,000.

Coon Canyon   Pima Co.
See Con Quien.

Coon Creek   Gila Co.   Map, Tonto N. F., 1927.
Stream rising at Aztec peak in sec. 4, T. 5 N., R. 14 E. Flows
southeast into Salt river at Redmond Flat in sec. 5, T. 3 N., R.
14 E.
"The story is told that when the first settlers came onto this
creek they found a large colony of coons along the lower part
of the stream." Fred Croxen, Forest Ranger.

Coon Creek Butte   Gila Co.   Map, Tonto N. F., 1927.
In sec. 23, T. 5 N., R. 14 E. Named for the creek on which it is
located. q.v.

Coon Mountain   Coconino Co.
See Meteor Mountain.

Cope Plateau   Coconino Co.
In Grand Canyon N. P. "After Cope the well known paleontologist." James.

Cooper Pockets   Coconino Co.
Several desert water holes at southern end Hurricane ledge,

about 30 miles northwest Mount Trumbull. Owned and used as a sheep camp by a man named Cooper who grazed sheep through here in the years 1862-1874.

Bolton says that Escalante camped here on his way to the ford across the Colorado, in October, 1776.

Copeka   Pima Co.   G. L. O. Map, 1921; U. S. G. S., 1923.

In T. 17 S., R. 2 E. Papago Ind. Res. Mountain and Indian village. Father Oblasser says this is an incorrect spelling of "Ko-opke" or "Kupk." q.v.

Copper   Yavapai Co.   Map, Prescott N. F., 1926.

Station Ash Fork-Phoenix branch A. T. & S. F. R. R. 19 miles north of Prescott. In Chino valley. "Just another name." A. G. W.

Copper Basin   Yavapai Co.   Map, Prescott N. F., 1927.

In sec. 21, T. 13 N., R. 3 W. Early copper and gold camp in Walnut Grove district. "Was quite a busy camp in 1887." P. O. established Aug. 4, 1888. Duncan M. Martin, P. M. He failed to qualify, no office opened.

Copper, Canyon   Yavapai Co.   Map, Prescott N. F., 1927.

Canyon and stream heading in sec. 12, T. 13 N., R. 4 E. Flows northeast into Verde river about a mile below Camp Verde.

Copper Center   Cochise Co.

P. O. established Nov. 14, 1901, Rengwold Blix, P. M. A short-lived copper camp.

Copper City   Pinal Co.

Early mining camp 3 miles northeast of Globe. *Silver Belt*, Nov. 24, 1884, mentions first election held there, Copper City, a few days before. Was cn north side of Birch or Black peak. Map is indistinct as to this name. It was undoubtedly the peak now on most maps as Copper Hill q.v. Town is now so called.

Copper Creek   Pinal Co.   U. S. G. S. Map, 1923

In T. 8 S., R. 17 E. Creek rises close to Pinal-Graham line, flows southwest into San Pedro river about 3 miles south of Mammoth. Town is at the mine near head of creek about 6 miles east of Mammoth. P. O. established as Copper creek Mar. 6, 1906, Belle Sibley, P. M.

Copper Hill   Gila Co.   Map, Crook N. F., 1926.

Copper camp and P. O. about 3 miles north of Globe. P. O. established June 18, 1908, Ruth Hayden, P. M. See Copper City.

Copper Mountains   Yuma Co.   U. S. G. S. Map, 1923.

In long. 114°, south of S. P. R. R., west side Mohawk valley.

Copperopolis   Pinal Co.

"Just a name for a hopeful little copper settlement and mine." P. O. established Oct. 17, 1884, Edward E. Hellings, P. M.

Copper Queen Mine   Cochise Co.

Owned by the Phelps Dodge Co. at Bisbee. Ore first discovered in 1877 by John Dunn, an old government scout. George Warren and Dunn made a deal whereby Warren was to prospect on a "grub stake" furnished by Dunn. In Dec., 1877, Warren located the Mercey (sic) mine later called the Copper Queen, together with several other claims. Dunn seems to have dropped out of the picture. Warren lived a riotous life; drank and gambled away all he had. In his last years was a pensioner of the Copper Queen Co.

Cordes   Yavapai Co.   G. L. O. Map, 1921, Gordes;
                                               Prescott N. F., 1926.

In sec. 12, T. 11½ N., R. 1 E. On branch road Prescott to Middelton. Important sheep shipping point. Named for John K. Cordes, first P. M. and early settler. Before the railroad came, known as Antelope station. They asked for that name for their P. O. but there already was an Antelope. Cordes then decided to name it after his family. Thomas Cordes, father of John K., was U. S. Internal Revenue Collector for Arizona at Prescott, 1882. P. O. established June 9, 1886, John K. Cordes, P. M.

Corduroy Creek   Navajo Co.   U. S. G. S. Map, St. Johns Sheet.

Short stream rising near North fork, White river, Fort Apache Ind. Res. flows northwest into Forestdale creek, which crosses the old road from Apache to Showlow. Where the road skirted the stream it was corduroyed with logs, in 1880, by troops from Apache.

Cork   Graham Co.   G. L. O. Map, 1921.

On Gila river across from Eden. On Arizona-Eastern R. R. from Bowie. "William Garland who built this branch R. R. was born in Cork, Ireland. He called this place Cork, another, Dublin, and still another, Limerick, in honor of his native country." Letter, Seth T. Arkills, Globe.
"A wide place in the road between Safford and Fort Thomas." Miami *Silver Belt*. P. O. established Nov. 22, 1916, Mary Stapley, P. M.

Corn Creek   Coconino Co.   G. L. O. Map, 1921.

Formed by junction Oraibi and Polacca creeks, Navajo Ind. Res. Flows south into Little Colorado about 6 miles above Leupp. The Hopi and Navajos have always raised considerable corn on this creek. Hence the name.

Cornet Peak   Pinal Co.

See Comet.

Cornfields   Apache Co.   U. S. G. S. Map, 1923.

On Navajo Ind. Res. In T. 3 S., R. 11 W. On Pueblo Colorado wash, eastern part of Navajo Ind. Res. Many Navajo corn fields are usually found here on this wash.

Cornville   Yavapai Co.   U. S. G. S. Map, 1923.

In T. 15 N., R. 4 E. First called "The Pitchner Place." P. O. and settlement near the mouth of Oak creek. "At a meeting of Verde Valley pioneers, one of them said it was the intention to name it Cohnville, for a family named Cohn that lived there. When the papers came back from Washington, they had read it Cornville, so the settlers accepted the name." Letter, L. J. Putsch, Forest Ranger.
Old settlers say the first P. M. was George A. Kingston, appointed July 9, 1885. P. O. records at Washington however show that the P. O. was established May 11, 1887, Samuel C. Dickinson, P. M.

Corona Mountains, and Mining Camp   Yuma Co.
ᶜ   G. L. O. Map, 1921.

Elevation, 1,675 feet.   In T. 8 N., R. 15 W.   On north side of Cunningham wash.   According to local history, this was called after a mine near here by this name, Corona.

Coronado   Greenlee Co.   G. L. O. Map, 1921.

Station, Arizona & New Mexico R. R. between York and Guthrie.   "Named after the Spanish explorer who is said to have come through here with his army on his way to the 'Seven cities of Cibola.'"   There is absolutely no historic basis or incident for this claim.   See Fort Apache Ind. Res.

Coronado   Greenlee Co.   G. L. O. Map, 1921.

Town south slope Coronado mountain, 10 miles west of Metcalf, on branch railroad known as "Coronado Incline."   An early day copper camp on Coronado Gulch.   First engine on this road was named after the camp and mine.   Name was printed on her boilers in large white letters, "Coronada" (sic).   See Morenci Quad., 1915.

Coronado Mountain   Greenlee Co.   Map, Crook N. F., 1927.

"So named by a miner named Grant who located claims here and named it for the Spanish explorer."   In Clifton mining district, about 4 miles west of Metcalf.

Coronado National Forest

National Forest lying in Pinal, Pima, Santa Cruz and Cochise counties; small part lies in southwest corner of New Mexico in Hidalgo county.   Forest now has within its boundaries parts of what originally were seven different Forests, or Forest Reserves, viz.: The Chiricahua, Peloncillo, Huachuca, Tumacacori, Dragoon, Santa Catalina and Santa Rita.   In 1910 these were again consolidated into three: the Chiricahua, Garces and Coronado Forests.   On June 6, 1917, these three were consolidated under the name Coronado after the great explorer and adventurer.   Total area, 1931, in Arizona 1,376,763 acres.   Supervisors headquarters, Tucson.

Coronation Peak   Yuma Co.   Smith Map, 1879; Eckhoff, 1880;
                                   U. S. G. S., 1923.

"At Mission camp, 14 miles beyond Gila City, a fine view of Coronacion (sic) peak is had.   On north side of Gila 10 miles from station.   The old Spanish explorers named and spelled it 'Coronacion' from its resemblance to a mitred crown.   Bartlett of the U. S. Boundary Commission calls it 'Pagoda.'"   Hinton. Is in the Muggins mountains about 25 miles northeast of Yuma.

Corta   Cochise Co.   G. L. O. Map, 1909.

Sp., to "cut or fell wood."   Station 2 miles east of Don Louis-Bisbee branch E. P. & S. W. R. R.   Station for loading fire wood cut near-by.

Cortaro   Pima Co.

Station S. P. R. R. 12 miles west of Tucson.   Spanish word derived from "cortar," to cut, to separate.   Station established 1890. "Many years ago this valley was covered with a heavy growth of Mesquite and Ironwood.   It was all cut off for local use.   The name means "cut off."   Letter Arthur Case.   P. O. established July 16, 1920, Richard C. Hunter, P. M.

Corva   Coconino Co.

Sp., "ham" or "hamshaped." Station A. T. & S. F. R. R. 12 miles west of Winslow. "There is an oddly shaped butte here which resembles a huge ham."

Corwin   Pima Co.   G. L. O. Map, 1921.

In T. 17 S., R. 14 E. about 18 miles south of Tucson, near Sahuarita Station S. P. R. R. P. O. established Oct. 7, 1912, Archibald W. Roberts, P. M.

Cosnino   Coconino Co.   Map, Coconino N. F.

Town and caves. Station on A. T. & S. F. R. R. 11 miles east of Flagstaff. ·Caves named for Cosnino or Havasupai tribe supposed to have lived in them years ago. See Havasupai.

" 'Rio Grande de los Cosninos.' This name was given by Escalante to the Grand Canyon of the Colorado." Coues.

Beale on Apr. 13, 1857, writes: "We travelled to Cosnino caves and stopped to noon. The stream was booming, filling the whole canyon."

"The caves seem to have been unoccupied for a long time. We called them Cosnino Caves, after the tribe that roams over this region." Wheeler, Dec. 19, 1853.

From all available information these caves are undoubtedly those in the present day Walnut Canyon National Monument, east of Flagstaff. See Colmorico.

Cottonia   Mohave Co.

"In early days Mohave Indians raised considerable cotton around here which I believe gave this name." Letter Edmund Lincoln. P. O. established May 12, 1910, Edmund Lincoln, P. M. Name changed in Apr., 1911, to Lincolnia for family of Lincolns who lived here.

Cottonwood Cliffs   Mohave Co.   U. S. G. S. Map, 1923.

In Ts. 21, 22, 23 N., Rs. 11, 12 W. Range south side A. T. & S. F. R. R., south of Truxton station. This is undoubtedly what Wheeler first called "White Cliffs." Name Cottonwood seems to have been adopted by him later, because he speaks of the vast groves of Cottonwood trees in the valley. See White Cliffs creek.

Cottonwood Creek   Yavapai Co.

One of the branches that form the Santa Maria river. Also called Connell gulch, q.v. See also White cliffs.

Cottonwood Creek   Pinal Co.   U. S. G. S. Map, 1923.

Rises near southwest boundary Crook N. F. in T. 3 S., R. 11 E. Flows southwest, enters Gila river about 4 miles west of Price. Called Cottonwood canyon on some maps.

Cottonwood Island   Mohave Co.   U. S. G. S. Map, 1921.

Island in Colorado river, opposite Mount Davis. So called by Ives because of dense grove of Cottonwoods on the island and along river.

"Isaac B. Jones, a young Mormon freighter and several settlers were killed at El Dorado Canyon near the Colorado river, May 12, 1897, by a Paiute Indian named Avote. The murderer was run down by Indian trailers and killed on this island where he had taken refuge." McClintock.

Cottonwood Mountain   Graham Co.   Map, Crook N. F., 1926.

In sec. 2, T. 7 S., R. 21 E. "Cottonwood mountain is at head of Cottonwood canyon, so called because of cottonwoods along the stream." Letter, C. E. Moore.

Cottonwood Springs   Navajo Co.   U. S. G. S. Map, 1923.

In T. 25 N., R. 21 E. "The water is sweet and cool. There are many cottonwood trees along here." Gregory.

Cottonwood   Pima Co.   Smith Map, 1879; Eckhoff, 1880.

Station on San Pedro stage road from Florence to Old Camp Grant. About 40 miles southeast of Florence. P. O. established Nov. 9, 1881, Charles D. Henry, P. M. Called Cottonwood springs on G. L. O. map, 1892.

Cottonwood   Yavapai Co.   U. S. G. S. Map, 1909, 1923.

Station in Verde valley below Clarkdale, west side Verde river. "Town is located in a grove of grand old cottonwoods." P. O. established July 8, 1895. George W. Willard, P. M.

Cottonwood Station   Mohave Co.

In T. 20 N., R. 12 W. At mouth of White Cliffs creek. This was probably a stage station on the old Hardyville-Prescott wagon road. Hinton lists it as a station "67 miles east of Hardyville. Good water, grass and wood."

"Stage station four miles east of Mineral Park. Station owned and run by Hugh White." *Arizona Gazetteer, 1881.*

Cottonwood Valley   Mohave Co.   Smith Map, 1879.

Valley on both sides of Colorado river south of Mount Davis and Mount Perkins. "Is formed by Black mountains on east and north and Dead mountains on south and southwest. Trees when we visited it were clothed in the vivid green of their spring dress and suggested a name for valley." Ives Report.

Cottonwood Wash   Navajo Co.   Map, Sitgreaves N. F., 1924.

Dry wash heading at line Apache Ind. Res. in T. 10 N., R. 19 E. Runs northeast enters Silver creek a short distance below Snowflake. In early days there were many cottonwoods along this wash near Snowflake which were soon cut off for house logs, fences, etc.

Cottonwood Wash   Navajo Co.   U. S. G. S. Map, 1923.

Rises northeast corner T. 23 N., R. 20 E. Navajo Ind. Res., flows southwest into Little Colorado about 6 miles east of Winslow.

So called for the many cottonwoods along its course. Early Mormon settlement called Sunset, was on the Little Colorado below mouth of this wash. All early travelers called this stream by this name.

Cottonwood Wash   Pinal Co.   U. S. G. S. Map, 1923.

In T. 6 N., R. 14 E. Heads in northern end Black hills, flows northwest into Donnelly wash about 4 miles from Gila river. Called "Big Wash" on U. S. G. S. Florence Quad. 1902.

Court House Butte   Maricopa Co.   G. L. O. Map, 1921.

In T. 1 N., R. 10 W. East side Eagle Tail range. "Because of its likeness to a court house. Sometimes called 'Cathedral Rock.' " Letter, Mrs. J. B. Martin, Salome.

Court House Butte   Yavapai Co.   Map, Coconino N. F., 1927.

In T. 16 N., R. 6 E., near Sedona. Descriptive name. "Rock has appearance of a large court house. Old man James, an early settler near Sedona is said to have named this butte, 1876." Letter, Ed. Miller, Forest Supervisor.

Court House Well   Maricopa Co.   U. S. G. S. Map, 1923.

In sec. 16, T. 2 N., R. 10 W. Station and watering place in Centennial wash. Named after near-by butte by this name. "A watering place belonging to Harqua Hala Live Stock Co." *Routes to the Desert.*

Courtland   Cochise Co.   U. S. G. S. Map, 1923.

In T. 19 S., R. 25 E. Mining camp on short spur Arizona-Eastern R. R. southeast corner Dragoon mountains. After Courtland Young, one of the owners of Great Western Mining Co. which operated several mines here. Town established, 1909, by W. J. Young, brother of Courtland Young. P. O. established March 13, 1909, Harry Locke, P. M.

Covered Wells   Pima Co.   U. S. G. S. Map, 1923.

On Papago Ind. Res. south of Brownell mountains, near lat. 32° 20′, long. 112° 10′. "A well, protected by a wooden cover. Papago name for this well is 'Maish-vaxia,' maish, to cover; vaxia, well. It is 15 miles west of Indian Oasis." Lumholtz.

According to Tucson *Citizen* this was originally owned by an Indian. About 1880, Pima county authorities had it dug out to improve supply for travelers. M. M. Rice and several others laid out a townsite here, 1883.

Cowlic   Pima Co.

Papago village about 15 miles north of Mexican line. There is a handsome Catholic Mission here built entirely by the Indians. Name is Papago and means "Little Mountain." There is a small mountain nearby. Village lies in Valshima wash, Papago Ind. Res. There were about 100 Indians living here in 1925.

Coyote Creek   Apache Co.   Map, Apache N. F., 1929.

Stream rising at Bear springs in sec. 12, T. 5 N., R. 30 E. Flows northwesterly into east fork Black river. So named by St. George Creaghe, early stockman who had a summer ranch on this stream. The author's recollection is that when Creaghe first went in here in 1880, he caught a number of coyotes which gave it the name.

Coyote Mountains   Pima Co.   U. S. G. S. Map, 1923.

In T. 16, 17 S., R. 8 E. Papago Ind. Res. At upper end Baboquivari range. Good map in Hornaday's *Camp Fires.*

Coyote Peak   Yuma Co.   U. S. G. S. Map, 1923.

In Copper mountains near long. 114°. South of S. P. R. R., about 12 miles southeast of Wellton.

Coyote Peak   Yuma Co.   U. S. G. S. Map, 1923.

North of Little Horn mountains, near long. 113° 30′, about 25 miles west of Maricopa county line. There is another Coyote peak southeast of Wellton on S. P. R. R.

Coyote Spring   Navajo Co.   U. S. G. S. Map, 1923.

In T. 26 N., R. 17 E. On Hopi Ind. Res. "The coyote is one of the mythical folklore animals of the Hopi."

Coyote Wells   Yuma Co.

"Watering place about 16 miles south of Vicksburg. One of Bales cattle camps and watering places." *Routes to the Desert.*

Coyoteros

A group of the Apache nation. "So called by the Spanish, meaning 'wolf men.'" Gregg, *Commerce of the Prairies.*

"A division of the Apache which is geographically divided into the Pinal-Coyoteros, and the White Mountain-Coyoteros. They comprised the White mountain group and the Pinal group. The name has been rather indiscriminately applied to various Apache bands." Hodge.

C. P. Butte   Yavapai Co.   Map, Tonto N. F., 1927.

In T. 9 N., R. 5 E. At head of Squaw creek." Col. C. P. Round-tree had a mine here some years ago from whose initials the butte took its name." Letter, Joe Hand, Forest Ranger.

Cox   Yavapai Co.

P. O. established July 18, 1883, William Durbin, P. M. P. O. records show it to be near Prescott but otherwise not located.

Crabb Well   Maricopa Co.

Desert watering place about 10 miles southeast of Aguila. "It was dug by, and belongs to D. D. Crabb." *Routes to the Desert.*

Craig   Apache Co.   G. L. O. Map, 1921.

In T. 11 N., R. 28 E. Summer camp of Dr. Craig who was once county physician of Apache county, prominent sheep man of the early Nineties.

Craig   Yavapai Co.   G. L. O. Map, 1909.

In T. 11 N., R. 3 W. Prescott N. F. On Hassayampa creek. P. O. records show it was named for E. G. Craig a local settler. George W. Craighead was appointed P. M. Aug. 13, 1894.

Cramm Mountain   Maricopa Co.   Map, Tonto N. F., 1927.

In sec. 1 T. 7 N., R. 4 E. Lies west of Ashdale Ranger station. "After an old miner and prospector by this name, who lived at the foot of this mountain in 1882." Letter, Joe Hand.

Crater Mound   Coconino Co.

See Meteor Mountain.

Crater Mountains   Maricopa Co.   U. S. G. S. Map, 1923.

In T. 9 S., R. 7, 8 W. West of Tucson-Cornelia and Gila Bend R. R. "This whole range shows volcanic origin."

Crater, The   Pima Co.   G. L. O. Map, 1921.

In T. 10 N., R. 6 W. In Crater mountains near Ajo, some 10 miles north of Childs station. An extinct crater.

Crest   Yavapai Co.   Santa Fe Folders.

Station on Drake and Clarkdale branch A. T. & S. F. R. R., 52 miles southeast of Ash Fork. "Station is at the very crest of the hill going down into the Verde valley."

Crittenden, Camp   Santa Cruz Co.   U. S. G. S. Patagonia Quad. 1905; G. L. O. Map, 1923.

In T. 20 S., R. 16 E. On Sonoita creek. According to Heitman's *Register,* Crittenden was built on site of old Fort Buchanan.

Established Mar. 4, 1868. Hinton says: "It is a ride of a dozen miles from the Fish ranch to Old Camp Crittenden, laid out on a hill from which we can look down on Old Fort Buchanan. Crittenden is now a useless ruin. There have been no troops here since 1867."

The State Highway Commission has a sign here which reads: "Camp Crittenden; Established, Aug. 10, 1867. Named Camp Crittenden by General Orders No. 57 Dept. California, Sept. 30, 1867. In honor of Thomas L. Crittenden, Col. 32nd U. S. Infantry, Major General U. S. Vols. Post abandoned June 1, 1873. Established to protect settlements of Babacomari; Sonoita; and Santa Cruz valleys against Indians. Leading a detachment of troops from this Post May 5, 1871, Lieut. Cushing was killed by one of Cochise's bands." See Crittenden P. O.

Crittenden   Santa Cruz Co.   G. L. O. Map, 1921.

In T. 21 S., R. 16 E. Early village on Sonoita creek. Station Nogales branch S. P. R. R. about 6 miles below Camp Crittenden from which it took its name. P. O. established June 11, 1873. Thomas Hughes, P. M.

Crook Canyon   Yavapai Co.   Map, Prescott N. F., 1926.

In Ts. 11, 11½ N., R. 2 W. Rises west side Longfellow ridge. Named for General George Crook.

"The military order assigning General Crook to Arizona, designated him as Lieut Col. 23rd Infantry, but authorized him to command under his brevet rank of Major General." Farish. See First Telegraph Pole.

Crook National Forest   Pinal, Graham, Cochise, Greenlee and
                                                          Maricopa Cos.

Created originally in 1902 as the Mount Graham Forest Reserve. Parts of the Apache and adjoining forests have been added to it from time to time. Created Crook National Forest in July, 1908. Named after General George Crook, U. S. A. Area approximately 452,590 acres. Supervisor's Headquarters, Safford.

Crook Station   Cochise Co.   R. R. Maps.

On E. P. & S. W. R. R., about 17 miles from Douglas. After Gen. Crook.

Crook Road, The

See Verde road.

Crookton   Yavapai Co.   U. S. G. S. Map, 1923.

Station A. T. & S. F. R. R., 17 miles west of Ash Fork, directly south of Mount Floyd. After Gen. Crook.

Cross Mountain   Yavapai Co.   Eckhoff Map, 1880; U. S. G. S., 1923.

In T. 20 N., R. 9 W. In northwest corner of county, north side of Trout creek. "We approached a mesa which, from its form was called 'Cross Mountain.'" Whipple Report Jan. 25, 1854. This was 20 miles below what Whipple called Aztec pass on a stream known to be head waters Bill Williams Fork.

Cross Canyon   Apache Co.   U. S. G. S. Map, 1923.

In T. 26 N., R. 28 E. Trading post and water hole about 12 miles west of St. Michaels on Navajo Ind. Res. "A well known Navajo trail crossed the canyon here, hence the name. The government sank a well here 301 feet into solid sandstone, but got no water." Gregory.

Crossing of the Fathers   Kane Co., Utah   G. L. O. Map, 1921;
Rand McNally, 1929.

Sp., "Vado de los Padres." "Vado," a ford, a crossing. Ford on
Colorado river in Glen canyon about 35 miles above Lee Ferry.
Used 1858 and later by Jacob Hamblin, Mormon missionary.
Sometimes called "Ute Crossing." The Ute Indians often crossed
here.

"During the year 1776, Hernando D' Escalante Fontaneda, a
zealous priest, made his memorable journey from Santa Fe returning to the Spanish settlements across the present western
Navajo Indian reservation to Hopi and Zuni. Tradition states
that he crossed Glen Canyon at a point designated on the map
as the 'Crossing of the Fathers.'" Gregory. Oddly enough, Gregory does not show this on his maps and it is found on only a few
others. It is about 5 miles north of the southern Utah state line.
For many years thought to be in Arizona. In 1926 Prof. H. E.
Bolton followed the trail made by Escalante from southern Utah
across the river and on to Santa Fe. He made the trip with a
translation of Escalante's rare diary in his hands. His recital
is of great interest. Charles Lummis says: "Escalante crossed
here on horseback without their horses having to swim. The
Padre states in his diary that 'the ford of the river is very good.
It must be more than a mile in width here at the crossing.'"
Lummis and Bolton on this crossing are both very interesting.

Crossman Peak (sic)   Mohave Co.   G. L. O. Map, 1921.

In T. 14 N., R. 18 W. At south end Chemehuevi mountains.
Shows on maps as Crossman but evidently should be Grossman.

"Named after A. G. Grossman now living at Quartzsite, Yuma
county, who once worked some placers here. He was a printer
and for a while ran a paper, *The Needle's Eye*, at the Needles."
Letter, Anson H. Smith, Kingman.

Croton Spring   Cochise Co.   G. L. O. Map, 1892, 1921.

In T. 24 E. R. 15 S. About 12 miles southwest of Willcox.
Spring of mineral water said to taste like croton oil. On Camp
Grant-Fort Bowie stage road. Hinton lists it as "82 miles from
Camp Grant, the water was very brackish."

Fish says: "It was owned by Thomas Steele in 1874 and was
then the stage station." See Steele's Station.

Crowley   Gila Co.

P. O. established July 20, 1907, James Lightfoot, P. M. Mining
camp near Globe. After Con Crowley, well known miner and
State Librarian, 1932.

Crozier Peak   Pinal Co.   G. L. O. Map, 1921.

In sec. 26, T. 5 S., R. 14 E. Elevation 4,276 feet, about 6 miles
due west of Dudleyville, east side Tortilla mountains.

"Mr. Giffin of Winkelman says a man named Crozier owned
and worked several mining claims on the peak. Hence the
name." Letter, P. M. Hayden.

Crown King   Yavapai Co.   G. L. O. Map, 1892, 1921.

In T. 10 N., R. 1 W. Important mining camp of early days.
At end of branch railroad from Prescott. Now abandoned.

P. O. established June 20, 1888, George P. Harrington, P. M.
This is also the name of station on branch railroad.

"The first mine here was called 'Crown King.'"

Crown Point   Yavapai Co.   Congress Quad., 1904.

In T. 9 N., R. 3 W. After Crown Point mine near here, east side Hassayampa river. Mine so named by the discoverers after Crown Point mine at Gold Hill, Nevada, from whence they came to Arizona. P. O. established Jan. 12, 1900, R. J. Bignell, P. M.

Crozier   Mohave Co.   G. L. O. Map, 1921.

In T. 24 N., R. 13 E. Station on A. T. & S. F. R. R. After Sam Crozier, early day Mohave county cattle raiser and legislator. He was a member of the Live Stock Sanitary Board of Arizona, 1898.

Cruice   Yavapai Co.

Station Ash Fork-Prescott branch A. T. & S. F. R. R., 4 miles south of Ash Fork. "After F. P. Cruice, Assistant General Freight Agent, Santa Fe R. R., Los Angeles, Calif." A. G. W.

Cruz   Pima Co.   G. L. O. Map, 1921; Crook N. F., 1926.

Station S. P. R. R., 7 miles east of Tucson. Established, 1912. On Santa Cruz river. "This is an abbreviation of the river's Spanish name." Station originally called Esmond. Shortened to save telegraphing." Letter, Supt. S. P. R. R., Tucson.

Crystal Peak   Graham Co.   G. L. O. Map, 1921; Crook N. F., 1926.

In sec. 5 T. 5 S., R. 20 E. At northern end Santa Teresa range. "So called because of presence of Silicon dioxide crystals, found in the rocks all over this mountain." Letter, Rosa Firth.

Crystoval

See Stoval.

Cubabi

See Cababi.

Curtiss   Cochise Co.

On E. P. & S. W. R. R. Station first called Kennard, 7 miles south of Benson. Named for Curtiss James of the Phelps Dodge Co.

Cub Headland   Coconino Co.

Grand Canyon N. P. in lat. 36° 13½', long. 112° 39½'. "On west side upper reach of Coconino plateau, in outline resembling a head of a bear cub." Named by Frank Bond.

Cubo   Pima Co.   U. S. G. S. Map, 1923.

Waterhole in Papago Ind. Res., 22 miles south of Ajo. Papago word meaning "Big Pond." Lumholtz says: "There is a good-sized artificial lake here filled by flood waters. Many Indians come here to farm in the summer. On east side Ajo mountains."

Cullen's Well (sic)   Yuma Co.   G. L. O. Map, 1892, Cullen; 1921, Collins.

In sec. 30, T. 7 N., R. 11 W., near Parker branch A. T. & S. F. R. R., about 38 miles west of Wickenburg.

"Named for Tom Cullen, an Englishman who kept a stage station on Ehrenburg-Wickenburg line, at forks where Ehrenburg road splits. He dug 240 feet for water. Sometimes called 'Cullings.' " Farish.

"The second day from Prescott brought us to Cullen's Wells. Mrs. Cullen cooked us an excellent dinner. She had a little boy named Daniel. She put my baby to bed in Daniel's crib. I was so grateful to her." *Vanished Ariz.*, May, 1875. Coues in his *Garces* gets this mixed up with Kerlins Well which is near the base of Mount Floyd, some distance from here.

In September, 1934, the author met at Fort Verde the child Daniel to whom Mrs. Summerhayes refers so kindly, now a man of over 60 years, who said his father's name was Charles C. Culling and the well should be so designated for historical accuracy.

McClintock has a delightful little story of this place well worth the telling. After Cullen, or Culling, died the station was kept by one Joe Drew. One night a man staggered into the station nearly dead from thirst. He had seen the dim light of the station through a window. After this Drew always kept a lantern burning on top of a tall pole so that anyone lost on the desert might see it if near enough. Drew called himself the "Keeper of the Desert Lighthouse."

Cumberland　　　Maricopa Co.　　　　　　Elliott Map, 1860.

Mining camp after mine by this name about 6 miles southeast of Vulture mine.

Cumero　　　Pima Co.　　　　　Map, Coronado N. F., 1927.

Sp., "hackberry." Southeast corner T. 22 S., R. 9 E. "Hackberry, a tree which covers the north slopes of mountain." Letter, A. S. Wingo, Forest Ranger.

Cumorah　　　Navajo Co.

First name for Allens Camp. Word doubtless misspelled but meant for Cumero, Spanish name for hackberry, a tree found occasionally in this vicinity. See Allen.

Cunningham Pass　　　Yuma Co.　　　G. L. O. Map, 1921; U. S. G. S., 1923.

In T. 7 N., R. 13 W. On south side Butler valley, in Harcuvar mountains. "After James Cunningham, who built a stone house here about 1885-1886. Located a group of claims near what was later 'The Critic' mine. Was a sailor in his younger days. A great friend of the Indians, who however ambushed and killed him in Bells Pass. It is claimed that later the Indians said they killed him by mistake." Letter, Mrs. J. B. Martin, Salome.

Cornutt

See Livingston.

Curtis　　　Graham Co.　　　U. S. G. S. Map, 1923; Crook N. F., 1927.

In sec. 21, T. 5 S., R. 24 E. Mormon settlement established 1881. On north side Gila river, now called Eden. Named for Moses M. Curtis.

Curtis (Camp Curtis)　　　Yavapai Co.　　　G. L. O. Map, 1891.

On Big Bug creek about 4 miles above Mayer. Origin not known. P. O. established Nov. 27, 1891, Marvin A. Baldwin, P. M.

Curvo　　　Cochise Co.

Sp., "crooked, curved." Station S. P. R. R., 6 miles east of Benson. The road here is very crooked, hence the name.

Cutter　　　Gila Co.　　　　　　G. L. O. Map, 1909.

In Gila valley, on Gila valley R. R., San Carlos Ind. Res., about 10 miles east of Globe. After an old stage station by this name

on wagon road, Willcox to Globe. It was also known as Gilsons
Well. "The station was named after Capt. E. A. Cutter of Cutter
and Leahy, who ran a general merchandise store at Camp Thomas
in the Eighties. At one time he was President of Gila Valley
R. R." Letter, Dan Williamson, Globe.

Cycloptic   Mohave Co.   U. S. G. S. Map, 1923.

In T. 28 N., R. 18 W. On Sacramento wash. "Meaning rough,
rugged, huge, from the name Cyclops. Named by Stanley C.
Bagg for a group of gold mines he owned and worked for some
years near here." Letter, O. D. M. Gaddis, Kingman. P. O. established July 7, 1905, Robert Nickel, P. M.

Cygnus Peak   Mohave Co.   Elliott Map, 1866;
                                          G. L. O., 1892, 1923.

Cygnus, a swan. In T. 19 N., R. 11 W. At head of Trout creek,
west of Baca Grant. "We are now (Jan. 25, 1854) 20 miles from
the summit of Aztec pass (which they later on discovered to be
Bill Williams Fork). About 10 miles south is a range of mountains with snow upon their summits. This has been termed Cygnus mountain." Whipple.

"Mr. Marcou calls this elevation 'Whipple mountain.' It was
called Cygnus mountain by Capt. Whipple." Report W. P. Blake,
Geologist with Whipple's party.

It was however called Mount Whipple by Ives, who evidently had
not heard of its first name, Cygnus. It is a fair guess to say
that Whipple got the name Cygnus, swan, from the snow-capped
peak and not from any fancied resemblance to the bird as some
writers have stated. Not shown as Mount Whipple on any
known map.

Dad's Lookout   Gila Co.   Map, San Carlos Ind. Res.

In T. 3 N., R. 20 E. Peak at north end Cassadora range. Indian Service has a fire lookout here. No one can tell who "Dad"
was or is.

Dahk   Pinal Co.

See Dock.

Dahl   Cochise Co.

P. O. established Sept. 19, 1905, John A. White, P. M. Origin
unknown.

Dana Butte   Coconino Co.   Map, Grand Canyon N. P., 1924.

South side Colorado river. Bold headland directly north of
Powell Memorial. Named by James, after the great geologist.

Danta Headland   Coconino Co.

Sp., "tapir." In Grand Canyon N. P., lat. 36° 16', long. 112° 40'.
West side upper reach of Coconino plateau. Its outline strongly
resembles head of a tapir, with wide-open mouth. Named by
Frank Bond.

Date   Yavapai Co.

In T. 11, N., R. 6 W. Station Ash Fork-Phoenix branch A. T.
& S. F. R. R. After Date creek which rises near here. Railroad
company shortened name to Date. Date creek, U. S. G. S. map,
1923.

Date Creek; Camp Date Creek   Yavapai Co.   G. L. O. Map, 1921.

Early military post on Date creek, Martinez Mining district. "Established by California Volunteers, 1866, as Camp McPherson. Changed to Camp Date creek, July 15, 1867. Abandoned Aug. 24, 1867." *Heitman's List.* In sec. 30, T. 11 N., R. 6 W., at junction north and south forks Date creek, about 2 miles west of railroad.

"Sixty-two miles from Prescott to the southwest lay the sickly and dismal post of Camp Date Creek in the creek of that name." Bourke. One cannot understand Bourke. The location on this creek is attractive and lovely. It was moved twice and he may have been speaking of the earlier ones.

Post was on high road to Prescott through Bells canyon. Present railroad station of this name is 8 or 10 miles north. P. O. established as Date creek Mar. 1, 1872, George H. Kimball, P. M.

Date Creek   Yavapai and Yuma Cos.   All Early Maps; U. S. G. S., 1923.

In T. 11 N., R. 12 W. North and south forks rise west side Weaver mountains. "Called by Indians 'Ah-ha-cassona,' pretty water. We all agreed it was the most beautiful place we had ever seen." Genung. Early settlers found the Opuntia bearing huge clusters of fruit which the Mexicans call "Da-til" or dates. Hence Date creek.

Date Creek Agency   Yavapai Co.

"In 1871 Vincent Collyer established a temporary reservation at Date Creek and about 225 Indians, mostly Apache-Mohaves, were gathered here. In June, 1871, government began to issue rations to Indians in this part of Arizona. They were transferred to Camp Verde reservation May, 1873. General O. O. Howard then abolished the Date Creek reservation or 'feeding station' as it was sarcastically referred to." Farish.

Date Creek Mountains   Yavapai Co.   Hinton Map, 1877; Eckhoff, 1880; U. S. G. S., 1923.

In T. 10 N. Rs., 6, 7 W. Small range north of Congress Junction, A. T. & S. F. R. R. See Date creek.

Davenport Hill and Lake   Coconino Co.   U. S. G. S. Map, 1923; Tusayan N. F., 1927.

Flat topped hill in sec. 5, T. 21 N., R. 2, E., about 4 miles southeast of Williams. Lake, in sec. 28 N., R. 3 E., about 6 miles east of Williams. On A. T. & S. F. R. R. See Davenport peak for origin.

Davenport Peak   Yavapai Co.   Map, Tonto N. F., 1926.

In sec. 36, T. 8 N., R. 7 E. "According to Henry Walport so called for an old timer, Jake Davenport, who lived on the Davenport wash in the Seventies." J. H. Sizer, Forest Supervisor.

Davenport Wash and Ranch   Maricopa Co.

Map, Tonto N. F., 1927.

Rises in sec. 16, T. 8 N., R. 8 E., Yavapai county, flows southwest, enters Verde river in Maricopa county, northeast corner of T. 7 N., R. 6 E.

Smith map, 1879, shows only the ranch at mouth Deadman's canyon, across Verde river from Mount Buford. See Davenport peak.

Davidson Canyon and Spring   Pima Co.   Eckhoff Map, 1880; Coronado N. F., 1927.

In T. 18 S., R. 16 E. Heads southern end Empire mountains, near Rosemount, runs north into Pantano wash, in T. 16 S., R. 17 E. Near Irene Station, S. P. R. R.

"Lieut. Reid T. Stewart and Corporal Black, 3rd U. S. Cavalry, were killed near Davidson spring in this canyon in 1871." Bourke. The Arizona *Sentinel*, Sept. 7, 1872, gives this as in August, 1872. "Lieut. Stewart and Corporal Black, Troop G, 5th Cavalry, left Crittenden post for Tucson in a buckboard early that morning. They were attacked by Apaches in the canyon some 22 miles from Crittenden and both killed August 22, 1872." Probably Bourke's dates are not correct.

Davis   Yavapai Co.   G. L. O. Map, 1909.

In T. 16 N., R. 1 E. Station, United Verde and Pacific R. R., about 8 miles east Jerome Junction. "This station now abandoned, was originally named after a teamster by that name who hauled lumber to it for shipment. Saw mill was at base of Mingus mountain." Letter, H. P. Hughes, Jerome.

Davis, Mount   Mohave Co.   Eckhoff Map, 1880; G. L. O., 1921.

In T. 25 N., R. 22 W. On Colorado river, west side Black range.

Is not clear who named this peak. Ives, 1858, speaks of it as "a conspicuous mountain which stands in solitude on left bank of river." His report shows a picture of it. Does not claim to have named it however although he named the Black mountains to the east.

If Ives named this peak it was undoubtedly for Jefferson Davis, Secretary of War, 1853-1857. Not on Sitgreaves map, 1851, nor does Sitgreaves mention it.

Ives says: "Mr. Davis, the Secretary of War, proposed to me to carry along some different seeds to the Mohaves for distribution among them." Davis was thus in Ives' mind while in this region. Why not the name for him?

Davis, Mount   Yavapai Co.   Map, Prescott N. F., 1927.

In southwest corner T. 12½ N., R. 1 W., north of Mount Union. "The Unionists of the mining camp near here first gave the name Mount Union to another near-by peak. The Southerners in the camp, not to be outdone, named this peak for President Jefferson Davis."

Davis Mountain

See Harris.

Daze Lake   Coconino Co.   Map, Coconino N. F., 1928.

Dry lake southern part T. 16 N., R. 11 E. Fills with flood waters in wet weather. Is an excellent stock watering place. So called after William Daze (pro. "Daw-zy") Santa Fe R. R. engineer of Winslow, who ran many sheep in this vicinity in the Eighties.

Dead   Apache Co.   U. S. G. S. Map, 1923.

River or dry wash about 10 miles long rising in T. 20 N., R. 25 E. Joins Rio Puerco one mile east of Adamana in T. 18 N., R. 24 E.

Dead Boy Point   Gila Co.   Map, Tonto N. F., 1927.

In sec. 4, T. 8 N., R. 11 E. In Cottonwood basin about 3 miles east of Tonto creek. "John Berry's sheep camp was attacked at this place Dec. 22, 1903, by Zack Booth, a cowboy of unsavory reputation from Gisela. Wiley Berry and Juan Rafael, two young boys in the camp, were killed. Zack Booth was tried for the crime and hung at Globe. Local settlers gave this name to the point just above the camp." Letter, F. W. Croxen, Forest Ranger.

Deadman Gap   Maricopa Co.   G. L. O. Map, 1921.

In T. 9 S., R. 7 E. Pass, in Crater mountains. Origin not known.

Deadman Tank   Yuma Co.   G. L. O. Map, 1921.

In T. 1 S., R. 12 W., upper end Nottbush valley. "An unknown man was found dead at this tank in the Eighties."

Deadmans Canyon   Gila Co.   G. L. O. Map, 1921.

Canyon on East Verde near main river. "On the morning of Mar. 23, 1873, one of our packers, Preciliano Monje, died. We buried him under a huge cottonwood by the side of two pretty springs." Bourke. Why not his name, Preciliano Canyon or Monje canyon?

Deadmans Creek   Yavapai Co.   Map, Tonto N. F., 1927.

Stream rising in T. 8 E., R. 8 N., on western slope Mazatzal peak. Flows southwest, enters Verde in northeast corner T. 7 N., R. 6 E. in Maricopa county. "Discovered and named by Boyd Dougherty and Judge Reiley who found the remains of an unknown man in the canyon." Letter, Margaret Platt, Payson.

Deadmans Flat, Wash, and Tank   Coconino Co. G. L. O. Map, 1921; Coconino N. F., 1928.

Flat about 20 miles north of Flagstaff, in T. 24 N., Rs. 7, 8 E. Wash rises north side San Francisco peak, flows northeast into Little Colorado, near Black falls.

C. J. Babbitt, Flagstaff, writes: "An old prospector who had been hanging round Flagstaff for some days, started for his camp. Navajo Indians found him dead several days later lying under a cedar tree. A clear case of suicide."

Dead Old Mans Pond   Pima Co.   Lumholtz Map.

Papago Ind. Res. About 8 miles southeast Brownell. Is exactly at long. 112° on east side Quijotoas. Papago name is "Kolipat-vooka" meaning "dead old mans pond, or well." " 'Koli,' Old man; 'Pad,' dead; 'Vawka,' a charco or water hole. The Pond belonging to the Dead Old Man. Usually such ponds were built and owned by the community. This was owned by the 'Old Man.' Hence the distinctive name." Father Oblasser.

"We arrived rather late at a summer rancheria with the somewhat disconcerting name of Dead Old Mans Pond." Lumholtz. Who the old man was nobody seems to remember.

Dean Peak   Mohave Co.   G. L. O. Map, 1921.

In T. 20 N., R. 15 W. East side Hualpai mountains. About 12 miles southeast Kingman. "After William, 'Bill,' Dean, an early day prospector who, 1877, recorded and located the Dean mine near this peak." Letter, O. D. M. Gaddis, Kingman. Decision U. S. G. B.

Debebe-kid Lake   Navajo Co.   Gregory Map, 1916;
G. L. O., 1921.

Southwest Chilchinbito spring. "Navajo word meaning Sheep lake." Haile.

Decker Wash   Navajo Co.   U. S. G. S. Map, 1923.

In T. 11 N., R. 18 E. Heading close to line Apache Ind. Res. west of Snowflake. Joins Phoenix wash and ends in Dry lake. After Z. B. Decker, Mormon stockman who ran sheep here in the Eighties.

Deer Creek   Pinal Co.   U. S. G. S. Map, 1923.

Rises west side Stanley butte in Deer Creek basin. Flows west into Gila river near Christmas.

Deer Creek, Basin, and Coal Mines   Pinal Co.   G. L. O. Map, 1921.

In T. 4 S., R. 18 E. South of Rockhouse mountain 12 miles east of Christmas. There are several coal mines in the basin which in the Eighties were said to be on San Carlos Ind. Res., and therefore not subject to entry. Coal was of little value and mines not worked even when survey decided they were off Indian land.

Deer Lake   Coconino Co.   Map, Sitgreaves N. F., 1924.

In sec. 25, T. 12 N., R. 13 E. Shallow lake near "Tonto Rim" usually holding water from rain or snow. Many deer watered at it in early days. Was a favorite camping place for travelers on Verde road. In 1882 after Big Dry wash fight with Apaches troops under Col. Evans came here to rest for a day or two. The writer as late as 1898 saw several names of soldiers whom he knew carved on aspen trees with date of fight. Lake was named by F. Pius who ran horses and camped here in early days.

Deer Spring Mountain   Gila Co.   Map, Apache Ind. Res., 1928.

In sec. 6, T. 7 N., R. 23 E. At county line. There is a large spring at its foot from which it gets its name.

Deer Valley   Maricopa Co.   G. L. O. Map, 1921.

In T. 4 N., R. 2 E. Open, fairly level valley north of Peoria. Origin unknown.

Defiance, Fort   Apache Co.   U. S. G. S. Map, 1923.

Elevation 6,862 feet. In T. 1 N., R. 6 W. Military post established on Bonito creek by Col. Sumner, 1852. About 60 miles north of Zuni villages, Navajo Ind. Res., and about 10 miles west Arizona-New Mexico line. In 1852 was center of Navajo's country. Now U. S. Indian school.

Lieut. Simpson, 1850, says: "It was established in defiance of, and to the Navajo Indians." Was first military post established in what is now Arizona. There was also a Fort Defiance in Yuma county q.v. Name "Defiance plateau" has been given by Gregory to area lying in southeast corner of Navajo reservation. See Gregory's report. P. O. established as Defiance Jan. 6, 1875, William F. M. Arny, P. M. D. M. Riordan, later of Flagstaff, came here in 1883 as agent for Navajo Indians. Appointed P. M. Mar. 12, 1883. See Camp Hualpai.

Defiance, Fort   Yuma Co.

"In 1849 a party of Americans dispossessed the Yuma Indians of the crude boat they used for a ferry boat; drove them away and established a ferry across the Colorado river. They then built a fort which in contempt for the Indians they called 'Fort Defiance.' "   Bartlett.

De la Vergne Park

See Fort Valley.

Delaware Spring   Mohave Co.

One of several springs which Beale mentions in 1857-58. Was somewhere on Truxton canyon but does not show on his maps. Beale says: "It is between Truxton springs and White Rock springs which is in Engles Pass north of the Aztec range." It is not always easy to locate Beale's places. He named it for the Delaware Indian with him, called Dick, who discovered it.

Del Che

See Del Shay.

Dellenbaugh, Mount   Mohave Co.

South end Shivwits plateau, elevation 6,750 feet. North side Grand Canyon near lat. 36° 6′ long. 113° 30′. Named by Major Powell after Frederick S. Dellenbaugh, artist, topographic engineer and historian of second trip through Canyon. "When they came down from Mount Logan Major Powell said he had seen a fine isolated mountain to the west which he had called after me. I naturally felt much pleased to have my name on the map." *A Canyon Voyage.*

DeLong Peak   Pima Co.   Map, Coronado N. F., 1929.

In T. 14 S., R. 17 E. In Santa Catalina mountains about 6 miles north of Oury peak. After Sidney DeLong, pioneer of southern Arizona, Mayor of Tucson, 1871.

Delesa   Yuma Co.   Old R. R. Folders.

Station S. P. R. R. about 95 miles east of Yuma. Origin unknown.

Del Rio   Yavapai Co.

In T. 17 N., R. 2 W. Ash Fork-Phoenix branch A. T. & S. F. R. R. Large springs are found here. Station on stage line Ash Fork to Prescott. Located 1866 by George Banghart; station first called after him. Location of "Postle ranch" where capital of Arizona was first located. The railroad bought Banghart out and called station Del Rio, "the river." "Just why so called no one can say unless because it is near the real head of the Rio Verde. For many years water from these springs was hauled by train to El Tovar Hotel." See Bangharts, also Postles.

Del Shay (sic) Basin and Creek   Gila Co.
Map, Tonto N. F., 1924.

In Ts. 7, 8 N., R. 11 E. Creek flows into Tonto creek. After Del-che, "red ant," Tonto-Apache chief who lived here with his band. "He was brave, able, bold and enterprising, and rightfully regarded as the worst enemy the white man ever had." Bourke. A letter written in 1924, by Col. W. H. Corbusier, U. S. Army, who served in Arizona in early days says: "Del-che's scalp with the long hair attached and one ear and part of his face, was brought to me at the agency some 15 miles above Camp Verde in May, 1874. There had been a price offered for his dead body, and three Tontos brought the scalp in to prove they had killed him. There was a large pearl button tied to the lobe of the right ear with the scalp."

Col. Corbusier sent the trophy to the Commanding Officer at Fort Verde for identification. He in turn sent it to Lieut. Schuyler, Indian Agent, 14 miles above Verde, present location of Cottonwood. His Indian scouts identified the affair as belonging to Del-che.

Fish has a wild story from Banta claiming that in 1869, he and Cooley on their way to Fort McDowell, had Del-che for a guide. Banta says: "By some hook or crook, Del-che was decoyed into camp by a white flag and shot to death by the camp doctor." Col. Corbusier's story is however amply verified and somewhat extended, by an article in the *Tucson Citizen* of August 22, 1874.

Stories of an Apache's head being brought into some military post for a reward, were very common in the early days. The Del-che incident is however the only one that has the least bit of historic or official background. Bourke once admitted to the author that he knew of the Del-che incident but evidently his soldierly instincts made him dislike to discuss it.

Dr. Warren S. Day, Post Surgeon at Camp Verde in the early Seventies, writes from Prescott, Sept. 3, 1913: "Schuyler and I had accidentally let Delche escape a few days before and were anxious to capture him. Gen. Crook gave me two sacks of 'dobies' holding 200 Mexican dollars. He told me to use them any way I wished to secure the return of the chief. We decided to try Delche's brother. He came to our tent and placing a Navajo blanket on the floor I tossed dollars into it until he counted a hundred. Then he grabbed the blanket, threw it over his back and left. Four or five days later he returned bringing Delche's head with him."

Cooley also told the author this same story; said he believed it was true but felt that the officers expected the Indians to bring Delche back alive, a prisoner. Cooley felt however that "the ends justified the means."

At Camp McDowell, Apr., 1931, Col. Schuyler verified this story, together with that of Corbusier, to the writer.

Deluge Wash   Mohave Co.   U. S. G. S. Map, 1923.

In T. 17 N., R. 15 W. Rises on east slope Hualpai mountains, flows east into Big Sandy. "So called by a prospector named Burch when, in 1873, a cloud burst swept his camp from the face of the earth." Letter, Louis Janc.

DeMotte Park   Coconino Co.

In T. 35 N., R. 3 W. Open park or valley on Kaibab N. F. on road to Grand Canyon. There is a hotel here. Favorite place to see deer feeding in the evenings. "So named by Powell Aug., 1872, after Prof. Harry C. DeMotte with Powell's party. He did not make the trip through the Canyon but left at Lee ferry and returned east." Letter, Frederick Dellenbaugh. Is locally called "V. T. Park" after cattle brand of Van Slack and Thompson. People of Orderville established one of the first herds of cattle grazed here. Cattle sold to Van Slack and Thompson in 1886 who ran the brand V. T. and made this park their headquarters. Herd eventually sold to Grand Canyon Cattle Co. of California. With the establishment of the National Park cattle were shipped out and range abandoned 1919. When National Park was created name De Motte was re-established. Decision U. S. G. B.

Dennison   Coconino Co.   U. S. G. S. Map, 1923.

On A. T. & S. F. R. R., Colorado Ind. Res. 6 miles southeast of Parker.

"After Assistant Roadmaster Denny, who had charge of track gangs on Santa Fe for many years, on this end of the road." Letter, P. M., Parker.

De Noon   Pinal Co.

Point where mill of Reymert mine owned by Judge J. D. Reymert was located, 1888. The "D" in Reymerts name was for De Noon which gave it the name. See Reymert mine.

Descanso   Cochise Co.

Sp., "Rest, repose." Was near present town of Turquoise. Not on any map, nobody knows its origin. P. O. established May 23, 1892. William O. Abbott, P. M.

Desert   Pima Co.   Eckhoff Map, 1880; G. L. O., 1892.

Station on old stage road and also on S. P. R. R., 20 miles northwest Tucson. P. O. established May 10, 1880. Charles H. Labarell, P. M. Labarell owned the station according to Hinton who spells the name Labaree. P. O. records at Washington, however spell it clearly Labarell.

Desert Station   Yuma Co.   Smith Map, 1879; Eckhoff, 1880.

On G. L. O. map, 1921, shows as Desert Well, 15 miles southwest of Vicksburg. Station Prescott-Ehrenberg stage line at head Granite wash in Hanegras plains.

"At midnight we reached Desert station. There was a good ranch there kept by Hunt and Dudley, two Englishmen. Their ranch was clean and attractive." *Vanished Arizona.*

Desert Peak   Pinal Co.   U. S. G. S. Map, 1923.

In T. 9 S., R. 12 E. Northern end Tortilla mountains. Elevation 1,969 feet. On G. L. O. map, 1886, shows as about 10 miles northeast of Red Rock station S. P. R. R.

Desert Range, Peak   Pinal Co.   G. L. O. Map, 1921.

In Ts. 6, 7 S., R. 10 E. About 6 miles south of Florence.

Desert View Point   Coconino Co.

Grand Canyon N. P. on south rim of canyon near lat. 36° 2′ N., long. 111° 49′ W. Not called Navajo. Decision U. S. G. B., 1933.

Desert Well   Maricopa Co.   U. S. G. S. Map, 1923.

In T. 1 S., R. 7 E., about 10 miles east of Gilbert. Well known early day watering place and station on road Mesa to Roosevelt dam.

Desert Wells   Pinal Co.

Hinton lists it as about 36 miles south of Florence, about where Desert station is shown on Eckhoff map, 1880, on road Florence to Tucson.

Detrital, Valley and Wash   Mohave Co.   Smith Map, 1879;
                                                     U. S. G. S., 1923.

In northwest corner county and State. Heads north end Black mountains, west side Cerbat range. Wash runs north, enters Colorado opposite Virgin river. Valley filled with debris washed down from the hills. Name given by U. S. G. S. party many years ago.

De Vargas Terrace   Coconino Co.   Map, Grand Canyon N. P., 1927.

In T. 33 N., R. 2 W., at southern end of Powell's plateau north side of Grand Canyon. De Vargas was one of Coronado's officers.

Devils Kitchen   Cochise Co.

In Skeleton canyon. "A mysterious old German appeared in Skeleton canyon early in the Nineties. He built a little hut at the forks above the Devils Kitchen and lived alone. Who he was or his name never was learned. He dug all over the canyon looking for buried treasure taken from Mexican smugglers. One day he was gone, vanished into thin air." *Tombstone.*

Devils Wind pipe   Yavapai Co.   Map, Coconino N. F., 1928.

In sec. 21, T. 13 N., R. 7 E. Narrow, deep canyon heading east of "13-mile rock." Runs west into West Clear creek in T. 17 N., R. 6 E. Its narrow deep character gives the name.

Devine, Mount   Pima Co.   Roskruge Map, 1893; U. S. G. S., 1923.

In T. 15 S., R. 5 E. East side North Comobabi range. On Papago Ind. Res. "Named by George Roskruge after John J. Devine, father of K. C. Devine, who about 1890 had several silver mines near this peak." Letter, Mrs. Geo. Kitt, Tucson.

Devin's Peak   Apache Co.

Named after Lieut. Col. T. C. Devin, 8th Cavalry, U. S. A., who commanded the Arizona District, 1868. Bancroft says: "He had two regiments of Infantry and nine troops of Cavalry to patrol and protect the whole Territory."

Dewey   Cochise Co.

Siding S. P. R. R. 4 miles east of Willcox. "Established, 1903, named after Admiral Dewey." Letter, W. T. Brinsley, Agent S. P. R. R.

Dewey   Yavapai Co.   G. L. O. Map, 1923.

In T. 13 N., R. 1 E. After Admiral Dewey. Family home of Miss Sharlot Hall, writer, and former State Historian. About 25 miles southeast of Prescott. P. O. established Jan. 18, 1898, Fred. Hiltenbraut, P. M.

Diablo Mountain   Santa Cruz Co.   G. L. O. Map, 1923.

In T. 20 S., R. 12 E. On Coronado N. F. map is called Diablito mountain.

Diablito Mountain

See Diablo.

Dial   Cochise Co.   G. L. O. Map, 1921.

Ranch in South pass, Dragoon mountains. Owned and run by Robert Dial according to an item in *Tombstone Epitaph* of June 3, 1882.

Diamond Butte   Gila Co.

In Ts. 9, 10 N., R. 12 E. North side Spring creek. Descriptive name, Diamond Point lies about 14 miles northwest.

Diamond Butte   Mohave Co.   G. L. O. Map, 1921.

Elevation 6,250 feet. West of Hurricane cliff, near lat. 36° 35', long. 113° 20'. "A conical butte near which we camped and found a large ant hill covered with small, perfect quartz crystals that sparkled in the sun like diamonds. I recorded it temporarily as 'Diamond Butte.' The name became fixed, which shows how unintentionally names are sometimes bestowed." Dellenbaugh.

Diamond Canyon   Mohave Co.

Heads Hualpai Ind. Res. northeast part of T. 28 N., R. 9 W. Enters Grand Canyon at Diamond peak. Coues says Garces called it Rio de San Alexo. Ives, 1857, called it Diamond canyon. He and his party explored it thoroughly.

"It was here at Diamond canyon," says Powell, "that Lieut. Ives and Dr. Newberry came down to the depths of the Grand Canyon." This was April 5, 1858. There is no known reason for this name. Ives does not give any origin for it. An attempt was made here to revive the great diamond swindle that was staged in the extreme northeastern corner of State in earlier years, but it failed to attract suckers. This however was long after Powell's time.

Diamond Creek   Navajo Co.   U. S. G. S. Map, 1923.

On Fort Apache Ind. Res. Rises east slope Mount Thomas (Baldy), flows west entering White river about 10 miles north-east Fort Apache. Origin unknown.

Diamond Fields   Apache Co.   Mallory Map, 1876; Smith, 1879.

In extreme northeast corner State. South of San Dune plateau. Origin not known. Captain Walker came through here 1854. This is the region in which lay the famous, or infamous, Diamond fields which in 1872 caused a vast amount of discussion and dis-appointment. Clarence King, the geologist, finally exploded the whole thing after a careful investigation. Bancroft gives a full account of it in his volume on Arizona. There are extensive articles in Los Angeles *Daily News*, Aug. 2, and October 16, 1872. A man named Edward is given as the discoverer. Banta, in his personal history states that he "was directed by Gov. Safford to investigate this so-called diamond discovery." He left Tucson, July 15, 1871, which makes this item rather doubtful. Banta, however, was often badly mixed on his dates. "My report to the governor, was FAKE." was his short official report.

Diamond Joe   Mohave Co.   G. L. O. Map, 1921.

In T. 17 N., R. 13 W. Mining camp on Big Sandy. After Dia-mond Joe Reynolds who owned the Congress mine. So called because he once owned the "Diamond Joe" line of Mississippi river steamers.

Diamond Mountain   Maricopa Co.   Map, Tonto N. F., 1927.

In T. 6 N., R. 8 E. West side Mazatzal range. So called after Diamond Cattle Co., which ran a large herd of cattle here in early days. Brand was diamond on left hip.

Diamond Peak   Mohave Co.   U. S. G. S. Map, 1923.

East side Diamond creek, at junction with Colorado river. Near western boundary Hualpai Ind. Res.

Diamond Point   Gila Co.   Map, Tonto N. F., 1927.

In upper Tonto basin. A so-called Diamond mountain about 10 miles below the Rim, in T. 11 N., R. 11 E. Due north of Little Green valley. "It is of limestone formation and crystals are found in the rock and on the ground which are locally called Arizona diamonds. They have no value as gems." Letter,

Forest Ranger, Fred Croxen. Forest fire tower and Lookout station located on this point.

Dick Pillar   Coconino Co.

"In honor of the indefatigable Robert Dick of Thurso, Scotland, whose labors in the Red sandstone added so much to our knowledge." Named by G. Wharton James who did not locate it, nor does it show on any map.

Dilkon Trading Post   Navajo Co.   U. S. G. S. Map, 1923.

In T. 23 N., R. 19 E. "I named this place Dilkon, which is a Navajo word meaning 'a bare surface of any kind.' There is a bare topped butte just back of this location." Letter, Justus W. Bush, P. M., Dilkon. P. O. established Dec. 17, 1920, Justus W. Bush, P. M.

Dinne Mesa   Apache Co.   Gregory Map, 1917.

Large mesa on Navajo Ind. Res. northeast corner State. Navajo word meaning "The People." The Navajos often speak of themselves as "dinne" as do also the Apaches.

Dinne-bito Spring and Wash   Navajo Co.   G. L. O. Map, 1921;
                                                        U. S. G. S., 1923.

In T. 28 N., R. 13 E. West side Dinne-bito wash. "A Navajo word dinne, his; bito, spring; the Indians spring." Gregory. Wash rises under Black mesa, flows southeast across Hopi Ind. Res. Enters Little Colorado river 6 miles south of Black Falls.

Dirty River

See San Pedro river.

Disappointment Creek or Valley   Gila Co.   G. L. O. Map, 1909.

The lower end of Dripping Springs valley or wash. East side Gila above Christmas. Called Dripping Springs wash on most maps. Old settlers say name Disappointment antedates name Dripping springs. No one can give its origin however. Bourke called it Disappointment as early as 1873, which should indicate its precedence. Opens into Gila river near Christmas. See Dripping Springs wash.

Divide   Maricopa Co.   R. R. Guides

Station Parker branch A. T. & S. F. R. R. 10 miles west of Wickenburg. On crest of watershed between Colorado on west and Gila on east and south.

Dix   Mohave Co.

On A. T. & S. F. R. R. about 28 miles east of Colorado river, between Haviland and Franconia. "This station is no longer in existence and there is nothing in our records to indicate origin of the name." A. G. W.

Dixie Canyon   Cochise Co.   Map, Coronado N. F., 1921.

North side Mule mountains above Bisbee. Flows northwest and is lost in Sulphur Springs valley. "In early days a colored man known as 'Nigger Dick' lived at some springs in this canyon and had a small farm and some cattle. The canyon came to be known as 'Dicks' and then 'Dixie' canyon." Letter, C. W. Hicks.

Dixie National Forest   Mount Trumbull division G. L. O. Map, 1921

On north side Colorado river, east of Cold Springs wash. First Mormons who came into this region called it "Dixie" because it was much warmer than farther up in Utah. They raised cotton, figs and other tropical products here. Area in Arizona at Mount Trumbull, which is but a division of the main forest, was named after this mountain. Area in Arizona, 1931, about 65,000 acres. Supervisor's headquarters, Cedar City, Utah.

Doak   Gila Co.   Map, Crook N. F., 1926.

In sec. 13, T. 2 S., R. 14½ E. Small settlement on Mineral creek. P. O. established Feb. 19, 1919, Margaret L. Tanner, P. M.

Doanville   Yuma Co.

After John Doan, old timer, once postmaster at Fortuna mine. P. O. established Nov. 22, 1889, Frank P. Schultz, P. M.

Dock   Pinal Co.

Station S. P. R. R. 14 miles south of Chandler, between Santan and Ohlberg stations. So called from nearby peak at western end Santan mountains. Americans call this "Dock."

"It is a Pima word meaning 'Nose' and according to Father Felix, should be spelled 'Dahk.' Pimas call the peak 'Amelican Dahk' i.e. American Nose, says Father Felix." McClintock.

Dodson   Navajo Co.   Map, Sitgreaves N. F., 1924.

Dry wash heading in T. 11 N., R. 20 E. About 3 miles southwest of Shumway town. Enters Cottonwood creek in sec. 5, T. 12 N., R. 21 E., about 3 miles west of Taylor. After Rube Dodson, early Mormon settler and cattleman who farmed at Taylor and ran cattle near there in the Eighties.

Dome   Yuma Co.   U. S. G. S. Map, 1923.

P. O. and railroad station, S. P. R. R. about 24 miles east of Yuma. "So called because famous Castle Dome mountain is in plain view from this point. Originally 'Castle Dome,' 1881." Letter, Supt. S. P. R. R. Tucson. P. O. established Apr. 24, 1900, William D. Luce, P. M.

Dome Rocks Mountain   Yuma Co.   G. L. O. Map, 1892;
                                           U. S. G. S., 1923.

In Ts. 3, 4, 5 N., R. 20 W. After large dome-shaped rock, a land mark in this region.

Doña Ana County   New Mexico and Arizona   Colton Map, 1855.

One of the four original counties placed by Mowry on his 1860 map of Arizona. Extended over present Graham, Cochise, and Greenlee counties eastward to Texas line and all south of Gila river. See Yuma.

Don Luis   Cochise Co.   G. L. O. Map, 1921.

Station Bisbee branch E. P. & S. W. R. R. about 6 miles from International Line. Named for Lewis Williams, early Copper Queen superintendent, called "Don Luis" by Mexicans. P. O. established Oct. 7, 1903, John J. Mercers, P. M. He declined to qualify and Mary A. Head was appointed.

Donnelly Wash   Pinal Co.   U. S. G. S. Map, 1923.

Heads in T. 5 S., R. 14 E., southwest of Hayden; runs northwest, enters Gila river about 4 miles east of Price. After a cattleman named Donnelly who ran stock here in the Eighties.

Dony Park   Coconino Co.   Map, Coconino N. F., 1930
Open park in yellow pine timber 12 miles northeast Flagstaff. After Ben Dony, Civil War veteran who lived here for many years. Died Oct., 1932.

Dos Cabezas   Cochise Co.   G. L. O. Map, 1892, 1923.
Sp., "two heads." In T. 14 S., R. 27 E. Station Mascot branch S. P. R. R. at south end Dos Cabezas mountains. About 15 miles east of Willcox. P. O. established Apr. 8, 1879, F. Beebe, P. M.

Dos Cabezas Mountains   Cochise Co.   Map, Coronado N. F., 1927.
Elevation 8,000 feet. In T. 14 S., R. 26 E. Two outstanding peaks east side Sulphur Springs valley, southeast of Willcox. Have always been noted land marks in this region.

Dos Narices Mountain   Gila Co.
Sp., "Dos narices," two noses. "Going down by the head of Deer creek and over into Rock creek which rises in the Dos Narises mountains, not more than 12 miles from Grant itself." Bourke. This must have been the head of the Deer creek south of Rockhouse mountains. The name was for two rather snub-nosed peaks like "noses."

Dosoris Mining Camp   Yavapai Co.
Located 12 miles south of Prescott in Hassayampa mountains. Discovered 1880 by Townsend Cox. Named after his mother's home town, Dosoris Island, N. Y. Hamilton, 1884, says: "It is a very rich mine but admittance was denied me, so I could not examine it."

Dos Palmas Well   Maricopa Co.   U. S. G. S. Map, 1923.
In T. 4 N., R. 4 W. On east bank Hassayampa, near White Tank mountains. According to *Routes to the Desert*, "This is incorrectly called, 'Dos Palms.' A watering place owned by the Flower Pot Cattle Co."
"Originally there were two large Yucca palms near the well. The place was abandoned years ago. A recent flood washed nearly the whole place away." Letter, P. M., Morristown.

Dot Klish   Navajo Co.   U. S. G. S. Map, 1923.
Navajo word, "dot-lesh"; blue clay or blue earth. Canyon Navajo Ind. Res. south of Black mesa. Is part of Moen Kopi wash. Known also as Blue canyon.

Double Buttes   Maricopa Co.   Scott Map, Maricopa County, 1929.
Two volcanic upthrusts about 4 miles south of Tempe. Well known land marks. Sometimes called Gregg buttes, after Dr. A. J. Gregg. Scene of killing of Tom Graham, 1892.

Double Buttes   Pinal Co.
Near Florence on Gila river. See North Butte, South Butte.

Double Circle Ranch   Greenlee Co.
In T. 1 S., R. 27 E. East side of Eagle creek near mouth of Willow creek. So called after brand of Double Circle Cattle Co. owned by Joe Hampson of Kansas City. One of the oldest cattle outfits in State. Brand was double circle on left ribs. See Woolaroc.

Doudsville   Mohave Co.   G. L. O. Map, 1909, 1912.
Station Mohave and Milltown R. R. to Oatman. Short stub railroad from Needles. Named for Milo Doud.

Douglas   Cochise Co.   G. L. O. Map, 1921.

Elevation 3,966 feet. Named for Dr. James Douglas, President Phelps Dodge Co. On E. P. & S. W. R. R. near Mexican border. Townsite located 1900 by W. H. Brophy and A. J. Cunningham on a tip from company officials that the new smelter was to be located here. Country then was all an open cattle range.

Dove Springs   Coconino Co.   U. S. G. S. Map, 1923.

Well known watering place where great flocks of wild doves are often seen. On Navajo Ind. Res. north of Kaibito plateau.

Dowling   Pima Co.   G. L. O. Map, 1909.

Southern end Sonoita mountains. At Mexican line, lower end Ajo valley. After Pat Dowling, early settler and prospector.

Dox Castle   Coconino Co.   Map, Kaibab N. F., 1926;
    G. C. N. P., 1927.

In sec. 21, T. 33 N., R. 1 E. North side Grand Canyon. "In honor of Miss Virginia Dox, pioneer visitor at this point." James.

Doyle Saddle   Coconino Co.

In secs. 4 and 5, T. 22 N., R. 7 E., Gila and Salt River meridian, Coconino National Forest, between Agassiz and Fremont Peaks. Named locally for Allen Doyle, a guide, 1850-1920.

Dragoon   Cochise Co.   Map, Coronado N. F., 1927.

Station S. P. R. R. 18 miles east Benson in Dragoon Pass. "Established 1880. First called Dragoon Pass but shortened to Dragoon to save telegraphing." Letter, Supt. S. P. R. R., Tucson. P. O. established as Dragoon, June 20, 1881, Cassius M. Hooker, P. M.

Dragoon Mountains   Cochise Co.   Map, Coronado N. F., 1927.

In Rs. 23, 24 E. South of S. P. R. R. Mountains took name from Pass, q.v. which appears to have been first point so named in this vicinity.

Dragoon Pass   Cochise Co.

In Rs. 23, 24 E. Pass through Dragoon mountains, east of Willcox. After U. S. Dragoon regiment which garrisoned many posts in territory, 1857-58.
Captain Ewell—"Baldy"—was called sharply to account for an action in the Dragoon Pass in 1857.
In 1930 the stone walls of the old Butterfield stage station were still to be seen here. Lieut. Parke, 1856, named it Railroad Pass because he felt here was a fine place for a railroad to get through without too much climbing. It was at a well known spring in this Pass that Gen. O. O. Howard, Oct. 12, 1872, ratified a treaty of peace with Cochise. See Ewell county.

Dragoon Peak   Cochise Co.   Map, Coronado N. F., 1927.

In T. 16 S., R. 23 E. Upper end Dragoon mountains.

Drake   Yavapai Co.   G. L. O. Map, 1921.

First called Jerome Junction. Station Ash Fork-Phoenix branch A. T. & S. F. R. R., 21 miles south Ash Fork. "After W. A. Drake, engineer who constructed the line. Mr. Drake was Chief Engineer of Atlantic and Pacific R. R." A. G. W.

Drews Station   Cochise Co.

According to *Arizona Gazetteer,* 1881, this was a stage station about 15 miles north of Tombstone on road to Benson. Drew Hansen was the owner and station keeper. After Hansen's first name.

Dripping Springs Mountain   Pinal Co.   Smith Map, 1879; U. S. G. S., 1923.

Range southeast of Globe on north side Gila, extending northwest from river. So called from springs by this name in this range. Called Mescal mountains on Ray Quad. 1910.

Dripping Springs   Yuma Co.   G. L. O. Map, 1921.

In T. 3 N., R. 18 W. Well known spring west side Plumosa range.

Dripping Springs   Gila Co.   Map, Crook N. F., 1926.

In sec. 30, T. 3 S., R. 15 E. Well known stage station and cattle ranch of early days. On stage road Florence to Globe. In foot hills of Dripping Springs range. At one time these springs were owned by "Idaho Bill" Southerland. In 1890 were property of U. S. Marshal Griffith, who had a large herd of cattle here.

"Name is derived from character of springs which issue from the rocky sides of a cliff and are really 'dripping springs.'

"Springs are about a mile south of Globe-Winkleman road. The ranch is some 4 miles west of springs." Letter, O. E. Clendenin. In the Pioneers' library, Tucson, is a printed copy of a report to the Military officer at San Carlos, dated Mar. 16, 1887, and signed by Al. Seiber, Chief of Scouts. He had been scouting after the Apache Kid in the region about these springs. It reads in part:

"I saw Mr. Bernard, the man who is taking care of Mr. Drippings stock, etc."

Was Al Seiber mistaken in this name or was there really a man named Dripping? The author doubts the latter very much. P. O. established Nov. 17, 1886, Mrs. Mary O. Strockley, P. M.

Dripping Springs Wash   Gila Co.   U. S. G. S. Map, 1923; Crook N. F., 1926.

In T. 4 S., R. 6 E. Wash or creek flowing from northwest to southeast, enters Gila a few miles above Christmas. In extreme southwest corner Gila county. Called Disappointment creek on Smith map, 1879, and Eckoff, 1880. Bourke also calls it that. Name of course comes from the well known springs. See Disappointment.

Dromedary Peak   Pinal Co.   Map, Crook N. F., 1926.

Descriptive name, from its peculiar shape. In sec. 18, T. 2 S., R. 11 E.

Drury   Cochise Co.   U. S. G. S. Map, 1923.

Station S. P. R. R. about 4 miles east of Willcox, at northern end Dos Cabezas mountains. Paul Shoup says: "Am unable to establish the meaning of this name. Station opened prior to 1900. There is no agent, nor does any one live there now."

Dry Beaver Creek   Coconino Co.   Map, Coconino N. F., 1928.

Rises in T. 16 N., R. 6 E., flows southwest, joins Wet Beaver in sec. 36, T. 14 N., R. 5 E., near Montezuma Well, where it forms Beaver creek. So called because this fork was often dry except a hole here and there as against Wet Beaver creek, the other fork, which was never dry.

Dry Lake   Navajo Co.   U. S. G. S. Map, 1923.

Large open basin often filled with flood waters most of it coming from the Phoenix wash. In N.W. corner T. 15 N., R. 19 E. Frequently goes dry. The Hashknife (Aztec Cattle Co.) outfit about 1888 dug several long ditches to drain into it flood waters from Pierce, Phoenix and other washes. More than six thousand range cattle and probably a third as many wild horses often watered here in dry seasons, 1888 to 1896. Quite a dry farming settlement here now called Zeniff. q.v.

Dublin   Graham Co.   R. R. Maps.

Station Globe division Arizona-Eastern R. R. 10 miles west of Safford. So called by William Garland who built this road. He was a native of Cork, Ireland. q.v.

Dude Creek   Gila Co.

In upper Tonto basin. "Small creek on East Verde draining into east side of that stream about 6 miles from its source. Frank McClintock had a ranch on this creek and gave it this name." Letter, Fred Croxen, Forest Ranger.

Dudleyville   Pinal Co.   Hamilton Map, 1866;
                                                     G. L. O., 1921.

In sec. 25, T. 5 S., R. 15 W. On San Pedro about one mile south Gila river. Stage station owned and run by the Harrington family about 1879. "Dudley Harrington was the father. Dudley was a family name and he wanted his post office so called. They compromised on Dudleyville." Letter, Fred W. Lattin, Winkelman. One authority says place was first called Wharton City but who Wharton was nobody knows. P. O. established May 8, 1881, as Dudleyville. P. O. records in Washington show it changed later to Feldman, q.v.

Dugas   Yavapai Co.

The Dugas family had a ranch here. P. O. established Nov. 11, 1925, Mrs. Gertrude H. Dugas, P. M.

Dunbar's

See Tres Alamos.

Duncan   Greenlee Co.   U. S. G. S. Map, 1923.

In T. 8 S., R. 32 E. Elevation 3,642 feet. An early settlement. Formerly a heavy cattle shipping point. On Gila river about 25 miles above Solomonville. Close to New Mexico line, on old Arizona and New Mexico R. R. Named in 1883 for James Duncan, a director Arizona Copper Co. Was first called Purdy, q.v. P. O. established as Duncan October 11, 1883, Charles A. Brake, P. M.

Duncan   Mohave Co.   G. L. O. Map, 1928.

In T. 29 N., R. 16 W. Early mining camp on head Grapevine creek. Close to line Hualpai Ind. Res. Origin not known.

Dunlap   Graham Co.   G. L. O. Map, 1892.

In T. 6 S., R. 19 E. P. O. and ranch headquarters on Aravaipa creek. After Hon. Bert Dunlap, who ran cattle here 1882 to 1896. Dunlap was several times elected to Territorial Legislature. P. O. established Mar. 22, 1883, Bert Dunlap, P. M. Changed to Aravaipa in Apr., 1892.

Dunn Spring   Cochise Co.   Map, Coronado N. F., 1927.

In sec. 24 T. 15 N., R. 30 E., east slope Chiricahua mountains. After Jack Dunn, early miner and prospector who had a cabin at the spring about 2 miles from mountains. One of first men to prospect the Bisbee region. See Bisbee and Copper Queen. "One was always sure to meet in Tucson men like old Jack Dunn, who wandered about all parts of the world and has since done such excellent work as scout against the Chiricahua Apaches." Bourke.

Dunn Butte   Coconino Co.

In Grand Canyon N. P., about 3 miles northeast of Lyell butte near lat. 36° 5′ N., long. 112° W. Named for William H. Dunn of Powell's first expedition, 1869. One of Howland brothers party, all of whom were murdered by Shivwits Indians, 75 or 80 miles beyond west boundary of present Park. Named by Frank Bond.

Duppa Butte   Coconino Co.

Grand Canyon N. P. On west wall of canyon about 5 miles southeast Point Imperial. "Named for Bryan P. D. Duppa, known as Darrell Duppa, of English birth, who settled in Arizona, 1863. Pioneer of Salt River valley. Secretary Swilling Canal Co., which, 1867, constructed first irrigating ditch tapping Salt river." Named by Frank Bond.

Little known of Duppa's early history. John McDerwin, one of his intimate friends, writes: "Was in the English army reaching the rank of Colonel. Fought a duel with a brother officer, resigned and found his way to Arizona. Was said to receive $3,000 from home every quarter. Lived in the Salt River valley, then moved to Agua Fria where he ran the stage station for some time."

Bourke describes this station as "a most unattractive place bare of every comfort, with only the most primitive furnishings." Banta says "Duppa spoke perfect English and half a dozen other languages, as well as reading Greek, Latin, etc." Capt. Hancock had a written agreement with Duppa which described him as "Darrell Duppa, Halsingbourne House, County of Kent, England." He suggested name of both Phoenix and Tempe q.v.

Duppa's name was first one on enumerator's sheet for Phoenix district of U. S. Census Report, 1870. His age is given as "36 years. Born in France."

Tucson Citizen, Mar. 30, 1872, states that Duppa was attacked and badly wounded by Apaches at his Agua Fria ranch Mar. 24, 1872. He died at Phoenix. A headstone was erected over his grave by the D. A. R. of Phoenix in 1910.

Duquesne   Santa Cruz Co.   G. L. O. Map, 1921;
                                               Coronado N. F., 1927.

In sec. 2, T. 24 S., R. 16 E. Old mining camp east side Patagonias about 4 miles from Mexican line.

"Named by Westinghouse interests after Fort Duquesne original name of Pittsburgh, Pa. This Pittsburg company had some claims at this point many years ago." Letter, Fred Croxen, Forest Ranger. P. O. established Aug. 17, 1904, Charles A. Bankhead, P. M.

Dutch Woman Butte   Gila Co.   Map, Tonto N. F., 1927.

In T. 5 N., R. 12 E., about 5 miles north Roosevelt lake. "Reputed origin of this name is that Apaches had captured a Dutch woman.   The troops in a fight rescued her.   One soldier was killed and buried here.   Officer who reported the fight called it, Dutch Woman Butte."   Letter, Margaret Platt, Payson.

Bourke also calls it by this name.   A writer in the *Phoenix Herald* of July 21, 1888, alludes to it as "resembling an old Dutch woman sitting down."

Dutton Hill   Coconino Co.   G. L. O. Map, 1921.

In T. 20 N., R. 5 E.   In Coconino N. F.   Station on old logging railroad near Mooney mountain.   After Major Clarence Dutton, geologist and explorer.   See Dutton Point.

Dutton Point   Coconino Co.   U. S. G. S. Map, 1923;
                                                       Kaibab N. F., 1926.

Elevation, 7,555 feet.   In sec. 2, T. 33 N., R. 1 W.   North side of river east side Powell plateau, about 15 miles north of El Tovar. James says: "Dutton point I named for the distinguished geologist, poet and brilliant writer, Major C. E. Dutton.   To the left is a hump on the surface of the wall and this we call 'Powell Arch,' for the great explorer."

Dzil

See Ziltusayan—Apache word.

Eager   Apache Co.   Map, Apache N. F., 1926.

Mormon settlement in T. 6 N., R. 29 E.   "In Mar., 1871, came John T. Eager who located in Water canyon 4 miles south of present Springerville, which first was known as Union, later called Eagerville or Eager, after the three Eager brothers." McClintock's *Mormon settlement*—See Round Valley.

Eagle City   Cochise Co.   G. L. O. Map, 1908.

Small hamlet, east side Chiricahuas.   On White Cap creek, about 10 miles north of Paradise Camp.

Eagle Creek   Greenlee and Graham Cos.   Smith Map, 1879;
                                                       U. S. G. S., 1923.

In T. 3 N., R. 29 E.   Greenlee county, about 5 miles west of Morenci.   Rises under Mogollon Rim in Rattlesnake basin. Flows south, enters Gila in Greenlee county, in southwest corner T. 5 S., R. 29 E.   Flows alternately in Graham and Greenlee counties.   So named because of many eagles' nests in cliffs along the river.   Spanish called it "Rio Aguila," Eagle river.

Eagle Eye Peak   Maricopa Co.   G. L. O. Map, 1927.

In T. 6 N., R. 9 W.   An opening near crest of mountain gives the effect of an open eye.   At extreme eastern end of Harqua Halas.   About 6 miles west of Aguilar station, Parker branch.

Eagle Landing   Yuma Co.   Clason Map, 1908;
                                                       G. L. O., 1921.

Early day steamboat landing for Planet mine and others in Cienega mining district.   Located about 16 miles above Parker, and 5 or 6 below mouth Bill Williams fork.

Eagle Mountain   Maricopa Co.   U. S. G. S. Map, 1923.

In T. 1, S., R. 3 W.   In Buckeye hills south of Gila river, about 3 miles southeast of Buckeye.

Eagle Nest Mountain Coconino Co. Map, Tusayan N. F., 1927.

In sec. 9, T. 23 N., R. 2 W. An outstanding butte. "The cattle-man who named this butte found an eagle's nest in its cliffs, hence the name."

Eagle Pass Graham Co. G. L. O. Map, 1921.

In T. 8 S., R. 23 E. At northern end of Pinalenos. See Stockton Pass.

Eagle Peak Mohave Co. G. L. O. Map, 1921.

In T. 25 N., R. 22 W. On Colorado river.

Eagle Ranch Greenlee Co. Smith Map, 1879; Apache N. F., 1926.

On Eagle creek, known in the Eighties, as "Stevens" or "Little Steve's" ranch q.v. Owned by George H. Stevens, prominent cattleman and politician during Governor Wolfley's term.

May 7, 1880, on Eagle creek near a point shown on Smith map, 1879, as "Little Steve's ranch," in T. 14 S., R. 28 E. Capt. Adam Kramer with E troop, 6th U. S. Cavalry, was ambushed by some of Victorio's band of Warm Spring Apaches. Sergt. Dan. Griffin was killed and several men wounded. Kramer was hurrying to the rescue of some of Stevens' men said to be surrounded by Apaches and in dire straits.

Eagle Rock Peak Graham Co. Map, Crook N. F., 1926.

In sec. 12 T. 9 S., R. 24 E. On east side Pinaleno mountains.

Eagle Tail Mountains and Peak Yuma Co. U. S. G. S. Map, 1923.

"So named for three columnar shafts resembling the tail feathers of an eagle." *Arizona Magazine*, Nov., 1915. Range runs from northwest to southeast in Yuma and Maricopa counties south side Harqua Hala plains. Peak is at southern end of mountains in T 1, S., R. 10 W. in Maricopa county.

Eagle Tank Maricopa Co.

In T. 9, S., R. 10 E. Sp., "aguila," an eagle. Watering place east side Aguila mountains. After nearby mountains.

Eagle Valley Pah Ute Co., Nevada

Settlement on Muddy river in northwest corner of that part of Arizona later transferred to Nevada. Settlement about 1865 was at upper end Muddy valley. One of earliest settlements by Mormons along that stream and its tributaries.

East Cedar Mountains Yavapai Co. Map, Tonto N. F., 1927.

In sec. 13, T. 9 N., R. 5 E. Small mountain well covered with cedar timber. On boundary between Tonto and Prescott Forests.

East Clear Creek Coconino Co.

See Clear creek.

East Fork of Black River Apache Co. Map, Apache N. F., 1926.

Rises in Seven Springs draw; flows south, joins West Fork in sec. 11, T. 4½ N., R. 28 E., to form Black river.

East Fork Little Colorado River Apache Co.
           Map, Apache N. F., 1926.

Rises east side Mount Thomas (Baldy) flows northwest, joins West Fork in sec. 14, T. 7 N., R. 27 E., to form Little Colorado river.

East Fork of Verde   Gila Co.   Map, Tonto N. F., 1927.

Rises under "Rim" near Rim Rock ranger station, in northeast part of T. 12 N., R. 10 E. Flows southwest, enters Verde river at sec. 28, T. 11 N., R. 7 E. at O. K. Ranch. "We joined the pack train upon a stream that we called the 'East Fork of the Verde.' " *Woolsey's Report* June 2, 1864. Also called East Verde.

East Fork of White River   Apache and Navajo Cos.
Map, Fort Apache Ind. Res.

Rises in T. 6 N., R. 26 E. on west slope Mount Thomas. Flows southwest, joins North Fork at Fort Apache to form White river.

East Peak   Cochise Co.   G. L. O. Map, 1921.

In T. 18 S., R. 19 E. West side Whetstone range, Coronado N. F. "So called from its location on the range."

East Phoenix   Maricopa Co.

This was first location of Phoenix. P. O. established Dec. 19, 1871. Edward K. Baker, P. M. E. E. Hellings who owned the flour mill here was P. M. from Oct. 22, 1874, to June 6, 1876, when the office was closed. See Mill City. Also Phoenix. Hinton says: "East Phoenix and Hayden's Mill are small settlements gathered about two large flour mills. The stage road passes through them both."

East Point   Coconino Co.   U. S. G. S. Map, 1923.

In T. 12 N., R. 9 E. Coconino N. F. Prominent point on the rim near Bakers butte.

Easter   Maricopa Co.   P. O. Route Map, 1929.

Station Arizona, Eastern R. R. about one mile north of Hayden Junction. "After Easter mine near here, discovered on Easter Sunday." P. O. established June 3, 1915, Della S. Miller, P. M.

Ebert Mountain   Coconino Co.   Map, Tusayan N. F., 1927

In T. 25 N., R. 4 E. Nothing known of its origin. Several authorities feel it was probably meant for Lieut. Abert who was with Emory's party 1846-47. It would be a comparatively easy matter to get the spelling of this name wrong. It was he, Abert, for whom the beautiful squirrel "Sciurus aberti" found on south side of canyon in Northern Arizona, was named.

Ebles Ranch   Yavapai Co.

See Skull valley.

E. C. C. Peak   Yuma Co.   G. L. O. Map, 1921.

In T. 8 N., R. 12 W. In Harcuvar mountains. Persistent inquiry among early settlers and others has failed to disclose the reason for, or origin of, this interesting and intriguing name.

Echo Canyon Bowl   Maricopa Co.

North side Camelback mountain. Large natural amphitheatre with fine acoustic properties, where some day Phoenix will have an out-of-doors theatre.

Echo Cliffs   Coconino Co.   G. L. O. Map, 1921.

Navajo Ind. Res. Range of cliffs extending north and southeast of Colorado river at Marble canyon, named by Powell. See Echo peak.

Echo Peak   Coconino Co.   G. L. O. Map, 1921.

Elevation, 5,360 feet. On Navajo Ind. Res., east side Colorado river opposite mouth of Paria, near Lee Ferry. "The echos were so remarkable we could call it nothing but Echo peak. Since then this name has been applied to the line of cliffs breaking to the south." Dellenbaugh.

Ecks Mountain   Apache Co.   Map, Apache N. F., 1926.

In sec. 14, T. 10 N., R. 24 E. "So called after Ecks Nicholls who had a ranch near it for some years. It is often called Ecks Knoll." Letter, Paul Roberts, Holbrook.

Eden   Graham Co.   G. L. O. Map, 1921.

Settlement north side of Gila, opposite Glenbar. Formerly called Curtis. After Moses Curtis, first settler September, 1881. They could not get a postoffice as Curtis, so changed the name. P. O. established May 23, 1892, William T. Oliver, P. M.

Edith   Maricopa Co.

P. O. at Judson mine, established July 6, 1888, Judson S. Todd, P. M. "Todd named the place for his wife, Edith."

Edna Needle   Navajo Co.   Gregory Map, 1916.

Sharp, isolated peak in Navajo Ind. Res. On Carson mesa about 10 miles west of Chinle station. So named for Edna Earl Hope by Gregory. See Hope Window for Gregory's statement.

Edwards Park   Gila Co.   Map, Tonto N. F., 1927.

"A fairly open park, covering about 400 acres, in T. 6 N., R. 9 E., south and east of Edwards peak after which it was named. It is said to be the largest open, fairly level area, in the entire Mazatzal range, which is one of the roughest in Arizona." Letter, Forest Ranger Fred Croxen.

Edwards Peak   Gila Co.   Map, Tonto N. F., 1927.

Elevation, 5,907 feet. In T. 6 N., R. 9 E. In Mazatzal mountains, south side Reno pass. Peak shown under this name on map, Tonto N. F., 1927. On some early maps is called Reno mountain, q.v.

"Named after Charles (Charley) Edwards, an early resident on Tonto creek, who lived here when region was surveyed. Edwards was afterwards murdered near Clines while returning from Globe." Letter, Forest Ranger, Croxen.

Egloffstein Butte   Navajo Co.   Gregory Map, 1916.

In T. 25 N., R. 18 E. Named by Ives after Mr. Egloffstein, artist and topographer with his party, 1858. On Hopi Ind. Res.

Ehrenberg   Yuma Co.   All Old Maps; G. L. O. Map, 1921.

Town on Colorado river a few miles south of Colorado Ind. Res. Early day shipping point for Prescott and other mining districts. Named by Michael Goldwater, who established a ferry over the river and opened the first store here in 1860, after Hermann Ehrenberg, German mining engineer who came to Arizona about 1854. Supposed to have been killed by Indians in 1866, at Palm Springs, Calif., while enroute to Los Angeles.

"Of all the dreary, miserable looking settlements that one could possibly imagine, it was the worst. It was an important shipping point for freight to the interior and there always was an army officer stationed there." *Vanished Arizona.* According to Hinton it was first called "Mineral City," in 1863; resurveyed, 1867; and named Ehrenberg.

Regarding Ehrenberg; J. Ross Browne has a statement 'from Poston as follows, "Ehrenberg migrated from Germany, worked his way to the United States, and landed at New Orleans. The Texas war for Independence was on, and he enlisted in New Orleans 'Greys'; fought at Goliad, and Fannings defeat in Texas. Went back to Germany but returned in 1840; went across the continent to Oregon from there to Honolulu from where he made his way again to Arizona."

Ehrenberg had some five hundred people in 1871. There is now a fine auto bridge over the river. P. O. established Nov. 24, 1871, J. M. Barney, P. M.

Ehrenberg Point   Coconino Co.

In Grand Canyon N. P., on west canyon wall, near northeast corner of Park, about 2 miles southeast of Point Imperial. Named for Hermann Ehrenberg. Decision, U. S. G. B.

El Capitan Canyon   Gila Co.   Map, Crook N. F., 1926.

Sp., "the captain." Heads south end Pinal mountains. Flows southwest into Dripping Springs wash, at northeast corner T. 4 S., R. 15 E.

El Capitan Mountain   Gila Co.   U. S. G. B. Map, 1923; Crook N. F., 1926.

Elevation, 6,564 feet. On boundary line between Gila county and San Carlos Ind. Res. At southwest corner of reservation. After El Capitan mine south end Pinal mountains.

El Cienega

See Pantano.

Elden Mountain   Coconino Co.   G. L. O. Map, 1921; U. S. G. S. Map, 1923, Elden Mesa.

Elevation 9,280 feet. In T. 23 N., R. 7 E., about 3 miles northwest of Flagstaff. "After an old pioneer named Elden who, with his family lived at the foot of this mountain for many years." *Coconino Sun*, Dec. 7, 1923.

El Dorado Camp   Mohave Co.

Army camp listed by Heitman as "North of the mouth of El Dorado canyon." This would locate it near Mount Davis, on Colorado river. Does not show on any maps. Probably a temporary camp.

El Dorado Canyon Ferry   Mohave Co.   G. L. O. Map, 1921.

Early day ferry across Colorado opposite El Dorado canyon. Road came down floor of El Dorado canyon on California or western side of river. P. O. established Jan. 17, 1865, called El Dorado canyon, Frank S. Alling, P. M.

El Dorado Ranch   Cochise Co.   Roskruge Map, 1893.

West slope Chiricahuas. "Ranch of Theodore White in 1883. He was a government surveyor and, with his two brothers, Thomas and Jared, ran quite a bunch of cattle on this range." Letter, Mrs. George Kitt, Tucson.

Elephant Butte   Navajo Co.   U. S. G. S. Map, 1923.

In T. 23 N., R. 17 E. "A tall, outstanding lava 'plug' that can be seen from all sides." Gregory.

Elephant Head   Santa Cruz Co.

"A rather unique formation that at a distance resembles the head of a huge elephant." Letter, Robert C. Rodgers, Nogales. P. O. established July 10, 1914, Henry W. Williams, P. M. See Pete mountain.

Elephant Hill   Mohave Co.

North of Mount Davis, northwest corner State. "A conical mound about 150 feet high which stands in a bend of the river. We found a large and perfect tooth of *Elephas primigenius* in the bed of coarse gravel and boulders which form its base." Newberry, 1857. Dr. Newberry says it was between camps 56 and 57, which would make it very close to the El Dorado ferry of later years. Near T, 26 S., R. 22 W.

Elephants Tooth   Mohave Co.

In T. 19 N., R. 20 W. Prominent feature near and southeast of Oatman. Prof. Ransome says, "It is a plug of rhyolite stripped bare by erosion."

Elevator Mountain   Greenlee Co.

In eastern part San Carlos Apache Ind. Res., along its western boundary, east side of Eagle creek.

"Known as 'Elevator' mountain since the oldest settlers have known it. General opinion is that it takes the name from the height of the mountain, as it is the highest in vicinity. Is generally supposed to have been referred to as 'the mountain of elevation' and later this was shortened to 'Elevator.'" Letter, J. W. Girdner, Forest Ranger.

Elfrida   Cochise Co.   U. S. G. S. Map, 1923.

In T. 20, S., R. 26 E. Station, E. P. & S. W. R. R., 24 miles east Tombstone. "Named for mother of G. I. VanMeter, a well known settler who donated the railroad right-of-way across his land for which they were to name the station for his mother." P. O. established July 24, 1915, Marie K. Leitch, P. M.

Elgin   Santa Cruz Co.   G. L. O. Map, 1921.

In T. 20 S., R. 18 E. Town and Station on Calabasas-Fairbanks Branch R. R. On Sonoita creek. P. O. established Feb. 12, 1910, Reubin (sic) E. Collis, P. M.

Elkhart   Yuma Co.   G. L. O. Map, 1909.

An early station on Parker branch, A. T. & S. F. R. R., 6 miles east of Wenden. "Said to have been a temporary siding put in at end of the tunnel here, while it was being bored. Elkhart was tunnel foreman for the company." Letter, J. B. Quinn, Los Angeles, Calif.

Elliott, Mount   Yavapai Co.   Map, Prescott N. F., 1926.

In sec. 11, T. 13 N., R. 1 W. Northwest of Chaparral, head of Eugene gulch. "After A. G. Elliott, early day miner who located the Accidental lode, September, 1874." Letter, Forest Supervisor Grubb.

Ellison   Gila Co.   Map, Tonto N. F., 1926.

In sec. 10, T. 8 N., R. 15 E. Named for Jesse W. Ellison, stockman, who grazed cattle in this region and on the Apache reservation and had his headquarters here. Came to Arizona, 1886, with a herd of cattle which he shipped by rail from Texas to Bowie Station where he unloaded and drove across to Tonto

Basin. Settled on Ellison creek, later moved to the "Q" ranch southwest of Pleasant valley. Died, Phoenix, Jan. 21, 1934. One of his daughters married Governor G. W. P. Hunt. P. O. established at ranch, July 27, 1897. Jesse W. Ellison, P. M.

Ellison Creek   Gila Co.   Map, Tonto N. F., 1926.

Stream rises near Apache Ind. Res. line, flows southeast into reservation and enters Canyon creek. Named for Jesse W. Ellison. See Ellison P. O.

Ellsworth   Navajo Co.

Settlement on Showlow creek, about 2 miles south of Showlow town. Located by and named for Edmund Ellsworth, first settler here.

Eloy   Pinal Co.   U. S. G. S. Map, 1923.

In T. 8 S., R. 8 E. Station on S. P. R. R. about 6 miles west of Picacho. Station established many years ago.

"In the year 1902 the Southern Pacific built a switch here, naming it Eloi, a word taken from the Syrian language, meaning 'My God.' It was soon called Eloy after the Spanish pronunciation. In 1916 a couple of men came from California, laid out a town site, promoted the planting of cotton and renamed the town Cotton City. The Southern Pacific would not accept the new name and carried all mail for Cotton City on through. After many disputes and some litigation the town became Eloy for good." Letter, Mrs. M. M. Fordham, President Woman's Club, Eloy. P. O. established May 1, 1919, George L. Stronach, P. M.

El Paso   Pima Co.

P. O. established June 19, 1879, Damacia Garcia, P. M.

El Sopori-Mexican Land Grant   Santa Cruz Co.

This Grant was rejected in toto by U. S. Land Court. Area claimed, 142,721 acres, declared fraudulent on ground that, "the original title papers were forged, antedated and otherwise invalid." McClintock.

El Tovar   Coconino Co.

Railroad station and hotel at end of Grand Canyon R. R. at the canyon. After Don Pedro Tovar, one of Coronado's captains. If this was intended merely as a name, it is perfectly correct. But if, as is generally supposed, the name was to honor the first European to see the Grand Canyon, it is a grievous error. The historical facts are, that Cardenas, another of Coronado's captains, and not Tovar, was the first real discoverer of the canyon.

Bancroft says: "In August, 1541, Captain Tovar with a small force was sent to explore the Cebolla country, especially the Province of Tusayan. They found the Moki villages and the Indians mentioned a great river several days' journey to the north. Thereupon, Don Pedro returned and reported to the General. Then Captain Cardenas was sent with twelve soldiers, to seek the great river. He marched north and west for twenty days and found the river. He spent five or six days trying to get down its precipitous banks, but could find no place to descend. This was the first visit of Europeans to the Canyon of the Colorado."

El Vado

The Crossing, See Crossing of the Fathers.

El Vadito

Sp., "the little ford." See St. Johns.

El Veit

See Growler Well.

Emery Graham Co.

Hinton mentions but does not locate this place, other than to say: "It was near Fort Thomas, on the Gila river." Dan Williamson says: "It was named after the first settler."

Emery City Cochise Co.

By *Arizona Gazetteer*, 1881, this was a mill site on the San Pedro 3 miles above Charleston, where Boston and Arizona smelters were located.

Emery Park Pima Co. Postal Route Map, 1929.

Station Nogales branch, about 8 miles south of Tucson. Place named for Emery family who live here. P. O. established Sept. 21, 1928, Camilla Emery, P. M.

Emigrant Springs Apache Co. G. L. O. Map, 1921.

In T. 21 N., R. 28 E., about 6 miles south of Sanders station, A. T. & S. F. R. R. "Here the westbound emigrants of early days found good water and a fine camping place."

Emma, Mount Mohave Co. G. L. O. Map, 1921.

Elevation, 7,700 feet. On north side Colorado river, south of Dixie N. F. Near lat. 36° N, long. 113° W. Named by Major Powell for his wife, Emma.

Empire Pima Co. Map, S. P. R. R., Sept., 1930.

Station on S. P. R. R., 29 miles east of Tucson. Originally called Pantano; name changed to Empire, 1912. So called for well known Empire ranch of Vail and Gates located about 15 miles south. See Empire mountains.

Empire Mine Santa Cruz Co.

This mine is mentioned by French engineer, F. Brerton, who examined Mowry's Patagonia mine, 1861. Mowry published Brerton's report in his book. Brerton says: "It is half way between Mowry mines and town of Santa Cruz. Was owned by a big New York company, which gave it the name 'Empire,' for their home state."

An old map of 1860 shows a mine in this same locality called the "New York mine." Probably the first name for this Empire mine.

This was quite apart from a similar action taken some years later by Walter Vail for his ranch some distance above here which he also called the "Empire" ranch.

Empire Mountains Pima Co. U. S. G. S. Map, 1923.

In Ts. 17, 18 S., Rs. 16, 17 E. Isolated range about 10 miles south of Pantano. East of Santa Ritas. Near here was the Empire ranch of Vail and Hislip Cattle Co., Walter L. Vail and Herbert R. Hislip. John L. Harvey entered the firm soon after. Several years later Mr. Gates bought in and firm became Vail and Gates.

Walter Vail came to this region from New Jersey in 1875. Established several large ranches one of which he called "The Empire Ranch"—"because we intended to found an empire."

From an old Ms. by Walter Vail. Mountains later took their name from ranch.

According to Ed Vail, a mining district was started here about 1881 called Empire district after nearby mountains. Camp of Total Wreck was in this district. Frank C. Schrader mentions this district in U. S. G. S. Bulletin 582 and says "it was so called after the Empire mountains."

The Empire mine owned by Mowry was some distance south of these mountains. Hinton lists it, as does Mowry in his book *Arizona and Sonora*. Mine was owned by New York parties and that name undoubtedly originated with them.

Apparently Vail and these New Yorkers both used this name "Empire" each without the knowledge of the other.

Empire Ranch   Pima Co.   Smith Map, 1879.

In sec. 17, T. 19 S., R. 17 E. In Empire gulch. East side Santa Ritas, about 15 miles south of Pantano. Gulch clearly took its name from ranch.

This ranch was first owned by E. N. Fish and went by the name of the "Fish ranch" on some old maps. When Vail and Hislip bought it from Fish they called it the Empire ranch. P. O. established May, 1879, John L. Harvey, P. M. Eckhoff map, 1880, has it Fish. See Sanford, Pima county.

Encarnacion

See Tucson & Tucsonimo.

Enebro Mountain   Greenlee Co.   Map, Crook N. F., 1926.

In sec. 17, T. 3 S., R. 29 E. "Enebro," Sp., "Juniper tree." Doubtless for these trees growing on its sides.

Engel Well   Yuma Co.

"A watering place belonging to Zagel Engel. In sec. 10, T. 7 N., R. 8 W." *Routes to the Desert.*

Engles Pass   Mohave Co.

This is evidently Beale's name for the present Truxton canyon or wash. He writes "Truxton and White Rock springs are in this pass." Further on he says: "Leaving White Rock spring which is in Eagles (sic) pass we came to Truxton spring in a mile and a half."

"Eagles pass is either a mistake or misprint as Beale named the pass for one of his party Captain Engle, U. S. Navy." Coues.

Enid   Maricopa Co.   G. L. O. Map, 1909.

On S. P. R. R. about 9 miles west of Maricopa.

Ennis   Maricopa Co.   G. L. O. Map, 1921.

In T. 3 S., R. 1 W. Town and station Prescott-Phoenix R. R. About 2 miles north of Peoria. "After a Mr. Ennis who once owned a large tract of land in this vicinity." Letter, J. M. Turner, Peoria.

Enrequita   Pima Co.   Smith Map, 1879.

Mining camp in Pajarito mountains. West of Nogales near Mexican boundary. P. O. established May 7, 1866, Charles H. Lord, P. M. Origin unknown. Sp. for "Harriet," which may be the origin.

Enterprise   Graham Co.

According to McClintock, this was a Mormon settlement near hamlet of San Jose in Gila valley about 15 miles east of Thatcher.

Entro (sic)   Yavapai Co.

Station Ash Fork branch, A. T. & S. F. R. R., 6 miles north of Prescott. "At entrance to small canyon through which road passes, hence the name." A. G. W. If Spanish, however, it should be "Entrar."

Equator   Yavapai Co.   G. L. O. Map, 1908.

"There was a mine here by this name located near head of Cherry creek, east side of Black hills. Was quite a lively camp in 1900." P. O. established Dec. 12, 1899, Arthur Woods, P. M.

Erastus   Apache Co.

Early Mormon settlement on Concho creek about 16 miles west of St. Johns. Mexican town of Concho was already started here but the Mormons, 1880, came in and called their side Erastus in honor of Erastus Snow, then President of the Stake. On Dec. 6, 1895, they gave up this name and adopted Concho. P. O. established, called Erastus, May 26, 1881, Sixtus E. Johnson, P. M. See Concho.

Erickson Peak   Cochise Co.

Altitude 7,990 feet. In T. 19 S., R. 30 E. Named for Neil Erickson, pioneer and forest ranger on this division of Coronado National Forest for twenty-five years. Decision U. S. G. B., 1933.

Erman   Pinal Co.   Railroad Maps.

Spur P. and E. R. R. about 2 miles east of Ray Junction.

Escala   Graham Co.   U. S. G. S. Map, 1923.

Sp., "a ladder." In T. 11 S., R. 28 E. Station Arizona Eastern R. R., in San Simon valley. "Station is on summit of a hill or pass. The road climbs 'zig-zag,' like a ladder, up one side, down the other, hence the name."

Escalante Creek   Coconino Co.

In Grand Canyon N. P. Rises at Canyon wall just below Escalante butte, flows into Colorado river. Named for Father Escalante, one of the leaders in an expedition from Mexico, 1775-76. See Escalante Crossing.

Escalante Crossing   (Utah)

See Crossing of the Fathers.

Escudilla   Apache Co.   Smith Map, 1879; Eckhoff, 1880.

Sp., "a porringer" or a "bowl." Prominent mountain near state line in Ts. 6, 7, N., Rs. 30, 31 E. Apache N. F. Hinton describes this mountain very fully. When viewed from a higher peak looks exactly like a huge bowl. Probably an old crater.

Escuela   Pima Co.   G. L. O. Map, 1921; U. S. G. S. Map, 1923.

Sp., "a school." In T. 14 S., R. 13 E. Settlement, Santa Cruz valley about 4 miles south of Tucson. Papago Indian school is located here, hence the name. P. O. established July 10, 1907, Haddington G. Brown, P. M.

Eskiminzin

Apache, "big mouth." Chief of Aravaipa Apaches, most of whom were killed in Camp Grant Massacre, 1871. About 1880, he took up a regular homestead on the San Pedro and ceased all tribal relations. The historians are none too kind to this Apache.

Esmond   Pima Co.

"Station, S. P. R. R. east of Tucson, now called Cruz. Origin not known." Letter, Supt. S. P. R. R., Tucson. See Cruz.

Espejo Butte and Creek   Coconino Co.

Five miles south of Little Colorado river, on east rim of canyon Near lat. 36° 7' N. long. 111° 48' W. Creek rises on west slope of Espejo butte. Named after Antonio Espejo, Spanish explorer who visited northern Arizona, 1582. Named by Frank Bond.

Espejo Spring   Coconino Co.   Gregory Map, 1916.

Navajo Ind. Res. near lat. 36° N. So named for Espejo by Gregory.

Esperanza   Pima Co.   Eckhoff Map, 1880.

Sp., "hope." In T. 18 S., on west side Sierrita range. Mining camp, Pima district, about 12 miles due west of Sahuarita. From the name of a mine here. P. O. established Feb. 26, 1884, W. Blaisdell, P. M.

Espero   Greenlee Co.   U. S. G. S. Map, 1923.

Sp., "hope." In T. 4 N., R. 29 E. Settlement, Apache N. F., on Beaver creek near line of Apache-Greenlee counties. "First settlers were Mexicans 'who hoped they would succeed' in making homes." P. O. established Jan. 11, 1919, Sophia J. Taylor, P. M.

Espinosa   Pima Co.

Sp., "thorny." Water hole on Papago Ind. Res. Letter in Pioneer Society, Tucson, says "It is named for an Indian family by this name who live on this water hole."

Esthwaite   Pinal Co.   U. S. G. S. Map, 1923.

Settlement on Queen creek about 12 miles west of Superior. On Crook N. F. P. O. established June 23, 1919, Richard W. Mattison, P. M. Origin unknown.

Estrella Hill

See Estrella.

Estrella, or Sierra Estrella Mountains   Pinal and Maricopa Cos.
                    G. L. O. Map, 1921; U. S. G. S. Map, 1923.

Sp., "a star," as the white spot in forehead of a horse. In Ts. 2, 3 S., Rs. 1, 2 E. "These mountains designated by the mongrel name of San Jose de Cumars, are the Sierra Estrella; Estrella or Star mountains. They are sometimes lettered Santa Estrella; on some maps, Maricopa mountains. Extend about 20 miles northwest and southeast parallel with the Gila on its left side. There is a similar range across the Gila running down to the point between this and Salt river." Coues. This latter range is now called Salt River mountains. Highest point, Montezuma peak, 4,000 feet. "This entire Estrella range is known to the Pimas as the Ko-matk, which means 'broad or thick' or even massive. From the east side of the Gila they have that appearance. None of our present-day older people among the Pimas know anything about a 'blue hazy mountain.'" Letter, Fr. Antonine, St. Johns Mission. An intelligent, elderly Pima woman speaking perfect English, when asked the meaning of Ko-mat-k said "thin, high—a high, thin mountain." She illustrated by placing a large, rather thin couch cushion on one edge on the floor.

Estrella Maricopa Co.   G. L. O. Map, 1921.

"Station S. P. R. R., 23 miles west of Maricopa. After Estrella range to east. Established, 1881." Letter, Paul Shoup. East side Maricopa mountains. P. O. established Jan. 29, 1919, called Estrella Hill, Ray L. Crowley, P. M.

Eugenie (sic) **Station and Stream** Yavapai Co.
               Map, Prescott N. F., 1926

Station Poland branch R. R. Named after Eugene creek on which it is located about 13 miles from Poland mine. Hinton spells this name Eugenia and lists a mine by this name at that point.

"Eugene is named for a man by that name who operated a placer mine in the gulch nearby which goes by the same name. My impression however is that he also spelled it Eugenia." Letter, P. M. Venezia. Stream rises near Mount Elliott, flows southeast into Big Bug creek in T. 13 N., R. 1 E.

Eureka Mountain Graham Co.   G. L. O. Map, 1921.

East side Galiuro range, north of Kilberg peak. Named after Leitch brothers' ranch, the Eureka Cattle Co., of the Eighties. See Eureka springs.

Eureka Springs Graham Co.   Eckhoff Map, 1880.

"Headquarters for an old cow ranch formerly owned by Leitch brothers, one of whom was territorial auditor for several years. On east slope Galiuro range about 15 miles west of Fort Grant." On Aravaipa creek.

Evans Graham Co.

In Gila valley. P. O. established April 4, 1897, Mungo R. W. Parks, P. M.

Evans Mountain Pima Co.   Map, Coronado N. F., 1927.

In sec. 32, T. 11 S., R. 17 E. East side Catalina range due west of Redington.

Ewell County

One of the four original counties Sylvester Morley placed on his map of 1860. Changed to Pima county, 1864. "After Captain R. S. Ewell, one of Mowry's partners. Ewell was known to the soldiers as 'Baldy' because of his lack of hair. Was a captain in First Dragoon regiment, later a Lieutenant General in Confederate Army. He commanded at Fort Buchanan, 1860. In 1857 was called sharply to account for an action with Apaches in Dragoon pass, in which he happened to kill a large number of women and children as well as bucks. 'How the devil can a soldier stop in the midst of a battle to summon a jury of matrons to determine whether the Indians pouring bullets into the soldiers are women or not?' was his answer." McClintock.

Ewell's Station and Spring Cochise Co. Smith Map, 1879;
                   Eckhoff, 1880.

Well known stage station in early days. Spring was a fine one, scene of many fights with Apaches. About 13 miles west of Camp Bowie, on old overland stage road, and a favorite camping place for travelers. Named after Capt. Ewell.

Excalibur Rocks Coconino Co. Map, Grand Canyon N. P.

In T. 33 N., R. 1 W. North side Grand Canyon. Word is of Celtic origin, name of King Arthur's favorite sword. Outlines of mountain resemble a sword lying flat on the ground hence the name was given it by U. S. G. S. party that covered this area.

Explorers' Pass or Canyon   Yuma Co.

Narrow canyon on Colorado river a few miles above Yuma. So called by Lieut. Ives, Jan. 12, 1857, for his steamer "The Explorer." This vessel only 54 feet over all was used by Ives in his exploration of the Colorado. Built in the east, carried to the coast; thence to the head of Gulf of California by ship, she was put together by Ives and his men and launched in Dec., 1857.

Fagan, Mount   Pima Co.   U. S. G. S. Map, 1923; Coronado N. F., 1925.

Elevation 6,715 feet. In T. 18 S., R. 16 W. North end Santa Rita mountains. About 6 miles northeast of Helvetia." Named after Michael Fagan, prospector and cattleman who operated in Huachucas and Santa Ritas in early days. Was a partner of Dave Harshaw. Sold his mine here about 1880 and invested in a cattle ranch." Letter, Fred Winn, Forest Service.

Fain Mountain   Coconino Co.   G. L. O. Map, 1921.

In sec. 35, T. 17 N., R. 8 E. In Coconino N. F. north of Stonemans lake. "After William Fain, father of Albert and Granville Fain. He ran the Sixteen brand at what was known as Sixteen springs." Letter, Link Smith.

Fairbank   Cochise Co.   G. L. O. Map, 1921.

In T. 20 S., R. 21 E. Station on San Pedro river, established in 1882 on E. P. & S. W. R. R. at junction Tombstone branch. Named for N. K. Fairbank, well-known Chicago merchant who was interested in mines around Tombstone, 1882. P. O. established May 13, 1883, John Dessart, P. M.

Fair Oaks   Yavapai Co.   Map, Prescott N. F., 1927.

In sec. 26, T. 16 N., R. 5 W. Early stage station and P. O. "There was a fine grove of Live Oaks here. The place was located by W. W. Ross, druggist of Prescott, and Henry Clay. They planted a fine orchard known as Fair Oaks orchard from the natural oak groves." Letter, Frank Grubb, Forest Service.

Fairview   Graham Co.

This was later called Glenbar. On the Arizona-Eastern R. R., on south side of Gila river. P. O. established Jan. 13, 1909, Ephraim Larson, P. M. Changed to Glenbar, Nov. 1, 1917.

Fairview   Navajo Co.

See Lakeside.

Fairview   Yavapai Co.   U. S. G. S. Map, 1923.

In T. 21 N., R. 1 W. Station A. T. & S. F. R. R. 8 miles east of Ash Fork. "There is a fine view of the country to the west from this point. So named by locating engineers." A. G. W.

Falfa   Maricopa Co.   Scott Map, Maricopa Co., 1929.

In T. 1 S., R. 5 E. Hay loading station, Chandler branch P. and E. R. R. "Falfa, a shortening of the word alfalfa, raised here in large quantities. About 3 miles north of Chandler."

Fan Island   Maricopa Co.

Butte in Grand Canyon N. P. One and half miles northwest of mouth of Shinumo creek. Small, isolated, fan-shaped, flat-topped butte, between Powell plateau and Colorado river. So named by Frank Bond.

Farrar Peak   Yuma Co.   G. L. O. Map, 1921.

Elevation 2,900 feet. About 15 miles east of Ehrenberg. In Dome mountains. Should undoubtedly be "Ferra," after Juan Ferra, a prospector who found rich gold placers near here, 1862-63. See Ferra gulch.

Feldman   Pinal Co.   U. S. G. S. Map, 1923; Post Route Map, 1929.

In sec. 33, T. 6 S., R. 16 E. East side San Pedro river, near site Old Fort Grant, 2 miles north of Aravaipa creek. "This was originally known as the 'Pusch ranch.' When the P. O. was established it was named for Henry Feldman, manager for Mr. Pusch. P. O. discontinued many years ago." Letter, C. C. Clark, Phoenix.

According to P. O. records, this was originally called Dudleyville q.v. P. O. re-established Nov. 22, 1911.

Fenner   Cochise Co.   Railroad Maps.

Station, S. P. R. R., about 3 miles east of Benson. For Doctor Fenner, many years chief surgeon, Tucson division, S. P. R. R.

Feroz Terrace   Coconino Co.

Sp., "ferocious." Formation on canyon wall, Grand Canyon N. P., near lat 36° 20', N. long. 112° 25' W. Spur with bench slopes descending west from north end of Powell plateau. Name refers to dragon-like form of feature. Named by Frank Bond.

Fern Mountain   Coconino Co.

In sec. 27, T. 23 N., R. 7 E. East of Humphrey's Peak. "A cinder cone called this for the heavy growth of bracken on its sides. Named by Otto Platten." Letter, Dr. H. S. Colton, Flagstaff.

Ferra Gulch   Yuma Co.

Very rich placer region 8 or 9 miles east of La Paz. Found by Juan Ferra, Mexican miner in March, 1862. Ross Browne says hundreds of men were at work when he was here in 1863. Mines gave out in a year or two, after over a hundred thousand dollars in gold dust had been taken out. See also Farrar peak, named for same man.

Fields   Yavapai Co.

Station on A. T. & S. F. R. R. about 11 miles east of Peach springs. "After Billy Fields, Santa Fe brakeman, who lost both arms in an accident near here." A. G. W.

Filibuster   Yuma Co.

Stage station, listed by Hinton as 44 miles east of Yuma. From here the famous Henry A. Crabb party of filibusters set out for Sonora, 1857. Crabb, according to McClintock, had some sixty-eight men, all but one of whom were captured and shot by the Mexicans. Crabb's head was cut off, preserved in mescal and sent to Mexico City in an olla to prove the Mexican commander's prowess. The idea of the affair seems to have been the capture of enough land across the line to give each member of the party a good-sized piece, and then have it all annexed to this country. Some early writers spell his name "Crabbe." Poston, east bound from Yuma, writes of this place.

"Filibuster camp, next we reach.
This camp can novel lessons teach.
Some brave, strong men, long years ago
From here, invaded Mexico."

Filmers Ranch

See Joe Filmers ranch.

Finney   Pinal Co.   R. R. Maps.

Spur on P. and E. R. R., Christmas branch; about 4 miles north of Winkelman.

Firebrand River   Apache and Coconino Cos.

Sp., "Rio del Tizon." This is the Colorado river. "The Indians carried firebrands to keep warm." So Coronado called it "Firebrand river." More likely it was to have the means for starting fires as they moved along. See Colorado river.

First Chance   Pima Co.   G. L. O. Map, 1892.

In T. 17 S., R. 8 E. Papago village, Papago Ind. Res. west side of Arivaipa (sic) valley according to G. L. O. map, 1892. On other maps is called Altar valley. This town and Last Chance were just south of Warren shown on G. L. O. map, 1921. Origin unknown.

First Hollow   Navajo Co.   Map, Apache Ind. Res., 1928.

A branch of "Big canyon," coming in from east. There are four short parallel canyons here, all running into Big canyon, and named consecutively, First, Second, Third and Fourth Hollow. All are in T. 8 N., R. 22 and 23 E.

First Knoll   Navajo Co.   Map, Sitgreaves N. F., 1924.

In sec. 4 T. 13 N., R. 21 E. Solitary, flat-topped knoll of moderate elevation. On open range about 5 miles northwest Snowflake, on old "telegraph road" to Holbrook. James Flake in 1882, so named this and two other near-by knolls because, "it was the first knoll from Snowflake towards Holbrook, out on the mesa." The others he called Second and Third knolls, but only this First knoll seems to have secured a place on maps.

First Mesa Wash   Navajo Co.   Gregory Map, 1916;
                                                 U. S. G. S. Map, 1923.

In T. 28 N., R. 18 E. Hopi Ind. Res. Rises southeast part of Black mesa, Navajo Ind Res., flows southwest, joins Polacca wash, 2 miles west of Walpi. In early days the Hopi villages were always spoken of by their consecutive number from Holbrook. We came first to Walpi from Holbrook and called it the First mesa. The others the same way, Second, Third, Fourth, etc., an easy way to designate them.

FIRST THINGS IN ARIZONA

First Anglo-Saxon settlement

"The first Anglo-Saxon settlement within the borders of the original Arizona, was founded by Mormons at Beaver dams in Mohave county in 1863." Farish.

First Arizona Christmas Tree

At Prescott, Christmas day, 1865. See Elizabeth Toohey's story in *Arizona Highway Magazine,* December, 1934.

First Arizona State Song

Called "Hail to Arizona, the Sun-kissed Land." Composed and written by Mrs. Frank Cox and Mrs. Elise R. Averill. Mrs. Cox sang it the first time in public, at dedication of new Territorial capital, Feb. 24, 1901. Under the law adopting this song, trustees of public schools were required to furnish copies free to each school.

First Arizonan Killed in the World War

Matthew B. Rivers, a Pima Indian of Company K, 28th Infantry, was first man killed in action. Killed at Cantigny, May 28, 1918. He was born at Sacaton.

First Artesian Well

Legislature, 1875, offered a reward of $3,000 to first person discovering artesian water in the Territory. This was paid to W. J. Sanderson, of Sulphur Springs valley, who in 1883 found flowing water there at easy depths.

First Artificial Ice Factory

"Samuel D. Lount at Phoenix, 1879, built first factory for producing artificial ice. Its daily capacity was 1,000 pounds. Product was peddled around town by wheel-barrow and sold for seven cents a pound." McClintock.

First Butterfield Stage into Territory

Sept. 15, 1858, Butterfield Stage Co. started a semi-weekly line from San Francisco to St. Louis via Arizona. Contract was for six years at a yearly cost to the government of $600,000. Running time was twenty-two days from end to end. Tipton, Mo., according to McClintock, was the railroad terminus at that time. Distance was 2,795 miles. There was not a break in this schedule until the Civil War stopped operations in 1861. Congress then passed a law changing it to the northern route.

Service was also changed to a daily run for which the government paid over a million dollars a year.

First Camp Meeting

"Held near Prescott, April 17 to 27, 1875, under auspices of Methodist church. Six ministers preached forty-five sermons." Farish.

First Capital

See La Paz; Aztlan; Camp Clark, Yavapai Co.; Walnut Grove.

First Cattle in Arizona

Father Kino probably brought to the missions near Tucson, between 1690 and 1700, the first livestock, cattle, sheep and horses, in what is now Arizona. In his diary of 1700, Kino says: "We gathered up after branding time, and sent alive to California, about seven hundred head of beeves, one thousand sheep and goats and some horses."

First Child born of white parents

"On Nov. 1, 1849, a flat boat going down the Gila from the Pima villages with a Mr. Howard and family arrived at Camp Calhoun, later called Fort Yuma. With them were two men, a doctor and a clergyman, fellow travelers. During the voyage a son was born to Mrs. Howard, said to have been the first white child born in Arizona, of American parents. They named the boy Gila Howard." Farish Notes.

Pancoast, in *A Quaker 49'er* tells of this birth. "They stopped the boat and the woman was taken ashore. After the child was born they resumed their journey. There were several rafts and one other boat. We all insisted that the child be called Gila. The second day after the birth, the mother cooked the meals for the party regularly."

First Copper Mine worked systematically in Arizona

This seems to have been the Ajo mine in Pima county. It has been worked almost continuously since 1855.

First Cotton grown by whites

A five-acre patch was said to have been raised near Phoenix, 1873, by John Osborn.

According to McClintock, "Felix G. Hardwick, 1883, received the $500 reward offered by the Legislature for the first bale of commercial cotton raised in Arizona. It was raised near Tempe and the bale exhibited at New Orleans Fair, 1884. The Pimas and Maricopas of course raised cotton for ages before white men came.

First Counties

Pima, Yuma, Mohave and Yavapai. See Pima Co. See Yuma Co.

First Delegate to Congress

Charles D. Poston was elected Delegate at first election July 18, 1864. He was then U. S. Superintendent of Indian Affairs for the Territory.

First Desert Land Entry

"First desert land entry in Arizona was made Apr. 13, 1877, by William A. Hancock at Florence for sec. 4, T. 1 N., R. 1 E. Desert Land Entry. Patent issued June 20, 1882. Final Certificate No. 1, Florence Series. Land lies near town of Tolleson." Letter U. S. Land Commissioner, Washington, D. C. Feb. 24, 1931.

First Election

The first general election in Arizona was held July, 1864. Town of Prescott cast one hundred forty-nine votes.

First European in northern Arizona

One writer says: "Therefore it can be truthfully claimed, that Father Marcos De Niza stands in history as the first European and earliest of the priestly explorers, who penetrated into the heart of the country in advance of all the old world explorers. He sent Estevan, the Negro, ahead of him. This was in May, 1530." Fish says however: "It is not absolutely certain that Friar Juan de la Asuncion did not reach the Gila the year before Estevan, the Negro from Morocco, who preceded De Niza by several weeks."

First European to see the Grand Canyon

There are several historic references to the first visitor to the Grand Canyon. See El Tovar for history.

First Flour Mill in Arizona

Authorities are not in full accord on this point. The writer after a careful study of all available information feels that the honor belongs to Adamsville, often called Casa Blanca.

Farish, Vol. 1, p. 346, says: "Solomon Warner established the first flouring mill in the territory at Tucson." He gives no date beyond the statement that Warner arrived in Tucson early in 1856.

However, he states in Vol. 4, p. 255: "It is claimed that as early as 1858, one R. Jackson put up a flour mill at Tucson. It was the property of Captain Rowlett and his brother." Could Tucson have had two grist mills at the same time?

District court records at Tucson for 1864 show that as early as 1865, "the mill site on the Santa Cruz river near Tucson, had been regarded from time immemorial as the property of the people of Tucson, as a right inseparable from their use of the water of this river for irrigation purposes.

"In this same year the Tucson people voted to grant the mill site with its water privileges to William Rowlett on certain conditions." These were: "The building of a mill and grinding wheat and other grain for the people of Tucson, they to have preference over all other persons.

"These court records go to show that in the spring of 1861, the mill and buildings were burned by U. S. troops as a military necessity.

"Later on, the Tucson people at a special election granted the mill site and its appurtenances to Gerald L. Jones and J. Riordan as successors to Rowlett. They rebuilt the mill on the ruins of the old one. Later they dissolved and Jones became sole owner. When he died, John W. Swilling and James Lee bought the mill from the Jones estate and so held it until the date of these proceedings in court, in June, 1864. The record unfortunately does not show how the suit ended.

"It is evident this Tucson mill was one of, if not the first, grist mills in Arizona although the same court records for 1864 show a suit involving a grist mill in the town of Tubac which may have antedated the Tucson mill." Condensed from *Cross Country News*, March 15, 1934, by P. H. Hayhurst.

However there were doubtless crude water power grist mills among the Pimas in their villages along the Gila about as early as either of these but there are no dependable records to prove their age.

Fish claims that: "The first flour mill was erected at Tucson in June, 1872, by James Lee and W. F. Scott." Where Fish got the item he fails to say. Probably from Governor Safford's Annual Report, 1874, which states: "James Lee produced over 600,000 pounds of flour at his steam flour mill in Tucson, in 1873. He also ran a saw mill in connection with it."

First Governor of Arizona

This was John A. Gurley of Ohio, appointed by President Lincoln March 4, 1863. He died in Washington D. C., Aug. 18, 1863, after a long illness and never assumed office. His sickness and death delayed the departure of the new territorial officials for the west.

First Homestead Entry

"The first homestead entry filing in Arizona was made at Prescott, Nov. 10, 1871, by Nathan Bowers for a homestead entry in sec. 11 T. 13 N., R. 1 E. Homestead entry No. 1. Prescott series. Patented March 30, 1880." Letter, Commissioner of Public Lands, Washington, D. C., Feb. 24, 1931. This land lies near Humboldt.

First Honey Bees

McClintock says that Joseph Ehle and his wife brought several hives to Prescott in 1865, the first tame bees to be brought in. The *Arizona Sentinel* of Yuma states that General J. B. Allen brought two hives from San Diego to Tucson in December, 1872. They swarmed often and hives were sold to persons in Salt River and Gila valleys. "One day," says the *Sentinel,* "some cows got into Allen's garden, upset the hives and the bees all escaped to the desert." There were of course wild honey bees here before that for trappers found honey bees in the San Carlos mountains in 1845.

First Indian Reservation

Gila River Indian Reservation, with an agency at Sacaton, was established by Act of Congress, dated Feb. 28, 1859.

First Indian School

"Arizona's first Indian school was established at Sacaton agency Feb. 15, 1871, Rev. Charles H. Cook, missionary teacher." Taken from Cook's *History.*

First Lawyer Admitted to Practice

Coles Bashford was first lawyer admitted to practice before Territorial courts at Tucson in May, 1864. He came to Arizona with the Goodwin party.

First Legal Hanging

Barney says this took place in Yuma, May 2, 1873, opposite the only school in town. The teacher, Miss M. E. Post, not wishing her pupils to witness it, dismissed school for the whole week. Entire town turned out, including undoubtedly the aforesaid school children, to witness the execution. The victim was a Mexican named Fernandez, who had been sentenced in the district court.

First Legislative Act

Passed Oct. 1, 1864. It empowered the Governor "to appoint a Commission to prepare and report on a code of laws for the use and consideration of the legislature of the territory."

First Livestock Sanitary Board

Established March 10, 1887, by an act of Fourteenth Legislature. On April 28, 1887, Gov. Zulick appointed Henry Smith of Apache Co., Thomas Halleck of Mohave Co., B. E. Norton of Graham Co., C. M. Bruce of Cochise Co., and Nathan Bowers of Yavapai Co., as members of the Board. Smith refused appointment. Zulick appointed C. O. Howe of Apache Co., who also refused it. Governor then appointed Will C. Barnes of Apache Co., who accepted. Later Norton declined and I. N. Town of Calabasas was appointed and accepted. Board met first time and organized at Prescott in July, 1887. C. M. Bruce was elected chairman. Later the board selected Dr. A. J. Chandler of Detroit, Mich., as veterinary surgeon. He arrived and assumed his duties Aug. 6, 1887.

First Marriage between Americans

William Kirkland married a Miss Bacon at Tucson, May 26, 1860. She was enroute to California with her parents, who stopped a few days in Tucson, when Kirkland persuaded her to marry him and remain in Arizona. Farish says their first child, a daughter, was born Aug. 15, 1871, in the second house built on the Phoenix townsite.

First Masonic Lodge

"Was opened in the upper room of the old log capital at Prescott on the evening of July 25, 1865, as Aztlan lodge No. 1." McClintock.

First Military Expedition into Arizona

Bancroft says: "In November, 1697, Lieut. Christoval Martin Bernal, with a sergeant and twenty soldiers marched form Fronteras, while Kino and Manje with ten servants came from Dolores and united with Bernal at Quiburi not far from site of modern Tombstone."

This party went on down the San Pedro and saw the Casa Grande ruins, which Kino described and pictured in his diary. This is said to have been the first formal expedition by the Spanish into Arizona.

First Military Post in what is now Arizona

Fort Defiance in Apache county, then part of New Mexico, was established, 1852, by Col. Sumner, U. S. Army, "In defiance of, or to, the Navajo Indians."

It was about 10 or 15 miles west of the present boundary between New Mexico and Arizona. In 1860 Navajos made a concerted attack upon it but were driven off with heavy losses.

First Mission

See Quebabi; which some believe to have been the first Spanish Mission in Arizona.

First Newspaper

This was *The Arizonian*, edited and published by Col. Ed. Cross at Tubac. Photostat copy in office of State Historian at Phoenix spells the name *"Arizonian."* Photostat shows it as No. 18, Vol. 1 of June 30, 1859. So the first copy must have been issued some time before. It had four pages and four columns to the page. According to McClintock, it was originally owned by the Salero Mining Co. Later Sylvester Mowry bought and ran the paper. See First Printing Press.

First Ostriches

Will Robinson says: "Josiah Harbert and M. E. Clanton, 1888, imported a pair of grown birds and twelve chicks and landed them in the Salt River Valley. Eleven of the chicks and the female adult bird died en route. This left the male and one single chick—a female. This young lady after three years study of the situation, laid an egg and kept it up with commendable regularity. By 1898 she had ninety-seven members of her family —a record to be proud of."

First Overland Mail

Was carried by saddle animals. It left San Diego in October, 1857, and was the first overland mail going east via Arizona. There is no reliable record as to how long this service was kept up, but it was turned into a regular stage line in November, 1858.

First Overland Stage Line

Started from San Diego, a four-horse coach being used, at noon Nov. 15, 1858. Company was the "San Antonio and San Diego Semi-monthly Stage Company." Coaches went right through to San Antonio without stopping other than for meals. The Mail Contractor was James Burch with I. C. Woods, Manager. Government paid at first $149,000 a year for the service.

An advertisement for this line in a San Antonio paper states that: "Passengers are forwarded in new coaches, drawn by six mules, excepting in the Colorado Desert, which we cross by mule-back for 100 miles. An armed escort travels with each mail train, through the Indian country. Each passenger is allowed 30 pounds of baggage, exclusive of blankets and fire arms."

First Penitentiary

Territorial legislature, 1874, authorized penitentiary commissioners to purchase "not less than 10 acres of land on which to locate the penitentiary at Yuma." It was ready and opened for business with seven prisoners July 1, 1876, according to Farish *Notes.*

First Pole set on Military Telegraph Line

According to the *Tucson Citizen,* Oct. 11, 1873, "the first pole on this military line to the west from Maricopa, was set Oct. 8, 1873, with cheers and a general rejoicing."

Fish says: "The first pole on the branch line from Prescott was set at Whipple Barracks, Sept. 2, 1873. The main line reached Tucson and opened for business Dec. 1, 1873. The *Tucson Citizen,* Dec. 6, 1873, tells of a grand ball given in honor of Capt. George F. Price, 5th U. S. Cavalry, in charge of the work. His men built an average of 7 miles a day."

First Postmistress

Records at Washington show that Miss Jane Oswald, of Walnut, was first woman to hold this position in Arizona. Appointed P. M. at Walnut, Yavapai county, June 24, 1874.

First Post Office Established in What is Now Arizona

According to official post office records in Washington, D. C., this was at Tucson, Doña Ana county, New Mexico, Dec. 4, 1856, Elias Brevort, P. M. The region was at that time part of New Mexico and the commission of the postmaster so locates it.

First Pre-emption entry

"The first pre-emption cash entry in Arizona, was made May 26, 1871, at Prescott Land Office by William Bicard, for land in sec. 8, T. 5 S., R. 9 E. His declaratory statement alleged settlement on or before June 15, 1866. Patent issued April 28, 1873. Cash certificate No. 1, Prescott series." Letter, U. S. Land Commissioner, Washington D. C., Feb. 24, 1931. This land lies southwest of Florence.

Some historians report that John B. Allen filed the first pre-emption claim in Arizona in the Tucson Land Office, and the land was that on which the old Maricopa Wells station was located. There is no record of any application by Allen at any of the land offices for the first entry of any kind.

First Presbyterian Church

Will Robinson says it was started in a log cabin at Prescott in 1864. Rev. William H. Reed was preacher. Reed was also the Prescott postmaster at the time.

First Printing Press

Was brought to Tubac, coming via Cape Horn and Guaymas, in 1858. Hauled by teams overland from Guaymas to Tubac consigned to William Wrightson. It was a Washington Hand Press No. 25, manufactured by the Central Type Foundry Co., of Cincinnati, Ohio.

It was used to print the first newspaper in Arizona, which was called *The Arizonian.*

Press is now in Pioneers Library, Tucson.

First Public Building

This was a log building at Prescott called the "Governor's Mansion." Proposals for its erection were published in *Arizona Miner,* June, 1864. It was to be of logs and 40 by 50 feet in size. Cost, according to the *Miner,* was not to exceed $6,000. The nails are said to have cost $1.75 a pound.

First Public Schools

First territorial legislature passed an act appropriating funds for public schools as follows: $250 each for the Prescott, La Paz and Mohave schools; $250 for the new school at San Xavier Mission; and $500 for the school at Tucson, "provided that instruction is given in the English language."

"The first public school in Tucson was opened in the fall of 1869, by Augustus Brichta. It had 55 pupils, all Mexicans. Brichta had been an assistant clerk in the legislature." Will Robinson.

First Public School in Phoenix

Opened September 5, 1872, J. D. Daroche teacher. In small adobe building on First avenue just south of Washington street. He resigned and in October, 1873, Miss Nellie Shaver, later Mrs. John Y. T. Smith, came to Phoenix from Wisconsin and was promptly appointed in his place. She taught in a one-room adobe on north Center street on the block where the San Carlos hotel now stands. Mrs. Smith says it was the second house in the town to have a shingle roof and board floor.

First Railroad Engine

While the railroad at Clifton was the first railroad—for it had rails upon which the cars ran—the first actual railroad engine, on a regular train running in the territory, was a Southern Pacific engine which pulled the train that crossed the bridge at Yuma at 11 o'clock p. m., September 29, 1877, and entered the territory in defiance of the United States authorities.

First Railroad in Arizona

The first railroad built and operated in Arizona was the narrow gauge affair built on Chase creek, 1873, to carry ore from the Longfellow mine to the smelter at Clifton. For several years the cars were hauled up by mules and then ran down by gravity. In 1880, a small engine was hauled in by wagons, put together and used. It was called the "Little Emma." Who Little Emma was no man knows today.

First Railroad Train into Phoenix

"Captain Hancock drove the last spike closing the track, and then the train came into the depot. Three little Misses, Mabel Hancock, Serena and Cora Goodrich, rang the engine bell as it moved along." From *Phoenix Herald,* July 7, 1887. This was the morning of July 3, 1887. Miss Hancock was the daughter of Capt. Hancock.

First Republican-Democratic election

Held, 1880. Grant Oury, Democrat, for Delegate to Congress, received 4,095 votes; M. W. Stewart, Republican, received 3,606 votes.

First Saw Mill

"In 1857 a party from Maine under Captain Tarbox, came to the Santa Ritas and established a sawmill where they 'whipsawed' lumber which sold for $150 a thousand feet. They built a house and corral and dug a well on the south side of the Santa Cruz at what was called the 'Canoa crossing.' This I found to be a very convenient stopping place on my travels between Tucson and Tubac." Letter from Poston, in Farish *Notes*.

The canyon has been variously called Madera—Sp., "lumber" —and Casa Blanca canyon. q.v. Present town and P. O. of Madera canyon southwest of Greaterville, just at the county line, is undoubtedly located about where this early day sawmill stood. The well and stopping place on the Santa Cruz was, of course, the point to which they hauled the lumber for sale.

First Sewing Machine in Arizona

Farish says that C. O. Brown brought the first sewing machine to Tucson and Arizona, in 1864 or 1865. The natives came many miles to see this wonderful machine which sewed like a "mujer" but much faster. Brown on the birth of his first baby, sent to St. Louis for the first baby buggy that ever came to the Territory. It was equally an object of wonder and admiration. Brown at that time was the leading saloon keeper of Tucson.

First Spanish Mission

Practically all writers agree that the first mission in Arizona was the Mission of Quebabi or Guevavi, on the San Pedro river about 1687. Bolton, however, locates it on the Santa Cruz.

First State Legislature

Convened at Phoenix, March 18, 1912.

First Steamer on Colorado river

Was the "Uncle Sam," Captain Turnbull. She was brought from San Francisco to mouth of river in sections on the schooner, "Capacity." Was put together and reached Yuma, Dec. 2, 1852. Was a side wheeler, 65 feet long and 16 feet wide. Sank at Pilot Knob, June 22, 1854.

First Stone on Roosevelt Dam

Laid on bedrock, Sept. 20, 1906. Last stone placed in position Feb. 5, 1911. Height from bedrock, 284 feet; width at base, 168 feet. Dedicated by Theodore Roosevelt, March 11, 1911.

First Southern Pacific Train into Tucson

Arrived March 17, 1880.

First Suspension Bridge

This was doubtless the home-made suspension bridge across Silver creek, 1887, at Shumway, Navajo county. Town was located on both sides of stream. During floods school children could not cross. It was a genuine suspension affair. Cable wires were made by twisting several strands of heavy number nine telegraph wire together.

First Telegraph Line into Territory

Fish claims that, "the first line was owned by Cerro Colorado Mine Company and ran from Frowita to Cerro Colorado mine." This was at an early date not given. He gives no authority for the statement. Its correctness is problematical.

Undoubtedly the first telegraph line in Arizona was the extension of the Deseret Telegraph Line; a Mormon church affair, from

Kanab, Utah, to Pipe springs, Arizona, 1871. Miss Ella Stewart was the operator. She later became the wife of D. K. Udall, of Mesa. See Pipe springs.

First Telegraph Pole at Prescott

Prescott Miner, Sept. 6, 1873. "Tuesday last, Sept. 3, we made our way to Fort Whipple to witness the erection of the first telegraph pole. We found a large crowd of citizens and soldiers with many ladies from the post. The 23rd Infantry band added sweet music to the occasion. At 10 o'clock, Mrs. General Crook broke ground for the first post hole. Mrs. General Dana, broke a bottle of champagne on the pole. In a few minutes, Lieut. J. F. Trout and his men had up the first three poles and the wires strung on them. The Editor, (John Marion), spoke a few words."

The *Yuma Sentinel*, Sept. 20, 1873, states that the first pole on that end was set at Yuma Sept. 19, 1873. "The line was completed between Yuma and Prescott Nov. 11, 1873, and the first message carried congratulations to General Crook on his being promoted to a Brigadier General that same day." Letter from General Crook in Farish *Notes*.

Before that date, Crook was Lieutenant Colonel, 21st U. S. Infantry Regiment, commanding department under his brevet of Major General.

First Telephone Line

This was probably at Tucson, when the Arizona Telephone Company, Dr. Charles H. Lord, president, advertised itself in the *Arizona Gazetteer*, 1881, as "ready for business."

In spring of 1881, a phone was cut in on the old military telegraph line at San Carlos and another at Camp Thomas and several Apaches talked over it. The regular military wire was used which worked successfully. The astonishment of the Indians when they recognized voices of friends over the wire was something interesting. As the author recalls it now a civilian operator named Robert Lord had just come back from the east bringing with him two phones which were used. Later the party talked between Globe and Camp Thomas with the same wire and instruments.

First Term of Court in Yavapai County

"Held at Prescott in September, 1866. Chief Justice Turner on the bench." Fish.

First Territorial Historian

Mulford Winsor, of Yuma, was appointed first historian, by Governor Kibbey, January, 1909.

First Territorial Legislature

Convened at Prescott September 26, 1864. Coles Bashford, President of Council; W. Claude Jones, Speaker of the House. Bashford had served one term as Governor of Wisconsin.

First U. S. Flag Raised

William H. Kirkland claims he raised the first flag in Arizona from the roof of an adobe house in Tucson, Feb. 20, 1856, the day the Mexican garrison evacuated Tucson.

Donald Page claims this was done first when Lieut. Col. Cooke marched his command into Tucson with the Mormon battalion in December, 1846. This, however, was but temporary, for Cooke marched on west in a few days and the Mexicans again took possession. Kirkland's flag doubtless remained permanently.

First United States Land Office

"First land office in Arizona opened at Prescott, Nov. 3, 1868. Florence office opened May 8, 1873; that at Tucson, July 12, 1881. Office at Prescott was therefore first U. S. Land office in Arizona." Letter, Commissioner Public Lands, Washington D. C., Feb. 24, 1931.

First University

"The 13th legislature passed an act March 12, 1885, authorizing establishment of a territorial University at Tucson, with a proviso that bonds to the amount of $25,000 could be issued for erecting buildings, provided that before the bonds were sold and on or before a certain date, the people of Tucson were to donate not less than 40 acres of land on which to erect the buildings. The matter ran along until the time limit had almost expired. Then, Charles M. Strauss, Superintendent of Public Instruction, interested himself in the matter. As a result three or four prominent gamblers and saloon men of the town got together and purchased 160 acres of land outside the city and gave 40 acres of it to the territory." Item taken from a printed address by Selim Franklin at Tucson on "Founders Day," March 12, 1922.

"The men who donated this land were W. S. 'Billy' Reed, B. C. Parker, Paddy Wood and a Mr. Griffith." Letter, Pioneer Society's files.

First Use of name Arizona

See Arizona.

First Women Legislators

In the Senate, Mrs. Francis W. Munds, Yavapai County; in the House, Mrs. Rachael Berry, Apache County. Second State Legislature, January, 1915.

Fish Creek and Station   Maricopa Co.   Map, Tonto N. F., 1927.

Creek rises in Pinal county in T. 1 N., R. 12 E. Flows northwest into Canyon lake on Salt river. Station originally established about 1881 by Jack Frasier, well-known cattleman of Pinal county. It is said that when he first went there he found the stream full of fish. McClintock says they were a red fish of a variety not known elsewhere in that region. On some maps as "Frasiers Station."

Fish Creek Mountain   Maricopa Co

In secs. 17, 18, 19 and 20, T. 2 N., R. 11 E. On Tonto N. F. Decision U. S. G. B., 1933.

Fishtail

See Paguek wash.

Fiske Wall   Coconino Co.

In Grand Canyon N. P. Huge rock-wall formation in canyon. "In honor of the able scientist John Fiske, born Edmund Fiske Green, who did so much to make known the works of Spencer, Huxley and Darwin to this country." G. Wharton James.

Fitz (sic) **Jefferson's Ranch**   Santa Cruz Co.   Smith Map, 1879;
G. L. O., 1892.

Early day station and ranch on San Pedro river. From the maps it was on the site of "The Old Presidio of San Pedro," q.v. It is marked plainly Fitz, not Fritz, on all old maps.

Fittsburg   Cochise Co.

In Pearce district, eastern slope Dragoon mountains. "About 1905, when the town of Pearce was enjoying a modest boom, George Fitts, a merchant of Tombstone, attempted to establish an addition to Pearce west of that town. It was to be called Fittsburg, but it never amounted to anything, and soon disappeared. There is now nothing to mark the spot." Letter, John A. Rockfellow, Tombstone.

Five Buttes   Navajo Co.   U. S. G. S. Map, 1923.

Group of five outstanding peaks in Ts. 21, 22 N., R. 21, 22 E. On Navajo Ind. Res., near head of Cottonwood wash.

Five Mile Lake   Coconino Co.   Map, Sitgreaves N. F., 1924.

In sec. 21, T. 12 N., R. 13 E., wet weather lake. Not one of the numbered lakes of Crook's time for it was not so called in early days or even as late as 1895. It was probably so called by travelers, because it was 5 miles from Rim.

Five Point Mountain   Gila Co.   Map, Crook N. F., 1926.

In sec. 18 T. 1 S., R. 14 E., mountain with five points or tips, 3 or 4 miles west of Bellevue.

Flag, de, Wash (River de Flag)   Coconino Co.

In Tps. 21-22 N., Rs. 6, 7, 8, 9, 10 E., Gila and Salt River meridian, flows southeasterly through Flagstaff, Coconino National Forest. Well established local name.

Flagstaff   Coconino Co.   G. L. O. Map, 1892-1923

Elevation, 6,935 feet. County seat at base of San Francisco mountains. The famous Lowell Observatory and one of the State Teachers' Colleges are located here. Latter was first erected as a Territorial Reform school but when completed was turned into a Teachers' College.

Lieut. Beale first camped at Leroux spring near the town, April 15, 1858. Banta says "it was first called Antelope spring, later known as 'Old Town Spring.'"

"I will tell you how the town came to be so named. We were trying to get a post office and had to have a name. The spring to the west was then called 'Flagpole spring.' Later known as 'Old Town Spring.' It was named Flagpole, because a flagpole had been put up some time before by the militia boys who came through here. It was about 50 feet long and was put into the top of the highest pine tree nearest the spring, and laced to the tree by rawhide thongs. Doc Brannen finally said, 'how about calling it Flagstaff?' We all agreed and so it was named. The original pole fell down shortly after I came here." Ed Whipple in *Coconino Sun*, Dec. 7, 1928.

Rev. J. T. Pierce, first minister in Flagstaff, writes: "I remember very well when I reached Flag in the fall of 1882 of hearing the flagstaff story. It was a young pine tree stripped of all its branches and a pole spliced to its top to which a flag was fastened. It stood close by the spring in Old Town." *Coconino Sun*, March 12, 1929.

The Flagstaff Chamber of Commerce gives the following, undoubtedly correct: "In June, 1876, a party of immigrants from Boston came on westward after a failure to settle in the Little Colorado valley. One of the party tells of stripping a small pine tree and raising a flag upon it. Around this extemporized flagpole the party celebrated on July 4, 1876. Thus the name

Flagstaff was attached to the spring and was retained on the establishment of a construction camp of the Atlantic and Pacific R. R., 1882. This same year, E. E. Ayer built a saw mill in the settlement." Read McClintock's story of the event.

Old timers at Flagstaff insist that "Doc" Brannen was the first postmaster. Washington records tell a different story. P. O. established at Flagstaff, Feb. 21, 1881, Thomas McMillen, P. M. P. B. (Doc) Brannen was his successor, May 23, 1881.

Town incorporated June 4, 1894. Atlantic and Pacific R. R. arrived in the summer of 1882.

It is an interesting coincidence that there is a town and post office in Somerset county, Maine, which received its name in exactly the same manner. Benedict Arnold, on his way to capture Quebec, 1775, erected a flagpole over his camp which later was snowed in for some months. The pole stood for many years marking the spot of Arnold's camp. A town gradually grew up about it which was and still is, called Flagstaff.

Flatrock Spring   Mohave Co.

In T. 25 N., R. 13 W., on south slope Music mountains. "There is a large flat rock standing on edge near this spring."

Flat Top Mountain   Apache Co.   G. L. O. Map, 1921.

In T. 8 N., R. 29 E. East of Eager. Descriptive name.

Flat Top Mountain   Gila Co.   Map, Crook N. F., 1926.

In T. 1 N., R. 14 E. About 6 miles northwest of Miami. A flat-topped mountain. Descriptive name.

Flax River—"Rio De Lino."

Sp., "flax, linen." This is one name for Little Colorado river. Ives speaks of it as "Flax river," for the plant that grew on its banks. Dr. Newberry, geologist with Ives, in his separate report always calls it "Little Colorado River." His report however, was written in 1861, which may explain the change. Beale, in 1859, always called it the "Colorado Chiquito."

Fleming Peak   Cochise Co.

See Swisshelm mountains.

Flint Creek   Coconino Co.   Map, Kaibab N. F., 1926.

In Grand Canyon N. P. Rises on west side Point Sublime, flows northwest into Shinumo creek. "So called for the geological formation along the stream." Letter, Ed Miller, Forest Service.

Florence   Pinal Co.   G. L. O. Map, 1909.

Elevation 1,493 feet. One of the first settlements in Pinal county. County seat. Levi Ruggles settled here, 1866, as Indian Agent. Elliot says: "Charles G. Mason built the first house, 1866. Town named by Governor Safford in honor of his sister, Florence." Hinton says: "Regular stages leave here for Silver City, Pioneer, Globe, San Carlos, Camp Apache; also East Phoenix; Wickenburg and Prescott." Of Florence, Poston writes:

> "Fair Florence wreathed in Gila green,
> A city yet to be, I ween.
> For here, e'en more than at Tucson
> It's always, always afternoon."

Florence Station   Pinal Co.   G. L. O. Map, 1909.

Railroad station north side of Gila river 2 miles from Florence, where passengers from Florence entrain.

Flores   Yavapai Co.

Spur, 10 miles north of Wickenburg. A. T. & S. F. R. R. "So called because when the road was building, the desert round here was covered with lovely desert flowers of every hue." A. G. W.

Flower Pot Ranch   Maricopa Co.

Headquarters ranch for "Flower Pot Cattle Co." "So called from their cattle brand. On the desert west of Arlington district. Established, 1899, by C. Warren Peterson." *Routes to the Desert.*

Floy   Apache Co.   U. S. G. S. Map, 1923.

In T. 11 N., R. 25 E. "When the settlers asked for a post office here they put up the names of several girls in the village and voted for them. Floy Greer won." Letter, Paul Roberts. P. O. established Nov. 28, 1919, Rosa Despain, P. M.

Floyd Mountain, Floyds Peak   Coconino Co.   Eckhoff Map, 1880; G. L. O., 1921.

In T. 23 N., R. 4 W. "We came through Tucker's pass into a valley at the head of which is Floyds peak, which I named after Dr. Floyd of our party." Beales report, April, 1857. About 6 miles north of Crookton station, A. T. & S. F. R. R.

Fluted Rock   Apache Co.   G. L. O. Map, 1921.

In T. 2 N., R. 7 W. Navajo name. Elevation, 7,000 feet. Prominent peak on Defiance plateau, Navajo Ind. Res. At State line near head of Pueblo Colorado wash. Gregory gives it as "Zil-klu-say-an"—a fluted rock. G. L. O. map, 1921, has it "Fluted Rock." Navajo dictionary says: "a fluted rock stream."

Flying Buttes   Navajo Co.   G. L. O. Map, 1921.

In T. 20 N., R. 20 E. In northern end of Marcou mesa, eastern side Cottonwood wash.

Fly's Peak   Cochise Co.   Map, Coronado N. F., 1925.

In T. 18 S., R. 30 E. In Chiricahua mountains. After John Fly, a Tombstone photographer with General Crook on several Apache campaigns. Took many excellent pictures of Indians, especially Geronimo.

Fontana

See Spring creek.

Fools Gulch   Yavapai Co.   Map, U. S. Congress Quad., 1904.

Post office for Planet-Saturn mine, northwest of Congress Junction. Camp was on gulch which headed in Weaver mountains near Yarnell. Runs southwest into Martinez creek above Congress Junction. "So called because when first prospectors came here they were called 'fools' for expecting to find gold in such a formation." P. O. established Jan. 18, 1897, Wm. H. Clark, P. M.

Fools Hollow   Navajo Co.   Map, Sitgreaves N. F., 1924.

Dry wash rising at Apache Ind. Res. line in northwest part of T. 9, R. 21 E., 3 miles west of town of Showlow. Flows northeast into Adair wash. Everybody said they were fools to try to farm there. See Bagnal and Adair.

Fordville   Pinal Co.

P. O. established March 15, 1880, William A. Cunningham, P. M. Origin unknown.

Forepaugh   Maricopa Co.   G. L. O. Map, 1921.

Station, Parker branch A. T. & S. F. R. R., 19 miles west of Wickenburg. Also Peak east side of Plomoso mountains, in T. 6 N., R. 17 W. In Yuma county. "So called for an old time 'desert rat' by this name, who had a mine near this point." Letter, P. M., Aguila. P. O. established, April 25, 1911, Charles B. Genung, P. M. Genung lived here during his later years.

Foresight   Yavapai Co.

See Hooper.

Forestdale   Navajo Co.   Smith Map, 1879; Eckhoff, 1880.

Mormon settlement on stream of same name which enters Carrizo creek on Fort Apache Ind. Res. Named by Llewellyn Harris, 1878, "because of its location in the forest." When reservation was extended, 1880, the settlers were removed by troops from Fort Apache. Sometimes called Apache springs q. v.

Forest Lagoons   Coconino Co.   Smith Map, 1879.

Near crossing of long. 113° N. and lat. 36° W., short distance north of Pine springs. On one of the trails made by Ives or Sitgreaves. They evidently were flood water lakes on Hualpai Ind. Res. amid the pine forest. Named by Ives.

Forrest   Cochise Co.   G. L. O. Map, 1921; Judge Map.

On E. P. & S. W. R. R., 12 miles east of Naco. After a rancher and old resident by this name. P. O. established May 8, 1914, Josie C. Clymer, P. M.

Forrest   Yavapai Co.

P. O. established by this name April 21, 1882, not far from Big Bug station, Henry A. Marsh, P. M. "After Henry F. Forrest, who ran a small cattle ranch here in early days."

Forster Canyon and Rapids   Coconino Co.

In Grand Canyon of Colorado, 2 miles above Fossil Bay. Named on recommendation of Geological Survey after the late W. J. Forster, who traversed this part of the river. Decision U. S. G. B.

Fort Apache Indian Reservation   Navajo-Gila-Apache Cos.

In east-central part of State. Original area established by War Dept., Jan. 31, 1870, "as a reservation for the roving Apache Indians of New Mexico and Arizona." Area laid out on advice of Col. Green, 1st. Cavalry, in consultation with Vincent Collyer, U. S. Indian Commissioner, who visited Camp Apache in Sept. 1871. Executive order establishing it issued by President Grant, Nov. 9, 1871.

Variously called "White Mountain Apache" or "Apache Indian Reservation." Used principally by the White Mountain (Coyoteros) and Tonto Apaches. The Warm Spring and Chiricahua Apaches also used it prior to their removal to Florida. Reservation later divided.

"The northern part was designated as Fort Apache Indian Reservation and the southern as the San Carlos Indian Reservation. These are the proper designations." Letter, Commissioner of Indian Affairs, Oct. 3, 1928. Area of both about 5,000,000 acres.

According to historians, Coronado came up the San Pedro river, 1539-40, bound for Cibola and passed a few miles east of Fort Apache. In his diary he calls the region "The Wilderness."

Fort Rock   Yavapai Co.   Smith Map, 1879; Eckhoff, 1880.

In T. 20 N., R. 10 W. Station on Hardyville-Prescott stage road. "We camped at Fort Rock and Lieut. Bailey shot an antelope. It was the first game we had seen. The sight of green grass and trees brought new life to us. *Vanished Arizona.* Sept., 1874.

"At Buckmans ranch his boy, about twelve years old, built near the house a circle of large rocks for a 'play fort.' Indians attacked the ranch and Pat MacAteer got inside the boy's fort and carried on a good fight with them. From that day on, the place was called 'Fort Rock.'" Letter, Orick Jackson, Prescott. P. O. established, May 12, 1879, L. Bacon, P. M.

Fortuna   Yuma Co.   U. S. G. S. Map, 1923.

In T. 10 S., R. 20 W. Mine and P. O. on west side Gila mountains, east of the Yuma desert, about 16 miles southwest of Yuma. After the Fortuna mine. P. O. established Sept. 30, 1896, John Doan, P. M.

Fortuna Station   Yuma Co.   Map, Fortuna Quad.

In sec. 31, T. 8 S., R. 21 W. Station S. P. R. R. After the Fortuna mine, 12 miles southeast.

Fort Valley   Coconino Co.

About 8 miles northwest of Flagstaff. Named for Fort Moroni. Built 1881, by John W. Young, son of Brigham, was headquarters for the Moroni Cattle Co., a Mormon church outfit. Later owned by A1 (A One) Cattle Co. After Moroni, character in book of Mormon. Forest Service has an experiment station here called "Fort Valley Station." Professor Lemon called it "De la Vergne Park" after one of the St. Louis owners of the A1 Cattle Company, who was here in 1885. On map Coconino N. F., 1923, as Southwest Experimental Station. See Fort Moroni.

Fossil Canyon   Coconino Co.   Map, Kaibab N. F., 1929; N. P. Map, 1927.

In Grand Canyon N. P. Near lat. 36° 17′ N. long. 112° 32′ W. Drains "Fossil Bay," an amphitheatre shown on map.

Fossil Creek   Gila Co.   Map, Tonto N. F., 1927.

In T. 12 N., R. 8 E. Rises in Coconino N. F. Flows southwest, enters Verde river in sec. 17 T. 11 N., R. 7 E. Woolsey's party from Camp Verde followed this stream about 18 miles into Tonto Basin after Apaches, June, 1864. Rock along the stream is filled with fossil remains, shells, etc.

Fossil Springs   Gila Co.   Map, Tonto N. F., 1927.

In secs. 14, 15, T. 12 N., R. 7 E. Several large springs break from banks of Fossil creek and form the stream. Water heavily charged with lime. Many fossil remains and shells found in rock.

Foster   Yavapai Co.

P. O. established April 26, 1887, Philander J. Schofield, P. M. Origin unknown.

Four Bar Mesa   Greenlee Co.   Map, Crook N. F., 1926.

In T. 1 S., R. 29 E. "So called after the 'Four Bar' brand of cattle that grazed on the range around here." Letter, J. W. Girdner, Forest Ranger.

Four Mile Peak   Graham Co.   U. S. G. S. Map, 1923.

In T. 8 S., R. 9 E. In Galiuro mountains, 4 miles southeast of Biscuit peak.

Fourmile Spring   Coconino Co.

In Grand Canyon N. P., near south rim. About 4 miles west of Grand Canyon station. Decision U. S. G. B., 1933.

Four Peaks   Maricopa Co.   U. S. G. S. Map, 1923.

Four large, rugged, granite peaks in Mazatzal range, about 10 miles west Roosevelt dam. They are notable landmarks.

Col. Schuyler, U. S. Army, who served at Ft. McDowell, 1868-69, when at McDowell, Mar., 1931, said the Apaches' sign for these peaks was one hand held up with fingers wide spread indicating it meant either four peaks or four spaces between them. At Phoenix Jan. 3, 1934, Mike Burns, who was born in the very shadow of these peaks, said his people called them, "Wee-ka-ja-hor," meaning "four notches or cuts, as with an axe." See Mazatzal range.

Fourth of July Butte   Maricopa Co.   G. L. O. Map, 1921.

See July 4th. butte.

Fourth of July Wash   Maricopa Co.

Rises on Fourth of July butte from which it takes its name. Flows southeast into Gila. "There is always fresh, sweet water a few feet under the sand." *Routes to the Desert.* See July 4th.

Fraesfield Mountain   Maricopa Co.   G. L. O. Map, 1921.

In T. 5 N., R. 5 E., about 8 miles southeast Cave creek P. O. Shows as Round mountain on Tonto N. F. map. Round mountain is purely descriptive. Origin for Fraesfield undiscovered.

Fraguita Peak   Pima Co.   Map, Coronado N. F., 1927.

T. 22 S., R. 10 E. On Cobre ridge; about 4 miles west of Oro Blanco. "Fraguita is a Spanish word, said to mean 'bellows.' So named because a small blacksmith bellows was found at the base of the mountain. Originally called Roderick after an old prospector and Indian fighter." Letter, A. S. Wingo, Forest Ranger.

Francis Creek   Yavapai Co.   G. L. O. Map, 1927.

In T. 18 N., R. 9 W. Rises south side Gemini peak, flows south into Burro creek. After John W. Francis, sheepman and citizen of Flagstaff.

Franconia   Mohave Co.   U. S. G. S. Map, 1923.

Station A. T. & S. F. R. R. 25 miles east of Needles. "After Frank, son of F. W. Smith, first Gen'l Supt. A. and P. R. R." A. G. W.

Frankenburg   Maricopa Co.   Postal Guide, 1929.

Station Phoenix and Eastern R. R. 4 miles east of Tempe. Established about 1902. After an early settler, cattleman and farmer by this name, who had large land holdings near the station.

Franklin   Greenlee Co.   U. S. G. S. Map, 1923.

In T. 9 S., R. 32 E. Station E. P. & S. W. R. R. Mormon settlement below Duncan. Settled 1895, by Thomas J. Nations. Named for Franklin D. Richards in 1898. P. O. established May 17, 1905, Nephi Packer, P. M.

Franklin Heaton Reservoir   Coconino Co.

Water hole and reservoir southern end Hurricane ledge 2 miles east of Cooper Pockets. Northeast of Mt. Trumbull. Located and used about 1865 as a stock watering place by Franklin Heaton of Pipe springs.

Frank Murrays Peak   Mohave Co.

"We camped at our old place under Frank Murrays Peak." Beale. Murray was one of Beale's party. Beale does not locate it.

Frasiers Station.

See Fish creek.

Fray Marcos Mountain

See Baker.

Fredonia   Coconino Co.   U. S. G. S. Map, 1923.

In sec. 17, T. 41 N., R. 6 W. Town east side Kanab creek. About 3 miles south of Utah line. "Name suggested by Erastus Snow because many of the residents were from Utah seeking freedom from Federal laws against polygamy."

The most northerly town in Arizona. Settled, 1865, by people from Kanab. It should probably have been spelled "Free-donia" but many years of usage has settled that.

"According to local authorities, Mormons living in Kanab, Utah, sent their extra wives across the state line to Fredonia in Arizona, to make it hard for U. S. Marshals to find and arrest them. The name is a combination of 'Doña'—a woman, and 'free' forming the word Fredonia. This information I secured from the *Daughters of the Pioneers* in Kanab. Said to have been first called Hardscrabble." Letter, W. G. Mann, Forest Service, Kanab.

P. O. established April 6, 1892, William S. Lewis, P. M.

Freezeout Creek   Graham Co.   U. S. G. S. Map, 1923.

Stream eastern part San Carlos Ind. Res. Rises west side of Freezeout mountain. Flows west into Black river. "In early days when the Chiricahua Cattle Company had cattle on the Reservation, the boys used to play a great deal of Freezeout poker. When they wanted a name for the camp, they called it thus." Letter, J. W. Girdner, Forest Ranger.

Freezeout Mountain   Graham Co.   U. S. G. S. Map, 1923.

Eastern part San Carlos Ind. Res. At head of Freezeout creek, east of Black river. Near west boundary Apache N. F. See Freezeout creek.

Freeze Wash   Mohave Co.

"About 14 miles east of Beales spring, a bare lonesome spot near some old silver mines." *Vanished Arizona*. Origin unknown.

Fremont Peak   Coconino Co.

Elevation, 11,940 feet. In sec. 4 T. 22 N., R. 7 E. A round peak southeast of Humphrey named for John C. Fremont, explorer, and pathfinder. Territorial governor of Arizona, 1878-1881. Peak has been known by this name in Flagstaff for many years. First mentioned by H. H. Robinson, U. S. G. S., 1912. But never placed on any map. Decision U. S. G. B., 1933.

French Joe Peak and Canyon   Cochise Co.   Map, Coronado N. F., 1927.

In T. 19 S., R. 19 E. In Whetstone mountains. "A man known as French Joe located a mine and lived in the canyon near the peak for many years." Letter, Elizabeth T. Merrill.

French Spring and Butte   Navajo Co.   U. S. G. S. Map, 1923.

Spring in T. 22 N., R. 18 E., butte in T. 22 N., R. 19 E. For an early day stockman and miner Franklin French, who married Emma Lee, one of the widows of John D. Lee. She lived with Lee at Lee Ferry. For several years she and French lived at Hardy station on Santa Fe R. R. 24 miles west of Holbrook, where they ran the section house. Later French lived and died at Winslow. Most of his last years were spent prospecting in the Grand Canyon.

Fresnal, Creek, Well and Papago Village   Pima Co.

Fresnal, Sp., "ash tree." Creek rises west slope Baboquivari mountains, flows southwest, enters Valshni wash in T. 19 S., R. 4 E. On Papago Ind. Res.
Well and village on west side of Baboquivari in Papago Res.
Pumpelly, 1860, says: "Fresnal, a Papago village with a fine spring of water in a ravine descending from Baboquivari peak. The spring was surrounded by fine ash and mesquite trees."
Mr. Washburn, one of Pumpelly's party was here seriously wounded by the accidental discharge of his pistol. Pumpelly tells an interesting tale of suffering, on one side, and devotion to a friend, on the other.

Fresno Spring   Santa Cruz Co.

In sec. 16 T. 22 N., R. 12 E. "Fresno consists of really three *ranchos* scattered along the foothills of Baboquivari mountain. Name derived from grove of ash trees growing in the wash or *arroyo*." Lumholtz.

Frisco   Mohave Co.   G. L. O. Map, 1921.

In T. 22 N., R. 12 E. Mining camp and peak, east side of Black range. First mine here was called "The Frisco" which named this peak. P. O. established May 5, 1913, Cornelius J. Falvey, P. M.

Fritchie (sic)   Yavapai Co.   U. S. G. S. Map, 1923.

In T. 19 N., R. 3 W. Small hamlet in Chino valley. West side Black mesa. Spelled as above on P. O. lists. "Named for H. W. Fritsche, a well known stockman of this locality. He spelled his name Fritsche." Letter, L. J. Putsch, Forest Service. P. O. established Oct. 26, 1912, Sidney Fritsche, P. M.

Fritz Springs   Cochise Co.

See Lewis springs.

Frog Peaks   Pinal Co.   Smith Map, 1879.

Two outstanding peaks south side Salt river, about 15 miles east of Maryville. Origin not known.

Frog Tanks   Maricopa Co.   Smith Map, 1879.

Station east side Agua Fria, below mouth of New river. Captain Calderwood once told the author it was so called because first persons here found the tanks full of very large frogs.

Fryes Canyon   Graham Co.   Map, Crook N. F., 1927.

Canyon heading west side Mount Graham, flowing northeast into Gila river near Solomonville.

After Albert A. Frye, who built a saw mill in this canyon, 1879. It is sometimes erroneously called Chlarsons canyon.

Fuller   Yavapai Co.

P. O. established here March 5, 1898, Oscar Townsend, P. M. Station and early ranch on East Verde river, after the Fullers, well known local cattlemen.

Fulton   Coconino Co.   G. L. O. Map, 1892.

In T. 17 N., R. 9 E. Station on old Arizona Central R. R. which was the logging road built by Riordan interests. After Harry Fulton of Flagstaff, well known sheepman of the early Nineties.

Gabriels Spring   Mohave Co.

Discovered by one of Beale's men for whom Beale named it. In lat. 35° 26' long. 113° 43', close to east side Cottonwood cliffs, probably in Truxton canyon. Beale says: "They were shaded by hackberry and locust trees." Unable to locate on any present day spring.

Gadsden   Yuma Co.   U. S. G. S. Map, 1923.

In T. 10 S., R. 25 W., station on Yuma Valley R. R., 19 miles south of Yuma on Colorado river. After U. S. Secretary of State Gadsden. P. O. established July 17, 1915, Wm. M. Davidson, P. M.

Gadsden Purchase.

After Secretary of State Gadsden who planned treaty of 1853 which authorized purchase from Mexico by U. S. of nearly thirty million acres of land. Purchase ratified Dec. 30, 1853.

Purchase covered "all the land south of the Gila from Rio Grande on the east, to a point twenty miles below mouth of Gila on the west." Bulk of it was within present state of Arizona. Cost, ten million dollars—thirty-three cents an acre. As many more acres could easily have been secured, but nobody then saw any future value in the land.

Gadsonia

One of the names suggested for Arizona. See Arizona, the name.

Gael   Yuma Co.   R. R. Maps.

Station S. P. R. R., 50 miles east of Yuma. "Station so called for Robert Gael, station pumper at this place." Letter, Paul Shoup.

Galeyville   Cochise Co.   Hamilton Map, 1886; Judge, 1916.

In T. 31 E., R. 17 S. Coronado N. F. Named for John H. Galey, Pennsylvania oil man, president of the Texas Consolidated Mining and Smelting Co. Near Paradise camp in Chiricahua mountains.

"Galeyville, Curley Bill's last capital, sprang up in the fall of 1880 as a boom silver camp on Turkey creek canyon, on the east side of Chiricahuas. Named for John H. Galey who owned the Discovery mine and established a small smelter there. Town totally deserted by 1882. Never had more than 300 or 400 people." *Tombstone.*

Arizona Gazetteer, 1881, says: "A weekly paper, the *Galeyville Bulletin,* is published here. Place occupies a picturesque site in the midst of shady oaks, in a cool corner of Chiricahuas." P. O. established January 6, 1881, Frank McCandless, P. M.

Galiuro Mountains   Pinal and Graham Counties. U. S. G. S. Map, 1923.

Crook N. F. Extends southeast from Arivaipa creek, to Graham-Cochise county line on eastern side of San Pedro valley. Bandelier says: "The name Galiuro is a curiosity. It can be traced on the maps through Saltire, Calitre, Calitro to Galiuro."

Galzville   Cochise Co.   Elliot Map, 1866.

Early day town shown on map spelled this way. On Turkey creek in San Simon valley and probably meant for Galeyville.

Gallagher Peak   Yuma Co.

See Klara.

Galleta Well   Yuma Co.

In sec. 24 S., T. 1 S., R 7 W. "Watering place of Flower Pot Cattle Co. So called for galleta (gai-et-ta) grass on ranges near here." *Routes to the Desert.*

Ganado   Apache Co.   U. S. G. S. Map, 1923.

Sp., "Cattle or live stock." In T. 2 S., R. 10 W. On Pueblo Colorado wash. Well known Indian trading post, established about 1875 by "Old man Leonard" on Navajo Ind. Res. He sold it to J. Lorenzo Hubbell of St. Johns about 1876 or 1877. Mr. Hubbell died here Nov. 11, 1930.

A careful study of the name and its origin following a conversation with Lorenzo Hubbell about 1886 results in the following conclusion: Name Ganado—meaning in Spanish, live stock, cows, sheep, horses and even bees—as applied to this trading post, seems to have originated many years ago when a Navajo Indian, called "Tom," who owned many horses, cattle and sheep, was nick-named "Tom Ganado," i. e., Cattle Tom. His camp on Pueblo Colorado wash gradually became known as Ganado. When Hubbell established his trading post on this stream, he called it Ganado after Tom. Name soon became well established. P. O. established Feb. 15, 1883, Charles Hubbell, P. M. See Hubbell butte.

Gannet Tower   Coconino Co.

In Grand Canyon. So called by James, after Henry Gannet, noted topographer and scientist.

Garces   Cochise Co.   U. S. G. S. Map, 1923.

In T. 23 S., R. 21 E. Hamlet east side Huachuca mountains, about eight miles west of Hereford. So named after Garces National Forest. P. O. established April 12, 1911, Richard M. Johnson, P. M.

Garces National Forest   Santa Cruz and Pima Counties.

First name of area now known as Coronado N. F., with headquarters at Nogales. Changed to Coronado about 1915, q. v. Named after Padre Garces who, after many years of tireless activity among the Indians of Arizona, was killed by them at Yuma, July 17, 1781.

Garden Canyon   Cochise Co.   G. L. O. Map, 1921.

Canyon and stream heading near Fort Huachuca, running northeast into San Pedro river. So called because post gardens were located on stream. P. O. established March 4, 1919. William Carmichael, P. M.

Gardiner Canyon   Pima Co.   Map, Coronado N. F., 1926.

Canyon heading at Granite mountain, east side of Santa Ritas. Flows into Cienega creek about three miles east of Empire ranch, in T. 19 S., R. 17 E. Spelled Gardiner on Roskruge map, 1893. He named it for Tom Gardiner and family who lived on this canyon for several years. On some maps spelled Gardner.

Gardiner Spring   Mohave Co.

Beale writes: "After one of my men who showed it to me." From Beale's account it was not far from Truxton spring. See Hackberry.

Gardner Canyon   Pima Co.

See Gardiner canyon.

Garland   Yavapai Co.   G. L. O. Map, 1892.

In T. 20 N., R. 5 W., station on P. and A. C. R. R., first railroad to Prescott. later abandoned and track torn up. After William Garland. See Garland prairie.

Garland Prairie   Coconino Co.   Map, Tusayan N. F., 1929.

In T. 21 N., R 4 E. Large open park in pine timber. After William Garland, contractor on Atlantic and Pacific R. R., who under firm name of Garland and Ross ran cattle in this vicinity between 1888 and 1895. Their brand was the O H Triangle iron. Garland first ran these cattle near St. Johns in Apache county, but moved them to this point. Died, Los Angeles, 1929.

Garland Spring   Coconino Co.   Map, Tusayan N. F., 1927.

In sec. 20, T. 21 N., R. 4 E. Headquarters ranch of Garland and Ross in early Nineties. See Garland prairie.

Gash Mountain   Coconino Co.   Map, Coconino N. F. 1928.

In sec. 24, T. 17 N., R. 8 E. North side Stonemans lake. "According to Link Smith, John Gash settled in Gash flat at foot of mountain in the Seventies and ran cattle. Later a Mr. Van Deren located here and named the flat and mountain for Gash." Letter, Ed. Miller, Flagstaff.

Gatagama Terrace   Coconino Co.

Benched or stepped mesa, in Grand Canyon N. P., just below Gatagama point, near lat. 36° 22', long. 112° 35'. South side Colorado river, two miles southeast mouth of Kanab creek. Name of an Indian family.

Gates Foundation   Gila Co.

In T. 8 N., R. 10 E. On Gun creek in Tonto basin. Named for Tom Gates, who 1880-1890 ran horses in the basin. He laid a foundation for a cabin consisting of four oak logs. He moved away when people became suspicious as to the ownership of some of his horses. Letter, Fred Croxen. See Gates pass.

Gates Pass   Pinal Co.

After Tom Gates, early character who drove stock through this pass. He came to this region in 1865. See Gates foundation.

Gatewood   Cochise Co.   G. L. O. Map, 1892.

Town in San Simon valley about twelve miles northeast of old Camp Bowie. Named for Lieut. Charles B. Gatewood, 6th U. S. Cavalry, who from 1878 to about 1887, was constantly in the field after hostile Apaches. He was an early commander of Apache Indian scouts.. The author knew him well. A tall, serious, grave-faced man, who spoke at least two Apache dialects fluently and had full confidence of the Indians. Conducted preliminary negotiations which eventually led to Geronimo's surrender. But for Gatewood's bravery and the confidence the Indians had in him and his faith in them, Geronimo might never have surrendered. Gatewood had a long, prominent nose, so the Apaches always called him "Bay-chin-day-sin" (Long Nose). P. O. established June 7, 1890, Joseph M. Hooker, P. M.

Gavilan   Maricopa Co.

Sp., "Hawk." Said to have been named for an Indian chief whom Mexicans called Gavilan. Twelve miles below Canyon station on Black Canyon stage road. Unable to locate station or learn who the Indian was.

Geike Monument   Coconino Co.

"On south side of canyon below Drummond point is a huge mass, like a couchant lion, which I named in honor of the well known British Geologist." G. Wharton James.

Gemini Peak   Eckhoff Map, 1880; U. S. G. S., 1923.

The Twins. In T. 17 N., R. 9 W. Two sharp buttes about four miles west of Baca Grant. In Mahon mountains.

"January 24, 1854, descending the smooth slope from Aztec pass, we encamped. South of the valley was a remarkable mountain rising 2,000 feet; its sides clothed with dark cedars. In the center it was cut in two equal peaks. Hence called 'Gemini.'" *Whipple's Report.*

Generals Springs   Coconino Co.   Smith Map, 1879; G. L. O., 1921.

In sec. 1, T. 12 N., R. 10 E. Coconino N. F. Fine large spring east of Baker's butte on Verde road, close to the rim. "Named after General Crook, which he discovered and near which he had such a narrow escape from being killed by Apaches." Bourke. Bourke always gives it the possessive and plural; i. e., Generals' Springs.

Generals Springs Canyon   Coconino Co.   Map, Sitgreaves N. F.,
1924.

In sec. 34, T. 14 N., R. 11 E. Rises at Generals springs, flows
north into Clear creek.

Gentle Spring   Mohave Co   G. L. O. Map, 1892.

About three miles south of Kingman. Also known as Railroad
spring. On some maps this is "Gentile" spring. Probably an
error in printing. Coues mentions this spring but says nothing
as to name.

Gentry Canyon   Coconino Co.   Map, Sitgreaves N. F., 1924.

In sec. 27, T. 12 N., R. 12 E. East of head of Leonard Canyon.
Flows northeast into Willow creek, in sec. 29, T. 13 N., R. 12 E.
See Gentry mountain.

Gentry Mountain   Gila Co.   U. S. G. S. Map, 1923.

In T. 9 N., R. 15 E. Near boundary Apache Ind. Res. After
"Old Man Gentry," an early sheepman, who grazed his herds
on the Indian reservation, with headquarters at Gentry spring
on Black canyon, Navajo county. He was born in Redding, California, and came to Arizona in 1880.

Gentry Spring   Navajo Co.   Map, Sitgreaves N. F., 1923.

In T. 10 N., R. 15½ E., about three miles south of early settlement of Wilford on Black canyon. See Gentry mountain.

Germa   Mohave Co.

Small place about 2½ miles southwest of Oatman, west side
of Ute mountains.
"First called Snowball. Name formed from names of company, 'German-American-Mining Company,' which operated here
at that time." Letter, J. H. Knight, Kingman. P. O. established
Jan. 20, 1903, Isaac D. Hilty, P. M.

German Colony

See Tubac.

Germann   Maricopa Co.   R. R. Maps.

Spur and loading point on P. & E. R. R. about 14 miles south
of Mesa.

Geronimo   Graham Co.   U. S. G. S. Map, 1923

In T. 4 S., R. 22 E. Station, Arizona-Eastern R. R., 6 or 8
miles southwest of Fort Thomas. On site of Old Camp Thomas.
After Geronimo, Apache Chief. Sp., "Jerome"; name given him
by Mexicans. Geronimo was a full-blooded Apache. Born at Janos,
Mexico. His name was spelled Eronimo, Herinomo, Hieronymo,
etc. His Apache name was "Goy-ath-lay" (one who yawns).
P. O. established April 30, 1896, George Rayfield, P. M.

Geronimo Mount   Coconino Co.   U. S. G. S. Map, 1923.

Elevation, 8,634 feet. In T. 18 N., R. 10 E., 6 miles east of Mormon lake. After Apache Chief.

Giant Chair   Navajo Co.   U. S. G. S. Map, 1923.

In T. 17 E., R. 27 N. Hopi Ind. Res. Resembles a gigantic arm
chair.

Gibson   Maricopa Co.

"This was Jack Gibson's cattle ranch, on lower New river." Gibson was a well known cattleman and race horse owner around Phoenix in early Nineties. P. O. established Aug. 15, 1900, W. D. Piles, P. M.

Gibson Peak   Gila Co.   Map, Tonto N. F., 1926.

In T. 10 N., R. 10 E. High point about 4 miles southeast of Payson. "Named for Joe Gibson, Mormon, who with his family settled here at lower end Round valley." Letter, F. W. Croxen, Forest Ranger.

Gila   Yuma Co.

Station S. P. R. R. originally called Gila Bend, qv.

Gila

Pattie spells it "Helay." Appears to be of Indian origin, meaning "spider." "Bancroft says name was first applied to a province in New Mexico, near source of this river. Previously known as Nombre de Dios." *Gila River Flood Control.*

"The name Gila, or Xila, was apparently originally that of an Apache settlement west of Socorro. As early as 1630 was applied to those Apaches residing part of the time on headwaters of Gila river." Hodge.

"The Yumas call the Gila river 'Hah-quah-sa-eel' with an accent on the last syllable which appears to be the basis for the word. It means 'running water that is salt.' Same name appears to have been given to the Salt river. A Yuman in my employ says 'e-el' with accent of the first syllable means 'salt,' and the 'hah' means 'water.' Literally 'salt water.'" McClintock.

Gila Bend   Maricopa Co.   G. L. O. Map, 1921.

Town on S. P. R. R., about 35 miles west of Maricopa. Elevation 736 feet.

"Named from its proximity to so-called 'Great Bend' on Gila river which comes in from north and resumes its westerly flow at this point. About 1925 railroad shortened it to Gila to save telegraphing.' Letter, S. P. Agent, Gila. The "Gila Bend" of 1877-1880, was a well known stage station on the river about 6 miles north of present railroad station. Poston in *Apache Land* says:

"Arrived at last at Gila Bend
Our river journey comes to end.
'Tis wise to stop here, wheels to tauter
To rest and fill the cans with water."

P. O. established May 1, 1871, Albert Decker, P. M.

Gila Bend Canal   Maricopa Co.
     G. L. O. Map, 1921; U. S. G. S., 1923.

In T. 5 S., R. 4 W. "Sometimes called Peoria canal because men who started it came originally from Peoria, Illinois." Name "Peoria Damsite" is shown on G. L. O. map, 1921, as in T. 2 S., R. 5 W. Often called the "Wolfley canal" because Governor Wolfley was heavily interested in it.

Gila Bend Mountains   Maricopa Co.   U. S. G. S. Map, 1923

Range extending from lat 33° 20', long. 113° 10'. After the Big Bend of Gila river.

Gila Bonita Creek   Graham Co.

Called thus on Smith map, 1879. See Bonita.

Gila Butte   Pinal Co.   U. S. G. S. Map, 1923.
Elevation, 1,657 feet.   In sec. 20, T. 2 S., R. 5 E. On Gila Ind. Res.

Gila Center   Yuma Co.
See Blalack.

Gila City   Yuma Co.   Smith Map, 1879; Eckhoff, 1880.
Stage station established about 1858, south side Gila river, about 24 miles east of Yuma.   Discovery of some placers at Laguna gave it a start as an outfitting point for Laguna and Picacho on the Colorado.
"In 1858 Jacob· Snively discovered gold placers at Gila City 24 miles northeast of Yuma.   Within three months over a thousand men were at work there."   Hinton.
"Gila City was our first camp.   Not exactly a city at that time. A few old adobe houses and the usual saloons."   *Vanished Arizona, 1878.*
J. Ross Browne, January, 1864, says: "It existed only in the memory of disappointed speculators.   At the time of our visit it consisted of three chimneys and a coyote."
Farish Notes say: "In October, 1873, Alvah Smith discovered a rich mine here which he called the Alvah mine."
P. O. established Dec. 24, 1858, Henry Burch, P. M.   Name changed to Gila, March 3, 1904.

Gila County.
Created in 1881 out of Pinal and Maricopa counties.   A year or two later a large piece of Yavapai county was added.   Named after river which forms part of its southern boundary.   A large acreage lies in Apache Indian Reservation.   County seat, Globe.

Gila Mountains   Graham Co.   U. S. G. S. Map, 1923.
In Ts. 2 and 3 S., Rs. 22, 23, 24 E.   On boundary between Graham county and San Carlos Ind. Res.   Parallel Gila river on north side, for about 40 miles.

Gila Mountains   Yuma Co.   U. S. G. S. Map, 1923.
Extend from S. P. R. R. at Dome station, southeast across Ts. 8, 10, 11 S., Rs. 21, 22 W.

Gila Peak   Graham Co.   U. S. G. S. Map, 1923.
On boundary line between San Carlos Ind. Res. and Graham county.   In Gila mountains on south side of Ash flat.

Gila River.
Coues says: "Rio Gila, Xila, Jila and Hela, has been longer known than the Colorado or any other river in Arizona, or New Mexico.   Probably discovered 1539 by two friars, Juan de Asencion and Pedro Nadal.   Name, Rio de la Asuncion has long been applied to its principal branch.   The Gila was certainly discovered by the Negro, Estevan, in 1539.   I do not know what name the Gila bore from 1539 to 1604, in which year it was named Rio Nombre de Jesus by Oñate.   Name Hila or Gila first appears as a river above the confluence of Salt river.   This date is said to be 1679.   Its present name is comparatively recent."
On Kino's map, 1701, it shows as Rio Hila for main stream above Salt river which later is marked Rio Azul.   It appears on Venegas map, 1757, as Rio Gila.   Rises in Cattron county, New Mexico, in Mogollon range, enters Arizona near lat 32° 40′, long.

109°, flows southwest and joins Colorado river a few miles east of Yuma.

"In 1699, Kino named it 'Rio de los Apostoles.' Its four branches the Salado, Verde, Santa Cruz and San Pedro, he called 'Los Evangelistas.' Oñate, 1604, called the Gila 'Rio del Nombre Jesus.'" *Franciscans in Arizona.* Bolton agrees with this.

Kino who was of German birth called it Gila or Hila Fluss or Spine Fluss on his map. McClintock thinks the word "Spine Fluss" may have been German for spring or perhaps spiderspinn. Several writers have given it the meaning of spider. McClintock who has studied these names very carefully thinks that "This name seems to have been used first in 1630 when Benairdes wrote of the Gila."

Dr. Lockwood, who has delved deep into Kino's origin, says he was born in Italy.

Gila River Indian Reservation.

See Pima and Maricopa Reservation.

Gila Valley Railroad   Bowie to Globe.

For nearly three years the Apaches positively refused to allow this railroad to cross their reservation. Finally on Feb. 8, 1898, the various bands signed an agreement for the crossing. They were given a cash payment of $10,000 to the entire group and each individual Indian was to be paid for any damage to his land, crops, fences, etc. The railroad also agreed to carry all Apache Indians free of charge, for thirty years from date of signing.

Gilbert   Maricopa Co.   G. L. O. Map, 1921.

Elevation, 1,273 feet. On Arizona-Eastern R. R. 7 miles southeast of Mesa. Named for Robert Gilbert, who gave the ground for railroad station. P. O. established Aug. 22, 1912, David H. Butler, P. M.

Gilbert   Yavapai Co.   U. S. G. S. Congress Quad., 1904.

In T. 9 N., R. 3 W. On King Solomon gulch, east side Hassayampa. At famous King Solomon mine, 3 miles south of Constellation. P. O. established Nov. 17, 1899, Wm. J. Gilbert, P. M., for whom the place was named.

Gilbert Terrace.

"So named for the accomplished geologist, C. K. Gilbert, who while with the Wheeler party made the ascent of Colorado river as far as Diamond canyon." James.

Gilenos.

"Term employed to designate the Pimas residing on Gila river in Arizona." Hodge. See Gila.

Gillespie   Graham Co.   Map, Crook N. F., 1927.

In T. 10 N., R. 25 E. Old settlement on Stockton creek, east side Peloncillo mountains. After an early day settler.

"Curly Bill got what men he had into the saddle. There were others of his band at the little town of Gillespie not far away from Clantons ranch." *Tombstone.*

Gillespie Dam   Maricopa Co.   P. O. Route Map, 1929.

In Buckeye hills south of Arlington. T. 2 S., R. 5 W. Across Gila below mouth of Hassayampa. After Frank A. Gillespie of

Oklahoma, chief engineer and president of Gila Water Co., which built the dam, 1921. P. O. established Aug. 24, 1925, Edward F. Holland, P. M.

Gillette   Maricopa Co.

Station on Black canyon stage road, Prescott to Phoenix. At junction Agua Fria and New river. On some maps Gillett, others, Gillette. P. O. established Oct. 15, 1878, John J. Hill, P. M. After D. B. Gillette, superintendent of nearby Tip Top mine.

Gilsons Well   Gila Co.   Map, San Carlos Ind. Res., 1917.

Station on old wagon road, Willcox to Globe, about 12 miles from Globe. North side Aliso creek in T. 1 S., R. 17 E. After Sam T. Gilson, early settler and stockman.

Gimletville   Yavapai Co.

See Goodwin, also Prescott.

Gisela   Gila Co.   G. L. O. Map, 1923.

Named by Mrs. Frederick Stanton, local school teacher, for heroine of a book, *Countess Gisela*, by E. Marlitt. Village on Tonto creek, in T. 9 N., R. 10 E. Dave McGowan settled here, 1881. Sold to Mort and John Sanders who made a permanent settlement. Gisela lies in what was first known as Grass valley. Also once called Tonto creek. P. O. established Apr. 9, 1894, Frederick Stanton, P. M. See Concho.

Glance   Cochise Co.   Map. Coronado N. F.

Mining camp on Glance creek about 6 miles southeast of Don Luis. At end of short railroad spur from E. P. & S. W. R. R. So called from character of ore.

Glassford Hill   Yavapai Co.

Altitude, 6,161 feet. In sec. 17, T. 14 N., R. 1 W., about 6 miles northeast of Prescott. Named for Col. William A. Glassford, Signal Corps, U. S. A., who, as a lieutenant in early Eighties used this hill as a heliograph station for sending messages to Baker butte, thence eastward to Fort Union, New Mexico. Col. Glassford was Chief Signal Officer to Gen. Miles in Geronimo campaign, 1886. He established system of heliograph stations all over southern Arizona and southwest New Mexico. See Bald hill. Decision USGB.

Gleed   Yavapai Co.   U. S. G. S. Map, 1923.

In T. 22 N., R. 2 W   Station A. T. & S. F. R. R. 13 miles west of Ash Fork. "After C. S. Gleed, director Santa Fe railway, 1900-1920." A.G.W.

Gleeson   Cochise Co.   U. S. G. S. Map, 1923.

In T. 19 S., R. 25 E. Named for John Gleeson who ran cattle here in early days. On Kelton branch E. P. & S. W. R. R. P. O. established Oct. 15, 1900, Frank A. O'Brien, P. M.

Glenbar   Graham Co.   U. S. G. S. Map, 1923.

In T. 6 S., R. 24 E. Station Arizona-Eastern R. R. On south bank of Gila. "First located by Joseph Matthews, Dec., 1880. Near settlement of Pima. First called Matthewsville; then Matthews, for its founder. For a while called Fairview. When it came to securing a post office, the officials would not give that name because there was already one Fairview in Arizona. So it was changed to Glenbar because some of the settlers were Scotch. As for Fairview, I cannot discover from any old timers just how it came to be called that." Letter, J. W. Ferguson, P. M., Glenbar.

Glen Canyon   Coconino Co.   U. S. G. S. Map, 1923.

Canyon in Colorado river, extending northeast from mouth of Paria river to mouth of San Juan. "We now entered a new canyon then called Mound, but afterwards it was consolidated with the portion below the Monument. It opened into many 'glens' or coves, and we decided to call it Glen canyon." Powell.

Glencoe   Cochise Co.

"This was probably first name of Lochiel, as Mrs. Rippey was postmistress there in early days. Originally Lochiel was called La Noria, 'the well.' At that time the national boundary had not been surveyed between Arizona and Sonora. When it was run the village was cut in two. The part in Arizona was called Lochiel, that in Sonora, La Noria, by which it is known today." Letter, Mrs. Caroline De la Ossa. Glencoe was near Lochiel but does not show on any map. P. O. established Jan. 12, 1889, Loretta A. Rippey, P. M.

Glendale   Maricopa Co.   U. S. G. S. Map, 1923.

Elevation, 1,154 feet. In T. 2 N., R. 2 E. On Ash Fork branch A. T. & S. F. R. R. 8 miles northwest of Phoenix. Important cotton, hay and farming center. *Arizona Magazine,* Aug., 1913, says: "Town established 1892 by New England Land Co. Settlement was made by some members of the 'Church of Brethern' from Illinois, who sent B. A. Hatzel out to locate a place for them. He chose this spot, named the town, and bought 360 acres of land for the site. There is a prohibition clause in every deed. On May 20, 1921, citizens donated 10 acres of land to the U. S. for a poultry experiment station."

Glenn, Mount (Mt. Glenn)   Cochise Co.   G. L. O. Map, 1921.

Elevation, 7,512 feet. In T. 17 S., R. 23 E. In Dragoon mountains. "After Calvin Glenn, manager Chiricahua Cattle Co., about 1888." Letter, Fred Winn, Tucson. It is believed that General Miles' "Stronghold Heliograph station" was on this peak. See Cochise Stronghold.

Glinns Falls   Yuma Co.   G. L. O. Map, 1921.

In T. 10 S., R. 14 W. West side Mohawk mountains, east side Mohawk valley. "Glinns Falls is a series of rock tanks pretty well up on the mountain. They hold water most of the year. These are natural rock tanks and there is a leak in the lower end which is perhaps why they are called 'Falls.' Why Glinn, nobody knows." Letter, Charles H. Hindman.

Globe   Gila Co.   Smith Map, 1879; Globe City, G. L. O., 1921, Globe.

Elevation, 3,507 feet. County seat, Pinal county. Originally called Globe City. An important copper mining center. Named for Globe mine, located in 1873 by Anderson brothers.

"First mines were silver and very rich. At a point on Pinal creek now called Radium, a prospector picked up a large globe or ball of silver, perfect in shape, and about 9 inches in diameter. It was 99 per cent pure, and valued at over $12,000. From this the camp received its name." The above is the commonly accepted story of the origin of the name Globe. Another and more likely story is to the effect that one of the discoverers when asked as to its extent said: "Why man, she's as big as the whole globe."

The *Silver Belt* of May 2, 1878, says: The town was laid out in 1876 by Surveyor A. J. Pendleton and officially designated by the name Globe on May 1, 1878. At first they sought only for silver, throwing aside as worthless ore that which later, as the silver veins played out, proved to be copper of high values. Up to 1929, district had produced over $10,000,000 worth of gold and silver, but over $360,000,000 in copper. P. O. established Dec. 22, 1877, Edwin M. Pearce, P. M.

Gobbler Peak   Apache Co.   Map, Apache N. F., 1926.

In sec. 12, T. 6 N., R. 29 E., about 6 miles west of Escudilla mountains, near Nutrioso. A well known wild turkey roost in the Eighties.

Gobbler Point   Greenlee Co.   Map, Crook N. F., 1920.

In sec. 5, T. 3 N., R. 28 E. North side of Bear Wallow creek in Apache N. F. "Mr. Cooper, an old timer, says so named because of the killing of an exceptionally large gobbler on this point. Wild turkeys have always been very plentiful on this mountain." Letter, D. H. Suite, Forest Ranger.

Goddards   Yavapai Co.

Station on Black Canyon stage route to Phoenix. On Agua Fria, at mouth of Squaw creek. After an old time goat owner, who lived here, whose son was supervisor of Tonto N. F. at Roosevelt in 1910. Also called Canyon, q.v.

Golconda   Mohave Co.   U. S. G. S. Map, 1923.

In T. 23 N., R. 17 W. Mining camp in Cerbat range. "Named for the Golconda, rich mine owned by John Boyle, Jr. Mill burned and the closing of the mine was the end of the camp." Letter, J. R. Livingston, Chloride. P. O. established Dec. 8, 1909, Wm. Pound, P. M.

Gold Creek Canyon.

See Canyon del Oro.

Golden   Maricopa Co.   U. S. G. S. Map, 1923.

Station on Parker branch A. T. & S. F. R. R., 36 miles west of Wickenburg. "Was named Golden for a small mining camp of the eighties, located in Harqua Hala mountains, about 20 miles south of present station. The early place has long been abandoned." Letter, Mrs. John Martin, Salome.

Golden Palisades   Pinal Co.

P. O. established by this name April 7, 1915. Unable to locate it, except it was near Casa Grande.

Golden Rule

See Manzora.

Goldfield   Pinal Co.   U. S. G. S. Map, 1921.

In T. 1 N., R. 8 E. Mining camp about 36 miles east of Phoenix on highway to Roosevelt dam. At foot of Superstition mountains. Mine owned and worked by Hon. George U. Young, last secretary of Territory. P. O. established Oct. 7, 1893, James L. Patterson, P. M. He did not qualify, and the office was not opened. November 17, 1895, an office was opened, Louis C. Wagner, P. M. Later called Youngsberg, q.v.

Goldfield Mountains   Maricopa Co.

In T. 2 N., Rs. 7, 8 E. Not Harosoma nor Orohai. Decision USGB, 1932.

Goldflat   Mohave Co.   G. L. O. Map, 1909.

Near Hancock on the A. T. & S. F. R. R. 10 miles south of Kingman. P. O. established Dec. 22, 1908, Jacob A. Hamme, P. M.

Gold Hill   Santa Cruz Co.

See Mt. Benedict.

Goldmine Mountain   Pinal Co.   U. S. G. S. Map, 1923.

North peak of Santan mountains, on Gila river Ind. Res. "I was told that many years ago there was a gold mine opened on this peak which gave it this name." Letter, P. M. Santan.

Goldroad   Mohave Co.   U. S. G. S. Map, 1923.

In T. 19 N., R. 20 W. In western part of county about 15 miles east of Colorado river. "Jose Jerez, a Mexican, grubstaked by Sheriff Levin in May, 1900, was camped on the Beale road. He idly tapped a rock near him with his hammer and developed one of the great gold mines of the west, hence the name." McClintock. Original papers for the mine call it "Gold Roads." The "s," however, was dropped in time. P. O. established March 4, 1906, E. A. Shaw, P. M.

Goldwater (Lake)   Yavapai Co.   Map Prescott N. F., 1927.

In sec. 34, T. 14 N., R. 2 W. "An artificial lake about 3 miles south of Prescott on Groom creek. Water is impounded for major portion of Prescott city water supply. After Morris Goldwater, one-time mayor of Prescott." Letter, Frank Grubb, Prescott.

Goodwin   Yavapai Co.   G. L. O. Map, 1909.

Mining camp about 4 miles north of Bueno in Prescott N. F. After Gov. Goodwin.

Goodwin, Camp   Graham Co.

Camp on Gila river for U S. troops. Heitman's List says: "Established June 21, 1864, vacated account of sickness March 14, 1871." Is about 6 miles below old Camp Thomas, just off San Carlos reservation. Named for Gov. Goodwin.

"The next day, (about July 10 or 12, 1864,) we moved down the San Carlos to the Gila about 10 miles and then by easy stages up the Gila about 30 miles to New Fort Goodwin. It is situated on a stream called 'Pulerosa.'" Woolsey, *Report to Gov. Goodwin,* June, 1864. Possibly Woolsey meant Tulerosa, but neither name is found on any map.

Sometimes this is called "Old Camp Goodwin." Fish says: "It was located by Lieut. Col. E. A. Rigg, U. S. A., June 18, 1864, near a beautiful spring about 3 miles south of Gila river and some 6 west of present Fort Thomas. It was very unhealthy. Out of two hundred and fifty men in the post not more than twenty were fit for duty. Col. H. C. Hooker had the contract for erecting the buildings. Every adobe cost $2.50" Fish may have this post mixed up with Camp Riggs, q. v. P. O. established Mar. 5, 1875, Thomas McWilliams, P. M.

G. L. O. Map, 1897, locates this camp on Goodwin creek about 4 miles from its junction with the Gila. It is difficult to reconcile some of these statements as to the location of this post, especially as to Camp Riggs.

Goodwin City   Yavapai Co.

Early day town a short distance up Granite creek. Named for Gov. Goodwin. Started, in December, 1863, to draw people from Prescott. Often called "Gimletville" by residents of Prescott. Was short lived.

Goodwin Spring   Cochise Co.   U. S. G. S. Map, 1923.

In southeast corner T. 14 S., R. 28 E. In Dos Cabezas mountains, at Apache pass. Early stopping place and camp of Gov. Goodwin.

Goodwin's Proclamation

See Navajo Springs.

Goodwin Wash   Graham Co.   Map, Crook N. F., 1926.

Rises in T. 5 S., R. 20 E. In Santa Teresa mountains, flows northeast into Gila near Geronimo town. So called after Old Camp Goodwin, which was located on the Gila at mouth of this wash. On G. L. O. map, 1866, wash shows as "Rio Santo Domingo."

Goodyear   Maricopa Co.   U. S. G. S. Map, 1923.

In T. 2 S., 5 E., on Chandler branch Arizona-Eastern R. R., 10 miles south of Mesa. Named after Goodyear Tire and Rubber Co. of Ohio, which bought large tracts of land near here upon which to produce cotton.

Gordes   Yavapai Co.

See Cordes.

Gordon   Gila Co.   Map, Tonto N. F., 1927.

Ranch and canyon, located "Under the Rim" at head of what was known as Gordon canyon, for owner of ranch in T. 11 N., R. 13 E. Stream heads under the rim, flows southwest into East Tonto creek. Gordon lived here 1885. P. O. established Sept. 10, 1913, Katie L. Payne, P. M.

Gothic Mesas   Apache Co.   G. L. O. Map, 1921.

In T. 14 N., Rs. 6 to 10 E. Along Colorado-New Mexico line. "This area south of the San Juan is cut into an intricate mass of mesas of various sizes and shapes, carved from red sandstone. For this geographical province the name 'Gothic Mesas' is proposed. Macomb noted the complicated pattern in 1860 and gave the name 'Gothic Wash' to the wide-mouthed canyon which joins the San Juan above Cambridge." Gregory.

Goudy Creek   Graham Co.   Map, Crook N. F., 1926.

Rises east side Merrill creek in Graham mountains. Flows southwest into Grant Creek Fort Grant Military Reservation. "A man named Goudy settled here and cultivated a small bit of ground for several years." Letter, Forest Ranger, Rowley.

Government Hill   Coconino Co.   Map, Tusayan N. F., 1927.

Elevation, 8,490 feet. In T. 23 N., R. 4 E., 6 miles due north of Maine station.

Government Hill   Pinal Co.   Map, Crook N. F., 1926.

Elevation, 5,445 feet. In sec. 25, T. 1 N., R. 12 E., about 12 miles west of Miami. "The U. S. G. S. established a bench mark on this hill, so the cowboys and settlers came to speak of it as Government Hill." Letter, Roy Painter, Forest Service.

Government Knolls   Coconino Co.   Map, Tusayan N. F., 1927.

Elevation, 7,593 feet. In T. 23 N., R. 5 E., about 12 miles north of Bellemont.

Government Mountain   Coconino Co.   G. L. O. Map, 1921; Tusayan N. F., 1927.

Elevation, 8,347 feet. In T. 23 N., R. 4 E., 9 miles northwest of Bellemont, on Government prairie. "Said to have been given this name 'Government prairie' and mountain, by early settlers because the old government road passed through the prairie and close to the mountain." Letter, George Kimball, Williams.

Government Prairie   Coconino Co.   U. S. G. S. Map, Flagstaff Quad.

In Ts. 22, 23 N., Rs. 4, 5 E., on north side Santa Fe track at Bellemont. See Government mountain.

Government Springs   Yavapai Co.

West side Williamson valley, Prescott N. F. "General Crook and troops that captured horses stolen from Camp Wallapai, camped at this spring. At Horse wash, mescal pits made by Apaches, and remains of old Indian camps are still to be seen." Letter, Frank Grubb, Prescott.

Grace Valley   Yuma Co.

Large, open valley south of Salome. Named for Grace Salome Pratt, wife of H. B. Pratt, who many years ago started an agricultural colony in Salome-Wenden section. See also McMullen valley and Salome.

Graham   Graham Co.

Mormon settlement. McClintock says: "It was across the Gila from Thatcher. Original settlers were Andrew Anderson, George Skinner, George Lake and others. They arrived here in Jan., 1881." For the Graham mountains. P. O. established March 17, 1882, Thomas J. Wins, P. M. Post office records show it as "near Clifton."

Graham County   G. L. O. Map, 1921.

In southeastern part of State, north of Cochise county. Created, 1881, from Pima and Apache counties. First settled, 1874, by members of California Volunteers, who left the service and went to farming in Gila valley. Named from Graham mountains near center of valley. County seat established first at Safford; legislature of 1883 changed it to Solomonville; in 1915, when Greenlee county was created, it went back to Safford.

Graham Mountain or Mount Graham   Sitgreave Map, 1851; Smith, 1879; Crook N. F., 1926.

Elevation, 10,516 feet. Peak in Pinaleno mountains, often called Graham mountains. On Oct. 26, 1846, Lieut. Emory, with the Kearney expedition says: "We camped at the base of Mount Graham." On October 28 he says: "We are again in the valley of the Gila which widened out gradually to the base of Mount Graham, abreast of which we are camped." He gives the location as lat. 32°, 53', 16", long. 109°, 31', 34", which would not be far from present town of Safford. Emory's notes are embellished with a sketch of Mount Graham showing it as a high, solitary, snow-capped peak. In 1851 Whipple speaks of it as Mount Graham. This indicates early use of this name.

As for whom it was named, no one can say definitely. There was Lieut. Col. James Duncan Graham, U. S. Topographic Corps, the astronomer with Bartlett survey of 1850, and doubtless in this region some years earlier. Again, it may have been named for George Graham, Secretary of War, 1830. Then there was Will A. Graham, Assistant Secretary of the Interior, 1848-1850. Which of these was honored? Bancroft thinks it was the Lieut. Colonel of Engineers. Hodge feels it was James Duncan Graham. Hinton speaks of "the able secretary of the Aztec Syndicate, Col. John D. Graham." This was possibly the Aztec Mining Syndicate of Col. Poston's days at Tubac. There are many theories as to this name Graham. The singular and very obvious point is that this entire region was wholly Mexican in 1846 when Emory called it by this American name. How did it get it? War was declared with Mexico May 13, 1846, and the Treaty of Peace was proclaimed July 4, 1848.

McClintock speaks of a "Major Lawrence P. Graham who led a squadron of Dragoons to California in the summer of 1848. He reached Yuma October 30, 1848. The old house on the John Slaughter ranch, later known as San Bernardino ranch, was built by this Graham's party who camped there on their way along the border." Apparently Arizona had some attraction for the Graham family if one is to judge by the number here at various times.

Bourke and other writers frequently called this peak and range "Sierra Bonita." It so shows on one or two early maps.

Grand Canyon   Coconino Co.   G. L. O. Map, 1902-21.

Elevation, 6,866 feet. Post office and town. Terminal Grand Canyon branch of Santa Fe, 64 miles from Williams. Originally called Hance's Tank. The famous Harvey hotel, "El Tovar," is here. Branch railroad originally built to reach a group of copper mines north of Williams. Plan failed and line was bought by Santa Fe and extended to canyon. P. O. established Mar. 14, 1902, Martin Buggeln, P. M.

Grand Canyon Forest Reserve   Coconino Co.   Map, Grand Canyon, N. P., 1923.

This reserve was created by presidential proclamation Feb. 20, 1893. It then included both sides of the canyon, that on north side being called Grand Canyon North and on the south side, Grand Canyon South. Later the area on the south became "The San Francisco Mountains Reserve," then changed to the "Tusayan" and "Coconino National Forests," while the area on north was changed to "Kaibab National Forest." Still later a strip on both sides of the canyon was taken from Kaibab Forest on north and Tusayan on south and called "The Grand Canyon National Park."

Grand Canyon National Park   Coconino Co.

Park lying on both sides of Grand Canyon. Created Feb. 26, 1919, from parts of Kaibab N. F. on north rim and part of Tusayan N. F. on south rim. Grand Canyon Game Preserve also covers this same area. Superintendent's headquarters, Grand Canyon, Arizona.

Grand Canyon of the Colorado River   Coconino & Mohave Cos.

"Its head at the confluence of the Little Colorado, its foot at the entrance of Nonnow Valley; its length 238 miles." Powell's report.

Father Garces named the canyon "Puerto de Bucareli," q. v., "for the great Viceroy of Spain." Coues. First European to see the canyon was Cardenas. See El Tovar. Dellenbaugh says: "Powell was responsible for most of the names in the Canyon. He called it Grand Canyon on the first trip. Previously it was the Big Canyon or Great Canyon by the few who knew of it." Letter, Feb. 14, 1933.

The U. S. Geographic Board made following decision on name Grand Canyon. "Nearly 280 miles long, extending from the Paria River and Lee Ferry nearly to mouth of Grapevine Wash." The author feels this definition was not justified by physical or historic facts.

Grand Cliff Range   Mohave Co.   U. S. G. S. Map, 1923.

Often called Grand Wash cliffs. Along west boundary Hualpai Ind. Res. East side Hackberry valley. Range begins at Iceberg canyon on Colorado river opposite Grand wash on Nevada side.

Grand Falls   Coconino Co.   U. S. G. S. Map, 1923.

On Little Colorado river about 45 miles below Winslow. Here the river pours over a cliff forming several falls.

Grand Gulch   Mohave Co.

P. O. established Oct. 20, 1916, Sam R. Galloway, P. M. Location unknown.

Grand Reef Mountain   Graham Co.   G. L. O. Map, 1921.

In T. 6 S., R. 20 E. Crook N. F., in Santa Teresa range. After Grand Reef mine.

Grand Scenic Divide   Coconino Co.   Map, Grand Canyon, N. P., 1923.

High divide on south side of river at Granite gorge between Bass and Serpentine canyons; heads at Darwin plateau near lat. 36° 12', long. 112° 16'. So named by George Wharton James.

Grand View Point   Coconino Co.   Map, Tusayan N. F., 1927; Grand Canyon N. P., 1929.

In T. 30 N., R. 4 E. Descriptive name given by John Hance. Now Piute point, q. v.

Grandview   Coconino Co.

Trail, Grand Canyon N. P., down south wall of canyon from Grandview point near lat. 36° N., long. 111° 59' W., to Colorado river. Decision U. S. G. B.

Grand View   Yavapai Co.   G. L. O. Map, 1921.

Point at top of divide on Ash Fork-Prescott-Phoenix R. R. Also near that point on auto highway at Yarnell Hill. From here there is a wonderful desert view.

Grand View Peak   Graham Co.   Map, Crook N. F., 1926.

In sec. 24, T. 8 S., R. 24 E. One of the peaks near Graham mountain. "There is a grand view of the Gila valley from this peak."

Grand Wash   Mohave Co.   U. S. G. S. Map, 1923.

Deep gorge in extreme northwest corner of State extending southwest from south side of Mount Bangs. Enters Colorado river near State line at Iceberg canyon.

Grand Wash Cliffs   Mohave Co.

See Grand Cliffs range.

Granite   Yavapai Co.   G. L. O. Map, 1921; Prescott N. F., 1926.

In sec. 7, T. 15½ N., R. 1 W. A. T. & S. F. R. R. station camp and recreation area about 10 miles north of Prescott, on Granite creek in mass of granite boulders and peaks. P. O. established April 10, 1903, Earl D. Norton, P. M.

Granite   Coconino Co.

Gorge of Colorado river in Grand Canyon, about 41 miles long, below mouth Little Colorado. Decision U. S. G. B.

Granite Creek   Yavapai Co.   G. L. O. Map, 1921.

So called by miners, 1864, because local rock was principally granite. Rises in mountains southwest of Prescott; flows north through Prescott, joins Chino creek near Del Rio.

Granite Dells   Yavapai Co.   Map, Prescott N. F., 1927.

In T. 14¼ N., Rs. 1, 2 W., 4 miles north of Prescott, on Granite creek, several miles in length. Santa Fe R. R. runs through it. There are lakes, shade trees, a clear mountain stream (Granite creek). Favorite place for picnic parties. P. & E. Junction station is about the center of area.

Granite Mountains   Pima Co.   G. L. O. Map, 1921; U. S G. S., 1923.

At western boundary of county in T. 10 W., Rs. 11, 12 S. West side of Growler valley.

Granite Park   Coconino Co.   U. S. G. S. Map, 1923.

In T. 30 N., R. 9 W. East of Colorado river, Hualpai Ind. Res.

Granite Peak   Cochise Co.   U. S. G. S. Map, 1923.

Elevation, 7,387 feet, in T. 19 S., R. 19 E. At southern end of Whetstone mountains. "Just another peak of granite formation."

Granite Peak   Mohave Co.   G. L. O. Map, 1921.

In T. 16½ N., R. 16 W., in Hualpai mountains.

Granite Peak   Yavapai Co.   U. S. G. S. Map, 1923.

In sec. 3 S., T. 14½ N., R. 3 W. Prescott N. F. Farish says: "It was once called Mount Gurley for the first Governor of the Territory." About 6 miles northwest of Prescott. Called Granite on Smith map, 1879.

Granite Point   Yuma Co.

Coues says: "This is a point on Ives' map a few miles above La Paz." According to Ives' location, it would be on Colorado River Ind. Res. On no other map.

Granite Spur   Yuma Co.   Fortuna Quad., 1903.

In sec 18, T. 8 S., R. 20 W. Spur about 26 miles east of Yuma on S. P. R. R. "We gave it this name because the native rock all around the station is granite." Letter, Paul Shoup.

Granite Wash Mountains   Yuma Co.   U. S. G. S. Map, 1923.

In Ts. 6, 7 N., Rs. 14, 15 W., north of Salome. These are marked plainly Granite Wash mountains on several maps, but oddly enough not one of them shows a Granite wash.

Grant, Camp or Fort   Graham Co.

According to various statements, this post was first established, 1859, as Fort Breckenridge after the Secretary of War. On San Pedro river at junction with Arivaipa creek where Camp Grant Apache massacre occurred. Of it Bourke says: "Beauty of situation or construction it had none. Its site was the supposed junction of the sand bed of the Arivaipa with the sand bed of the San Pedro which complacently figured on maps of that time as a creek and river respectively. They were generally as dry as a lime burner's hat. It was a hot-bed of fever and ague."

Old Camp Grant or Breckenridge was abandoned, 1861. Re-established 1862 by the California Column and named Fort Stanford for Governor of California.

Gen. O. O. Howard says: "It was renamed Fort Grant 1866, for Gen. U. S. Grant."

In 1872, fort was transferred to a point on west side of Graham mountain, 25 miles north of Willcox.

There seems to be some doubt about first location, however, Gen. Mason says: "Fort Grant as a separate post was originally placed on the Gila at the mouth of San Pedro. Floods washed it out in 1865 and it was moved up the river to site of old Fort Breckenridge." Report of Gen. John Mason, Apr. 29, 1866.

Owing to the unhealthy location, old Fort Grant was abandoned in Oct., 1866, and a new post established Dec. 19, 1872, at base of Graham mountain, in sec. 24, T. 9 S., R. 23 E. Later it was also abandoned as a military post. When statehood was granted, Congress authorized State "to select not to exceed 2,000 acres of land within the Fort Grant Military Reservation in partial satisfaction of its grants for state, charitable, penal, and reformatory institutions." This was done and the State set up the reform school which had previously been located at Benson. P. O. established at foot of Graham mountain, Mar. 5, 1875, Warner Buck, P. M. P. O. changed from Camp Grant to Fort Grant, Mar. 28, 1881, Henry A. Morgan, P. M. Post office at first Camp Grant on San Pedro established Aug. 19, 1869, George Cox, P. M.

Grant Co., New Mexico.

Governor Safford of Arizona in his message Jan. 5, 1877, informs the Territorial Legislature that "the people of Grant county, New Mexico, have petitioned to be annexed to Arizona, alleging that our laws are superior to theirs and better executed. The Grant county merchants and business men are already in close business contact with the business men of southern Arizona and feel that by annexation both communities will prosper and improve." The Governor recommended a petition to Congress approving this annexation. Nothing was done about it however.

Grant Creek   Graham Co.   Map, Crook N. F., 1926.

Formed on Fort Grant Military Res. by junction of Goudy, Big and Post creeks, which furnished post water supply. Flows southwest into Sulphur Springs valley where it is lost.

Grant Hill   Graham Co.   Map, Crook N. F., 1926

In sec. 10, T. 9 S., R. 24 E., about 5 miles north east of Fort Grant in Graham mountains, west side. After military post.

Grant Wash Camp.

See Camp.

Granville   Greenlee Co.   Map, Crook N. F., 1926.

In sec. 5, T. 3 S., R. 29 E. Old station on Chase creek about 6 miles above Metcalf. Granville, Metcalf and Chase were three pioneer prospectors in this vicinity. All had towns named for them.

Grapevine Canyon   Coconino Co.   Map, Coconino N. F., 1928.

Long, narrow canyon rising west side T. 17 N., R. 10 E., running northeast into west side Canyon Diablo in sec. 26, T. 18 N., R. 12 E. Takes its name from Grapevine springs at its head.

Grapevine Creek   Mohave Co.   U. S. G. S. Map, 1923.

In T. 29 N., R. 16 W. Rises in Grand Wash cliffs, flows north into Colorado river in Iceberg canyon.

Grapevine Spring   Gila Co.   Smith Military Map, 1879.

On Tonto creek about 6 miles north of old Camp Reno. In Woolsey's Report, June, 1864, he writes: "Here is a large spring of pure water and grass in abundance. We moved there and named it Grapevine spring."

Grapevine Spring   Maricopa Co.   Map, Tonto N. F., 1927.

In T. 6 N., R. 4 E., 3 miles northeast of Cave Creek P. O. "So called because when first visited it was completely surrounded by huge wild grape vines."

Grasshopper   Navajo Co.   U. S. G. S. Map, 1923.

Spring and Camp on Fort Apache Ind. Res., at head of Salt River draw. So called as early as 1880 after a lame Apache squaw whom the Indians called "Naz-chug-gee" (Grasshopper) from her peculiar limp. She had one short leg which caused the limp.

Grass Mountain   Mohave Co.   G. L. O. Map, 1921.

Elevation, 1,700 feet, in Andrus canyon east of Shivwits plateau. "So called because unusually well covered with good nutritious grass." Grassy Mountain on U. S. G. S., 1923.

Grass Valley

See Gisela.

Grayback Mountains   Yavapai Co.   G. L. O. Map, 1921.

In Ts. 13, 14 N., Rs. 9, 10 W., north side of Santa Maria river. Northwest of Hillside station A. T. & S. F. R. R. Origin not known.

Grayback Peak   Pinal Co.   G. L. O. Map, 1921.

Elevation, 3,558 feet. In T. 4 S., R. 12 E., about 2 miles south Gila river upper end Tortilla mountains. Origin not known.

Gray Mountain   Maricopa Co.

"South of the Sierra Estrella Coyote stopped and laid the heart upon a bush. Near Ki-ha-toak Coyote stopped again upon a mountain to eat the heart. He shook it, and the ashes fell and covered the mountain, which to this day is called Gray mountain." From the *Pima Myths*, by Frank Russell. 26th Report Bu. Eth., page 214.

This Gray mountain does not show on any modern map. Father Antoine of St. Johns Mission on the Gila river, locates it as follows: "Gray mountain or 'Karo-mak,' lies some 20 or more

miles south and a little west of Montezuma Head at the extreme
south end of the Estrella range. I am quite sure it is in the Sand
Tank Range." Letter, March 10, 1934. See Sand Tank mountains,
which are in the extreme southeastern corner of Maricopa county.

Greasewood Mountain   Graham Co.   Map, Crook N. F., 1926.

In sec. 3, T. 11 S., R. 25 E., southern end Pinaleno mountains.
"The mountains are covered with a dense stand of brush that is
called locally 'greasewood.' Unable to learn by whom named."
Letter, Forest Ranger, Rowley.

Greasy Mountain

See Salt River mountains.

Greaterville   Pima Co.   U. S. G. S. Map, 1923.

In sec. 19, T. 19 S., R. 16 E. Coronado N. F. Named after
Greater, early settler. Called Santa Rita in 1873. Ed Vail says
that about 1880 a group of his cowboys went over here to a
dance. They were drunk and the local people refused to admit
them. They withdrew to discuss the situation. House in which
dance was held was an adobe with dirt roof. It was winter and
cold. A man climbed to roof and dropped a handfull of six-
shooter cartridges down the chimney into the blazing fire. This
ended the dance. P. O. established Jan. 3, 1879, Thomas Steele,
P. M.

Great Thumb Mesa   Coconino Co.

Tableland, Grand Canyon N. P. near lat. 36° 20', long. 112° 31'.
An eastward extension of extreme northern end of Coconino
plateau within great bend of Colorado river. Descriptive name;
looks like a huge thumb. Named by Frank Bond.

Greenback Peak, Creek and Valley   Gila Co.   G. L. O. Map, 1921;
                                                        Tonto N. F., 1927.

Elevation 6,505 feet, in sec. 12, T. 6 N., R. 13 E. In Tonto basin.
Valley lies northeast of butte at head of Greenback creek. Shows
on nearly all maps as Greenback. Called locally Green valley.
Creek enters Tonto creek from the east a few miles above head
of Roosevelt lake near Cline post office. "Said to have been
named by U. S. troops that first camped there and found it so
green and lovely that they called it Greenback Valley." Farish.
The author's recollection is that Capt. Bourke once told him
troops scouting through here found a roll of greenbacks at an
abandoned Apache camp. Supposition was that Apaches had
found the money on the body of some murdered settler and, not
knowing its value, had thrown it away. Hence the name.

"It was in Greenback valley, in the spring of '65, that my father,
Wm. A. Hancock, a lieutenant of Arizona Volunteers, with a band
of Pima scouts, started from Fort Reno, crossing the Tonto north
of Roosevelt dam where Cline post office was later established,
and up a narrow valley.

"Coming upon an abandoned camp, father picked up a bit of
paper and started to light his pipe with it when he saw it was a
hundred dollar greenback.

"It was suggested the valley be named Greenback valley and
the creek Greenback creek. It was officially called so from then
on. Evidently the Apaches had killed a prospector and as paper
money had no meaning to them, it was thrown away." Letter,
Harry A. Hancock, Phoenix.

Gregg Buttes   Maricopa Co.

See Double buttes.

Greggs Ferry   Mohave Co.   G. L. O. Map, 1921; U. S. G. S., 1923.

In T. 31 N., R. 17 W., on Colorado river between Arizona and Nevada, at Virgin canyon. Well known ferry crossing owned by a man named Gregg.

Greenes Reservoir   Pinal Co.   U. S. G. S. Map, 1923.

Reservoir on eastern side Sawtooth mountain, in Ts. 9, 10 S., Rs. 6, 7 E., a part of Santa Cruz Irrigation project. Named after William Greene, of Cananea fame, who took out a ditch here in the Eighties.

Greenlee County.

Created by Twenty-fifth Territorial Legislature, January, 1909. Owing to many questions of settlement between Graham and the new county, it was not organized until Jan. 1, 1911. Named after Mace Greenlee, one of first prospectors to explore this region.

Green's Peak   Apache Co.   Map, Apache N. F., 1926.

Elevation 10,115 feet, in sec. 2, T. 8 N., R. 20 E. After Col. John Green, 1st Cavalry, U.S.A., who commanded at Camp Apache, 1873.

Green Valley   Gila Co.

See Little Green valley, also Payson.

Greenwood   Mohave Co.   Smith Map, 1879; G. L. O., 1921.

McCracken mining town on Big Sandy, near Signal mine. Named for palo verde (green tree), plentiful here. Abandoned many years ago. "Four or five miles above (Signal City) on Big Sandy is Greenwood where a 10-stamp mill has for some time been working ores from McCracken mine from which it is about 12 miles distant." Hinton.

Greenwood Peak   Mohave Co.   G. L. O. Map, 1921.

In T. 13 N., R. 12 W. Peak named after milling town of Greenwood. East of Big Sandy.

Greer   Apache Co.   G. L. O. Map, 1921.

In T. 27½ E., R. 8 N. Town on head waters of Little Colorado river. After Mrs. Ellen Greer, whose family established this settlement about 1880. They ran many cattle and horses on the range for years.

Grey's Peak   Greenlee Co.   U. S. G. S. Metcalf Quad., 1915, Grey; G. L. O., 1921, Gray.

Elevation 7,077 feet in sec. 30, T. 2 S., R. 29 E, west side Chase creek. "Named for an early prospector who lived near foot of peak. Nobody can say how he spelled it." J. W. Girdner, Forest Ranger, Clifton.

Grief Hill   Yavapai Co.   Map, Prescott N. F.

In southern part T. 14 N., R. 4 E. "The summit of Grief hill on road Prescott to Camp Verde is 32 miles from Prescott. There is water at right of road one mile below the summit, except in dry seasons. Grazing is good and plentiful." Hinton.

"Well-known hill of early freighting days. It was long, steep and rough. Wash joins Verde river about a mile above Camp Verde, heads at Piute mesa." Letter, L. J. Putsch, Forest Service.

Griffin Flat   Gila Co.

"This was an area belonging to C. C. Griffin, stockman and farmer who lived on what is now the bottom of Roosevelt lake. He ran the 76 brand of cattle." Bud Farmer.

Griffith   Mohave Co.

Station A. T. & S. F. R. R. 10 miles west of Kingman. "First called Sacramento Siding, then changed to Drake, which shows on maps as early as 1883. Drake was at that time chief engineer, A. & P. R. R. Nov. 14, 1930, name was again changed to Griffith for a former clerk who was killed in action in France." Letter, S. W. Simpson, Supt. A. T. & S. F. R. R.

Grinnells Station   Yuma Co.

According to J. Ross Browne, this was a station some 6 miles from Agua Caliente on the Gila.

Groom Peak   Mohave Co.   U. S. G. S. Map, 1923.

In T. 15 N., R. 13 W. Southern end Hualpai mountains, on Big Sandy. "After Bob Groom who probably made the first settlement at Prescott, 1863. He had several mining claims near this peak." Letter, T. Levy, Signal.

Groom Creek and Settlement   Yavapai Co.   G. L. O. Map, 1921.

Prescott N. F. about 8 miles south of Prescott. After R. W. (Bob) Groom, who lived and mined near here for many years. He surveyed the townsite of Prescott. Groom discovered the Stirling mine near Prescott. Was a councilman from "Groomdale" in First and Second Territorial Legislatures. Was buried at Wickenburg. Old records show that over three million dollars in gold was taken from placers on this creek. P. O. established as Groom creek, Aug. 19, 1901, Clara B. Riley, P. M.

Grossman Peak   Mohave Co.

See Crossman peak.

Grosvener Hills   Santa Cruz Co.   Map, Coronado N. F., 1927.

In T. 21 S., R. 14 E. Group of hills in eastern part of Baca Grant; No. 3. After H. C. Grosvener, English mining engineer, superintendent of Salero and Santa Rita mines, 1860-61. Was killed by Apaches, 1861.

"To the east and south of Mount Wrightson rises another and smaller peak which has been called Mount Grosvener in honor of another bold pioneer who in 1861 was murdered by Apaches." Hinton. This seems to cover the present-day Josephine peak. Pumpelly gives an interesting account of Grosvener's death.

Grove of Robinson   Gila Co.   Smith Map, 1879; Eckhoff, 1880.

On east side Tonto creek about 10 miles below a stream called Camp River on the map. See Catalpa.

Growler Mountains and Valley   Pima Co.   U. S. G. S. Map, 1923.

In extreme western part of county. See Growler peak.

Growler Pass   Pima Co.   U. S. G. S. Map, 1923.

In T. 14 S., R. 6 W. At southern end Growler mountains.

Growler Peak   Pima Co   G. L. O. Map, 1921, Sheep Peak;
                                              U. S. G. S., 1923, Growler.

West side Growler mountains. So named by Frederick Wall,
who discovered and named Growler mine after John Growler,
an early miner.

Growler Well   Pima Co.

See Bates well.

Guadalupe Canyon   Cochise Co.   U. S. G. S., Perilla Quad.

In Guadalupe mountains, extreme southeast corner, Arizona.
Comes in from New Mexico, crosses a corner of Arizona, enters
Old Mexico in T. 34 S., R. 32 E., near Mile Post No. 73, at town
of Estes. Favorite runway in Seventies and early Eighties for
bands of Mexican and American cattle thieves and smugglers.
Old man Clanton, with four of his gang, was ambushed and
killed in this canyon.

Guadalupe   Maricopa Co.   U. S. G. S., Mesa Sheet.

In sec. 5, T. 1 S., R. 4 E. Yaqui Indian village, with church,
about 4 miles southeast of Tempe. "So named in honor of
Nuestra Señora de Guadalupe, the especially Mexican manifes-
tation of the Virgin Mary." Hinton. Easter and Christmas services here are most interesting.

Guajolote Wash   Santa Cruz Co.   Roskruge Map, 1893.

Rises west side of Patagonia range. Runs southwest into Santa
Cruz river. The guajolote is a small reptile known to Mexicans
under that name. It is commonly called "water puppy," "water
dog," or "newt." It is the salamander (Ambystoma) of the
ancients. These reptiles are very common in old dry lakes or
water holes and name probably came from their presence.

Guebavi   Santa Cruz Co.

Name is also Mexican for turkey.
See Quebabi.

Gun Creek   Gila Co.   Map, Tonto N. F., 1927.

In sec. 7, T. 8 N., R. 11 E. Flows northwest into Tonto creek
near Howell ranch. "It is said to have been so named because
one of the early settlers found an old gun somewhere along the
creek many years ago." Letter, Fred Croxen, Forest Ranger.

Gunsight Hills   Pima Co.   U. S. G. S. Map, 1923.

West of Quijotoa valley, near lat 32° 20′, long. 112° 30′. Named
from Gunsight mine. "Mine got its name from an alleged story
about one of the men who discovered it. Having no sight on his
gun he whittled one from a piece of almost pure silver which he
fastened to the barrel of his rifle."

Gunsight Well   Pinal Co.   G. L. O. Map, 1921

In T. 14 S., R. 3 W., in Gunsight hills. "Named from the mine."
P. O. established June 27, 1892, Samuel W. Sutherland, P. M.

Gurley Mountain   Yavapai Co.

First name of Granite peak, northwest of Prescott. After Gov.
John A. Gurley, first Governor of Arizona. Appointed by Lin-
coln, Mar., 1863, but died before he could assume office.
Gurley street in Prescott is the only other place named for him.
See Granite.

Gust James, Wash   Pinal Co.   Map, Crook N. F., 1926.

Rises west side Galiuro mountains, flows southwest into San Pedro, in T. 9 S., R. 17 E. Origin unknown.

Guthrie   Greenlee Co.   U. S. G. S. Map, 1923.

In T. 5 S., R. 30 E., on Gila river. Mining town, E. P. & S. W. R. R. "Guthrie is at the Gila river crossing about 59 miles north of Lordsburg. The Arizona Copper Co., which built the railroad here, named it after a Scotch stockholder." Letter, J. H. Brown, Clifton.

Guthrie Mountain   Pima Co.   G. L. O. Map, 1921; Coronado N. F. 1927.

In sec. 20, T. 12 S., R. 17 E. After John D. Guthrie, U. S. Forest Service, former Supervisor, Coronado N. F.

Guthrie Peak   Greenlee Co.   U. S. G. S. Map, 1923.

In Peloncillo mountains west of York, near county line. See Guthrie, town.

Gypsum Creek   Navajo Co.   U. S. G. S. Map, 1923.

In Navajo Ind. Res. Rises northeast of Marsh pass; flows northeast into Colorado river near lat. 37°, long. 109°, 55'. There is a huge bed of gypsum on this stream which gives the water a strong taste, and its name.

Hackataid River

"Said to be the Wallapai Indian name for Colorado river." James.

Hackberry   Mohave Co.   G. L. O. Map, 1921.

In T. 23 N., R. 14 E. Town on A. T. & S. F. R. R. west of Peach springs on Truxton wash, east side Peacock mountains. "For the Hackberry mine which took its name from a large hackberry tree near a spring where the camp was." As nearly as the author can work it out this is Beale's "Garden Spring," q.v. P. O. established July 9, 1878, Alonzo E. Davis, P. M.

Hackberry Mountain   Yavapai Co.   Map, Tonto N. F., 1927.

In sec. 15, T. 12 N., R. 6 E. of Coconino N. F. "So named about 1878 because of the many large hackberry trees upon it."

Hacks Canyon   Mohave Co.   U. S. G. S. Map, 1923.

Short canyon, north side of Colorado river, rising on eastern side Uinkaret plateau; drains east, enters Kanab creek in T. 36 N., R. 4 W.

"Briggs A. Riggs of Kanab says 'A man named Haskell Jolly bought a spring near the head of this canyon from Chris Heaton. Jolly improved the spring and raised horses in the vicinity for a number of years. Jolly's nickname among the settlers was Hack, and all the old timers know it as Hack's canyon.'" Letter, Walter G. Mann, Kanab.

Hado   Cochise Co.   G. L. O. Map, 1921.

Station on S. P. R. R. about 5 miles west of Willcox at edge of Willcox playa, a huge level dry lake which is very hot and dry. From its climate, said to be called Hades or Hell by local Mexicans.

Haeckel   Graham Co.   U. S. G. S. Map, 1923.

In T. 8 S., R. 26 E. Station on Arizona-Eastern R. R. Upper end of San Simon valley. Origin unknown.

Haigler Creek   Gila Co.   Map, Tonto N. F., 1927.

In sec. 6, T. 10 N., R. 13 E. Formed by Naeglin and Colcord creeks. Flows southwest into Marsh creek. After Joseph Haigler, early day cattleman.

Halfmoon Valley   Cochise Co.   Map, Coronado N. F., 1927.

In T. 21 S., R. 29 E. in Pedrogosa mountains. "Named by William Lutley of Tombstone, who lived here in the early Eighties, because the valley is the shape of a half-moon or crescent." Letter, Forest Ranger Bentley.

Hall Butte   Coconino Co.

Grand Canyon N. P., 3 miles across Colorado river, northeast from Lyell butte, near lat. 36° 5′ N., long. 111° 59′ W. Named for Andrew Hall, member Powell's first expedition through Grand Canyon, 1869. Named by Frank Bond. Decision U. S. G. S.

Hall Creek   Apache Co.   Map, Apache N. F., 1926.

In sec. 6, T. 8 N., R. 26 E. One of several forks of Little Colorado. Rises on east flank of Mount Ord; flows northeast into Little Colorado at T. 8 N., R. 27 E. "Named after John Hall, early settler on this stream. He now lives at Eager." Letter, Forest Supervisor Hussey, Springerville.

Hall Well   Yuma Co.   U. S. G. S. Map, 1923.

In T. 5 S., R. 11 W. Water hole about 6 miles northeast of Agua Caliente. "Dug in 1914 by a Mr. Hall. Well is 151 feet deep." *Routes to the Desert.*

Halloysite   Apache Co.   Postal Route Map, 1929.

Station on A. T. & S. F. R. R., 7 miles east of Navajo springs. "Formerly called Chambers. On June 1, 1930, this name was abandoned and the name Chambers restored. Halloysite is a clay similar to kaolin, used in manufacture of fine china. There was a mine of this material worked near here for several years." Letter, R. W. Cassady. P. O. established Dec. 9, 1926, Spencer Balcomb, P. M.

Hamblin Creek   Coconino Co.   Gregory Map, 1916; G. L. O., 1921.

Navajo Ind. Res. Rises lower end Echo cliffs; flows south into Moenkopi canyon and wash. After Jacob Hamblin, Mormon missionary. So named by Gregory. McClintock calls Hamblin "The Leather Stocking of the Southwest."

Hamburg   Cochise Co.   G. L. O. Map, 1921.

In sec. 9, T. 23 S., R. 20 E. Coronado N. F. Settlement and peak on Ramsay canyon, Huachuca mountains. South of Huachuca Military Reservation.

"Many years ago an old German, Henry Hamburg, had a mine here called the Hamburg mine. Locally the mines were called 'Stromberg and Hamburg' group of copper mines." Letter, P. M., Sunnyside. P. O. established Oct. 5, 1906, Louise de Vera Hamburg, P. M.

Hancock Butte   Coconino Co.

In Grand Canyon N. P. one mile south of Point Imperial, near lat. 36° 16' N., long. 111° 58' W. Northeast corner of park. Named for Capt. William A. Hancock, pioneer. He surveyed the Phoenix townsite and erected first building there, 1870. First Sheriff, Maricopa county; Probate Judge; County School Superintendent; Asst. U. S. District Attorney, Phoenix. Born in Massachusetts; crossed plains to California, 1853; went to Fort Yuma, 1865, as Second Lieut. California Volunteers; mustered out as First Lieut. in 1866. Named by Frank Bond. Decision U. S. G. B.

Hanegras Plain

See Ranegras.

Hannigan Creek   Greenlee Co.   Map, Apache N. F., 1926.

In sec. 3, T. 3 N., R. 29 E. Rises in Hannigan meadows, flows north into Beaver creek, a branch of Black river. See Hannigan meadows.

Hannigan Meadows   Greenlee Co.   Map, Apache N. F., 1929.

In sec. 3, T. 3 N., R. 29 E. Beautiful open meadow at head of Hannigan creek. On state highway between Springerville and Clifton. After Robert Hannigan, cattleman, who, as early as 1886, ran the X V brand both in Arizona and New Mexico, with summer headquarters at this meadow.

Hano   Navajo Co.

One of the Hopi villages located on First or East mesa at Walpi. "These people are of Tewa origin who in the Eighteenth Century migrated from the upper Rio Grande at the solicitation of the Hopi who wanted them for 'guards' at their village. Name in Hopi and means 'Eastern People.'" Hodge.

Hansbrough Point   Coconino Co.

"Ten miles below Point Retreat we discovered the body of Peter M. Hansbrough, one of the men drowned on our trip last summer. We buried him under an overhanging cliff and named a magnificent point opposite 'Point Hansbrough.'" *Stanton's Story,* Jan., 1890. Point Retreat was 30 miles below Lee Ferry.

Hansen   Maricopa Co.   G. L. O. Map, 1921.

In sec. 35, T. 1 S., R. 4 E. Flag station and loading switch on Arizona-Eastern R. R. Hansen was a farmer near here.

Happy Camp   Yuma Co.   Smith Map, 1879.

Early day stage station on old overland route east from Yuma. On south side of Gila where road cuts across Gila Bend. Water was hauled from the river.

Writing of this place in 1877, E. Conklin in *Picturesque Arizona* says: "At this station water was brought 15 miles across as desolate a waste as one could well imagine. A charge of 25c a head was made for watering horses. It was originally one dollar but for some reason was reduced recently." Further along Conklin wonders just why it was called by such a jovial name. He says, "Contrary to its name the spot was a dreary one."

Harcuvar   Yuma Co.   U. S. G. S. Map, 1923.

Peak, 1,200 feet elevation, in T. 7 N., R. 13 W. Mountain range and peak. Range parallels Parker branch of A. T. & S. F. R. R. from Salome to Forepaugh. Mountains are in northeast corner of Yuma and Maricopa counties, on north side of McMillen valley, about 60 miles east of Colorado river. Vicksburg lies at southern end of range. Mohave word for "sweet water." Genung says: "It was an Indian word for 'cottonwood water.'"

Harcuvar   Yuma Co.

Station, Parker branch of A. T. & S. F. R. R. about 3 miles south of Salome. After nearby mountains.

Hardimui   Pinal Co.   U. S. G. S. Map, 1923.

In T. 16 S., R. 1 E. Indian village, Papago Ind. Res.

Hardin   Maricopa Co.

P. O. established Mar. 9, 1898, Frank Moody, P. M. "This place, just a store and saloon, was located on Black Canyon stage road where it crossed the Arizona canal. Who it was named for cannot now be learned." Letter, John M. Turner, P. M., Peoria.

Hardscrabble   Coconino Co.

According to McClintock the first name of Fredonia, q.v.

Hardscrabble Mesa   Gila Co.   Map, Tonto N. F., 1927.

In Tonto basin. "High open mesa of black volcanic rock. Lies between west end of Strawberry valley and Fossil creek. The Camp Verde-Tonto Basin trail crossed it. Soldiers of old army days so named it for its extreme roughness." Letter, Fred Croxen, Forest Ranger.

Hardscrabble Wash   Apache Co.   U. S. G. S. Map, 1923.

Affluent of Zuni river rising in T. 18 N., R. 29 E. Flows southwest into Zuni below Hunt, in T. 14 N., R. 25 E. Origin unknown.

Hardy   Navajo Co.   U. S. G. S. Map, 1923.

In T. 18 N., R. 17 E. Station A. T. & S. F. R. R. 12 miles east of Winslow. "Hardy was the first superintendent of telegraphs on A. & P. R. R. Later changed to Havre." A. G. W.

Hardys Colorado

In the summer, 1826, Lieut. R. W. H. Hardy, English Navy, came up the Gulf of California into the lower Colorado. He claimed to be on a pearl fishing expedition, chartered the schooner Bruja (owl or witch) at Guaymas and made his way up to a slough or stream which he erroneously thought was the Gila. This has since been called Hardys Colorado. It was neither the Gila nor the Colorado, merely a side slough. It seems well to make this explanation as many suppose it to be after Hardy, the pioneer who located Hardyville.

Hardys Landing   Mohave Co.

See Hardyville.

Hardyville   Mohave Co.   Smith Map, 1879;
                                                                    Eckhoff, 1880.

On Colorado river about 10 miles north of Fort Mohave. After Capt. W. H. Hardy who established a trading post and ferry here in 1864. Important river point often called Hardys Landing. Was at head of steamboat transportation.

McClintock says: "Hardy had an extensive place here. There was a store, warehouse, hotel, blacksmith shop and several dwellings." *Arizona Sentinel,* Mar. 20, 1873, mentions the total destruction of Hardyville by fire on Mar. 18, 1873. P. O. established June 7, 1865, Wooster M. Hardy, P. M.

Harosoma

See Goldfield mountains.

Harper   Mohave Co.   G. L. O. Map, 1909.

Settlement on the Colorado about 6 miles above Hardyville, at lower end of Pyramid canyon. "Named after first settler at this place, 1872." *Arizona Sentinel,* Sept., 1872.

Harqua   Maricopa Co.

This was Harqua Hala camp but the post office, established June 6, 1927, was simply called Harqua, Mrs. Margaret E. Ward, P. M. See Harqua Hala.

Harqua Hala   Yuma Co.   U. S. G. S. Map, 1923.

Mountain range, peak, plains. Mohave for "running water," or "always water." "Ah-ha-quahla." Mountains about 35 miles long, on south side Parker branch of A. T. & S. F. R. R. 30 miles southwest of Wickenburg in Yuma and Maricopa counties in Ts. 5, 6 N., Rs. 10, 11 W. Peak, elevation 2,200 feet in T. 5 N., R. 11 W. Plains, south of mountain range between Big Horn and Eagle Tail mountains in Yuma and Maricopa counties. Name derived from a never-failing spring in Harqua Hala mountains, which the Indians so called.

The official spelling of this name has never been definitely settled. The author has followed the majority of modern writers in making it two words, "Harqua Hala."

Harqua Hala   Yuma Co.   Smith Map, 1880; G. L. O., 1892.

In T. 4 N., R. 12 W. Mining camp on east side of Harqua Hala mountains, about 2 miles south of Salome. Mine owned by Hubbard and Bowers of Prescott in the Nineties. After extracting a fortune, they sold to an English corporation for $1,335,000 cash. P. O. established Mar. 5, 1891, Horace E. Harris, P. M. Later called Harqua, q.v.

Harrington   Pinal Co.   All Early Maps.

Station and ranch on San Pedro between Dudleyville and Winkelman. The Harringtons located here 1879, and ran the 76 brand of cattle for many years. They also lived at Dudleyville.

Harrington   Yavapai Co.   G. L. O. Map, 1909.

On Rock creek, in Prescott N. F. "Named for George P. Harrington, well known early day mining man who operated the Tiger mine near this place." Letter, Frank Grubb, Prescott. P. O. established Apr. 4, 1904, Robert G. Scherer, P. M.

Harris   Mohave Co.

Station A. T. & S. F. R. R., five miles south of Kingman. "For G. W. Harris, Chief Engineer, Santa Fe System." A. G. W.

Harris Cave   Apache Co.

After "Uncle John Harris," who had a shingle mill on Mineral creek near which was this cave. Harris and two sons discovered and explored the cave, 1882, finding a large number of Indian relics, pottery, arrow heads, etc. Sometimes called Pottery cave.

Harris Lake   Apache Co.   U. S. G. S. Map, 1923, Hardy, an
                                                error; Apache N. F., 1927.

In sec. 30, T. 9 N., R. 26 E. At head of East Fork Concho creek, near line of Fort Apache Ind. Res. Named after Harris Greer, son of Mrs. Ellen Greer, who had a summer ranch here in the Nineties.

Harris Mountain Cochise Co.   G. L. O. Map, 1921.

In T. 17 N., R. 31 E. on east side of Chiricahua mountains, at head of Turkey creek, about 4 miles north of Paradise. "There is the grave of a man named Harris, his wife and two children, murdered by Apaches, 1873. Indians carried off Harris' 15-year old daughter. She was rescued by the Second Cavalry, 1876. "After 20 years of puzzling over Davis mountain I have at last identified it as Harris mountain. Is at the eastern gate post of Turkey Creek canyon near old Galeyville." *Tombstone.*

A lot of treasure, diamonds, etc., was taken from Mexicans by Zwing Hunt, and others, and buried here, according to Noble's book. He says: "Buried here in this canyon, according to the story, is the pillage of many robberies in Old Mexico and the southwest. The value of $3,000,000 was placed on it by the dying outlaw supposed to have taken part in the robberies and burial of loot." *Tombstone.*

Harrisburg Yuma Co.   G. L. O. Map, 1921.

In southwest corner of T. 5 N., R. 12 W. "Named for Capt. Charles Harris, Canadian, who served in U. S. Regulars in Civil War. He, with Gov. Tritle, started the town, 1886. They packed a 5-stamp mill from Prescott and operated on ores from the Socorro mine as well as milling such custom ores as came their way." About 4 miles southeast of Salome, south of Parker branch. P. O. established Feb. 9, 1887, William Beard, P. M.

Harry Edwards Mountain Mohave Co.

Named by Beale. "At this point I have sent back my first assistant, H. B. Edwards Esq., in order to superintend the construction of bridges over the streams we have crossed." Later he writes: "Leaving Armistead's creek we came by a beautiful pass . . . . to a great valley. Harry Edwards mountain lay directly in front of us, its lofty summit covered with great pines." Beale's Report, Nov. 15, 1858.

"It is not over 45 or 50 miles from Beale's Crossing of the Colorado river," writes F. E. Nagle, Asst. to Beale. Cannot be located definitely.

Harry J. Jones (Camp) Cochise Co.

Military camp established in Douglas during the 1910 trouble with Mexico.

At one time more than 15,000 troops were stationed here. Named after Private Harry J. Jones, U. S. soldier, killed Nov. 1, 1915, by a stray bullet from "Villistas." Shot was probably meant for one of the Mexican defenders of Agua Prieta, across the border. Camp abandoned Jan., 1933, and troops removed to other posts.

Harshaw Santa Cruz Co. G. L. O. Map, 1923; Coronado N. F., 1927.

Mine on east side Patagonia mountains, on Harshaw creek. So named for David Tecumseh Harshaw, who settled here, 1875. "First called 'Peach,' 'Durasno' by the Mexicans because of venerable peach trees probably planted by some early padre." P. O. established April 29, 1880, Dan R. Gillette, P. M.

Hart Mountain Coconino Co.

After D. F. Hart, cattleman who ran cattle on upper Oak Creek range, 1887.

Hart Spring and Prairie   Coconino Co.   Eckhoff Map, 1880.

Head of Fort valley. Headquarters ranch of Frank Hart, well known sheep man in 1880. In T. 23 N., R. 7 E. East of Humphrey peak.

Hartt   Pima Co.   R. R. Maps.

Station on S. P. R. R. in Santa Cruz valley, 30 miles south of Tucson. After William Hartt, who came to Arizona with J. A. Rockfellow, January, 1878. Located ranch here, where he lived for many years.

Harvard Hill   · Coconino Co.   U. S. G. S., Map, 1923.

Evidently an error of mapmaker. See Howard hill or butte.

Harwood   Yuma Co.

"Landing place on Colorado river, head of Colorado and Gila canal, 28 miles above Yuma. So named by Capt. Mellon for Col. Harwood of the Gila Canal Co." Farish Notes.

Hashbidito Creek   Apache Co.   G. L. O. Map, 1921.

Rises in T. 10 N., R. 8 W. on Navajo Ind. Res. north of Gigante butte, flows west into Agua Sal creek, east of Carson mesa. " 'Hash-bi-to,' Navajo word meaning 'turtle,' or 'mourning dove,' " Father Haile.

Haskell Spring   Yavapai Co.

In Verde valley from which Clarkdale gets its water supply. About 1873, some Apache-Mohave and Apache-Yuma Indians were moved from this spring, where they had been located for years, to the San Carlos Agency. "So called after Lieut. Harry Haskell, Twelfth U. S. Infantry, in charge of Indians at the time."

Hastings   Pinal Co.

Found on old map, 1882, of Pioneer Mining district. On Queen creek. First name of Superior, q.v.

Hassayampa   Maricopa Co.   U. S. G. S. Map, 1923.

Town on Hassayampa river, in T. 1 S., R. 5 W., western end of Buckeye branch A. T. & S. F. R. R. P. O. established Mar. 28, 1881, Mrs. Matilda E. Spence, P. M.

Hassayampa River

Originally spelled "Assamp" in old mining notices. Later, "Hassamp" or "Hasiamp." Rises in Yavapai county on north slope of Mount Union; flows south, enters Gila at Powers butte, Maricopa county, in T. 1 S., R. 5 W.

According to D. E. Connor: "Was first called 'Haviamp.' Wheelhouse, secretary of the mining district, did not like the spelling; said it was not Spanish enough and in the district notices he spelled it 'Hassayamp.' "

"Said to have been named by Pauline Weaver and to mean 'beautiful waters.' " James, *Arizona the Wonderland.*

"According to a Yuma Indian employed by me, this name 'Hasa-yamp' means 'water that is hidden' or 'water that is in a dry bed.' " Letter, J. H. McClintock.

> "You've heard about the wondrous stream
>   They call the Hassayamp.
> They say it turns a truthful guy
>   into a lying scamp.

And if you quaff its waters once
It's sure to prove your bane
You'll ne'er forsake the blasted stream
or tell the truth again."

—Orick Jackson.

"Those who drink its waters bright
Red man, white man, boor, or knight
Girls or women, boys or men,
Never can tell the truth again."

—Anon.

Hat Mountain   Maricopa Co.   U. S. G. S. Map, 1923.

West side of Sauceda mountains in T. 9 S., R. 5 W. Origin unknown.

Hatchton   Yuma Co.

Origin undetermined. P. O. established Nov. 30, 1921, Frank E. Black, P. M.

Hattan Point   Coconino Co.

Canyon wall projection, Grand Canyon N. P. about 2 miles west of north of suspension bridge, on left bank of Phantom creek, near lat. 36° 8', long. 112° 6' W. Named for Andrew Hattan, hunter and cook for Powell's Second expedition through Grand Canyon. "It was Andy's first experience as a cook although he had been a soldier in the Civil War." Dellenbaugh. Named by Frank Bond. Decision U. S. G. B.

Havasupai Ind. Res.   Coconino Co. Map, Grand Canyon N. P., 1927.

Small area lying on both sides of Cataract creek where it joins the Colorado. Set aside June 8, 1880, by President Hayes for Havasupai Indians. Increased later. Indians live part of year in Cataract canyon, their main village being about 8 miles from its junction with the Colorado.

John D. Lee, executed by the U. S. Government for complicity in the Mountain Meadows massacre, hid in this canyon for a number of years. He is said to have introduced the growing of peaches and alfalfa to the Havasupai.

Hodge says: "The word means 'blue or green water people.' " Undoubtedly so called from color of water in huge springs that break out from canyon's side 10 or 15 miles from its junction with Colorado. These springs furnish the water which Indians use for irrigation. It is highly charged with lime which has formed many water falls or cataracts.

These Indians, also called "Cosninos," were living here when Whipple visited it, 1854. According to Major Powell, they claim to have lived at one time on the Little Colorado east of San Francisco mountains. See Cosnino.

Havasupai Point   Coconino Co.   Map, Tusayan N. F., 1927;
                                            Grand Canyon N. P., 1927.

Point in side canyon in sec. 1, T. 32 N., R. 1 W., 3 miles northeast of point. After local Supais. Name brought into use by George Wharton James. Previously called "Supai."

Havasu Canyon and Creek   Coconino Co.
Map, Grand Canyon N. P., 1927.

Name commonly given to lower end of Cataract canyon. Coues says Padre Garces called this creek and canyon "Rio Jabesua" which he thinks was merely Garces' way of spelling their name. He sometimes called the Indians "Agua Azul" (Blue Water) for the color of the water in the springs. After the Havasu or Supai Indians. See Cataract and Supai.

Haviland   Mohave Co.   U. S. G. S. Map, 1923.

Station on A. T. & S. F. R. R. 29 miles south of Kingman. In T. 18 W., R. 16½ N. "There is some question about this name but it probably was so called because there is near here a deposit of the clay from which Haviland china is made." Letter, G. W. Simpson, Supt. Santa Fe.

Havre   Navajo Co.

On A. T. & S. F. R. R. 11 miles east of Winslow. Just another name. Formerly called Hardy, q.v. Changed because of another Hardy on the Santa Fe.

Hawkins Butte   Coconino Co.

Grand Canyon N. P., 2 miles across Colorado river, northeast from Lyell butte, near lat. 36° 5' N., long. 112° W. Named for W. R. Hawkins, hunter and cook for Powell's first expedition, 1869. Named by Frank Bond. Decision U. S. G. B.

Hay Lake   Coconino Co.   G. L. O. Map, 1921;
Coconino N. F., 1928.

In sec. 30, T. 16 N., R. 11 E. Holds water nearly entire year. In early days hay was cut here for the stage teams of the Santa Fe-Prescott stage line.

Hayden   Gila Co.   U. S. G. S. Map, 1923.

Elevation 2,051 feet. Mining camp on Arizona-Eastern R. R. on Gila river about 35 miles east of Florence. Named for senior member of Hayden, Stone & Co., operating mines here.

Hayden Junction   Pinal Co.   G. L. O. Map, 1921.

On S. P. branch of Arizona-Eastern R. R., east of Florence, on Gila river. Junction point for Hayden, q.v. P. O. established Nov. 8, 1913, Joseph C. Boughton, P. M.

Hayden Mountain   Coconino Co.   G. L. O. Map, 1921.

Peak in Grand Canyon N. P. near west canyon rim at northeast corner of park. Near lat. 36° 16' N., long. 111° 58' W; about one-half mile southeast of Point Imperial. "Named for Charles T. Hayden, Arizona pioneer. Born in Connecticut, 1825, came to Arizona, 1858, on first Overland stage to Tucson. In 1870 established first ferry across Salt river and first store at Tempe. Called 'The Father of Tempe,' where he erected and operated the first flouring mill and organized a milling and ditch company. The mill still exists. Probate Judge at Tucson. Died at Tempe, 1907." Farish. Father of Hon. Carl Hayden, U. S. Senator, 1927. Named by Frank Bond.

Hayden Peak   Pinal Co.   G. L. O. Map, 1921.

In T. 4 S., R. 6 E. Triangulation station, Gila River Ind. Res. After Charles T. Hayden of Tempe. Named by field party, U.S.G.S.

Haydens Butte   Maricopa Co.

Named for Charles T. Hayden. So called on several early maps. See Tempe butte.

Haydens Ferry   Maricopa Co.   Smith Map, 1879.

On Salt river at Tempe. Established by Charles T. Hayden in 1870 or 1871. Place later became Tempe. Ed Irvine, in letter to State Historian, says: "This place was first, 1872, called Butte City." P. O. established as Haydens Ferry April 25, 1872, John J. Hill, P. M. Mrs. Sallie D. Hayden, mother of Sen. Carl Hayden, appointed P. M. Dec. 19, 1876. See Tempe.

Hayes Mountains   Gila Co.   U. S. G. S. Map, 1923.

San Carlos Ind. Res. Three peaks about 15 miles southeast of Globe, north of Gila river. "After Zee Hayes who ran cattle in this vicinity for many years."

Haynes   Yavapai Co.

"R. R. station for Big Stick mine of which Lloyd C. Haynes was superintendent." Letter, Supt. Santa Fe R. R., Needles. P. O. established April 4, 1908, John R. Roberts, P. M.

Haystack Butte   Navajo Co.   Gregory Map, 1916; U. S. G. S., 1923.

In T. 23 N., R 18 E. On Hopi Ind. Res., between forks of Corn creek. Descriptive name.

Haystack Peak   Yuma Co.   G. L. O. Map, 1921; U. S. G. S., 1923.

In T. 4 S., R. 18 W. East side Plomosa mountains. Descriptive name.

Hearst Mountain   Coconino Co.   Map, Tusayan N. F., 1927.

In sec. 22, T. 22 N., R. 1 E. About 4 miles northeast of Williams. Hearst-Perrin Co., for whom it was named in 1887, had large cattle interests here.

Heaton   Pima Co.   R. R. Maps Only

Siding on S.P.R.R. about 4 miles west of present Maricopa station. Company once intended to build branch to Phoenix from this point because it was several miles shorter. For a time was called Maricopa; also Maricopaville. See Maricopa, Tempe, Maricopa wells.

Heaton Reservoir

See Franklin Heaton.

Heber   Navajo Co.   G. L. O. Map, 1921;
Sitgreaves N. F., 1927.

In sec. 13, T. 12 N., R. 16 E. Mormon settlement of about 1880, on Black canyon, 50 miles southwest of Holbrook. After Heber C. Kimball, Chief Justice, State of Deseret, 1883.

John Bushman was first settler. It was quite a settlement up to about 1883 when several years of drought drove most of the settlers away. About 1883 John Hoyle, former cook for the Hashknife outfit, opened a store here, which he ran for several years. P. O. established Sept. 11, 1890, James Shelley, P. M.

Hecla   Yavapai Co.   Map, Prescott N. F., 1927.

In sec. 3, T. 13 N., R. 2 E. "There was a Hecla mine here from which the camp took its name. It is now known as the 'Stone Corral' from a big stone corral here." Letter Frank Grubb, Forest Service. P. O. established Mar. 3, 1893, John H. Hudson P. M. It was near Cherry P. O.

Heintzelman Mines   Santa Cruz Co.

These were undoubtedly named and in part owned by Gen. Heintzelman, U. S. Army, who commanded troops in southern Arizona in the early Sixties. McClintock locates them in Santa Cruz county 8 miles from Tubac. Heintzelman was president of the Sonora Exploring and Mining Co., of Cincinnati, Ohio, which owned this mine. Poston says Heintzelman was on official leave while at the mines. See Cerro Colorado.

Helena   Maricopa Co.   U. S. G. S. Map, 1923.

In T. 1 S., R. 4 E. Station on Arizona-Eastern R. R. 6 miles south of Tempe. Origin not known.

Helena Canyon   Apache Co.

See Quirinal canyon

Helen's Dome   Cochise Co.   G. L. O. Map, 1921; Smith, 1879.

Elevation 4,956 feet. In sec. 14, T. 15 S., R. 29 E. Near Chiricahua mountains, in Apache pass. Local tradition says it was named for a young woman who jumped to her death from a bluff here during an attack by Apaches.

Sidney DeLong, who was post trader at Fort Bowie about 1880, says: "It was named for Mrs. Helen Hackett, wife of Capt. Hackett of Fort Bowie. She and a party of friends climbed the peak for the first time. It is very close to the post." Doubtless correct.

Heliograph Peak   Graham Co.   Map, Crook N. F., 1926.

In sec. 13, T. 9 S., R. 24 E. East side of Grahams, west of Arcadia Ranger station. During Miles' Geronimo campaign this was one of several peaks on which heliograph stations were established. See Glassford peak.

Hell Canyon   Yavapai Co.   Map, Prescott N. F., 1927.

Deep canyon rising on southwest slope of Bill Williams mountain. Drains into Verde river in sec. 29, T. 18 N., R. 1 E. In early days Ash Fork stage line came down and across this canyon. It was very rough and name was easily applied to it. Now crossed by bridge.

Hellings Mill   Maricopa Co.

William B. Helling built a flour mill here in 1871. Machinery came by steamer up the gulf and river to Ehrenberg, thence to mill site. Said to have cost $70,000 when ready for business. Location about 6 miles east of Phoenix. Ruins of three-story adobe were standing as late as 1890, when the author first saw them.

"The old Hellings Mill on Salt river, once the scene of openhanded hospitality to all travelers, still existed, 1881, under changed ownership." Bourke, *On the Border.* Later became Mill City, q. v.

Hells Hole   Gila Co.   Map, Tonto N. F., 1929.

"That part of Wertman, or Workman Creek canyon lying between Reynolds creek and up the stream for about a mile in a deep gorge, is locally known as 'Hell's Hole.'" Letter, M. R. Stewart, Forest Service. See Wertman creek.

Hells Hole   Gila Co.   Map, Tonto N. F., 1932.

In sec. 4, T. 11 N., R. 7 E. Rough area in western part of Tonto basin, at forks of Hardscrabble canyon. Close to Fossil creek. About 4 miles southwest of Twin buttes. So called by local cattlemen because of its extremely rough character.

Hells Hole   Greenlee Co.   Map, Crook N. F., 1926

Peak in T. 5 S., R. 32 E. "Hells Hole was a small area lying under the peak so very rough and inaccessible that it was a difficult matter to get cattle out. So the stockmen gave it this name." J. W. Girdner, Forest Ranger.

Hells Hollow

See Red Rock country.

Helvetia   Pima Co.   U. S. G. S. Map, 1923.

In T. 18 S., R. 15 E. An old silver mine so called by Ben Hefti, local Swiss miner, after his native country. P. O. established Dec. 12, 1889, Charles M. Coon, P. M.

Hendershot Place   Gila Co.   Map, Tonto N. F., 1926.

In T. 11½ N., R. 10 E., upper Tonto basin, on East Verde. "This was an early day ranch. At time of Apache raid, July, 1882, Old Man Meadows, his wife and two sons were living here. Indians attacked the place killing the father and badly wounding both boys. Men from Payson came to their relief, took the father's remains to the Siddle ranch and buried them under Siddle's cabin floor to keep Indians from finding and mutilating them." Letter, Fred Croxen, Forest Ranger.

Henning   Mohave Co.   G. L. O. Map, 1892.

Station on A. T. & S. F. R. R. in Sacramento valley, east of Needles. Named after A. E. Henning, for several years in charge of general water service on Santa Fe R. R., Needles to Gallup. See his cattle ranch near Billings under that name. P. O. established Feb. 28, 1884, John H. Mollering, P. M.

Herder Mountain   Maricopa Co.   Map, Tonto N. F., 1927.

In sec. 28, T. 5 N., R. 8 E., west side of Sycamore creek. "This mountain is near the government sheep trail across Tonto Basin. It is an outstanding peak which sheep herders climb to locate other flocks on the trail to prevent mix-ups." Letter, Joe Hand, Forest Ranger.

Hereford   Cochise Co.   G. L. O. Map, 1921.

In T. 23 S., R. 22 E. In San Pedro valley, on E. P. & S. W. R. R. Named for Ben Hereford, father of Frank Hereford of Tucson.

"Col. Herring of Tucson and others built a smelter at this place which they named for Ben Hereford, Frank's father. Smelter was shut down, later burned and place deserted for several years. About 1892, Col. Bill Greene (Cananea Greene) located a ranch here for his cattle interests and reestablished the place under its old name."

Hermit Basin, Creek and Trail   Coconino Co.

Map, Grand Canyon N. P., 1923; Tusayan N. F., 1927.

Named for Louis P. Brown, miner and prospector who, in the Eighties lived a hermit's life here. Large open basin on south side of canyon; about half way down to river. Trail leads to it from rim. Starts down the canyon in sec. 21, T. 31 N., R. 1 E. Creek rises at canyon rim near Santa Maria spring in T. 31 N., R. 2 E. Flows north into river in Granite gorge.

Hermo   Maricopa Co.

Location or history of this postoffice appears completely lost. Records at Washington show that it once existed. P. O. established May 17, 1901, Lewis D. Nelson, P. M.

Hermosillo   Pinal Co.

This was a new town in 1891, about 3 miles east of Casa Grande.

Hess Creek   Gila Co.   Map, Crook N. F., 1926.

Rises northeast part T. 4 N., R. 17 E., flows south and northwest into Salt river in sec. 7, T. 4 N., R. 16 E. "After a man named Hess who settled and ran cattle on this creek in early days. His ranch was east of Jackson butte. The flat there is still known as Hess Flat." Letter, Ray Painter, Safford.

Hewitt   Pinal Co.   Florence Quad., 1900.

Canyon rising near Iron mountain; flows southwest into Queen creek in T. 2 S., R. 11 E. After a local settler by this name who had a ranch at mouth of canyon.

Hibbard   Coconino Co.   U. S. G. S. Map, 1923.

On main line A. T. & S. F. R. R. "After I. L. Hibbard, Gen'l. Supt. Santa Fe R. R., later, Gen'l. Mgr." A.G.W. About 8 miles west of Canyon Diablo.

Hickey Mountain   Yavapai Co.   Map, Prescott N. F., 1927.

In sec. 4, T. 15 N., R. 2 E. at south end of Woodchute mountain, about 2 miles west of Mingus mountain. "After Dennis Hickey, later of Prescott, who had a potato ranch near this mountain in the early Eighties.

Hidden Canyon   Mohave Co.   U. S. G. S. Map, 1923.

North side Shivwits plateau; runs through Grand Wash cliffs in northwest corner of State. "So called because of its inaccessibility."

Hieroglyphic Canyon   Maricopa Co.

Notable canyon in what is now Phoenix Mountain park, in Salt River mountains, some five miles south of Phoenix. The dark volcanic rocks are covered with hieroglyphics or pictographs cut in the rock by some long-forgotten race. Favorite resort for tourists, archaeologists, and others interested in prehistoric era of the valley.

Hieroglyphic Mountains   Maricopa and Yavapai Cos.
U. S. G. S. Map, 1923.

West of Castle Hot springs. There are many hieroglyphic records on the rocks here. Ives speaks of them as common everywhere.

Higgins Tank   Navajo Co.

Well known watering place of late Eighties about 10 miles southwest of Holbrook. Originally a series of rock tanks in the canyon. About 1888, J. M. Higgins of Holbrook made a dirt tank in the flat near-by and caught flood waters. Was Higgin's horse ranch for some years.

Highest point in Arizona.

Humphrey mountain, in San Francisco group, 12,611 feet.

Higley   Maricopa Co.   U. S. G. S. Map, 1923.

In T. 1 S., R. 6 E., 12 miles southeast of Mesa. Named for S. W. Higley at one time owner of *Phoenix Republican*. Interested in

the construction of Phoenix and Eastern R. R. P. O. established
Jan. 11, 1910, Lawrence A. Sarey, P. M.

Hi Jolly

See Quartzsite.

Hi-ki-bon   Pima Co.

See Peregua.

Hill Camp   Gila Co.   Post Route Map, 1929.

Camp and store at top of grade from Rice into Fort Apache
Ind. Res. About 25 miles from Rice. P. O. established May 19,
1927, Mrs. Zona Lee Hill, P. M. Named after Mrs. Hill.

Hillers Butte   Coconino Co.

Grand Canyon N. P. 3 miles north of suspension bridge, near
lat. 36° 9' N., long. 112° 5' W., one mile west of Bright Angel
creek. Named by Major Powell for John K. Hillers, photographer, second expedition, 1872. "The Major returned to our camp
from Salt Lake bringing a new member of the party, Jack Hillers. He had an excellent voice and often sang popular songs.
He did all the photographic work." Dellenbaugh. Decision
U.S.G.B.

Hillside   Yavapai Co.   G. L. O. Map, 1921.

Elevation 3,853 feet. In T. 13 N., R. 7 W. Station on Ash Fork-
Phoenix branch A. T. & S. F. R. R. On Date creek. Descriptive
name. Town is on hillside. P. O. established July 31, 1888, John
W. Archbald, P. M.

Hilltop   Cochise Co.   Map, Coronado N. F., 1927.

In T. 16 S., R. 30 E. Town and mine, Chiricahua mountains.
Small summer settlement on Chiricahua range above Paradise.
P. O. established June 26, 1920, Raleigh O. Fife, P. M.

Hitt Wash   Yavapai Co.   Map, Prescott N. F., 1926.

Rises in sec. 6, T. 17 N., R. 5 W. East slope of Santa Marias.
Flows east into Williamson valley near Simmons in T. 17 N.,
R. 3 W. "Named after James Hitt who squatted on land in unsurveyed sec. 26, T. 17 N., R. 5 W., about 1880 and lived there
for several years. Spelling was changed one way, one 't'
being dropped." Letter, Forest Supervisor Grubb, U. S. G. S. map
spells it "Hit." Decision U.S.G.B., "Hitt."

Hobble Mountain   Coconino Co.   U. S. G. S. Map, 1923;
                                                  Tusayan N. F., 1927.

In T. 25 N., R. 4 E. "Many years ago a man named Kinsey
found a bunch of stolen calves hobbled out near this mountain.
This gave it the name." Letter, G. W. Kimball, Williams.

Hobson   Navajo Co.   U. S. G. S. Map, 1923.

Flag station on A. T. & S. F. R. R. 6 miles east of Winslow.
Opened during Spanish war. After Lieut. Hobson of Spanish
war fame.

Hobson Mountain   Pinal Co.

See Rawhide mountain.

Hogansaani Spring   Apache Co.   Gregory Map, 1916.

In T. 12 N., R. 9 W. Navajo Ind. Res. On Walker creek, east of
Carrizo mountains. "Navajo word 'Hogan-saa-ni' meaning 'the
lone hogan.'" Haile. Spanish called it "Ojo de Casa."

Hokum Ranch   Navajo Co.   Map, Sitgreaves N. F., 1924.

In T. 11 N., R. 17 E. This is incorrect spelling. Ranch was owned by Daniel Boone Holcomb, familiarly called "Red" because of his complexion. First called Phoenix Park, q. v.

Holbrook   Navajo Co.   G. L. O. Map, 1921.

Elevation 5,080 feet. County seat. Formerly known as Horsehead Crossing. "Named, 1880, after H. R. Holbrook, first chief engineer of Atlantic and Pacific railroad. He was the builder of the Rocky Ford Colorado Irrigation system." A.G.W. James H. Wilson was the first P. M., Sept. 18, 1882. Orestes P. Chaffee, brother of Gen. Adna R. Chaffee, U.S.A., was P. M. and quartermaster agent here from March 4, 1888, to Sept. 9, 1889. He was a crippled Confederate soldier.

Holden Lake   Coconino Co.   Map, Tusayan N. F., 1927.

In sec. 23, T. 22 N., R. 1 E. Lake about 2 miles northwest of Williams.

Holder   Gila Co.   Map, Tonto N. F., 1926.

On East Verde between Payson and Pine. "Named after John Holder who ran a herd of goats here up to about 1905 when he moved out because of a decision against sheep and goats in Tonto Forest." Letter, J. W. Girdner. P. O. established Sept. 5, 1896, John T. Holder, P. M.

Hole-in-the-Rock   Maricopa Co.   U. S. G. S. Mesa Quad., 1916.

Elevation 1,450 feet. An odd rock about 6 miles east of Phoenix. Has a large hole through which is framed a wonderful view of the valley below. On March 15, 1915, it was created into the Papago-Saguaro National Monument. This was recalled by Act of Congress Aug. 7, 1930. See Papago-Saguaro.

Holmes Creek and Canyon   Yavapai Co.   Map, Prescott N. F., 1927.

In sec. T. 9 N., R. 4 E. Short stream in Bloody basin, Prescott N. F. Rises southern end of Hutch mesa, flows southeast into Lime creek in T. 9 N., R. 5 E. Named after R. J. Holmes, Jr., who ran cattle for many years in Bloody basin. Died at Phoenix Apr. 26, 1931.

Holt   Cochise Co.   Early Maps and R. R. Folders.

Station on S.P.R.R. about 4 miles east of Bowie station. Named for Col. J. M. Holt of Montana who purchased and shipped a large number of cattle from this vicinity from 1887 to about 1892.

Holy Joe Peak   Pinal Co.   G. L. O. Map, 1921; Crook N. F., 1932.

In T. 7 S., R. 18 E. Galiuro mountains. About 5 miles west of Graham county line. " 'Holy Joe' was the nickname for an old man who prospected over these mountains for many years and preached sermons as a side line." Letter, S. A. Lowell, Jr., Forest Ranger.

Homedas Station   Pinal Co.   G. L. O. Map, 1892.

In T. 5 S., R. 7 E. Station on stage road from Sacaton to Tucson, about 6 miles southeast of Casa Grande ruins. Origin unknown.

Honeymoon Cabin   Greenlee Co.   Map, Crook N. F., 1926.

In sec. 31, T. 2 N., R. 28 E. On Eagle creek. "One of our earliest forest rangers was sent here to open a ranger station. He had just been married and took his young bride with him. She gave it this name."

Hookers Butte   Graham Co.   U. S. G. S. Map, 1923.

In northeast corner T. 11 S., R. 22 E., east slope Winchester mountains. After Col. H. C. Hooker, pioneer cattleman.

Hookers Hot Springs   Cochise Co.   G. L. O. Map, 1921; U. S. G. S., 1921.

In T. 21 E., R. 13 S. about 30 miles west of Willcox and 8 east of Cascabel. In Galiuro mountains. Flows into Hot Springs creek. Favorite point for invalids in early days. Named for Col. H. C. Hooker of Hookers ranch, who was a relative of Gen. Joe Hooker of the Confederate Army.

"Out of a flat smooth rock about 10 feet across came a column of steam through a large hole in the center. The water was always about 160 degrees. Range horses and cattle seemed to prefer it to the cooler water in the creek below. Dr. King lived here in the Eighties and ran a sort of hospital." Read Forrestine Hooker's book, *Just George.*

Hooper   Yavapai Co.   G. L. O. Map, 1921.

In T. 10 N., R. 1 W., Prescott N. F. Mining camp on Towers creek. First called Foresight (sic) for Foresythe family who lived here. P. O. established Feb. 8, 1900, John Foresythe, P. M. Office incorrectly spelled Foresight.

Hoover   Maricopa Co.   P. O. Route Map, 1929.

On A. T. & S. F. R. R. north of Marinette. P. O. established Feb. 1, 1915, Norman H. Morrison, P. M.

Hoover Dam

See Boulder dam.

Hop Mountain   Navajo Co.   G. L. O. Map, 1921.

In T. 10 N., R. 20 E. Fort Apache Ind. Res. "Under the rim" at extreme head of Hop canyon, a fork of Carrizo creek. Noted for vast areas of wild hops in the canyon.

Hope, Mount   Yavapai Co.   G. L. O. Map, 1921.

Elevation 7,000 feet. Located on private land grant, "Luis Maria Baca Float No. 3," western side of Yavapai county. Elliott map, 1866, shows it southeast of Gemini peak.

"Towards the southwest there is a conical peak that appears to be a volcanic cone. This we have called Mount Hope." *Whipple's Report,* 1847. He failed to give the origin or meaning of name. Sometimes called Hope peak.

Hope Window   Apache Co.   Gregory Map, 1916.

In T. 6 N., R. 11 W. Hole in a large rock, i.e. "a window," about 8 miles west of Chinle village. "I named it for Edna Earl Hope, student in Columbia University who served as a volunteer assistant in my geological survey work in the Navajo country." H. E. Gregory, Jan. 31, 1931.

Hopi   Coconino Co.   G. L. O. Map, 1921.

Station on Grand Canyon branch A. T. & S. F. R. R. 50 miles north of Williams. Between Anita and Apex stations. After Hopi Indians.

Hopi Buttes   Navajo Co.   Gregory Map, 1916.

"Group of mesas which since the days of Spanish explorers have been known as the Hopi buttes. Called Rabbit Ear mountains on early maps." Gregory. Also called Moqui or Moki. Visitors often call the several Hopi mesas or villages by number. See First mesa, also Seven pueblos.

Hopi Indian Reservation   Coconino and Navajo Cos.
Gregory Map, 1916; U. S. G. S., 1923.

Reservation for Hopi pueblos inside Navajo Ind. Res. Set aside by President Arthur, Dec. 16, 1882. Agency and school at Keam canyon.

Hopi Indians

"A contraction of Hopitu, 'peaceful people.' They speak a Shoshonean dialect and occupy several separate pueblos in northeastern Arizona. Spanish called them Moki, or Moqui, which means 'dead' in their language and was keenly resented by them. The region was called 'Tusayan' by the Spanish and is undoubtedly the Tontonteac of de Niza." Hodge.

First visited by Spanish, 1540. Celebrated for their snake dance ceremony. Name Moki or Moqui was generally used until about 1895 when Hopi was adopted by the Smithsonian and gradually took its place. Was probably the early Spanish understanding of the word Hopi. Old maps all show it "Moqui" or the "Moquis Pueblos." Occasionally spelled Moki.

The Franciscan *Navajo Dictionary* says " 'Mogi,' a Navajo word meaning monkey; a word of contempt for the Hopi which the Navajos had for these Indians." One wonders if this was not the genesis of the Spanish name for them, Moki or Moqui.

Eckhoff map, 1880, shows Moki; G.L.O., Arizona, 1921, Hopi and Moki. One or two old maps show the entire region as "Los Moquenos."

Hopi Point   Coconino Co.   Map, Kaibab N. F., 1927.

Formerly Rowes point. In Grand Canyon about 2 miles northwest of El Tovar hotel.

Hopi Villages

See Seven Pueblos of Tusayan.

Hopkins, Mount   Santa Cruz Co.   G. L. O. Map, 1921;
Coronado N. F., 1927.

In sec. 14, T. 20 S., R. 14 E. Santa Rita mountains. "After Gilbert W. Hopkins, mining engineer with Santa Rita Mining Co. Killed by Apaches near here Feb., 1865. Member of first Territorial Legislature." Bancroft.

"To the north and west of Mount Wrightson is a bold but lesser cone which it is proposed to call Hopkins peak in honor of Gilbert Hopkins, slain in 1861 by Apaches within the shadow of the mountain." Hinton.

Pumpelly and Farish both give 1864 as the year. Hinton must be wrong. Arizona records show Hopkins a member of the Legislature from "Maricopa Line," 1864.

Horse Canyon   Gila Co.   Map, Fort Apache Ind. Res.;
Tonto N. F., 1927.

In T. 7 N., R. 15 E. Rises in Tonto N. F. near Pine butte, flows into Canyon creek in T. 6 N., R. 16 E. On Tonto N. F. map marked "Rock House canyon," q.v.

Horse Mesa   Maricopa Co.   Map, Tonto N. F., 1927.

Outstanding mesa sometimes called Horse mountain. South side of Salt river. In T. 3 N., R. 10 E. below Roosevelt dam about 35 miles. So called because when sheep were trailed down this way the herders took their saddle and pack horses to this mesa where feed was always good. Not Vaquero mesa.

Horse Mesa Dam, Lake and P. O.   Maricopa Co.
                        Map, Tonto N. F., 1927; P. O. Route Map, 1929.

Dam is in sec. 21, T. 3 N., R. 10 E., across Salt river. Lake is formed by waters so impounded. Temporary post office established Dec. 20, 1926, at damsite while work was progressing. Daniel J. Jones, P. M. Named after well known mesa on south side of river. Water coming from the dam above is caught and used again for power purposes.

Horsehead Crossing   Navajo Co.

Point 2 miles above present town of Holbrook. Just below junction Little Colorado and Puerco rivers. All travel south to St. Johns, Concho, Fort Apache, Showlow and Snowflake in early days crossed the Puerco here. When the railroad came to Holbrook it lost out.

Started as early as 1870 as a trading post for settlers and Indians. Owned by a Mexican named Berado Frayde or simply Berado. About 1882 his wife eloped with a local stockman and Berado returned to Albuquerque. His old store and dwelling house stood there in 1882 upon the author's first visit.

Hinton says: "There were two stores here, neither owned by Mormons. Berado Frayde was the merchant and storekeeper in 1876." None of the old timers knew the reason for this name.

Horseshoe Bend   Gila Co.   G. L. O. Map, 1921; Crook N. F., 1926.

In sec. 2, T. 3 N., R. 15 E. Horseshoe curve in Salt river, about 10 miles east of Livingston P. O. "Old man Gleason was killed by the Apaches at this point in 1881, during the Cibecue outbreak." Letter, Fred W. Croxen.

Horseshoe Canyon   Cochise Co.

On east slope of Chiricahua mountains opening into San Juan valley. U. S. troops fought a battle with Apaches here Oct., 1871, under Capt. Gerald Russell, Third U. S. Cavalry. *Report Comdg. Gen'l. Dept. Arizona,* 1871. Surely meant for Cochise Stronghold, q.v.

Horseshoe Lake   Coconino Co.   Map, Sitgreaves N. F., 1924.

In sec. 34, T. 12 N., R. 12 E. On "Rim" of Tonto basin. Wet weather lake of horseshoe shape at head of Turkey creek.

Horseshoe Mine   Pima Co.

Lumholtz says: "Well and Indian camp at south end Quijotoa range. There was once a gold mine here. Papago word meaning 'grey soil,' alluding to the prevalence of caliche."

Horseshoe Station   Yavapai Co.   G. L. O. Map, 1909.

In T. 16 N., R. 2 E. Station United Verde and Pacific R. R. about 16 miles east of Jerome Junction. "So called because the road here was so crooked it made a regular horseshoe."

Horse Thief Basin and Creek   Yavapai Co., Map, Prescott N. F., 1931.

Creek rises in Bradshaw mountains, in southeast corner T. 9½ N., R. 1 E., flows northeast into Poland creek.

Basin is a small open area on east side of Lane mountain about 5 miles southeast of Crown King. In secs. 30, 31, T. 9½ N., R. 1 E. Many years ago this was called Horse Thief ranch because several noted characters made it a "hide out" for traffic in stolen horses.

Horse Wash　　Yavapai Co.　　Map, Prescott N. F., 1927.

"In pioneer days Wallapai Indians stole a number of horses from Camp Wallapai. Troops overtook them on this wash and recovered the horses which gave it the name." Letter, Forest Supervisor Grubb. Rises at Seepage mountain; flows east into Pine creek near Cross Triangle ranch.

Horton Creek　　Gila Co.

Short stream emptying into Tonto creek, one mile above crossing of Payson-Gordon Canyon road. "Named for an early settler who, about 1882, located on the creek. State has a fish hatchery at Horton springs, at head of creek." Fred Croxen.

Hosfelt Peak　　Gila Co.　　Map, Tonto N. F., 1927.

Elevation 5,770 feet. In T. 6 N., R. 10 E. East side Mazatzal range, near Edwards peak. "After Charles Hosfelt who lived here and for many years ran the 'butcher hook' brand on this range." Letter, Fred Croxen.

Hospital Lagoons　　Maricopa Co.

"We returned to camp and having gone two leagues, arrived at some pools of bad water where some of the party were made sick. For that they were called 'Las Lagunas del Hospital.' To the west of these lagunas is the 'Sierra de San Joseph de Comers' which ends on the Gila close to (junta) the place where this river is united to the Rio Asumpcion." Garces Diary, Nov. 3, 1775; Coues translation.

Coues says: "The Hospital Lagoons are hardly identifiable but I cannot doubt they are the place well known since American occupation as Maricopa Wells, 6 miles west of Sacaton on Maricopa and Phoenix R. R." See Maricopa wells.

Hotevila (Not Hoteville)　　Navajo Co.　　U. S. G. S. Map, 1923.

In T. 29 N., R. 15 E. Name of springs; Indian village; trading post and P. O. Hopi Ind. Res. P. O. is spelled Hotevilla. "Navajo word meaning 'springs at head of canyon,'" Gregory.

"The meaning or translation in Hopi is 'skinned back,' or 'scraped back.' There is a spring here used for centuries in a sort of rocky ledge or cave. One has to stoop in going in or his back is bumped. Hence the name 'Sore back,' 'Skinned back,' 'Scraped back.'" Letter, Edgar K. Miller, Supt. Hopi Agency. Another meaning given is "springs in the cave."

This village originated about 1907 when a number of disgruntled Hopi from Oraibi located here. Later they split into two factions part leaving Hotevila and moving to a new village called Bacabi, 8 or 10 miles east of Hotevila. P. O. established July 14, 1916, Emory A. Marks, P. M. Gregory spells it Hotevila, which is a decision of U.S.G.B.

Hot Springs　　Yavapai Co.　　G. L. O. Map, 1909-1921.

In T. 7 N., R. 1 W. P. O. address for Castle Creek Hot springs. P. O. established as Hot springs, April 22, 1890, Minnie Grove, P. M.

Hot Springs Creek   Cochise Co.   G. L. O. Map, 1921.

Rises in Winchester or Galiuro mountains, flows southwest, joins San Pedro river near Cascabel in T. 13 S., R. 19 E. The flow from Hooker Hot springs, q.v.

Hot Springs Junction   Maricopa Co.   G. L. O. Map, 1921.

Formerly post office and station on A. T. & S. F. R. R., 11 miles south of Wickenburg. Point of departure by stage for Castle Hot springs. Known now as Morristown P. O. and R. R. station, q.v.

Houck   Apache Co.   U. S. G. S. Map, 1923.

On A. T. & S. F. R. R. Third station west of New Mexico line. After James D. Houck, sheepman, who also ran a trading post here, 1877 to 1885. Later lived at Holbrook. Member of famous Thirteenth "Bloody Thirteenth" legislature from Apache county. Committed suicide at Cave creek, Arizona, March 21, 1921. First called Houcks tank, from the stock watering tank belonging to Houck. Navajos called it "Ma-it-go" "coyote water." Houcks tank P. O. established Dec. 16, 1884, James W. Bennett, P. M. Established as Houck Nov. 23, 1895; discontinued for years, re-opened Dec., 1930, as Houck.

Houdon Mountain   Gila Co.   Map, Tonto N. F., 1926.

In T. 9 N., R. 12 E. Upper Tonto basin. Is really a mesa on south side of Spring creek, 4 miles northwest of Diamond butte. "After Louis Houdon, Swiss prospector, who mined on the creek. He and Bob Sigsbee were killed by Apache Indians at the Bar X near Diamond Butte in July, 1882." Letter, Fred Croxen, Forest Service.

House Mountain   Yavapai Co.   Map, Coconino N. F., 1927.

In T. 16 N., R. 5 E., east of Oak creek. Descriptive name, from its resemblance to a huge house.

House Rock and Spring   Coconino Co.   Map, Kaibab N. F., 1930.

In sec. 3, T. 39 N., R. 3 E. East of Kaibab N. F. "About sunset we passed two large boulders which had fallen together forming a shelter under which Riggs or some one else had slept. They had printed above it with charcoal the words 'Rock House Hotel.' Afterwards Jacob Hamblin and others referred to it as 'House Rock' or 'House Rock valley.' So we called it by that name. A few yards away at the head of a gulch was a fine spring." Dellenbaugh, 1871.

Practically all Arizona maps have this place located wrong by confusing it with what is known as the "Rock House" a large stone building, the headquarters of an early day cattle company which stands on the main highway where it turns westward and up onto the Kaibab plateau. The original "House Rock" of Powells party is six or seven miles farther up the valley to the north and near the well known "House Rock Spring," mentioned by Dellenbaugh.

House Rock Valley and Canyon   Coconino Co.
     Map, Kaibab N. F., 1927.

Heads a few miles south of the northeast corner of the Kaibab N. F., extends southeast to Colorado river. Large open valley on east side Kaibab plateau, west of Vermillion cliffs.

Houston Mesa　　　Gila Co.

In upper Tonto basin, rocky juniper-covered mesa, 6 miles northeast of Payson. Named after Houston family, early settlers, who grazed cattle near here in the Eighties. They were great people for racing horses.

Houston Pocket　　　Gila Co.

In T. 10 N., R. 11 E. On upper Tonto basin, about 6 miles south of Starr valley. "Well grassed range surrounded by rocky ridges. The Houstons used it for their winter horses range." Letter, Fred Croxen.

Howard Hill　　　Coconino Co.　　　Map, Tusayan N. F., 1927.

In T. 28 N., R. 1 E., west side of Grand Canyon R. R. about 6 miles south of Anita. After Charles Howard. See Howard lake.

Howard Lake　　　Coconino Co.　　　Map, Tusayan N. F., 1927.

In sec. 34, T. 25 N., R. 1 E. about 10 miles east of Quivero (sic) station, Grand Canyon R. R. Named for Chas. E. Howard, stockman, who lived at Ash Fork, grazing cattle and sheep in this vicinity for many years.

Howard Mountain　　　Coconino Co.　　　Map, Coconino N. F., 1928.

Peak at corner of T. 19 N., R. 7 E. After Chas. E. Howard.

Howell　　　Navajo Co.　　　U. S. G. S. Map, 1923.

In T. 29 N., R. 14 E. Mesa in Hopi Ind. Res. on Moenkopi plateau; sometimes called Cedar mesa. Named for E. E. Howell, geologist with Wheeler survey party.

Howells　　　Yavapai Co.　　　G. L. O. Map, 1892.

In T. 13 N., R. 1 W. about 12 miles southeast of Prescott, near head of Agua Fria. "A man named Howells built and ran a smelter here for several years. Place named for him." Frank Grubb.

P. O. established Feb. 15, 1883, William Adams, Jr., P. M. Adams and Col. Frank Hatch organized the Petrified Wood or Chalcedony Co. near Holbrook about 1884.

Howlands Butte　　　Coconino Co.

Grand Canyon N. P. On lower wall of canyon about 3 miles northeast of Newton butte. Near lat. 36° 5' N., long. 112° 1' W. Named for Seneca and W. R. Howland, brothers, members of first Powell party, 1869. With Wm. H. Dunn they left the party below mouth of Cataract, now Havasu creek. All three were murdered by Shivwitz Indians shortly afterward. Decision U.S.G.B.

Huababi　　　Santa Cruz Co.

"Early day ranch on upper Santa Cruz. In April, 1866, Apaches attacked the place killing several persons. Rafael Saavedra, a Mexican, was shot when he ran from the house to save a woman the Indians were killing." Statement by Charles Shibell, Nov. 8, 1888. Meaning unknown.

Huachuca, Fort　　　Cochise Co.　　　U. S. G. S. Map, 1923.

Military post 12 miles from Mexican line, at northern end of Huachuca mountains. "First occupied by U. S. Troops March 3, 1877." Heitman *List*. Gen. Leonard Wood came to this post in 1877, a young army surgeon, his first station. P. O. established as Camp Huachuca Nov. 21, 1879, Fred L. Austin, P. M.

Huachuca Mountains Cochise Co. U. S. G. S. Map, 1923.

On Coronado N. F., in southwest corner of Cochise county at Mexican line. Short range, heavily timbered. Chiricahua-Apache word meaning "thunder." Mowry spells this "Wa-chuka" in his book. An unsigned manuscript in Arizona Pioneers Historical Society, Tucson, gives it "Indian for Gum mountains."

Huachuca Peak Cochise Co. G. L. O. Map, 1923.

Elevation 8,406 feet. In north part of T. 23 S., R. 19 E. In Huachuca mountains on Huachuca Mil. Res.

Hualpai Mohave Co. U. S. G. S. Map, 1923.

Station on A. T. & S. F. R. R. 15 miles east of Kingman. So called for Hualpai Indians.

Hualpai, Camp Mohave Co. Smith Map, 1879; Eckhoff, 1880.

Upper end Santa Maria mountains in what Whipple called "Aztec Pass." On Prescott-Fort Mohave road. Established, 1869, as Camp Tollgate, on Walnut creek. "There was a piece of road along here for which a small toll was charged by the man who did some work improving it. He collected at this gate." Hinton. Rand-McNally map, 1877, shows it as "Defiance." The notation on this map says, "Defiance was the first name of the camp." Heitman *List* says: "On Mohave creek, east of Aztec pass. Established May 9, 1869, as Camp Tollgate; changed to Hualpai Aug. 1, 1870, abandoned Aug. 21, 1870." P. O. established Jan. 13, 1873, Dewitt P. Foster, P. M.

Hualpai Ind. Res. Coconino and Mohave Cos.

Strip about 20 miles wide on south side of Colorado River canyon set aside by executive order for Hualpais in Jan., 1883. Spelled in various ways. Official legal form in Federal Appropriation bills is Hualapai. Hodge says Walapai. Several writers, James, and others, say Hualpai. Decision U.S.G.B., Hualpai.

Hualpai Indians

"Pine tree folk." Undoubtedly because much of their reservation in Mohave and Coconino counties is covered with a fine growth of yellow pine. They are of the Yuman tribe and originally lived along the Colorado below Fort Mohave.

Hualpai Mountains Mohave Co. U. S. G. S. Map, 1923.

In Ts. 16-20 N., Rs. 15-16 W., southeast of Kingman, east side of A. T. & S. F. R. R. After Hualpai tribe.

Hualpai, Old Fort Yavapai Co. Smith Map, 1879; Eckhoff, 1880.

Hinton, 1877, lists this as "a stage station on the road to Prescott; an excellent road; water plentiful but no wood." P. O. established as Hualpai Nov. 28, 1882, Charles A. Behn, P. M. See Juniper.

Hualpai Peak Mohave Co. G. L. O. Map, 1921.

Elevation 8,268 feet in T. 20 N., R. 15 W., northeast part of Hualpai mountains. After Hualpai Indians.

Hualpai Valley Mohave Co.

Northern part of county, east of Cerbat range. Drained by Truxton wash.

"So called for local Indians. Noted for the canaigre plant which grows luxuriantly all over valley." McFarland, *History of Arizona*.

Hualpai Wash   Mohave Co.   U. S. G. S. Map, 1923.

Rises in T. 28 N., R. 17 W., enters Colorado river near Scanlon ferry.

Hubbard   Graham Co.   G. L. O. Map, 1921.

In sec. 23, T. 6 S., R. 25 E. Early settlement on east side of Gila 4 miles north of Thatcher. Named for Elisha F. Hubbard, Sr. P. O. established June 13, 1902, John Hancock, P. M.

Hubbell Butte   Coconino Co.

Grand Canyon N. P. On west wall near northeast corner of park. Named for J. Lorenzo Hubbell, who settled on Navajo Res. 1871. He was a pioneer Navajo trader, county sheriff and a member of the Seventeenth Territorial and First State Senates. Defeated for U. S. Senate by Mark Smith, 1914. Named by the author. Mr. Hubbell was born at Pajarito, N. M., in Nov., 1853, died at Ganado, Nov. 11, 1930, aged 77. Was buried on a hill near his store where more than 20 years before his friend Chief Many Horses of the Navajos was buried with the understanding between them that Hubbell would be buried by his side. His paternal forebears were of eastern birth. See Ganado. Decision U.S.G.B.

Hudson   Maricopa Co.   G. L. O. Map, 1892.

Stage station in T. 7 N., R. 2 E. West side of Agua Fria about 15 miles above Gillett station. P. O. authorized April 23, 1891, Henry C. Hodges, P. M. He failed to qualify; office not opened.

Huerfano   Pima Co.   Map, Coronado N. F., 1927.

Sp., "orphan." In sec. 8, T. 18 S., R. 15 E. On Santa Rita Range reserve. Lone peak about 3 miles directly west of Helvetia. "This butte stands on the plain solitary and alone. Hence its name."

Huethawali Mountain   Coconino Co.

Elevation 6,280 feet. Grand Canyon N. P. Huethawali is the Indian name for Observation point. Decision U.S.G.B.

Hughes, Mount   Santa Cruz Co.   U. S. G. S. Patagonia Quad., 1905.

In T. 21 S., R. 16 E. In Canelo hills about 2 miles east of Sonoita creek. After Samuel C. Hughes of Tucson. See McLaughlin Peak.

Huggins Peak   Gila Co.   Map, Crook N. F., 1926.

In sec. 19, T. 4 S., R. 18 E. "Huggins peak is about 3 miles from my old ranch on Deer creek. We first called it Quartzite peak until about 1910 when Albert Crockett began to call it Huggins peak for a peak by that name in New Mexico. When the government surveyors were surveying in 1915, I gave them this name and some others which all went down on the maps they made." Letter, Bud Ming, Ray.

Humboldt   Yavapai Co.   U. S. G. S. Map, 1923.

In T. 13 N., R. 1 E. Well known mining and smelter camp. Named for Baron Alexander von Humboldt. Southwest of Prescott on Crown King branch of A. T. & S. F. R. R. First called Val Verde. P. O. established Aug. 18, 1905, William F. Buckingham, P. M.

Humboldt Mountain   Maricopa Co.   G. L. O. Map, 1921;
U. S. G. S., 1923.

In sec. 1, T. 7 N., R. 5 E. "This is known as Mount Buford by all old timers." Letter, Joe Hand, Forest Ranger. See Buford. Old Base map, undated, Tonto N. F., shows it as "Humboldt."

Humbug Creek   Yavapai Co.

In T. 8 N., R. 1 W., Prescott N. F. Near Wasson peak. About 2 miles southwest of Crown King. Flows southeast entering Agua Fria in T. 6 N., R. 1 E.

"About 1879 presence of placer gold was reported causing more or less of a gold rush. No gold was found and name 'Damn Humbug Creek' resulted; later shortened to Humbug. There is quite a lot of pyrites of iron or 'fool's gold' to be found there, which probably was the cause of placer being reported." Letter, Frank Grubb, Forest Supervisor.

Humming Bird Spring and Mine   Yuma Co.

"Furnished water for nearby Humming Bird mine. Belongs to E. R. Cartwright." *Routes to the Desert.*

Humphreys Peak   Coconino Co.   Smith Map, 1879;
Coronado N. F., 1928.

Elevation 12,611 feet. The highest peak in Arizona. In sec. 29, T. 23 N., R. 7 E. About 10 miles north of Flagstaff. Named in 1870 for Gen. A. A. Humphreys, Chief of Engineers, U. S. A. by Wheeler. On some maps as San Francisco peak, which was an early decision of U.S.G.B.

Hundred and Fifty Mile Canyon   Mohave Co.
Map, Grand Canyon N. P., 1923.

Stream and canyon on north side of Colorado; enter river at "Upset" rapids near lat. 36° 21' N., long. 112° 41' W. So named by Powell because that distance from their starting point.

Hunt   Apache Co.   G. L. O. Map, 1921.

Settlement on Little Colorado at mouth of Concho creek. After Col. James C. Hunt, retired army officer, who served at Camp Apache, 1872. He resigned June 20, 1872, went first to St. Johns, but located here and called it Hunt.

First Mormon settler was Thomas L. Greer, 1879. The old Greer ranch still stands about a mile east of present post office. Later it became known as Greer valley.

According to another authority it was named for Capt. Jefferson Hunt of Mormon Battalion; an admitted error.

In Nov., 1930, the author was given the following information by Mrs. Amelia Garcia of St. Johns, daughter of Col. Hunt: "Col. James Clark Hunt was born in New Jersey, July 21, 1836. Served as 1st Lt., 1st New Jersey Cavalry Aug. 15, 1861, to March 22, 1862. Appointed 2nd Lt., 1st U. S. Cavalry, Feb. 19, 1862, 1st Lt., July 17, 1862, and captain June 28, 1864. Commanding Co. M, 1st Cavalry, Comdg. officer at Fort Apache, Arizona, at time of resignation June 20th, 1872.

Brevetted Captain, May 6, 1864, for gallant and meritorious service at Battle of Todd's Tavern, Virginia; Brevetted Major, April 1, 1865, for gallant and meritorious service at Five Forks, Virginia; brevetted Lt. Colonel, January 29, 1867, for gallantry in an engagement with a band of Indians at Steens Mountain, Oregon, January 29, 1867. Wounded at Gettysburg. Regimental

comrade and friend of Gov. Brodie of Arizona. Asst. Engineer under Brodie in building Walnut Grove Dam. Died at Damsite and was buried there Mar. 29, 1890."
P. O. established July 12, 1902, John H. Greer, P. M.

Hunts Canyon   Cochise Co.   Map, Coronado N. F., 1925.

In T. 20 S., R. 29 E., Coronado N. F., in Pedrogosa mountains. Short canyon rising under Limestone peak, runs southwest into Sulphur Springs valley, east side of Swisshelm mountains. After Zwing Hunt, killed here by Apaches about 1880. "He was buried at the foot of a juniper tree and they cut his name on the trunk and the date of his death. The tree still stands, the epitaph still decipherable. Canyon known ever since as Hunts canyon." *Tombstone.*

Huron   Yavapai Co.   U. S. G. S. Map, 1923.

In T. 13 S., R. 1 E. Station on Prescott-Middelton branch A. T. & S. F. R. R., 27 miles southeast of Prescott. After Huron mine of the Sixties. P. O. established Aug. 27, 1901, Harvey M. Stamp, P. M.

Hurricane Cliff or Ledge   Mohave Co.   U. S. G. S. Map, 1923.

Western portion Uinkaret plateau, north of Colorado river. Southern end is in Uinkaret mountains.
Powell says: "It is over 2,000 feet high. It is related that a regular hurricane overtook a party of Mormon officials while exploring a route for a wagon road up the gulch. Hence its name, 'Hurricane Ledge.' "

Hurricane Creek   U. S. G. S. Map, 1923.

Apache Ind. Res. rises south slope of Baldy; flows southwest into Bonita creek. So called because as early as 1880, pine timber on both sides of this creek had been blown down by a tornado or hurricane.

Hutch Mountain   Coconino Co.   Map, Coconino N. F., 1928.

In sec. 36, T. 17 N., R. 9 E. About 8 miles south of Mormon lake. After Hutchinson, well known sheepman, generally called "Hutch."

Huttman Well   Yuma Co.

In sec. 18, T. 7 N., R. 9 W. "Watering place belonging to Hugo Huttman." *Routes to the Desert.*

Hutton Butte   Coconino Co.

Grand Canyon N. P. 5 miles southeast of Point Imperial. Near lat. 36° 14' N., long. 111° 54' W., northeast corner of park. Named for Oscar Hutton who, according to Farish; "has the reputation of having personally killed more Indians than any other man in Arizona." See Hutton peak. Decision U.S.G.B. Named by Frank Bond.

Hutton Peak   Gila Co.   Smith Map, 1879; Crook N. F., 1920-1926.

Elevation 5,608 feet. In T. 1 S., R. 13 E., about 12 miles southwest of Globe. After Oscar Hutton, packer and guide at Old Camp Grant, 1870.
Bourke says: "Oscar Hutton was one of the post guides at Camp Grant. A very good man. He had six toes on each foot. He died from the kick of a mule which crushed in the whole side of his face."

He was the Lieut. Hutton of Co. F, Arizona Volunteers, 1865-66. They were all Arizona Indians except the officers and did fine service against hostile Indians at Camp Verde (Lincoln) and Fort McDowell. See McClintock and Farish.

Tucson Citizen, Nov. 10, 1873, contains a notice of Hutton's death at that place, Nov. 1, 1873.

Hyder   Maricopa Co.   R. R. Folders

Station on Phoenix-Wellton branch S. P. R. R. about 78 miles west of Phoenix. Established 1927. Station nearest Agua Caliente Hot springs. "An Egyptian derivative meaning 'warm springs,' for the adjacent Agua Caliente springs." Letter, Agent, S. P. R. R. Co., Tucson.

Ibex Peak   Yuma Co.   U. S. G. S. Map, 1923.

Elevation 2,125 feet. East side Plumoso range, near long. 114. Origin unknown.

Iceberg Canyon   Mohave Co.   U. S. G. S. Map, 1923.

Colorado canyon from Greggs ferry to mouth of Grand Wash. "Passing through a small, unnamed canyon, we applied this term 'Iceberg' to it on account of the contour of its northern walls." *Wheeler's Report,* 1871.

Ice Caves   Coconino Co.   Map, Coconino N. F., 1927.

In T. 23 N., R. 8 E. About 10 miles from Flagstaff. Remarkable caves which, a few feet below the surface, are filled with ice the year round. In early days, 1880-1890, ice from them was used in the saloons and elsewhere in Flagstaff. East side of San Francisco mountains.

Ice House Canyon   Gila Co.

Northwest slope of Pinal peak. Extends northeast and enters Pinal creek about a mile south of Globe.

"Years before any artificial ice was made in Globe, some shallow cement ponds were built at the head of the canyon. These were filled with water and when ice froze it was cut and stored in an ice house near the ponds. At the Pinal ranger station we still have one of the old plows used to cut the ice." Letter, C. V. Christensen, Globe.

Ilges Camp   Yavapai Co.

Early army camp which Heitman's *Register* locates as "on the Verde." Named undoubtedly for Colonel or Major Guido Ilges, U. S. Army officer who served with distinction in Arizona in the early Seventies.

Independence, Camp.

See Fort Yuma.

Independence Rock

See Painted rock.

Indian Garden   Coconino Co.

Camping place for tourists on the trail into the Grand Canyon, below El Tovar.

"About eleven o'clock today, we discovered an Indian garden just where a little stream with a narrow flood plain comes down through a side canyon. The Indians have planted corn, and squashes, using water from springs for irrigating. The corn is not ready to eat but we carried a dozen squashes to our boat. Never was fruit so sweet as those stolen squashes." Powell, Aug. 16, 1869. He was then about 35 miles below the mouth of the Little Colorado.

Indian Gardens   Gila Co.   Map, Tonto N. F., 1927.

In sec. 5, T. 11 N., R. 12 E. Small valley about 4 miles southeast of Promontory butte. "Here the Apaches formerly farmed, raising corn, pumpkins, beans, etc. Forest ranger station here is called Indian Garden Ranger Station." Letter, Fred Croxen, Forest Service.

Indian Hot Springs   Graham Co.   Map, Crook N. F., 1931.

In sec. 16, T. 5 S., R. 24 E. Series of hot springs in Gila valley, north side of Gila river, opposite Fort Thomas. A popular health resort.

Indian Oasis   Pima Co.

P. O. established under this name Aug. 11, 1909. Joseph Menager, P. M. Name changed to Sells Dec. 14, 1918. See Sells.

Indian Springs   Cochise Co.   U. S. G. S. Map, 1923.

In T. 12 S., R. 32 E. In Peloncillo mountains at head of Indian Springs canyon.

Indian Wells   Navajo Co.   G. L. O. Map, 1921.

In T. 23 N., R. 21 E. P. O., and watering place. Well dug by Navajos for camping purposes on Keam Canyon road forty miles north of Holbrook. P. O. established April 1, 1910. Hubert Richardson, P. M.

Ingalls Lagoon   Yuma Co.   U. S. G. S. Map, 1923.

In T. 9 S., R. 24 W. Overflow lake about 8 miles south of Yuma. After Capt. Frank Ingalls, Surveyor General of Territory, 1903, pioneer resident of Yuma county.

Ingleside   Maricopa Co.   Scott Map, Maricopa Co.

Elevation 1,300 feet. About 6 miles northeast of Phoenix, near Camelback. An early settlement by William J. Murphy, who about 1884-85, set out olive and orange trees, one of the first large plantings in Arizona. Later on, he built a winter resort hotel here. "Just a fanciful and somewhat poetic name invented by Mr. Murphy."

Initial Point   Maricopa Co.

Surveyors' monument built by Mexican Boundary commission in 1851 to mark the beginning of all government surveys in Arizona. Located at the confluence of Salt and Gila rivers. "This monument is a substantial structure of stone about 8 feet high. Is on the summit of a hill about 150 feet high, on south side of Gila and opposite mouth of Salt. In lat. 33° 22' 57", long. 120° 18' 24". *U. S. Government Report.*

Inscription House Ruin   Coconino Co.   G. L. O. Map, 1921.

On Navajo Ind. Res. Part of Navajo National monument. At head of Navajo creek near Navajo county line.

An old, well preserved, Pre-Columbian ruin in the Nitsie canyon. On the mud wall some venturesome traveler carved an inscription which reads, "S-hapiero Ano Domo 1661." Its author and meaning have as yet not been determined. From this the ruin takes its name.

Inspiration   Gila Co.   Map, Crook N. F., 1927.

In T. 1 N., R. 15 E. Mining town and important copper camp about 3 miles west of Globe. "At one time the owners, being in hard straits for money, had the 'inspiration' to borrow money from a bank. Being successful they called the mine 'Inspiration,' after the thought."

Inspiration Point   Gila Co.   Map, Tonto N. F., 1927

West side of Roosevelt lake at north end of dam. From the hotel here one gets the finest view in this vicinity.

Irene   Pima Co.

Flag station on S. P. R. R. about 21 miles east of Tucson. Origin not known.

Iretebas   Mohave Co.

Name of Mohave sub-chief who guided Whipple through the Mohave country. He made a memorable trip to Washington, 1863. Whipple named a canyon in Mohave county for him but it is not marked on any map. Ives gave his name to a mountain in the Mohave valley but did not map it. See Ives' report for its picture. The chief died at Fort Mohave, 1874.

Iron Butte   Cochise Co.

See Orange butte.

Iron King   Yavapai Co.

After a mine here by that name. P. O. established June 11, 1907, Alfred W. Glenn, P. M. Place first called Blanchard, q.v.

Iron Mountain   Pinal Co.   G. L. O. Map, 1921; Tonto N. F., 1927.

Elevation 6,020 feet. In T. 1 N., R. 11 E. On boundary between Crook and Tonto national forests. In extreme northeast corner of Pinal county.

Iron Spring   Navajo Co.   G. L. O. Map, 1921.

Sitgreaves N. F. At head Black canyon about 2 miles above old settlement of Wilford. Water strongly impregnated with iron. First located and named by Will C. Barnes, 1887, as ranch headquarters.

Iron Springs   Yavapai Co.   G. L. O. Map, 1921; Prescott N. F., 1926.

Station and summer resort on A. T. & S. F. R. R. Old time station on Prescott-Wickenburg stage line. Six miles southwest of Prescott. When it was a stage station, they said the water contained considerable iron, hence the name. About 1890 some Phoenix residents organized a "summer outing club" and built a number of cottages here. They had the water analyzed, but found no iron in it. Investigation however, did develop the fact that the sands about the spring were full of iron. This gave the name to the springs. P. O. established June 22, 1900, Elmer Hawley, P. M.

Isaacson   Santa Cruz Co.

P. O. established here May 31, 1882, under this name; Jacob Isaacson, P. M., had a store here. Site was near present Nogales. Isaacson wanted to keep the name for the new town but the new residents objected.

This may have been the same place later called Isaactown, after Hon. Isaac N. Town, q.v.

Isaactown   Santa Cruz Co.

Also called Line City because located on International line. So called after Hon. Isaac N. Town who managed a cattle company here which owned the Calabasas Land Grant on the line. Was a member of first Cattle Sanitary Board of Arizona, 1888.

Fish says in his ms.: "This place was named for two brothers named Isaacson who had a small store here in very early days." I am inclined to feel that Fish mixed this place and another early settlement named Isaacson in the immediate vicinity. He says: "Isaacson was named later Nogales." This seems to have been one of those interesting and often perplexing co-incidents that occasionally happen. There were undoubtedly two men concerned. One Isaacson, the other Isaac N. Town. Both locally well known and both eligible to have a town named for them. The author's opinion is that there were two small settlements by these two names, i.e. Isaacson and Isaacton or Isaactown. Both of them, however, disappeared when the railroad came along, in favor of Nogales, which was the old Mexican name for the point on the International line where the canyon crossed it. See Nogales and Isaacson.

Island Mesa   Yavapai Co.   G. L. O. Map, 1920.

In T. 18 N., R. 4 E. In Coconino county. "On east side of Sycamore creek which flows on both sides of it, hence the name." Letter, Ed Miller, Flagstaff.

Ivalon   Yuma Co.   G. L. O. Map, 1921; U. S. G. S., 1923.

Station on S. P. R. R., 7 miles east of Yuma. "Ivalon was just a name. The switch is now called East Yard." Letter, Paul Shoup.

Ivanpah (sic) Spring (Ivanpatch)   Mohave Co.

At head of Andrus canyon into which it flows. About 20 miles west of Dixie N. F. "Known as 'Ivanpatch spring' and called so by all the natives. An old Indian pronounced it for me but it was little different from the way we use it. It is a Piute word meaning 'a small spring coming out from a white saline soil, with grass growing all round the place.' This description fits the location very nicely." Letter, Orange A. Olsen, Forest Ranger.

Ives Peak   Yavapai Co.   U. S. G. S. Map, 1923.

Elevation 3,856 feet. In T. 11 N., R. 9 W. East side of Santa Maria river. Named for Hon. Eugene S. Ives, who owned several mines in Yuma county, including the King of Arizona (Kofa). He was State senator and quite a politician. Some claim it was named after Lieut. Ives, but there seems to be no good foundation for the idea.

Ives Mesa   Navajo Co.   G. L. O. Map, 1921; U. S. G. S., 1923.

In Ts. 20, 21 N., R. 18 E. On Cottonwood wash at southwest corner of Navajo Ind. Res. Named after Lieut. Ives who was here in May, 1858.

Jackrabbit Well   Pima Co.   Lumholtz Map, 1916; U.S.G.S., 1923.

In T. 9 S., R. 5 E. Papago Ind. Res. West of Sawtooth mountains. After nearby Jackrabbit mine. On West slope of Black range about 40 miles northwest of Silver Bell mine, south of Casa Grande station on S. P. R. R.

Jacks Canyon Coconino Co. G. L. O. Map, 1902-21; U. S. G. S., 1923.

Rises in T. 14 N., R. 10 E. Flows northeast entering Clear creek in T. 18 N. R. 16 E. Upper end is known as Sunset canyon. Lower 5 miles is generally called Salt creek from its strong saline character. Mrs. W. S. Bennett of Winslow states that "From 1879 through 1881 there lived on what is now known as Jacks canyon a certain Jack DeSchradt or Dischrat; locally 'Jack Dishrag.' He built the cabin in Jacks canyon which was named for him." Where this Jacks canyon breaks through the mesa it forms the Sunset pass, q.v.

Jacks Canyon Yavapai Co.

Short canyon rising in north end of Munds mountain; runs southwest into Dry Beaver creek. "Canyon first known as Jacks trail, then Jacks canyon. Trail from Jacks ranch to Big park was built by C. M. (Jack) Montgomery, Al Doyle, and John Marshall between 1882-84. The present Clay park was named for J. W. Clay and is where Jacks ranch was formerly located." Letter, Ed. Miller, Forest Service.

Jacks Mountain Gila Co. Map, Tonto N. F., 1926.

In sec. 23, T. 6 N., R. 13 E. Near head of Reynolds creek. "Bill Lewis had a mule he called 'Jack' which often ran away and was always found on top of this mountain. So he called it Jacks mountain after the mule." Letter, Fred Croxen.

Jackson Butte Gila Co. Map, Crook N. F., 1926.

In T. 3 N., Rs. 16, 17 E. On north end of Seven Mile mountain, about 15 miles north of McMillenville. "A stockman named William Jackson had a ranch at this butte which was given his name." Letter, Frank Nunekley, Chrysolite.

Jackson Butte Maricopa Co. U. S. G. S. Map, 1923.

Elevation 1,266 feet. In T. 2 S., R. 3 E. South of Salt river, on Gila River Ind. Res. Origin unknown.

Jackson Mountain Graham Co. G. L. O. Map, 1921; Crook N. F., 1926.

In sec. 7 T. 6 S., R. 22 E. "Named after Bill Jackson, who, about 1900, had a ranch and ran a bunch of cattle near its base." Letter, C. E. Moore, Forest Ranger. Jackson was wagon boss and range foreman for the "Hashknife Outfit," Aztec L and Cattle Co., at Holbrook, 1890 to 1895. Butte in Gila county was also named for him.

Jacksonville Maricopa Co.

Early Mormon settlement. Now called Nephi, q.v.

Jacobs Pools Coconino Co.

In approximately T. 38 N., R. 5 E. North of Grand Canyon, near Vermillion cliffs, in House Rock valley. "Named after Jacob Hamlin, noted missionary and guide. He found good water here by digging, and was the first white man to camp here." Dellenbaugh.

Jacobs Lake Coconino Co. Map, Kaibab N. F., 1926.

In T. 38 N., R. 4 W. Flood-water lake in Kaibab Forest which seldom goes dry although kept full only by snow and rain waters. Well known stock-watering place. A sawmill was located here for several years in early Eighties. After Jacob Hamlin.

Jacob's Well   Apache Co.

Mentioned by Domenech in 1860, who wrote "It is called by the Navajos 'Ouah-nok-ai-tin-naie,' or 'Ouah-nok-aitin,' meaning 'Blessing of the Desert.'" Mentioned by Whipple, 1850. It is a crater about 300 feet across and 100 feet deep. There is always water in it from the floodwaters although there may be some under ground supply. Notable camping place for travelers on the east-west road across the territory. Also valuable water supply for cattle using adjacent ranges.

Beale camped here September, 1857. He says: "It is a hole 125 feet deep surrounded by a perfectly level plain. If you did not know its location you might easily pass it at a distance of a quarter of a mile. Its circumference I measured at about 650 feet."

About 4 miles south of Navajo springs where the Goodwin party camped and proclaimed the establishment of the Territory, Dec. 29, 1863.

Jadito Wash, Springs and Station   Navajo Co.
G. L. O. Map, 1921; U. S. G. S., 1923.

"Jadi" is the Navajo word for Antelope, "to," water. Navajo word meaning "Antelope spring," or "water." Wash heads about 12 miles east of Keam canyon on Navajo Ind. Res. Flows southwest, joins Corn creek in T. 23 N., R. 15 E. Water eventually reaches Little Colorado about 6 miles east of Leupp, in T. 27 N., R. 20 E. P. O. established Feb. 16, 1921, Alma G. Roberts, P. M.

James Canyon   Yavapai Co.   Map, Coconino N. F., 1927.

"After Bill James, (Old Man James) who settled here in 1876." Letter, Ed. Miller, Flagstaff.

Jaques Mountain   Navajo Co.   Map, Apache N. F., 1926.

In sec. 24, T. 10 N., R. 23 E. On Sitgreaves N. F. Isolated butte named for Sanford Jaques, sheepman and early settler of this region. His home ranch was above Showlow town.

Jarvis Pass

See Chavez.

Jaycox Mountain   Coconino Co.   Map, Coconino N. F., 1928.

In sec. 19. T. 17 N., R. 11 E. Isolated butte on north side of Canyon Diablo. See Jaycox tank.

Jaycox Tank   Coconino Co.   Smith Map, 1879; G. L. O., 1921.

On Coconino N. F., east of Stonemans lake, on road to Chaves pass. After Henry Jaycox who camped here as early as 1860. "Our stock of provisions was running low. I started a pack train for the Pimo (sic) villages, consisting of 23 men under the command of Henry Jaycox." *Report King Woolsey,* June, 1864.

Jaynes   Pima Co.   G. L. O. Map, 1921.

Station S. P. R. R. established about 1890, some 8 miles northwest of Tucson. "After Allen B. Jaynes, local railroad man and official." Letter, Supt., S. P. R. R., Tucson. P. O. established July 21, 1922. Herbert E. Hunts, P. M.

Jeffords Point   Coconino Co.

Huge projection on west wall of Grand Canyon at lat. 36° 13' N. long. 111° 54' W. At northeast corner Grand Canyon N. P. "Named for Thomas J. Jeffords, pioneer, government scout, Indian trader, miner, etc. He was a personal friend of Cochise, noted Apache. Spoke the Apache language fluently. In 1870, he took Gen. O. O. Howard to Cochise's camp in the 'Stronghold' where peace was made and a reservation created for these Indians. Jeffords was made Indian agent much against his wishes. Cochise died, but during four years of Jefford's control, the peace was not broken by the Chiricahuas. Jeffords died at Tucson, 1914, 82 years old." Farish. Named by Frank Bond.

Jerked Beef Butte   Gila Co.   Map, Tonto N. F., 1927, Jerkey Butte; Eckhoff Map, 1880, Jerked Beef Butte.

In T. 8 N., R. 13 E. At lower end of Pleasant valley, in Sierra Ancha mountains. "Raiding Apaches once ran off every head of oxen owned by Tully and Ochoa of Tucson. They never stopped till they crossed Salt river. Then they killed and jerked the meat on the slope of the high mesa, which is today called 'Jerked Beef Butte.'" Bourke.

Jerome   Yavapai Co.   U. S. G. S. Map, 1926.

Elevation 5,435 feet. On Prescott N. F. "After Eugene Jerome, New York attorney, one of the organizers of the United Verde Copper Co., 1883." Letter, Robert E. Talley, Jerome. Headquarters for Senator Clark's well known United Verde mine on Verde Tunnel and Smelter R. R. Smelters were located here first but removed to Clarkdale where there was more room. P. O. established Sept. 19, 1883, Frederick Thomas, P. M.

Jerome Junction.

See Chino Valley Post Office.

Jersey   Yavapai Co.   G. L. O. Map, 1919.

On Slate creek about 18 miles south of Prescott. Named for "Jersey Lily" mine which in turn was named after the celebrated English actress. Owner of the mine was a great admirer of her. P. O. established March 6, 1895, William N. Ferguson, P. M.

Jerusalem Peak   Pinal Co.   Map, Crook N. F., 1929.

In sec. 11, T. 4 S., R. 17 E. Three miles south of Gila river. Bud Ming says: "This hill was close to the Apache reservation line. The boys used to hold the extra saddle horses there while we scouted the reserve for stray cattle. They got to calling the trip 'Going to Jerusalem.' This eventually was shortened to Jerusalem." Letter, J. W. Girdner, Forest Ranger.

Ji-qui-bo   Pima Co.

See Peregua.

J. K. Mountain and Spring   Gila Co.   Map, Crook N. F., 1929.

In T. 1 N., R. 13 E. On west side of Pinto creek. "This was so called from the brand on cattle that used this range in the early Nineties." Letter, Dan Williamson, Globe.

Joe Filmers Ranch   Pima Co.

On San Pedro river, 3 miles above old Camp Grant. "Filmer, the post blacksmith, was married to an Apache squaw. He was present at the Caves fight on Salt river." Bourke.

Joe's Hill   Yavapai Co.   Map, Prescott N. F.

In sec. 8, T. 10 N., R. 2 E. On west side of Bumble Bee. Origin unknown.

John Howells Pass   Mohave Co.

See Union pass; Sitgreaves pass.

Johnson   Cochise Co.   U. S. G. S. Map, 1923.

Station and mining camp, on Dragoon branch railroad, east side of Little Dragoon mountains. In T. 15 S., R. 22 E. P. O. established April 5, 1900, William De H. Washington, P. M.

Johnson Creek or Wash   Coconino Co.   U. S. G. S. Map, 1923.

Rises in Utah, flows southwest into Arizona, enters Kanab creek in southeast corner of Kaibab Ind. Res. Called Johnson's run on some maps. "Named for W. D. Johnson of Powell's second party, 1872. He was a photographer with the party for only a few weeks." Dellenbaugh. "Johnson, with his four brothers, first located on this creek in the spring of 1871, about 10 miles northeast of Kanab. The settlement lasted only a few years but the name of the creek and canyon remained." Letter, Church Historian, Salt Lake, 1933.

Johnson Point   Coconino Co.

Altitude 5,100 feet. In Grand Canyon N. P. About 2 miles north of suspension bridge across Colorado river. On west side of Bright Angel creek. Named for Fred. Johnson, park ranger, accidentally drowned, 1929, just below this point in Colorado river in performance of official duty. Decision U.S.G.B., 1933.

Johnson Spring   Mohave Co.   G. L. O. Map, 1892; Camp Mohave Sheet, 1911.

In T. 21 N., R. 17 W. About 5 miles north of Kingman in Cerbat mountains. Coues mentions this spring but there is nothing to indicate for, or by whom, it was named. Most likely for Captain Johnson of the Steamer General Jessup, who, on Jan. 23, 1858, ferried Beale's party across the river at Mohave. Reported to have been named for an old settler and pioneer named J. J. Johnson. This is somewhat doubtful for no definite record can be found of him.

Johns Well   Maricopa Co.   U. S. G. S. Map, 1923.

In T. 1 N., R. 10 W. On east side of Eagle Tail mountains. Unable to learn origin.

Jokake   Maricopa Co.

A winter resort on the desert eleven miles northeast of Phoenix on the southern slope of the Camelback mountain. The group of buildings first erected were of sun dried adobes made right on the site. When finished a Hopi Indian who worked on the job was asked to suggest a name. He said "Jokake"—pro., Jo-Cocky—a Hopi word meaning "mud house."

Jones Peak   Cochise Co.

Altitude 8,415 feet. In T. 19 S., R. 30 E. on Coronado N. F. Named for local man who lost his life in this vicinity while enroute to join a fire-fighting crew on the forest in 1923. Decision U.S.G.B., 1933.

Jones Point   Coconino Co.

Elevation 5,300 feet. In Grand Canyon N. P. about 2 miles north of Suspension bridge, half mile east of Bright Angel creek. "Named for S. V. Jones of Powell's second expedition, 1871-72." Named by Frank Bond. Decision U.S.G.B., 1933.

Jonesville   Maricopa Co.

Mormon settlement first called Utahville. Changed to Fort Utah. Now called Lehi. Jonesville was named after President Daniel W. Jones who was in the original party coming to this place. According to Fish: "Jones was a man of poor judgment, rather hasty in his actions, and always in trouble with the rest of his party. Every one was against him."

Joppa   Navajo Co.   G. L. O. Map, 1921.

In T. 12 N., R. 18 E. about 15 miles east of Heber. Early Mormon settlement. "It was just a Bible name given by Mrs. Flake to this place. It was closed for several years and then opened under name of 'Aripine.'" Letter, John Murray, Snowflake.

Jornado   Yuma Co.

Sp., "journey." This term was applied in early days to the 42-mile ride across the desert between Maricopa wells and Gila Bend. The Spanish used this word to indicate any long journey or route where water was scarce.

Jose Pedro River

See San Pedro river.

Joseph City   Navajo Co.

Settlement on A. T. & S. F. R. R. The first settlement, made about March, 1876, 3 miles farther up the Little Colorado river, was called Allen City or Allens camp. That fall, however, the settlers abandoned Allens, moved down the river 3 or 4 miles, and established a new town which they called St. Joseph after the prophet, Joseph Smith. There was then a weekly mail buckboard service through this place on the Santa Fe—Prescott Star Route line. It was the author's post office address for his cattle ranch at the mouth of Chevelon Fork, from 1883 to 1888.

About 1900, St. Joseph was moved 2 miles southwest and a new town was built. The railroad company changed the station name to Joseph City because of another St. Joseph on their line. Of all the lower Little Colorado settlements this is the only one now in existence. P. O. established as Saint Joseph, Feb. 21, 1878, John McLaws, P. M. On Smith and Eckhoff maps this shows as St. Joe. Also it shows in both locations Arizona and Nevada. A town by this name was first established, 1865, on Muddy river in Pah Ute Co., Arizona, later Nevada. See Overton and St. Thomas.

Josephine Canyon   Pima Co.

On east side of Josephine peak. Canyon heads near Josephine peak but flows southeast into Sonoita creek. 4 miles above Crittenden. There is another creek by this name rising on west side of this peak but flowing southwest into Santa Cruz about a mile south of Tumacacori mission. Both are on the Roskruge map, 1893. This must have been an error of the compiler for according to all authorities the stream by this name flowing southwest is the real Josephine creek, or canyon. Map, Coronado N. F., 1925, shows it on west side of Josephine peak only.

Josephine Peak   Santa Cruz Co.

Elevation 8,435 feet. In T. 20 S., R. 15 E. In Santa Rita mountains about a mile southeast of "Old Baldy," or Mount Wrightson. Mrs. George Kitts says: "It was so named by George Roskruge after Josephine, daughter of a local settler." W. E. Balcom of

Tubac, writes: "Named for Josephine, daughter of Tom Gardiner. Balcom and Gardiner were partners in a mining venture near this peak." Others claim it was for Josephine Pennington of that early family. On Smith map, 1879, and Eckhoff, 1880, it shows as "Pichaco del Diablo." On Coronado N. F. map, 1921, and G.L.O. map, 1921, as Josephine. Oddly enough it does not show at all on Roskruge map, 1893. See Picacho del Diablo.

Josh, Mount   Yavapai Co.   Map, Prescott N. F., 1929.

In sec. 17, T. 15 N., R. 4 W. "Named after Joshua Draper, whose sons, Edward and Clint, between 1870 and 1880, located on the D1 (D One) ranch about a mile southwest of this mountain." Letter, Frank Grubb, Prescott.

Joys Camp   Greenlee Co.

See Morenci.

Joy Valley and Town   Graham Co.   G. L. O. Map, 1921.

In T. 10 S., R. 30 E. In southeast corner of Graham county east of Whitlock hills. After Capt. Joy, early settler and miner. Morenci was first called after him. Valley is a corner of the lower end of Whitlock valley.

July 4th Butte   Maricopa Co.   U. S. G. S. Map, 1923.

In T. 2 S., R. 8 W. At north end of Gila Bend mountains. Also called Fourth of July butte. Near head of wash by same name. "A group of local people held a big picnic here on the 4th of July in the early Nineties." Letter, H. C. Gable, P. M. See Fourth.

Jump up Canyon   Coconino Co.   Map, Kaibab N. F., 1926.

Rises T. 37 N., R. 2 W. flows southwest into Kanab creek in sec. 32, T. 36 N., R. 3 W. Origin unknown.

Junction   Yavapai Co.

Junction point, Jerome narrow gauge road and Ash Fork-Prescott branch. P. O. established as Junction, June 7, 1895, George G. West, P. M. Changed to Jerome Junction, Dec. 23, 1914.

Junction City   Nevada.

In Clarke county, Nevada. The first name of Rioville, q.v. In the old Pah Ute county, later given back to Nevada.

Juniper   Navajo Co.

See Linden.

Juniper   Yavapai Co.   Map, Prescott N. F., 1926;
G. L. O. Map, 1921.

In T. 18 N., R. 5 W. About 6 miles east of Baca grant on Walnut creek, Prescott N. F. East side of Santa Maria mountains. Formerly called "Old Camp Hualpai." "Our next stop was at the Old Camp Hualpai. We drove through groves of oaks, cedars and pines." *Vanished Arizona.* P. O. first named Hualpai, 1873. On Feb. 8, 1883, name was changed to Juniper. See Hualpai, Camp.

Juniper Mesa   Yavapai Co.   Map, Prescott N. F., 1927.

In T. 18 N., R. 6 W. East of Baca grant. Called "Juniper mountain" by local people. Part is shown as Santa Maria range on several maps. Originally the entire range was called Santa

Maria but seems to have been changed "because there were so many juniper trees on its sides, that this name became quite common locally." Origin of name Santa Maria as applied here cannot be traced. See Santa Maria.

Kabito Plateau, Spring and Creek   Coconino Co.
U. S. G. S. Map, 1923.

In Navajo Ind. Res. on east end of Marble canyon near long. 111° 10′ N. "Navajo word meaning 'Willows at a Spring.'" Gregory. Father Haile spells it "Kaibito" (Willow Springs).

Kadmon   Pima Co.   G. L. O. Map, 1909.

In T. 17 S., R. 18 E., about 5 miles east of Pantano. Origin unknown.

Kafa (sic)   Yuma Co.

Station on S. P. R. R., 43 miles east of Yuma. This is an error, should be Kofa, q.v.

Kaibab Forest   Coconino Co.   P. O. Route Map, 1929.

First called Kaibab; changed to "Kaibab Forest" for some unknown reason. Summer post office at Bright Angel point near old Bright Angel Ranger station, Grand Canyon N. P. P. O. established June 6, 1926, Woodruff Rust, P. M.

Kaibab Ind. Res.   Mohave Co.   G. L. O. Map, 1921.

West side of Kanab creek or wash, near lat. 37°, long. 112° 40′ W. Small reservation for remnant of this Pah Ute race.

Kaibab National Forest   Coconino Co.

Originally established Feb. 20, 1893, as Grand Canyon Forest Reserve, North. Name changed to Kaibab National Forest, July 2, 1908. Lower end lying along Grand Canyon and covering some 320,000 acres, formed into Grand Canyon National Park, Feb. 26, 1919. On Feb. 25, 1925, 46,400 acres more were eliminated from forest and added to park area. Kaibab was also designated by act of Congress, as the Grand Canyon Game Preserve, without in any way changing its status as a national forest. Total area of forest in 1931 was 724,137 acres. Supervisor's Headquarters, Kanab, Utah.

Kaibab Plateau   Coconino Co.   G. L. O. Map, 1921.

Large flat-iron shaped mountain or mesa, on north side of Grand Canyon. "So named by Powell after local Indians. Pah Ute word meaning, 'mountain lying down' or 'on the mountain.'" Hodge.

Powell states that: "This is called by the Indians 'Kaibab' or 'the mountain lying down,' so we adopted the name." See Buckskin mountain.

Kaka   Pima Co.   G. L. O. Map, 1921; U. S. G. S., 1923.

In T. 1 S., R. 1 W. Village on Papago Ind. Res. " 'Ka' denotes a clearing for a field. 'Ka-Ka' is the plural. One of the oldest Papago settlements. Probably one of the four original pueblos of Papago traditions." Father Oblasser.

Kana-a Valley and Wash   Coconino Co.

Heads in sec. 24, T. 23 N., R. 8 E. "Runs northeast from base of Sunset crater into Little Colorado river. Named for the Hopi Kachinas of this cult, who are supposed to make their homes in Sunset crater. Valley contains the Kana-a lava flow." Letter, Dr. Harold Colton.

Kanab Creek   Coconino Co.   U. S. G. S. Map, 1921.

Rises in southern Utah above Kanab, flows south into Arizona, enters Colorado river in Grand Canyon. Upper end has many willow trees along its course. "Kanab," a Piute word meaning "willow."

Kangaroo Headland   Coconino Co.

Table land projection into Grand Canyon, near lat. 36° 20′, long. 112° 37′ W. West side upper reach Coconino plateau. Its outline resembles a kangaroo. Named, 1929, by Frank Bond. Decision U. S. G. B.

Karo-mak

See Gray mountain.

Karro   Cochise Co.

Station on S. P. R. R., 12 miles east of Bowie station. "Named after Mr. Carr, grading contractor." Letter, Paul Shoup.

Kaster   Mohave Co.   U. S. G. S. Map, 1923.

Station on A. T. & S. F. R. R. 12 miles south of Kingman. "After Dr. Kaster, Santa Fe surgeon of the Eighties. First called Drake after General Manager Drake. This name, Drake, was transferred to Jerome Junction about 1900." A.G.W.

Katherine   Mohave Co.   P. O. Route Map, 1929.

On east side of Colorado river about 20 miles north of Mohave City. "Given this name from the nearby Katherine mine, immediately west of Secret Pass." P. O. established Dec. 21, 1921, Alva C. Lambert, P. M.

Kayenta   Navajo Co.   G. L. O. Map, 1921.

"Trading post founded by John Wetherill in 1909." Father Haile says this word is "Tye-nde" meaning "at the pits where animals fall in." He thinks Kayenta was derived from this word. This is possible for the Navajos and Zunis had many game pits dug to trap wild animals such as deer, antelope, etc. On Tyende creek in the Navajo Ind. Res. near lat. 36° 45′, long. 110° 15′. P. O. established Mar. 21, 1911, John Wetherill, P. M. Originally called Oljato, q.v. See Tyende.

Keam   Navajo Co.   Gregory Map, 1916; U. S. G. S., 1923.

Canyon and spring on Navajo Ind. Res.; also trading post and headquarters U. S. Indian School. Located 1878 by Thomas Varker Keam. U. S. Government later bought land and improvements and established the school.

Keam was born in Truro, Cornwall, England, in 1843. He was a salt water sailor for some years; landed in San Francisco, Calif., late in 1861.

"January 22, 1862, enlisted as private in Co. C, 1st. Calif. Vol. Infty. Transferred to Co. B, Oct., 1864. Honorably mustered out at expiration of service at Santa Fe, New Mexico, Jan. 22, 1865. Age at enrollment given as 19 years." War Dept. records.

Keam remained free less than a month. The War Dept. records read: "Reenlisted at Ft. Bascom, N. M., Cavalry and Infty., Co. C. Sergeant in First Battalion, N. M. Cavalry and Infty., Col. C. Carson commanding. (This was evidently a temporary organization.) Transferred after six months as Second Lieut., 1st. New Mexico Cavalry, Col. Carson commanding. Mustered out at

Santa Fe, New Mexico, Sept. 29, 1866. Age at enlistment, 22 years."

"In 1877 Thomas V. Keam was employed as Post Interpreter at Fort Wingate, New Mexico, for about a year. Was also Chief Packer at the post and on duty with Indian prisoners at Ojo Caliente, N. M. until Mar. 15, 1878, when he left the army and moved to the Hopi reservation." Letter from Quartermaster General's office, Jan. 5, 1929.

Keam died at Truro, Cornwall, England, Nov. 30, 1904, age 61 years. Cultivated, and refined, Keam was a fine type of English gentleman. His home at the Canyon was open to all on an equal footing; the scientific explorer and wandering Indian shared his generous hospitality alike. According to Gregory, "Keam went into the White Mesa copper district, some 60 miles north of Tuba City, in 1882, with Elias S. Clark of Phoenix. They located a number of copper claims." Clark verified this fact at Phoenix in January, 1931. A letter from Keam to Dr. Washington Matthews dated from Albuquerque, N. M., April 6, 1914, says: "I first went among the Navajos as Spanish interpreter in 1874. Was subsequently appointed special agent for the tribe." P. O. established under name Keams Canon, (sic) March 12, 1882, Alexander M. Steven, P. M. U.S.G.B. Decision, Keam Canyon.

Kelley   Yavapai Co.

P. O. established Nov. 12, 1888, Charles I. Kelley, P. M. Kelley did not qualify and office was not opened. Kelley had a small mine and ranch here.

Kellogg, Mountain   Pima Co.   Map, Coronado N. F., 1927.

In T. 12 S., R. 16 E. Elevation 8,385 feet. On east side of Catalina range. "After Alexander Kellogg, miner and prospector, who had a cabin on this mountain, 1897." Letter, Fred Winn, Tucson.

Kelly   Gila Co.   Smith Map, 1879; Eckhoff, 1880.

In T. 5 N., R. 22 E. Butte on Fort Apache Ind. Res. about 6 miles west of Fort Apache. Nobody could tell the author for whom this was named when he went to Apache in 1880, nor has he succeeded in tracing its origin or meaning.

Kelton   Cochise Co.   U. S. G. S. Map, 1923.

In T. 19 S., R. 25 E. In Sulphur Springs valley, on Arizona-Eastern R. R., 33 miles from Douglas. Named for Capt. C. B. Kelton, sheriff of Cochise county. Established, 1909. Town originally named Tyler after the first settler. P. O. established Feb. 10, 1915, Bailey A. Taylor, P. M.

Kelvin   Pinal Co.   G. L. O. Map, 1921; Tonto N. F., 1926.

In sec. 1, T. 4 S., R. 13 E. Mining camp at junction of Mineral creek and Gila river. On S.P.R.R. Named by mining company after Lord Kelvin of England. When Ray began to develop, the railroad company changed Kelvin to Ray Junction. P. O. is still called Kelvin; established Apr. 25, 1900, Sarah Hockett, P. M. See Ray.

Kendall   Maricopa Co.

Spur on old P. and E. R. R. about 6 miles from Phoenix across the river from Tempe. After Frank Kendall, Treasurer, Phoenix and Maricopa R. R. of early days.

Kendrick Mountains   Yavapai Co., Mallory Map, 1876; G. L. O., 1892.

South side of Kirkland creek, about 25 miles due west of Prescott, east of Santa Maria river. Probably named after Major H. L. Kendrick. See Kendrick peak.

Kendrick Peak   Coconino Co.   G. L. O. Map, 1921; Coconino N. F., 1927.

Elevation 10,418 feet. In sec. 3, T. 23 N., R. 5 E. Named for Major H. L. Kendrick, 2nd U. S. Artillery, who commanded the escort with the Sitgreaves expedition, 1853. Peak named by Whipple the following year. Major Kendrick was commanding officer at Fort Defiance, Arizona, for several years from 1855. He was an uncle of Rev. J. Mills Kendrick, Episcopal bishop for Arizona and New Mexico, 1889-1911.

Kenilworth   Pinal Co.   G. L. O. Map, 1909.

Headquarter ranch of Kenilworth Cattle Co., owned by Hon. Tom Davis, cattleman and politician, about 1889. On Gila river about 7 miles west of Florence. "Davis, an Englishman, named the place for his ancestral home." Letter, Bud Ming, Ray. P. O. established Sept. 20, 1891, Thos. C. Graham, P. M.

Kennard   Cochise Co.   Judge Map.

Station on E. P. & S. W. R. R., 6 miles south of Benson. Origin unknown. Later called Curtis, q.v.

Kentuck   Pinal Co.

Stage station on Butterfield route a few miles east of Tres Alamos road station. "Kentuck" was the nick name for Marcus H. Herring, one of the five first miners in Bisbee, 1879. Station was named after him. Listed as a stage station, 1873, by Hinton. Hamilton says: "Kentuck Edleman, another old 'Kentuck,' was one of the locators of the Copper Queen mine." This must have been Herring, but no one seems able to explain how or where Hamilton discovered the name "Edleman."

Kentuck Mountain   Maricopa Co.   Map, Tonto N. F., 1927.

In sec. 31, T. 7 N., R. 6 E. On east side of Camp creek two miles south of Maverick butte. "Said to have been named after an old pioneer, Jim Kentuck, who ran cattle here in early days." Letter, Joe Hand, Forest Ranger. There is nothing to prove it but it is likely this mountain was named for Marcus Herring, whose nick name was "Kentuck." He lived in many parts of southern and central Arizona. See Kentuck Station.

Kenyon Station   Maricopa Co.   Smith Map, 1879.

South side of Gila river 15 miles west of Gila Bend. "Stage station named after the man who ran it, Henry Kenyon."

Kerlins Wells   Coconino Co.   G. L. O. Map, 1892.

Near Floyds peak. After F. C. Kerlin, clerk for Beale. So named by George Beale. In his report George Beale says: "July 13, 1859. Our newly discovered watering place, is in a deep rocky ravine about 700 yards from our last camp. It has been named Kerlins Wells." George Beale, a brother of Lieut. Beale, was with his party. Coues writes: "I was camped here with an army command in June, 1881. Kerlin's name was then to be seen scratched in the rocks at the spring."

Shows on Smith map, 1879, as Collins Well; unquestionably an error. Should not be confused with Cullens well in Yuma Co., q.v.

Kerrigans Peak   Yuma Co.

See Klara peak.

Keystone   Mohave Co.

Station on Chloride branch A. T. & S. F. R. R., 22 miles north of Kingman. "So named for mine by this name near the station in 1900, when the road was built." Letter, Division Supt. Simpson.

Kibbey Butte   Coconino Co.

In Grand Canyon N. P. near its northeastern corner. Near lat. 36° 15' N., long. 111° 59' W., 2 miles south of Point Imperial. Named for Joseph H. Kibbey, born in Indiana, who came to Arizona in 1887. Appointed member of Arizona Supreme Court, Aug. 5, 1889. Specialized in laws relating to irrigation. Resigned judgeship to accept appointment as governor of Arizona May, 1905. Served until May, 1909. Kibbey originated the plan for formation of the "Salt River Valley Waters Users Association" and carried it successfully through the many intricate points when water rights were in a chaotic condition. Recognized at his death as foremost authority on irrigation law in U. S. Named by the author. Decision U.S.G.B.

Ki-ha-toak

See Gray mountain.

Kilberg Creek   Graham Co.   U. S. G. S. Map, 1923.

In T. 10 S., R. 18 E. Rises north side of Kilberg peak, flows southwest into San Pedro in Pinal county. See Kilberg peak.

Kilberg Peak   Graham Co.   G. L. O. Map, 1921; U. S. G. S., 1923.

In T. 10 S., R. 20 E. Crook N. F. In Galiuro mountains, east side of San Pedro river. "Kilberg peak and canyon were named after a man who prospected in this region many years ago. There are some low grade gold deposits in Kilberg canyon, where the 'Powers Boys' killings' occurred about 12 years ago." Letter, Rex King, Forest Supervisor.

Kim   Yuma Co.

Station on S. P. R. R. about 65 miles east of Yuma. "Somebody evidently admired Kipling's hero." Letter, Division Supt., S. P. R. R.

Kimball Peak (Mount Kimball)   Pima Co.

On southwest slope of Santa Catalinas, about 3 miles southwest of Cathedral rock, Coronado N. F. "So named for Fred E. A. Kimball, 1863-1930. Prominent citizen of Tucson, deeply interested in wild life and conservation. Decision U.S.G.B., 1933.

Kinder Spring   Coconino Co.   U. S. G. S. Map, 1923.

In T. 13 N., R. 10 E. In Long valley. After Runyon C. Kinder, well known sheepman who in latter Eighties, ran sheep near here. Lived for some years at Holbrook, in business as Brown and Kinder, Livery.

King Canyon   Yavapai Co.   Map, Prescott N. F., 1927.

Stream and canyon heading in sec. 30, T. 17 N., R. 1 E. Flows west into Verde river. After King brothers, well known horseraisers in this vicinity, 1898-1910.

King of Arizona Mine   Yuma Co.

See Kofa.

Kingman   Mohave Co.   G. L. O. Map, 1921.

In T. 17 N., R. 21 W. Elevation 3,336 feet. Second county seat of Mohave county, 1880. Mohave City was first. Important mining and business town. After Lewis Kingman, locating engineer, Santa Fe R. R. See also Mohave City, Mineral park and Cerbat, each of which has at some time been the county seat. P. O. established March 22, 1883, Edward F. Thompson, P. M.

Kings Creek   Coconino Co.

"July 14, 1859, we reached Kings creek by way of Bishops cut-off at about seven o'clock. We found no water. The grass was excellent." Beale's Report. This was not far from Kerlins well, q.v.

Kings Ranch   Yavapai Co.   Map, Prescott N. F., 1933.

A noted horse ranch in Upper Chino valley. In T. 18 N., R. 3 W. About 3 miles southeast of Fritsche P. O. Established about 1883 by Thomas R. King of California who later brought his three nephews to Arizona. They succeeded him and took over the ranch and managed it for many years. The uncle, Thomas R. King, died Feb. 2, 1932.

Kinney Mountain   Navajo Co.   Map, Ft. Apache Ind. Res., 1928.

In sec. 23, T. 8 N., R. 23 E., 2 miles west of McNary. So called after J. P. Kinney, forest officer, U. S. Indian Service.

Kinter   Yuma Co.

Station S. P. R. R. about 21 miles east of Yuma.

Kirby   Gila Co.

In sec. 2, T. 3 N., R. 13 E. Tonto N. F. "Town on south side of Roosevelt lake. Land here patented in 1876 as homestead by a man named Kirby. There was a small post office and store before Roosevelt dam was built." Letter, Forest Ranger Sizer. P. O. established as Kirby, Sept. 21, 1914, Amelia Kirby, P. M.

Kirby   Yavapai Co.

Mining camp near Tip Top. P. O. established May 23, 1883, William C. Dawes, P. M. Origin unknown.

Kirkland   Yavapai Co.   U. S. G. S. Map, 1921.

Town, valley and stream, in T. 12 N., R. 4 W. On line of Ash Fork-Phoenix R. R., west part of Yavapai county. After William H. Kirkland, who came to Arizona in 1856. He and his wife are said to have been the first white couple married in Arizona. Marriage took place in Tucson, May 26, 1860. Stage station here was hidden away in a grand grove of cottonwoods. The meals for those times and circumstances, about 1888, were epicurean feasts. P. O. established April 5, 1871, James W. Kelsey, P. M.

Kitchens Ranch   Pima Co.   Smith Map, 1879; Eckhoff, 1880.

Well-known place before 1870. "Short distance below Calabasas, near Fort Mason on Santa Cruz river. He called the ranch 'El Potrero.' Sp., 'pasture ground.' Farmed, raised hogs, corn, cattle, potatoes, etc." Farish. Every old Arizonan will recall the old gag about the man who "got what Pete Kitchen got in Sonora."

"Approaching Kitchens ranch, one finds himself in a fertile valley with a small hillock at one end. Upon the summit of this has been built the house from which no effort of the Apaches has ever yet succeeded in driving our friend. Pete Kitchen has had more battles with the Indians than any other settler in America." Bourke.

"Pete Kitchen was the connecting link in 1854, between savagery and civilization in Arizona. His hacienda was as much of a fort as a ranch house, and was the safest place between Tucson and Magdalena, Sonora." Lockwood's, *Arizona Characters*.

Hinton lists this place as: "On the road from Tucson to Libertad, Mexico. Revanton (Kitchens ranch) is located 24 miles south of Tucson, about 25 miles from the Sonora line." Hinton, undoubtedly has confused it with the Revanton ranch belonging to William Rhodes, which was about 25 miles north of the Sonora line. Kitchen never lived there as far as this investigator has been able to discover. A letter from Gov. Safford, who was there Oct. 11, 1873, says: "Pete Kitchen's ranch is about 4 miles this side of the Sonora line on a small stream they called 'the Potrero.'"

McClintock says: "Pete Kitchen's ranch is now kown as Saxon's Dairy ranch about 5 miles north of Nogales, after its present owner, John Saxon. Kitchen has been well called the "Daniel Boone of Arizona."

According to early writers, Kitchen was born in Covington, Ky., in 1822. He came to Arizona from San Francisco about 1854. Lockwood says: "He lived for some years at Canoa, Santa Cruz county. When the Civil War broke out he went into Sonora. Came back after the War and settled on his Potrero ranch near Calabasas. Died at Tucson, Aug. 5, 1895, and is buried there." Poston in his poetic *Travelogue*, writes of
"Pete Kitchen on his skew-bald horse."

Kitchin (sic) Springs   Apache Co.   Map, Apache N. F., 1926.

In sec. 4, T. 9 N., R. 26 E. "There was a story years ago to the effect that old Pete Kitchen camped on this spring for some time, which gave it the name. It was an open watering place for many years until some one filed on it as a homestead." Letter, A. F. Potter. Mr. Potter could not give any information as to the part Kitchen played in the naming. The map spells it "Kitchin"

Kits (sic) Peak   Pima Co.   G. L. O. Map, 1921.

In T. 17 S., R. 7 E. Sometimes spelled "Kitts." U.S.G.B. decided it as "Kitt." In Quinlan mountains, Papago Ind. Res. "So named by county surveyor, George J. Roskruge, who made the county survey in 1893. After his sister, Mrs. William F. Kitt. Roskruge, however, spelled it 'Kits' on his original map. Kitt came from England to Tucson in 1881. Died in Tucson 1904." Letter, Mrs. George F. Kitt, Tucson.

Kivagunt   Coconino Co.

"This was a lovely valley in the Grand Canyon. So called by Powell on his first trip through the canyon. Kivagunt was the name of a Pai-Ute Indian who said he owned the valley." Dellenbaugh.

Klara Peak   Yuma Co.   G. L. O. Map, 1921.

In T. 4 S., R. 21 W. 5 miles east of Colorado river, on southern end of Chocolate mountains.

"Was formerly known as Gallagher peak, then Kerrigan, and now Clara after Clara Consolidated Mining Co. When Sterling

Winters located this mine he named it after a woman." Letter, Mrs. Nettie Kuehn. But she did not know how it came to be spelled Klara on all the maps.

Klethla   Navajo and Coconino Cos.   U. S. G. S. Map, 1923.

Valley on Navajo Ind. Res. Extends southwest from Marsh pass, joins Moenkopi wash at Blue canyon in Coconino county just over Navajo county line. Father Haile says he knows no meaning in Navajo for this word.

Klondyke   Graham Co.   U. S. G. S. Map, 1920.

In T. 7 S., R. 19 E. ,So named by men returning from Alaska to commemorate their experiences there. P. O. and general trading center on Aravaipa creek about 2 miles south of Bert Dunlap's old cattle headquarters. P. O. established July 22, 1907, John F. Greenwood, P. M.

Klondike Mill   Mohave Co.   G. L. O. Map, 1909.

In T. 24 N., R. 22 W. Small mining camp and mill town, on east side of Colorado river, upper end of Pyramid canyon, below Cottonwood island. Origin unknown.

Klotho Peak   Yuma Co.   G. L. O. Maps, 1912-1921.

Elevation, 1,422 feet. ʼ In T. 8 S., R. 19 W. In Muggins mountains. This word is spelled with a "K" on some maps and a "C" on others. Its origin here is unknown. Clotho was the youngest sister of the Three Fates. She is represented as the "Spinner" which the name means in Greek. Some Greek student probably named the peak. On G.L.O. map, 1912, is marked Klothos Temple.

Knight Creek   Mohave Co.   U. S. G. S. Map, 1923.

Rises near Fort Rock, flows southwest into Big Sandy in Round valley, at T. 20 N., R. 13 W. Is apparently the same stream, but with another name, as White cliffs, and Cottonwood creek, q.v.

Knob Mountain   Apache Co.   G. L. O. Map, 1921.

Prominent peak about 8 miles northwest of Greer, on edge of Fort Apache Ind. Res. Descriptive name.

Kofa   Yuma Co.   U. S. G. S. Map, 1923.

Town, mine and butte, in central Yuma county. A coined word worked out by Col. Eugene Ives for his "King of Arizona" gold mine. Mine discovered by Charles Eichelberg; sold to Ives, 1899, for $250,000 after Eichelberg had taken out several times that sum. There is also a short range of hills nearby with this name. P. O. established June 5, 1900, Lewis W. Alexander, P. M.

Kohinoor Spring   Mohave Co.   U. S. G. S. Map, 1923.

On west slope of Grand Wash cliffs, in T. 26 N., R. 15 W. "There was once a Kohinoor mine near here." Letter, Postmaster, Kingman.

Ko-ho-nino   Coconino Co.

This is the spelling for Coconino used by George Wharton James, and some other western writers.

Koli-pat-vooka   Pima Co.   Lumholtz Map.

Papago village 8 miles southeast of Brownell. See Dead Old Man's Pond.

Komatke   Maricopa Co.   G. L. O. Map, 1921.

In sec. 5, T. 2 S., R. 2 E. On east side Gila river in Gila River Ind. Res. This is St. Johns Catholic Mission, q.v., 12 miles southwest of Phoenix. Pima word meaning "a blue hazy mountain." P. O. established Dec. 22, 1915. Herman P. Allis, P. M. This name is by some spelled thus "Ko-mat-k" giving the last syllable an aspirated effect. See Phoenix Mountain Park.

Komatke Mountains

See Estrella mountains.

Ko-op-ke   Pinal·Co.   G. L. O. Map, 1921.

In T. 8 S., R. 4 E. On Papago Ind. Res. Indian village. See Copeka. "From the Papago 'Kup,' a dam. Hence the 'place of the dam.' The 'K' ending in Papago simply denotes 'place.' The Papagoes built a dam here years ago," Father Oblasser.

Krauss Creek   Gila Co.   Smith Map, 1879; Eckhoff, 1880, Krauss.

Stream flowing south, entering East Fork of Verde river, about 15 miles west of Mazatzal City. Shown on Tonto N. F. map as "The Gorge."

Kuarchi   Pima Co.

Often called Archi. Known also as Santa Rosa. Indian village Santa Rosa valley, Papago Ind. Res. Lumholtz says it means, "Big Peak" or "Point of Peak." See testimony in case of Papago Indians vs. A. B. Fall. See Santa Rosa.

Kwagunt Hollow   Coconino Co.   Map, Kaibab N. F., 1927.

Rises in sec. 32, T. 36 N., R. 1 W. Grand Canyon N. P. Flows westerly into Jump Up creek opposite Jump Up point, in sec. 35, T. 36 N. R. 3 W. "Name of an old Piute Indian, dead some years since. Was very friendly and honest with the settlers. Lived all his life on the Kaibab forest and around the Grand Canyon." Letter, Walter Mann. "Kwagunt Hollow or Valley, was so named because a Pai-Ute Indian by this name said his father owned this valley." Letter, Frederick Dellenbaugh, Feb., 1933.

Kydestea   Navajo Co.   U. S. G. S. Map, 1923.

Spring on Navajo Ind. Res., south side of Black Mesa, in Dot Klish canyon, Navajo word of unknown meaning.

Kymo   Yavapai Co.

"The two first families to settle here came, one from Kentucky, the other from Missouri. Hence the name 'Ky-Mo' (Kimo)." P. O. established April 29, 1893, Robert H. Ferguson, P. M.

Kyrene   Maricopa Co.

In sec. 14, T. 1 S., R. 4 E. Former station on Maricopa branch Arizona-Eastern R. R., about 6 miles south of Tempe. Not on recent maps. From 1888 to about 1896 was quite a local hay and cattle shipping point. Named for Cyrene, a Carthagenian province but spelled with a "K" when adopted. Now called West Chandler.

La Abra   Pima Co.   G. L. O. Map, 1921.

In T. 17 S., R. 7 W. Valley east of Quitobaquito mountains. Near Mexican border. Sp., "a haven, valley." Decision U.S.G.B.

La Barge Creek   Maricopa Co.   Map, Tonto N. F., 1927.

Rises in T. 1 N., R. 11 E., flows north, joins Tortilla creek about one mile from Salt river. "According to Walter Martin, local settler, La Barge was a French prospector whose camp was at a spring at base of Weavers Needle. He was a friend and companion of the Dutchman of The Lost Dutchman Mine. After the Dutchman's death, La Barge spent all his time and money searching for the mine. Creek was named for him." Letter, Leo E. Anderson, forest ranger, Phoenix.

La Jara

See La Xara spring.

La Lesna Mountains   Pima Co.   Map, Coronado N. F., 1927.
Lesna Peak; U. S. G. S., Alisna; Papago Ind. Res., 1922, La Lesna.

Sp., "awl." Lumholtz says it is Papago for "hanging wolf." On line of Papago Ind. Res., on west side of Tecolote valley. At Boundary Post 153 in T. 22 S., R. 9 E.

La Noria   Pima Co.

Sp., "a draw well, one operated with a wheel." About 3 miles from Luttrell, where Holland mine smelters were located. P. O. established July 24, 1882, Richard Harrison, P. M.

La Osa   Pima Co.   G. L. O. Map, 1921.

Sp., "the bear." In T. 22 S., R. 8 E. Ranch at Mexican line. Headquarters La Osa Cattle Co., 1885. Known also as the Sturges ranch, after Col. W. S. Sturges, prominent cattleman and politician, 1885-1897.

"Mr. Ronstadt, of Tucson, states that a Mexican vaquero roped and killed a silver tip bear and her cub near where ranch is now located. After that it was always called 'La Osa' Ranch." Letter, Fred Winn, Tucson. Sturges was proud of the name and had a bear and three cubs on his letter-heads.

P. O. established May 28, 1894, James Finley, P. M. Name was changed to San Fernando, 1919, q.v.

La Paz   Yuma Co.   Smith Map, 1879; G. L. O. Map, 1921.

Mining town established, 1862, on Colorado river about 10 miles above Ehrenberg. Probably named by Pauline Weaver, whose party discovered rich gold placers near the town, 1862. J. Ross Browne says: "Weaver went to La Paz in 1862, attracted by the rich placers."

On Oct. 24, 1864, first Territorial Legislature attempted but failed to move the capital from Prescott to La Paz.

Fish says: "La Paz in 1863 had probably 5,000 men at work in its rich placers. Was then one of the largest places in the Territory." First county seat of Yuma county until 1870. According to all reports they took out over eight millions dollars worth of gold in eight or nine years.

Capt. Isaac Polhamus wrote: "County seat was moved to Arizona City (later Yuma) by an act of the Legislature, 1869. Records were shipped down the river on steamer Nina Tilden, which I commanded, early in January, 1870."

Court first opened at La Paz, June 24, 1864. Sylvester Mowry said it then had 155 houses.

In 1870 the river during a rise cut away from the place and left La Paz without a landing. After that event it lost its prominence. McClintock says: "The first gold was found in the Arroyo de la Tenaja about 7 miles from the river."

It seems fairly clear that the first comers made their way up here via the river stopping at La Paz, Mexico, which was then an important town in Lower California. Hence it was natural to use the name here. Otherwise no reason for this name can be learned.

"On Oct. 18, 1862, the county being under martial law, Gen. Carleton commanding, an election was ordered held at La Paz. Pedro Badillo, known as 'Six-toed Pete,' was elected Sheriff; F. G. Fitts, Alcalde." *Tucson Citizen*, Sept. 21, 1895. P. O. established July 12, 1865, Christopher Murr, P. M.

La Paz Arroyo   Yuma Co.   G. L. O. Map, 1921.

Rises on west side of Dome mountains; runs northwest into Colorado river at lower end of Colorado River Ind. Res. After La Paz, town.

La Paz, Camp   Yuma Co.

Fish says: "Camp La Paz was established as a temporary military camp Apr. 20, 1874, on left bank of Colorado. Garrison moved into and occupied deserted houses of the old Mexican town of La Paz." This must have been for a short time, as there is no such camp or post in War Dept. records at Washington.

This may be "Camp Colorado" in Heitman's List, on Colorado Ind. Res. La Paz town was at lower end of this reservation.

La Paz Mountain   Yuma Co.   U. S. G. S. Map, 1923.

In T. 4 N., R. 20 W. West side of Dome Rock mountains. After La Paz mining camp.

La Posa Plain   Yuma Co.   U. S. G. S. Map, 1923.

Sp., "a well." In Ts. 1 S., 1, 2 N., R. 19 W. "Doubtless so called because of the number of wells in this valley."

La Puente   Apache Co.

Sp., "the bridge." Small settlement, 1873, at the bridge on Little Colorado river 3 miles below St. Johns. Does not show on any map but is spoken of in an old clipping from a St. Johns paper. See St. Johns.

La Quituni   Pima Co.   Bryan Map, 1920; U. S. G. S., 1923.

Indian village and valley near Mexican line, Papago Ind. Res. Near lat. 31° 30' N., long. 112° 30' W. Meaning and origin unknown.

La Ventana   Pima Co.

Sp., "the window." A great upstanding rock in the desert about 3 miles east of Papago village of San Miguel at base of Baboquivari mountains about 90 miles from Tucson. Is notable for many prehistoric fortifications and old ruins found all over it. On its top is a large natural tank which holds considerable rain water. Lumholtz says the rock is about 400 feet high. Nobody has ever explained the name.

La Ventano (sic)

See Window.

La Xara Spring   Navajo Co.   G. L. O. Map, 1866.

At head of Leroux wash. Ives mentions camping at and naming it but gives no explanation of its origin. Also spells it La Zara. Shows "Jara," on old Military map, New Mexico, 1864.

Lady Bug Peak   Graham Co.   Map, Crook N. F., 1926.

In sec. 29, T. 9 S., R. 24 E. In Graham mountains. "So called because of the lady bugs always found on it. These bugs congregate on the rocks and trees in such quantities that they can literally be scooped off in handsful." Letter, Rex King, Safford.

Laguna   Yuma Co.   U. S. G. S. Map, 1923.

Sp., "lake." In T. 7 S., R. 22 W. Town on Colorado river at site of dam, west end of Laguna mountains. This was a camping place along the river since early times. Shows as a "laguna" or lake near river on many early maps. An item in an old Tucson paper speaks of "the valuable placer mines here." P. O. established Aug. 3, 1909, Robert G. Weatherstone, P. M. Site of Laguna dam which furnishes water for Yuma and Imperial valley in California.

Laguna Canyon or Stream   Apache Co.

Rises near Keet Seel ruins, flows south into Tyenda creek at Marsh pass. On Navajo Ind. Res.

Laguna Mountains   Yuma Co.   G. L. O. Map,. 1921.

In T. 7 S., Rs., 21, 22 W., on Colorado river, 15 miles above Yuma. "Gold was discovered here in May, 1854." Farish. After town by this name.

Lake No. 1   Coconino Co.   Map, Sitgreaves N. F., 1924.

In sec. 33, T. 11½ N., R. 14 E. Wet weather lake close to Crook road. Favorite camping spot for travelers and cowboys during roundups. On edge of Tonto rim. "When the soldiers built the Crook road they began at this lake and numbered them consecutively to the east. There were many of them and this seemed easier than coining names." Gradually, however, the numbers have given way to names as settlers ·came in. Only a few numbered lakes remain today.

Lake No. 4   Coconino Co.   Map, Coconino N. F., 1924.

In sec. 30, T. 12 N., R. 11½ E. Coconino N. F. on edge of Tonto Rim on Crook road. One of the lakes numbered and named by army officers who built this road, 1873.

Lake Pleasant   Maricopa Co.   P. O. Route Map, 1929.

In T. 6 N., R. 1 E. Lake formed by waters impounded by a dam across the Agua Fria. At lower end of Hieroglyphic mountains. So called after Carl Pleasant, engineer who worked out this irrigation plan. Dam is called "Carl Pleasant dam" and the lake, "Lake Pleasant." P. O. established Sept., 1926, James G. Tripp, P. M.

Lake San Carlos

See San Carlos lake.

Lakeside   Navajo Co.   G. L. O. Map, 1921.

In T. 10 N., R. 22 E. On road to Fort Apache. First called Fairview, also Woodland. Name changed about 1890 when Showlow creek was dammed here and a lake or reservoir created. Small Mormon settlement started about 1880. There are Boy and Girl Scout camps here, dedicated to these organizations. P. O. established Oct. 5, 1906, John L. Fish, P. M.

Lambey   Maricopa Co.   Smith Map, 1879.

Station east side Hassayampa about 10 miles south of Wickenburg. Origin unknown.

Lambing Lake   Coconino Co.   G. L. O. Map, 1921.

In sec. 26, T. 20 N., R. 8 E. Immediately east Lake Mary. "In early days this was a great lambing place. However when Jim Vail began running his cattle on Anderson mesa and had a cow camp at the lake, the name was changed to Vail lake by which it is now known." Letter, E. G. Miller, Flagstaff.

Lancha   Cochise Co.

Sp., "thin piece of stone." Station on S.P.R.R. about 18 miles east of Benson. Origin unknown.

Land   Cochise Co.

Station E. P. & S. W. R. R. on San Pedro river, 9 miles southeast of Benson. After Col. W. C. Land, early day cattle man and part owner Babocomari Land Grant. First P. O., July 15, 1911, Lou C. Woolery, P. M.

Lane Mountain   Yavapai Co.   Map, Prescott N. F., 1926.

In sec. 1, T. 10 N., R. 1 W. West side Bradshaws. After James Madison Lane who mined in Turkey creek district, 1876.

Langhorne   Pima Co.   G. L. O. Map, 1909; Post Route, 1929.

In T. 12 N., R. 12 E., settlement on Rillito near S. P. R. R. Railway station named for Langhorne family who have homesteads near. P. O. established Apr. 21, 1908, Catherine E. Langhorne, P. M.

Las Jarillas   Pima Co.   Map, Coronado N. F., 1927.

In T. 22 S., R. 10 E. Old cattle ranch headquarters, meaning unknown.

Las Moras   Pima Co.

Sp., "mulberry." On east slope Baboquivari range. Also known as Sturges ranch. Camp of Sturges Cattle Co. on Papago Ind. Res. "There were a number of mulberry trees at this place which gave the name."

Las Playas   Pima Co.   G. L. O. Map, 1921.

Sp., "sandy beach or shore." Small village, half Mexican, half Indian, in extreme southeast corner of county; almost on county line. This place is in a sandy flat, hence the name. Lumholtz locates it near Boundary Monument 180.

Last Battle with Indians in Arizona

See Big Dry Wash.

Last Chance   Pima Co.   G. L. O. Map, 1892.

In T. 17 S., R. 8 E. Papago Ind. Res. near present village of Warren, near Warren butte. Origin unknown. See First Chance.

Laub   Cochise Co.

Located near Dos Cabezas. P. O. established Nov. 15, 1900, Earl S. Peet, P. M.

Lauffer Mountain   Gila Co.   G. L. O. Map, 1909.

Peak Sierra Anches range. After Jake Lauffer, early day cattleman and prospector who had a fine ranch here in the Eighties. His orchard was the wonder of the region. Near head of Sally May creek. Lauffer and a man named Livingston were ambushed and badly wounded by outlaws here, Aug. 3, 1888.

Lava   Yuma Co.

Station S. P. R. R. about 93 miles east of Yuma. "Country near station is covered with lava rock, hence the name." Letter— Paul Shoup.

Lava Beds   Coconino Co.   Map, Coronado N. F., 1928.

In T. 22 N., R. 10 E. A large area here is covered with lava from nearby volcanic peaks.

Lava Creek   Coconino Co.

Grand Canyon N. P. Rises near Atoko point and lat. 36° 12′ N., long. 111° 56′ W. Runs through Lava canyon flowing southeast into Colorado river. Members U.S.G.S. called this Lava canyon because of the formation. Creek rises on plateau a quarter mile south of Atoko point; drains south into Grand Canyon west of Naji point; then southeast as above. Sometimes called Chuar, q.v. Decision U.S.G.B., 1933.

Lava Spring   Maricopa Co.   U. S. G. S. Map, 1923.

In T. 1 S., R. 6 W., southern end Palo Verde hills. Spring is in a lava formation.

Lava Springs   Navajo Co.   G. L. O. Map, 1921.

T. 24 N., R. 21 E., east side. Just off Navajo Ind. Res. "Springs burst from under a great lava cap or flow."

Laveen   Maricopa Co.

In T. 2 E., R. 1 S. Named for Roger Laveen, an early settler. Small settlement 12 miles southwest of Tempe.
"St. Johns Indian Mission School is located 6 miles south of Laveen."

Laws Spring   Coconino Co.

Somewhere west of San Francisco mountains. Named by Beale after Major W. L. Laws, Chairman Congressional Committee, 1858. "July 15, 1859, we started for Breckenridge spring but find an abundance of water at Laws spring where we arrived about 5 A. M." Beale.

Layton   Graham Co.

On Gila river 3 miles east of Thatcher. After Christopher Layton, of the Mormon church, who laid out town of Thatcher in May, 1883, where he lived for many years. Layton was an Englishman of force and character, although illiterate.

Leather Stocking of the Southwest
See Hamblin.

Lebanon   Graham Co.
First name for Algodon, q.v.

Lecheguilla (sic)   Cochise Co.   Map, Coronado N. F., 1927.

In sec. 17, T. 14 S., R. 19 E. Peak or hill in northwest Cochise county at Pima line east of Rincon mountains. "According to local authorities it is a Mexican name for the so-called agave or century plant, very abundant on its sides." Letter, Tom P. Neavitt, P. M. Cascabel. There is also a short range by this name in Yuma county south of Wellton, q.v.

Lechuguilla   Yuma Co.   G. L. O. Map, 1921.

Sp., "frill or ruff." Short range of hills on Mexican boundary. Lechuguilla desert and mountains south of Wellton on Mexican line near long. 114°. "Said to be so called after Spanish name for agave or century plant, plentiful here." J. S. Pomroy, Forest Ranger. The base of a good sized century plant is very like a ruff on a woman's neck. See also peak by same name in Cochise county. The above is spelling in all Spanish dictionaries. "Botanists agree that *Agave americana* (the true century plant) is a native of Central America and does not exist *naturally* in the United States. There are nearly a dozen different agaves in southwestern U. S., but not the real century plant." Letter, William A. Dayton, U. S. Forest Service, Washington, D. C.

Lee   Cochise Co.

Station E. P. & S. W. R. R., 9 miles from Douglas.

Lee Canyon and Stream   Coconino Co.   Map, Tusayan N. F., 1926.

In sec. 31, T. 32 N., R. 3 W. Flows southwest, enters Supai canyon on west side. Named after John D. Lee, who for several years lived in this canyon hiding from government officers because of his connection with the Mountain Meadows Massacre. See Lee Ferry.

Lee Ferry   Coconino Co.   Smith Map, 1879; U. S. G. S., 1923.

Elevation 3,170 feet. In T. 8 E., R. 4 N. On Colorado river, at mouth of Paria river.

Established about 1872 by John D. Lee then hiding to escape arrest. He was executed Mar. 23, 1877, by U. S. Government for complicity in Mountain Meadows Massacre. There was some crossing previous to 1872. Lee had a good boat and the crossing was safe and rapid. He called the place "Lonely Dell." Jacob Hamblin, Mormon missionary, crossed here in Oct., 1869. Bishop Roundy of the Mormon church was accidentally drowned here while crossing, May 28, 1876.

Dellenbaugh describes Lee, his wives and the surroundings at Lonely Dell with great fidelity and humor. P. O. established Apr. 23, 1879, Warren M. Johnson, P. M.

Lee Ferry Bridge   Coconino Co.

Steel bridge over Colorado river about 6 miles west of the old Ferry site. In T. 7 E., R. 40 W., 130 miles almost due north of Flagstaff. On Highway No. 89; 834 feet long; 467 feet above the river. Cost $350,000. Opened to traffic Jan. 12, 1929.

This bridge has never been named, officially. The Arizona legislature tried to pass a bill calling it "Hastele-Hamblin" after Hamblin and Hastele, his favorite Navajo guide. It failed of passage. It appears on the maps variously as "Grand Canyon," "Navajo," "Lee Ferry" and simply "Bridge." There is a strong sentiment against the name Lee Ferry because of Lee's unfortunate history. However to all old timers it will always be the "Lee Ferry Bridge" from its location.

Lee Ferry History

Fish gives this history of Lee Ferry: "The first real ferry boat was built by John J. Blythe in Oct., 1873. It carried two wagons and teams. Lee first called it 'Saints Ferry' but it soon became known as Lee Ferry from its owner. His widow sold the ferry which Lee left here to John Taylor of Salt Lake, in trust for the Mormon church. She turned it over on May, 1879, for $3,000 for everything at the ferry including privilege of landing on the property. In Aug., 1909, the church authorities sold the property to the Grand Canyon Cattle Co., a California firm then grazing cattle on the Kaibab and House Rock ranges to the north.

"In 1910 Coconino county bought the ferry from the Grand Canyon Co. and operated it about 3 years as a public property. In 1913 the Grand Canyon Co. contracted with the county to operate the ferry for so much a year. In 1916 the county took it over until the highway bridge was finished, when the ferry became useless for crossing purposes." Fish Ms. "Lee's first boat was one of Powell's boats, the 'Nellie Powell,' which was in poor shape for the trip. So the Major turned it over to Lee." Letter, Frederick Dellenbaugh, July, 1933. Not *Lee's* Ferry, "Lee Ferry." Decision U.S.G.B. See V. T. Park.

Lee Ranch   Yavapai Co.   Eckhoff Map, 1880.

Hinton lists it as a "stopping place on the Prescott stage road. Water, grass, and wood. Road excellent." East side Mint creek, near present settlement of Simmons. Who Lee was, not known.

Lee Spring and Mountain   Coconino Co.   Map, Coconino N. F., 1927.

In T. 17 N., R. 8 E. "Link Smith says both these were named after John Lee and his brother who lived at the spring for several years in the Seventies." Letter, Ed Miller, Flagstaff.

Le Fevre Canyon and Ridge   Coconino Co.   U. S. G. S. Map, 1923.

Rising western side Kaibab plateau; flowing northwest into Johnson creek, in T. 40 N., R. 1 W.

"After a family named Le Fevre who grazed sheep in winter on this ridge and canyon." Walter G. Mann, Kanab, Utah.

Lehi   Maricopa Co.   McClintock Map, 1916; G. L. O., 1921.

In T. 1 N., R. 5 E. Settlement on south bank, Salt river. About 3 miles north of Mesa. Originally called Utahville. An item in *Phoenix Herald*, Jan. 30, 1880, calls it "Bottom City."

"Settlement made Mar. 6, 1877, by Mormons under Daniel W. Jones. In July, 1877, Fort Utah was built as a place of refuge. It was formed by an adobe wall, enclosing considerable land with a well in the center. Called Camp Utah or Utahville. Later, called Jonesville after the leader. Brigham Young, Jr., suggested name Lehi, which was promptly accepted. The ditch they built was and is today known as the Utah ditch." McClintock.

Lehi was one of the Prophets in the Book of Mormon. He was the father of Nephi whom the Lord commanded "to take his family and go into the wilderness away from his enemies, who would slay him."

An item in *Prescott Miner*, 1878, says: "Lehi, which was sometimes called Mayville." See Jonesville. P. O. established May 26, 1882, James L. Patterson, P. M.

Lemmon, Mount   Pinal Co.   U. S. G. S. Map, 1923;
                                                      Coronado N. F., 1927.

Elevation 9,150 feet. In sec. 26, T. 11 S., R. 15 E., in Santa Catalinas, northeast Tucson. Prof. J. G. Lemmon is said to have named it for his wife, first white woman to reach its summit. In 1881 Lemmon discovered the wild potato growing in these mountains.

Leonard Canyon   Coconino Co.   U. S. G. S. Map, 1923.

Heads in T. 12 N., R. 12 E., Coconino N. F., about 4 miles west of Promontory butte. Runs northeast into Clear creek in T. 14 N., R. 12 E.

After W. B. Leonard well known early day sheepman who lived and died near Navajo springs. County commissioner of Apache county about 1883.

Leonard established a trading post near Fort Defiance about 1875 where he lived for some years. See Ganado.

Leroux Spring   Coconino Co.   Map, Coconino N. F., 1928.

In sec. 14, T. 22 N., R. 6 E., short distance above old Fort Maroni (Fort Valley) about 7 miles from Flagstaff. Spring is often mentioned by travelers. Named for Antoine Leroux, French hunter, guide and explorer, with Capt. Sitgreaves' expedition, 1851, when Sitgreaves visited this region.

"We turned the west point of San Francisco mountain and after travelling about 7 miles reached a permanent spring. In honor of the guide it was called Leroux Spring. Is the same to which he conducted Capt. Sitgreaves two years ago." Whipple, Dec. 17, 1853.

Lieut. Beale writes: "May 20, 1854, 189 miles west of West Port we overtook Mr. Antoine Leroux on his way to Taos and considered ourselves fortunate in securing the services again of so excellent a guide."

April 15, 1858, Beale, on his second visit, says: "This spring is 7 miles west of the Cosnino Caves. Rises in San Francisco mountains, flows into the valley on western side. Overland Mail Company has ditched the spring into their station." Antoine Leroux was also a guide for the Mormon Battalion, 1845, and one of Major St. George Cooke's guides, 1847, in southern Arizona. Emory's Report says: "There was a landing on Colorado river above Yuma in the 1860's known as Leroux Landing." According to Hinton, "LeReux (sic) was guide to the U. S. Boundary Survey Commission under Bartlett, 1849-51."

Leroux Wash   Navajo Co.

Formed by junction Cottonwood and Wide Water washes in T. 21 N., R. 23 E., flows west joins Little Colorado river 2 miles west of Holbrook. After Antoine Leroux. See Leroux spring. "Named by Whipple in 1853-54, 'Leroux Fork' for Antoine Leroux, guide for Whipple and Sitgreaves." Gregory.

Leroy   Pinal Co.   G. L. O. Map, 1879.

Mining camp in Bitterwell mountains. Headquarters Great Eastern Mining Company. Townsite surveyed and laid out by L. O. Chilson. One correspondent says: "So named because the surveyor's first name was Leroy."

LeSage (sic)   Yuma Co.   Post Route Map, 1929.

Station S.P.R.R., about 7 miles west of Aztec. "A farming town watered by pumping plants in land well adapted to tropical crops. Named after Pierre Lesage, a Frenchman. Settlers came and committed the unpardonable sin of changing it to LeSage.

"Pierre Lesage is a Frenchman from Brittany; he wanted to travel, came here 32 years ago and could never make up his mind to go away, except once. Then he went back and joined the French Army." Arthur Brisbane. See Musina. P. O. established Sept. 22, 1928, Sylvester H. Jansen, P. M.

Leslie Creek   Cochise Co.   U. S. G. S. Map, 1923.

Rises west slope Swisshelm mountains; flows southwest and is lost in Sulphur Springs valley below McNeal station. After Frank Leslie, scout and guide under Crook and Miles, 1880-1886. "Buckskin Frank Leslie was a jovial fellow in fringed buckskin with two six-shooters at his belt. He murdered a woman, 'Diamond Annie,' and was sent to Yuma for 25 years. Was pardoned after serving four years." *Tombstone.* The author saw him in his buckskins at Fort Apache in the Army pack train about 1882. Very picturesque chap.

Leupp   Coconino Co.   G. L. O. Map, 1921.

Navajo settlement on Little Colorado, northwest of Winslow. Near mouth San Francisco wash. Indian boarding school was established here about 1907. Named for Francis E. Leupp, U. S. Commissioner, Indian Affairs, 1905-1908.

Lewis, Camp   Yavapai Co.

Temporary military post on Fossil creek, on trail that led from Verde valley towards Tonto Basin. Capt. Bourke mentions it but says nothing as to its origin or exact location. It shows on GLO Map, 1866, as near head of Salt river. Probably named after Col. Charles H. Lewis, 7th. Infty. California Volunteers, who made several campaigns around here against Apaches, 1865-66.

Lewis and Pranty Creek   Maricopa Co.

In T. 2 N., R. 11 E. Intermittent stream. Flows into Fish creek in sec. 11, T. 2 N., R. 10 E. Not Arroyo Verde. Lewis and Pranty were two old timers who settled and prospected on this creek in early days. Decision U.S.G.B.

Lewis Springs   Cochise Co.   G. L. O. Map, 1921.

In T. 21 S., R. 22 E. Station established 1889 on E. P. & S. W. R. R. on San Pedro river. Originally called Fritz springs, having been located by Fritz Hoffman. Later owned by Alpheus and Robert A. Lewis, for whom it was named.

Liberty   Maricopa Co.   U. S. G. S. Map, 1923.

In T. 1 N., R. 2 W. Town in Buckeye valley. P. O. established Feb. 15,.1901, James Phillips, P. M.

Lichton   Maricopa Co.

See Litchfield Park.

Light   Cochise Co.   G. L. O. Map, 1921.

In T. 18 S., R. 27 E, on Turkey creek, Sulphur Springs valley. Named after John W. Light one of first dry farmers to settle here about 1909. Native of New York and Civil War veteran.

Lighthouse Rock   Yuma Co.   G. L. O. Map, 1921.

In T. 3 S., R. 23 W. East bank Colorado river, lower end Cibola valley.

"Not far above is a circular pinnacle of rock which resembles a lighthouse. It blocks the center of the river leaving a very narrow passage." Ives.

Ligurta   Yuma Co.   G. L. O. Map, 1923.

In T. 9 S., R. 20 W. Station S. P. R. R., about 30 miles east of Yuma. Paul Shoup says: "Origin not known; established about 1880."

Lime Creek   Yavapai Co.   Map, Tonto N. F., 1927.

Rises west side T. 9 N., R. 5 E., east end Cook mesa. Flows southeast into Verde river, in sec. 35, T. 8 N., R. 6 E.

Lime Mountain   Apache Co.   U. S. G. S. Map, 1923.

In T. 19 N., R. 24 E. On Lithodendron wash, 6 miles north of Adamana. So called because in early days, settlers burned lime here.

Limerick   Graham Co.

Station Globe-Gila Valley R. R. east of Geronimo. "So named by William Garland, contractor, who built the railroad. He was Irish by birth." Letter, Seth T. Arkills, Globe. See Dublin and Cork.

Limestone Mountains   Cochise Co.

See Little Dragoon mountains.

Limestone Tanks   Coconino Co.   G. L. O. Map, 1926.

On old Mormon road to Lee Ferry, west side Echo cliffs, about 27 miles south of river. On Navajo Ind. Res. "The tank is in a limestone formation."

Lincoln Camp   Yuma Co.

"A sub post, 140 miles north of Fort Yuma, on Colorado river, near La Paz. Established, 1864." Farish. Not in any War Dept. list of posts.

Lincoln Fort or Camp

Original name of Camp Verde. See Verde Camp. Also Camp La Paz; Lincoln Camp.

Lincolnia   Mohave Co.   G. L. O. Map, 1921.

Indian settlement Fort Mohave Ind. Res. Colorado river. First called Cottonia. Changed Apr. 13, 1911, to Lincolnia after Edmund Lincoln, an Indian trader located here.

Linden   Navajo Co.   G. L. O. Map, 1921.

In sec. 7, T. 10 N., R. 21 E. Formerly called Juniper. About 8 miles west of Showlow. Small Mormon hamlet in 1888. See Linden wash. P. O. established Apr. 28, 1893, John H. Hansen, P. M.

Linden Wash   Navajo Co.   Map, Sitgreaves N. F., 1924.

Dry wash heading in sec. 30, T. 10 N., R. 21 E. Near Apache Ind. Res. line. Runs northeast, enters Showlow creek in sec. 23, T. 12 N., R. 21 E.

First settlers called the long leaf cottonwood trees that lined the wash, "lindens." Hence the name.

Linskey   Yuma Co.   U. S. G. S. Map, 1923.

Station Parker branch A. T. & S. F. R. R. near east line Colorado River Ind. Res. "After Pat Linskey, track foreman, Arizona-Chloride R. R." A.G.W. Fifteen miles east of Parker.

Lirin   Pinal Co.

Station S.P.R.R. about 5 miles east of Maricopa. "Origin not known." Letter, Paul Shoup.

Liscum   Maricopa Co.   G. L. O. Map, 1921; Tonto N. F., 1927.

In T. 7 N., R. 4 W. On Cave creek. "The post office 'Liscum' was established, 1900, for the old Phoenix mine. Named by Sam Hunnington, manager of the mine, for an army officer, Col. Liscum. Postoffice only existed for eight or ten months. Nothing left now but the old stamp mill." Letter, Joe Hand, Cave Creek. Probably for Lieut. Col. Emerson H. Liscum, 9th. U. S. Infantry, killed at Tientsin, China, July 13, 1900. Served in Arizona, 1880-84 as First Lieut. 12th U. S. Infantry.

Litchfield Park   Maricopa Co.

In T. 2 N., R. 1 W. Town about 18 miles northwest of Phoenix. Named for Paul W. Litchfield, Goodyear Rubber Co. official. P. O. originally established as Lichton Jan. 7, 1910. Changed to Litchfield Park, July 16, 1926. On G.L.O. Map, Litchfield—others, Lichton. P. O. Guide, 1929, "Litchfield Park."

Lithodendron Wash   Apache Co.   Smith Map, 1879; G. L. O., 1921.

Greek word meaning "stone." Rises in T. 21 N., R. 25 E., flows southwest, enters Rio Puerco at Carrizo R. R. station in T. 18 N., R. 23 E.

"The camp was located on a creek to which Whipple gave the name Lithodendron." Whipple's report. Name appears on army maps, 1883.

Little Colorado River   Apache Co.   G. L. O. Map, 1921.

Sp., "Colorado chiquito." Stream in east part of State. Heads in Apache N. F. Formed by West and East Forks, in sec. 14, T. 7 N., R. 27 E., flows northwest, joins Colorado river in Coconino county at Cape Solitude, Grand Canyon N. P. in T. 35 N., R. 5 E.

Coues says: "Rio de Lino or Flax river was a name of the Little Colorado in Coronado's time. Garces also called it 'Colorado Chiquito.'" Gregory says: "The Navajo Indians called it 'Tol-Chaco,' 'Red stream or Red Water.'" Ives called it Flax river, 1861.

"What we know as the Little Colorado (Colorado Chiquito) was first called the 'Collorado' by Oñate in 1604." Chas. F. Lummis. When full the Little Colorado is of a dull red color due to the soil through which it flows.

Little Dog Mountains

See Perilla mountains. Somebody's mistake. Perilla does not mean "little dog" but "a small pear, a knob, or a goatee."

Little Dragoon Mountains   Cochise Co.   Smith Map, 1879;
U. S. G. S., 1923.

Short range north of Dragoon pass and north of S. P. R. R. Called also Limestone mountains, q.v.

Littlefield   Mohave Co.   Map, McClintock, "Mormon Settlement."

In T. 15 W., R. 40 N. "West side Virgin river, mouth of Beaver Dam creek. The people wanted a postoffice but authorities would not call it Beaver Dams so they compromised on Littlefield." Letter, Walter Cannon, P. M., St. George, Utah.

Settled by Mormons, 1864. Extreme northwestern settlement of present Arizona. Five miles south of Utah line and three miles east of Nevada line. Founded by Henry W. Miller. For a time called Millersburg in his honor. Formerly Beaver Dams. No one seems to know for whom it was finally named. P. O. established Oct. 25, 1894, Matilda Frehner, P. M.

Little Giant   Gila Co.

Arizona Gazetteer, 1881, lists this as a "P. O. and stage station 18 miles south of Globe." After George H. Stevens, noted politician of the Eighties, generally known as "the little Giant." P. O. established April, 1879, Samuel A. Lowe, P. M. See Stevens Ranch.

Little Gila River   Pinal Co.   U. S. G. S. Map, 1923.

Heads in T. 5 S., R. 8 E. Flood branch of main Gila. Runs parallel with Gila for about 35 miles; enters it at northwest corner T. 3 S., R. 5 E., about 3 miles north of Sweetwater, Gila Ind. Res.

Little Granite Mountain   Yavapai Co.   Map, Prescott N. F., 1927.

In sec. 9, T. 14 N., R. 3 W. Mountain about 2 miles north of Iron springs. In Granite Basin near head of Mint wash. Called "Little Granite" as against nearby main Granite mountain.

Little Green Valley   Gila Co.

In sec. 3, T. 10 N., R. 11 E. Valley and stream about 14 miles northeast of Payson, below Promontory butte. Flows northeast into Tonto creek. "Originally a lovely grass-covered 'cienega' or meadow surrounded by timbered hills. The valley north of Payson was first called Big Green valley, being the larger of the two. Naturally the smaller was called Little Green valley." Croxen.

"William Burch and John Hood were the first settlers in Green valley in 1876. They built a small stockade house at forks of creek. Creek went dry and they moved to the spring at its head." Letter, I. M. House, Mesa. See Payson.

Little Gust James Creek   Pinal Co.   Map, Crook N. F., 1926.

Rises west side Galiuro mountains, flows southwest into San Pedro river in T. 9 S., R. 18 E. See Gust James.

Little Harqua Hala Mountains   Yuma Co.   G. L. O. Map, 1921.

In Ts. 4, 5 N. Rs. 12, 13 W. South side of railroad extending from it to Martin peak and town of Harqua Hala.

Little Horn Mountains   Yuma Co.   U. S. G. S. Map, 1923.

In T. 1 S., Rs. 12, 13 E. About 25 miles west of Maricopa line. "So called because they are smaller than Big Horn range to northeast." Letter, O. G. Kelser, Quartsite.

Little Nankoweap Creek   Coconino Co.

Grand Canyon N. P. Rises in lat. 36° 19', long. 111° 55' W. Flows southeasterly into Colorado river. Creek drains Little Nankoweap canyon. Pah Ute Indian name. See Nankoweap.

Little Red Horse Wash   Coconino Co.   Map, Tusayan N. F., 1926.

Wash rising at old ruins near Hull Ranger station. Runs southwest into Red Horse wash in sec. 19, T. 26 N., R. 3 E. Small edition of well known Red Horse wash.

Little Squaw Creek   Yavapai Co.   U. S. G. S. Map, 1923; Tonto N. F., 1927.

Rises New River mountains; flows southwest; enters Agua Fria in T. 8 N., R. 2 E., near Canyon or Goddards station on old stage road. So called to distinguish it from the larger Squaw creek nearby.

Little Trough Creek   Gila Co.   Map, San Carlos Ind. Res., 1917.

Stream rising in T. 4 N., R. 19 E. Flowing into Salt river in T. 5 N., R. 19 E. "Indian Service placed a watering trough in this canyon for stock and persons traveling the road, which gave it this name."

Little Tucson   Pima Co.   Map, Indian Service, 1915; G. L. O., 1921.

Sp., "Tucsonito." In T. 18 S., R. 5 E. On Papago Ind. Res. Indian village about 20 miles southeast of Sells P. O. West side Baboquivori valley.

Lumholtz says: "On the north side of the road between Fresnal and Indian Oasis. Papago name is Alit-ju-kson, meaning 'at the foot of a small black hill.'" This Papago name proves fairly well the origin of name Tucson.

Live Oak   Gila Co.

"There is a fine grove of live oaks here." P. O. established Nov. 3, 1905, Rey A. Hascal, P. M.

Liverpool Landing   Mohave Co.

See Pittsburg Landing.

Livingston   Gila Co.   Map, Tonto N. F., 1927.

In sec. 36, T. 4 N., R. 13 E. Settlement on Salt river eastern end Roosevelt lake. After an early cattleman and settler. "Norman Howard Livingston moved into Arizona in late Seventies from Washington state with his step-father, Simon W. Kenton, locating in Globe. In 1888 Livingston filed on a homestead on Salt river at mouth of Pinto creek where a small town started. Some residents wanted to call it 'Curnott' to honor another old settler but they finally decided upon Livingston. With the completion of the dam the place was abandoned; dense thickets of Gila willow and mesquite now cover the area." Letter—A. L. Alexander, Forest Ranger, Roosevelt. P. O. established as Livingston, Sept. 7, 1896, James Curnott, P. M.

Lochiel   Santa Cruz Co.   G. L. O. Map, 1892-1921.

So named by Colin and Brewster Cameron, who owned the San Rafael Land Grant and ran a large herd of cattle here. P. O. established under this name Oct. 6, 1884, Abner B. Elder, P. M. First called La Noria; then Glencoe, q.v. See San Rafael Grant.

Lockett Lake   Coconino Co.   Map, Tusayan N. F., 1927.

Near Grand Canyon in sec. 35, T. 30 N., R. 4 E. Well known sheep watering place located and improved by Henry "Hank" Lockett, pioneer sheep owner of this region.

Lockhart   Yuma Co.   Map, G. L. O., 1921; U. S. G. S., 1923.

In T. 6 N., R. 12 W. Station Parker branch S. F. R. R. Changed to Love, q.v.

Locomotive Butte   Pima Co.   G. L. O. Map, 1921.

In T. 13 S., R. 6 W., in Little Ajo mountains about 6 miles south of Ajo. Descriptive name.

Locust Canyon   Coconino Co.   U. S. G. S. Map, 1923.

In T. 18 N., R. 9 E. Heads near Mormon lake; runs northeast, enters Canyon Diablo about 8 miles north A. T. & S. F. R. R. station by that name. So called because of many fine locust trees along its course.

Logan   Pah Ute Co.   G. L. O. Map, 1928.

One of the settlements in Pah Ute county originally in Arizona but later added to Nevada. On the Muddy a few miles above St. Joseph. Now called Logandale, station on Salt Lake and Los Angeles road. Said to have been named after Logan, Utah. McClintock calls it West Point.

Logan City   Pima Co.   G. L. O. Map, 1892.

In T. 15 S., R. 2 E. Townsite near Quijotoa, 1872. McClintock says: "This was the name of original townsite of what later became the Quitojoa Mine site."

Hamilton says of this place and its neighbor, New Virginia: "The principal avenue of Logan City forms the main street of New Virginia so that the two towns will eventually become one."

Tucson Star, May 23, 1885, says: "Logan City is nestled on the slope of Ben Nevis mountain."

"Logan City, or Allen, was so called after two brothers, J. T. and W. R. Logan, who dug a well here, 1893. Was on east side of Ben Nevis. George Roskruge surveyed and plotted it." The Quitojoa *Prospector* was published here for a while in Feb., 1884, by Harry Brook of San Francisco." Letter—in files *Arizona Pioneers Historical Society*. See Virginia, New Virginia, Brooklyn, Allen.

Logan Mine   Yavapai Co.   G. L. O. Map, 1921; Prescott N. F., 1927.

In sec. 27, T. 14 N., R. 3 E. Mine and stage station at lower end of Black Hills near town of Cherry. On Race Track wash north side of Onion mountain. "Mine originally called the Isabel and operated by John J. Gosper. Place named after an old chap named Logan." Letter, Frank Grubb, Prescott.

Logan, Mount   Mohave Co.   G. L. O. Map, 1921.

Elevation 7,700 feet. In T. 34 N., R. 9 W., Dixie N. F. North side Colorado river. Named by Powell for Gen. John A. Logan. "The next mountain I have called Mount Logan and the one standing nearest to the Grand Canyon, 'Mount Emma.'" Powell. "I climbed the peak, later named after Senator Logan and attempted some triangulation." Dellenbaugh.

Lokasakad Spring   Navajo Co.   Gregory Map, 1916.

About 25 miles south of Keam canyon and 3 west of Bidahochi trading post. Father Haile says it means "at the bunch of tules." Not to be confused with Lokasakal spring north of Keam canyon.

Lokasakal Spring   Navajo Co.   Gregory Map, 1916; U. S. G. S., 1923.

Near lat. 36° 10′ N., long. 110° 10′, Navajo Ind. Res., about 18 miles north of Keam canyon. Gregory spells it as above, locating it 27 miles south of Chilchinbito. But on his map, 1910, he spells it Lokasaka, "Navajo word meaning place where reeds grow," not to be confused with Lokasakad spring 25 miles south of Keam.

Navajo Dictionary of the Franciscan Fathers spells the word reed, "lu-ka," which is doubtless the proper spelling of this name.

Lolo-mai   Navajo Co.   Gregory Map, 1916; U. S. G. S., 1923.

Navajo Ind. Res. On south side east end of Marsh pass, Black mesa. Hopi word for "good." Also name of a well-known Hopi chief. Gregory wanted to call this for John Wetherell, but he was a living person. See Solo-mi.

Lompoc   Graham Co.   G. L. O. Map, 1921.

In T. 11 S., R. 23 E. Early day station in Sulphur Springs valley. About 12 miles south of Fort Grant. "The people who first settled here came from Lompoc, California, and called it for that place. Name is that of an old Indian village near Purisima Mission, Santa Barbara county, California." Letter, Mary J. Mills, P. M., Lompoc.

Lonely Dell

See Lee Ferry.

Lone Mountain   Cochise Co.   Map,. Coronado N. F., 1927.

In T. 23 S., R. 19 E., 8 miles south of Huachuca peak. "Descriptive name. The mountain stands out all alone."

Lone Mountain   Maricopa Co.   Map, Tonto N. F., 1927.

In sec. 19, T. 6 N., R. 5 E. Located about 4 miles northeast of Cave creek post office. "Just a name for a single peak standing alone." Letter—Joe Hand.

Lone Mountain   Yuma Co.   U. S. G. S. Map, 1923.

In T. 3 N., R. 11 W. Isolated peak in Harqua Hala plains north of Eagle Tail mountain.

Lone Mountain Well   Yuma Co.

In sec. 17, T. 3 N., R. 11 W. "In Harqua Hala plain. Watering place Harqua Hala Cattle Co., close to mountain by this name. Not far from it there is an abandoned well 465 feet to bed rock and not a drop of water." *Routes to the Desert*

Lone Pine Crossing   Navajo Co.

Early name for the "Reidhead place" on Showlow. There was a single yellow pine tree at crossing of creek when the author first saw the place, 1880. It was also known as "the Reidhead Crossing," q.v.

Lonesome Peak   Yuma Co.   G. L. O. Map, 1921.

In T. 1 N., R. 18 W. At southern end Plomosa mountain.

Lonesome Valley   Yavapai Co.   G. L. O. Map, 1921.

On Granite creek. Jerome Junction is in the center. Large rolling treeless valley with excellent grass. So called by first stockmen because of its extent and lonesomeness due to lack of settlers.

Lone Star   Graham Co.   R. R. Maps.

Station Globe-Bowie branch Arizona-Eastern R. R. So called after mountain and mine by this name about 8 miles north of Solomonville.

Lone Star Mountain   Graham Co.   U. S. G. S. Map, 1923.

In T. 6 S., R. 27 E., west of Bonita creek and 8 miles north of Solomonville. San Carlos Ind. Res. "There was a Lone Star mine near it. Whether the mine or the mountain was first named no one can say." Letter—Rex King, Safford.

Long Lake   Navajo Co.   Map, Sitgreaves N. F., 1927.

In T. 10 N., R. 22 E. Wet weather lake about 3 miles northeast of Showlow. Fed by several washes that run occasionally. Favorite lambing ground in the Eighties. A. F. Potter says: "It was so called because it was a long narrow lake."

Longfellow Coconino Co.   G. L. O. Map, 1892.

Station Central Arizona R. R. about 20 miles south of Flagstaff, near Mount Longfellow or Mormon mountain.

"When the Central Arizona was called upon to issue a tariff sheet my brother, D. M., and I applied the name 'Longfellow' to station at Mormon mountain. We both had a New England literary brainstorm about that time, hence the name." Letter—M. J. Riordan, Flagstaff.

Longfellow, Mount Coconino Co.   G. L. O. Map.

In T. 18 N., R. 8 E. About 2 miles northwest Mormon lake. Often called Mormon mountain. So called on Coconino N. F. Map, 1928. See Longfellow.

Longfellow Ridge Yavapai Co. Map, Prescott N. F., 1927.

In Ts. 11, 12½ N., Rs. 1, 2 W., south of Mount Union. There was a Longfellow mine at this point from which it undoubtedly took its name. Hinton listed it, 1877.

Longs River Apache Co.

"Leaving the springs (Navajo springs) we camped on a small creek. The creek is marked by scattering cottonwoods. I have called it Longs river after one of my party, E. P. Long." Beale, 1859. Not mapped.

This may have been our present Rio Puerco.

Long Tom Canyon Coconino Co. Map, Sitgreaves N. F., 1924.

Rises in T. 11½ N., R. 14 E., at the Crook-Verde road, about 2 miles from rim. Enters Chevelon in sec. 14, T. 12 N., R. 14 E. So called by an old hunter and sheep herder named Woolf who camped here as early as 1882. The author located in the valley and built the first cabin here, 1885. It was then a beautiful place. A clear stream flowed down the valley through dense willows; there was grass everywhere. Inside of fifteen years the creek was about dry, its floor cut down 10 feet or more, most of the willows were gone. Too many cattle. Cabin later on used as a forest ranger station.

Long Valley Coconino Co.   U. S. G. S. Map, 1923.

In T. 13 N., R. 10 E. Long open valley at head East Clear creek. Descriptive name. There is a Long Valley ranger station here. See Payson.

Lookout Mountain Gila Co.   G. L. O. Map, 1921.

Tonto N. F. In Sierra Ancha range, south of Horse mountain "This is sometimes called Lookout mountain because of its fine view. Correct name is Baker mountain." Letter, Theodore T. Swift, Forest Supervisor.

Lopeant Mohave Co.   G. L. O. Map, 1921.

Mormon settlement west of Cane Beds, in Antelope valley. P. O. established Jan. 26, 1921, Mrs. Mattie W. Ruesch, P. M. See Topeat.

Lord, Mount Pima Co.   G. L. O. Map, 1921.

Isolated peak about 5 miles southeast Silver Bell. "Name was put on map of Pima county by George Roskruge, 1893. Mrs. Roskruge, his widow, believes mountain was named for Frank H. Lord, a neighbor, who came to Arizona in the early Seventies. Member of Tucson firm of Lord & Williams. Lordsburg, New Mexico, was named for him." Letter, Mrs. Geo. F. Kitt, Tucson.

Los Comates (sic)   Pima Co.   Lumholtz Map.

Sp. camote "sweet potato." Papago name, "Shaat-kam," an edible root of the desert. Papago camp about 3 miles west of Mesquite range near boundary line. Almost due north of La Nariz in Sonora.

Los Gigantes Butte   Apache Co.   G. L. O. Map, 1921.

Sp., "the giants." In T. 10 N., R. 9 W., Navajo Ind. Res., on Hashbidito (turtle dove) wash.

Los Martires

Sp., "The martyrs." Name first given Colorado river by Father Kino. See Colorado.

Los Moros (sic) **Well**   Pima Co.   Bryan Map, 1920; G. L. O. Map, 1921.

In T. 20 S., R. 7 E. Sp., "mulberry." Also called Sturges ranch. Should be spelled Las Moras. East side Baboquivori mountains, in Altar valley. Also called La Osa, q.v.

Los Muertos   Maricopa Co.

Sp., "the dead." In T. 1 S., R. 4 E. Name applied by Frank H. Cushing to Pre-Columbian ruins excavated by him, 1886, 7 miles south Tempe. About 5 miles east of Salt river mountains. Shows on a small map issued by The Curio Co., Phoenix, 1902.

Los Reales   Pima Co.

"A new town called Los Reales is just started about 12 miles south of Tucson." *Tucson Citizen,* Aug. 11, 1888. Nothing known of it in 1930.

Lost Basin   Mohave Co.   G. L. O. Map, 1921.

Town in a large open valley extreme northern end county. Valley on south side Colorado river, east of Detrital valley. Town started many years ago on north side of river at lower end Granite wash, across canyon from valley. P. O. established July 11, 1882, Michael Scanlon who operated the ferry for several years, was P. M. See Scanlon Ferry.

Lost Creek   Mohave Co.   U. S. G. S. Map, 1923.

In Hualpai Ind. Res., rising east slope Grand Wash cliffs. Flows into Colorado river in T. 28 N., R. 14 W.

Lost Dutchman Mine

See La Barge.

Lost Spring   Mohave Co.   G. L. O. Map, 1921.

In T. 24 N., R. 21 W., western slope Black range.

Lotus Valley

See Ranegras Plain.

Louise   Mohave Co.   U. S. G. S. Map, 1923.

Station A. T. & S. F. R. R. about 5 miles east of Kingman. "After daughter of A. G. Wells, Gen'l. Manager and Vice President of Santa Fe Co." A.G.W.

Lousley Hill   Maricopa Co.   Scott Map, Maricopa Co., 1929.

Elevation 2,050 feet. In sec. 8, T. 4 N., R. 6 E. At northwest corner Salt River Ind. Res. Origin unknown.

Lousy Gulch   Gila Co.   Map, Tonto N. F., 1926.

In T. 10 N., R. 9 E. On upper Tonto creek, about one mile southeast of Payson.

"In the Eighties Ben Cole and his two sons, Emer and Link, had a mine here. They worked it during one winter and all became lousy. So they called it by that name." Fred Croxen, Payson.

Love   Yuma Co.   Santa Fe R. R. Maps.

Station Parker branch A. T. & S. F. R. R., 45 miles west of Wickenburg.

"This station was first called Lockhart, q.v. After World War renamed Love in memory of Ernest Love who died in France. His father was a Santa Fe engineer for many years. Station is 5 miles west of Wenden." Letter—P. M., Salome.

Low Mountains   Yuma Co.   U. S. G. S. Map, 1923.

In T. 7 N., R. 12 W. East side Harcuvar mountains.

Lowell   Cochise Co.   G. L. O. Map, 1921.

In T. 23 S., R. 24 E. Station Bisbee branch E. P. & S. W. R. R. About 3 miles south of Bisbee.

"As the canyon at Bisbee became congested people moved down to mouth of the canyon for room on which to build homes. So named by parties from Lowell, Mass., who opened a mine here which they called after their native city." Letter—P. M., Lowell.

Lowell, Camp or Fort   Pima Co.   Smith Map, 1879-80, "Camp Lowell."

Well-known military post near Tucson. Named for Gen. C. R. Lowell, U. S. A., killed May 21, 1862, at Cedar Creek, Va. First camp established by California Volunteers under Lieut. Col. West immediately after Tucson was abandoned by Confederates, Sept. 15, 1864. Reestablished, Aug., 1866. "On Mar. 19, 1873, post was moved about 8 miles out and located on the Rillito. It was originally built close to Tucson and all unmarried officers boarded in town." Bourke.

Was first located on Military plaza in what is now center of city. The post on the Rillito and its adobe ruins are now included in Tucson Memorial Park.

Lowest place in Arizona

In southwestern Yuma county; 137 feet above sea level.

Lucky Cuss Mine   Cochise Co.   Eckhoff Map, 1880.

One of the Tombstone group. Ed Schieffelin rode into camp. "I've struck it rich this time," to his brother. "You're a lucky cuss," his brother Al flung back. And so it was named. *Tombstone.*

Luis Maria Baca Grant   Yavapai and Santa Cruz Counties.

"Two rights or 'Floats' for the selection of five tracts of approximately 100,000 acres each were placed in Arizona. One of the Arizona 'Floats' is in western Yavapai county near Walnut creek, owned by Dr. E. B. Perrin. The other was placed, June 20, 1863, upon lands in upper Santa Cruz valley, including settlements of Tubac, Tumacacori and Calabasas." McClintock.

"These grants were made by the Mexican Government in Jan., 1821, to heirs of Luis Maria Cabeza de Vaca. They were authorized to select land near Las Vegas, New Mexico, then called Las Vegas Grandes. Sp., vega, 'a meadow.' They were unable to secure all the land owing to conflicting grants. Congress passed an Act, June 21, 1860, authorizing the heirs to select an equal acreage in square bodies not exceeding five in number, they being available on any public lands in New Mexico, part of which later became Arizona. The Yavapai tract, Float No. 2, contains 92,160 acres; the Santa Cruz tract, No. 3, over 200,000 acres. The U. S. Supreme Court validated these tracts in 1914." *Arizona Tax Payers Magazine,* Dec., 1919.

Lukachukai Creek   Apache Co.   Gregory Map, 1916.

In T. 11 N., R. 10 W. Navajo Ind. Res., rises near Matthews peak; flows northwest into Chinle creek. Navajo word meaning "streaks of white spruce." Haile.

Luka-chu-kai Mountains   Apache Co.   U. S. G. S. Map, 1923.

In T. 9 N., Rs. 6, 7 W. Navajo Ind. Res., near New Mexico line. "Navajo word meaning 'patches of white rocks.'" Gregory. Navajo dictionary also calls these mountains "White Spruce."

Lupton   Apache Co.   U. S. G. S. Map, 1923.

On A. T. & S. F. R. R. First station in Arizona west of New Mexico line.

"For G. W. Lupton, train master at Winslow, 1905, later Santa Fe superintendent at San Francisco. In 1929, assistant to vice president, Chicago." A.G.W. P. O. established May 25, 1917, Joseph D. Gorman, P. M.

Luttrell   Pima Co.

"Mining camp 80 miles southeast Tucson, near the line. Named after J. K. Luttrell, superintendent Holland mines located here." *Arizona Gazetteer,* 1881. According to post office records was near La Noria. P. O. established Aug. 23, 1880, Harrison Fuller, P. M.

Luzena   Cochise Co.   U. S. G. S. Map, 1923.

In T. 12 N., R. 27 E. North of Dos Cabezas mountains. Station S. P. R. R. Paul Shoup says: "Origin unknown, established about 1880, 15 miles east of Willcox."

Lyman Dam   Apache Co.

Dam for impounding water on Little Colorado river above St. Johns. After Francis M. Lyman, Mormon bishop. Originally called "Slough Reservoir." Destroyed by floods, 1903. Some $200,000 was spent to rebuild it, most of which was contributed by Mormon Church. Second dam went out April 1915. Then a law was passed appropriating State funds taking for security mortgages on dam and farm land. At last accounts the State had nearly $800,000 invested here. *Mormon Settlement.*

Lyonsville   Mohave Co.

"Below Virginia City, half a mile is Lyonsville, sarcastically said by Virginians to consist of one house to be built and the skeleton of a corral." J. Ross Browne. See Virginia City.

Lynx Creek   Yavapai Co.   U. S. G. S. Map, 1923.

Stream on which much gold was mined in early days. Rises in vicinity of Walker; flows northeast, enters Agua Fria near Dewey in T. 14 N., R. 1 E. So called because a lynx was killed here by Sam C. Miller.

There is also a story that the first miners found several *links* of an ox chain. Some writers feel the name should be spelled "links."

Dr. Elliott Coues who served with the army for many years, mostly at Prescott, says: "So called for the number of these animals killed along the creek in early days." Article by Coues in *American Naturalist*, 1867. Undoubtedly correct. Several say it was first called Walker creek. See Walker.

McAllister   Cochise Co.   G. L. O. Map, 1921; U. S. G. S., 1923.

In T. 12 S., R. 23 E. Sulphur Springs valley on road Willcox to Fort Grant, about 10 miles northwest Willcox. Named after family which settled here about 1884. P. O. established March 3, 1911. Mary T. McAllister, P. M.

McCabe   Yavapai Co.   G. L. O. Map, 1921.

In T. 13 N., R. 1 E. Named for McCabe mine about 5 miles southeast of Prescott. P. O. established Dec. 31, 1895. Mrs. Marion C. Behn, P. M.

McCartys Canyon   Coconino Co.

See Millers Canyon.

McCleary Peak   Pima Co.

Elevation 7,000 feet. In Santa Rita mountains about 6 miles north of Pima county line. Named after William B. McCleary, pioneer cattleman and miner who located in this vicinity about 1879. Decision USGB.

McClellan Tank   Coconino Co.   G. L. O. Map, 1921.

Natural tank or reservoir Navajo Ind. Res., east side Echo range, near lat. 36° 30′ N., long. 111° 30′ W. Named for William C. McClellan, member Mormon battalion, who settled at Sunset on Little Colorado in 1876.

McClellan Wash   Pinal Co.   U. S. G. S. Map, 1923.

Rises in T. 4 S., R. 7 E. Gila River Ind. Res., near Blackwater, runs southeast into Picacho reservoir in T. 6 S., R. 8 E. "The McClellans were a pioneer family and lived on this wash."

McClellan Well   Yuma Co.

In sec. 36, T. 1 N., R. 6 W. "Watering place of Flower Pot Cattle Co. west of Buckeye." *Routes to the Desert.*

McClintock Ridge   Coconino Co.   Map, Coconino N. F., 1928.

In T. 12 N., R. 11 E., between Barbershop and Dane canyons. "After homesteader and cattleman, W. W. McClintock who, 1904 located a place on this ridge." E. R. Smith, Forest Ranger.

McCloud Mountains   Yavapai Co.   U. S. G. S. Map, 1923; G. L. O., 1921.

In T. 13 N., R. 7 W. North and west of Hillside A. T. & S. F. R. R. Settler by this name lived for many years at a spring east side of these mountains which were named for him. Probably the original spelling was McLeod, but above is usual spelling around here." E. A. Putnam, Hillside.

McConnico   Mohave Co.   U. S. G. S. Map, 1923.

Station A. T. & S. F. R. R. 4 miles west of Kingman junction Chloride branch. "Mr. McConnico was railroad contractor who built the branch line Kingman to Chloride. A fine man. The company did well to name the station for him." Letter, O. D. M. Gaddis, Kingman.

McCracken Mine   Mohave Co.   Smith Map, 1879; G. L. O., 1921.

In southern part Mohave county, near Bill Williams river. After Jackson McCracken, member Walker party who, according to Hinton, located this mine in August, 1874. McCracken was a member first and second territorial legislatures, coming from Lynx creek, Yavapai county.

"The McCracken is 30 miles from Aubrey's landing, via Planet. There are over 100 persons employed and resident at McCracken. The capacity to produce seems limited only by the number of men employed and the milling capacity." Hinton. P. O. established here as McCracken May 16, 1908, John L. Witley, P. M.

McCracken Peak   Mohave Co.   G. L. O. Map, 1921.

Elevation 3,410 feet. In T. 13 N., R. 15 W. About 6 miles north of Bill Williams river. After McCracken mine.

McCullum Ranch   Coconino Co.

P. O. established here Feb. 24, 1881. Robert McCullum, P. M. Shows on Smith map, 1879 as McColloms Ranch. See Coleman lake.

McDonald   Yavapai Co.

P. O. established April 4, 1904, Fred H. Gorham, P. M. Did not remain in operation more than a year.

McDonald, Fort   Gila Co.

"Small flat-topped sandstone butte, east of Payson, approximately 100 feet above town. During an Indian scare in 1882 people of Payson and Marysville 'forted up' on this butte. Old fort still to be seen, 1930. It was named after William McDonald for whom McDonald mountain and pocket are named." Letter— Fred W. Croxen, Payson.

McDonald, Mountain and Pocket   Gila Co.

East side Tonto creek. "Named for William McDonald, one of first settlers in Payson. He and William Burch came from Mohave county, 1870, with a bunch of cattle. McDonald wintered his saddle horses in the so-called 'pocket' which is enclosed by the mountain to form a basin or 'pocket.' Thus the name." Letter—Fred W. Croxen.

McDowell, Fort   Maricopa Co.   Smith Map, 1879; G. L. O., 1921; U. S. G. S., 1923.

Military post west bank Verde river about 7 miles above junction with Salt. Established Sept. 7, 1865 by five companies California Volunteers. After Gen. Irvin McDowell, U. S. A., then commanding U. S. troops in California and Arizona. Abandoned by G. O. No. 43 April 10, 1890. Known in early days as Campo Verde, Sp., "Green Camp." Known also as Camp McDowell.

G. O. No. 22, March 2, 1891, turned the reservation of 25,688 acres over to the Department of Interior for an Indian school. P. O. called McDowell established Dec. 12, 1873, John Smith, P. M. This was John Y. T. Smith who later lived in Phoenix for many years. Smith was then the post sutler.

McDowell Mountain   Maricopa Co.   G. L. O. Map, 1892-1921; U. S. G. S., 1923.

Elevation 4,330 feet. At lower end McDowell range. West of Verde river at junction with Salt. After Gen. Irvin McDowell,

U. S. A. On Camelback Quad., 1906, it is McDowell peak. Other maps show a McDowell peak north of this mountain at head of Paradise valley, q. v.

McDowell Mountains   Maricopa Co.   G. L. O. Map, 1892-1921; Camelback Quad, 1906.

Short range extending from McDowell peak southeasterly to McDowell mountains lower end of T. 3 N. On west side Verde river at junction with Salt. After Gen. Irvin McDowell.

McDowell Peak   Maricopa Co.   Scott Map, Maricopa Co., 1929.

In sec. 2, T. 4 N., R. 5 E. Small peak elevation 4,022 feet upper end Paradise valley. Peak separate and distinct from the other McDowell mountain near junction Salt and Verde.

McFadden Horse Mountain   Gila Co.   G. L. O. Map, 1921; Tonto N. F., 1927.

North end T. 6 N., R. 14 E., Sierra Ancha range. "In early days, Bill McFadden, a cattleman, used the flat top of this mountain for a horse pasture. Hence the name. He ran the Circle brand." Letter, Forest Supervisor Swift, Phoenix.

McFadden Peak   Gila Co.   U. S. G. S. Map, 1923.

In T. 7 N., R. 14 E. In Sierra Ancha mountains. After William McFadden, an early settler and cattleman.

McIntosh Ranch   Gila Co.

See Black Mesquite.

McKay   Apache Co.   Map, Apache N. F., 1926.

In T. 7 N., R. 24 E., Apache Ind. Res., close to western line Apache county. After Alex McKay, former supervisor, Sitgreaves, N. F., later a prominent cattleman in this region.

McKee, Camp

See Camp Mason.

McLaughlin Peak   Santa Cruz Co.   G. L. O. Map, 1892.

In Canillo range northeast of Harshaw. Corresponds very closely with Mount Hughes on Patagonia quad, 1905, q.v. As near as can be worked out they are the same.

McLellan   Coconino Co.   Tusayan N. F. Map, 1927.

In sec. 5, T. 21 N., R. 1 E. Station A. T. & S. F. R. R. 8 miles west of Williams. "After C. T. McLellan, Supt. Arizona Division old A. & P. R. R." A.G.W.

McMillen   Gila Co.

Present P. O. name of McMillenville.

McMillenville   Gila Co.   G. L. O. Map, 1921; Crook N. F., 1926.

In T. 16 E., R. 2 N. Named for Charles McMillen, discoverer of famous "Stonewall Jackson" silver mine. About 10 miles northeast of Globe. Here 1882 the Globe Rangers, hot on an Apache trail, went into camp; were attacked by Indians and lost nearly all their horses.

"About 20 miles from Globe City, a mining village named McMillenville has recently sprung up which already contains three hundred inhabitants; three blacksmith shops; one carpenter shop; a bakery; barber shop; two stores; saloons; and post office." Hinton's *Hand Book.* On October 10, 1878 name changed to McMillen. Ante-dated Globe by several years and was quite a mining camp when Globe was discovered, 1876. P. O. established November 12, 1877, Charles T. Martin, P. M.

McMullen Valley or McMullen Wash   Yuma and Maricopa Cos.
Smith Map, 1879; G. L. O., 1892.

Directly south of Harcuvar range, north side Parker branch R. R. Santa Fe Mining district. Extends northeast from vicinity of Salome to near Forepaugh. "Sometimes called Grace valley. McMullen was an old prospector in this region." Letter, P. M. Salome. McMullen station shows on Ehrenburg-Prescott stage road on map.

McNary   Apache Co.   U. S. G. S. Map, 1923.

Sawmill town Apache Ind. Res. Original name was Cooley, after the old pioneer scout. When McNary Lumber Co., of Louisiana, bought the mill and cutting contract name was changed to McNary after James G. McNary of the lumber company. Never should have been changed. P. O. established under McNary April 8, 1925. Drue T. Diel, P. M. See Cooley, and Clough Cienega.

McNeal   Cochise Co.   G. L. O. Map, 1921; U. S. G. S., 1923.

In T. 21 S., R. 26 E. Station E. P. & S. W. R. R. 7 miles from Douglas. Named after Judge Miles McNeal, one of first settlers here. P. O. established October 1, 1909. Josephine A. Lane, P. M.

McNutt Mountain   Mohave County

See Nutt.

McPherson, Camp   Yuma Co.

Temporary military post on road La Paz to Prescott, 1866-67. About 60 miles southwest Prescott. After Gen. McPherson, U. S. Army. Established 1866 to protect travel on road. Changed to Camp Date Creek, q.v.

McQueen   Maricopa Co.

Spur and loading station Phoenix and Eastern R. R. about 2 miles south of Mesa. After A. C. McQueen, for many years Live Stock Agent A. T. & S. F. R. R. Has a large stock ranch and farm near this point. Member Arizona Live Stock Sanitary Board 1899.

McVay   Yuma Co.   U. S. G. S. Map, 1923.

Station Parker branch A. T. & S. F. R. R. about 10 miles northwest of Vicksburg. "Named for man who drilled the first well here for the railroad company." Alma Beeler, P. M. Bouse.

MacDonald   Cochise Co.

Settlement on San Pedro river. "Established 1882 by Henry J. Horne and others. Named for Alexander F. MacDonald, then President of Maricopa Stake, L. D. S. Was upon lands then claimed as part of San Juan de Boquillas Grant, later rejected by U. S. Land Court. Was really an extension of St. David settlement." *Mormon Settlement.*

Mack   Yavapai Co.   Santa Fe folder.

Station, Drake and Clarksdale branch A. T. & S. F. R. R., 28 miles southeast of Ashfork; 6 miles south of Drake.

Macnab   Mohave Co.

Nobody knows origin of name. Only record is that of the post office. P. O. established January 4, 1903. Francis L. O'Dea, P. M.

Maddox Ranch   Navajo Co.

First called Stiles, after Barnett (Barney) Stiles, cattleman. Later called Maddox after a man by this name who located here 1914. P. O. established January 15, 1914. McPherson C. Maddox, P. M. See Stiles.

Madero (Sic) Canyon   Santa Cruz Co.   Postal Route Map, 1929

Sp., "lumber." Should be spelled Madera. P. O., store and sawmill town, southwest of Greaterville at county line. First sawmill in Arizona was erected here, q.v. Canyon originally called "Casa Blanca," q. v. P. O. established April 29, 1929. Catherine M. Dusenberry, P. M.

Magma   Pinal Co.   U. S. G. S. Map, 1923

In T. 3 S., R. 8 E. Junction point on Arizona-Eastern R. R. 30 miles southwest of Superior.

"Word Magma means molten rock material, from which igneous rock, or lava is formed. I presume name was so given to the Magma mine. There is much igneous rock in the mine." Letter, William Koerner, Supt. Magma mine.

Mine first known as "Silver Queen." P. O. established Aug. 13, 1915. George H. Parker, P. M.

Mahan Mountain   Coconino Co.   Map, Coconino N. F., 1928.

In northern part of T. 16 N., R. 9 E. "A. J. T. Mahan was a settler who took up and patented a location on a spring on east slope this mountain 1889." Letter. Ed Miller, Flagstaff.

Maine   Coconino Co.   U. S. G. S. Map, 1923.

Station A. T. & S. F. R. R., 18 miles west of Flagstaff. "The station was established shortly after sinking of battleship Maine and was named for her." A.G.W.

There is a story that John Dennis who owned the sawmill here came from Maine and gave it that name. Mr. Wells, however, is undoubtedly correct for he had the naming of these places while superintendent of Atlantic and Pacific R. R.

Maish   Pima Co.   G. L. O. Map, 1892-1909.

In T. 16 S., R. 8 E. Ranch Papago Ind. Res. One of the ranches of the Maish and Driscoll Co. of Tucson which ran many cattle in Pima county in early days. Their brand was 73 on left ribs. On some old maps it is "Marsh," an error.

Maley   Cochise Co.

According to records in Washington this was first name of Willcox. P. O. was established as Maley on September 13, 1880, John F. Roll, P. M. Changed to Willcox, q. v., October 19, of same year.

Malpais Spring   Navajo Co.

Sp., "bad land"; so named because of volcanic formation around it. In T. 22 N., R. 21 E., Navajo Ind. Res.

Mam-a-tok Mountain   Pima Co.   G. L. O. Map, 1921; U. S. G. S. Map, 1923.

In T. 18 N., R. 2 W., in Mesquite range about 12 miles north of Mexican Boundary line. In La Quituni valley. Meaning unknown.

Mammoth   Pinal Co.   U. S. G. S. Map, 1923.

In T. 8 S., R. 17 E. Copper camp on San Pedro river east of Black Hills. "Mammoth mine was located here by Frank Schultz in 1881. It was a 'mammoth' copper ledge." P. O. established here May 24, 1895, Felix C. McKinney, P. M.

Manila   Navajo Co.   U. S. G. S. Map, 1923.

In T. 18 N., R. 18 E. Flag station A. T. & S. F. R. R., 15 miles west of Holbrook. Named during Spanish-American War after city in Philippines. P. O. established June 6, 1912, Clarence G. Wallace, P. M.

Manje Springs

See Monkey.

Manlyville   Pinal Co.   G. L. O. Map, 1892.

Old stage station about 15 miles southwest Old Camp Grant, west of San Pedro river. So called after Manly C. Chamberlin, first post master. Appointed April 18, 1881.

Mansfield Camp   Apache Co.

Heitman's *List* gives this as "Seven miles south of Fort Defiance." Unable to locate.

Manzana   Santa Cruz Co.   Map, Coronado N. F., 1927.

Mountain in sec. 35, T. 23 S., R. 11 E. There is a Manzanita spring at foot of mountain on south side. According to Forest Ranger A. S. Wingo, "The Mountain is named for the dense cover of manzanita all over its slopes." Manzana or Manzano, Sp., "apple," may have been the origin.

Manzanita Creek   Coconino Co.

Grand Canyon N. P. Intermittent stream rising lat. 36° 11', long. 112° 1'. Flows west into Bright Angel creek. Named and located in Park Service pamphlet at base of Manzanita point. Spanish for shrub of the genus *Arctostaphylos*, common in this region. Decision U.S.G.B.

Manzora   Cochise Co.   U. S. G. S. Map, 1923.

In T. 16 S., R. 23 E. Station S. P. R. R. East side Dragoon pass. "Unable to determine significance of this name. Station established prior to 1900. Probably a combination of letters and has no meaning." Letter, Paul Shoup.

"For some years it was known as Golden Rule but was later on changed to Manzora. Meaning of Manzora unknown." Letter, P. M. Dragoon. P. O. established December 13, 1916, Harry O. Miller, P. M.

Maple Peak   Greenlee Co.   U. S. G. S. Map, 1923.

Elevation 8,302 feet. In sec. 14, T. 1 S., R. 31 E., Crook N. F. "There are large numbers of maple trees in the canyons of this mountain."

Marana   Pima Co.   G. L. O. Map, 1909; Postal Guide, 1929.

Sp., "jungle or tangle." Railroad station S. P. R. R., 22 miles west of Tucson. Established 1890. Probably because of dense thickets of mesquite, cat claw, and other desert trees around here. "First called Postvale after Mr. Post of Battle Creek, Mich., who was interested here for a time. In 1920 it began to grow due to the erection of a fine pumping plant. Much cotton is now raised here." P. O. established May 17, 1924, Jesse W. Dells, P. M.

Marble Canyon   Coconino Co.   Post Route Map, 1929.

P. O. established Oct. 12, 1927 by this name at east end of bridge across the Marble canyon about 6 miles from Lee Ferry. Florence L. Lowrey, P. M.

Marble Gorge   Coconino Co.   U. S. G. S. Map, 1927.

Canyon or gorge in Colorado river between mouths of Paria and Little Colorado, so named by Major Powell 1869. "We have cut through the sandstones and limestones met in the upper part of the canyon and through one great bed of marble a thousand feet in thickness. So we call it 'Marble Canyon.' It is 65½ miles long." Powell.

Dellenbaugh writes: "As the formation was mainly a fine-grained grey marble, Powell concluded to call this division by a separate name and gave it the title Marble Canyon." Decision U.S.G.B.

Marcos Terrace   Coconino Co.   Map, Grand Canyon N. P., 1927.

In T. 33 N., R. 2 W. North side of canyon. After Fray Marcos, the Spanish Padre. So named by members of U.S.G.S. who mapped the canyon.

Marcou Mesa   Navajo Co.

Mesa about 6 miles north of St. Joseph. Named for Jules Marcou, geologist with Whipple's party. See Rabbit hills.

Maria Santissima de Carmen Land Grant

See Buena Vista.

Maricopa   Pinal Co.   Smith Map, 1879; Eckhoff, 1880.

In sec. 28, T. 4 S., R. 3 E. Station, S. P. R. R., 10 miles south of Gila river. When Southern Pacific reached here in 1880 the military telegraph station was moved here, the railroad station was opened under this name, and gone was the glory of the old Maricopa Wells Stage station 3 miles south of the Gila river and some 7 miles northwest of present Maricopa station.

Later on when they started to build the branch to Phoenix, the company planned to abandon this Maricopa station and run a branch from a point on the line 4 or 5 miles west of present Maricopa. They first called it Maricopaville, then Heaton, which is its present name.

Maricopa was a very lively village when the author was there in February, 1880. It was where a change was made to stages for Tucson and the east. Travel to Tombstone was at its peak. Huge twenty-passenger stages rolled away with every seat, inside and out, filled. Great twenty-four-mule freight teams lined the road to Tucson and Tombstone. Maricopa was also the getting-off place for Phoenix, Prescott, McDowell, and points north, to which military telegraph line ran. Was a busy place, day and night, with special emphasis on the night life. P. O. established here November 26, 1880. Perry Williams, P. M. See Maricopa Wells, Maricopaville, and Heaton.

Maricopa County

Created out of Yavapai county by Sixth Legislature February 12, 1871, sixth county in Territory. Since that date portions have been taken from it to form Pinal, 1875, and Gila, 1881. Named after Maricopa Indians.

Maricopa County Recreation Park   Maricopa Co.

In T. 3 N., R. 5 E. Area in McDowell mountains about 30 miles northeast of Phoenix. Purchased from Federal Government by county in 1929 for future recreational use. Contains 5,100 acres of rough desert mountain land. Covers crest of McDowell range, looking down into Verde valley on one side and area about Phoenix on the other.

"An important Yuman people living along Gila river in southern Arizona. Maricopa is their Pima name. Their own name for themselves is 'Pipatsje' meaning 'people,' a common tribal name among Southwest Indians." Hodge.

Maricopa Cheriquis says, "It means 'butterfly.'"

The early Spaniards found the Indians with no clothes, but as they had their faces and hair painted yellow, red, and black, they called these Indians "Maricopa," or "butterfly." As the Spanish word for butterfly is "mariposa," this seems plausible.

Maricopa Indian Reservation   Pinal Co.   U. S. G. S. Map, 1923.

Small outlying reservation for these Indians. South of Maricopa station S. P. R. R.

Maricopa Indians

Maricopa Mountains   Maricopa Co.   G. L. O. Map, 1921.

Short range about 30 miles west of Maricopa station on S. P. R. R., which crosses range through an open pass. See Estrella mountains.

Maricopa Point   Coconino Co.

See Rowes Point.

Maricopa Villages   Maricopa Co.

War Dept. map, 1864, shows a "Military Post" at the Maricopa Villages on Gila river not far from old Maricopa Wells station. Not found on any list of military camps, or posts, however. There is a more recent village by this same name, on south side Salt river, in secs. 2, 3, T. 1., R. 1 E.

Maricopaville   Pinal Co.

Station opened by S. P. R. R. as a new station apart from all former stations by that name. This was about 4 or 5 miles west of old Maricopa station. They were preparing to build a branch line to Phoenix and from this point it was a straight run into Phoenix. They named the new place Maricopaville and on May 12, 1879, ran a large excursion from California points and had a big sale of town lots.

Phoenix papers of that date say that 216 passengers came to the auction. John Sutherland bought first lot sold, Lot No. 1, Block No. 1. It brought $1,000 cash.

Phoenix Herald correspondent says: "As a political and commercial point Maricopaville has a great future." But the movement failed. Proposed line was 8 or 9 miles shorter and the Gila Crossing had solid banks on each side. The company planned to go almost due north to Phoenix, passing near present town of Laveen. This, however, left Tempe off the line. The representative in the Territorial Legislature of that town blocked the bill, offering the road a subsidy, unless it came through his town. The railroad company accepted this change rather than lose the subsidy.

It proved a poor trade for the present crossing of the Gila being very wide with low sandy banks, has cost the company many thousands of dollars for new bridges to replace those washed out by floods, and many days of interrupted traffic.

"The Gila bridge is washed out" was an oft' told tale in Phoe-

nix in those days. But they got the subsidy and the road went via Tempe. Later this place was called Heaton, q. v.
See Maricopa and Maricopa Wells.

Maricopa Wells   Pinal Co.

In sec. 17, T. 3 S., R. 3 E. Early stage and Indian trading station located southwest corner Salt River Ind. Res., some 28 miles from Phoenix. South side Gila river 3 miles from Morgans Ferry. About 6 or 8 miles northwest of present railroad station of Maricopa.

There was here in the Santa Cruz wash a well of good water which was sold to travellers. Water was raised by a mule or ox team at the end of a long rope. The bucket had a trap valve in the bottom, which filled it when lowered into the water and emptied it on top when dropped on a long wooden peg in the trough. A Mexican boy drove the team with much belaboring and shouting.

The military telegraph line had an office here with a branch northward to Phoenix and Prescott. In 1869, according to one record, there was a customs house here in charge of Col. Poston. He moved it to Florence, 1871.

From all accounts there have been two different points by this name in this vicinity. First, the original Maricopa Wells, mentioned above. Second, the present railroad station of Heaton, first called Maricopa, then Maricopaville, and finally Heaton, about 4 or 5 miles west of present Maricopa. They planned to run the branch line to Phoenix from Heaton, q. v. Then came the present station of Maricopa on S. P. line at junction of branch road to Phoenix.

Barney says that on July 27, 1864, John B. Allen filed a pre-emption claim on land about this place in the Land Office at Tucson. Barney claims this was the first land filing in the territory. The records, however, do not show this to be a fact. First land office in Territory was not opened at Prescott until 1868. Tucson office was not opened until 1881. See First U. S. Land Offices, First Homestead Entries, Maricopa, Heaton, Maricopaville.

Marinette   Maricopa Co.   U. S. G. S. Map, 1923.

In T. 3 N., R. 1 E. Station 12 miles northwest Phoenix on A. T. & S. F. R. R. "So named by people who homesteaded land in that vicinity and came originally from Marinette, Wis." A.G.W.

Marion Point   Coconino Co.

Grand Canyon N. P., near northeast corner of Park. Named for John H. Marion, pioneer of 1865, public spirited citizen and editor who published a newspaper at Prescott for many years. Born in Louisiana, 1835; died, in Prescott, July 27, 1891.

"Week after week in the columns of the *Miner*, John H. Marion fought out the battles of America for Americans. Not so much as a Spanish advertisement could be found in its columns." Bourke. Named by the author. Decision USGB.

Marsh   Coconino Co.   Map, Grand Canyon N. P.

Butte, south side of Colorado river on Granite gorge. Near lat. 36° 10', long. 112° 15'. G. W. James says: "I called it Marsh Plateau after Prof. Marsh of Yale, the great paleontologist."

Marsh   Gila Co.   Map, Tonto N. F., 1927.

Creek rising in T. 10 N., R. 14 E. Flows westerly into Tonto creek at Hells Gate in T. 10 N., R. 12 E. Origin unknown.

Marsh   Navajo Co.   U. S. G. S. Map, 1923.

Pass in north part of Navajo Ind. Res., in Klethla valley. Near Lolamai peak, in lat. 37° 38', long. 110° 30'. After Marsh of Yale University.

Marsh (sic)   Pima Co.

Settlement in T. 15 S., R. 11 E. About 8 miles southwest of Tucson. Is called Maish on G.L.O. map, 1892, which is correct. But is plainly Marsh on G.L.O. map, 1909. After Maish of firm of Maish and Driscoll of Tucson.

Marsh Pass   Apache Co.

On Navajo Ind. Res. So called because many years ago when first explored the stream through this pass had many swampy places where travel was difficult. For this reason the pass was so named. Some authorities claim it was named for Prof. Marsh, the scientist, but this is denied by those who should know.

Marshall Lake   Coconino Co.   G. L. O. Map, 1921;
                                              Coconino N. F., 1928.

In secs. 10, 20, T. 20 N., R. 8 E., north of Lake Mary. "So called for John Marshall, who homesteaded lake site, 1892, and received a patent for the land. Marshall was at one time superintendent of Flagstaff Water Works." Letter, E. G. Miller, Flagstaff.

Martin   Yavapai Co.   Map, Prescott N. F., 1927

In T. 16 N., R. 2 E. Canyon heading west side Woodchute mountain. Runs northwest into Lonesome valley. Origin unknown.

Martin Mountain   Yavapai Co.   Map, Prescott N. F., 1927.

In T. 14 N., R. 5 W. On west side of Skull valley at corner Prescott N. F. After Hon. John C. Martin of Prescott. Mr. Martin came to Prescott, November 1882, and purchased the Arizona *Journal*, which was consolidated with the Arizona *Miner*, and published as *Journal-Miner* for many years. Register U. S. Land Office at Prescott, 1890 to 1893. Member 18th Arizona Legislature, 1895.

Martin Peak   Yuma Co.   G. L. O. Map, 1921.

Elevation 2,300 feet, about 12 miles south of Salome, Parker branch A. T. & S. F. R. R., west of Harqua Hala in Little Harqua Hala mountains. After Hon. John B. Martin, who lived at Salome and worked the Harqua Hala mine for many years. See Brayton.

Martinez   Yavapai Co.   U. S. G. S. Map, 1923.

In T. 10 N., R. 6 E. Old mining camp on Prescott-Phoenix R. R., east side Date Creek mountains. In Martinez canyon. P. O. established October 3, 1896, Edward Ziegler, P. M.

Martinsville   Graham Co.

Settlement one mile south of Bonita. "After Joseph M. Martin, discharged colored soldier 10th U. S. Cavalry. He settled here on a little place and quite a Negro settlement grew up around him." Letter, Rex King, Safford.

Martyres, Rio de los

Sp., River of the Martyrs. Kino's name for Colorado river, q. v.

Mary Lake   Coconino Co.   G. L. O. Map, 1921;
                                                  Coronado N. F., 1927.

In T. 20 N., R. 8 E., artificial lake about 8 miles southeast of Flagstaff. At lower end Clark valley. Dam built, 1905, by Arizona Lumber and Timber Co. Lake thus formed named for Mary Riordan, eldest daughter of T. A. Riordan. Its outlet is through Walnut ·canyon into Little Colorado river through San Francisco wash.

Marysville   Gila Co.   Eckhoff Map, 1880.

"This town was settled in March, 1880, and only lasted about three years. Named after first woman settler, Mrs. Mary Pyeatt. Mining camp of 1880 on Webber creek, about 3 miles west of Payson." Letter, F. W. Croxen, Forest Ranger.

Maryville   Maricopa Co.   Smith Map, 1879.

"The town of Maryville, often called Rowes station, was located in early days on north bank Salt river, opposite Lehi. Founder was Wm. Rowe, who came to valley 1868. When McDowell was abandoned, Maryville became of no importance and was gradually deserted." Farish. Barney says it was often called "Maryville Crossing of Salt river." But why Maryville, no one seems to know. P. O. established April 25, 1873, Charles Whitlow, P. M.

Mascot   Cochise Co.   Judge Map, 1916; U. S. G. S., 1921.

Station and mining camp, end of Mascot & Western branch Arizona-Eastern R. R., 15 miles southeast of Willcox in Dos Cabezas mountains. After Mascot mine. P. O. established December 11, 1916, Lillie A. C. Hauser, P. M.

Masies Canyon   Cochise Co.

See Turkey Creek canyon.

Mason Fort   Santa Cruz Co.

On Santa Cruz river near Calabasas; named for Gen. John Mason, of California Volunteers; commanding Military Dept. Garrisoned by California Volunteers during Civil War, with a sub-post at Tubac.

According to Eckhoff map, 1880, this post was located close to Kitchens ranch. *Heitman's Register* says: "Established Aug. 21, 1865, 12 miles southeast of Tubac. Changed to Camp McKee September 6, 1866. Abandoned October 1, 1866."

Masons Valley   Gila Co.   Smith Map, 1879.

North side Pinal mountains about 10 miles north of Huttons peak. Old military outpost of Camp Pinal was in this valley. "We crossed the lofty Pinal range over into the beautiful little nook known as Masons valley." Bourke, 1870. Named, perhaps, after Col. Julius W. Mason, 5th U. S. Cavalry, operating in this region with Crook in 1871-73. Possibly named after Charles G. Mason, one of the discoverers of Silver King mine.

Massicks   Yavapai Co.

P. O. established March 6, 1895, Peter Meade, P. M. Origin unknown.

Mastens Peak   Pinal Co.

Named for N. K. Masten, president, Maricopa and Phoenix R. R. Said to lie on divide between Superior and Pinal mountains. The author knows there was such a peak but it is not found on any map.

Matkatamiba Mesa and Canyon   Coconino Co.
Map, Tusayan N. F., 1927.

Grand Canyon N. P., near lat. 36° 20′ N., long. 112° 42′ W. Low table land on left bank Colorado river partly filling a small bend. Bordered on southwest by Sinyala canyon, on northeast by "Matkatamiba canyon." Name of an Indian family. Decision, USGB. Short stream flowing northwest into Colorado river near 150 Mile creek.

Matthews   Graham Co.   Judge Map, 1916.

In T. 6 S., R. 24 E. Early Mormon settlement on Gila river. Founded December, 1880, by Joseph Matthews and family. Also called Matthewsville for its locator; then `Fairview; and lastly Glenbar, q. v.

On south side Gila river. Station on Arizona-Eastern R. R., 5 miles below Pima. P. O. established February 9, 1897, Hulda A. Blaine, P. M. There was a flour mill here in 1883.

Matthews Peak   Apache Co.   G. L. O. Map, 1921;
Gregory Map, Navajo Ind. Res., 1916.

Elevation 9,403 feet. In T. 7 N., R. 6 W., Navajo Ind. Res. West side Chuska mountains. "So named in memory of Dr. Washington Matthews, author of many papers on Navajo anthropology." Gregory.

Matthewsville   Graham Co.

See Glenbar and Matthews.

Matthie   Yavapai Co.

Station, Ash Fork-Phoenix branch A. T. & S. F. R. R., about 5 miles north of Wickenburg. "Formerly A. & C. Junction. In honor of a superintendent of the Santa Fe R. R., who lost his life at this point in a motor car accident." A.G.W.

Maverick Butte   Maricopa Co.   Map, Tonto N. F., 1927.

In sec. 13, T. 7 N., R. 5 E., near head Camp creek about 5 miles north of Kentuck mountain. "J. M. Cartright says this peak was so named because years ago he and some other men discovered a bunch of mavericks in the rough country around it. After branding them they named the mountain to commemorate the event." Letter, Fred Croxen.

Maverick Hill   Greenlee Co.   Map, Crook N. F., 1926.

Elevation 7,457 feet. In T. 5 S., R. 32 E., near New Mexico line. "Maverick Hill is in a basin of the same name. Basin was very brushy and rough and in early days came to be a fine place for mavericks. Hence the name." Letter, J. W. Girdner, Forest Service, Clifton.

Maverick Mountain   Apache Co.   Map, Fort Apache Ind. Res., 1928.

At southwest corner of T. 4 N., R. 26 E. Fort Apache Ind. Res., east side Big Bonita creek. Indian Service maintains a fire lookout here.

"This mountain was between Slaughter range on one side

and Springerville range on the other. It was a very rough region and before the stockmen realized it was full of big long-eared mavericks." Letter, A. F. Potter.

Mayer   Yavapai Co.   G. L. O. Maps, 1892-1921.

In sec. 23, T. 12 N., R. 1 E. Named for Joe Mayer who built a ranch and kept the stage station at this place in late Seventies. Was on Black Canyon Stage line, Prescott to Phoenix. Famous for excellence of its meals. On Big Bug creek, also present station on Prescott and Middleton branch A. T. & S. F. R. R., located near old station, 32 miles southeast of Prescott. P. O. established as Mayer, January 11, 1884, Sarah B. Mayer, P. M.

Mays Hill   Cochise Co.   Map, Coronado N. F., 1927.

In sec. 7, T. 20 S., R. 22 E. Lone peak about 4 miles directly west of Tombstone. Origin unknown.

Max   Apache Co.

Town somewhere in southern Apache county. P. O. established February 24, 1881, Redden Allred, P. M. The author's recollection is that it was Reuben Allred, but the name is plainly spelled Redden in the P. O. records in Washington.

Maxey   Graham Co.

In T. 4 S., R. 23 E. Small settlement on Gila river near Fort Thomas Military Reservation. In 1880 it consisted of a miscellaneous collection of "shacks," mostly saloons and houses of prostitution. Possibly two hundred and fifty people lived here, making their living off the soldiers.

"At a meeting held last evening, it was voted that the future name of this settlement be Maxey and that a petition be sent in for a post office with Judge Meany as postmaster." *Tucson Citizen* June 24, 1880.

"The town was named by J. B. Collins, often called the 'Father' of Maxey, who served in the Confederate army. Major General Samuel B. Maxey was born in Kentucky, graduate of West Point Academy, and took part in the Mexican War. He raised the 9th Texas Infantry and served in Civil War with great distinction. Elected U. S. Senator from Texas, two terms, 1874-1887. P. O. established June 21, 1886. William Hibberd; P. M. Name changed to Fort Thomas February 8, 1887."

Maxton   Yavapai Co.   G. L. O. Map, 1908; Prescott N. F., 1927.

Settlement in sec. 11, T. 12½ N., R. 2 W., about 3 miles north of Venezia. P. O. established July 6, 1901, Marilla T. Alwens, P. M.

Mazatzal City   Gila Co.   Smith Map, 1879; G. L. O. Map, 1921.

Early Mormon settlement south side East Fork of Verde, about 10 miles west of Payson, at upper end Deadman canyon. About 7 miles above mouth of Pine creek.

"Settlement was made by Mormons in late Seventies. They abandoned it about 1882 and moved to Pine. Called Mazatzal City for want of a better name." Fred Croxen. Location must have been at point where City creek, on map of Tonto N. F., 1927, enters east fork of Verde in sec. 17, T. 10 N., R. 9 E.

Mazatzal Mountains   Gila and Maricopa Cos.
                              U. S. G. S. Map, 1923; Tonto N. F., 1927.

Forms a dividing line between Gila and Maricopa counties, west of Roosevelt lake. Range is about 40 miles long, extending north and south. Salt river breaks through the range at Four Peaks. Here the Roosevelt dam is located.

Early settlers said the word was Apache and meant "bleak, barren." Some early writers spell it "Mat-a-Zell." McClintock says Apaches named it "Maz-at-zark," meaning "space between." An Indian held up his four fingers to represent the peaks and between them it was "Maz-at-zark," the space between. See Four Peaks.

Mazatzal Peak   Gila Co.   Map, Tonto N. F., 1927.

In sec. 5, T. 8 N., R. 8 E., east side Mazatzal range.

Meadow Creek   Mohave Co.   Camp Mohave Sheet, U. S. G. S., 1892.

Coues says: "Beale in Oct., 1857, went from Meadow creek down into Sacramento valley. He named it because of the lovely green grassy meadow at its head." Rises in "Sitgreaves Pass" in T. 19 N., R. 9 E., immediately south of Mount Nutt, and flows east into Sacramento valley where it is lost.

Meadows, The   Apache Co.

Large grassy flat on Little Colorado below St. Johns. Purchased 1878 by Mormon church for location by settlers. First settler, Ira Hatch, arrived November 28, 1879. Later it was abandoned. In 1884 was owned by Twenty-four Cattle Co., Smith Carson & Tee, as a headquarters ranch and so used for many years.

Meadow Valley Creek   Gila Co.   Smith Map, 1879; Eckhoff, 1880.

Stream rising Sierra Ancha mountains flows northwest, enters Tonto creek, 35 miles northeast of Fort McDowell. So called by troops that camped on this creek in 1872 "because of the lovely meadows." Military outpost of McDowell was established here in 1866. Inclined to think this is the present Spring creek.

Meath   Yavapai Co.   Map, Tusayan N. F., 1927.

Station Ash Fork-Phoenix branch A. T. & S. F. R. R. 9 miles south of Ash Fork. "An old English name. Suggested by the Rev. Meany of Prescott." A.G.W.

Medicine Valley   Coconino Co.

In secs. 5, 6, 7, 8, T. 23 N., R. 8 E. "Medicine valley was named for Medicine Cave, excavated by Museum of Northern Arizona, 1929. So called because a Medicine Man's kit was found in the cave." Letter, Dr. Harold Colton, Flagstaff.

Meesville   Yavapai Co.   Prescott Sheet, U. S. G. S., 1902.

In T. 10 N., R. 1 W. Settlement in Bradshaw mountains east of Del Pasco mountain about 2 miles southwest of Alexander. Named for James Mee, who located here, 1880, and did some mining. P. O. established November 28, 1881, James Mee, P. M.

Melendreth Pass

See Melendrez Pass.

Melendrez Pass or Canyon   Pima Co.   Map, Coronado N. F., 1925.

Pass through lower end Santa Ritas directly west of Greaterville. North of Mount Wrightson (Old Baldy). Greaterville is at its eastern end. Canyon runs northwest into Santa Cruz at Continental. "This canyon or pass took its name from an old-time Mexican whose first name was Melendrez. Ruins of

stone and adobe house he lived in can still be seen." Letter,
Carl Schofield, Forest Ranger. G.L.O. map, 1909 spells it Melendreth.

Mellen   Mohave Co.   G. L. O. Map, 1909.

Station, A. T. & S. F. R. R., just at Colorado river. After
Capt. Mellen, early day steamboat captain on the river. P. O.
established March 26, 1903. Emelie O. Holstein, P. M.

Meridian   Maricopa Co.

Settlement in Buckeye valley, near crossing of Salt and Gila
river base line, and Gila and Salt river meridian, hence the
name. About 12 miles southwest of Phoenix. P. O. established
July 16, 1895, Harriet Toothaker, P. M.

Meridian Butte   Apache Co.   U. S. G. S. Map, 1923.

Butte near 110th Meridian. At northwest corner of county.
So called because it lies close to the Meridian. On Navajo Ind.
Res.

Merijilda Canyon   Greenlee Co.   Map, Crook N. F., 1926.

Canyon heads east side Mount Graham; runs northeast into
Gila about one mile east of Safford. After a Mexican, Merijilda
Grijalva, one of Gen. Crook's trusted scouts who lived in Gila
valley for some years. When the author knew him in 1880-82, he
was a handsome, dignified Mexican of the old type, who appeared
to be a native Californian.

Meriwitica (sic)   Mohave Co.   U. S. G. S. Map, 1923.

In T. 28 N., R. 13 W. Spring and creek on Hualpai Ind. Res.
Runs into Spruce canyon. "This name Meriwitheca had its
origin from the Hualpai word Muth-widi, meaning 'Hard dirt
or hard ground.' This is the character of the soil in the canyon."
Letter, Supt., Hualpai Ind. Res.

Merriam Crater   Coconino Co.

In secs. 35, 36, T. 23 N., R. 10 E. About 2 miles northeast of
Coconino N. F. Named in honor of C. Hart Merriam, naturalist,
author, and Chief of U. S. Biological Survey at Washington,
D. C. for many years. Decision U.S.G.B.

Merrill Crater   Coconino Co.

In sec. 12, T. 21 N., R. 10 E., about 2 miles north A. T. & S. F.
R. R. Named in honor of Dr. George P. Merrill, 1854-1929,
formerly head curator of geology in the U. S. National Museum,
the first scientist to visit and describe Meteor mountain, which is
in this vicinity. Decision, U.S.G.B.

Merrill Peak   Graham Co.   Map, Crook N. F., 1926.

In sec. 25, T. 8 S., R. 24 E. One of the peaks near Mount
Graham. "This peak was named after Forest Ranger Gerald
Merrill who erected the first forest fire lookout tower on its
top." Letter, Rex King, Forest Supervisor.

Mesa   Maricopa Co.   Smith Map, 1879; Eckhoff, 1880;
                                          G. L. O., 1921.

Sp., "table." Elevation 1,273 feet. Town in T. 1 N., R. 5 E.,
about 20 miles southeast of Phoenix on Arizona-Eastern R. R.,
3 miles from Salt river. Established Feb. 1878 by Mormon colonists from Salt Lake City, Utah. So called because it was located on a plateau or mesa somewhat above the valley. Incor-

porated July 5, 1883. P. O. established as Mesa Jan. 19, 1889, George Passey, P. M. First called Zenos, q. v. Then Mesaville. Mesa City on Smith map, 1879.

The land on which the town now stands was located first in May, 1878, by T. C. Sirrine who deeded it to three Trustees: C. I. Robson, G. W. Sirrine, and F. M. Pomeroy who named and platted it. All streets were 130 feet wide. Incorporated July 15, 1883. A. F. McDonald, first mayor. First called Hayden, because for a time mail went to Hayden Ferry. Postal authorities first refused to allow the name Mesa for a postoffice because of a Mesaville in that region. That town died however and Mesa came into its own. Census of January 4, 1894, gave it 648 persons.

Mesa Butte　　　Coconino Co.　　　U. S. G. S. Map, 1923.

In T. 26 N., R. 6 E. Descriptive name.

Mesa de la Avansada

See San Bernardino.

Mesa La Vaca　　　Navajo Co.　　　Mallory Map, 1876; Smith, 1879; Eckhoff, 1880.

Sp., "Cow Mesa." Northeast of Hopi villages, Navajo Ind. Res. Doubtless mesa now shown as Black Mesa, q. v. Capt. Walker went clear around it 1854 and probably named it.

Mesa Redondo　　　Apache Co.　　　U. S. G. S. Map, 1923.

Sp., "Round Mesa." Large, round table land in T. 12 N., R. 24 E. Noted landmark about 15 miles southeast of Snowflake.

Mesaville　　　Maricopa Co.

One of the first names for present town of Mesa, q. v.

Mesaville　　　Pinal Co.　　　Hamilton Map, 1886; G. L. O. Map, 1892.

On San Pedro river mouth of Aravaipa creek. Early day town located near Old Camp Grant. Probably an outpost of Grant. According to *Pinal Drill*, October 16, 1880: "This place was first called Dodsons after the first postmaster but they could not get a post office under that name so they changed it." P. O. established June 6, 1878, Joseph N. Dodson, P. M.

Mescal　　　Cochise Co.　　　U. S. G. S. Map, 1923.

Railroad station E. P. & S. W. R. R., 6 miles west of Benson; established 1881. Spanish meaning, "a species of maguey or Mexican agave, which is very common about this station." P. O. established April 25, 1913. Frank E. Black, P. M. There is a station by this name on S. P. R. R. near this same point.

Mescal Gulch　　　Yavapai Co.　　　Map, Prescott N. F., 1927.

Rises east side Woodchute mountain, runs northeast into Verde river above Cottonwood. "There were many so called 'mescal pits' in this gulch used by Apaches for baking mescal in early days."

Mescal Mountains　　　Gila Co.　　　U. S. G. S. Map, 1923; Crook N. F., 1926.

In southwest corner county, east of Dripping Springs wash. "So called from abundance of mescal found on its sides." Hinton. On October 29, 1846, Lieut. Emory was in the Gila valley near base of Mount Trumbull. He says: "The crimson-tinted Sierra Carlos skirted the river on the north side the whole day." This must have been the range we now call Mescal mountains, as it is the only range on north side of Gila near this point. See Dripping springs.

Mesilla County.

One of the four Arizona counties placed by Mowry on his first map of Arizona. It extended eastward clear to the Rio Grande, and covered all of eastern Arizona, north of Cochise county. See Yuma county.

Mesquite   Maricopa Co.

An item in *Arizona Sentinel* at Yuma says: "The school at Mesquite, near Haydens Ferry, was discontinued on January 7, 1876." Farish *Notes.* There is no other record of any such settlement or P. O.

Mesquite   Pah Ute Co.   G. L. O. Map, 1921; McClintock Map.

Early Mormon settlement north side Virgin river about a mile above and across river from Bunkerville. Almost on Nevada line. Established 1880. This was another of the many settlements in Pah Ute county, once in Arizona, but eventually turned over to Nevada.

Mesquite Creek   Maricopa Co.

In T. 2 N., R. 9 E. Much branched intermittent stream joining Tortilla creek from north, Tonto N. F. So named from the mesquite trees along its course. Decision U. S. G. B.

Mesquite Flat   Maricopa Co.

In unsurveyed sec. 12, T. 2 N., R. 9 E. Small flat covering about 640 acres bordering Mesquite creek crossed by the Apache Trail. Covered with a dense stand of mesquite timber. Decision U. S. G. B.

Mesquite Mountains   Pima Co.   U. S. G. S. Map, 1923.

In Ts. 16, 17, 18 S., Rs. 1, 2 E. Lumholtz spells it Mezquite. On Papago Ind. Res.

Mesquite Springs.

See Black Mesquite.

Mesquite Wells   Yuma Co.

Stage station on road about 45 miles east of Ehrenberg. "There was a deep well worked by a Mexican and a mule. Water was bought for our animals at so much per head." *Vanished Ariz.,* 1875.

Metcalf   Greenlee Co.   U. S. G. S. Morenci Quad., 1915.

Elevation 4,431 feet, copper camp on branch railroad up Chase creek. About 8 miles northwest of Clifton. Named for Robert B. Metcalf, an early mining man who came to this camp 1872. One of the first owners of the Longfellow mine.

Meteor Mountain   Coconino Co.   U. S. G. S. Map, 1921; Coconino N. F., 1927.

In T. 19 N., R. 12½ E., known commonly as "Coon butte" or mountain. Shown on some maps as "Crater Mount." Origin of name Coon butte unknown. All old timers knew it as Coon butte when the author first saw it in 1883. About 20 miles west of Winslow near Canyon Diablo.

Farish quotes Banta: "I discovered this crater in 1861 while a guide with Wheeler who investigated it and called it Franklin's Hole. I was known then as Charley Franklin." There is however not a word in Wheeler's *Report* on this alleged discovery.

It is a distinct hill or small mountain on the open plain. The opening or crater is about 4,000 feet across and almost perfectly round. The walls are from 500 to 600 feet high and, excepting the eastern side, almost perpendicular.

The writer believes' that he and two friends, S. I. Frankenfield of Philadelphia, and Tom Trimble, grazing sheep on this range in 1889, first brought this crater to the attention of the scientific world. A sheep herder who was a trained German geologist, brought into our camp several pieces of soft iron of an unusual character. The assayer reported it as "Meteoric iron worth a dollar a pound." Pieces sent also to the Smithsonian Institution at Washington brought to the camp their expert Dr. George P. Merrill. After a long examination he gave a rather guarded report that it was possibly made by the impact of a huge meteor which had fallen and buried itself in the solid rock of the plain.

We organized a mining company and dug a shaft seeking the main body but finally gave that up as hopeless. The author sent a large piece of it to the World's Fair at Chicago in 1893. A few years later D. M. Barringer and his associates spent large sums drilling holes and sinking an open shaft in an effort to determine whether the meteor was really buried there. They got no satisfactory results and discontinued work after an expenditure of over $100,000. About 1925, another company renewed the search sinking drill holes outside the rim of the crater.

To date, nothing definite has been discovered. Present theory is that the meteor drove in on an angle and is buried off from the floor of the crater under the solid rock of the plain.

P. O. established April 27, 1906, Samuel J. Holsinger, P. M. The Barringer Co. then had a large number of men at work and needed postal facilities. See *Pacific Monthly Magazine* for 1905 for complete history.

Methodist Creek and Mountains   Gila Co.   Map, Tonto N. F., 1927.

Creek heads in the mountains, flows southwest into Roosevelt lake in sec. 25, T. 5 N., R. 11 E. Mountains are a group of rough hills in Ts. 5, 6 N., R. 12 E. West side Salome creek.

"From the best authorities around here this name was given these mountains because a young fellow, Will Vineyard, about 1890 robbed a bee tree on this creek and had a pretty rough reception from the bees. 'The way they went after me would have made a Methodist preacher swear,' was his report when he came home. So they called it Methodist creek and mountains." Letter, R. I. Stewart, Forest Ranger.

Mexican Water   Apache Co.   G. L. O. Map, 1921.

Trading post junction of Walker and Chinle creeks, Navajo Ind. Res. Almost on Colorado-Arizona boundary line. "This is on the 'Mormon Road' of 1879, which here crosses Chinle creek." Gregory.

Miami   Gila Co.

Elevation 3,408 feet. Town about five miles west of Globe. Named by James F. Gerald for stockholders of Miami Milling Co., who were from this valley in Ohio. Settled, 1907. The *Arizona Republican*, August 30, 1929, says: "The name was for a girl, Mima Tune, who married 'Black Jack' Newman, who claimed to have discovered the mine. Jack sold his claims to the Lewissohn interests and asked that it be named for his wife. Jack could not write very well and the word Mima looked like Miami, so it was named that way." A rather doubtful story.

Mica   Pima Co.   Map, Coronado N. F., 1927.

Elevation 8,950 feet, at eastern end Tanque Verde mountains, directly east of Tucson. "There are large amounts of mica here."

Midmont   Maricopa Co.   G. L. O. Map, 1912.

P. O. established January 7, 1919, Louise Osborne, P. M. Was about 4 miles northwest of and midway between Phoenix and Phoenix mountains (Camelback).

Midnight Mesa   Gila Co.   Map, Tonto N. F., 1926.

In T. 9 N., R. 8 E. Black looking mesa west side Mazatzals. "Is covered with dark oak brush. The formation is of black volcanic rock. Hence the name."

Midway   Cochise Co.   G. L. O. Map, 1921.

"Station Arizona-Eastern R. R., midway between Pearce and Kelton. Established 1909. Road abandoned 1926." Letter Supt. S. P. R. R. Co.

Midway   Maricopa Co.   U. S. G. S. Map, 1923.

Station, Tucson-Gila Bend R. R., west of Sauceda mountains. "It was half way between the two terminals." Letter, R. R. Agent, Tucson.

Midway   Yuma Co.   U. S. G. S. Map, 1923.

Station, Arizona and Swansea R. R. "It is halfway between the two ends of road."

Middelton   Yavapai Co.   Map, Prescott N. F., 1927.

In T. 11 N., R. 1 E. Station, Prescott and Middelton branch A. T. & S. F. R. R., 47 miles southeast of Prescott. P. O. established May 8, 1903, George W. Middelton, P. M. Named for this family.

Middle Cedar Creek   Navajo Co. Map, Fort Apache Ind. Res., 1928.

Rises in T. 8 N., R. 21 E., at Big mountain, flows southwest into Gila county, entering Cedar creek in sec. 23, T. 7 N., R. 21 E.

Middlemarch   Cochise Co.   G. L. O. Map, 1921; Coronado N. F., 1927.

Mining camp in sec. 8, T. 24 E., R. 18 S., middle pass Dragoon mountains about 6 miles southwest of Pearce. One writer says: "Said to have been the 'middle march' of the military in early days between Fort Bowie and Fort Huachuca."
The fact is, it was named for "The Middlemarch Copper Company," which operated here for some years. P. O. established May 10, 1898, Charles M. Lawrence, P. M.

Middle Well   Yuma Co.   U. S. G. S. Map, 1923.

In T. 4 S., R. 16 W. "Well dug originally to supply King of Arizona mine (Kofa) in the S. H. mountains. About 28 miles from Palomas." *Routes to the Desert.*

Miles Butte   Coconino Co.   G. L. O. Map, 1921.

In T. 18 N., R. 8 E., west side Dry Beaver creek, Coconino N. F. Origin not known.

Military Posts in Arizona*

Apache, Fort
Arivaipa—see Breckenridge
Beale Springs, Camp
Bowie, Fort; Camp
Breckenridge, Fort
Buchanan, Fort
Canyon Chelly, Fort
Colorado, Camp
Connor, Camp
Crittenden, Camp
Date Creek, Camp
Defiance, Fort
El Dorado, Camp
Grant, Fort
Goodwin, Camp
Green, Camp
Huachuca, Fort
Hualpai, Camp
Ilges, Camp
LaPaz, Camp
Lewis, Camp
Lincoln, Camp
Little, Stephen A., Camp
Lowell, Fort
McDowell, Camp

McKee, Camp
McPherson, Camp
Mansfield, Camp
Mason, Camp
Mogollon, Camp
Mohave, Fort
Moore, Camp
Ord, Camp
Picket Post, Camp
Pinal, Camp
Price, Camp
Rawlins, Camp
Rigg, Camp
Rucker, Camp
San Carlos, Camp
Stanford, Fort
Supply, Camp (2)
Thomas, Camp
Tollgate, Camp
Verde, Camp
Wallen, Camp
Whipple Barracks
Whipple, Fort
Willow Grove, Camp

*List compiled from government official lists and other sources.

Military Telegraph Line

Government line built to connect military posts in Arizona, New Mexico, and western Texas. In 1872 Congress voted the first money, $50,311.80, for line from San Diego, Cal., east to Yuma and on east via Maricopa, Tucson, Silver City, etc. Branch lines to be erected to Prescott, Fort Apache, Santa Fe, etc. No less than 540 miles of line, seventeen poles to mile, were erected. Much of this work was done under supervision of Lieut. Philip Reade, 3rd U. S. Infantry, and Capt. George F. Price, 5th U. S. Cavalry. See First Telegraph line.

Milk Ranch Point   Gila Co.   Map, Tonto N. F., 1926.

Point in T. 12 N., R. 9 E., extending out from Mogollon rim northeast of Pine, Coconino N. F. "In early days, a Mormon family lived at a spring on the point and milked a number of cows selling butter and cheese to construction camps along the Atlantic and Pacific R. R." Letter, Fred Croxen, Forest Ranger.

Milkweed Creek   Mohave Co.   U. S. G. S. Map, 1923.

Stream rising in approx. T. 25 N., R. 14 W., east slope southern part Grand Wash cliffs, flows northeast, enters Colorado river through Spencer canyon. "So called from abundance of milkweed that grows in this locality." P. M. Valentine.

Milkweed Spring   Mohave Co.   U. S. G. S. Map, 1923.

Spring in T. 26 N., R. 13 W., east side Milkweed creek, q.v.

Milkweed Tank   Mohave Co.   U. S. G. S. Map, 1923.

In T. 26 N., R. 11 W., on Peach Springs draw. See Milkweed creek.

Milky Wash   Apache Co.   U. S. G. S. Map, 1923.
Rising in T. 19 N., R. 29 E., near State line. Runs southwest across Petrified Forest, enters Little Colorado about 8 miles southeast of Woodruff in T. 15 N., R. 23 E. So called because in rainy weather water is white or milky, due to color of the soil along its course.

Mill City   Maricopa Co.
Point about 6 miles east of Phoenix where in 1871 Hellings & Co. built a flour mill. Was also called East Phoenix. Ruins still visible, 1934. Mill was in sec. 1, T. 2 N., R. 3 E. Farish says it turned out daily about 12,000 pounds of flour. Burned by incendiaries. P. O. established, 1872, Ed. K. Baker, P. M.

Miller Peak and Canyon   Cochise Co.
Map, Coronado N. F., 1927.
Elevation 9,445 feet. In sec. 34, T. 23 S., R. 20 E. "Many years ago a saw mill was established here and the canyon was called Mill canyon. Later it came to be known as Miller canyon. Eventually peak took same name." Letter, J. B. Williams, Hereford.

Millersburg   Mohave Co.
Early name for Littlefield. After Henry W. Miller, who founded the town. See Littlefield.

Millers Canyon   Coconino Co.   Map, Coconino N. F., 1926.
In T. 12 N., R. 10 E. Stream heading at the "Rim." Sometimes called McCarty's canyon for state game warden found dead here a few years ago. After Supervisor Ed Miller U. S. Forest Service.

Millers Ranch   Yavapai Co.
Well known ranch belonging to Samuel Miller. About 7 or 8 miles northeast of Prescott. In 1865, Indians surrounded the ranch. Miller killed seven of them and escaped to Prescott. Indians then burned the place which was always known afterwards as "Burnt Ranch," q.v.

Millett Point   Coconino Co.   Map, Kaibab N. F., 1926.
In sec. 18, T. 35 N., R. 1 W. Grand Canyon N. P. After the artist, Frank Millett, who was lost at sinking of Titanic.

Milligan, Fort   Apache Co.
Early camp in Round valley about a mile west of present town of Eager. Home of Jacob Hamblin for a time. So named for Anthony (Tony) Milligan who built first saw mill in Round valley. In those early days nearly every Mormon settlement was a fort built around a hollow square for protection against Indians. See Round valley and Springerville.

Milltown   Mohave Co.   G. L. O. Map, 1909.
Town, Mohave-Milltown branch R. R. from Needles to Oatman. It was a logging road. Timber was cut near Oatman and mill was located here.

Mill Point   Pah Ute Co.
Small early day settlement on Muddy river in Nevada between St. Joseph and Overton.

Millville   Cochise Co.

Listed, *Arizona Gazetteer* 1881, as "a milling town on San Pedro about 10 miles from Tombstone." *Tombstone Prospector* says: "Here the great mills of the Tombstone Mining and Milling Co., and the Tombstone and Corbin Quartz mill were located in 1880." Undoubtedly an early name for Charleston.

Millville   Coconino Co.

According to McClintock, "a settlement on Mogollon plateau 35 miles south of Flagstaff."

Millville   Navajo Co.

Fish says: "This was first name of Forestdale, q.v. A saw mill was the first building here."

Millville   Pima Co.

P. O. established May 26, 1879, John B. Allen, P. M. This was the same Allen who once had a store at old Maricopa Wells.

Milpa Creek   Navajo Co.   Smith Map, 1879; Eckhoff, 1880.

Short stream about 3 miles south Fort Apache, Fort Apache Ind. Res. Flows southwest and enters what is called Salt river on Smith map, but is really Black river. Stream unknown to anyone today.

Milton   Coconino Co.

Settlement, A. T. & S. F. R. R., about one mile west of Flagstaff. "The name was changed from Mill Town to Milton in honor of the poet Milton, by M. J. Riordan." Letter, M. J. R.

Mineral   Mohave Co.   Eckhoff Map, 1880.

In T. 22 N., R. 18 W., town in Sacramento valley, Kingman branch A. T. & S. F. R. R., about 12 miles northwest of Kingman. Originally called Mineral Park. Changed to Mineral about 1889.

"Mineral Park was second county seat of Mohave county, Mohave City being first. Originally called Mineral Park because of a little park-like group of cedars near the town site and mine." McFarland.

"At Mineral Park, county seat 8 miles north of Cerbat, there is a 5-stamp quartz mill and a population of about 200. Water strongly impregnated with unpalatable minerals. Drinking water brought from a canyon some miles distant." Hinton. P. O. established as Mineral Park, Dec. 23, 1872, Alder Randall, P. M.

Mineral City   Mohave Co.   G. L. O. Map, 1892.

Said by Hinton to have been the first name given Ehrenberg, q.v. Shows as a post office by this name on map.

Mineral Creek   Apache Co.   Map, Apache N. F., 1926.

Stream rising southern part T. 9 N., R. 26 E. Flows northerly and loses itself in open country to north. Mexicans pronounce the name "Miner-*al*." In its lower stretches it often carries considerable alkali, hence the name.

Mineral Creek   Pinal Co.   Map, Crook N. F., 1926.

Rises in T. 1 S., R. 13 E., north of Signal mountain. Flows south, enters Gila river near Kelvin.

McClintock says: "So named by Col. Emory himself, 1846, because of croppings and stains of copper seen. He predicted that the time would come 'when the Gila will carry flat boats loaded with copper ore for reduction.'" "From the many indications of copper and gold here I have named it Mineral Creek." Emory, 1847.

Mineral Hill   Yuma Co.   G. L. O. Map, 1921.

Elevation 1,855 feet. In T. 10 N., R. 17 W. About 8 miles east of the Colorado river.

Mineral Mountain   Pinal Co.   G. L. O. Map, 1921.

Elevation 3,350 feet. In T. 3 S., R. 11 E. North side Gila river, 10 miles northeast of Florence. Mountain probably named by Lieut. Emory, who wrote so enthusiastically about the copper deposit here. See Mineral creek.

Mineral Park   Mohave Co.

Second county seat. See Mineral.

Ming Spur   Yuma Co.   Wellton Quad.

In sec. 30, T. 8 S., R. 21 W. Station S. P. R. R. about 7 miles east of Wellton. According to railroad people was so named after Dan Ming, well known early day Graham county politician and cattleman.

Mingus Mountain   Yavapai Co.   U. S. G. S. Map, 1923.

Elevation 7,720 feet, in Black Hills, south of Jerome, on Verde slope in sec. 2, T. 15½ N., R. 2 E.
"In early days, Dominguez brothers located on the mountain. They farmed and raised sheep and cattle. Indians shortened named Dominguez to 'Mingus.' " Letter, R. H. Cunningham, Postmaster, Camp Verde.

Mingville   Graham Co.

In sec. 28 T. 6 S., R. 19 E. Named for "Big" Dan Ming, prominent politician and cattleman. His cow ranch was in the Aravaipa canyon. Summer of 1885 and preceding winter had been very dry all over southern Arizona. The cattlemen held a meeting at Willcox. Some wag suggested Ming be invited to open with a prayer. Nothing daunted Ming accepted.
He said: "Oh Lord, I'm about to round you up for a good plain talk. Now Lord, I aint like these fellows who come bothering you every day. This is the first time I ever tackled you for any thing and if you will only grant this I'll promise never to bother you again. We want rain, good Lord, and we want it bad, and we ask you to send us some. But if you can't or don't want to send us any, for Christ's sake don't make it rain up around Hookers or Leitch's ranges but treat us all alike. Amen." From *Range News*, Willcox. Ming died in San Francisco in Nov., 1926, age 84. "We only got mail twice a week. It came by horseback 60 miles from Willcox." Letter, Bud Ming, Ray. P. O. established Jan. 26, 1881, Thomas I. Hunter, P. M.

Minnehaha   Yavapai Co.   G. L. O. Map, 1921.

In T. 10 N., R. 1 W. Mining camp on Minnehaha Flat. The Minnehaha Mine is listed, 1878, in Hinton's *Hand Book*. Town and flat named after the mine. P. O. established June 21, 1880, Charles Taylor, P. M.

Mint Creek   Yavapai Co.   U. S. G. S., 1923.

Rises south side Little Granite peak, Prescott N. F. Flows northwest into Williamson valley near Simmons. "Tradition says there were large beds of fragrant mint near head of this stream." Eckhoff map, 1880, calls it "Mint Valley."

Miramonte   Cochise Co.   G. L. O. Map, 1921.

Sp., "mountain view." In T. 17 S., R. 19 E. North of Whetstone Range, west of Benson, on E. P. & S. W. R. R. "It was 9 miles west of St. David settlement on San Pedro. Settled by the St. David people, 1913." P. O. established May 4, 1918. Rebecca Lofgreen, P. M.

Misery, Fort   Yavapai Co.

Joseph Fish says: "This name was given first house built in Prescott because Judge Howard here held court and dispensed justice."

According to Farish, name was given the house by a woman known as the "Virgin Mary" who kept in it the first miners boarding house in Prescott. From all accounts the lady was the originator of this name but Judge Howard made it stand for something definite.

Mishongnovi   Navajo Co.   Gregory Map, 1916.

In T. 28 N., R. 17 E. Hopi, "The Hill of Boulders," one of the Hopi villages located on second or middle mesa. U.S.G.S. Tusayan Sheet 1906 spells it "Mi-shong-i-nivi."

Mistake Peak   Gila Co.   Map, Tonto N. F., 1927.

In sec. 30, T. 7 N., R. 12 E., 6 miles east of Hackberry Ranger Station. "Peak is in Juniper basin west side Sierra Ancha. From Tonto Basin side it seems part of main range. On the other side, changes completely and looks like a separate peak standing well out from range. Hence people called it Mistake peak." Letter, Fred Croxen, Forest Ranger.

Mission Camp   Yuma Co.   Smith Map, 1879; Eckhoff, 1880.

Station, old Butterfield stage route 32 miles east of Yuma. A road from here led south to Papago country and on into Old Mexico. Hinton lists it as a stage station. According to Charles D. Poston, this place was so called because U. S. Boundary Commission camped here. Poston says, in his *Apache Land*, (he was traveling east from Yuma):

> "Our first night was in Mission camp
> Where the river bed was somewhat damp.
> The Camp was named for the Commission
> In early days sent on a mission
> The Nations boundary to run."

J. Ross Browne, January, 1864, says: "At Mission camp 14 miles east of Gila City we had a fine view of 'Corrunnacion mountain,' (sic) about 10 miles distant. It was on the north side of Gila and resembled strongly a mitred peak or crown." His spelling was evidently phonetic.

Mitchell Peak   Greenlee Co.   U. S. G. S. Map, 1915; Crook, 1926.

Elevation 7,947 feet. In sec. 34, T. 2 S., R. 29 E., about 6 miles north of Metcalf.

"Named for a man named Mitchell, who once ran a sawmill at foot of this peak. He was shot and killed with a pistol at his mill. The Mexicans call the peak 'Pistola Peak' because of this." J. W. Girdner, Forest Ranger.

Mitten Butte   Navajo Co.   U. S. G. S. Map, 1923.

Elevation 6,210 feet, Navajo Ind. Res. on Arizona-Colorado state line near lat. 37°, long. 110°. From a distance resembles a huge mitten.

Mitten Peak   Navajo Co.   G. L. O. Map, 1921.

In T. 20 N., R. 22 E. Tall butte shaped very like a mitten. On east side Leroux wash about 15 miles north of Holbrook. So named by Frank A. Zuck of Holbrook, 1897.

Moa Ave   Coconino Co.   Map, Navajo Ind. Res.

In T. 32 N., R. 10 E. Settlement Navajo Ind. Res. east of Little Colorado, about 6 miles west of Tuba City. There is a series of fine springs here coming from Echo cliffs, water from which supports the settlement.

Father Haile says: "This word is Hopi. Navajo name for it is 'To-zai.' "

Mobile   Maricopa Co.   Postal Map, 1929.

In T. 4 S., R. 1 E. R. R. station S. P. R. R. about 14 miles west of Maricopa. P. O. established here August 5, 1925, Mrs. Elsie B. Lung, P. M. Origin unknown.

Moccasin Spring   Mohave Co.   U. S. G. S. Map, 1923.

Elevation 4,500 feet. Kanab Ind. Res. in Vermillion cliffs, north of Pipe springs.

"Occupied before 1860 by William B. Maxwell, who left in 1864 because of Indian troubles. Located and abandoned several times by the Mormon pioneers." McClintock.

Name said to have been given because when the first white men came they found fresh moccasin tracks around the spring.

P. O. established June 11, 1909, Charles C. Heaton, P. M. Closed in two years but re-established in 1930 as Moccasin for a small settlement in sec. 31, T. 41 N., R. 4 W.

"Some ten or a dozen families settled here before the reservation was set aside and therefore got patents for their lands. Indian School established for local Indians 1914." Letter, Walter G. Mann, Kanab, Utah.

Moenkopi   Coconino Co.   G. L. O. Map, 1892; Gregory, 1916;
                                                      U. S. G. S., 1923.

In T. 31 N., R. 11 E. Small farming settlement, Navajo Ind. Res. Hopi, meaning "running water." "Oñate visited this place, 1604, apparently calling it 'Rancheria de los Gandules'; gandul, Sp., 'disreputable.' Was headquarters for a large milling enterprise by the Mormons." Hodge. Hodge and Father Haile spell it Moen Kapi. Above is official spelling. Lot Smith lived here for many years. Was killed at Tuba City, 1892, by Navajo Indians.

Fish says: "John W. Young built a woolen mill here, 1879, and spent over $12,000 in the undertaking. He depended upon Navajo Indian wool. It was not a success." Roundy visited this place, 1873, and described it as "A good deal like St. George, having springs breaking out from the hills. The land is partly impregnated with salt." Hamblin was also here the same year.

The home of Tuba, famous Navajo chief. Mormons made a permanent location here December 4, 1875, the place being established by James S. Brown. In 1900 had about 150 inhabitants. Government wanted the land for an Indian school. There was only a squatter right to the land. Settlers finally sold for $45,-000 in February, 1903. Money was divided according to holdings.

Moenkopi, Wash and Plateau   Coconino and Navajo Cos.
                                      Gregory Map, 1916; G. L. O., 1921.

Rises south side Black mesa, flows southwest across Hopi Ind. Res., enters Little Colorado about 10 miles below Cameron bridge in Coconino county. "Hopi word meaning 'Place of the running water.'" Hodge. One of the few living streams in this region. The Navajos called the wash 'where they plant cotton.'" The plateau lies east of Little Colorado, western part of Navajo Ind. Res. Father Haile says: "The word is Hopi. The Navajo name for it is xayaj' meaning 'Little Oraibi.'" Moenkopi is a decision of U.S.G.B.

Mogollon, Camp   Navajo Co.

One of early names for Fort Apache, q.v.

Mogollon Mesa   Navajo and Coconino Cos.

Called this on G.L.O. map, 1921. Generally known as Black mesa, q.v.

Mogollon Mountains   Smith Map, 1879.

The high region in northern Arizona, principally Coconino and Navajo counties, extending east and west about 100 miles known commonly as "The Rim" or the "Tonto Rim." On U.S.G.S. map, 1923, is shown as Mogollon plateau. There is also a range of mountains in western New Mexico by this name.

Gannett says: "Spanish word meaning 'hanger-on, a parasite.'" "Named for Don Juan Ignacio Flores de Mogollon, Captain General of New Mexico, 1712-15. Commonly called Governor Flores." Coues.

Mo-ha-tuk

See Salt River mountains.

Mohave and Milltown R. R.   Mohave Co.   G. L. O. Map, 1909.

Logging railroad about 25 miles long. "Ran from Needles northeast to Oatman. Here they cut the timber, such as it was. Mill was about half way down the road at Milltown."

Mohave and Prescott Toll Road

See Wagon Roads.

Mohave City   Mohave Co.   G. L. O. Map, 1892; U. S. G. S., 1927.

In T. 19 N., R. 22 W. About one mile above Fort Mohave, on Colorado river. Established by California Volunteers about 1863. First county seat of Mohave county. P. O. established October 8, 1866, James P. Bull, P. M.

Mohave County

In northwest corner of State along Colorado river. One of the four original counties. After local Indians. "An Indian word meaning 'three mountains' from their proximity to the 'Needles.'" Hodge.

An Act of the 13th Legislative Assembly of Arizona contained a clause to the effect that: "The county seat of Mohave county shall be at Mineral Park or some place located on the Atlantic and Pacific railway within said county."

The Howell code originally spelled this word "Mojave," but according to authorities of that day, "due to an ignorant clerk," the legislative act above quoted spelled it "Mohave." Word now seems to be uniformly spelled Mohave, excepting the post office in California which has always used the "j."

Mohave Creek   Mohave Co.   G. L. O. Map, 1921.

In T. 14 N., R. 17 W. Rises east slope Chemehuevi mountains, flowing south entering Bill Williams river in T. 11 N., R. 17 W.

Mohave, Fort   Mohave Co.   Smith Map, 1879; G. L. O., 1892-1921.

Established 1858 by Col. Hoffman, 6th U. S. Infantry, near point where Beale crossed Colorado river on his way to California. Whipple is said to have selected this site. "Was abandoned in May, 1861, at beginning of Civil War but reestablished in May, 1863, by two companies of 4th California Regiment." McFarland. Land was set aside as a "Military, hay, and wood reservation" by G. O. War Dept., August, 1871. President Harrison in September, 1880, turned it over to the Interior Dept., for Indian school purposes. P. O. established in June, 1881, Paul Breon, P. M. Breon had a large store here and was Post Trader.

Mohave Indians

"From Mohave words 'hamol,' three; and 'avi,' 'mountains.' They lived on Colorado river near the Needles, hence the name. The most populous and warlike of the Yuman tribes." Hodge.

Mohave Mountains   Mohave Co.

Coues says: "Garces called the Mohave mountains 'Sierra de San Ildefonso.'" Neither of these names can be found on any map. From his description of their location they are probably the present Ute or Black mountains. See Sierra de San Ildefonso.

Ives says: "This important chain bounds the Chemehuevi valley on the east. Where it crosses the Colorado its remarkable pinnacles were called "The Needles" by Whipple. Newberry report in Ives, 1858.

Mohave Peak   Mohave Co.   G. L. O. Map, 1921.

In T. 15 N., R. 20½ W. An outstanding mountain on the Colorado river.

Mohawk   Yuma Co.   Smith Map, 1879; G. L. O., 1921.

In T. 8 S., R. 15 W. Stage station established as early as 1877. Railroad station, S. P. R. R., 66 miles east of Yuma, established in early 1900. Located at northern end of Mohawk mountains. "A man named Kilbright, the station keeper, jumped into the well here, after taking poison with suicidal intent. Later, leaders of a six-horse stage coach team fell into the same well, which was then abandoned and a new one dug." McClintock. P. O. established here June 25, 1890, George W. Norton, P. M. When Poston was here about 1864, he wrote: "Mohawk station with its misplaced name." He evidently felt such a name did not belong here.

Mohawk, Canyon and Creek   Coconino Co.   U. S. G. S. Map, 1923.

In T. 29 N., R. 7 W. Rises in "Laguna," flows north, enters Colorado river in T. 33 N., R. 6 W., Hualpai Ind. Res. Origin not known.

Mohawk, Mountains and Peak   Yuma Co.   Smith Map, 1879; G. L. O., 1921; U. S. G. S., 1923.

In Ts. 8, 9, 10 S., Rs. 13, 14, 15 W. Southeast of Mohawk station, S. P. R. R. Origin unknown. See Mohawk Station.

Mohawk Valley   Yuma Co.   Smith Map, 1879; G. L. O., 1921.

West side Mohawk Mountains.

Mohon Peak　　　Yavapai Co.　　　G. L. O. Map, 1921; U. S. G. S., 1923.

In Mohon mountains west of Baca Grant, in approximately T. 18 N., R. 10 W. At head of Burro Creek.

Anson H. Smith says: "After Jim Mahone, a Wallapi Indian. He was a scout for Crook and had a letter from the General certifying to his bravery. Mohon is an error." Some maps show "Mohone."

Moki

See Hopi.

Mollies, Mountain　　　Yuma Co.　　　G. L. O. Map, 1909.

Southern end Granite Wash mountains, about 6 miles west of Salome. North side of railroad. Origin unknown.

Monitor　　　Yuma Co.　　　G. L. O. Map, 1892.

Station S. P. R. R., about 20 miles east of Yuma. First called Gila City, q.v. P. O. called Monitor established Dec. 3, 1895, Albert S. Potter, P. M. "Named after Monitor mine near the place."

Monkey Springs　　　Pima Co.

Shows thus on Roskruge map, 1893, and earlier maps. On Sonoita river below old Fort Buchanan. Said to have been originally located by Tom Hughes. Story goes that "Hughes had a half-witted man working for him. The cowboys started a yarn that Hughes had bought a monkey and trained him to be a cowboy and sent him down there to work. Ranch was first claimed by a Mexican named Apodaca who called it Cuevacita (Little Caves), because there were a number of small caves above the springs. When Hughes got hold of it he called it the Pennsylvania ranch because he came from that state. When Ashburne and Vail bought it they changed name to Monkey springs." Letter, Mrs. Mary Gardner Kane, in files of Arizona Pioneer Historical Society, Tucson.

Modern students, however, have another story. "Captain Manje or Mange, Kino's historian friend and companion, was here about 1694-95, and saw the springs. They soon became known as "Agua de Mange"; Manjes Springs. Mange's name was pronounced with a hard j—Man-ke. With the coming of the Americans this was soon translated into 'Monkey.'" Letter, Frank C. Lockwood.

Monnow Valley

See Grand Canyon.

Montana Peak　　　Santa Cruz Co.　　　Map, Coronado N. F., 1927

In secs. 4 and 9, T. 23 S., R. 11 E. After Montana mine near here, located by a Montana man. See Ruby.

Monte Cristo　　　Pima Co.　　　U. S. G. S. Map, 1923

In T. 11 S., R. 1 E. Settlement, west side Cimarron mountains, southwest of Vekol mine. "After the Monte Cristo mine near here." P. O. established August 14, 1922, Mattie L. Megron, P. M.

Monte Vista Peak　　　Cochise Co.　　　G. L. O. Map, 1921;

Elevation 8,373 feet, in Chiricahua mountains in T. 18 S., R. 30 E. Monte Vista, meaning "mountain view," descriptive name.

Montezuma Pinal Co. Smith Map, 1879.

Stage station and village, south side of Gila river 6 miles west of Casa Grande ruins. About 10 miles east Sacaton. "Just another of the many Montezumas." P. O. established, 1880, Joseph Collingwood, P. M.

Montezuma Yavapai Co. Verde Quad., 1902.

Settlement at Montezuma Well on Beaver creek above Camp Verde. P. O. established October 20, 1892, Amaňda Mehrens, P. M.

Montezuma Castle Yavapai Co. G. L. O. Map, 1921; Coconino N. F., 1928.

In T. 14, R. 5 E. Well preserved prehistoric ruin, on Dry Beaver creek, about 4 miles north of Fort Verde. Created National Monument Dec. 8, 1906. Name given by early visitors.

"The name Montezuma," says Emory, "is as familiar to every Indian Pueblo, Apache and Navajo, as is that of the Saviour or Washington to us."

Montezuma Head Maricopa Co. G. L. O. Map, 1921

In T. 3 S., R. 9 W. Point about 18 miles north of Agua Caliente. Resembles a huge head.

Montezuma Head Pima Co. G. L. O. Map, 1921.

In T. 15 S., R. 5 W. Ajo mountains, one of several peaks by this name. Resembles a human head at a distance.

Montezuma Head Pinal Co. G. L. O. Map, 1921.

Elevation 2,406 feet, in T. 3 S., R. 2 E., Gila River Ind. Res., southeastern extremity Sierra Estrella, bearing some resemblance to a gigantic head. Resemblance is strongest when seen from the east. There are three Montezumas in this immediate vicinity.

Montezuma Peak Pinal Co. G. L. O. Map, 1921.

Elevation 4,000 feet, in sec. 7, T. 3 S., R. 2 E., northwest of Maricopa station in Estrella range.

Montezuma Cave Pima Co.

Very ancient cave about 6 miles from Fresnal settlement on Papago reservation. According to Lumholtz, is abiding place of the "Elder Brother," one of the Papago deities. Is called by them "The Elder Brother's House." Located 1,000 feet up on mountainside. Lumholtz visited it and says: "It was not particularly interesting."

Montezumas Chair Navajo Co. Gregory Map, 1916; G. L. O., 1921.

In T. 24 N., R. 17 E. Rock shaped like a huge chair, southern line Navajo Ind. Res.

Montezuma Sleeping Maricopa Co. G. L. O. Map, 1921.

In T. 2 S., R. 1 E., Estrella mountains, west side Gila river, prominent peak from all sides. Descriptive name.

Montezuma Store Pinal Co.

Stage station listed 1877 by Hinton "about 12 miles below Florence on old Tucson stage road. Austin and Dempsy ran the store and station."

Montezuma Well   Yavapai Co.   G. L. O. Map, 1921;
Coconino N. F., 1927.

In Sec. 31, T. 15 N., R. 6 E. Isolated limestone mesa about 100 feet above Beaver creek. In this mesa is a huge open depression or crater about 600 feet across. Of great depth in which clear fresh water stands at all times about 75 feet above stream. There is a small opening through wall at one side from which a constant stream flows into Beaver creek. Lake always stands at same level. Water is used to irrigate adjacent fields. In the walls are a number of cliff dwellings. About 1884 a crazy man took up his abode in these caves. Was finally captured and placed in an asylum.

Montgomery   Maricopa Co.   G. L. O. Map, 1921.

Station about 12 miles north of Phoenix. After the Montgomerys who have a ranch here. P. O. established November 20, 1913, Arminta J. Montgomery, P. M.

Montrose   Pinal Co.

On S. P. R. R., about 36 miles west of Tucson.

Monument   Santa Cruz Co.   Smith Map, 1879; Eckoff, 1880.

Station on Mexican border at corner boundary monument about 12 miles west of Nogales. P. O. established in May, 1876, Albert C. Benedict, P. M. Later Peter Kitchen was appointed P. M., June 11, 1876.

Monument Canyon   Apache Co.   U. S. G. S. Map, 1923.

In T. 3 N., R. 7 W., rises east end Defiance plateau near line of New Mexico. Runs northwest about 18 miles, joins Canyon de Chelly in T. 5 N., R. 8 W., Navajo Ind. Res. There are many monument-like formations of sandstone in this canyon, hence the name. Called by Navajos "The flow of the Fluted Rock," *Navajo Dictionary.* Not to be confounded with Monument valley in Navajo county near Colorado line.

Monument Canyon   Mohave Co.   U. S. G. S. Map, 1923.

Canyon on Colorado river. "Extends from 'Corner Rock' to mouth of Bill Williams fork. A canyon of wild, picturesque scenery with vivid colors," writes Newberry of Ives party.

Monument Mountain   Coconino Co.   G. L. O. Map, 1921.

In T. 25 N., R. 14 E., west side Corn or Oraibi creek, Hopi Ind. Res. "So called for a government cairn or monument on its top."

Monument Valley   Navajo Co.   Gregory Map, 1916; U. S. G. S., 1923.

On Colorado state line, near long. 110° 20', Navajo Ind. Res. "On the valley floor—the most conspicuous features are the 'monuments' which rise nearly 1,000 feet above crest of the Dome." Gregory.

Moody Point   Gila Co.   Map, Tonto N. F., 1926.

In secs. 1, 2, T. 5 N., R. 14 E., Sierra Ancha range. "An old timer named Moody had a horse ranch in this vicinity. Peak was named for him. He ran the Circle H brand." Letter, Bud Armer.

Mooney Falls   Coconino Co.   Map, Grand Canyon N. P., 1927.

In Supai or Cataract canyon. Named after James Mooney, prospector accidentally killed here by a fall. In his younger days, Mooney had been a sailor. He accompanied a number of men of whom Edward L. Doheny was one, on a visit to Supai or Cataract canyon in January, 1880, on a prospecting trip.

"Mooney joined us at Williamson valley," writes Mr. Doheny on April 6, 1929, from Los Angeles. "Party consisted of James Mooney, who had been a sailor; Fowler, a school teacher; Billy Beckman, prospector; Warren Potts, a carpenter; Alex Davidson, an engineer; Matt Humphreys, an Indian scout and trailer under Gen. Crook; Alphonso Humphreys, his brother and two nephews of the Humphreys named Budd and Bob Schultz; Young, a house painter; and myself, Edward Lawrence Doheny, then 23 years of age; youngest member of party.

"Mooney was very reckless and fell over the cliff to his death as he started to go down on a small rope. We called the falls 'Bridal Veil Falls.' Some months later an effort was made to recover the body, but it was not done at that time."

W. W. Bass says the body was still at the foot of the cliff in 1884. The writer visited the spot with J. W. Benham and Frank Rogers of Williams in December, 1886. A broken rope ladder with rounds of cottonwood sticks was still hanging over the cliff. Some one had brought Mooney's body up and buried it at the top of the falls. The author took a photo of the grave which had a headstone with Mooney's name scratched on it. George Wharton James, *In and Around the Grand Canyon*, gives an extended account of this tragedy which in the main agrees with Mr. Doheny's story.

Mooney Mountain   Coconino Co.   G. L. O. Map, 1921; Coconino, 1928.

Elevation, 7,666 feet, in sec. 6, T. 20 N., R. 5 E., about 6 miles southwest of Rogers lake. "According to Harold Linn, an old resident, this was made for an early day stockman who had a camp at base of this mountain." Letter, Ed. Miller. It is generally believed, however, that it was after Mooney of the Falls.

Moonlight Creek   Navajo Co.   U. S. G. S. Map, 1923.

Navajo Ind. Res., rises west side of Tyende mesa, flows north into Colorado near lat. 37°, long. 110° 20'. Joins San Juan river. "Short stream of intermittent flow about 44 miles long." Gregory.

"The Navajo name for this stream is Olja (moon) and To (water)—Olgato most commonly spelled Olja. There is a store on the creek on Colorado side by this name—Olja, by which the stream is best known." Letter, Keith Warren, P. M., Kayenta. *Gregory* map spells it Oljeto.

Moor Camp   Maricopa Co.

Mining camp operated about 1877 by William Moor (sic). Located about 5 miles east of Gilette station on Agua Fria. Listed in *Arizona Gazetteer*, 1881.

Moore, Camp

Original name of Fort or Camp Buchanan, q. v.

Moore Creek   Gila Co.   Map, Tonto N. F., 1927.

"Stream heading under rim, just west of old Ellison place. After Walter Moore, who built a cabin here and ran cattle on this range about 1886." Letter, Fred Croxen.

Moores Spur   Cochise

Short side track, E. P. & S. W. R. R. P. O. established as Moores spur, October 25, 1913. James R. Phillips, P. M.

Moqui

See Hopi.

Moqui Coconino Co. G. L. O. Map, 1921.

Station, A. T. & S. F. R. R., 7 miles west of Winslow. After Moqui or Hopi Indians.

Moqui Spring Coconino Co. Map, Sitgreaves N. F., 1924.

In sec. 21, T. 14 N., R. 11 E. Named by E. R. Carr, manager of Waters Cattle Co., that used this range from 1884. Favorite camping place. There was always plenty of water. After Moqui or Hopi Indians who often hunted eagles about here in early days.

Moran Point Coconino Co. Map, Tusayan N. F.

Point, Grand Canyon N. P., southwest corner T. 31 N., R. 5 E., eastern end of park, about 6 miles east Grand View hotel. After Peter Moran, artist, who was here in 1881 with Captain Bourke. James called this Ute Point, but maps show it as Moran.

Morenci Greenlee Co. G. L. O. Map, 1892-1921; U. S. G. S., 1923.

Elevation 4,838 feet, in T. 4 S., R. 29 E. Mining camp on Gold Gulch about 6 miles northwest Clifton at end Morenci Southern Narrow Gauge R. R. Named by Mr. Church of Detroit Copper Co., who came from Morenci, Mich. First called Joys Camp after Capt. Joy, early settler and prospector, q. v. P. O. established Mar. 3, 1884, George W. Davidson, P. M.

Morenci Hot Springs Greenlee Co. G. L. O. Map, 1921.

In secs. 26, 27, T. 5 S., R. 29 E., north side Gila river above mouth San Francisco river. After the town and mine.

Moreno Pima Co. G. L. O. Map, 1892.

Papago village in T. 20 S., R. 10 E, east side Arivaca valley. Sp., "brown or swarthy." Origin unknown.

Morgan, Mountain Navajo Co. Map, Apache N. F., 1926.

Sitgreaves N. F. in sec. 11, T. 9 N., R. 23 E. After William Morgan, local sheepman, politician, and settler of early Eighties. Was County Commissioner; member, Territorial and State Legislatures; Sheep Sanitary Board, etc.

Morgans Ferry Pinal Co. Hinton Map, 1877; Maricopa Co. Map,. 1891.

Stage and camping station on Gila river. Henry A. Morgan ran a trading store and a ferry for travellers when the Gila was in flood. On road from Camp McDowell to Maricopa Wells, about 3 miles from latter. Station southwest side of river, in sec. 5, T. 3 S., R. 3 E.

Moritz Hill Coconino Co. Map, Tusayan N. F., 1927.

In sec. 2, T. 23 N., R. 4 E. See Moritz lake.

Moritz Lake Coconino Co. G. L. O. Map, 1921; Tusayan N. F., 1926.

In sec. 34, T. 24 N., R. 4 E. Named for Joe Moritz, pioneer stockman. Well-known watering place.

Mormon Buttes Maricopa Co.

"East of Mesa—named in memory of pioneers of Mormon Battalion, who colonized Mesa. The buttes have seven peaks, one for each of the Presidents of the church." McClintock.

Mormon Crossing

See Chevelon Fork and West Chevelon.

Mormon Dairy   Coconino Co.

In T. 18 N., R. 9 E., Coconino N. F. West side Mormon Lake, southeast of Flagstaff. Here on a large "wet-weather lake," known as Mormon lake, the settlers from Sunset and Brigham City established, 1877, a summer camp to which they moved their dairy cattle every spring.

McClintock says: "They first called it Pleasant valley. Under Bishop Lot Smith, about 80 people came up in 1878, bringing more than one hundred cows with them. They made butter and cheese and it was known as The Mormon Dairy." Near by was Pine Spring, q. v.

Mormon Flat   Maricopa Co.   Map, Tonto N. F., 1926.

In sec. 4, T. 2 N., R. 9 E. South side of Salt river. Large open flat place where the canyon of Salt river opens out on one side making a good stock watering place. Early day stage drivers over road to dam told passengers weird tales of Mormons being massacred here by Apaches.

There is also a story that Mormon families hid in this secluded spot during days of federal activity against plural wives. Hence the name. These historians to the contrary, the Mormons from Mesa and below often brought their surplus stock to graze here. It is now the location of the second of three additional supplementary dams built by Salt River Valley Water Users Association to conserve waters flowing from Roosevelt Dam above. Named Canyon lake from its location in canyon of Salt river.

Mormon Lake   Coconino Co.

In T. 18 N., R. 9 E. In Coconino N. F., 25 miles southeast of Flagstaff. Largest body of water in Coconino county. Discovered by Casner brothers, 1873. Later a small Mormon colony from Brigham City, headed by Lot Smith, settled here and it became known as Mormon Dairy, q. v. Lake has gone dry several times during past forty years. Absolutely dry on roundup of 1888. P. O. established May 18, 1925, Chauncey D. Lewis, P. M.

Mormon Lakes   Navajo Co.   Map, Sitgreaves N. F., 1924.

In T. 10 N., R. 22 E., about 4 miles east of Showlow. There are several wet weather lakes here where in the early Eighties some Mormon families tried to make homes. Water failed them.

Mormon Mountain   Coconino Co.

Elevation 9,500 feet, in secs. 1, 2, T. 18 N., R. 8 E., Coconino N. F. Also called Longfellow mountain, q. v. On most maps it is Mormon mountain. On G.L.O. map, 1892, is Longfellow.

Mormon Wagon Road   Coconino Co.   Smith Map, 1879.

An early road over which went all travel between Mormon settlements on Little Colorado river, and southern Utah. It crossed the Puerco at Horsehead, 3 miles east of Holbrook, followed down Little Colorado into Moenkopie wash along Echo cliffs to Lee Ferry and on north through House Rock valley. For years, highway was used by young Mormon couples in Arizona going back by teams to Saint George, Utah, over 350 miles to "go through the temple." They usually went in November and came back in March or April.

Moroni, Fort   Coconino Co.

Built about 1882 by Mormons working on Atlantic and Pacific R. R. About 6 miles northwest of Flagstaff. Moroni was a prophet of the Mormon church.

Fort was abandoned, and about 1885 became headquarters of A1 (A One) Cattle company, so called from its brand. Captain Bullwinkle, ex-chief of Insurance Fire Patrol of Chicago, was its general manager for some years. He ran the cow outfit as if it was a fire department. Was accidentally killed one dark night by his horse falling on him in one of his mad races from Flagstaff to the ranch. Is now an experiment station of the U. S. Forest Service. See A1—"A One." Also Fort Rickerson.

Morris Canyon

See Turkey Creek.

Morristown   Maricopa Co.   G. L. O. Map, 1921.

On A. T. & S. F. R. R., originally known as Hot Springs Junction. P. O. and original point of departure for Hot Springs stages. Named after first inhabitant, George Morris, who had a store here. P. O. established Dec. 30, 1897, Lee H. Landis, P. M.

Morse Canyon or Creek   Cochise Co.

See Turkey Creek.

Mortensen   Navajo Co.

One of the early names of Pinedale, q. v. So called because Nels Mortensen and his sons lived here about 1880.

Mortensen Wash   Navajo Co.   Map, Sitgreaves N. F., 1924.

Dry wash heading in T. 10 N., R 19 E. At line Fort Apache Ind. Res. Runs northeast, enters Dodson wash southeast corner of T. 12 N., R. 20 E., about 7 miles southwest of Taylor. After Nels Mortensen. See Mortensen.

Mound

See Glen canyon.

Mount   (Not towns or settlements.)

See these under right name—thus, Mount Fagan under Fagan, etc.

Mount Buford

See Buford mountain.

Mount Hope   Yavapai Co.

Settlement not on any map. From its name was probably in vicinity of Mount Hope peak. In Santa Marias west of Williamson valley, on Baca Grant. P. O. established June 23, 1876, George D. Smith, P. M. See Hope, Mount.

Mowry Mine   Pima Co.

Old mining camp, Patagonia mountains about 20 miles east of Calabasas. Named after Lieut. Sylvester Mowry, U. S. Army, who in 1857 was elected first and again 1859, second delegate to Congress, but not admitted. Mine discovered, 1857, called the Patagonia. Bought by Mowry, 1860. Seized by Gen. Carleton, 1862, who charged Mowry with disloyalty and confined him in Yuma. Released, Nov. 4, 1862, but eventually lost his mine. Mowry graduated from West Point, 1852. Resigned, 1859, while stationed at Fort Yuma. See McFarland for Mowrys history. Smith map, 1879, calls it Mowry; also Eckhoff, 1880. G. L. O. map, 1892, calls it Old Mowry Mine; G. L. O., 1921, Mowry.

Muav Canyon   Coconino Co.

Deep gorge in Grand Canyon N. P. On north wall of canyon between Powell and Rainbow plateaus, drained by White creek. Origin of name not known. Powell speaks of it as Muav canyon, 1869. Has a picture of it in his report but says nothing as to why so called. Dellenbaugh mentions canyon by name but writes, January, 1933, that he is unable to give its meaning or origin.

Muchos Cañones   Yavapai Co.

Sp., "many canyons." "In 1872 troops under Crook had a hard fight with the Hualpais at this point. Here five canyons unite to form the Santa Maria," writes Bourke. "The enemy had to record a loss of more than forty. It was a terrible blow—upon a band which had causelessly slaughtered a stage full of our best people." Bourke here refers to the Loring Massacre, Nov. 4, 1871, about 9 miles west of Wickenburg. There is, however, some reason to believe that possibly Mexican outlaws, and not Indians, were responsible for this slaughter.

Mud Tanks   Yavapai Co.   Map, Coconino N. F., 1928.

Wet weather tank, west slope of range about 30 miles east of Camp Verde. Arnold Hugle, cattleman and beef contractor at Fort Verde, had a ranch here 1879 and 1880. He gave it this name. It was first located and owned by David Horst of Camp Verde, known as "Uncle Davy."

Muddy Canyon   Yavapai Co.

Stage station on road Willow Grove to Prescott, 20 miles southeast of Willow Grove. Valley called Round Valley on Smith map, 1879. Hinton says: "Three miles beyond Muddy canyon is an old government camping ground with wood and water all the year round. Grass is abundant." The canyon up which the road led was very wet in the spring, and the road was terribly soft and muddy, which gave it the name.

Muddy River   Nevada.

Stream in Pah Ute county, once a part of Arizona. Was settled in January, 1865, with several good sized Mormon towns. Oddly enough, stream was never one that could be called muddy. Probably it was first seen in a time of high water when it could well have been discolored by silt. Ordinarily, a clear mountain stream. Rises in southeastern Nevada, flows southeast, enters Virgin river about 40 miles above its junction with Colorado.

Muggins Tank   Yuma Co.

"Natural rock tank in Muggins mountains. Has an unusually large capacity." *Routes to the Desert.* See Muggins mountains for location.

Muggins Mountains   Yuma Co.   U. S. G. S. Map, 1923.

In Ts. 7, 8, Rs. 19, 20, W., northeast Dome station, S. P. R. R., about 25 miles east of Yuma. Origin unknown. See Coronation Peak.

Muldoon Canyon   Yavapai Co.   Map, Prescott N. F., 1927.

In T. 17 N., R. 1 W., south side Verde river flowing north into it near Bald Hills.

"For Muldoon, a soldier at Camp Verde, whose real name was Farrell Teirnen, who, when discharged, remained in the country and ran a bunch of cattle on the Verde at this canyon." Letter, Harry Hartin, Prescott.

Mule Gulch   Cochise Co.

In Mule mountains. Bisbee is built on this gulch. Named from mountains in which gulch is located. But why "mule" is an unsettled question.

Mule Mountains   Cochise Co.   U. S. G. S. Map, 1923.

Short range extending from T. 21 S., to Mexican line. Bisbee and the copper mines of Phelps Dodge Co. are located in the Mule mountains. Called Mule Pass mountains on early maps. Smith map, 1879, calls this range thus, but the pass is marked "Puerta de las Mulas." Origin of name seems to be lost to history.

Mule Pass

See Mule mountains.

Mule Shoe Bend   Yavapai Co.   G. L. O. Map, 1921.

On Verde river about 5 miles below where East Verde enters main Verde. A large peculiarly shaped bend in river.

Mullen   Mohave Co.   G. L. O. Map, 1908.

Small town on Colorado river near present town of Topock. "Said to have been named after the same John Mullen who established Mullens wells in Arlington valley." Letter, Mrs. John Martin, Salome.

Mullen Wells   Maricopa Co.   G. L. O. Map, 1921.

In T. 1 S., R. 7 W., in Centennial wash about 4 miles west of Arlington. Early day station and watering place. After John Mullen, the owner.

Mulligan Peak   Greenlee Co.   Map, Crook N. F., 1920.

Elevation 5,615 feet. In sec. 21, T. 4 S., R. 30 E., about 6 miles northeast of Clifton, turning point at corner Crook N. F. "Named for a man by this name who lived at foot of the peak." Letter, J. W. Girdner, Forest Ranger. G. L. O. map, 1921, spells it "Muligan."

Munds   Mohave Co.   Railroad Maps.

Station, Chloride branch A. T. & S. F. R. R., 8 miles north of Kingman. After John L. Munds. See Munds Draw.

Munds Draw   Yavapai Co.   Map, Prescott N. F.

In T. 16 N., R. 1 E. Rises near St. Matthews mountain. Flows north into Verde near Perkinsville. After John L. Munds, early day stockman and for two terms sheriff of Yavapai county.

Munds Park   Coconino Co.   Map, Coconino N. F., 1928.

In T. 18 N., R. 6 E. An open park in yellow pine forest.

Munn   Pinal Co.   Railroad Maps.

Spur and loading station about 8 miles east of Florence on Pacific & Eastern R. R. "After a railroad man named Munn in charge of construction work on this branch, 1903." Letter, Bud Ming, Ray.

Murrays Spring   Mohave Co.

Located by Beale near head of Meadow creek. He named it for one of his men, Frank Murray, but there is no record in his report as to who he was or his duties with the expedition. Coues mentions the spring in his work on Garces' travels.

Music Mountains   Mohave Co.   U. S. G. S. Map, 1923.

Elevation 3,971 feet, in T. 25 N., R. 13 W., about 10 miles west of Peach springs.

"Named in 1854 by Ives, because of regularity of the strata of which it is composed and singular erosive work on the face which gives it distinct appearance of a huge sheet of music, carved on mountain." Hinton.

"After James Music, an old time prospector." Letter, Anson H. Smith.

Musina   Yuma Co.

Siding on main S. P. R. R., about 7 miles west of Aztec. "P. O. is called LeSage, and the people have asked the railroad to change Musina to that name." Origin unknown. See LeSage.

Mustang Mountains   Cochise and Santa Cruz Cos.
      Smith Map, 1879; Eckhoff, 1880; U. S. G. S., 1923.

Elevation 6,915 feet, in approx. T. 20 S., Rs. 18, 19 E. Short range south of Whetstone mountains.

"So called from the fact that a herd of wild ponies were to be found there or not far off, They did not number more than sixty when I last saw them in 1870, and were probably the last wild horses within limits of the United States." Bourke.

Muth-widi-tha

See Meriwitica.

Myrtle Lake   Coconino Co.   Map, Tonto N. F., 1927.

On old Verde road. On the rim, above Pyle ranch. After Myrtle, daughter of Mr. and Mrs. E. F. Pyle. One of the many wet weather lakes found along Verde road. See Myrtle P. O.

Myrtle Point   Gila Co.   Map, Tonto N. F., 1926.

In T 12 N., R. 11 E., extending south from Tonto Rim. See Myrtle P. O. for origin.

Myrtle Ranch   Gila Co.   G. L. O. Map, 1909.

In T. 12 N., R. 11 E., in Tonto N. F. "So called after Myrtle, daughter of Mr. and Mrs. E. F. Pyle, who died here and is buried at Pyle ranch on Bonito creek." Letter, Fred Croxen. P. O. established December 23, 1890, Alphonso Landry, P. M.

Mystic Spring   Coconino Co.   Map, Kaibab N. F., 1927.

In Grand Canyon N. P., on plateau above river. A much sought spring secreted in a sandstone cavern immediately over a deep gorge of the Colorado on Bass' Trail. Well known to Supai Indians but for years not discovered by whites. It is a mere seep, but by making a cement and stone basin every drop is saved, furnishing an ample supply of water for local needs. See Bass spring for history. Decision U. S. G. B.

Na-at-tee Canyon   Navajo Co   G. L. O. Map, 1921.

In T. 24 N., R. 21 E. Just below south line Hopi Ind. Res., "Navajo name for loco plant." Letter, Richard M. Murphy. P. O. established November 27, 1916, Harry W. Wetsel, P. M.

Naches   Graham Co.   G. L. O. Map, 1921.

On San Carlos Ind. Res. Station, Arizona-Eastern R. R., about 6 miles east of San Carlos. "Naches, Nachis, Nachez, or Natchi. Son of Cochise and hereditary chief Chiricahua Apaches. A leader among the Indians and principal talker in Crook's councils with Geronimo's party when they surrendered March 25, 26, 27, 1886." *Truth About Geronimo.* Waters of San Carlos lake will cover this station, road having been moved to higher ground. See Natchi.

Naco   Cochise Co.   U. S. G. S. Map, 1923.

Village on International boundary line 7 miles southwest of Bisbee. Many believe this was a coined word worked out by B. A. Packard who had an early cattle ranch here. Said to be a combination of last two letters of Arizona and Mexico. The author at Phoenix, April 15, 1931, asked Mr. Packard for the facts. He said, "When they were figuring on building this railroad the engineers asked me to suggest a name for the first station on the line then called Southern Pacific of Mexico. As the road was being built principally to reach mines at Nacozari, Mexico, I suggested the first half of the name, Nacozari, and Naco was the result.

"The story of the last two letters of Arizona and Mexico is pure fiction but very plausible."

J. S. Williams, Douglas, says: The name Nacozari is of Indian origin and means "bear hills" or "hills of the bear." P. O. established Dec. 1, 1899, John E. Curry, P. M.

Naco Hills   Cochise Co.   U. S. G. S. Map, 1923.

Range of low hills about 12 miles long, directly west of Bisbee. After nearby town of Naco, q. v.

Nadaburg   Maricopa Co.   Map, U. S. G. S., 1923.

Sp., *nada,* "nothing." Station Ash Fork-Phoenix branch road. About 25 miles northwest of Phoenix. So named by General Manager, A. G. Wells. "Sometimes called 'Nada' for short. There was absolutely nothing here." A.G.W. In 1929, name was changed to Wittman for the man who financed re-building Walnut Grove dam. P. O. established Dec. 2, 1920, John P. Berry, P. M.

Naeglin Creek   Gila Co.   Map, Tonto N. F., 1927.

In T. 10 N., R. 14 E. Stream flowing into Haigler creek. After Naeglin brothers, William and Lewis, who located here about 1886. They drove a herd of cattle from Mora, New Mexico, via Holbrook to the basin that spring, 1886. Bill, the elder, was a blacksmith.

Nail Canyon   Coconino Co.   Map, Kaibab N. F., 1926.

In T. 36 N., R. 4½ W, stream and canyon; flows almost due north into Snake gulch. Big Spring flows into this stream. Named after an early settler whose name was Nagel. His sons, Alvin and Casper, anglicized the name, i.e., Nail. They moved to Apache county, settled near Concho, where they ran cattle for many years.

Nankoweap Creek   Coconino Co.   U. S. G. S. Map, 1923.

Northeast corner Grand Canyon N. P., west side Marble canyon. Enters Colorado river about 10 miles above mouth Little Colorado.

"Pah Ute word meaning literally 'singing' or 'echo' canyon, because of the deep echo." Dellenbaugh says Powell gave it this name on his second trip. Decision U. S. G. B., 1932.

Nariz Mountains   Pima Co.   Bryan Map, 1920; U. S. G. S., 1923.

Sp., "nose." On Mexican border at boundary post, No. 160. Descriptive name.

Nash Creek   Navajo and Gila Cos.

Map, Fort Apache Ind. Res., 1920.

Small stream about 8 miles south of Fort Apache. After man who had government beef contract at Apache about 1892.

Stream rises in Turkey Creek flat and flows southwest into Black river in Gila county, in T. 3 N., R. 21 E.

Natanes Peak   Gila Co.   U. S. G. S. Map, 1923.

Southern part Natanes plateau, south of Black river. San Carlos Ind. Res. From Apache word Natan or Nantan, a chief.

Natanes Plateau   Gila Co.   Smith Map, 1879; U. S. G. S., 1923.

Plateau, western part San Carlos Apache Ind. Res. West of Black river.

Natchi Canyon   Coconino Co.

Grand Canyon N. P., about half a mile southwest of Natchi point. Drains southeast into Bright Angel creek near lat. 36° 12' N., long. 112° 2' W. Small canyon tributary to Bright Angel canyon from west. See Natchi point.

Natchi Point   Coconino Co.

Grand Canyon N. P. West side Bright Angel canyon about 10 miles east Bright Angel Ranger Station. Near lat. 36° 12' N., long. 112° 2' W. On Kaibab plateau. Natchi was second son of Cochise. Name means "mischievous or meddlesome." In 1886 he was sent with other Chiricahuas to Florida. Hodge spells this name Nache. Britton Davis, and others, Naches, q. v. Decision U. S. G. B., Natchi. See "Uncle Jim."

National Canyon   Coconino Co.   U. S. G. S. Map, 1923.

Canyon extending north from T. 31 N., R. 6 W., to Colorado river. Hualpai Ind. Res.

Natural Bridge   Apache Co.

In T. 17 N., R. 24 E. In Petrified forest. Bridge is formed by a petrified log about 75 feet long spanning small canyon. We were camped here on the round-up in 1886 or 1887. A cowboy named Paine bet $10 he could ride his pony across this bridge. Pulled the shoes from his pony, rode safely over and won the money. Several months later he was killed in Pleasant Valley war.

Natural Bridge   Gila Co.   G. L. O. Map, 1892-1921; U. S. G. S., 1923.

Elevation 4,750 feet. In T. 11 N., R. 9 E. About 80 miles south of Flagstaff. Remarkable example of limestone creation. Waters of springs along the side of Pine creek, here, have gradually "built out" a formation entirely across the creek, creating the bridge. An object placed in water soon becomes encrusted with lime. There are some pre-Columbian ruins under bridge. On top is an orchard planted by the original settler, David Gowan. Top of span covers about 25 acres, measures nearly 400 feet north and south. Arch is from 125 to 150 feet high and that many wide.

In the center of "roof" top, is a hole about a foot in diameter, "weathered" through the rock. One can lie flat on ground and look down through the hole into the cool, dark depths below.

"This is the only case in North America, in which a valley has been spanned by a travertine deposit. Springs on east side contain lime in solution which deposits as it flows." *Bulletin, Geol. Society of America*, July 2, 1910.

"Bridge discovered July 23, 1880, by L. W. Snow, William Nelson, and Irvin L. House. In spring, 1881, Snow and David Gowan located area as a homestead. Gowan moved onto claim and later became sole owner. First printed description of it was prepared by D. D. Lake, who sent it to his daughter in Golden, Colo. Was printed in local paper and copied extensively. Gowan's relations in Scotland saw it in an English paper. They wrote him and later on migrated to Arizona and lived with Gowan, succeeding him as owner." Letter, L. M. House, Mesa. Gowan died in his cabin on Deer creek, Gila county, December, 1929.

Natural Corral Creek   Gila Co.   Map, San Carlos Ind. Res., 1917.

Stream rising extreme southeast corner T. 3 N., R. 18 E. Flows south into San Carlos river, southeast corner T. 1 N., R. 18 E., about 8 miles north of Rice. "There is a large natural corral on this stream used by reservation stockmen and Indians in handling their stock."

Navajo   Apache Co.   U. S. G. S. Map, 1923.

Trading station, A. T. & S. F. R. R., in T. 20 N., R. 26 E. First called Navajo springs, but shortened by railroad people to save telegraphing. Lynch brothers, Lewis and Hugh, owned a trading post here for many years. P. O. established July 13, 1883, J. A. Smith, P. M. See Navajo springs.

Navajo County

Created by Territorial Legislature at midnight, March 21, 1895, after two months fight against a hostile minority. Bill was held up until the last moment by a filibuster. Two members took turns in holding the floor, reading page after page of Arizona court decisions, histories of Arizona, decisions U. S. Supreme Court, etc. Finally the writer, who was author of the bill, managed to get it before the house on a parliamentary question and it was passed only a few minutes before adjournment at midnight, the last day of session. There was a strong sentiment for calling it Colorado county, but the writer insisted on adhering to names of Indian tribes or individual Indians and spelling it with a "J"—Navajo.

Navajo Creek   Coconino Co.   U. S. G. S. Map, 1923.

Navajo Indian Res. Rises north end White Mesa, flows northwest into Colorado river at State line in Glen canyon.

Navajo Indian Reservation   U. S. G. S. Map, 1923.

In Apache, Coconino and Navajo counties, Arizona, extending east into New Mexico, north into Utah. First established by President Hayes, 1878, added to later by various proclamations.

Navajo Indians in Arizona and New Mexico

These are one of our largest so called "Blanket tribes." Reservation is in northeast corner Arizona and northwest corner New Mexico. Origin of name has been interpreted as coming from Spanish word "Navaja" "a clasp knife—a razor." This because of their keenness in trade with the Spanish.

Hodge, who is generally so correct in his deductions along such lines says: "The word Navajo is possibly the corruption of Wichita Indians' name for themselves. The Navajos are an important Athapascan tribe. First to mention them by name was Zarati-Salmeron about 1629. Grammatical structure of their language shows majority of their words to have counterparts in dialects in Alaska, British Columbia and California. Spanish knew them as Apaches de Navajo. Navajos call themselves 'Dine' meaning simply 'people.' It is similar to the Apache name for themselves." *Hodge Hand Book.*

Others believe real origin of name is probably the Tewa word for the tribe meaning "a place of large plantings," referring to the vast cornfields of the Navajo. This may again have come from Spanish word "navajo," "a large piece of level ground."

Spelling of this word is not well defined. Congressional appropriation bills for the Navajo Indians spell it Navajo.

Authorities differ on it. Hodge says Navajo, while others write it Navaho. Broadly speaking, scientists and ethnologists have decided on the spelling Navaho and Mohave as most satisfactory and it is gradually coming into use. As long as Congress uses a certain form, that is legal for that particular place or thing. The writer has a deep-seated aversion to this abandonment of the Spanish "j" in preference to the English "h." Navajo, decision U. S. G. B.

Navajo Mountain   Coconino Co.

Navajo Indian Reservation. Navajo name means "Enemies' Hiding Hole." Located at Colorado state line near long. 110° 50′ N. Almost due south of junction San Juan river with the Colorado.

"Professor Powell climbed up 800 feet and had a fine view of Navajo mountain, now very near. The major then called it Mount Seneca Howland, in memory of that unfortunate person, but it having been known as Navajo mountain for years that name was finally adopted." Dellenbaugh.

Gregory writes: "From whatever quarter it is viewed, Navajo mountain always presents the same profile. It is quite solitary, without even a foothill for society. Its very loneliness is impressive. Called 'Sierra Panoche' on the Macomb-Newberry map, 1859." Gregory map, 1916, shows it Sierra Panoche, as does Eckhoff, 1880. G. L. O. and late maps have it Navajo.

Navajo National Monument   Coconino Co.   G. L. O. Map, 1921.

Navajo Ind. Res. at headwaters of Navajo creek, west of Marsh pass. Series of large, well-preserved pre-Columbian ruins set aside March 2, 1909, as National Monument by Secretary of Interior to preserve them from spoliation.

Navajo Spring   Coconino Co.   G. L. O. Map, 1923.

Navajo Ind. Res., on old Mormon road about 10 miles south Lee Ferry. Well-known camping place in early days when this road was main highway from Arizona to southern Utah.

Navajo Springs   Apache Co.   U. S. G. S. Map, 1923.

In T. 20 N., R. 29 E. Apache county. Number of small springs about 3 miles southeast of Navajo Station, A. T. & S. F. R. R.

Here, Tuesday, December 29, 1863, the newly appointed federal officials raised the flag and formally inaugurated the government of Arizona Territory. Oath of office was administered to Governor Goodwin and others by Secretary McCormick. Navajo Springs was the first point party was sure was within geographical limits of Arizona. They were forced to act at this time because their commissions as federal officials, as well as salaries, called for their taking oaths of office in the new territory within calendar year, 1863. Governor Goodwin's original proclamation is in state historian's office at Phoenix. It is dated at Navajo Springs. On the lower part he has written in his own handwriting as follows:

"The seat of government will for the present be at or near Fort Whipple."

He also changed the date with a pen from December 23—date originally decided on—to December 29, 1863. Original proclamation was evidently printed in advance, on the supposition they would arrive inside the Territory on first date set. On the bottom is written in lead pencil:

"Found among ancient papers. It may possibly be of some interest." Signed, but not dated, R. L. Richmond, Grand Rapids, Michigan.

Naviska   Pinal Co.

Station, S. P. R. R., about 25 miles west of Tucson. No record of its origin or meaning. See Navajo and Nevissa for possible origin.

Nazlini Stream and Canyon   Apache Co.   Gregory Map, 1916; U. S. G. S., 1923.

In T. 3 N., R. 10 W. According to Gregory, this is a Navajo word meaning "running crooked" or "crooked canyon." Navajo Ind. Res., 10 miles south of Chinle.

Needles   Graham Co.   G. L. O. Map, 1921.

In Pinaleno range, Crook N. F. Ten miles south of Mount Graham. Descriptive name. There are several sharp points or peaks which give the name.

Needles   Mohave Co.

Town first established as a P. O. in Mohave county, Arizona, on Atlantic & Pacific R. R., February 18, 1883, August A. Spear, P. M.

On October 11, 1883, name changed to Powell, q.v., according to P. O. records and name Needles taken by the new town across the river on California side. In early days, a paper was published here called *The Needle's Eye*. See also "The Needles" on the Arizona side.

"Was first located on Arizona side of river but later moved over to California side where there was more room for town which the railroad wished to lay out for a division point." Letter, Supt., Santa Fe Railroad.

Needles Eye   Pinal Co.   U. S. G. S. Map, 1923.

San Carlos Ind. Res. Narrow place in canyon of Gila river about 10 miles below San Carlos, where Coolidge dam is located.

Needles Mountain   Gila Co.   Map, Crook N. F., 1926.

In Sec. 34, T. 1 N., R. 14 E. About 10 miles west Globe. "We camped on top of Pinal mountain—from it the following observations were made. Needles, N. 86′ W.; Tonto Peak, N. 60° 30′ W.; Casa Blanca, near Pimos, 70° W." Woolsey's report, July 4, 1864. On Smith map, 1879, and Eckhoff, 1880, this is called "Weaver Needle." Woolsey's figures, however, do not check up with any modern maps. Possibly his instruments were not correct.

Needles, The   Mohave Co.   G. L. O. Map, 1892.

Group of three sharp peaks on Arizona side, Colorado river. About 5 miles below point where A. T. & S. F. R. R. crosses river. So called by Whipple, 1853.

Ives says: "A cluster of slender, prominent pinnacles named by Lieut. Whipple, 'The Needles.'" In close proximity to river.

Nelson   Coconino Co.   G. L. O. Map, 1921.

In T. 25 N., R. 10 E. Station A. T. & S. F. R. R. Ten miles east of Peach Springs. "After Fred Nelson, former division superintendent of roadway, A. & P. R. R. 1886." A.G.W. P. O. established March 23, 1904, William Carey, P. M.

Nephi   Maricopa Co.   G. L. O. Map, 1892.

A "ward" of the Mormon church. Two miles west of Mesa. Settled, 1883—mainly by people from Tempe. Also called Jacksonville at one time for Frank J. Jackson, first postmaster, February 20, 1889. Nephi was one of the Mormon prophets. He wrote the record of the Mormon people on plates of gold and, in general, is considered as the historian of the Mormon people and church."

Nero   Apache Co.

In T. 11 N., R. 28 E. Shows on map, 1884, as on Colorado river 12 miles below Springerville, near mouth Coyote creek. "It was a small colony of Mormons about 1883. A few families are still living there today—1931. None of them can say why it was so called." Letter, Gustave Becker, Springerville. P. O. established February 15, 1883, James H. Wilkins, P. M.

Nestor, Mount   Coconino Co.   G. L. O. Map, 1921.

In T. 18 N., R. 8 E. On Coconino N. F., about 6 miles southwest of Mormon lake.

Nevin   Coconino Co.   U. S. G. S. Map, 1923.

In T. 21 N., R. 5 E. "So named for A. G. Nevin, general manager Santa Fe R. R." A.G.W.

Nevissa River   Pinal Co.

McFarland's history says, "Fort Breckenridge was located, 1856, at junction of San Pedro and Nevissa rivers." No such stream found on any early maps, nor is it known to any of the old timers in that region. In all probability, was a misprint or error and meant for Aravaipa. See also Naviska—Ft. Breckenridge.

New Creek   Mohave Co.

See Peach Springs draw.

Newberry Mesa   Mohave Co.   G. L. O. Map, 1921.

East side Little Colorado north of Leupp. Named after Dr. J. S. Newberry, physician and geologist with Lieut. Ives' party, who visited this spot, 1858.

New London   Mohave Co.   Smith Map, 1879;
                                                         Mohave Sheet, 1892.

Small mining town, southern end, Cerbat mountains north of Kingman. "The road passes through Stockton, Cerbat and New London." Coues.

"The New London was a well-known lead mine from which camp took its name. In Hualpai mining district and a very prosperous camp in 1883." Hinton.

Newman Peak   Pinal Co.   G. L. O. Map, 1921;
                                                         U. S. G. S., 1923.

In T. 8 S., R. 9 E., southern end Picacho mountains.

New Osborne   Cochise Co.

See Osborne Junction.

New River Mountains   Yavapai Co.   Map, Tonto N. F., 1927.

In T. 8, S. R. 3, 4 E.   Short range after stream by this name.

New River   Maricopa Co.   G. L. O. Map, 1921.

In T. 9 N., R. 4 E.   Stream rising, Yavapai county. Heads at Cook Mesa. Flows southwest into Agua Fria river in T. 2 N., R. 1 E., about 5 miles west of Glendale. Just why called New River cannot be learned. Listed in *Arizona Gazetteer*, 1881, as "A stage station at New River, 35 miles north of Phoenix. Station is kept by George Hall." P. O. established May 9, 1898, Ephraim Tomkinson, P. M.

New Virginia   Mohave County

See Virginia City, Mohave county. There is one in Pima county also.

New Water Mountains   Yuma Co.   U. S. G. S. Map, 1923.

West side Ranegras plains. Near lat. 33° 30′ N., long 113°. No one can explain this name.

New Water Pass   Yuma Co.   G. L. O. Map, 1921; U. S. G. S. Map, 1923.

In T. 1 N., R. 17 W. Pass between Little Horn and New Water mountains, lower end Plomosa range.

New Years Spring   Coconino Co.

Powell's report says: "New Years Spring is 30 miles southwest of San Francisco mountains. Whipple camped on it in 1854, and named it."

Whipple writes, December 31, 1853: "We bivouaced upon a hillside. Leroux spring lay due east at an estimated distance of 20 miles. From south to southwest about 10 miles from us was Bill Williams mountain. North and northwest were black volcanic hills and a high prairie devoid of snow."

The next day his men found a fine spring, "about a mile west of camp. They called it New Years spring for the day." This spring may be present Volunteers spring which lies almost exactly here, according to Whipple's locations.

Only map which shows this spring under name New Years is Smith, 1879. This locates it 18 miles southwest of Leroux spring. Shows it as due south of Sitgreaves mountain at Pitman's ranch. Doubtless this is Pitman valley of today. There is an unnamed spring in sec. 17, T. 22 N., R. 4 E., on Flagstaff quad, 1912, that fits it nicely.

Niblack Peak   Apache Co.

Peak near Arizona and New Mexico line, Navajo Ind. Res., described by Wheeler, but not located on any map. So called after meterologist by this name with Wheeler expedition.

He was son of Congressman Niblack of Indiana, well-known politician and congressman of those days.

Nic-dot-soe Peak   Apache Co.

See Wild Cat peak.

Nigger Well   Maricopa Co.

"Well dug by a Portuguese said to have been part Negro, lying between Hassayampa and Salt rivers, about 12 miles from the 'sink' of Hassayampa north of White Tank mountains. The Negro ran a bakery shop at Wickenburg for a while." Farish.

Nigger Well was so called because it was dug by several men, one of whom was a Negro. They quarreled when water was not found and threw rocks in on the Negro while he was down in the bottom and killed him.

"It was here that Frenchy Debaud exploded 2,600 pounds of giant powder stored along the road by a freighter, whose wagon had broken down. He covered the stuff with a heavy canvas; Frenchy came along, saw a coyote smelling around the canvas, stopped his team and took a shot at the animal. Shot exploded powder leaving a huge hole to mark the spot. Powder belonged to Goldman Brothers of Phoenix, who sued Frenchy for damages but got nothing. The freighter in turn sued the Goldmans for his work—but got nothing. 'Did you kill the coyote?' Frenchy was asked. 'Not for cer-taine,' said the Frenchman, 'but I got one dam beeg hole to bury him een.'" J. M. Barney. The author, with Buckey O'Neill, came along on the stage a few days later. It was surely "one dam beeg hole."

Nine Mile Peak   Pima Co.   G. L. O. Map, 1921; U. S. G. S., 1923.

Papago Ind. Res. Near lat. 32° 20' N., long. 112° 30' W. "It is 9 miles east of Gunsight mine."

Nine Mile Station   Yuma Co.   Smith Map, 1879.

First stage station east of Yuma, on old road to Tucson.

Nine Mile Valley   Mohave Co.   G. L. O. Map, 1921.

West side Kanab creek, south of Kaibab Ind. Res. "Valley extends south from Fredonia about 9 miles." Letter, Walter Mann, Kanab.

Nipples, The   Cochise Co.

See College peaks.

N. O. Bar Mesa   Greenlee Co.   Map, Crook N. F., 1926.

In T. 2 S., R. 29 E. "An old ranch headquarters of N.O. Bar Cattle Co., which used this range and gave this brand for many years." Letter, J. W. Girdner, Clifton.

Noble Mountain   Apache Co.   Map, Apache N. F., 1926.

In sec. 21, T. 6 N., R 30 E. Solitary mountain at head Nutrioso creek. After John Noble, one-armed Englishman who, in 1885-1909, grazed large numbers of sheep on this range. About 1909, Noble, for some reason never known, abandoned his sheep and left the country under an assumed name. Although discovered in New York before sailing, he went his way without any explanation as to his behavior.

Nogales   Santa Cruz Co.   Smith Map, 1879; Eckhoff, 1880; U. S. G. S., 1923; G. L. O., 1921.

Sp., "Nogal—walnut." Elevation 3,869 feet. An old settlement first known as "Los Nogales" postoffice. Known also as "Line City," then "Isaactown," "after the owner of one of its saloons," according to McClintock.

Land grant on which town stood was owned by a Topeka Cattle Company, with Isaac N. Town, citizen, politician and stockman, as president and general manager. Nogales was the name agreed upon in 1882. Nogales, Sp., "walnut trees." First settlers say stream was lined with these trees. When Santa Cruz county was created, Nogales became county seat. Emory, with U. S. Boundary commission, held a conference here with Indians June 26, 1853.

Morley Avenue, the main street in Nogales, was named after William R. Morley, Chief Engineer, A. T. & S. F. R. R. P. O. established Oct. 29, 1897, Albert J. Griswold, P. M. See Isaactown and Isaacson.

No-Kai   Navajo Co.   U. S. G. S. Map, 1923.

Creek Navajo Ind. Res. Rises north Marsh pass, flows north into Colorado river near lat. 37', long. 110' to 40'. Gregory says, "It is a branch of San Juan river in Colorado. No-Kai is Navajo name applied by them to Mexicans." Father Haile says, "No-Kai is a personal or general, not a geographical name."

Noon Camp   Pima Co.

See Noonville.

Noonville or Noon Camp   Pima Co.

Mining camp and settlement 18 miles west Nogales and about 3 miles from Mexican line. Named after Captain John A. Noon, mining man who located first near Oro Blanco, November, 1879. Moved here 1887.

Noria   Pima Co.

Sp., "a deep well." Rancheria on Papago Ind. Res. Commonly used for a well where a rope and wheel is used. Papago name is Vi-penoi, meaning, "Where a small cactus is growing." Hornaday says: "Very old Papago village or rancheria northwest Indian Oasis." See La Noria, on Lumholtz map, 1916.

North Butte   Pinal Co.   G. L. O. Map, 1921.

Elevation 2,980 feet. In sec. 2, T. 4 S., R. 11 E. About 10 miles northwest of Florence, north side Gila river. Reservoir site holding Gila flood waters. There are two prominent buttes, one on each side of river, which flows between them, known locally as North and South buttes.

North Canyon and Creek   Coconino Co.   Map, Kaibab N. F., 1926.

Rises in sec. 21, T. 34 N., R. 3 E., near head South canyon. Flows northeast, enters Colorado river in sec. 8, T. 37 N., R. 6 E. The two canyons, North and South, rise near each other, run nearly parallel.

North Fork of White River   Apache and Navajo Cos.
Smith Map, 1879; Fort Apache Ind. Res., 1928.

Rises in T. 7 N., R. 26 E., in "Big Cienega"; flows west and southwest, joins East Fork at Fort Apache to form White river.

North Peak   Gila Co.   Map, Tonto N. F., 1927.

East side Mazatzal range near head Rye creek. "This peak is at north end Mazatzal range, hence its name." Letter, Fred Croxen.

Norton   Yuma Co.   G. L. O. Map, 1921.

In T. 7 S., R. 15 W. Town and farming community east of Yuma on north bank Gila river. Named for George W. Norton, member Eleventh Territorial Legislature, 1881, from Yuma county. P. O. established June 4, 1883, Jacob D. Dettelbach, P. M. See Norton's Landing.

Nortons Landing   Yuma Co.

Colorado river, 52 miles north of Yuma. *Arizona Gazetteer*, 1881, says, "It is a landing place for freight for the Silver District and reduction works of Red Cloud Mining Co." Named for Captain George W. Norton.

Nottbush Butte   Yuma Co.   U. S. G. S. Map, 1923.
South end Cemetery ridge near Yuma county line, near lat.
113° 30'. "After Fred Nottbush of Palomas, who lived here in
early days." Letter, Mrs. John Martin, Salome.

Nottbush Valley   Yuma Co.   G. L. O. Map, 1921.
Valley lying between Cemetery ridge and Clanton hills. Same
origin as Nottbush butte.

Novinger Butte   Coconino Co.
Grand Canyon N. P. About 3½ miles southeast of Imperial
point. Near northeast corner of Park in lat. 36° 15' N. long. 111°
to 56'. "Named for Simon Novinger, pioneer of Salt River valley.
Born in Pennsylvania, 1832, crossed plains to Montana, 1863, to
California, 1868, in 1871 went to Arizona when Phoenix had but
two or three houses. Prospected, attacked by Indians and wounded. Settled near Phoenix, 1873, where he died January 24, 1904.
Decision U. S. G. S. Named by Frank Bond.

Nugents Pass   Cochise Co.   G. L. O. Map, 1882.
East of old "Tres Alamos"—"Three Cottonwoods"—stage station on road through Galiuro mountains.

Nuggett   Gila Co.
P. O. for mining camp of Richmond Basin, "named after Nug-
gett mine, discovered and worked for some time by Chilson
brothers." Letter, Dan Williamson, Globe. P. O. established
January 7, 1881. George Santan, P. M.
One wonders if this postmaster's name was not the origin of
Pima name, "San-Tan," for which there has been found no sat-
isfactory meaning or origin.

Nuñez   Pima Co.   G. L. O. Map, 1921.
In T. 6 S., R. 5 E. Station, S. P. R. R. "About 16 miles east of
Maricopa. Established about 1900. Spanish proper name." Letter Paul Shoup.
Named after Ventura Núñez, who, according to Farish: "On
July 7, 1874, murdered G. R. Whistler at Burkes station, q. v., on
lower Gila west of this station, and for whose capture, alive or
dead, King Woolsey offered $500. Was caught and hung at this
station by Woolsey himself."

Nutrioso   Apache Co.   Map, Apache N. F., 1926.
In T. 7 N., R. 30 E. Town and stream. Originally located by a
man named Jones. Then came James G. H. Coulter, lumberman
from Wisconsin, who in 1875 settled at Round valley. He and a
man named Murray located part of Jones valley and settled there
near him. First settlers here killed a beaver and a bear. Hence
they named it rather picturesquely. "Nutria," beaver, and "Oso,"
bear, e.g., "Nutrioso." For a time called Bush valley, q.v.
Stream rises in T. 6 N., R. 30 E., near Nobles mountain, flows
south into Little Colorado at Eager.
Hintons map, 1883, shows this stream as "Neute Rossa," evidently a corruption of real name. Coulter family later on founded town of Coulter, near Springerville. P. O. established April 12,
1883, John A. Clark, P. M. See Reservation creek.

Nutt Mountain   Mohave Co.
Elevation 5,065 feet. In T. 20 N., R. 19 W. "Nothing in any
official reports to indicate origin of this name." Letter James
McCormick, U. S. G. S., Washington, D. C.

"Name should be McNutt, who was a surveyor with the engineering corps that made the 35th parallel survey under Whipple." Letter, Anson H. Smith, Kingman. Name McNutt is not to be found in Whipple's list of his command. Mountain shown as Nutt on every map published until 1921 edition of G. L. O. map of Arizona, which has it McNutt. Evidently a misprint.

Oak Creek   Coconino Co.   Map, Coconino N. F., 1928.

In T. 18 N., R. 6 E. Stream in Munds park flows southeast, enters Verde river 4 miles below Clemenceau. "So called for number of fine oak trees in canyon." Letter, M. J. Riordan, Flagstaff.

Oak Creek   Gila Co.   Map, Tonto N. F., 1929.

Stream rising near Boneyback peak, Sierra Ancha mountains. Enters Tonto creek above Greenback creek in T. 6 N., R. 11 E. So called by Capt. Sanford, 1st U. S. Cavalry, who in November, 1866, had a fight at upper end this stream inflicting great damage to the Apaches. "I called it Oak creek because of a number of beautiful oak trees where we camped." Sanford's report.

Oak Creek   Gila Co.   U. S. G. S. Map, 1923.

Apache Ind. Res., rises near reservation line, under "Rim," flows south into Gila county. Joins Canyon creek in T. 8 N., R. 15½ E., about 10 miles northeast Sombrero butte. William Young had a camp on this creek when he grazed his cattle on the Apache reservation. Camp shows on Reservation map.

Oak Creek   Graham Co.   U. S. G. S. Map, 1923.

Small stream southwest corner San Carlos Apache Ind. Res. Rises near southern edge Natanes plateau, flows south, enters San Carlos one mile below Blue river.

Oak Spring   Coconino Co.   G. L. O. Map, 1921.

In approx. T. 28 N., R. 8 W. Hualpai Ind. Res. Under upper rim of Grand Canyon.

Oakdale   Yavapai Co.

Settlement P. O. established July 1, 1901, Clara B. Riley, P. M. "The town is a pretty oak grove." Item Prescott *Journal-Miner*, August, 1901.

Oak Grove   Cochise Co.   Smith Map, 1879; Eckhoff, 1880.

Early-day ranch and stage station about 8 miles north of present Willcox.

"At Oak Grove about 8 miles beyond Point of Mountain, White brothers have a 12-foot well with a fine flow of water for many thousands of cattle." Hinton.

The author passed here February, 1880. Point of Mountains was station where one left the overland stage and took a buckboard for Fort Grant.

Oak Grove   Pinal Co.

Hinton lists this station "about 22 miles south of Globe on new road to Florence."

Oaks and Willows   Yavapai Co.   Smith Map, 1879; Eckhoff, 1880.

Early day stage station on Fort Mohave-Prescott road. In Round valley, south of Anvil Rock. In later years was headquarter camp for Perrin Livestock Co., of Williams, which owned nearby Baca grant. Mrs. Summerhayes, in *Vanished Arizona*, tells of her joy at seeing the groves of oaks, willows, cedar and pine along here in 1874.

Oatman   Mohave Co.   G. L. O. Map, 1921; U. S. G. S., 1923.

In T. 19 N., R. 20½ W. Town and mining district, Black moun-tains. First called Vivian according to post office records. Named after Olive Oatman of the family massacred by Apaches on Gila river, March, 1851. See Oatman Flat. P. O. established June 24, 1909, Lenore M. Clark, P. M.

Oatman Flat   Maricopa Co.   Territorial Maps, 1877.

Open valley south Gila river Maricopa county. South end Big Horn (later called Painted Rock) mountains about 18 miles east Agua Caliente. On March 28, 1851, Royce Oatman, his wife and five children were attacked at this point by Apache-Mohave In-dians. All but two girls and a boy were killed. Were buried near Burke's station about 11 miles northeast of Sentinel. Lorenzo, the boy, was left for dead but made his way to safety. Girls taken captive and traded later to Mohaves. Taken to Mohave county on Bill Williams river. One girl, Mary Ann, died, 1852, in captivity. Olive, the elder, was finally rescued in 1856 after five years of captivity and restored to her brother at Fort Yuma. See Oatman, Mohave county.

Oatmans   Maricopa Co.   Hinton Map, 1878; Smith, 1879.

Stage station, Yuma-Tucson road, 1879. About 120 miles east of Yuma. So called for Oatman massacre which occurred close to this spot. Hinton says: "At Painted Rock, near this station (Oatman's), the road from Phoenix comes in."

Obed   Navajo Co.   G. L. O. Map, 1882.

In T 17 N., R. 19 E. Mormon settlement 3 miles south of Little Colorado, opposite present town of Joseph City. According to Mormon history was located and named by Bishop George Lake in March, 1876. Name "Obed" in Hebrew means "servant." Obed was the son of Boaz and Ruth and a character in the Book of Mormon. Settlers built a fine stone fort here at edge of a large ciénega or swamp. Walls were 10 feet high, 3 feet thick at base, tapering to one foot. There were round bastions at two oppo-site corners. These and the walls were loop-holed for rifle firing. Inside were comfortable stone houses, with stone floors and roofs. Water piped from a spring outside. Only opening was a gate on east side 8 feet wide of planks hewn from cottonwood logs.

Fort was a masterpiece of stone mason's art. Bishop Owen of Woodruff was said to have been in charge of its building. Used for years as a cattle corral. Should have been preserved as an example of pioneer work, but was torn down about 1895, by Aztec Cattle Co. There is almost a replica of it at Beaver, Utah. On G.L.O. map, 1892, only, which places it in T. 18 N., R. 19 E. *Mormon Settlement* has a good account of it.

Obi Canyon and Point   Coconino Co.

Flows south and drains into west side Clear creek near lat. 36°, 7′ N. long. 112° W. Small canyon below Obi point on north canyon wall. First called Indian point, changed by U.S.G.B., 1906. Obi is Supai or Pah Ute, for nut pine (piñón) tree. Point shows on Grand Canyon map, 1928, as Observation Point. See Hue-thawali mountain.

Observatory Hill   Coconino Co.

Hill west of Flagstaff on which, 1894, Percival Lowell erected and equipped an observatory. First called Schulz or Schultz hill.

Ocapos   Maricopa Co.   G. L. O. Map, 1921.

Station, S. P. R. R., about 12 miles east of Gila Bend, east side Maricopa mountains. Paul Shoup says: "Is the name So. Pac. Co. reversed. Established about 1890."

Ocatillo (sic)   Pinal Co.

Station S. P. R. R., about 43 miles west of Tucson. After well-known desert plant by this name. Correct spelling is Ocotillo. See Ocotillo.

Ochoa   Cochise Co.   G. L. O. Map, 1892.

Station, S. P. R. R., about 15 miles east of Benson. After Esteban Ochoa, junior member Tully, Ochoa & Co., Tucson. See Ochoa point. "Ochoaville" on S. P. R. R. folders.

Ochoa Mount   Maricopa Co.

In T. 5 N., R. 2 E., between New River and Cave creek. On G. L. O. map, 1921, this is Mount Ogoa. Origin of either name unknown. U.S.G.S. map, 1923, is Ochoa.

Ochoa Point   Coconino Co.

Grand Canyon N. P., near Basalt cliffs, lat. 26° 6', long. 111° 52'. "Named for Esteban Ochoa, born New Mexico, educated Kansas City. Before Civil War, interested in large mercantile establishments in Tucson and elsewhere in Arizona. Driven out of Tucson by Confederates on refusing to swear allegiance to Confederacy, his property was confiscated except one horse which he rode to the Rio Grande 200 miles away alone through Apache infested country. When Union troops retook Tucson, Ochoa returned and resumed business." Farish. Named by Frank Bond. Decision USGB.

Ochoas Ranch   Pima Co.   Eckhoff Map, 1880.

In T. 16 S., R. 13 E. Named after Esteban Ochoa of Tucson. Well-known ranch, 1870, on San Pedro about 6 miles south San Xavier. See "Ochoas" on the Sonoita.

Ochoas   Santa Cruz Co.   Eckhoff Map, 1880.

Station, Sonoita river, about 20 miles northeast Nogales. Named for Don Esteban Ochoa of Tucson. Ochoa who had large livestock holdings, doubtless had more than one ranch bearing his name. P. O. established under name Ochoas, November 11, 1879, Esteban Ochoa, P. M.

Ocotillo   Yavapai Co.   G. L. O. Map, 1921.

Prescott N. F. Station and mine, Crown King branch railroad from Prescott, about 6 miles south of Mayer station. Hills about the station are covered with the desert shrub known as ocotillo, *Fouquiera splendens*, "Candlewood." P. O. established January, 13, 1917, Pearl Orr, P. M.

Ocotillo   Yuma Co.   U. S. G. S. Map, 1923.

Mining camp east side Kofa mountains. "So named for plant by this name, very plentiful here."

Octave   Yavapai Co.   U. S. G. S. Map, 1923.

In T. 9 N., R. 4 W. Mining camp and mine, on Weaver creek about 10 miles southeast of Congress. "So called because it was owned by eight men." P. O. established April 19, 1900, David J. Jones, P. M. First called Weaver, but as there already was a post office by that name, they called it Octave.

Odart Mountain   Apache Co.   Map, Fort Apache Ind. Res., 1928.

Peak in T. 5 N., R. 26 E. "An outfit from New Mexico ran cattle near this mountain for a time, and made it their summer headquarters. Their brand was O-dart, hence the name. Letter, A. F. Potter, Los Angeles.

Ohnersorgen Stage Station   Cochise Co.

"Beyond the old Ohnersorgen stage station when they crossed the San Pedro river they found the fresh graves of two men killed by Indians." *Tombstone.*

Ojo Bonito   Apache Co.   Map, Apache N. F., 1926.

Sp., "pretty eye." In T. 10 N., R. 25 E. Sitgreaves N. F. Well known spring and sheep watering place. Mexicans commonly speak of a spring as an "ojo"-eye.

Ojo Caliente Apaches

See Apaches.

Oldberg   Pinal Co.   Post Route Map, 1929.

Station, Mesa-Picacho branch R. R., about 10 miles south of Santan. "This is the Sacaton diversion dam, sometimes called Sacaton bridge. Named after Major Olberg, chief engineer, Sacaton Dam and Bridge Co." Letter, J. O. Willett. Oldberg P. O. established June 2, 1927, Joseph O. Willett, P. M.

Old Camp Thomas

See Thomas.

Old Dominion   Gila Co.

One of earliest copper mines in Globe district. About 3 miles north of Globe.

"Named by Mrs. Alex Pendleton for her native state, Virginia. About 1881, this was a village called Old Dominion. It was near Bloody Tanks, where mine smelter was located."

Old Fort Goodwin

See Goodwin.

Old Fort Hualpai   Yavapai Co.

See Juniper.

Old Glory   Santa Cruz Co.   G. L. O. Map, 1921.

In T 22 S., R. 11 E. Early day mining camp about 2 miles south of Ruby, close to Mexican line. Mine first called "American Flag." When they asked for a P. O. they wanted it named for this mine. Authorities at Washington compromised on Old Glory. Name first spelled Oldglory, one word. Considerable comment was made and Postal authorities changed it to Old Glory, November 23, 1895. P. O. first established Jan. 15, 1895, William E. Ward, P. M.

Old Pete Mountain   Pima Co.

See Pete mountain.

Old Town Spring

See Antelope spring.

Old Trails   Mohave Co.   G. L. O. Map, 1921;
                                                  U. S. G. S. Map, 1923.

In T. 19 N., R. 20½ W., in Black mountains, near Oatman. Believed to have been so called because of location of Beale and Sitgreaves trails near here. P. O. established February 29, 1916, Ernie L. Stratton, P. M.

O'Leary Peak   Coconino Co.   U. S. G. S. Map, 1923;
                                                  Coconino N. F., 1928.

Elevation 8,925 feet. In T. 23 N., R. 80 W. Named for Dan O'Leary, scout and guide for Gen. Crook. "Over on the Colorado river, Dan O'Leary still dealt out to expectant listeners tales of the terrible days when he 'fit with Crook.'" Bourke.

"Dan O'Leary was a Hualpai interpreter at the camp on Date creek at the time the Indians tried to kill Gen. Crook, Sept. 8, 1872. He probably saved Crook's life when the shooting began by killing the leaders of the attack while Crook was looking in a different direction." Farish. Decision USGB.

Olga   Cochise Co.   G. L. O. Map, 1909.

Station, S. P. R. R., 21 miles east of Bowie. In T. 13 S., R. 29 E.

Olive Camp   Pima Co.   G. L. O. Map, 1892.

In T. 17 S., R. 12 E. West of Santa Cruz river. After Olive mine located here. Said to have been largest mining camp in Pima county, 1889. P. O. established March 4, 1887, Owen J. Doyle, P. M.

Olive City   Yuma Co.   Smith Map, 1879; Eckhoff, 1880.

Settlement on Colorado a few miles above Ehrenberg. Ferry established here, 1863, by Wm. Bradshaw. Was authorized as a toll ferry by First Territorial Legislature. "Olive City consisted of one house covered with brush and sided up with willow poles." Chas. B. Gening, 1863. First called Olivia. Very likely after Olive or Ollie Oatman. See Oatman. Bancroft says it was called Olivia in 1864. See Bradshaw ferry.

Olja-Oljato

See Moonlight creek, Kayenta.

Olo Canyon   Coconino Co.   Map, Grand Canyon N. F., 1928.

Rises in T. 34 N., R. 3 W., flows northwest, enters Colorado river about 2 miles west of Kanab creek. "Hava Supai word for 'horse.' The Supai grazed their horses in the canyon." G. Wharton James.

Olo Mesa   Coconino Co.   U. S. G. S. Map, 1923.

Grand Canyon N. P. near lat 36° 23', long. 112° 26', between Olo and Hundred and Forty Mile canyon. One of the low tablelands on left (south) bank of Colorado river, north end Coconino plateau. Indian name meaning "horse." See Olo canyon.

Omer   Apache Co.

One of the two wards out of which settlement of Eager was formed. "Omer was a Mormon prophet, king of the Province of Omer and a son of Shule." See Eager, Round Valley and Springerville.

O'Neal Spring   Coconino Co.

In sec. 20, T. 21 N., R. 7 E. About 8 miles south Flagstaff. "It was on land taken up as a homestead by Oscar O'Neal, March, 1888. City of Flagstaff bought property and ran a pipe line from it to the town reservoir. Now used only in dry times." Letter E. G. Miller, Forest Service.

O'Neil Hills and Pass   Pima Co.   G. L. O. Map, 1921; U. S. G. S., 1923.

In T. 16 S., R. 11 W. Western boundary of county at Mexican line. "After William J. O'Neil, who came to southern Arizona, 1867. He was a miner and ranchman in Pima county, represented that county in 8th Territorial Legislature." Farish. On all maps as Oneil.

O'Neill Butte   Coconino Co.   Map, Tusayan N. F., 1928; Grand Canyon N. P., 1929.

Southern side of river about 6 miles above El Tovar, opposite mouth Bright Angel creek.

Named for William O. (Buckey) O'Neill, captain of Rough Riders in Spanish-American War. Killed at El Caney. Born, Washington D. C., buried Arlington National Cemetery. Was a printer and type setter. Came to Arizona 1879, studied stenography, became court reporter at Prescott where he established and ran for several years as a side issue, a livestock paper, *Hoofs and Horns*. Probate judge, Yavapai county, 1886; sheriff, 1888; mayor of Prescott, 1889. Spent two years exploring wilds of Brazil. Returned and ran for Congress on Populist ticket, 1894, and again, 1896. Defeated both times. An unusual man in every way. Brilliant, scholarly, but very eccentric. One of Arizona's most picturesque, historic figures.

O'Neill Spring   Coconino Co.

Grand Canyon N. P., near Cottonwood creek, 1¼ miles below Grandview point. Named for "Bucky" O'Neill. Decision U. S. G. B.

Onion Spring   Navajo Co.   Gregory Map, 1916; U. S. G. S., 1923.

In T. 30 N., R. 17 E. Hopi Ind. Res., at second mesa. Often confused with well-known Wipo spring. Wipo is Hopi name for Onion. They are two separate springs.

Ookilsipava River   Pinal Co.

"Miners meeting on the Ookilsipava river in the Pioneer mining district, May 10, 1863. Signed V. Wheelhouse, Secy." *Farish Notes*. The Pioneer district was in Pinal county but the name of this stream is not found on any map nor in any other connection. History or origin unknown.

Oracle   Pinal Co.   U. S. G. S. Map, 1923; Coronado N. F., 1925.

In T. 9 S., R. 15 E. Town at northern end Santa Catalinas. "Alexander McKay, who first prospected the region, says name Oracle was given to the mine southwest of village by Weldon who in 1875 came around Cape Horn on a ship named 'The Oracle.' Many years later, a post office was desired at this point, then known as Acadia ranch. A neighboring ranch was called 'American Flag.' Government instructed both ranches to get together on one name. Oracle was chosen." Letter, Frank C. Lockwood, Tucson. P. O. established Dec. 28, 1880, James Branson, P. M.

Oracle Hill   Pinal Co.   U. S. G. S. Winkelman Quad;
                                              Coronado N. F., 1925.

Elevation 5,290 feet. South of Oracle, on northeast slope Santa Catalina mountains. Named after town.

Oraibi   Navajo Co.   G. L. O. Map, 1921; U. S. G. S., 1923.

In T. 29 N., R. 16 E. One of the several Hopi pueblos; on "third," or west mesa, Hopi group. Hopi word said to mean "eagle traps." On Oraiba wash, Hopi Ind. Res. P. O. established August 11, 1900, as Oraiba (sic.). Later changed to Oraibi, Herman Kampmier, P. M. Decision U. S. G. B.

Oraibi Wash   Navajo Co.   U. S. G. S. Map, 1923.

Navajo Ind. Res., rises south side Black mesa, flows southwest across Hopi Ind. Res., into Tolapi lakes in T. 24 N., R. 14 E. See Oraibi village.

Orange Butte   Cochise Co.   Smith Map, 1879; G. L. O., 1921.

Elevation 5,257 feet. In T. 12 S., R. 31 E. East side San Simon valley about 12 miles southwest of San Simon on S. P. R. R. "So called from its shape and color." Letter, M. S. Scott, P. M., San Simon.
"Sometimes called Iron Butte, q.v., because one side of the peak looks like iron." Letter, Lena Hemstead, P. M., Bowie. Not mapped by this latter name.

Ord, Mount   Apache Co.   G. L. O. Map, 1892; U. S. G. S., 1923;
                                              Sitgreaves N. F., 1927.

Elevation 10,850 feet. In T. 6 N., R. 26 E. Apache Ind. Res., northwest of Baldy. After Major Gen. Ord, U. S. A. There is another Mount Ord in Tonto N. F., near old Fort Reno.

Ord, Mount   Gila Co.   G. L. O. Map, 1921; Tonto N. F., 1927.

Elevation 7,350 feet. In T. 7 N., R. 9 E. North side Reno Pass. On boundary line between Gila and Maricopa counties. After General Edward O'Connel Ord, who commanded U. S. troops in Arizona, 1869. Camp Reno is located at foot of this mountain on eastern slope. In 1886, Gen. Miles opened a heliograph station on this peak in his Geronimo campaign. There is also another Mount Ord on the Apache Ind. Res., east of Fort Apache.

Orderville Canyon   Coconino Co.

Heading in sec. 34, T. 38 N., R. 2 E., flows northwest into White Sage wash, in T. 41 N., R. 1 W. After Mormon village by this name.
"Name comes from what was known in the early days of Mormon settlement in this region as 'The United Order.' This was not a church movement, although it had the full approval of the church authorities. A communistic movement designed to help its membership, but while it spread over most of the northern Arizona Mormon settlements it eventually died out."
McClintock says Edward Bellamy, the writer, was so much interested in it that he made a special journey to Utah, 1886, to see how it was working. Soon after his return east his book *Looking Backward* was issued. *Arizona Gazetteer,* 1881, shows Joseph H. Richards of St. Joseph, Apache county, as "President of the United Order at that place." Mr. Richards once explained to me that the order was purely a cooperative movement.

Orizaba   Pinal Co.

"This station was called after an old Papago by this name. He worked around this vicinity when they were building the road in 1903. They called the mine here 'Orizaba,' also after him." Letter, Bud Ming, Ray. Camp was about 25 miles southeast Casa Grande, near Jack Rabbit mine. P. O. established here Sept. 25, 1888, John Riess, P. M.

Oro   Greenlee Co.   G. L. O. Map, 1892.

Village Graham county when established. Was called Oroville on all early maps. Was about 6 miles above Clifton on the San Francisco river.

"The place was named by George Wells who homesteaded it in early days and found gold. He called it Oroville, but authorities would not establish a post office by this name, so it became Oro." Letter, Forest Ranger Girdner. Wells had a farm here in 1888 which supplied fruit and vegetables to Clifton. P. O. established October 19, 1880, Joseph T. Yankie, P. M. Map shows it as Oroville.

Oro   Yavapai Co.

Mine in nearby Minnehaha flat. P. O. established June 20, 1904, Benjamin Heller, P. M.

Oro Blanco   Santa Cruz Co.

Sp., "white gold." In sec. 1, T. 22 S., R. 10 E. Town, southwest part of county. After the mine here. P. O. established Oct. 2, 1879.

Oro Blanco, Mountain and Peak   Santa Cruz Co.
                                        G. L. O. Map, 1921; Coronado N. F., 1925.

In T. 24 S., R. 12 E. Formerly called Pajarita, Sp., "a little bird," q.v. In extreme southwest corner of county. After Oro Blanco.

Oronai Mou tain   Maricopa Co.   Map, Tonto N. F., 1927.

In T. 2 N., R. 8 E. South side Salt river opposite Stewart mountain. Origin or meaning unknown.

Orrville   Yuma Co.

Station on Gila river near Palomas. P. O. established February 2, 1888, William B. Ready, P. M. Origin unknown.

Ortega Lake   Apache Co.   Map, Sitgreaves N. F., 1927.

Sp., "hazel grouse." In T. 10 N., R. 24 E. After Leandro Ortega of Concho, prominent Mexican citizen and sheep owner of this vicinity. This was a famous sheep lambing ground in the Eighties.

Osborne Junction   Cochise Co.   G. L. O. Map, 1921.

Point where branch of E. P. & S. W. R. R. leaves for Bisbee. Formerly New Osborne. Named for William Church Osborne of Phelps Dodge Corporation. Once called Bisbee Junction, q. v.

Osborne Spring Wash   Yavapai Co.   Map, Prescott N. F., 1927.

Rises in T. 14 N., R. 1½ E., flows southeast into Ash creek at V Bar ranch. East side Agua Fria. After John P. Osborne, who first claimed these springs before 1876.

Osborne Well   Yuma Co.   G. L. O. Map, 1921;
U. S. G. S. Map, 1923.

About 12 miles east of Parker, southwest of Planet peak.
"After E. S. Osborne who located a mine near here and dug the
well. Later on T. J. Carrigan bought the mine from Osborne and
drilled a new well. It is often called locally 'Carrigan camp.'"
Letter, J. B. Roberts, Parker.

Otero Creek   Maricopa Co.   U. S. G. S. Map, 1923.

Named for Jesus Otero, cattleman who had a ranch on this
stream, 1884-90. West side, Mazatzal range. Rises north of Four
Peaks, flows southwest into Sycamore creek.

Otis   Pinal Co.

P. O. established here January 13, 1893, Thomas C. Carry, P. M.

Outlaw Mountain and Spring   Cochise Co.   G. L. O. Map, 1921;
U. S. G. S., 1923.

Elevation 5,070 feet. In sec. 24, T. 20 S., R. 24 E., west side
southern end Dragoon mountains about 8 or 10 miles southwest
of Tombstone. It is said that "Old Man" Clanton and his bunch
of renegades made this spring a hiding place, hence the name.

Oury, Mount   Pima Co.   Map, Coronado N. F., 1929.

Peak in Rincon mountains about 12 miles northeast of Pantano.
Immediately north of Catalina peak. Named for the Oury brothers, well known early citizens of Tucson.

Overton   Cochise Co.

Believed to have been so called after Capt. Gilbert E. Overton,
6th U. S. Cavalry, who camped at this spot with his command in
Geronimo campaign, 1886. P. O. established November 26, 1917,
Jean C. Wilder, P. M.

Overton   Maricopa Co.   G. L. O. Map, 1921.

Listed in *Arizona Gazetteer*, 1881, as post office for Cave creek,
30 miles north of Phoenix. There is no record of such an office
in files of P. O. department at Washington.

Overton   Pah Ute Co.

One of three towns, originally in Arizona. An early Mormon
settlement on Muddy river about 1865. Abandoned, 1871, accord-
ing to Fish, "because Pah Ute county was cut off in 1866 from
Arizona and added to Nevada." First called Patterson's ranch.
Origin of Overton not known. P. O. established April 25, 1870,
James Farmer, P. M. See Joseph City.

Owen   Mohave Co.   Eckhoff Map, 1880; G. L. O., 1921.

In T. 15 N., R. 13 W. Mining camp. Named for John Owen,
otherwise "Chloride Jack." Letter, O. D. M. Gaddis, Kingman.
Near town of Greenwood in Owens mining district. P. O. established April 4, 1899, Nellie C. Cornwall, P. M.

Owens Lake   Coconino Co.

See Stoneman's lake.

Owls Head Camp   Pinal Co.

About 45 miles south of Florence and 12 miles from Desert station.

Charles P. Mason says, "Owls Head was started about 1882 by two mines, the Arcade and Jesse Benton. Name came from two buttes close by, which, at a distance, had the appearance of two huge owls' heads."

Oxbow   Gila Co.   Map, Tonto N. F., 1928.

Mine and well-known hill on road to Payson from Roosevelt. Road made two large loops up the mountain, forming perfect oxbow. "According to Land Office records this mine was first located May 21, 1880, by D. C. Moreland, William St. John, and Al Sieber, the scout." Letter, Fred Croxen. See also Ox Yoke.

Name of hill undoubtedly came from name Ox Yoke given it by Genung. See Ox Yoke mountain. P. O. established, named Oxbow, March 7, 1895, Elizabeth H. St. John, P. M.

Ox Yoke Mountain   Gila Co.

Tonto N. F. "We got to the top of Ox Yoke mountain in June, 1881. There we found several ox yokes taken from oxen that had been run off in the raids by Indians." Letter, Charles B. Genung, *Mining Record,* May 13, 1911. Oxbow Hill is in T. 10 N., R. 9 W., on Rye creek above Rye. This is doubtless the place Genung refers to. They were out from Prescott on a scout after Indians who had stolen horses and cattle. See Oxbow.

Pacheto Creek   Apache Co.   Map, Fort Apache Ind. Res., 1928.

Rises at Mount Thomas, flowing south into Black river southeast corner, T. 4 N., R. 27 E., extreme eastern side reservation.

Pacific   Yuma Co.

Settlement on Colorado river above Yuma. According to *Arizona Gazetteer,* 1881, was originally called Silent. *Gazetteer* calls it Pacific City. See Silent. P. O. established Nov. 30, 1880, Paul Billicke, P. M.

Packsaddle Mountain   Cochise Co.   Map, Coronado N. F., 1927.

In sec. 17, T. 21 S., R. 29 E. Peak west of Dragoons. "From a distance this peak has a strong resemblance to a pack saddle." Letter, Forest Ranger Mettler.

Packwoods' Ranch   Mohave Co.

Early ranch on road, Camp Mohave to Prescott. "About noon Sept. 3, 1874, we reached a forlorn mud hut known as Packwoods ranch. The place had a bar which was cheerful to some of the poor men. I shall always remember Mr. Packwoods' ranch because we had milk to drink and some delicious quail to eat." *Vanished Arizona.*

Paddy Creek   Apache Co.   Map, Fort Apache Ind. Res., 1928.

T. 4 N., R. 26 E. Fort Apache Ind. Res. Rising northeast corner, flows south into Black river in sec. 16, T. 3 N., R. 26 E.

"After Paddy Creaghe, brother of George Creaghe, killed by Apaches in early Eighties." Letter, A. F. Potter, Los Angeles.

Padilla Mesa   Coconino Co.   U. S. G. S. Map, 1923.

In Ts. 27, 28 N., Rs. 14, 15 E. West side Hopi Ind. Res. "Named for Juan de Padilla, Franciscan priest who discovered Hopi villages, 1540. Killed by Indians in a revolt against white people and their religion." Gregory.

Padres Mesa   Apache Co.   G. L. O. Map, 1921.

In T. 22 N., Rs. 25, 26 E., south side Wide Ruin wash, Navajo Ind. Res. Named by Gregory, 1916, "to remember the early Spanish priests."

Pagoda Peak   Yuma Co.

See Coronation.

Paguekwash Point   Mohave Co.

Butte, north rim, Grand Canyon, 2½ miles southwest of mouth of Kanab creek. (Not Fishtail.) "Name changed from Fishtail to an Indian equivalent on recommendation of Geological Survey. Both this and another rim point, 6 miles northeast, have been known by descriptive name Fishtail Point." Decision U. S. G. B.

Pah Coon Springs   Coconino Co.

Pah Ute word meaning "water that boils up" or "boiling water, or spring." Mentioned by early Mormon writers.

Pahreah River   Coconino Co.   Map, Kaibab N. F., 1926.

Stream rising in southern Utah, flows southeast, enters Colorado river at Lee Ferry. The old Utah-Arizona road came down this stream for many miles. Pah Ute word for "dirty water." See Paria.

Pah Ute County   Map, McClintock, Mormon Settlement.

Established by Second Territorial Legislature; annexed to Nevada, 1866. Act creating this county repealed by Sixth Legislature, February, 1871.

One of the four original Arizona counties, northwest corner of State. Part was in Nevada and was finally attached to that State by act of Congress, May 9, 1866.

Painted Canyon   Mohave Co.   U. S. G. S. Map, 1923.

On Colorado river about 24 miles north of Mohave City.

"Just above Painted canyon is a prominent peak, Mount Davis." Ives' report. He has a picture of canyon on p. 80. Ives called it by this name because of the beautiful colors on canyon walls.

Painted Desert   Coconino and Navajo Cos.

A vast region lying north and east of Little Colorado river, extending for many miles. Often called "bad lands"; locally—Mal pais.

Powell writes: "The marls and soft rocks of the Painted Desert are of many colors, chocolate, red, vermillion, pink, buff, and grey."

Region about Petrified Forest in Navajo and Apache counties is an excellent reproduction of the Painted Desert, much of which lies in Navajo Ind. Res.

First so called by Lieut. Ives, 1858. The Hopis call it "Assama-unda"—country of departed spirits.

The geologic formation name "Painted Desert" was used by Ward (U. S. G. S. Mon. 48) for strata in this same area. Applied by Ives and Newberry to east side Little Colorado river between Sunset crossing (Winslow) and Tanner crossing.

Gregory says: "The use of name Painted Desert on portions of the Puerco is not justified." Although often claimed, there is no record of Coronado's use of the expression "El Desierto Pintado."

Painted Rocks   Yuma Co.   Smith Map, 1879; G. L. O., 1892-1921.

Small area in Ts. 5, 6 S., Rs. 8, 9 W., south side Gila river, 18 miles east of Agua Caliente. The "Painted Rocks" themselves cover not over an acre and rise 40 to 50 feet. They are covered with carvings of every description. Some very old; others recent. This was undoubtedly the rock which Kit Carson with California column under Kearney called "Independence Rock." "Nov. 18, 1846; passed close to a rock of basalt upon which various persons had scratched their initials and names. This point Carson called 'Independence Rock.' " *Journal, Capt. A. R. Johnston,* aide to Gen. Kearny. The next day Carson killed a big horn a few miles above this and Johnston called it Big Horn mountain. See Big Horn.

Hinton's *Hand Book* has a very good picture. They are the usual hieroglyphics of the Southwest.

Emory speaks of and has a picture of them in his report, 1854. He calls them "Picture rocks." His latitude and longitude are exactly right: Lat. 32° 55′ 52″; long. 113° 25′ 25″.

Poston in *Apache Land,* says:
"The Painted Rocks claim notice next
All covered o'er with Indian text."

J. Ross Browne visited them Dec., 1863. He says "many of the marks were of late date. Many were merely painted on the rocks." He has a good sketch of them made by himself.

Pajarito   Pima Co.

In Pajarito mountains west of Calabasas. P. O. established Jan. 3, 1881, John McArthur, P. M.

Named spelled Pijarito on P. O. records in Washington.

Pajarito Mountains and Peak   Santa Cruz Co.
      Smith Map, 1879; Coronado N. F., 1927.

Sp., "small bird." In T. 24 S., R. 12 E. Early name for Oro Blanco mountains, q. v. Emory, 1854, while on Boundary Survey, calls them "Arizona mountains."

"Small rugged range extending east and west along Mexican border between International monuments 126 and 129." Letter, Fred Winn, Tucson.

"According to local authority sometimes called Bear valley mountains." Letter, P. M., Ruby.

Palisades Creek   Coconino Co.

In Grand Canyon N. P. Rises in lat. 36° 1′, long. 111° 48′; flows northwest into Colorado river. Rises on canyon wall near south end "Palisades of the Desert," after which it was called.

Palisades of the Desert Mountains   Coconino Co.

Range of bold cliffs, east side Colorado river, extending south from Cape Solitude near mouth Little Colorado to Comanche Point, near lat 36° 10′, long. 111° 47′.

Name given by U. S. G. S. party about 1886.

Palmerlee   Cochise Co.   G. L. O. Map, 1904.

In T. 23 S., R. 20 E. Coronado N. F. about 12 miles west Hereford. At Reef mine. On Miller creek. Named for J. L. Palmerlee, owner of land on which P. O. was located. P. O. established Dec. 7, 1904, Joseph L. Palmerlee, P. M.

Palo Alto Valley and P. O.   Pima Co.   G. L. O. Map, 1921.

Sp., "tall or high tree." In T. 18 S., R. 9 E. In Altar valley. "There is no town or high tree, just a large cattle ranch headquarters in the valley." Letter, O. Huffman. P. O. established Aug. 3, 1925. Walter A. Jost, P. M.

Palomas   Yuma Co.

Sp., "doves." Early settlement in T. 6 S., R. 12 W., north bank Gila river. P. O. established Apr. 18, 1891, S. Schuerman, P. M. G. L. O. map, 1892, shows it on south side river; G. L. O., 1921, and U. S. G. S., 1923, on north side.

Located about 7 miles north of Aztec station, S. P. R. R. "So called because of flocks of white wing doves that always come here in summer." Letter, O. G. Keiser, Quartzsite.

Palomas Mountains and Plain   Yuma Co.   U. S. G. S. Map, 1913;
                                                 G. L. O., 1921.

In T. 5 S., Rs. 13, 14 W. Mountains, 12 miles north of Texas hill. Plain: north of Agua Caliente on Colorado river, in T. 4 S.

Palomas Peak   Yuma Co.

Same as Nottbush peak, q. v.

Palo Verde Town and Hills   Maricopa Co.   U. S. G. S. Map, 1923.

In T. 1 N., Rs. 6, 7 W. Town in Palo Verde hills. At head of Buckeye valley. So called because first settlers found many palo verde trees growing here. P. O. established Jan. 4, 1910, William Walton, P. M.

Palo Verde Mountains   Pinal Co   U. S. G. S. Map, 1923.

Sp., "green stick," or "wood." In Ts. 4, 5 S., R. 2 E., west of Maricopa Ind. Res. Common desert tree in this region.

Pamela   Yavapai Co.

P. O. by this name established Nov. 28, 1881, Fernando Nellis, P. M. According to post office records, was close to Prescott. Unknown today.

Pan   Yavapai Co.   U. S. G. S. Map, 1923.

Station A. T. & S. F. R. R., 5 miles east Seligman. "So called, 102, because it was a short name for a short switch." A.G.W.

P. and E. Junction   Yavapai Co.   G. L. O. Map, 1921.

Junction, Santa Fe-Ash Fork R. R., with branch to Humboldt and Stoddard known as Prescott and Eastern R. R. Leaves main line about 5 miles north Prescott.

Pantano   Pima Co.

Station S. P. R. R., 18 miles west of Benson. First called "La Cienega," Sp., "a swamp—marsh—pool of stagnant water." Later Tulleyville, lastly Pantano. Well known early stage station and ranch.

Farish says: "W. A. Smith (Shotgun Smith) had a great fight here with Apache Indians in 1867."

"In 1912 it was changed to Empire." Letter—Supt. S. P. R. R. Ed Vail writes: "The old cemetery at or near station was filled with graves of men killed by Indians."

P. O. established as Pantano July 2, 1880, Lyman W. Wakefield, P. M. Origin of Pantano unknown.

Cienega-La Cienega on Smith map, 1879; Pantano, G. L. O., 1892-1921.

Pantano Wash   Pima Co.   U. S. G. S. Map, 1923.

Rises in Pima county, north slope Whetstone mountains. Flows northwest, enters Rillito at old Fort Lowell, southeast corner T. 13 S., R. 14 E. "Originally called 'Cienega creek.' In later years creek cut a deep channel and name wash was given it." Letter— E. Cummings, P. M., Pantano.

Panya Point

On south rim Grand Canyon, 3½ miles south of Supai village. So named on recommendation U. S. G. S. from name of Indian family here. Decision U. S. G. B.

Papago   Maricopa Co.

McClintock says: "This was an 'Indian Ward' of Mormon church, lying on both sides of river just northwest of Mesa."

Papago Creek   Coconino Co.

Grand Canyon N. P. Rises in lat. 36° 1', long. 111° 54', on canyon wall, one-half mile southwest Papago point. Named by Frank Bond.

Papago Indian Reservation   Pinal and Pima Cos.

Reservation for Papago Indians. Papago word, from papah, "beans," and ootam, "people"; "beanspeople." Spanish called them "Frijoleros," bean eaters. Pimas call them Too-no-oo-tain, "desert people," very appropriate.

"The word 'Papago' is said to be a corruption of the word 'christian' or 'baptized,' in their language. These Indians have always worn their hair short, unlike their Pima neighbors." Farish. There is little to support this idea.

July 1, 1874, President Grant created the Papago Reservation, a small area at San Xavier Mission, Tucson. June 16, 1911, President Taft created a new and very large Papago reservation in Pima county, west of Tucson.

Fish says name "was because of Indians' readiness to accept Christianity. The Padres called them 'Bap-coina, Pima word for baptized. From this came the name." One must rather question this statement.

Papago Point   Coconino Co.   Map, Grand Canyon N. P., 1927.

Bold point projecting into Grand Canyon near lat. 36° 1', long. 111° 54', northern edge Coconino plateau, Grand Canyon. Named for Papago Indians.

Papago-Saguaro National Monument   Maricopa Co.
                                                G. L. O. Map, 1921.

Name suggested by Prof. O. A. Turney. About 2,000 acres of land lying 6 miles east of Phoenix, opposite Tempe. At camp and picnic grounds known as "Hole in the Rock."

Act of Congress setting area aside was recalled Apr. 7, 1930, principally because area was not considered suitable for a national monument.

Act authorized sale and gift of certain parts to Tempe, the State of Arizona, and the Water Users Association. Federal government reserved all oil, coal or other minerals.

Papagueria, The Country of the Papagoes

Name appearing on many early Spanish maps.

"Area between Pimeria Alta and Apacheria, south and west of San Pedro and Gila rivers in what is now mainly Pima county where the Papagoes maintain a severe struggle against the Apaches whom they usually defeat, and still another struggle against Nature's aridity by which they are often worsted." Hamilton.

Paradise   Cochise Co.   U. S. G. S. Map, 1923.

In T. 17 S., R. 31 E. Coronado N. F. Mining camp and P. O.

"Paradise was a boom camp that went up like a rocket and came down like a stick in the early years of present century." *Tombstone.*

"Along about 1903 prospectors up here had to cross the valley on their way to San Simon station to get their supplies and mail. Was about 28 miles, no water on the way, and awfully dry and hot in summer. When they would get back up here they would take a drink of spring water and lay back in the shade and say, 'well, this is Paradise all right.' When Geo. Walker and Geo. Myers went to shipping ore, it made a camp large enough for a post office. When the department asked what name, they all said 'Paradise.' " Letter, J. C. Hancock, Paradise.

P. O. established Oct. 23, 1901, George A. Walker, P. M.

Paradise Valley   Maricopa Co.   U. S. G. S. Map, 1923.

In Ts. 2, 3 N., Rs. 4, 5 E. Broad valley lying east Phoenix mountains and west of McDowell mountains. So named by Frank Conkey, Manager, Rio Verde Canal Co., 1899.

"When the promoters of this Rio Verde canal project first saw this broad level valley in the early spring covered with flowers and the palo verdes in full blossom, they all said, 'this is Paradise Valley.' " They planned a ditch 140 miles long with laterals and water to cover 250,000 acres. Failed because of financial troubles.

Paria   Kane Co., Utah

Under name Pahreal (sic.) a post office was established here according to post office records, when it was assumed to be part of Arizona. Was a Mormon settlement on the Paria river. P. O. established May 20, 1892, Allen F. Smithson, P. M.

Place later found to be in Kane county, Utah. See Paria creek, Coconino county. Paria is a decision of U. S. G. B.

Paria Creek   Coconino Co.   U. S. G. S. Map, 1923.

Stream rising Garfield county, Utah, flowing south into Colorado river at Lee Ferry. An early route into Arizona. Escalante with his party undoubtedly came down the Paria to the canyon in 1776. McClintock gives some very interesting history of this locality.

Paria is said to be a Ute word meaning "elk water." Sometimes spelled "Pahrea."

Paria Plateau   Coconino Co.   U. S. G. S. Map, 1924.

On west side Marble canyon at State line at long. 112 W. Bold escarpment east side House Rock valley.

Parishawampitts Canyon   Coconino Co.   Map, Kaibab N. F., 1926.

In sec. 25, T. 35 N., R. 1 E. Flows west into Tapeats creek. "Name is of Piute origin and means 'boiling water.' Spring in canyon bubbles or boils out of the ground." Letter, Walter Mann, Kanab, Utah.

Parashont

See Shivwits.

Parker Butte   Gila Co.   Map, Tonto N. F., 1927.

In T. N., R. 11 E. East side Tonto creek below Del-che basin. "This was called after a Texan named Parker who settled on a ranch near the butte in the Eighties. Ranch now owned by George Felton." Letter, R. I. Stewart, Forest Ranger. See Reno mountain.

Parker Canyon   Santa Cruz Co.   U. S. G. S. Map, 1923.

In T. 24 S., R. 18 E., Coronado N. F. Settlement on canyon of same name.

"The Parker family from Texas were early settlers in this region. They were commonly referred to as 'The Kinfolks.' " Carl B. Scholefield, Forest Ranger, Tucson.

P. O. established Apr. 14, 1912, Louis K. McIntyre, P. M.

Parker's Peak   Pinal Co.   G. L. O. Map, 1892.

West side of Mineral creek about 10 miles north of Riverside. Name given peak by U. S. G. S., 1906, presumably after Tom Parker, an old prospector who had claims not far from it.

Parks   Coconino Co.   G. L. O. Map, 1921; Tusayan N. F., 1927.

Settlement in sec. 22, T. 22 N., R. 4 E., about 8 miles north Maine station.

"So called because located near a number of open areas, locally called 'parks.' " Letter, Forest Supervisor Kimball, Williams.

Parks Lake   Graham Co.   U. S. G. S. Map, 1923.

In T. 10 S., R. 30 E., west side Peloncillo mountains. After J. B. Parks, well known San Simon cattleman.

Parker   Yuma Co.

Elevation 370 feet. In T. 9 N., R. 20 W. The first stake of new town of Parker was driven June 6, 1906, by James Haddock, Otis E. Young and C. W. McKee. On Colorado river at Arizona end, Parker branch, A. T. & S. F. R. R.

"This town was named for old Fort Parker." Letter, P. M. Parker. There is no War Dept. record of any such post.

"In 1905 and 1906, I located the Santa Fe railroad line to the river where Parker is now located. There was an old Indian settlement on the river 2 or 3 miles below railroad crossing then known as Parker. William A. Drake who was then Gen'l. Superintendent and Chief Engineer said to me 'Parker, we will give you this town and call it Parker.' So it was put on railroad maps that way." Letter, Earl H. Parker. Phoenix, Mar. 3, 1931.

Several old timers agree that long before the railroad a Captain Parker lived with the Indians a few miles below present Parker. Who he was or what his business nobody seems to know. Some claim he was Indian Agent but records in Washington do not show this to be a fact. Earl Parker's explanation is, of course, correct as to the modern town. P. O. established Aug. 24, 1876, Wm. E. Morford, P. M.

Parsee Hill

See Poston Butte.

Parsons Peak and Canyon   Graham Co.   G. L. O. Map, 1909.

In T. 8 S., R. 30 E. East side Peloncillo range. "Named after Parson Alexander Graves, a real sure enough minister who settled on Parson canyon 1871 where he made butter and sold milk from a few cows. He married my father and mother in 1879." Letter, Bud Ming, Ray.

Partridge City   Maricopa Co.   U. S. G. S. Map, 1923;
                                                  Tusayan N. F., 1927.

Hinton lists this as a "stage station 17 miles north of Wickenburg and 10 to Antelope valley." Origin unknown.

Partridge Wash or Creek   Coconino Co.   U. S. G. S. Map, 1923;
                                                 Tusayan N. F., 1927.

Rises in T. 24 N., R. 2 W. Tusayan N. F. Flows southwest into Chino valley in T. 20 N., R. 4 W. Very old name. Ives called it "Partridge Ravine," 1858. Later he called it Partridge creek as does Whipple 1854. Mollhausen, *Diary of a Journey*, 1858, says: "So called from the numerous pretty creatures of that kind." "January 10, 1854: Many partridges were killed today. Upon their heads are tufted plumes like those of the California partridges." Whipple Report. Evidently our common tufted quail.

Pass Mountain   Yuma Co.   U. S. G. S. Map, 1923.

Near long. 113° 25'. In Palomas plain, 17 miles north of Agua Caliente. See Turtle Back Mountain.

Pastora Peak   Apache Co.   G. L. O. Map, 1921; U. S. G. S., 1923.

Elevation 9,420 feet. Navajo Ind. Res. west side Pastora mountains. Sometimes called Pastura.

Gregory says: "Name given it by Dr. W. H. Holmes, 1875, due to the fine stock feed, grasses, etc., he found here."

Pat Hills   Cochise Co.   G. L. O. Map, 1921; U. S. G. S., 1923.

In T. 16 S., R. 27 E., Sulphur Springs valley.

"After a man named Pat Bierne—sometimes spelled Burns—who in 1878 located at a small spring or cienega still called Pat Burns cienega. He ran cattle here for years; finally sold out and removed to Trinidad, Colorado, where he died." Letter, Wm. C. Riggs, Dos Cabezas.

Pat Mountain and Creek   Greenlee Co.   Map, Crook N. F., 1928.

In sec. 15, T. 2 S., R. 30 E. After Pat Trainor, early stockman who had a headquarter ranch near Nutrioso, but grazed his cattle to the south along the Blue.

Patagonia   Santa Cruz Co.   G. L. O. Map, 1866, 1921.

In T. 22 N., R. 16 E. Original name of Mowry mine, once owned by Capt. Snell, located 1858. Sold, 1860, to Lieut. Mowry, who changed the name.

Station on Sonoita creek and S. P. R. R., north end Patagonia mountains. P. O. established May 7, 1866, Chas. E. Mowry, P. M. See Mowry.

J. Ross Browne says: "Mine first called the 'Patagonia,' but when Mowry got possession of it, he called it 'Mowry's.' "

Mowry's book, *Arizona and Sonora*, makes the statement that the origin of the name Patagonia was to him, Mowry, unknown.

F. Brerton, a mining engineer who examined and reported on Mowry's mines, 1861, says: "But why is it called the Patagonia? Is it because it is situated in a desert inhabited by wild Indians?"

Patagonia Mountains   Santa Cruz Co.   U. S. G. S. Map, 1923.

In southern part of county, near Mexican border, northeast of Nogales. See mine for origin.

Pat Burns Cienega   Cochise Co.

See Pat Hills.

Patio   Yuma Co.

Sp., "court or yard." Station S. P. R. R., 5 miles east of Yuma. "When the company built quite a good sized yard here some one suggested the name be turned into Spanish, which was done." Letter, Paul Shoup.

Pat Knolls   Apache Co.   Map, Apache N. F., 1926.

In sec. 30, T. 7 N., R. 29 E. Several smooth prairie hills. After Pat Trainor, settler and cattleman who ran cattle over this region as early as 1881.

Pat Mullen Peak   Navajo Co.   Map, Apache N. F., 1926.

In sec. 11, T. 9 N., R. 23 E. East end Blue Ridge mountains. After Pat Mullen, pioneer stockman.

Pattie Butte   Coconino Co.

Elevation 5,400 feet. On south wall near lat. 36° 4', long. 112° 3'. Named for Sylvester Pattie, first American citizen to visit Grand Canyon. Leader of a prospecting party, 1825. Decision USGB. Named by Frank Bond.

Paulden   Yavapai Co.

Station, Prescott-Ash Fork R. R., 8 miles south of Puntenney. "Sometimes called 'Midway Grocery.' So named for Paul, son of O. T. Pownall, who was accidentally killed here." Letter, P. M., Paulden.

P. O. established Feb. 13, 1926, Orville T. Pownall, P. M.

Paya Point   Coconino Co.

South rim Grand Canyon, 6 miles south of mouth, Kanab creek. After name of a local Indian family. Recommendation USGS. Decision USGB.

Payson   Gila Co.   G. L. O. Map, 1921; U. S. G. S., 1923.

In T. 10 N., R. 10 E. On Tonto N. F. On Payson creek. Lively mining camp and livestock region.

F. W. Croxen, Forest Ranger, says: "Payson was founded, 1882, as Union Park. Was also called Long valley. C. C. Callahan laid it out. John Hise, first Surveyor General of Territory, 1885 to 1889, with his brother Frank, built first house and started a store."

Named after Senator Payson of Illinois, chairman Congressional Committee, Post Offices and Post Roads. P. O. established Mar. 3, 1884, Frank C. Hise, P. M. An advertisement in Globe *Silver Belt*, Jan. 15, 1887, calls it "Payson (Green Valley)." Evidently Green valley was a common name for Payson.

Peach Orchard   Pinal Co.

"Mining camp by this name across canyon from Silver King camp, 1877." Hinton.

George Lobb, 1931, writes: "Hinton was right. About 1877 there were a few rock houses and a mining claim or two about a mile northwest of Silver King. One of the miners planted a dozen or so peach trees around the spot and the place came to be called by that name."

Peach Springs   Mohave Co.   Smith Map, 1879; G. L. O., 1892-1921.

Station A. T. & S. F. R. R. in extreme southern part Hualpai Ind. Res. Springs are about 6 or 7 miles north of railroad station. So named by early explorers because some peach trees were found growing at the springs.

Spanish tradition says at one time the Jesuit missionaries from San Bernardino, Calif., sought a silver mine in that neighborhood. These missionaries planted fruit trees.

Dr. Coues says: "This was Peach Springs which Garces called Pozos de San Basilio—St. Basilios Wells. Garces was here June 15, 1776." He writes: "June 15, I set out up the arroyo northeast and north. We followed this arroyo and came upon some wells which I named Pozos de San Basilio."

Coues says further: "Peach Springs is so called from the fact that trees of that name are planted there. Some of them were in evidence when I was there on June 18-19, 1881." *On the Trail of a Pioneer.*

Several writers have credited Sitgreaves, 1851, with calling these springs by this name, Peach Springs. A careful review of everything Sitgreaves or any of his party wrote does not justify this claim.

The Navajo and Hopi Indians had great numbers of peach trees which they undoubtedly secured originally from the Spanish settlements along the Rio Grande in New Mexico. Carson, for instance, in his official report of his campaign against the Navajos in western New Mexico and eastern Arizona in 1862-63 speaks of having "destroyed many thousands of peach trees owned by the Navajos as a reprisal against them for their constant raids on the Mexican settlement."

When Elder Brigham F. Duffin, missionary for the Mormon Church, came to Moenkopi in April, 1878, he found "several small groves of peach trees bearing a heavy crop of fruit." He estimated the trees to be at least six years old at that time. Letter, Nov. 24, 1934.

The writer feels that all these plantings in western Arizona were done by Mormon missionaries who were in this region as early as 1859-60; Hamblin, Haight, Roundy and others.

Hon. Anson H. Smith of Mohave county writes that the accepted story as to the origin of the peach trees at Peach Springs is that the planting was done by a party of Mormon pioneers who were on the south side of the Colorado looking for an easy crossing back into Utah.

This was in 1852. 'They camped at these springs for several days while exploring the region. A little girl who later became Mrs. Thomas Logan, planted some peach pits near the springs. They came up and from them came the orchard."

Several descendants of the original trees were flourishing when the author visited these springs in October, 1934.

Mormons are credited with having brought the peach trees to the Supai Indians in the Cataract canyon many years ago.

The interesting thing about these trees at Peach Springs is the fact that although the place was visited by many early explorers, at least three of whom were accompanied by well known botanists, not one of them noted the presence in this far land of the stranger trees or wondered how and when they were planted.

Peach Springs Draw   Mohave Co.   U. S. G. S. Map, 1923.

Canyon and stream rising near Peach Springs in T. 25 N., R. 12 W. Enters Diamond creek near Colorado river at Diamond peak in T. 27 N., R. 10 W. The author found, in 1886, a so-called wagon road down this canyon from Peach Springs clear into Diamond creek. Peach Springs draw was named New creek by Ives. It was his Camp 66 and shows as that on some early maps.

Peachville Mountain   Pinal Co.   Map, Crook N. F., 1926.

In T. 1 S., R. 12 E. Northeast of Silver King. Named from nearby mining camp of early days. See Peach Orchard.

Peacock Mountains, Peak, and Spring   Mohave Co.

Smith Map, 1879.

Elevation of peak 6,268 feet. In T. 22 N., R. 14 W. North of Hackberry. Mountains, eastern side Hualpai valley. Spring discovered by G. H. Peacock, member of Ives party. Named by Lieut. Ives, 1858.

"Mr. Peacock, the trainmaster, discovered a large spring of clear sweet water. Ireteba even did not appear to have known of its existence." Ives, Mar. 31, 1858.

Coues, *On the Trail*, believes that Peacock spring and Truxton spring are one and the same. He says: "It is near present Hualpai station on Santa Fe railroad." He thinks the USGS and GLO maps incorrect on Truxton springs location. He writes further: "To judge from Ives Map, Truxton springs are the same as that called Peacock spring by Ives for one of his men."

Pearce   Cochise Co.   R. R. Maps; G. L. O., 1921.

In T. 25 E., R. 18 S., Cochise branch Arizona-Eastern R. R. Town at Pearce or Commonwealth mine, discovered by and named after James Pearce, miner and cattleman, 1894. One of richest mines ever found in Arizona. Said to have produced over fifteen million dollars in gold. R. R. station opened, 1903.

McFarland's *History* says it was first called Fittsburgh. This is not correct. See Fittsburg. P. O. established Mar. 6, 1896, Thomas Chattman, P. M.

John A. Rockfellow tells this interesting story: "Pearce and his wife had worked hard for some years at Tombstone, he as a hard rock miner: she, managing a miner's boarding house. They had saved considerable money. Their two sons were crazy to invest in cattle. They started a ranch in Sulphur Springs valley near my ranch. One day the old man scouting round on the range got off his horse on top of a small hill. Sitting there he idly hammered a rock against a nearby ledge. The break showed gold. An assay proved it to be very rich. He and his wife and the three children all filed claims and worked it for a time as a family affair. This was too slow for the boys.

"John Brockman of Silver City coaxed an agreement of sale from Pearce. Brockman was to have 90 days to work the mine. At the end he was to pay Pearce $250,000 cash, or leave all the work and ore as it was. Inside of 60 days Brockman took out enough to pay the $250,000 and some still left on the dump. Money was divided into five equal shares, a fifth for each. The old lady however refused to sign for her fifth until new owners had signed an agreement giving her sole right to run the only miners boarding house in camp for ten years. She didn't propose to be without a job." Letter, John A. Rockfellow.

Pearce Ferry

See Pierce Ferry.

Pearce Mountain   Navajo Co.   Map, Sitgreaves N. F., 1928.

Peak southwest corner T. 9 N., R. 25 E., edge Fort Apache Ind. Res. After Pearce family, sheepmen, who lived in this vicinity for many years. James Pearce, the father, was first Mormon settler on Silver creek. See Pierce (sic) Ferry.

Peck Canyon   Santa Cruz Co.   Map, Coronado N. F., 1925, "Piskorski Canyon."

In sec. 4, T. 23 S., R. 11 E. Stream and canyon. Rises near Montana peak. Enters Santa Cruz river from west on Baca grant about 4 miles above Calabasas. After A. L. Peck, who lived near upper end of canyon in early days. His wife was killed by Apaches, with her baby in her arms near the place, Apr. 27, 1886. A second child was carried off by the Indians, but recovered later by Bob Leatherwood.

Peck then left and a Pole named Piskorski settled there and canyon gradually took his name. It was also known as Palaco canyon. Why, nobody seems to recall. See Pecks pass, west of canyon.

Peck Mine   Yavapai Co.

About 30 miles southeast Prescott in Bradshaws. Discovered Dec., 1875, by, and named for Ed. G. Peck, at one time scout and general guide for troops at Whipple. Peck was a brother-in-law of George Banghart. Peck district which appears on all early maps was established, 1875. Mine, however, does not show on them nor does Peck creek, mentioned in filing certificates as one boundary of district.

Peck Pass   Santa Cruz Co.   G. L. O. Map, 1921.

In Pajarita mountains, about 6 miles northwest Nogales, near Mexican line. "Peck Pass is very appropriate because Mrs. A. L. Peck was killed by Indians at their ranch home at this point in pioneer days." Letter, A. S. Wingo, Forest Ranger. This pass appears on this map, but is unmistakably an error; meant for Peck canyon.

Pecks Lake   Yavapai Co.   All early maps.

In sec. 8, T. 3 E., R. 16 N. A comparatively small body of water on east bank of Verde river about 3 miles east of Clark-dale. The Apache-Mohave Indians living in this region called it "Crooked Water" from its shape. Probably so named after the well known Army scout and prospector Ed. G. Peck for whom the Peck mine and Peck mining district of this vicinity were named in 1875. See Tu-zigoot.

Pedregosa Mountains   Cochise Co.   Smith Map, 1879; G. L. O., 1892-1921.

Sp., "stony—rocky." In T. 22 S., R. 28 E., north side E. P. & S. W. R. R., about 10 miles northeast of Douglas. See Swisshelm mountains.

Pedricks   Yuma Co.   Ives Map, 1858; G. L. O., 1866.

Early settlement on Colorado river 15 or 20 miles below Yuma. Unable to learn its origin.

Peeples Valley   Yavapai Co.   Smith Map, 1879; G. L. O., 1892-1921.

West of Kirkland valley about 25 miles southwest Prescott. After A. H. Peeples, early pioneer who, with Weaver, explored a large part of western Arizona and discovered Rich hill. Owned a ranch in Kirkland valley for many years. P. O. established Dec. 15, 1928, Joseph C. Coupal, P. M.

Peloncillo Mountains   Smith Map, 1879; Coronado N. F., 1927.

Sp., "hairless or bald." Low range lying along line, Arizona and New Mexico, in Greenlee, Graham and Cochise counties, extending from about T. 22 S., to Mexican boundary. Smooth round hills with little timber and no outstanding peaks. On some maps shown as Black Hills, q.v.

Pembroke   Yuma Co.

Station S. P. R. R. about 58 miles east of Yuma.

Pen Pockets   Mohave Co.

See Ambush Water Pockets.

Penrod

See Pinetop.

Penzance   Navajo Co.   G. L. O. Map, 1921.

On A. T. & S. F. R. R. Name given, 1888, by officers of Santa Fe R. R. to sandstone quarry 4 miles west of Holbrook. It is understood that this name was given for the Gilbert and Sullivan opera "The Pirates of Penzance," very popular about that time.

Peoria   Maricopa Co.   G. L. O. Map, 1892-1921; U. S. G. S., 1923.

In T. 3 N., R. 1 E. On A. T. & S. F. R. R., about 10 miles northwest Phoenix. So called because first settlers came from Peoria, Illinois. The Greenhuts, distillery owners of that city, made large investments in land here about 1890. Named by Chauncey Clark. P. O. established Aug. 4, 1888, James McMillan, P. M.

Peoria Canal

See Gila Bend Canal.

Pepper Sauce Wash   Pima Co.   Map, Coronado N. F., 1927.

In sec. 34, T. 10 S., R. 17 E. "Picturesque canyon or wash, 10 miles east of Oracle. On trail to Mount Lemmon. Named by Alex. McKay about 1880, who camped on wash while prospecting. The pepper sauce bottle was stolen from their camp. So they called it for this incident. Rises, Coronado N. F. near Apache peak; flows southwest into San Pedro river." Letter, Frank C. Lockwood, Tucson.

Percheron   Navajo Co.

Early Mormon settlement in pine timber southwest of Snowflake. So called because first settlers, the Mortensens and Petersons, brought with them a number of fine horses of this breed. Settlement afterwards called Pinedale, sometimes Mortensen. See Pinedale.

Perea Canyon   Coconino Co.

Navajo Ind. Res. "Originally called Dortch for an agency employee, Josiah N. Dortch; changed to Perea in honor of Fray Estevan Perea under whose custodianship first missions were established among the Hopi." F. W. Hodge.

Peregua (sic)   Pima Co.   Lumholtz Map; G. L. O., 1921; U. S. G. S., 1923.

In T. 12 S., R. 2 W. Indian village, Papago Ind. Res. Lumholtz spells it "Perigua" and says, "It is a summer home of the Papagoes. Situated in a 'llano' in a kind of basin, northeast of Ajo. There are several water holes here." Papago name is Ji-qui-bo, meaning, "Where there is a rough mountain."

Perhaps Mine   Maricopa Co.

Mine east side Gila Bend mountains near Woolsey peak. "Perhaps we will find gold, perhaps not," is said to have been origin of name.

Peridot   Graham Co.   R. R. Maps.

Station 7 miles east San Carlos on Globe division Arizona-Eastern R. R. So called for the semi-precious stones of this name found near the place. When full, the waters of San Carlos reservoir will cover this station. Road moved, 1930, to higher ground and station abandoned.

Perilla Mountains   Cochise Co.   G. L. O. Map, 1892;
                                              U. S. G. S., 1923.

Sp., a "goatee." Elevation 5,937 feet. In Ts. 23, 24 S., Rs. 28, 29 E. East of Douglas. Eckhoff, 1880, and Smith, 1879, spell it Peria and locate them south of line in Mexico.

Perkins, Mount   Mohave Co.   G. L. O. Map, 1921.

In T. 25 N., R. 21 W. In Black range. Ives or Wheeler must be responsible for this name, but neither mention it.

Perkinsville   Yavapai Co.   Map, Prescott N. F., 1927.

In sec. 31, T. 18 N., R. 2 E. After M. A. Perkins, well-known, local cattleman. Station, Drake and Clarkdale branch A. T. & S. F. R. R., 39 miles southeast Ash Fork. P. O. established Aug. 29, 1925, Mrs. Annie Perkins, P. M.

Peroxide Well   Maricopa Co.

In sec. 15. T. 1 N., R. 5 W., west side Hassayampa creek, Buckeye valley.,
"This well was dug, 1910, by Flower Pot Cattle Co. for stock water. It tasted of soda and other chemicals so the cowboys called it Peroxide." Letter, W. M. Walton, Palo Verde.

Pete Mountain   Santa Cruz Co.   Map, Coronado N. F., 1927.

In sec. 6 T. 20 S., R. 14 E., on county line between Pima and Santa Cruz counties. On Roskruge map, 1893, is shown as "Old Pete Mountain." He says, "It was named after Old Pete Gabriel." "Locally known as Elephant Head (q.v.). Huge bare rock, 1,200 feet high that looks like the head of a great elephant." Letter O. J. Olsen, Forest Ranger.

Peters Mountain   Gila Co.   Map, Tonto N. F., 1927.

In sec. 34. T. 5 N., R. 11 E., west side Payson road above Roosevelt lake.
"After a man named Peters, often called Dr. Peters, who started and for years ran the "Three Bar" brand now owned and run by Fred L. Bixby." Letter, Forest Ranger, Croxen.

Peterson   Maricopa Co.

Loading station, P. & E. R. R., for stock and hay about 4 miles south of Tempe. After Charles Peterson, farmer and stockman, who gave the land for station. He came to the valley in 1872.

Petrified Bridge   Apache Co.

See Natural Bridge.

Petrified Forest   Navajo and Apache Cos.   U. S. G. S. Map, 1923.

About 15 miles southeast of Holbrook. A vast deposit of petrified trees of beautiful colors and extreme hardness. Set aside as Petrified Forest National Monument, April 7, 1900. "We learn that Col. Hatch has purchased the interest of Ex-Governor Tritle in the Petrified Forest in Apache county." *Phoenix Herald*, June 3, 1887. Hatch shipped the stone to Sioux Falls, South Dakota, where it was polished. Whipple's party visited it, 1853, calling it Lithodendron Park. "Where trees have been converted into Jasper."

In 1896 Denver men erected a small stamp mill at Adamana for grinding up these logs. The author went to Washington, 1897, and with Hon. Oakes Murphy, our delegate, protested against such vandalism. Secretary of Interior Noble took prompt steps to stop it—cancelled all the "mineral claims" the company had filed and eventually it was withdrawn as a National Monument. Al Stevenson, a local cowboy, was first government guard over it. The Denver outfit was called "The Angell Abrasive Company." They used it as emery for fine polishing, etc. The stamp mill they were using was standing near Adamana as late as 1920. See Natural Bridge.

Phoenix   Maricopa Co.

Elevation 1,080 feet. North bank Salt river. "A mass meeting of the citizens of Salt River Valley was held on October 20, 1870, for purpose of selecting a suitable piece of unimproved public land for a town site. Darrell Duppa, John Moore, and Martin P. Griffin were appointed as a committee to make the selection. They recommended the North ½ of sec. 8 T. 1 N., R. 3 E. and that the town be called Phoenix." Elliott's *History of Arizona.*

"The earliest settlement was probably early in 1868 about 4 miles east of the present town where the flour mill was later erected. First called Swillings, then Helling Mill, after the mill owner, then called East Phoenix. When the question of a name came up Jack Swilling wanted to call it 'Stonewall,' after Stonewall Jackson, because he had been a Confederate soldier. 'Salina' was also suggested. These were turned down. Then Duppa, pointing to the evidence of a former civilization and occupation suggested the name 'Phoenix.' He declared, 'A new city would spring Phoenix-like upon the ruins of a former civilization.' The name was accepted." McClintock.

On some early military maps name was spelled "Phenix." Many army officers and others believed it was after the noted army officer and writer John Derby, who wrote under pen name of John Phenix. Derby was for some time commanding officer at Fort Yuma. Theodore Roosevelt once told Col. McClintock that he, Roosevelt, had always supposed the city was named after Derby. According to Farish, "The name Phoenix was first used officially when the Board of Supervisors of Yavapai county formed an election precinct by the name, May 4, 1868."

P. O. established as Phoenix, June 15, 1869, Jack Swilling, P. M. He served until July 8, 1870. John W. Olvany was the second. Captain Hancock was the third, taking charge February 13, 1871, retiring December 12, 1872.

Prescott *Miner* of August 27, 1870, has an advertisement as follows:

"Phoenix Station, Phoenix, Yavapai County.
Hay and Grain and Best Accommodations
for travelers. Patronage of the
public solicited.
E. K. Baker, Owner."

Barney says this station was on the McDowell to Wickenburg
road a little north of present State Insane Asylum.

Captain Hancock was employed to make the first survey. It
covered 98 blocks, each 300 feet long. The announcement of
sale of lots says:

"One-third of the purchase money will be required at time of
sale, balance when title is made. Phoenix, Arizona. December
10, 1871."

"Bicard's Flour Mill was built in March, 1871, on what was
later known as the Commercial Hotel corral block lying between
Center and First Avenues, and Jefferson and Madison Streets.
City gave them this block on condition that they erect a steam
flour mill as soon as machinery could be brought in. Steam
raised it on July 4, 1871, and first flour made that day." Barney.

Prescott Miner of December 7, 1870, carried following advertisement:

"GREAT SALES OF LOTS AT PHOENIX, ARIZONA
on the 23rd and 24th of December."

First lot sold was on corner of Washington and Montezuma
streets, to Judge Berry of Prescott for $104. City was incor-
porated by the Legislature, 1880.

Vanished Arizona says, "December, 1878, we took supper in
Phoenix at a place known as Devine's. Even then its gardens,
orchards and climate were becoming famous."

Phoenix Mountains   Maricopa Co.   U. S. G. S. Map, 1923.

Small group of hills of which Camelback is southern point.
West side Paradise valley. After the city.

Phoenix Mountain Park   Maricopa Co.

Tract of some 15,880 acres of mountain land five miles south of
Phoenix at end of South Central avenue. Embraces most of
Salt River mountains. Purchased by city from Federal government. Tract covers nearly every form of cacti, trees, and shrubs
peculiar to Southern Arizona. Doctor Turney was anxious to
have this park called "Komatke" Pima word meaning a "blue
hazy mountain." His idea did not get over, however. See Salt
River mountains.

Phoenix Park   Navajo Co.   U. S. G. S. Map, 1923.

In T. 11 N., R. 17 E. Ranch and watering place at head Phoenix Park wash near Apache Ind. Res. So named by James
Stinson, 1882, who ran cattle here for some years. He had a
farm near Phoenix and called this park for that place. Known
now as the Holcomb or Hokum ranch, q.v.

Phoenix Park Canyon   Navajo Co.
Map, Fort Apache Ind. Res., 1928.

Fort Apache Ind. Res. Stream rising at boundary line, Fort
Apache Indian Reservation near north end of T. 10 N., R. 17 E.,
above Phoenix Park ranch. Flows south into Carrizo creek on
reservation. After park by this name to the north in Sitgreaves
N. F.

Phoenix Park Wash   Navajo Co.   Map, Sitgreaves N. F., 1924.

In T. 10 N., R. 17 E. Dry wash heading near line Fort Apache Ind. Res. Runs northeast into Big Dry lake in T. 14 N., R. 19 E. So named by James Stinson, who first owned Snowflake valley and ran cattle all over this region as early as 1873. See Phoenix Park.

Pica   Yavapai Co.   G. L. O. Map, 1921; U. S. G. S., 1923.

Station A. T. & S. F. R. R. 23 miles west Seligman. Originally called Picacho after nearby mountain.

"There was a station by this name, Picacho, on Southern Pacific, which made confusion in shipments. Officers of Santa Fe and Southern Pacific matched coins to see which road would change—Santa Fe lost. Hence Pica." A.G.W.

Picacho   Pinal Co.   Smith Map, 1879;
                                    G. L. O. Map, 1921.

Sp., "peak or point." Station S. P. R. R. opened about 1881, 46 miles northwest of Tucson. Well-known stage station in early days. Located in Picacho Pass, q.v. P. O. established June 26, 1881, Manuel S. Ramirez, P. M.

Poston marching from Yuma east writes poetically, "We camped at night at old Picache, a peak for which you'll find no match."

Picacho   Coconino Co.   Map, U. S. G. S., 1923.

Sp., "peak." Peak in northwest corner T. 21 N., R. 4 W. south of Crookton station A. T. & S. F. R. R.

It is difficult to say who named this peak. From a point near our present Ash Fork; Whipple on January 3, 1854, writes, "Nearly west is Picacho." On page 85, he has a sketch showing this peak as "north of Aztec Pass." This was at his camp 93 or 94. Marcou, the geologist, says, "The Picacho mountain is in the north and appears to be of granite." He was writing from somewhere near head of Chino valley. It is evident, therefore, that the peak was named by some one before Whipple. Sitgreaves, 1851, however, makes no mention of it.

Picacho Colorado   Gila Co.   Map, Crook N. F., 1926.

Sp., "red peak." In T. 5 N., R. 16 E., south side Salt river. "A brilliant red peak which naturally gave it this name by the early settlers." Letter, Roy Painter, Forest Ranger.

Picacho del Diablo   Pima Co.   Smith Map, 1879;
                                    Eckhoff, 1880; Patagonia Quad, 1905.

Sp., "devil's peak." Southwest slope Santa Ritas near Alto. Hinton describes it as "A bold striking feature rising like a massive fortress. Juts out into the valley—a favorite post from which the Apache watches to make a raid."

This now appears to be Josephine peak, q.v., near lat. 31° 40', long. 110° 50'.

Picacho Mountains   Pinal Co.   G. L. O. Map, 1921; U. S. G. S., 1923.

Short range in Ts. 7, 8 S., R. 9 E. north side S. P. R. R. near Picacho station about 25 miles northwest Tucson.

Picacho Pass   Pinal Co.   G. L. O. Map, 1921.

In Ts. 8, 9 S., R. 9 E., between Picacho mountains on north and peak on south. S. P. R. R. runs through it. There was a stage station here in early days.

"April, 1862, Arizona witnessed its only skirmish of the Civil War. A small detachment of the Union soldiers encountered the Confederates at what is known as Picacho Pass. The brief battle claimed the lives of three Union soldiers, Lieutenant James Barrett, Company A; Private George Johnson, Company A; and Private William S. Leonard, Company D, of the First California Volunteer Cavalry.

"Spot where the three men fell has been marked by an appropriate monument by the Arizona Pioneers Historical Society, and the S. P. R. R. Co. It is on state highway about midway between Picacho and Red Rock." *Arizona Republican*, Dec. 30, 1928.

Picacho Peak   Pinal Co.   Smith Map, 1879; G. L. O. Map, 1892-1921.

Elevation 1,765 feet. In T. 9 S., R. 9 E., near Wynola station S. P. R. R., about 25 miles northwest of Tucson. Owing to its shape it is sometimes called "Saddle mountain."

"Still nearer is the 'Picacho' marking line of the Great Southern Mail road. At its base the ranch of Charlie Shibell where stages changed teams and travelers stopped for suppers. The scene of as many encounters with Apaches as any other spot in the whole southwest." Bourke.

Peak south of pass is often called Saddle peak, from its fancied resemblance to a large saddle.

Picacho Reservoir   Pinal Co.   U. S. G. S. Map, 1923.

Water storage reservoir on Casa Grande canal system, located northern end Picacho mountains.

Pica Chica   Pima Co.

Sp., "little peak." Stage station on Butterfield route about 5 miles from Tucson. Near a small butte or peak, hence the name. On 1880 and 1881 lists of stage stations.

Picket Post   Pinal Co.   Smith Map, 1879; G. L. O., 1892-1921.

Small early day settlement on Queen Creek canyon about 10 miles southwest of Silver King mine. Troops were stationed here to protect mines in the Seventies. Silver King mill was located here and the town flourished while mine was in full blast. Hamilton says it was established by the military as an outpost or picket post of old Camp Pinal.

"That blighted and desolate place called Picket Post. Forsaken by God and Man it might have been an entrance to Hades." *Vanished Arizona.* Mrs. Summerhayes, evidently had no admiration for this place. P. O. established April 10, 1878, William H. Benson, P. M.

Picket Post Mountain   Gila Co.   G. L. O. Map, 1921; Crook N. F., 1926.

Elevation 4,370. In sec. 18, T. 2 S., R. 12 E. Mountain named for nearby military post. Sometimes called Picket Post butte. On an old map of Pioneer mining district, 1882, this is called "Picket Post or Tordillo mountain."

Picture Rocks   Yuma Co.

See Painted Rocks which Emory called Picture Rocks.

Piedmont   Yavapai Co.   G. L. O. Map, 1912.

Station Ashfork-Phoenix branch A. T. & S. F. R. R., 23 miles north of Wickenburg, between Congress Junction and Haynes. So called because of variety of colors on nearby mountains.

Piedra   Maricopa Co.

Sp., "stone or rock." Station in T. 6 S., R. 7 W., S. P. R. R., 15 miles west Gila Bend.

Paul Shoup says, "Established about 1890. The region in this vicinity is covered with rocks of volcanic origin. It is the station nearest the well known 'Painted Rocks.'"

There is a railroad station called Painted Rock on G.L.O. map, 1892.

Pierce Ferry (sic)   Mohave Co.   G. L. O. Map, 1921.

In Iceberg canyon, Colorado river, at Nevada-Arizona boundary.

"In December, 1876, a regular ferry was here established by Harrison Pearce which bears the name of Pearce Ferry, although the maps give it as Pierce. Pearce's son, James Pearce, was first settler at Taylor on Silver creek." This ferry is marked "Colorado Crossing" on both Smith, 1892, and Eckhoff, 1880, maps.

Pierce Wash (sic)   Navajo Co.   Map, Sitgreaves N. F., 1926.

Dry wash heading near "Rim" in northern part T. 10½ N., R. 17 E., runs generally north entering Black canyon in sec. 22, T. 14 N., R. 17 E. An open grassy draw with water only in times of heavy summer rains or melting snows in spring. Named, by an error in spelling, after the Pearce boys, Joe and Jim, who as early as 1885 ran cattle along here. Sons of James Pearce: see Pierce ferry.

Pierce Wash   Mohave Co.   Clason Map, 1908.

Wash rising at Cave spring near Vermillion cliffs close to Utah line. Flows west into Virgin river. Named after Fort Pierce, Utah, camp just across Utah-Arizona line.

Pigeon Canyon and Spring   Mohave Co.   U. S. G. S. Map, 1923.

Rises west side Shivwits plateau, runs northwest through Grand Wash cliffs, enters Grand Wash near lat. 36° 20', long. 113° 55'. According to Forest Supervisor, "When the first Mormons went in here, they found large flocks of wild pigeons."

Pilar River

Bolton says, "Father Escalante gave this name to the Virgin river," q.v.

Pilot Knob   Mohave Co.   U. S. G. S. Map, 1923.

East side Black range, east of Colorado river, northwest of Mount Perkins. Point used by travelers and steamboat captains as a guide in navigating river.

Pilots Peak   Navajo Co.   G. L. O. Map, 1921; U. S. G. S., 1923.

Northeast corner of T. 20 N., R. 23 E., at Apache county line. "A tall outstanding volcanic shaft, a landmark from every side." Gregory.

Pilot Rock

See Mitten Peak.

Pima   Graham Co.   G. L. O. Map, 1921.

Mormon settlement of 1879 or 1880, 2 miles below Central on Gila river. Station Arizona Eastern R. R. in T. 6 S., R. 25 E. First called Smithville. Originally in Pima county. Named for Pima Indians. P. O. established Aug. 23, 1880, Wm. R. Teeples, P. M.

Pima Agency and Indian Reservation   Pinal and Maricopa Cos.

In T. 4 S., R. 5 E., originally called Pima and Maricopa Ind. Res. Established by Act of Congress, Feb. 28, 1859. Enlarged by subsequent executive orders. Name changed to Gila River Ind. Res., q.v. P. O. established June 21, 1859 under name "Pima Village." Cyrus Leuman, P. M.

Pima Butte   Pinal Co.   U. S. G. S. Map, 1923.

Elevation 1,169 feet. In T. 3 S., R. 3 E. On Gila River Ind. Res.

Pima County

Originally called Ewell county, after Capt. R. S. Ewell. On Mowry's map, 1860, which showed only four counties. Was called Pima in Act of First Legislative Session, 1864, which created four counties, Pima, Yuma, Mohave and Yavapai.

Pima Indians

These Indians called themselves Otama and Ohotoma or A-a-tam—"men" or "people," to distinguish themselves from the Papagos. Name Pima was given these Indians by the early Spanish and is a Pima word to express negation as "pia" or "pimatc."

When the Indians were questioned they said "pia" ,or "pimatc," "I do not know" or "I don't understand." Spanish took this to be their name and so used it.

Pima Villages   Pinal Co.

Early day stage station and Indian trading post, 12 miles east of old Maricopa Wells and some 200 from Yuma.

Hinton says, "There is a good store and a flour mill here." There were several grist mills in the valley which produced a good grade of flour from native wheat. Emory visited these villages in 1846 and speaks of their fine crops of cotton, wheat and other products.

J. Ross Browne says: "There were ten Pima and two Maricopa villages in this group known as the Pima villages. They were scattered along the Gila for several miles and produced large crops of wheat, cotton and other materials. In 1859 they sold 250,000 pounds of wheat to the local trade much of it for horse feed to travelers and the government. In 1860, 400,000 pounds; in 1863 when the war was on and there were many moving troops, some 600,000 pounds."

Of the character and methods of the Pimas, Col. Poston writes most poetically and interestingly:

> "The Pima's name's much controverted,
> And many still remain unconverted
> To this or that man's theory,
> As we learn naught of history.

> You ask a Pima how to go,
> Or something that he does not know,
> He's sure to answer you 'pima'-ch'
> If favors asked he says 'pia'-ch.'

The Pimas took us in their hands,
Like good and kind samaritans;
Fed us with dainty chicken broth
And gave us clothes of cotton cloth
Of fibre woven by their hands,
From cotton raised upon their lands."

Mapped under "Pima Villages" by Smith, 1879, and Eckhoff, 1880.

Pimeria Alta

Sp., "upper pimeria." This was the region lying south of Gila river extending into northern Sonora. Included Pimas, Papagoes and Sobaipuiras on both sides of line. So called by early missionaries and Spanish padres who explored this region. Kino and his party entered here, 1687.

Bancroft calls it "Pimeria Alta or Arizona" and says: "This name would have been far more appropriate than Arizona." As a matter of fact, it was suggested as a name for this State as early as 1854. Bolton says: "Pimeria Alta, home of the upper Pimas, extended from the valley of the Altar river to that of the Gila." See Arizona, the name.

Pinacate Lava Flow and Valley   Yuma Co.
                                    Lumholtz Map, 1916; U. S. G. S., 1923.

This lava flow lies at Mexican boundary, extreme southeast corner Yuma county. Runs over into Mexico for many miles culminating in a range of considerable size and height. Hornaday describes and pictures it in *Camp Fires on Desert and Lava*.

Named for a beetle found here called Pinacate by the Mexicans. Scientists call it "Eleodes armata." The Papagos call it, "The bug that stands on its head," which sounds remarkably like our ordinary western "Tumble bug." Papago name for this region is "Tjuk-toak," meaning Black peak.

Pinal   Gila Co.   G. L. O. Map, 1909.

Station, Gila Valley R.R., about 6 miles east of Globe. After Pinal mountains.

Pinal County   G. L. O. Map, 1921.

Formed, 1875, out of Pima, Maricopa and Yavapai counties. There seems to be no definite explanation of the meaning of Pinal. It means "deer" in the Apache language. Spanish called the Apaches who lived in the Pinal mountains "Pinalenos," probably from their name for deer, "pinal."

Pinal Creek   Gila Co.   Map, Crook N. F., 1928.

Rises in sec. 20. T. 2. N., R. 15 E., east side Pioneer mountains. Flows northwest joins Salt river a few miles from Salt river end Roosevelt lake.

"A beautiful valley covered with corn and wheat fields. A fine stream of water, which was named Pinal creek." King S. Woolsey's report to Gov. Goodwin, Aug. 28, 1864.

Pinal Camp or Fort Pinal   Gila Co.

Temporary post established by Gen. Stoneman, 1870. Shows first time on Lieut. Mallory's map, 1875. In Mason's valley near head of Pinto creek, north side Hutton peak, 30 miles northeast of Florence. Globe does not show on this map at all. Heitman's Register says name was later changed to "Infantry Post." On Smith Military map, 1879, is on Queen creek road, Florence to

Globe, about 12 miles southwest of Globe. On Rand McNally's map, 1883, Old Camp Pinal has now become Pinal post office and is located about 4 miles west of original point. Is shown as Pinal Post Office, 1892. Not shown on any maps later than 1902.

McClintock says: "For a while there was a Camp Pinal in the early Seventies at headquarters of Mineral creek. Abandoned, 1871. Was in same locality as Gen. Stoneman's Picket Post near Picket Post butte when town of Pinal was later established around Silver King mill."

Hinton, 1877, speaks of "Camp Pinal and a Picket Post thereto attached; the latter recently developed into a village."

It is fairly evident the original camp at Hutton peak in Mason valley was eventually moved to Queen creek at Picket Post butte or mountain and became Pinal Post Office. When Silver King mine was at its best, Pinal claimed to have 2,500 people. Mine said to have produced over sixteen millions in ore and paid over a million and a half in dividends. Ruins of King mill are still to be seen, 1930, on Queen creek above the town.

Gazetteer of 1881 lists this as Pinal P. O., saying "It was called 'Picket Post' from 1878 up to 1880 when it was changed to Pinal. It was 3 miles southwest of Hastings," q.v.

Pinal Mountains   Gila Co.   G. L. O. Map, 1921; Crook N. F., 1926.

In Ts. 1, 2 S., Rs. 14, 15 E., southwest of Globe. Signal peak is about the center of range.

Pinal Peak   Gila Co.

Elevation 7,850 feet. In sec. 4 T., 2 S., R. 15 E. Southwest of Globe, south end Pinal mountains. Named by King Woolsey, who climbed it on his scout after Apaches and took observations. "We camped July 4, 1864, on the top of Pinal mountain." Woolsey's report, Aug. 28, 1864.

Pinal Peak   Greenlee Co.

Elevation 6,488 feet. In sec. 9. T. 12 S., R. 29 E., near Granville, q.v. East of Chase creek, turning point corner Crook N. F. Called Pinal point on map Crook N. F. 1926. G.L.O. map, 1921. Pinal Peak.

Pinaleno Mountains   Graham Co.

Smith Map, 1879; Crook N. F., 1926.

U.S.G.S. map, 1923, has it Pinalino. Sometimes called Graham mountains, q.v. and again, Sierra Bonita mountains. Graham is its highest peak. Whipple calls it "Pinal-Llano." Emory, 1864, gave it the name Pino Leno. Evidently a corruption of Whipple's name.

Pinalenos

"A branch or group of the Apache nation. They were the Pinal Coyoteros and lived mainly in Pinal mountains near Globe. They ranged, however, generally over present Fort Apache or White Mountain Ind. Res. Are officially classed with Coyoteros or White Mt. Apaches." Hodge.

Pinaveta   Yavapai Co.   U. S. G. S. Map, 1923.

Station, A. T. & S. F. R. R., 7 miles west of Ashfork. "The end of the pines. Here the road leaves the pines and enters the cedar country." A.G.W.

Military map, Division New Mexico, 1864, calls it Pineveta (sic). The peak is near here, q.v.

Pine   Gila Co.   U. S. G. S. Map, 1923.

In T. 12 N., R. 8 E. Settlement about 6 miles north of Natural Bridge. So called because cf its location in pine timber. As early as 1866, two men, Paul and Bill Gregg, came to this vicinity, built a log cabin and cleared some land. S. M. McDonald brought in and erected a saw mill a few years later. Mormons moved here in 1878. P. O. established April 2, 1884, Mary D. Fuller, P. M.

Pine Butte   Gila Co.   Map, Tonto N. F., 1926.

In sec. 4 T. 7 N., R. 9 E., upper Tonto basin, on boundary line between Gila and Maricopa counties. Prominent pine-covered butte in Mazatzal range. Not to be confused with Pine mountain farther south in same range.

Pine Creek   Gila Co.   G. L. O. Map, 1921; Tonto N. F., 1928.

Stream rising under "Tonto rim." Flows southwest under Natural Bridge, enters East Verde about 8 miles west of Payson. So called because in midst of a great pine forest.

Pine Creek   Yavapai Co.   Map Prescott N. F., 1927.

Stream rising southeast corner Baca Float No. 5. Flows west into Burro creek.

Pine Creek   Yavapai Co.   Map, Prescott N. F., 1927.

In sec. 3 T. 16 N., R. 6 W. "Stream rising at Hide mountain near Camp Wood. Flows north and east into Chino valley.
"Two Pine creeks are in this immediate vicinity. Other flows west to Colorado river." Letter, Forest Supervisor Grubb, Prescott.

Pine Creek   Maricopa Co.

Tributary to Salt river near sec. 15 T. 3 N., R. 11 E., unsurveyed. On Tonto N. F. (Not Pinyon.) Decision USGB.

Pine Hollow   Coconino Co., U. S. G. S. Map, 1921; Kaibab N. F., 1926.

Rises near Big Spring running southwest into Colorado river. "The point where it rises near Big Spring is heavily timbered with yellow pine and was therefore called by this name."

Pine Mountain   Yavapai Co.   Map, Prescott N. F., 1927.
                        Tonto N. F., 1927; Prescott N. F., 1927.

Elevation 5,761 feet. In T. 5 N., Rs. 9, 10 E. In Mazatzal range. There is a Pine butte a few miles north.
In sec. 18, T. 11 N., R. 6 E. Northern end Skeleton ridge, west side, Verde river. Isolated peak on Prescott National Forest with forest of yellow pine on its slopes.

Pine Springs   Coconino Co.   G. L. O. Map, 1921.

In T. 28 N., R. 8 W., under upper rim Grand Canyon. Hualpai Ind. Res. There is a fine growth of yellow pine around this spot. According to Coues, Garces named this "Posa de la Rosa," or "Rose Well" because he found it "Crowned with wild roses." P. O. established Mar. 20, 1879, Hugh Marshall, P. M.

Pine Ridge

See Zil-tadin.

Pine Springs   Coconino Co.

Near Mormon lake. Fish says: "Nearby at Pine springs was a saw mill which came from Mount Trumbull in Mohave county. Mill was sent by the Mormon church to Lee Ferry, for Little Colorado settlements. Settlers from St. Joe and Sunset sent to the ferry for it in August, 1876, and took it up near Mormon lake where it was set up. Later sold to William Flake, who moved it to a place southwest of Snowflake." See Mormon Dairy and lake.

Pineair   Maricopa Co.

Sixty miles from Mesa in Salt River range. "Just a fancy name for the old Reavis ranch, q.v."

Pinedale   Navajo Co.   G. L. O. Map, Pinedale, 1892; U. S. G. S., 1923.

In sec. 32, T. 11 N., R. 20 E. Sitgreaves N. F. Mormon settlement of 1879. Descriptive name. Located in a little glade amid yellow pines. First settlers, Niels Mortensen and sons. They brought with them a fine Percheron stallion. Town first called Percheron, q.v.; also Mortensens, q.v. P. O. established Apr. 18, 1888, Lydia C. Bryan, P. M.

Pinery Creek   Cochise Co.   Smith Map, 1879; Coronado N. F., 1927.

Rises Chiricahua mountains near Buena Vista peak, in T. 17 S., R. 29½ E., flows west and is lost in Sulphur Springs valley. Upper end called Pine creek on some maps. Is in yellow pine country.

Pinetop   Navajo Co.   Map, Sitgreaves N. F., 1924.

In T. 8 N., R. 23 E. Mormon settlement started about 1888. First called Penrod after David Penrod, local settler. On edge of Fort Apache Ind. Res. The Penrods built and ran a saw mill here as early as 1891. P. O. established Dec. 9, 1891, Edward E. Bradshaw, P. M.

Pineveta Peak (sic)   Yavapai Co.   Military Map, New Mexico, 1864; G. L. O., 1883.

In T. 23 N., R. 4 W., about 4 miles directly north of Crookton station A. T. & S. F. R. R. One mile north Floyd peak, which does not appear on some later maps. Probably named by early travellers. See Pinaveta Station.

Pineyon (sic)   Apache Co.   U. S. G. S. Map, 1923.

In T. 10 N., R. 24 E. Settlement in southern part of county, about 10 miles northeast of Pinetop. Incorrect spelling of Spanish "piñon." Located in heavy piñon timber. Spelling still incorrect in Postal Guide, 1929. First P. M., Mary A. Calloway, June 29, 1918. See Pine Creek.

Pinyon Mountain   Maricopa Co.

Elevation 5,256 feet, in sec. 21, T. 3 N., R. 12 E., south end Two Bar ridge, Tonto N. F. So named by early residents because a few pinyons grew on its north slope. Decision U.S.G.B.

Pinnacle Mountain   Maricopa Co.   G. L. O. Map, 1921; Tonto N. F., 1926.

Elevation 3,170 feet. In sec. 32, T. 5 N., R. 5 E., about 4 miles north of McDowell mountain. Descriptive name.

Pinnacle Ridge   Graham Co.   Map, Crook N. F., 1926.
In T. 6 S., R. 21 E. Descriptive name.

Pinole
See Bloody Tanks.

Pinoleno or **Pinon Leno**
See Pinoleno mountains.

Pinta Mountains
See Sierra Pinta.

Pinto   Apache Co.   U. S. G. S. Map, 1923.
Flag station and trading post, A. T. & S. F. R. R., southeast
corner of T. 20 N., R. 25 E., on Puerco River. Sp., "painted—
spotted." P. O. established Feb. 27, 1902, Celia F. Henning, P. M.
See Billings.

Pinto Creek   Gila Co.   Map, Crook N. F., 1920.
Rises in T. 1 S., R. 14 E., near Bellevue. Flows north into
Roosevelt lake, 2 miles west of Livingston. Said to have been
named by early settlers on account of varied colorings of hills
on either side. See Pinta.

Pinto Mesa   Yavapai Co.   Map, Prescott N. F., 1927.
Isolated butte in sec. 4, T. 13½ N., R. 4 E. On north side Copper canyon, west of Camp Verde. "George Young of Verde says
it was named after a pinto horse or cow which ran on this mesa."
Letter, Harry Hartin, Prescott.

Pioneer   Gila Co.   Smith Map, 1879.
Mining camp and stage station in Pioneer District, near old
Silver King mine, west of Globe. P. O. established Apr. 24, 1882,
Thomas A. Lonergan, P. M. See Tucson *Weekly Citizen*, June
29, 1889.

Pioneer, Mountain and Basin   Gila Co.   Map, Crook N. F., 1926.
Elevation 2,504 feet, in T. 2 S., R. 15 E. After Pioneer mines
and Pioneer Mining District.

Pipe Springs   Mohave Co.   G. L. O. Maps, 1892-1921.
In T. 40 N., R. 4 W. Kaibab Ind. Res. Three miles south of
Moccasin spring. Powell says: "The local Indians had a name
for these springs meaning 'Yellow rock springs.'" A fitting
name, for the rocks around are bright yellow in color. First
settlement here, 1863, made by Dr. James M. Whitmore, killed
by Indians, 1866. Bought from his heirs by Brigham Young who,
1870, established here the "Church Herd" of cattle. Place called
"Winsor Castle" because A. P. Winsor, 1870, built a large stone
house here; later owned and used as ranch headquarters. Cattle
company was known as the "Winsor Castle Stock Growing Company." Brigham Young was a director and owned controlling
interest in the corporation.
In 1871, Deseret Telegraph Co. extended its line to Pipe Springs
from Kanab. This is said to have been first telegraph office
opened in Arizona. Miss Ella Stewart, later wife of D. K. Udall,
St. Johns, was first operator.
May 31, 1931, Mrs. Udall wrote: "In March, 1870, my father,
Levi Stewart, was called as a missionary to colonize Kanab,
Utah. President Brigham Young asked him to have one of his
daughters learn telegraphy as they intended to extend the line

of the Deseret Telegraph Co. to Kanab and Pipe Springs. In
May, 1870, father on his way to Kanab, left me at Toquerville,
Utah, to study telegraphy. I practiced on a wooden key for
over a year. The line was finished in Dec., 1871. Miss Rosalia
Haight was selected as operator at Kanab and I was sent to Pipe
Springs. A. M. Musser was superintendent of the line. I worked
as operator from that time until we left for St. Johns in 1880."
    "According to A. W. Ivins, William Hamblin bet that he could
shoot the bottom out of Dudley Leavitt's pipe at 25 yards, which
he did. For this the place was named Pipe Springs. Ivins and
Leavitt were camped here with Jacob Hamblin's party." Mc-
Clintock.

Pirtle   Cochise Co.

    See Pirtleville.

Pirtleville   Cochise Co.   Map, Coronado N. F., 1927.

    Old ranch and mining camp one mile north of Douglas. P. O.
established Feb. 8, 1908, under name of Pirtle, Cassius C. Hockett,
P. M. Named for Elmer Pirtle, early settler who died August,
1920.

Pisinimo   Pima Co.   Bryan Map, 1920; U. S. G. S., 1923.

    Papago Ind. Res. Indian village in Quijotoa valley. Lumholtz
says word means "bear's head" in Papago. Located about 15
miles northwest of south point of Quijotoas.

Piskorski Canyon   Santa Cruz Co.   Coronado N. F., 1926.

    Stream and canyon rising in sec. 4, T. 23 S., R. 11 E. At foot
of Montana Peak. Stream flows northeast into Santa Cruz about
4½ miles above Calabasas. Originally called Pecks canyon.
When Peck left after his wife was killed by Apaches, Joseph
Piskorski settled there and it soon took his name. It was also
called Palaco canyon, although nobody seems to know how it
got the name. On June 24, 1930, U.S.G.B. ordered name of A.
L. Peck restored to this canyon. See Peck canyon. Piskorski
canyon on map.

Pistola Peak   Greenlee Co.

    See Mitchell.

Pitahaya Region.

    Several early writers speak of parts of southwestern Arizona as
"The Pitahaya Region." It seems to have been applied to an area
lying east of Yuma along the International boundary and extending as far east as the Santa Ritas.
    The Pitahaya was the fruit of several cacti of this region and
was a staple article of food among both Indians and Mexicans.
In Sonora the Organ cactus is known commonly as "Pitahaya
Dulce" or Sweet Pitahaya.
    The name may perhaps be traced to the Spanish word "Pita"
a strong thread made from the fibre of the Agave. The full word
is generally accepted as of Indian origin.
    Davis *Conquest of New Mexico*, 1869, says, writing from
Northern Sonora: "The men drank a liquor made from the fruit
of the cactus called the 'wine of Pitihaya (sic.).' It was very in-
toxicating."
    Bartletts *Personal Narrative* says: "Today we saw for the
first time since leaving Fort Yuma, our friend the Pitahaya or
Giant Cactus. The early priests speak of the 'three Pitahaya
months when the fruit is ripe.'"

Lumholtz says: "The Pitihaya (sic) fruit is the size of a large hen's egg. Does not possess as much flavor as the related and famous Pitahaya fruit of Mexico."

Dr. Woodhouse, with Sitgreaves in 1851, calls it the "Pitahaya or Cereus gigantea."

Pitt   Coconino Co.   Map, Tusayan N. F., 1927.

In sec. 32, T. 23 N., R. 2 E. Livestock loading station, Grand Canyon branch A. T. & S. F. R. R., 7 miles north of Williams. After William Pitt, local sheepman.

Pittsburgh   Cochise Co.

P. O. established June 18, 1906, Harry Alexander, P. M. Exact location unknown.

Pittsburgh Landing   Mohave Co.

In T. 13 N., R. 20 W. On Colorado river, former landing for river steamers. Also called Liverpool, q.v. On Smith map, 1879, Hinton, 1886, and G.L.O., 1892, is called Liverpool Landing. On G.L.O., 1921, called Pittsburgh. No record found of origin of either name. Probably point where supplies for mines in Owens district and near Signal were unloaded.

Piute   Navajo Co.   U. S. G. S. Map, 1923.

Creek, northwest corner Navajo Ind. Res. Flows north into Colorado river near lat. 37°, long. 110° 50'.

Piute Point   Coconino Co.   Map, Grand Canyon N. F.,
                                                         Tusayan N. F., 1927.

Elevation 6,632 feet. In T. 32 N., R. 1 E., south side Colorado river, about 6 miles due west of Granite Falls. First called Grand View. Piute, decision U.S.G.B.

Pivot Rock   Coconino Co.   Coconino N. F., 1928.

In sec. 21, T. 13. N., R. 9 E., 2 miles northeast of Baker butte. "A rock that sits on a pivot with a small 8-inch pine tree growing on it. There is a Pivot rock, Pivot Rock canyon and a Pivot Rock spring. Spring comes out of a cave and drops about 30 feet. Cave can be entered to about 400 feet. Pivot Rock is in the canyon about half a mile from spring." Letter, W. J. Brown, Forest Ranger.

Placerita   Yavapai Co.   Congress Quad, 1904.

In T. 11 N., R. 4 W., mining camp about 8 miles east Peeples valley on Placerita gulch. This is a word brought in by early miners from California, Placerita, diminutive of placer. Sp., "the place near a river bank where gold dust is found and washed out." P. O. established February 1, 1896, Lewis H. Herron, P. M.

Planchas de Plata

See Bolas de Plata.

Planet, Town and Peak   Yuma Co.   G. L. O. Map, 1921.

Mine discovered, 1863, by a man named Ryland. Claimed to be the first copper mine worked by Americans in Arizona. Town was at the mine, east of Aubrey landing, about 15 miles northeast of Parker, on Bill Williams river.

Peak in T. 10 N., R. 17 W., in Buckskin mountain west of Swansea about 20 miles from Colorado river. P. O. established March 28, 1902, Edward Webb, P. M. See Ajo.

Plateau of Arizona   Coconino Co.

"An area bound on north by Grand Canyon, on east by Little Colorado desert, on south by Mogollon escarpment, on west by Aubrey cliffs. Includes Coconino plateau, San Francisco Mountain plateau and Mogollon mesa." Decision U.S.G.B. Name decided on, and approved May 3, 1910, by a special committee of this Board, consisting of C. Hart Merriam, Henry Gannett and Frederick G. Plummer." Report U.S.G.B.

Platten Springs   Coconino Co.   Map, Tusayan N. F., 1927.

In sec. 23 T. 23 N., R. 3 E. Group of springs in Spring valley northeast of Sitgreaves mountain.

After Fred Platten, former forest ranger on this forest for several years, about 1918. Now retired. Platten holds the Congressional Medal of Honor "for gallantry in action with hostile Indians at Sappa Creek, Kansas, while a sergeant in Troop H, Sixth U. S. Cavalry, April 23, 1875."

Plattsville   Coconino Co.   G. L. O. Map, 1909.

P. O. established April 7, 1900, Ethel S. Sharpnack, P. M.

Pleasant Valley   Gila Co.   Map, Tonto N. F., 1927.

Large open valley on Cherry creek, northern end Tonto Basin. So called because of its beauty. About 15 miles west of Fort Apache Ind. Res. Scene of many stirring events in "Pleasant Valley War." 1887. See *Arizona Historical Review*, Dec., 1930.

Plomosa   Yuma Co.

There must have been such a town, for post office records at Washington show an office established by this name, Apr. 8, 1880, J. Coleman, P. M. Probably a mining camp at base of Plomoso range where early prospectors mined considerable lead.

Plomosa Mountains and Peak   Yuma Co.

Sp., "leaden"; plomo, "lead." Mountains running north and south along Rs. 17, 18 W., east of Colorado River Ind. Res. Peak, at south end of mountains in T. 35., R. 18 W. There seems to be no uniform spelling. On late maps it is Plomoso. Earlier ones, Plumas, Plomas and Plomosa. Range is full of lead-bearing ores and mines were located here as early as 1865. Plomosa, decision U.S.G.B.

Point

See the real name for such places, i.e. Point Sublime, under Sublime.

Pointed Butte   Gila Co.   G. L. O. Map, 1921.

Fort Apache Ind. Res., north side Salt river and west of Carrizo creek. Very sharp pointed peak or butte.

Point of Mountain   Cochise Co.

Also known as Steeles station because for a time it was owned and run by Tom Steele.

In 1876, station was owned and run by a man named Tom Williams, according to John P. Clum, who stopped there over night while moving the Chiricahuas from Bowie to San Carlos. Known as Point of Mountain when the author stopped there enroute to Fort Grant in February, 1880. Stage that dropped the writer was attacked a few hours after the author left it by Victorio and his Apaches, about 25 miles east of the station, and two passengers who had been with us from Tucson as well as the driver and the horses were killed.

Point of Mountain   Pima Co.   Hinton Map, 1877; Eckhoff, 1880.

Another early day station on main stage road across southern part of Territory. Was about 18 miles northwest of Tucson where road crossed Santa Cruz wash. Plenty of well water here. Was important stage and freighting point of those days.

Point of Rocks   Pima Co.

Station Butterfield stage road 8 or 10 miles west of Tucson. Poston was here, 1863, and writes of it:
"Next we rested at the Point of Rocks
Where Tucson keeps her herds and flocks."
Hinton lists it as a stage station, 1873.

Point of Rocks   Yavapai Co.   G. L. O. Map, 1892.

About 10 miles north of Prescott. "The Apaches attacked the ranch of Hon. Louis A. Stevens here Sept. 20, 1867. Mr. Stevens, councilman from Yavapai county, was in Prescott at the Legislature. The story goes that Mrs. Stevens sent him word to send her ammunition and she could hold the ranch. He sent it and followed." Fish.
The Fourth Ter. Legislature met on Sept. 4, 1867, an unusual date.

Poker Mountain   Apache Co.   G. L. O. Map, 1921.

On Fort Apache Ind. Res., west side Black river, south of Burnt Corral creek. "About 1885, several large cow outfits had a winter horse camp in the gap or pass between the two mountains. The boys used to play poker to pass the time away. Hence it became Poker gap, Poker mountain, and Freezeout creek." Letter, Arthur Slaughter, Springerville.

Polacca   Navajo Co.   U. S. G. S. Map, 1923.

In T. 28 N., R. 18 E. Settlement and trading post on Hopi Ind. Res., near Walpi.
After Tom Polacca, Hopi Indian boy who lived with Thomas V. Keam for many years as a sort of personal body guard. A very handsome, intelligent chap, a favorite with everybody. Keam so named him.
"Polacca was started about 1890, when Tom Polacca, for whom it was named, came down from the mesa and built a cabin on the flat below. The government built several houses near him in an endeavor to coax the Hopi to move down and settle in the valley, but they would not do it. They stole the windows and doors from the cabins and carried them to the top." Letter, J. W. Hoover, Keam Canyon. P. O. established Feb. 16, 1901. Richard J. Barnes, P. M.

Polacca Wash   Navajo Co.   Gregory Map, 1916; U. S. G. S., 1923.

Wash formed by junction First mesa and Wepo washes, about 10 miles northwest Polacca, Hopi Ind. Res. Flows southwest across reservation into Oraibi wash, in T. 24 N., R. 14 E. Course of this wash is not clear on many maps. Gregory is followed because he probably made a closer study of these streams than anyone else.

Poland   Yavapai Co.   G. L. O. Map, 1921.

In T. 12½ N., R. 1 E. Mining camp near Big Bug, at western end branch road from Poland Junction, Prescott and Eastern R. R.

"After Davis R. Poland, who found and named the mine, 1872. He filed on a homestead, 1882, in sec. 20, T. 12 N., R. 3 E." Letter, Frank C. Grubb, Forest Supervisor. Frank Lecklider was appointed P. M., Jan. 6, 1902. Refused to give bond. Office not opened.

Poland Creek   Yavapai Co.   U. S. G. S. Map, 1923.

Rises near Crown King, flows northeast into Black canyon.

Poland Junction   Yavapai Co.   Map, Prescott N. F., 1927.

Junction point, Prescott and Eastern R. R., of branch to Poland mine about 15 miles southwest.

Polaris   Yuma Co.   U. S. G. S. Map, 1923.

Well known mine south side Kofa mountains, near long. 114°. "The story is that the discoverer located the mine by the north star." P. O. established June 17, 1909, William R. Wardner, P. M.

Pole Knoll   Apache Co.   Map, Apache N. F., 1926.

Timbered knoll where settlers from valley cut many poles for corral and house logs. On mountains south of Springerville.

Polhamus   Mohave Co.

Landing on Colorado river about 300 miles north of Yuma. Found only in *Arizona Gazetteer*, 1881. Named after Captain Polhamus of early steamboat days on river.

Polles Mesa   Gila Co.   Map, Tonto N. F., 1926.

In T. 10 N., R. 8 E., upper Tonto Basin. Mesa lying north of East Verde and west of Pine creek. "Named for an old timer, Polle Chilson, who grazed cattle here many years ago. This name appears as Rolles on the maps but this is an error, the name is Polle." Letter, Forest Ranger Croxen, Payson.

Polvo   Pima Co.

Station, S. P. R. R., about 4 miles east of Tucson. Polvo, Sp., "dust, powder." "The country here is very dry and dusty, hence it took this name." Letter, Supt. S. P. R. R., Tucson.

Pomerene   Cochise Co.   G. L. O. Map, 1921.

In T. 17 S., R. 20 E. Settlement, San Pedro river about 3 miles north of Benson. "Originally called Robinson. Said to have been named for Senator Pomerene of Ohio." Letter, Edith A. Macia, P. M., Cochise. P. O. established October 27, 1915. Henry A. Kimmell, P. M.

Pool   Cochise Co.   G. L. O. Map, 1921.

"Small settlement on San Pedro about one mile south of Cascabel. After Dr. Josiah Pool, who located here about 1900." Letter, Edith A. Macia, P. M., Cochise. P. O. established February 12, 1902, John J. Pool, P. M.

Pool Knoll   Apache Co.   Apache N. F., 1926.

In sec. 21, T. 7 N., R. 28 E. Isolated knoll in White mountains. So called because in early Eighties the "Pool Wagon" or outfit formed by representatives of the large cattle companies, the U. S., the 24's, the Greers, St. George Creaghe, Woods and Potter, William Garland, Rudds, Pat Trainor and others, met here to start spring roundups.

Popper Well   Yuma Co.

"Watering place belonging jointly to Richard Popper and Harqua Hala Cattle Company. "It is merely a cow camp." *Routes to the Desert.*

Porras Dikes   Navajo Co.   Gregory Map, 1916.

Some peculiar geological dikes east of Kayenta, southern end Comb ridge. Named by Gregory after a Franciscan Missionary, Francisco de Porras, killed by Hopis, 1633.

Portal   Cochise Co.   G. L. O. Map, 1921; Coronado N. F., 1927.

Sp., "el portal," the entrance, the opening. In T. 17 S., R. 31 E. Village on Cave creek, east side Chiricahua mountains. Located at entrance to Cave creek canyon. U. S. Forest Ranger Station is here. P. O. established June 14, 1905, Edward F. Epley, P. M.

Porter Creek   Navajo Co.   Map, Sitgreaves N. F., 1928.

In T. 9 N., R. 25 E. Stream rising north side Pearce mountain near line Fort Apache Ind. Res. Flows northwest into Showlow creek about 2 miles north of Lakeside reservoir. Named after James Porter, well known sheepman of this neighborhood.

Porter Mountain   Navajo Co.   Map, Apache N. F., 1926.

In sec. 6. T. 9 N., R. 23 E. Sitgreaves N. F. An isolated point. See Porter creek for origin.

Porter Tank and Wash   Navajo Co.   U. S. G. S. Map, 1923.

In T. 16 N., R. 19 E. Dry wash running north from high ridge above the "Dry Lake." Eventually lost in Little Colorado valley. Named after "Jack" Porter, a sheepman who about 1887, located these rock tanks for a sheep camp. A man was shot and killed about 1887 in a quarrel over the ownership of these tanks.

Post Creek   Graham Co.   Map, Crook N. F., 1926.

Rises west side Mount Graham, flows south into Grant creek, Fort Grant Military Reservation. So called by military because it furnished water for Grant.

Posta Quemada Canyon   Pima Co.   Map, Coronado N. F., 1927.

Quema, Quemada—Sp., "burned." Heads at Wrong mountain runs southwest into Pantano wash about 3 miles southeast Vail station.

"Here in very early days an old stage station was burned in the canyon near Mountain springs. Hence Posta quemada—"Burnt station." Nobody ever knew date it was burned, but it was before we came here in 1875." Letter, Ed Vail, Tucson.

Postals Ranch

See Postles ranch.

Postles Ranch   Yavapai Co.

In big Chino valley on old stage road, Ash Fork to Prescott, about 5 miles south of Bangharts. Spelled Postals on Mil. maps, 1877, 1879. This was the first Fort Whipple location.

"Ft. Whipple was established 24 miles northeast of Prescott at what was then Postals Ranch." McFarland's History: "Postle seems to be the correct word." Farish. Hinton calls it Postals Ranch. Says it is 22 miles from Prescott, "Good water, but wood and grass poor."

Letter from A. F. Banta in State Historian's office says, "Bob Postle was a lieutenant of N. M. Volunteers. When the first

Whipple in Chino valley was abandoned, Postle squatted on and farmed it for several years." Banta was right. War department records at Washington show that: "Robert Postle was mustered into the 1st New Mexico Cavalry as 2nd Lieut. Co. L, Feb. 7, 1863. Appointed 1st Lieut. Co. G, Sept. 4, 1863. Dismissed Dec. 31, 1863, by sentence General Court Martial." Postle's company was part of escort under Lieut. Col. Chavez to Governor Goodwin and party. Postle seems to have followed the party westward to Yavapai county where he settled on this ranch.

Some of Postle's descendants are now living in the Salt River valley.

Post Office Canyon and Creek   Gila Co.

Short canyon and stream rising southwest corner of T. 8 N., R. 23 E., Fort Apache Ind. Res. Flows southeast enters North Fork of White river below Ft. Apache. So called from nearby Post Office Hill, q.v.

Post Office Hill   Navajo Co.   Map, Fort Apache Ind. Res.

In sec. 2 T. 7 N., R. 23 E. Well known place on Ft. Apache-Holbrook road north side of Post Office canyon, Ft. Apache Ind. Res.

Here in early days passing Apaches always placed a stone with some leaves, twigs or grass on the big pile of such materials that had accumulated. They told me it was "talk" (yosh-ti) to the next Indian passing. No doubt it had some meaning long ago, but in 1880 it was a mere "function." In 1880 the pile was possibly 50 feet round at the base and 8 or 10 feet high. Often people tore the top off looking for valuables.

Poston Butte   Coconino Co.

Grand Canyon N. P., on west canyon wall, near northeast end of Park and lat. 36° 11', long 110° 54'. Named for Charles D. Poston, by Frank Bond. Decision U.S.G.B. See Poston butte, Pinal Co., for full history.

Poston Butte   Pinal Co.   G. L. O. Map, 1921; Florence Quad, 1921.

In T. 4 S., R. 9 E. An outstanding point across river and about 2 miles northwest of Florence.

After Charles D. Poston, who first came to Arizona, 1857. Appointed Superintendent Indian Affairs for Arizona by President Lincoln. Elected delegate to Congress at first Territorial election, 1864. About 1877, appointed Register, U. S. Land Office at Florence. His official life was always rather turbulent. An educated, refined gentleman, yet with certain marked peculiarities, through which he made enemies as well as friends.

While at Florence he built a road to the top of a nearby butte which came to be called "Poston's Butte," also "Primrose Hill," q.v. Locally called "Poston's Folly." He asked to be buried on this hill but due to financial difficulties he was buried at Phoenix, where he died January 24, 1902.

In 1906, D. A. R. of Phoenix erected a headstone over his grave. His was a very pathetic figure on the streets of Phoenix from 1890.

April 25, 1925, the Phoenix D.A.R., in cooperation with State officers, placed Poston's remains in an iron case and buried it under a monument on top of this butte. The copper plate says, "Charles D. Poston, born April 20, 1825, died June 24, 1902. First Arizona delegate to Congress in 1864."

Elliott's History states that this butte was called "Primrose Hill" by Poston, but I have been unable to find a single item as to why so called. Charles B. Mason, of Florence says: "It was first called Stiles Hill after William Stiles, an early settler near its base and father of Billy Stiles, the noted train robber, who was born at this ranch."

George A. Brown of Florence insists that Poston called it "Parsee Hill" because he secured from that sect most of the funds for the erection of the proposed temple. See Primrose Hill.

McClintock's story of the "Father of Arizona," is well worth reading.

Postvale   Pima Co.   Railroad Folders.

Small farming community, established 1910, by Mr. Post of Battle Creek, Mich. Shows on Post Route map, 1924, about 21 miles northwest of Tucson, on Santa Cruz river. Also a station, S. P. R. R. P. O. established Oct. 15, 1920, Frank Clark, P. M. Name changed to Marana in Feb., 1925, q.v.

Potato Butte   Gila Co.   G. L. O. Map, 1921; Tonto N. F., 1927.

In sec. 28, T. 9 N., R. 12 E., on west side Pleasant valley, about 5 or 6 miles west of Young P. O.

"Not positively known but on account of its striking resemblance to a potato standing on end, it is likely this gave the name." Letter, Walter J. Pinson, Forest Ranger.

Potato Wash   Navajo Co.   U. S. G. S. Map, 1923.

Dry wash heading at county line in T. 12 N., R. 15½ E., running north into Chevelons Fork, in T. 16 N., R. 16 E. Named by Will C. Barnes, who planted and raised potatoes in this wash, 1888-95.

Pot Holes   Coconino Co.   Map, Tusayan N. F., 1927.

In T. 29 N., R. 7 E. In Tusayan N. F. Several deep crater-like openings, probably of volcanic origin. Common name for this sort of opening which often holds water from rains or melting snow. Frequently they are used for holding round-up herds where there is a sloping entrance into them.

Potter Mountain   Cochise Co.   Map, Coronado N. F., 1927.

In sec. 16, T. 22 S., R., 24 E., about 5 miles north of Bisbee, in Mule mountains.

"Mr. J. A. Rockfellow, County Engineer, says it was so named for an early cattleman who had his ranch at foot of mountain." Letter, E. S. Mettler, Forest Ranger.

Pottery Cave   Apache Co.

See Harris Cave.

Potts Mountain   Mohave Co.   G. L. O. Map, 1921.

Elevation 3,101 feet. In T. 12 N., R. 14 W. "After John Potts, who located and developed a lead mine on this mountain." Letter, G. Levy Signal.

Poverty Knoll   Mohave Co.

Elevation 6,000 feet. Near lat 36° 30', long. 113° 25'. Shown on G.L.O. map, 1892 and 1921, also on Mount Trumball Quad of 1892 as Solitaire Butte. U.S.G.S., 1923 as Poverty.

Powell   Mohave Co.   G. L. O. Map, 1892, 1921.

Station A. T. & S. F. R. R., 6 miles east of Colorado river, on Arizona side.

Named for Major J. W. Powell, noted geologist, first explorer to pass through Colorado river canyon. According to official records this was first called Needles, and P. O. was established by that name February 18, 1883. August A. Spear, P. M. October 11, 1883, it was renamed and called Powell. See Needles.

Powell, Lake   U. S. G. S. Map, 1923.

In T. 16½ N., R. 21 W. Flood lake, due north of Topock station, A. T. & S. F. R. R., 2 miles east of Colorado river. Named after Major J. W. Powell

Powell Plateau   Coconino Co.   U. S. G. S. Map, 1921.

After Major Powell. North side Colorado river, about 20 miles northwest of El Tovar, Grand Canyon N. P. Powell was a one-armed veteran of Civil War. On trips through the canyon he was strapped in an arm chair fastened to the boat. "Ka-pu-rats," meaning "Arm off" is the name by which I am known among the Utes and Shoshones. Powell Report.

Powell made two trips through canyon. Dellenbaugh says, "Powell's first trip was financed in part by the University of Illinois, which gave him $500. The Illinois Academy of Science gave him an additional $250. Only thing the United States Government did was to furnish a letter from War Department to all commanding officers authorizing them to issue Government rations for exact number of persons in his party." Powell was later Director of the U. S. Geological Survey and the Bureau of Ethnology.

Powers   Cochise Co.   G. L. O. Map, 1892.

After a local family by this name. Station, west slope of Chiricahuas in what would be T. 18 S., R. 28 E., on a fork of White river. P. O. established December 1, 1887, Mrs. Jane M. Powers, P. M.

On June 20, 1891, name of P. O. was changed to Rucker, Joseph H. Coggswell, P. M., to commemorate death here of Lieut. Rucker, U.S.A. This was where Camp Rucker was originally located. After it was broken up, Powers family settled here. In later years the well known Rak ranch was established here on the old Camp Rucker military reservation. See Rucker.

Powers Butte   Maricopa Co.   U. S. G. S. Map, 1923.

In T. 1 S., R. 4 W. South side Gila river. After Gov. Powers of Mississippi, who started quite a colony at Arlington, southwest of Phoenix, and built first canal there.

Pozo Blanco   Pima Co.   U. S. G. S. Map, 1923.

Sp., "white well." Papago Ind. Res. Papago name is "Kom-Voxia," "where the Kom tree grows." Eight miles south of Burrills, upper end Quijotoa mountains.

Pozo Redondo Mountains and Indian Village   Pima Co.
                                        U. S. G. S. Map, 1923.

Sp., "round well." Near lat. 32° 30′, long. 112° 40′. Papago Ind. Res.

Pozo Verde Pima Co. G. L. O. Map, 1921.

In Papago, "Tjui-takvaxi"—green well, Tjuitak, green, vaxi, a well, water-hole, or spring. Spring and Indian village, extreme southeast corner Papago Ind. Res., west slope Baboquivari mountains, near International boundary line and La Osa ranch.

"And you can see the Great Spirit's footprints there today. The place is in the Baboquivari mountains near the Indian village called in these days Poso Verde, which means Green Well." Harold Bell Wright, in *Long Ago Told.*

Pozos de San Basilio (St. Basil's Wells) Mohave Co.

Name given by Garces to Peach springs, q.v.

Pozos Muchos Pima Co. Lumholtz Map, 1912.

Sp., "many wells." About 20 miles southeast of Gila Bend R. R. station. In Saucida mountains near Pima-Maricopa county line. There are a number of "wells" (pozos) or water holes in this valley.

Prado Coconino Co. G. L. O. Map, 1909.

Sp., "a meadow, or a pasture ground." Station, Grand Canyon R. R., about 20 miles north of Williams.

"All about here is one of the best grazing areas in northern Arizona." Letter, Fred Platten, Forest Ranger.

Prairie Siding Yavapai Co. Map, Tusayan N. F., 1927.

In sec. 24, T. 20 N., R. 2 W., station, Ash Fork-Phoenix branch, A. T. & S. F. R. R., about 12 miles south of Ash Fork. Descriptive name. Station is on an open, fairly level prairie.

Pranty Creek Maricopa Co. Map, Tonto N. F., 1924.

Small stream entering Fish creek about 3 miles east of Fish creek station.

"After Old Man Pranty, early settler, miner, and cattleman, who had a ranch on the stream in early days. About 1900, Pranty located in Tonto basin and prospected and mined for many years. In 1925, he disappeared. His cabin was found empty and locked, his glasses and 'four-bits' lying on the table and nothing disturbed. He was well along in years and probably overcome by some physical attack died alone." Letter, Dan Williamson, Globe.

Pratt Maricopa Co. G. L. O. Map, 1892.

In T. 6 N., R. 1 E. Station, west side Agua Fria, above Gillett. Named after William B. Pratt of Pratt Bros., stationers and book sellers in Phoenix, 1890-96. Pratt had a mine back in the hills and this was the mail and supply station. P. O. established May 5, 1890, Eugene E. St. Clair, P. M.

Prescott Yavapai Co.

Elevation 5,346 feet. One-time capital, county seat and mining town. On Granite creek. On Ash Fork-Phoenix branch A. T. & S. F. R. R. Originally a branch railroad was built to Prescott "on the sod" from what was then called Prescott Junction, later Seligman, A. T. & S. F. R. R. When Santa Fe built from Ash Fork, this line was abandoned.

Name Prescott was selected at a public meeting on May 30, 1864. Suggested by Secretary of Territory, McCormick, in honor of the historian. Was the capital until November 1, 1867, when it was moved to Tucson. Later on taken back to Prescott. In January, 1899, was moved to Phoenix. Has at times been called Granite, Gimletville, and Goodwin City.

McClintock says: "The official records in State Adjutant General's office show that J. Ross Browne, the writer, was appointed a Captain in the First Arizona Volunteers from 'Prescott, Socorro County, New Mexico.'"

Judge Wells says the first Apache attack on Prescott was March 16, 1864, when Joseph Cosgrave was killed while herding stock, almost in the town itself. P. O. established May 18, 1865, Calvin White, P. M.

Prescott Junction

See Seligman.

Prescott National Forest	Yavapai Co.

Created May 10, 1898, as Prescott Forest Reserve. Renamed Prescott National Forest, 1908. In February, 1908, Verde Forest Reserve was combined with it. Total area Prescott Forest, 1933 —1,207,112 acres. Named after William H. Prescott, historian. Supervisor's headquarters, Prescott, Arizona.

Prescott, Walnut Grove and Pima Toll Road

See "Wagon Roads."

Presidio of San Pedro	Cochise Co.

Also called Fitz (sic) Jeffersons ranch, q.v., on Smith and Eckhoff maps. East side San Pedro river, south of Broncho creek.

Hinton says that this was or is the site of present Camp Huachuca. He must have meant the first temporary camp, for the post lies some fifteen miles to the west.

Preston Mesa	Coconino Co.	U. S. G. S. Map, 1923.

Prominent mesa, Navajo Ind. Res., about 21 miles north of Moen-kopi. Named for Sam Preston, Navajo trader. In lat. 36° 25', long. 111° 10'.

Price, Camp	Cochise Co.

Temporary military camp established about 1881, southern end Chiricahua mountains, during campaign against Apache chief Victorio. Named after Lieut. Col. Price, 6th Cavalry.

A temporary camp "in the field," not found on any map. There was a military telegraph office here, for in 1880-81, the author sent and received messages to and from it.

Price	Pinal Co.	U. S. G. S. Map, 1923.

Station, Arizona-Eastern R. R. about 12 miles east of Florence. On Gila river. P. O. established March 18, 1909, Henry Zeuner, P. M.

From two authorities the author has the following. Take your choice.

"So named for the foreman of concrete construction gang, B. S. Price, who worked on the road along here, 1903, under George Tisdale, general contractor." Letter, Dan Williamson, Globe.

"After William Price of Florence, merchant who did considerable business with railroad contractors at the time of building the railroad, 1903." F. N. Pool, Superior.

Prieta	Yavapai Co.	Railroad Maps.

Sp., prieto "dark or black." Station, Phoenix-Ash Fork branch R. R., 9 miles southwest of Prescott, near Iron springs.

Primrose Hill   Pinal Co.

"Near Florence is Primrose Hill, a solitary peak. Poston conceived the idea of building upon it a Temple to the Sun and establishing the Parsee religion. He spent several thousand dollars in constructing a road to the top where he planted a flag, bearing a huge disk upon its ample folds. It is known as "Poston's Folly." Elliott's *History*.

This is undoubtedly Poston Butte, q.v., near Florence. How Elliott came to give it this name "Primrose" is not known.

Professor Creek   Yavapai Co.   Map, Tonto N. F., 1927.

Rises in sec. 8 T. 8 N., R. 5 E. Flows southwest about 4 miles into Lime creek, about 2 miles northeast Rover peak. Unable to learn its meaning although it must have had one.

Promontory Butte   Coconino Co.   Smith Map, 1879; U. S. G. S. Map, 1923.

In T. 11 N., R. 12 E. An outstanding point on "Tonto Rim."
"It has borne this name since very early days. No one seems to know who first used it." Letter, Forest Ranger Croxen, Payson.

Prospect   Cochise Co.   G. L. O. Map, 1892.

Mining camp, east side San Pedro valley above mouth of Turkey creek.
"Some enthusiastic miners had some prospect holes here which gave the name to the short lived camp." Letter, Forest Ranger Medler.

Prospect Canyon   Coconino Co.   U. S. G. S. Map, 1923.

In approximately Ts. 29, 30, 31 N., R. 8 W. East of Colorado river, Hualpai Ind. Res. Franklin French and John Conners of Holbrook once had a prospect hole here. They named it thus; "just to identify it."

Providence Wells   Pima Co.

See Sasabe Flat.

Providence   Yavapai Co.   Bradshaw Mountain Quad, 1903.

In T. 12 N., R. 1 W. Mine on Big Bug creek about 6 miles east of Poland mine near Big Bug mine. P. O. established April 4, 1899, Bradford M. Crawford, P. M.

Pueblo Colorado, Wash and Valley   Navajo and Apache Cos.
                     Gregory Map, 1916; G. L. O., 1921.

Sp., "red village." Near T. 21 N., R. 23 E., Navajo Ind. Res. Rises west side Defiance plateau, Apache county; flows southwest, joins Leroux wash, west of Tanner springs.
Village is an old ruined Tano pueblo of red sandstone. Hence the wash was given this name by pioneers who discovered it.

Pueblo Creek

See Walnut Creek.

Pueblo Viejo   Graham Co.   Smith Map, 1879; G. L. O., 1921.

Sp., "old town." Small Mexican hamlet about 2 miles southeast Safford. So named because of the many "Pre-Columbian" ruins in its vicinity.
Fish says "the first store at this place was started in 1872 by a man named Munson. He later sold the store to I. E. Solomon who moved it a few miles to present site of Solomonville."

Puerco River   Apache and Navajo Co.   Smith Map, 1879;
    U. S. G. S., 1923.

Sp., "dirty, nasty." Because of the character of water; vile smelling and dirty when at "flood" stage. Rises McKinley county, New Mexico, flows southwest, enters Arizona with A. T. & S. F. R. R. at Lupton, joins Little Colorado about 3 miles east of Holbrook. Most of the year is a dry sandy wash. Often called "Rio Puerco of the West" to differentiate it from another Puerco which rises in same vicinity but flows east into Rio Grande.

Puerto Blanco Mountains   Pima Co.   G. L. O. Map, 1921;
    U. S. G. S., 1923.

Sp., "white door or gate." Southeast of Growler mountains, near lat. 32°, long. 113°

Puerto de Bucareli   Coconino Co.

"So named by Garces for the great viceroy by this name. This was the Grand Canyon of the Colorado itself." Coues.

Puerto de Las Mulas   G. L. O. Map, 1892.

See Mule Pass.

Pulerosa River   Graham Co.

This undoubtedly was meant for Tulerosa, but it is spelled as above on early maps. See Camp or Fort Goodwin.

Puntenney   Yavapai Co.   G. L. O. Map, 1921.

In T. 18 N., R. 2 W. Ash Fork-Prescott branch, A. T. & S. F. R. R. Named for George Puntenney, who built first lime kilns here. P. O. established April 26, 1892, under name Puntew (sic). Spelling was mistake of P. O. Department and changed later. George Puntenney, P. M.

Puntew   Yavapai Co.

See Puntenney.

Purcell   Pima Co.

Located south of Purcell mine and named after it. According to local authorities, it was once called Aguajito, "little water." Item, *Tucson Star*.

Purdy   Greenlee Co.

The first name of Duncan, q.v. P. O. established under name Purdy, April 2, 1883, George G. Batchelder, P. M. Post Office record says, "Changed to Duncan, October 11, 1883."

"Purdy was an old timer. Post office was first on east side of Gila. When the railroad came it was moved to west side and named Duncan." Letter, J. H. Brown, Duncan.

Purple Hills   Yuma Co.

These were some mountains close to Colorado river about 40 miles above Yuma and just above "Lighthouse rock." Newberry, Ives' geologist, says: "From their general color this name was given them."

Pusch Ridge   Pima Co.   Map, Coronado N. F., 1927.

In T. 12 S., R. 14 E. Short ridge west of Santa Ritas northeast of Tucson about 10 miles. After Hon. George Pusch, well-known citizen and cattleman of Tucson.

Pyramid Canyon and Peak   Mohave Co.   G. L. O. Map, 1921.

In R. 22 W., on Colorado river about 18 miles north of Mohave City, west side Black range. So named by Lieut. Ives, 1858, who writes: "So called from a natural pyramid of symmetrical proportions, 20 or 30 feet high, near the rapids." Ives' *Report* has pictures of it.

Pyramid Mountain   Navajo Co.   U. S. G. S. Map, 1923.

In T. 23 N., R. 18 E., southwest corner of county. Descriptive name.

Pyramid Peak   Maricopa Co.   U. S. G. S. Map, 1923.

In T. 5 N., R. 2 E. About 2 miles south of Mount Ochoa. Descriptive name.

Pyramid Peak   Yuma Co.   G. L. O. Map, 1921.

In T. 4 N., R. 13 W. West of Little Harqua Halas. Descriptive name.

Quajote   Pinal Co.   G. L. O. Map, 1921; U. S. G. S., 1923.

In T. 9 S., R. 4 E. Village, Papago Ind. Res. The Papago pronunciation is "Koatk." Kino called it "Co-at." The word signifies "a curved hill or other formation." "From 'Ko,' something that curves up. Village is near a curved formation in the Vekol mountains." Father Oblasser. One of several Papago villages involved in Hunter suit again Pueblo of Santa Rosa. See Con Quien.

Quartsite Mountain   Pinal Co.   G. L. O. Map, 1921.

In T. 4 S., R. 18 E. At eastern end Deer Creek basin. After the peculiar ore in a mine near here.

Quartsite Peak   Gila Co.   Map, Crook N. F., 1926.

In T. 2 N., R. 15½ E. About 2 miles east of Ramboz peak. "So called from character of ore in mine."

Quartz King   Yuma Co.   G. L. O. Map, 1909.

Mining camp 3 or 4 miles south of Bill Williams river. P. O. established Oct. 24, 1907, Willard McCune, P. M.

Quartzite Canyon   Apache Co.   Gregory Map, 1916.

On Navajo Ind. Res. Branch of Bonito canyon, near Fort Defiance. Gregory wished to call it "Paquette" for Peter Paquette, local resident. U.S.G.B. first called it Blue canyon, but later changed it to Quartzite due to Gregory's urging that blue was not appropriate to the formation. P. O. established Sept. 19, 1896, George U. Ingersoll, P. M.

Quartzsite (sic)   Yuma Co.

Elevation 900 feet. In T. 4 N., R. 19 W. East of Dome Rock mountains. Early day mining camp and post office near old Ehrenberg-Prescott stage station of Tyson's Wells, q.v. According to N. H. Darton, U.S.G.S.: "The local people wish it spelled Quartzsite." Hi Jolly is buried here in an unmarked grave. Philip Tedro, called "Hi Jolly" by most people, was a Greek, who took the name "Hadj Ali," when converted to Islam. He came to U. S., 1857, with shipment of camels for U. S. government. His name was soon "Americanized" to "Hi Jolly."

When plan for using camels for army packing purposes was abandoned, he turned prospector and spent rest of his life along Colorado river in western Arizona. Died at Quartzsite, Jan. 23, 1903, 75 years old. Decision U.S.G.B. U.S.G.S. map, 1923, spells it Quartsite; *Postal Guide*, 1923, Quartsite.

Quayle   Coconino Co.   Post Route Map, 1924.

Hamlet on Fork of East Clear creek near its head. Coconino N. F. Named for the Quayle family who lived here for several years. P. O. established Oct. 19, 1914, Selma H. Quayle, P. M.

Quebabi   Santa Cruz Co.

An old mission called "Mission Santos Angeles de Guevavi," by Franciscans. Also known as "San Miguel de G"; also "San Rafale de Quevavi." On early Spanish maps is spelled variously: Quebabi, Quevavi, and Guebavi.

In Santa Cruz valley between San Xavier and Nogales, about 10 miles below Tumacacori, near Calabasas. The Apaches raided it, 1769.

Kino says: "On the 27th day of October, 1699, we arrived at Guebavi, where we counted 90 souls." Bolton says: "The ruins of the Quebavi mission were still visible when this spot was visited by the editor a few years ago." Some historians believe it to have been the first mission in Arizona. Also it seems to mark the farthest point north of the Jesuits.

Queen   Pinal Co.

Station on Queen canyon, east of Florence, near Silver City, probably near old Silver Queen mine. Place listed, *Arizona Gazetteer,* 1881, as "Queen City Post Office, 31 miles northeast of Florence and 3 east of Pinal City. At the mouth of Queen creek canyon." P. O. established April 21, 1881. Charles Miller, P. M.

Queen Canyon   Gila Co.   Map, Crook N. F., 1926.

In T. 1. N., R. 11 E. After Silver Queen, first mine located in Pioneer district near Globe. Stream flows southwest and is lost in desert near Higley, Maricopa county. Thompson Arboretum is located on this creek, 4 miles below Superior.

Queen Creek   Maricopa Co.   G. L. O. Map, 1921; P. O. Route, 1929.

Station, Chandler-Magma branch, Arizona-Eastern R. R. After Silver Queen mine. On Queen creek in corner Pinal and Maricopa counties. P. O. established March 21, 1913, Frank Ross, P. M.

Querino   Apache Co.

Station, A. T. & S. F. R. R., about 15 miles west of Arizona State line. Named for Querino canyon, down which railroad runs for several miles. Origin unknown.

Prof. Reginald Fisher, University New Mexico, writes: "Stream which flows through this canyon is known only as the 'Rio Puerco of the West.'" Name shows on maps of early 1860's. However, on maps of 1883 and 1885, stream and canyon are marked Quirini. Again in 1912, is shown as Helena canyon. Helena seems to have disappeared, however, and the canyon is now called Quirino and stream flowing through it "Rio Puerco of the West."

Querino Canyon   Apache Co.   Elliott Map, 1884.

Lies between stations of Allantown and Sanders A. T. & S. F. R. R. in Apache county. Heads in New Mexico and ends about 25 or 30 miles west of Arizona line. See Querino station.

Quien Sabe Peak   Maricopa Co.   Map, Tonto N. F., 1927.

In sec. 14 T. 7 W., R. 5 E. On west side Bronco canyon. "So called after nearby mine by this name." Letter, Joe Hand.

Quijotoa Pima Co. Lumholtz Map, 1920; U. S. G. S., 1923.

In unsurveyed T. 15 S., R. 2 E. Indian village, old mining camp, and range of mountains near lat. 32°, 10′, long. 112°, 20′. Papago Ind Res. The peculiar carrying basket used by the Papagos and Pimas is called a "Kiho" (Key-ho). McClintock says: "One of the ephemeral boom mining camps of Arizona, by the side of a mountain, 'shaped like a carrying basket.' From the Papago word 'kiho' or 'qui-ho,' carrying basket, and toa, mountain. Hence 'Carrying basket' mountain. First locations were made early in 1879." McClintock's story of this camp is well worth reading. Hamilton calls it "Basket mountain."

Original Quijotoa town was divided or added to by sub-divisions called, respectively Virginia, New Virginia, Brooklyn, and Logan. New Virginia was located and surveyed, 1884, by U. Johnson. Quitojoa City, or Allen, after General "Pie" Allen, who had a hotel here; was on west side of mountain.

P. O. established Dec. 11, 1883, Ransome Gibson, P. M.

Quinlan Mountains Pima Co. G. L. O. Map, 1921; U. S. G. S., 1923.

In T. 17 S., R. 7 E. At northeast corner Papago Ind Res. Short range at upper end Baboquivari range. Kitt peak is in this group.

"James Quinlan, for whom these mountains were named, was an early day freighter, known all over Arizona. Born Bangor, Maine, landed in Tucson, 1865. Died, Naco, Ariz., 1892. Named by George Roskruge on his map, 1893."

Quitobac or **Quitovaquito**

See Saint Louis de Vacapa.

Quitobaquito Mountains and Settlement Pima Co. G. L. O. Map, 1921.

In T. 17 S., R. 8 W. Close to Mexican boundary. Decision, U.S.G.B. Hodge, *Hand Book*, spells it Quitovaquito.

Quivero or **Quivera** Coconino Co. G. L. O. Map, 1921.

In sec. 32, T. 25 N., R. 2 E. Station, Grand Canyon branch, A. T. & S. F. R. R., north of Williams. "After a mythical province of Cibola called Quivera." A.G.W. Of Quivera, Hodge says: "An Indian province of which Coronado learned from a plains Indian, a Pawnee known as the 'Turk.' Coronado sought for but never found it. After many siftings, name finally settled on the place known as 'La Gran Quivera' at ruins of a Piro settlement on Rio Grande in New Mexico, where a Franciscan mission was established, 1629. This is in central New Mexico, east of Rio Grande."

Rabbit Pinal Co.

P. O. established Jan. 13, 1893, Hon. Andrew J. Doran, who later ran for Congress, P. M. Doran failed to qualify and office was not opened.

Rabbit Hills Navajo Co.

Range of hills between Cottonwood wash and Leroux fork, on north side Little Colorado. Two or 3 miles north of St. Joseph.

When Beale was journeying along Little Colorado west of present Holbrook, Apr. 4, 1857, his diary has the following:

"San Francisco with its frosty head is in sight this morning. Also the Rabbit Hills to the north. These are curious looking points of considerable height which seem to rise straight up out of the plain." This is all we have as to this name. See Marcou Mesa.

Smith map, 1879, "Rabbit Hills"; G.L.O., 1921, "Marcou Mesa."

Raburnie, Mount	Graham Co.	G. L. O. Map, 1921.

In T. 11 S., R. 31 E. On line between Graham and Greenlee counties. Origin unknown.

Raccoon Creek	Gila Co.	G. L. O. Map, 1921.

South slope Sierra Ancha mountains. U. S. troops had a hard fight on this creek with Apaches, 1872. "This fight was on or near the head of a little stream marked on the maps 'Raccoon Creek,' on south slope of Sierra Ancha. Close by was a huge prehistoric ruin." Bourke.

Radium Hot Springs	Yuma Co.	U. S. G. S. Wellton Quad.

In sec. 12, T. 8 S., R. 18 W. Series of hot springs said to have radium qualities. North side Gila river. Directly north of Wellton station.

Raft River or **Rio de las Balsas**

See Salt river.

Ragged Top	Gila Co.	U. S. G. S. Map, 1923.

Peak, Fort Apache Ind. Res., about 10 miles south of Navajo county line. "This is strictly a descriptive name." Letter, Fred Croxen, Forest Ranger.

Railroad Pass	Cochise Co.	Smith Map, 1879; Eckhoff, 1880.

Elevation 4,291 feet. Lies between Pinaleno mountains on north and Dos Cabezas on south. This is pass now known as Dragoon pass, through which S.P.R.R. runs. So named by Lieut. J. G. Park, 1856, on a survey for a railroad to the coast. See Dragoon Pass and Raso.

Railroad Pass	Mohave Co.

In Cerbat mountains. So named by Ives who thought it would be a practicable railway location. A. T. & S. F. R. R. uses this pass.

"The next day (Mar. 30, 1858), after proceeding one or 2 miles along the pass which was first like a canyon, then a regular pass, we emerged from the Cerbat range. We called it Railroad Pass." Ives. There is a picture of this pass on p. 95 of Ives' *Report*. Hartley map, Arizona, "R. R. Pass."

Railroad Spring	Mohave Co.

See Gentle spring.

Rainbow	Navajo and Apache Cos.	U. S. G. S. Map, 1923.

In Ts. 16, 17 N., Rs. 23, 24 E. Unit of Petrified Forest southeast of Holbrook. So called by early visitors because of the brilliant colors in adjoining hills.

Rain Tank	Coconino Co.	Smith Map, 1879; U. S. G. S., 1923.

In sec. 36, T. 30 N., R. 2 E. On Tusayan N. F. Flood water tank and stock watering place, near Apex Siding, Grand Canyon R. R. Owned by Babbitt Bros., Flagstaff.

Rain Tank Wash   Coconino Co.   Map, Tusayan N. F., 1927.

Heads in sec. 29, T. 29 N., R. 1 E. Near Anita station, Grand Canyon R. R. Flows northeast into Rain Tank. Name given this tank and wash by pioneer stockmen.

Ramah City

Named for the hill where: "The army did despatch their tents by the hill Ramah, and it was that same hill where my father Mormon did show the records unto the Lord." Book of Mormon. See Allen Camp.

Ramanote Peak   Santa Cruz Co.   Map, Coronado N. F., 1927

In sec. 8, T. 23 S., R. 12 E. East side Atasco mountains.

"Ramanote Peak is so called for a Mexican of early days who, so his neighbors said, was unable to tell the ownership of cattle and horses on ranges near his camp. His name was Ramon. The 'ote' was a Spanish suffix meaning big, large, grand, i.e. Big Ramon." Letter, A. S. Wingo, Forest Ranger.

Ramboz Peak   Gila Co.   Map, Crook N. F., 1926.

In sec. 1, T. 1 N., R. 15 E., 6 miles north of Globe. After an early mining man, Henry Ramboz. The name Henry Rambo appears in Hinton's *Handbook*, 1876, covering a recorded mine in Pinal county near Globe.

"Rambo, or Ramboz, came to Arizona in 1875-76 with Billy Ransome. Ramboz is the way his name was spelled when he entered the Pioneers Home in Prescott where he died a few years ago." Letter, Forest Supervisor T. T. Swift.

Ramer Ranch   Gila Co.   U. S. G. S. Map, 1923.

On Tonto N. F. In T. 10½ N., R. 15 E. On Canyon creek, close under rim, on Pleasant valley road. Owned by H. J. Ramer who, about 1887, bought the place from one Andy Cooper, later killed by Sheriff Owens at Holbrook. Originally called Cooper ranch.

Ramsey Peak   Cochise Co.   Map, Coronado N. F., 1925.

In T. 23 S., R. 20 E., on Ramsey Canyon. "Named for Frank Ramsey, pioneer and prospector, who lived in this canyon for many years." Letter, J. B. Williams, Hereford, Arizona.

Ramsgate   Yavapai Co.

Station 6 miles west of Iron Springs, Ash Fork-Phoenix branch, A. T. & S. F. R. R., but not over 2 miles by air line. "Road is very crooked. Like a ram's horn."

Ranch Creek   Gila Co.   Map, San Carlos Apache Ind. Res.

In southern part of T. 3 S., R. 16 E. On San Carlos Ind. Res. Stream rising on north slope Mescal mountains. Flows north into Aliso creek at Gilson's well. So called because of the Hayes ranch, located on west bank near Aliso creek.

Rancheria de San Juan Capistrano

See Sacaton.

Randolph   Pinal Co.   Postal Route Map, 1929.

Station, Arizona-Eastern R. R., about 15 miles north of Picacho. After Col. Epes Randolph, for many years vice-president and general manager of S. P. lines in Arizona. P. O. established July 18, 1925, Channing E. Babbitt, P. M.

Ranegas Plain   Yuma Co.

Near lat. 33° 50′, long. 114°, west side Parker branch, A. T. & S. F. R. R. Bouse wash runs through the plain. Meaning unknown. Smith map, 1879, "Hanegras"; undoubtedly an error. G.L.O., 1892, 1912, 1921, "Ranegras."

Rankin   Pima Co.

Station S. P. R. R., 10 miles east of Tucson. Origin unknown.

Raso   Cochise Co.   G. L. O. Map, 1921; U. S. G. S., 1923.

Sp., "a flat plain." In T. 13 S., R. 25 E., at west end of pass. Flag station established 1881. On S. P. R. R., in Dragoon Pass, 7 miles northeast of Willcox. "This was originally called Railroad Pass, shortened to Glade in 1903, and about 1910 again changed to Raso to save telegraphing." Letter, W. T. Brinley, Agt., S. P. R. R.

Rattle Snake Basin   Greenlee Co.   Map, Crook N. F., 1926.

In T. 9 S., R. 29 E. Under Mogollon Rim. "So named by Tolles Cosper, local cattleman, who states that many years ago while camped here he and a companion killed 60 or 70 rattlesnakes in one week." Letter, Rex King, Supervisor, Crook N. F.

Rattlesnake Canyon   Yavapai Co.   Map, Coconino N. F., 1928.

Rises north of Stoneman's lake, runs southwest of Woods canyon in sec. 16, T. 16 N., R. 6 E. See Rattlesnake Tanks.

Rattlesnake Creek   Graham Co.   Map, Crook N. F., 1926.

Stream rising Galiuro mountains, flows northeast into Aravaipa creek in sec. 25, T. 7 S., R. 21 E.

"The usual story of rattlesnakes having been plentiful. There are a number of very old graves said to be of soldiers, in a side canyon of Rattlesnake, but nobody knows who they were or when they died. It was in Rattlesnake that the Powers boy killed three peace officers in 1916." Letter, Rex King, Forest Supervisor.

Rattlesnake Tanks   Yavapai Co.   G. L. O. Map, 1921.

In sec. 17, T. 16 N., R. 7 E. "Formerly called Updyke Tanks for Geo. Updyke, pioneer. Later a party camped in the canyon above this tank killed several rattlesnakes. Then began to be called Rattlesnake tanks and canyon, and name Updyke gradually fell into disuse." Was called Rattlesnake Tank when the author camped on it, 1885.

Raven Butte   Yuma Co.

North end Tinajas Altas mountains, 20 miles south of Wellton station, S. P. R. R. Ravens (corvus) are plentiful in this region. Of them Hornaday says: "The ravens that flocked round us were so tame and trustful. We were not willing to kill even one for a specimen."

Rawhide Mountains and Village   Mohave Co.   U. S. G. S. Map, 1923.

In T. 11 N., R. 14 W. North of Bill Williams river. Anson Smith says: "The mountain was so called because it was so exceedingly rough and ragged. The mine was named for the mountain."

Tucson Star, July 2, 1909, says: "This camp lies between Harcuvar mountains and Colorado river. Was opened, 1879, by Bill Hearts. Ore was called 'petanque.' It was native silver combined with copper. A furnace was built on the Big Sandy 7 miles away. Coke was hauled from Maricopa. Ore was packed out of mine on backs of Mexican miners. Then the Calico mines opened and every one left."

Rawhide Mountain   Pinal Co.   Map, Crook N. F., 1927.

In sec. 36, T. 4 S., R. 19 E., south end Mescal range, on boundary between Graham and Pinal counties. After an old Mexican goat herder who wore rawhide "teguas," (Sp. "shoes, sandals") and lived like a miser. Slept on a rawhide.

Sometimes called Hobson mountain for Lieut. Hobson of Spanish War fame. Decision U.S.G.B. "Rawhide."

Rawlins Camp   Yavapai Co.   Smith Map, 1879; Elliott, 1884.

Sub-post, Whipple Barracks, about 1870. In Williamson valley about 27 miles northwest of Prescott, on old road, Hardyville to Prescott. Located east of Aztec Pass, east side Santa Marias. About 17 miles southeast of Camp Hualpai.

Heitman's *List* says: "Established Feb., 1870—abandoned Sept. of same year. After Gen. Rawlins of Civil War fame."

Ray   Pinal Co.   G. L. O. Map, 1921.

Elevation 2,100 feet. Station, Phoenix-Christmas branch, Arizona-Eastern R. R. Seven miles north of Ray Junction. "A man named Bullinger named a mine for his sister, Ray, in 1870. The town took its name from the mine. He also named a copper camp a few miles up Copper Creek for another sister, Esperanza." The Ray Copper Co. was organized, 1882. Not on early maps. P. O. established Sept. 8, 1899, Charles R. Clanberg, P. M.

Ray Junction   Pinal Co.   G. L. O. Map, 1909.

Station Arizona-Eastern R. R. where branch line goes up to Ray mine. Town and postoffice, however, both called Kelvin, q.v.

Reamer Draw   Yavapai Co.   Map, Prescott N. F., 1927.

Rises in sec. 6, T. 13 N., R. 4 E. Flows south into Spring creek. See Reamer peak for origin.

Reamer (sic) Peak   Yavapai Co.   Map, Prescott N. F., 1927.

In sec. 1, T. 12 N., R. 3 E. After well-known local stockman, Gus Reamer or Reimer, who grazed sheep in this vicinity for many years. Spelled as above on maps. Official records at Phoenix show that he spelled his name Reemer in his letters.

Reavis   Maricopa Co.

See Reevis.

Red Butte   Coconino Co.   Map, Tusayan N. F., 1927.

Elevation 7,600 feet, in T. 28 N., R. 3 E. Southeast Anita station Grand Canyon R. R. Brilliant red sandstone peak.

"To our right in solitary stateliness rises 'Red Butte' which the Havasupais call Hue-ga-da-wi-za or 'the mountain of the clenched fist.' " James, *Around the Grand Canyon.* See Red mountain.

Coues locates this and says: "Its former and probably earliest name was Mt. Thorburn, given it by Beale for a member of his party, Lieut. C. E. Thorburn, U. S. Navy, Sept. 15, 1857." On north side Red House Wash. See Thorburn.

Red Butte   Yavapai Co.   Map, Tusayan N. F., 1927.

Elevation 4,563 feet. In sec. 16, T. 18 N., R. 1 E. West side Verde valley R. R., about 2 miles north Verde river. One of several outstanding red sandstone buttes common in this region.

Red Butte   Yavapai Co.   G. L. O. Map, 1921.

Southwest corner Baca Grant southern end Mohon mountains. "Purely a descriptive name."

Red Hill   Coconino Co.   G. L. O. Map, 1921; Tusayan N. F., 1927.

Elevation 7,750 feet. West of Slate mountain in T. 24 N., R. 4 E. Descriptive name. See Red mountain.

Red Horse Wash   Coconino Co.   Map, Tusayan N. F., 1927.

Dry wash, rising in north part of T. 29 N., R. 3 E. Flows south and west into Cataract creek, 6 miles west of Anita.

Coues thinks Garces camped on this wash in July, 1776. He says: "Garces called this water hole 'Pozo de Santa Isabel.'"

Redington   Pima Co.   U. S. G. S. Map, 1923.

In T. 11 S., R. 18 E. On east slope Santa Catalinas, on San Pedro river. Early ranch and post office.

"Named after two brothers, Henry and Lem Redfield, who located here, 1875. Lem was hung by a mob at Florence, 1883, for alleged part in a stage robbery and killing. They wanted a post office, but could not get Redfield so coined the word 'Redington.'" Letter, Fred W. Lattin. P. O. established Oct. 7, 1879, Henry F. Redfield, P. M. Spelled Reddington on some maps.

Red Lake   Coconino Co.   G. L. O. Map, 1921.

In T. 23 N., R. 2 E. Station Grand Canyon branch A. T. & S. F. R. R. North of Williams. "There is a large dry lake at this point where a number of dry farmers alternately starve and exist. The soil is very red." P. O. established June 16, 1888, Adah F. Stone, P. M.

Red Lake   Coconino Co.   U. S. G. S. Map, 1923.

On Navajo Ind. Res. Near Wild Cat peak.

Red Lake   Mohave Co.   U. S. G. S. Map, 1923.

Large "dry lake" west of Grand Wash cliffs in Ts. 26, 27 N., Rs. 16, 17 W.

Redlands   Graham Co.   Map, Tonto N. F., 1926.

According to McClintock this was an early name for Ashurst, q.v.

Redman (sic) **Mesa** (Redmond)   Gila Co.

In sec. 22, T. 7 N., R. 12 E. After Joe Redmond who ran "J.R." cattle brand here for many years. According to Bud Armer it should be spelled "Redmond."

Red Mountain   Coconino Co.   Map, Tusayan N. F., 1927.

In T. 25 N., R. 5 E. Not to be confused with Red hill, about 6 miles northeast; or Red butte, southeast of Anita station Grand Canyon R. R., north side Red Horse wash. We thus have in this immediate vicinity Red hill, Red mountain, Red butte, all somewhat alike in color and general appearance and very near the same height.

Red Mountain   Greenlee Co.   Map, Crook N. F., 1926.

In T. 3 S., R. 28 E., Coronado ridge. About 5 miles northwest of Metcalf. From color of its top. There is another peak by this name not far from here in T. 1 N., R. 30 E.

Red Mountain   Greenlee Co.   G. L. O. Map, 1921; Crook N. F., 1926.

Elevation 8,174 feet. In sec. 7, T. 1 N., R. 30 E. There is another peak by this name a few miles distant in T. 3 S., R. 28 E.

Red Mountain   Santa Cruz Co.   G. L. O. Map, 1923;
Coronado N. F., 1927.

Elevation 6,350 feet. In T. 22 S., R. 16 E., about 6 miles southeast Patagonia.

Redmond Mesa

See Redman.

Red Peak   Greenlee Co.

See Rose peak.

Red Rock Country   Yavapai Co.   G. L. O. Map, 1921.

Rough broken region covering more than a township on east side Chino valley. Rocks are red in color, hence the name. James says: "The cowboys call this country 'Hells Hollow.'"

Red Rock   Yavapai Co.

P. O. established as Red Rock Nov. 28, 1879, Amos C. Stedman, P. M. Not on any map.

Redrock (sic)   Pinal Co.   G. L. O. Map, 1921.

Station S. P. R. R., 33 miles west of Tucson. Established about 1881. Named for prominent red butte nearby. P. O. established Nov. 30, 1895, Mrs. Catherine E. Langhorne P. M.

Red Rock   Apache Co.   U. S. G. S. Map, 1923.

Short valley Navajo Ind. Res. Opening into New Mexico near State line in T. 10 N., R. 6 W. "There is a huge red sand stone peak in center of this valley."

Red Top Mountain   Navajo Co.   G. L. O. Map, 1921.

In T. 9 N., R. 20 E., on Fort Apache Ind. Res. near head of Hop canyon. A fork of Carrizo creek. "The top strata of this mountain is a brilliant red sand stone."

Reef   Cochise Co.   Judge Map, 1896.

Southwest corner of county close to Mexican line. Named for a conspicuous reef of rock, a noted landmark. Mining camp in Huachuca mountains. Later called Palmerlee, q.v. P. O. established Jan. 7, 1901, Mark Walker, P. M.

Reevis Ranch (Reavis)   Maricopa Co.   Map, Tonto N. F., 1927.

In sec. 19, T. 2 N., R. 12 E. Now called Pineair. Once owned for many years by a hermit recluse named E. A. Reavis. Generally spelled Reevis on maps. He often came to Mesa, where his long beard, hair hanging to his shoulders and a long rifle he always carried, made him an object of curiosity. Little is known of his history. He was called the "Hermit of the Superstitions," although his place was not in the Superstition mountains but several miles to east. About Apr. 20, 1896, his dead body was found near his home. Why, or by whom killed, was never discovered. His two burros were found tied to a tree near by perishing from hunger and thirst. Clemens Cattle Co. now owns the place.

Reidhead   Navajo Co.

Ranch and stopping place in early Eighties. On stage road to Horsehead crossing and Holbrook. Crossing marked by a large lone pine. About 12 miles south of Snowflake where Apache road crossed Showlow creek. John Reidhead, a Mormon, settled here 1878, where he lived until 1883. The author camped with him,

1882, on his way to Holbrook. Reidhead bought the claim from a man named Woolf who in turn got it from an unknown Mexican. On June 1, 1882, Apaches killed a freighter named Nathan B. Robinson at this place. The author's recollection is that it was done for robbery and was not an outbreak. Also called Woolfs Crossing. Also Lone Pine.

Reileys (sic) **Mountain, Canyon, and Ranch**   Cochise Co.
                                        Elliott Map, 1896, "Reileys Ranch."

In T. 12 S., R. 22 E., in Winchester mountains. Canyon heads at mountain, flows northeast and is lost in western side Sulphur Springs valley. "These three points are all named after an old timer known as 'Well-digger Riley' who located there in early days." Letter, E. G. Mettler, Forest Ranger. This is spelled Rilay on map, Crook N. F., which is doubtless an error as there is no local record of any one by that name.

Reliable   Yavapai Co.   G. L. O. Map, 1892.

Prescott N. F. Mining camp 6 miles south of Mayer, in Bradshaw mountains. "There was a mine here named 'Old Reliable' which gave the camp its name." P. O. established May 13, 1890, Margaret C. Liston, P. M.

Reno, Camp   Maricopa Co.   Smith Map, 1879; G. L. O., 1921.

An out post of Fort McDowell 1866-1868. On Tonto creek near Reno mountain. East side Mazatzal range. Named for Gen. Marcus A. Reno. P. O. established as Reno Oct. 20, 1880, Isaac R. Prather, P. M.

Reno Creek   Gila Co.   Map, Tonto N. F., 1927.

Western side Tonto Basin. Stream coming out of Reno pass, east side of Mazatzals. Old Fort Reno was built on this creek which enters Tonto creek where postoffice of Tonto Basin is located. Reno Ranger Station also located here. In T. 6 N., R. 10 E.

Reno, Mount   Gila Co.   G. L. O. Map, 1921.

In T. 7 N., R. 10 E. Eastern side Mazatzal mountains. After Gen. Marcus A. Reno, Civil War Commander. On Tonto N. F. map this peak shows as Parker butte but is placed on east side of Tonto creek. This map has no Reno mountain. See Parker. Undoubtedly Reno and Parker are for the same mountain.

Reno Pass   Gila Co.   G. L. O. Map, 1921; Tonto N. F., 1927.

Elevation 4,724 feet. In sec. 11, T. 6 N., R. 9 E., on crest of Mazatzal range between Mount Ord on north and Edwards peak on south. Named after Camp Reno. "The old military road over this pass called the Reno road, built originally by U. S. troops, was one of the roughest and most difficult bits of road in all Arizona. Its way was strewn with wrecks of old wagons. It was built in 1863 at a huge cost in money and labor but it gave the troops a wagon crossing into Tonto Basin. Rebuilt, 1877, by Maricopa county with King Woolsey, John Y. T. Smith and Jerome Barton as county commissioners."

Reppy   Gila Co.   R. R. Maps.

Station, Globe division Arizona-Eastern R. R., about 14 miles east of Globe. After Charles Reppy, early editor of Florence *Enterprise.* Member State Legislature, well known local politician.

Reservation Creek   Apache Co.   Map, Fort Apache Ind. Res., 1928.

Stream rising southeast side Mount Thomas; flows almost due south, enters Black river in Apache county, in T. 27½ N., R. 27 E. On an old military map, 1864, shows as Rio Nutrioso, which causes one to wonder if the story about Nutrioso creek farther north is altogether reliable.

Revanton   Santa Cruz Co.

Revanton ranch according to Coues is about 40 miles south of Tucson. Is now a ruin. Settlement made shortly after Gadsden Purchase. Mrs. Bogan says it was the fortified ranch of William Rhodes.

Under date of Santa Fe, N. M., Nov. 3, 1877, Elias Brevort, who was an army post sutler, writes: "I went from here in 1856 as sutler for the U. S. troops ordered to establish a military post on Gadsden Purchase. About 1859, I sold my sutlership and went to reside at Revanton."

J. Ross Browne, 1863, says: "The Revanton, about 40 miles south of Tucson, was once owned by Elias Breevort who built a fine adobe house at the crossing of the river. This palatial edifice is perhaps the largest and most imposing private residence in Arizona; $16,000 was spent in the building and improvements."

Hinton, 1877, says: "The Revanton is now a ruin. Revanton is (Kitchen's Ranch) also known as 'El Potrero.'" He writes as if they were one and the same thing. All the maps however show Kitchen's as below old Fort Mason, near Calabasas.

This place shows as Revanton on a map of New Mexico dated 1854. The Hacienda del Revanton was not a Spanish grant but was held by preemptions under the U. S. laws. It has been impossible to determine origin of this name. It is on Rand McNally's map, 1877, as El Riverton, but on most maps it is Revanton and sometimes El Revanton. See Kitchens ranch.

Reward   Pinal Co.   G. L. O. Map, 1921.

In T. 9 S., R. 3 E. Mine in Vekol mountains, Papago Ind. Res. "The miners who discovered and developed this mine so called it for a mine here."

Reymert   Pinal Co.   G. L. O. Map, 1921.

Lower end Superstition mountains. Named for Reymert mines, located here, by J. D. Reymert. About 12 miles southeast of Pinal. Reymert was a lawyer and newspaper man. He ran the *Pinal Drill*, 1881. Listed *Arizona Gazetteer*, 1881, as "J. DeNoon Reymert, editor and publisher *Pinal Drill.*" P. O. established June 6, 1894, Thomas P. Carson, P. M.

Reynolds Creek   Gila Co.   Map, Tonto N. F., 1927.

Rises Sierra Ancha mountains; flows northwest into Salome creek near Greenback peak, in T. 6 N., R. 12 E.

"After Glenn Reynolds, early Apache county cattleman; later sheriff Gila county. Killed by Indians Nov. 2, 1889, while taking the 'Apache Kid' and several other Apache prisoners to Alcatraz Island, Calif. Reynolds built first log house on this stream." See Tanner springs.

Rhoades   Coconino Co.   G. L. O. Map, 1909.

Early station, A. T. & S. F. R. R., near present town of Maine. "Meaning or origin cannot be learned." A.G.W. P. O. established Apr. 26, 1898, William D. Bliss, P. M.

Rhodes Ranch   Pima Co.

"About 18 miles from Tubac on road to Tucson. Owned by William Rhodes, an American ranchero." J. Ross Browne.

Browne also visited Mohave county, 1866, and writes of Rhodes ranch as extending some 16 miles along east bank of Colorado above "The Barriers" which were some rapids in the river about half way between Yuma and La Paz.

"Rhodes was drowned in the Colorado near La Paz while crossing it when at full flood." *Arizona Sentinel*, Apr. 29, 1870.

See Revanton, which at times was called Rhodes ranch.

Poston says: "Wm. H. Rhodes came to Arizona from Kentucky in 1855 and settled first at Sopori and went to raising cattle."

On Smith map, 1879, about 5 miles north of Revanton.

Rice   Gila Co.   G. L. O. Map, 1921.

On Aliso creek at junction with San Carlos river. U. S. Indian School located here on San Carlos Apache Ind. Res. "So named after Lieut. Sedgwick Rice, 23rd. U. S. Infantry, who, in 1873 had charge of one of the first bands of hostile Apaches brought to the reservation." Bourke. Station, Arizona-Eastern R. R. here is also called Rice. Was first called Talklai, q.v.

"In 1880, and earlier, Rice was known as the 'Twelve Mile Post'; 12 miles from Globe on Globe-Willcox road. There was then a white sign attached to a telegraph post here, reading, '12 miles to Globe.'" Letter, Charles M. Clark, Phoenix.

On Sept. 1, 1930, name was again changed to San Carlos, a most unfortunate and unsatisfactory official trifling with well established names. See Talklai. P. O. established as Rice Sept. 7, 1907, James H. Stevans, P. M.

Rice, Mount   Pima Co.   Map, Coronado N. F., 1927.

In T. 16 E., R. 10 S. Named for Gen. Rice of Iowa, in early days interested in some mines on north side of Catalinas. On boundary line Pima and Pinal counties.

Richards Lake   Navajo Co.   U. S. G. S. Map, 1923.

Crater or "sink hole," into which a local cattleman, J. W. Richards "Billie Saint Joe" about 1902, led flood waters from Black canyon forming a good sized lake or tank. About 5 miles east of Chevellons Fork, near the "Potato Field," q.v.

Richey   Apache Co.   U. S. G. S. St. Johns Sheet.

Originally called Walnut Grove, q.v. About 12 miles south of Springerville. Also known as Richville, q.v. Named for Joseph B. Richey early settler here.

Rich Hill   Yavapai Co.

In T. 10 N., R. 4 W. About 4 miles northeast of Stanton at head Weaver creek. So named by a Mexican with Peeples' party, 1863, who discovered rich gold deposits on this hill. It is claimed that in 1862-63 over $500,000 in gold nuggets was taken from a single acre of the summit of this hill. Later workers probably took out as much more during the following years. In Oct., 1890, William Johnson, a miner, was buried alive here by a cave-in and could not be rescued. Body was left in mine.

Richinbar   Yavapai Co.   G. L. O. Map, 1921.

In T. 10 N., R. 2 E. Mine on Agua Fria river. About 4 miles east Bumble Bee station.

"This mine was located in early days by a man named Zika, who named it Richinbar; coined from Rich Bar." Letter, W. J. Martin, P. M. P. O. established July 30, 1896, John A. Webb, P. M.

Richmond Basin   Pinal Co.

Early day mining camp, 12 miles north of Globe. Globe *Silver Belt*, May 16, 1878, tells about the fine mines located there, mostly silver mines.

Bancroft says: "This basin was remarkably rich having yielded over $100,000 in nuggets picked up on the surface."

"It was so named after the Richmond mine in the basin, one of the first to be located here." Letter, Dan Williamson, Globe. See Nugget.

Richville   Apache Co.

Small Mormon hamlet settled by a family named Richey. P. O. established June 23, 1892, William H. Sherwood, P. M. First called Walnut Grove from the walnut trees found here, and at one time, Richey, q.v.

Rickerson, Fort   Coconino Co.

On Coconino N. F. Said by McClintock to have been an early name for Fort Moroni, q.v. (Fort Valley) about 7 miles from Flagstaff. He says: "the name was given by the manager of the Arizona Cattle Co., Capt. Bulwinkle, in honor of the treasurer of that company, Charles L. Rickerson, of Chicago." See Moroni and Fort Valley.

Riego Valley

See Ranegras Plain.

Rigg, Camp   Graham Co.

McClintock says: "This was a temporary camp on San Carlos river." King Woolsey in his report to Governor Goodwin, Aug. 28, 1864, says: "I had gone to Camp Rigg, 40 miles from Goodwin, to hurry up supplies. Camp was on the Gila, about 3 miles above Fort Goodwin. I reported to Col. Edwin A. Rigg, First California Infantry." Woolsey was then somewhere between what he called Fort Goodwin and Signal mountain. He says: "The next day we marched to old Camp Pinal in a day and a half."

Impossible to locate this post any closer. It does not show on any map and was probably a temporary scouting camp out from Goodwin. Not in any list of military posts.

The G.L.O. map, 1866, shows this post on San Carlos river, a short distance above Goodwin. See Camp Goodwin.

Rilay Mountain and Creek   Cochise Co.

See Reileys ranch, mountain and canyon.

Rillito   Pima Co.   G. L. O. Map, 1921.

Sp., "small stream." Station, S. P. R. R., 17 miles west of Tucson, near Santa Cruz river. After stream by this name, which enters Santa Cruz, about 6 miles east of station. P. O. established July 13, 1905, Catharine E. Langhorne, P. M. P. O. changed to Langhorne, Apr. 21, 1908.

Rillito Creek   Pima Co.   Smith Map, 1879;
                              G. L. O. Map, 1892; U. S. G. S., 1923.

Sp., "a little creek." Dry wash heading in Tanque Verde mountains. Flows northwest into Santa Cruz river in T. 13 S., R. 13 E., near Jaynes station, S. P. R. R. Pronounced "ree-yee-toe."

Rim, The

See Black mesa.

Rimrock   Yavapai Co.

"Ranch and station about 12 miles southeast Cornville, on Beaver creek. There is a long and rather high rim rock along Beaver creek from which it gets its name." Letter, Ella I. Loudermilk, P. M.

Rincon Creek   Pima Co.

On Coronado N. F. Rises north side Rincon peak. Flows west into Pantano wash in T. 15 S., R. 16 E. Sp., "a corner—a nook."

Rincon Peak   Pima Co.   U. S. G. S. Map, 1923;
                                                Coronado N. F., 1927.

Elevation 8,465 feet. In Rincon mountains, southeast of Tucson.

Rincon Mountains   Pima Co.   Eckhoff Map, 1880;
                                                       G. L. O., 1921.

On Coronado N. F. Fifteen miles southeast of Tucson, north of Pantano. On some early maps they appear as "Sierra El Rincon."

Rincon Valley   Pima Co.   Smith Map, 1879, "El Rincon";
                                                U. S. G. S., 1923.

Fairly level valley, opening on to desert from west slope Rincon mountains, about 18 miles southeast of Tucson, on Pantano wash.

Rio de Flag

See River de Flag.

Rio de las Balsas

See Salt river.

Rio de Lino

See Little Colorado river.

Rio de los Apostoles

See Apostoles.

Rio Jabesua

See Havasu canyon.

Rio Puerco of the West   Apache Co.

See Puerco river.

Rio de Santa Maria

See Santa Cruz river.

Riordan   Coconino Co.   G. L. O. Map, 1921.

On Coconino N. F. Station A. T. & S. F. R. R., 6 miles west of Flagstaff. Named for D. M. Riordan, who, with his brothers, built large saw mills at Flagstaff, and also branch logging railroad extending south. D. M. Riordan first came west as U. S. Indian Agent for the Navajos at Fort Defiance, 1880 to 1884.

Rio San Domingo

See Goodwin wash.

Rioville   Clarke County, Nevada   G. L. O. Map, 1923.

One of early settlements in Pah Ute county when that region was part of Arizona Territory. First called Junction City because at junction of Virgin and Colorado rivers.

Ripsey Hill   Pinal Co.   Ray Quad., 1910; G. L. O. Map, 1921;
Crook N. F., 1926.

Elevation 3,973 · feet. Upper end Tortilla mountains, mine, ranch, spring, and wash, in southwest corner T. 4 S., R. 14 E. Wash heads near mine and enters the Gila in sec. 10, T. 4 S., R. 13 E. Ranch is a few miles south of old Florence wagon road. Takes the name from Ripsey family who ran cattle here for many years.

Rita (sic)   Pima Co.   Railroad Folders.

Station E. P. & S. W. R. R., about 14 miles east of Tucson.

River de Flag   Coconino Co.   Map, Tusayan N. F., 1927.

On Coconino N. F. Local name for stream flowing through Flagstaff. Carries a huge body of water in times of melting snows or summer rains.

Rises in T. 22 N., R. 6 E. Near Leroux Springs. Flows southeasterly round city, entering San Francisco wash east of Flagstaff near Turkey Tanks in T. 22 N., R. 10 E. Frequently called "Rio de Flag."

Rivera   Pinal Co.

Station north bank of Gila where road crosses that stream. So called for its location.

Riverside   Pinal Co.   Smith Map, 1879; G. L. O., 1892.

On Gila river about 30 miles east of Florence. "It was by the side of the Gila river." P. O. established Oct. 17, 1877, Charles D. Putnam, P. M.

Robbins Butte   Maricopa Co.   G. L. O. Map, 1921; U. S. G. S., 1923.

Should be Roberts butte, q.v.

Roberts Butte   Maricopa Co.

In T. 1 S., R. 4 W. Prominent butte about 6 miles west of Buckeye, south side Gila river, north of Buckeye hills. This butte appears on Hamilton map, 1866, G.L.O., 1921, and U.S.G.S., 1923, as Robbins Butte, q.v.

"It was named for J. W. Roberts, one of the pioneer farmers of the Buckeye district, who was the nearest settler. It has been so called since 1885. He homesteaded at the foot of butte in 1885." Letter, P. M., Buckeye. Decision U.S.G.B.

Roberts Cienega   Cochise Co.

"In Sulphur Springs valley 6 miles from mouth of West Turkey creek canyon." *Tombstone.*

It was always the author's understanding this was named after Lieut. Col. Roberts, one of Gen. Crook's aides, 1870-1873.

Roberts Mesa and Draw   Gila Co.   Map, Tonto N. F., 1926.

In sec. 29, T. 11½ N., R. 11½ E. In upper Tonto Basin. "Named after Jim Roberts, who once had a ranch under the mesa. Roberts was concerned in Pleasant Valley war. In 1928, when 72 years old, and Deputy Sheriff in Clarkdale, he shot and killed a bank robber, escaping in a fast moving auto. Ranch is now owned and lived on by Zane Grey, the writer." F. W. Croxen, Forest Ranger.

Robinson   Cochise Co.

See Pomerene.

Robinson Crater   Coconino Co.

Near sec. 9, T. 23 N., R. 8 E., one-half mile southwest of O'Leary peak. Coconino N. F. Named for Henry H. Robinson, U.S.G.S., 1873-1925. His book *San Franciscan Volcanic Field* is the leading source of information regarding craters in this region. Decision U.S.G.B.

Roblas Butte   Pinal Co.   Map, Crook N. F., 1926.

In T. 1 S., R. 11 E. "Many years ago a Mexican by this name, Robles or Roblas, had a ranch on eastern side this butte." Letter, Roy Painter, Forest Ranger.

Robles   Pima Co.   Hornaday Map; G. L. O., 1921.

Ranch and pass east side of Roskruge mountains, about 20 miles southwest of Tucson. "Mr. Robles was at home and let us water our horses and burn up two camp fires of his wood, all for the moderate price of 50 cents." Hornaday, *Desert and Lava.*

Letter in Pioneer Library, Tucson says: "This was the ranch of B. Robles, a well known stage man, operating between Tucson and Quijotoa."

Rock Butte   Pinal Co.   G. L. O. Map, 1921.

In T. 3 S., R. 7 E., eastern end Malpais hills, north side Gila river.

Rock Buttes   Yavapai Co.   G. L. O. Map, 1921.

Two outstanding buttes near mouth Hell canyon, east of Prescott branch, A. T. & S. F. R. R. Railroad station here in T. 2 W., R. 20 N., is also called Rock buttes.

Rock Creek   Gila Co.   Map, Tonto N. F., 1927.

In sec. 15, T. 9 N., R. 15 E. Small stream near Nail ranch. Flows southeast into Canyon creek, Fort Apache Ind. Res. On Fire Control map, Fort Apache Ind. Res., 1927, this is Rock canyon.

Rockfellow Dome   Cochise Co.   Map, Coronado N. F.

Elevation 6,542 feet. In T. 17 S., R. 23 E. In Dragoon mountains at eastern entrance to Cochise Stronghold. After J. A. Rockfellow, mining engineer and pioneer.

Rockhorse Canyon   Gila Co.

See Rock House.

Rock House Creek and Canyon   Gila and Coconino Cos.
Map, Tonto N. F., 1927.

In T. 7 N., R. 15 E. Stream and canyon rising on Tonto N. F., about one mile southeast Castle peak. Flows southeast, enters Fort Apache Ind. Res., and joins Canyon creek in T. 6 N., R. 16 E.

"So called from an old stone or rock cabin located near head of creek. Is also called Tank House creek, Rock Tank canyon, and Rock House canyon; but the above is correct name according to all old timers." Letter, T. T. Swift, Forest Supervisor.

Rockhouse Mountain   Pinal Co.   G. L. O. Map, 1921;
                                                U. S. G. S., 1923.

In T. 4 S., R. 18 E. At lower end Mescal mountains, south of Gila river. "There was a rock house at foot of this mountain in early days." Letter, P. M., Christmas.

Rockinstraw Mountain   Gila Co.   Map, Crook N. F., 1926.

In sec. 21, T. 3 N., R. 15 E. About 15 miles north of Globe. "After a one-armed German, an early settler, who farmed in the Horse Shoe bend of Salt river a few miles from the mountain. Later lived between Globe and Miami. He spelled his name Rockenstrough." Letter, Rex King, Safford.

Rock Point   Apache Co.   Map, Navajo Ind. Res.;
                                        Postal Route, 1929.

Indian trading post in northeast part of State, about 15 miles west of Lukachukai mountains. On Lukachukai creek. Navajo Ind. Res. P. O. established June 16, 1916, Raymond C. Dunn, P. M.

Rock Tank Canyon   Gila Co.

See Rock House.

Rock Top Mountain   Coconino Co.   G. L. O. Map, 1921.

In T. 17 N., R. 8 E. On Coconino N. F., near head Dry Beaver creek. Descriptive name.

Rocky Butte   Mohave Co.   G. L. O. Map, 1921.

In T. 25 N., R. 13 W. On boundary Hualpai Ind. Res.

Roden Spring   Coconino Co.   G. L. O. Map, 1921;
                                            Coconino N. F., 1927.

In T. 24 N., R. 10 E., about 5 miles west of Little Colorado river. Fine spring owned by William Roden, headquarters for his cattle operations in early Eighties.

Roderick Mountain   Pima Co.

See Fraguita.

Rogers Lake   Coconino Co.   G. L. O. Map, 1921;
                                            Coconino N. F., 1927.

In southwest corner T. 21 N., R. 6 E. An artificial lake created by Charles T. Rogers, early-day cattleman of Williams, 1880-1890, who ran the 111 brand in this vicinity for many years. One of the first dams built by stockmen on this range to impound stock water.

Rok   Yavapai Co.   R. R. Folders.

Station Ash Fork-Phoenix branch A. T. & S. F. R. R. 16 miles south Ash Fork. "It is near Rock butte and named after that point, but shortened to save telegraphing." A.G.W.

Roll   Yuma Co.   Postal Map, 1929.

Railroad station Buckeye branch S. P. R. R. About 11 miles northeast of Wellton. "Named for John H. Roll, who had a homestead nearby." P. O. established Nov. 3, 1926, John H. Roll, P. M.

Rolles

See Polles mesa.

Rollintown   Pima Co.   Roskruge Map, 1893.

Village on old Crittenden military reservation. There was a mine and smelter here built and owned by R. R. Richardson. Town was about 2½ miles distant from Fort Crittenden. Was named Rollin after the mine superintendent.

Roods Ranch   Santa Cruz Co.

In a letter to Farish, Col. Poston calls this the "William B. Roods ranch." See Rhodes, also Revanton.

Roof Butte   Apache Co.   G. L. O. Map, 1921.

Navajo Ind. Res. Elevation 9,575 feet. North end Tunicha mountains, near New Mexico line. Descriptive name.

Roosevelt   Gila Co.   Map, Tonto N. F., 1927.

Town, south side Roosevelt lake. First located on Salt river at entrance to canyon in which dam was built. With the rise of water, town was moved to higher ground. P. O. established July 22, 1904, William A. Thompson, P. M.

Roosevelt Lake and Dam   Gila Co.   Map, Tonto N. F., 1927.

Lake created by Roosevelt dam, erected to impound waters of Salt river and Tonto creek to irrigate land in Salt River Valley. Dedicated by Theodore Roosevelt, Mar. 18, 1911.

"First stone laid Sept. 20, 1906. Cap stone placed 284 feet above it Feb. 6, 1911. Every stone used was washed as clean as a new button before being set in place."

Rose Creek   Gila Co.   Map, Tonto N. F., 1927.

Stream rising east side Armer mountain. Flows into Salome creek east of Greyback peak. In Tonto Basin. After Al Rose, killed in Pleasant Valley War, Oct., 1887. Rose, an old timer, was one of the Graham faction. Bud Armer says it was first called Connor canyon or creek after old Sam Connor, first man to locate on the creek.

Rosemont   Pima Co.   U. S. G. S. Map, 1923; Coronado N. F., 1927.

T. 18 S., R. 16 E. Settlement and mining camp. "For L. J. Rose, who came to this region about 1896 from California; bought the McCleary group of mines and sank a fortune in them. Born in Scotland; came to U. S. a boy of 16. Raised and raced the celebrated stallion, 'Stamboul.' Died in Los Angeles about 1915." Letter, Carl Scholefield, Forest Ranger, Globe. P. O. established Sept. 27, 1891, William B. Cleary, P. M.

Rose Peak   Greenlee Co.   G. L. O. Map, 1892; Apache N. F., 1927.

In northwest corner T. 1 N., R. 29 E. "So called because of the presence on its north slope of large quantities of wild roses, which attracted attention of early settlers." Letter, Rex King. On some old maps shows as Red peak.

Roskruge Mountains   Pima Co.   U. S. G. S. Map, 1923.

In T. 13 S., Rs. 8, 9 E. On Papago Ind. Res. After George J. Roskruge of Tucson, U. S. Surveyor General of Arizona, 1896-97. "Pioneer, champion sharp-shooter, civil engineer and father of masonry in Arizona. Came to Prescott from England, 1872. Was cook, packer, and chainman for surveying party that established fifth standard north. One of Arizona's outstanding citizens." Died July 27, 1928.

Ross Spring   Coconino Co.   Map, Tusayan N. F., 1927.

In sec. 13, T. 21 N., R. 3 E. After Tom Ross of Garland and Ross who ran cattle here from about 1888 to 1895 when they sold the cattle and went out of business. See Garland prairie.

Round Knob   Yuma Co.   G. L. O. Map, 1921.

On east side S. H. mountains. Descriptive name.

Round Mountain   Cochise Co.

See Chiricahua peak.

Round Mountain   Coconino Co.   U. S. G. S. Map, 1923.

In T. 24 N., R. 4 W., about 12 miles north of Crookton station, A. T. & S. F. R. R. Purely descriptive name.

Round Mountain   Greenlee Co.   U. S. G. S. Map, 1923.

In T. 10 S., R. 32 E. In southeast corner county near New Mexico line. See Fraesfield.

Round Peak   Apache Co.   G. L. O. Map, 1921.

Elevation 6,020 feet. In T. 9 N., R. 10 W. On Navajo Ind. Res., east side Chinle creek. Shown as Round rock on Geologic map, Navajo county, 1916. "It is a very symmetrical, well-rounded peak."

Roundtop Cone   Navajo Co.   U. S. G. S. Map, 1923.

In T. 24 N., R. 17 E. "Descriptive name for a rather odd looking peak or volcanic cone."

Round Valley   Apache Co.   Smith Map, 1879.

Valley, Little Colorado river, settled by Wm. R. "Tony" Milligan, 1870. Called Round valley because of its shape. Early Mexican settlers, 1870, called it "Valle Redondo." Also called Milligans or Milligans fort. Tony Milligan built a saw mill here, 1870, and also had a large farm. In 1882, was chief sawer at Fort Apache saw mill.

"Round Valley was organized into a Mormon 'ward' in 1879, called Round Valley Ward; Jacob Hamblin, bishop, Oct. 29, 1882. Was also called Amity and for a time Omer. In 1888, the people united on a new townsite first named Union, later Eager, for the three Eager brothers who were among the first settlers in the district." McClintock.

Round Valley   Yavapai Co.

See Muddy canyon.

Roundy Creek   Coconino Co.   Gregory Map, 1916; U. S. G. S., 1923.

In lat. 36° 35', long. 111° 40'. East side Marble canyon. Flows from Echo cliffs at Cedar mesa into Colorado river.

"Named for Bishop Lorenzo Roundy, drowned crossing Colorado river at Lee Ferry May 28, 1876." Gregory.

Rounsensock Creek   Greenlee Co.   Map, Crook N. F., 1926.

In sec. 36, T. 1 N., R. 30 E. Heads at Rose peak, flows southeast into Blue river. "Frank Fritz whose father knew Rounsensauc (sic) says it was for this old settler and should be spelled that way." Letter, J. W. Girdner, Forest Ranger.

Rover Mountain   Yavapai Co.   Map, Tonto N. F., 1927.

Peak in sec. 22, T. 8 N., R. 5 E. After Red Rover mine, opened 1880, which is at its base and was named first.

Rowe Knob   Coconino Co.   Map, Kaibab N. F., 1926.

Elevation 7,071 feet. In T. 31 S., R. 2 E. In Grand Canyon N. P. About 2 miles northwest of El Tovar. Solitary butte in canyon. After Sanford Rowe, early settler and prospector in region.

Rowes Point   Coconino Co.   Map, Tusayan N. F., 1927.

South side Colorado river, in Grand Canyon N. P., near El Tovar R. R. station. Also Rowes Well ranger station in T. 21 N., R. 2 E. Named for Sanford Rowe. Now known as Hopi point.

Rowes Station   Maricopa Co.

See Maryville.

Rowood   Pima Co.   G. L. O. Map, 1921.

In T. 12 S., R. 6 W. Mining camp at end Tucson, Cornelia, and Gila Bend R. R.

This place lies about 2 miles from Ajo. Parties who desired to start a town away from Ajo finally got title to some mining ground and divided it into town lots. They wanted a post office and asked for the name "Woodrow Wilson." Postal authorities would not grant it. Then they tried successively Woodrow and Wilson. Finally, in disgust they reversed the word Woodrow which was approved. P. O. established June 21, 1918. Kallulah H. Holcomb, P. M.

Royal, Cape   Coconino Co.   Map, Kaibab N. F., 1921.

In northern part of T. 31., R. 4 E. So called by members U.S.G.S. party because of its commanding site.

Ruby   Santa Cruz Co.   U. S. G. S. Map, 1923.

In Oro Blanco mountains, southwest corner of county. Ranch, mining camp and post office.

"Post office first located at Montana mine, operated by Eagle, Pilcher Mining Co., of St. Louis. Post office named after Ruby Andrews, who lived at the camp." Letter, Fred Winn, Tucson. P. O. established April 11, 1912, Julius S. Andrews, P. M.

Rucker, Camp   Cochise Co.

In Rucker or White River canyon sometimes called White Water canyon. In T. 19 S., R. 28 E. After Lieut. John A. (Tony) Rucker, 12th U. S. Infantry, accidentally drowned here during Victorio campaign of 1879, while his company had a camp on this stream.

List of Military posts says: "Originally called Camp Supply and then Powers." Is called "Old Camp Supply" on G.L.O. map, 1892. Is close to Mexican line. See Powers.

On Elliott's map, 1884, Rucker is shown as at upper end White river, at north end Swisshelm mountains, while Camp Supply is close to the line on same stream. Two entirely different locations. The writer has an idea that Supply was first established and later on when they determined to make it a semi-permanent camp it was located higher up on the creek, perhaps for strategic purposes.

Military reports, July 21, 1876, show that "Rucker rode his horse into the stream when in heavy flood to rescue his comrade, Lieut. Henley, and was drowned." Rucker was then in command of a company of Indian scouts.

Heitman's *List* says: "It was established as Camp Supply, Apr. 29, 1878. Changed to Rucker, Apr., 1879."

P. O. established here called Powers, q.v. Mar. 3, 1891, Joseph H. Coggswell, P. M. Name changed to Rucker, June 20, 1891.

Rudd Creek   Apache Co.   Map, Apache N. F., 1926.

Stream rising at Rudd Knoll, flowing southeast into Nutrioso creek in sec. 28, T. 8 N., R. 30 E. After Dr. William Rudd, local physician, who lived in this region and ran cattle along this stream in early Eighties.

Dr. Rudd was first district attorney for Apache county, 1881. See Rudd Knoll.

Rudd Knoll   Apache Co.   Map, Apache N. F., 1926.

In sec. 26, T. 7 N., R. 28 E. An isolated butte in mountains above Springerville. See Rudd creek.

Ruggles and Ewings Ranch   Pinal Co.   Smith Map, 1879; Eckhoff, 1880.

In T. 4 S., R. 10 E. On road Florence to Old Camp Grant, on San Pedro river. Levi Ruggles kept a store here. It was about 5 miles south of Florence. Hinton says: "It was a good stopping place. The last ranch before leaving the river." Col. Levi Ruggles was receiver, U. S. Land Office, at Florence, 1877.

Russel   Yavapai Co.   G. L. O. Map, 1909, 1921.

In T. 16 N., R. 1 E. An early station, Jerome narrow gauge railroad, east side of Lonesome valley.

"A side track on the old M. V. and P. R. R., for unloading mine and ranch supplies for local people. Road since abandoned and not a sign of place left. Not even a road to it. Named for a Mr. Russel, an early superintendent of this road." Letter, R. S. Cunningham, Jerome.

Russell Butte   Coconino Co.

In Grand Canyon N. P. Mentioned in James' *Canyon Book*. He says: "After the geologist who traced the beaches of the prehistoric lake Lohanton." Unfortunately for Geologist Russell and geographers, Mr. James forgot to locate this butte.

Russel Camp   Cochise Co.

An early day mining camp. "It is in Cochise county and numbers already nearly 100 souls." Item *Tombstone Epitaph*, June 3, 1882. Nothing more known of it.

Russet Hills   Gila Co.   Smith Map, 1879.

Low range of brown hills, on Tonto creek, a few miles southeast of Mazatzal City.

Rutherford   Yavapai Co.

P. O. established Sept. 14, 1907. Elizabeth Hopper, P. M. Unable to locate.

Ryan   Coconino Co.   U. S. G. S. Map, 1923.

In T. 38 N. Mining camp on Warm Springs creek, western side Kaibab N. F. First P. M., Roy N. Davidson, July 26, 1902.

"Aquilla Nebeker of Salt Lake and a man named Ryan located and worked some mines near this place about 1900. Camp first called Coconino. Nebeker sold out to Ryan who then called it Ryan. He was father of Paddy Ryan, the prize fighter, who was interested with his father in the mines." Letter, W. G. Mann, Forest Supervisor.

Rye   Gila Co.   G. L. O. Map, 1909; U. S. G. S., 1921.

In T. 9 N., R. 10 E. Town and P. O. on Rye creek. At the old Sam Haught ranch. P. O. established Nov. 14, 1883. Mary E. Boardman, P. M. Named after the creek.

Rye Creek   Gila Co.   Smith Map, 1879, "Wild Rye";
                                              U. S. G. S., 1923, "Rye."

In T. 9 N., R. 9 E. Rises east side North peak, upper end Mazatzal mountains, some 4 miles northwest of Rye settlement. "So called because when the first settlers came the range along the creek was covered with a luxurious growth of wild rye."

Saavedra Springs   Mohave Co.

After one of his Mexican guides of whom Beale says, "He was absolutely worthless as a guide or anything else." Shows on Beale's map, 1857-58, as a little north of lat. 114°. West side Cerbat range, at its northern end. They were suffering for water when the guide discovered this spring.

Sabino Canyon   Pima Co.   Map, Coronado N. F., 1927.

In T. 12 S., R. 16 E., heads on Bigelow mountain. Runs southwest into Rillito, near Fort Lowell. Named after Sabino Otero, of Tucson, well known merchant in the early days. He had a cattle ranch in this canyon.

Sacate (sic)   Pinal Co.   G. L. O. Map, 1921.

Indian village and station S. P. R. R. south side Gila river, in T. 3 S., R. 4 E., 8 miles north of Maricopa. "Formerly called Sacaton, shortened, 1904, to Sacate." Letter, S. P. R. R. Agent, Tucson.

Sacaton (sic)   Pinal Co.   Smith Map, 1879; G. L. O., 1921.

Very old Indian settlement on Gila, 16 miles north Casa Grande station, S. P. R. R., Gila River Ind. Res. Seat of Pima and Maricopa Indian Agency. According to Hodge word comes from the Nahuatl—Sacaton "small grass." Sp., zacati or sacate, "grass" or "hay." Word saccaton means a coarse, perennial grass (Sporabolus wrightii), found along the Gila. Early explorers all spoke of the grass along here. Word saccaton, or sacaton as it is often incorrectly spelled, was undoubtedly the origin of this name, due probably to some wandering botanist.
"Garces visited it in Nov., 1775. He calls it Rancheria de San Juna de Capestrano, otherwise Uturictuc." Coues.
Sacaton was made division headquarters for the Military District of Arizona, 1867.
Poston writes poetically:
                   "Leaving the stream at Sacatone
                   So named for grass of Arizone."
P. O. established Jan. 3, 1876, John C. Loss, P. M.

Sacaton   Pinal Co.   Map, Coronado N. F., 1927.

Station and store on San Pedro river in T. 10 S., R. 18 E. There is another Sacaton on Gila river, 16 miles north of Casa Grande, q. v. P. O. established Sept. 23, 1895, Nannie B. Young, P. M.

Sacaton Buttes   Pinal Co.   U. S. G. S. Map, 1925.

Elevation 1,520 feet. In T. 4 S., R. 4 E. In Salt River Ind. Res.

Sacaton Mountains   Maricopa Co.   G. L. O. Map, 1921;
                                                    U. S. G. S., 1923.

In T. 5 E., R. 5 S., Gila River Ind. Res., south side Gila river.

Sacramento Hill   Cochise Co.

Noted hill or mountain in city limits of Bisbee. Is part of Mule mountains. Contains large quantities of copper which are mined by steam shovels, hence easily handled. For years they have worked on it and eventually it will be but a hole in the ground.

Sacramento Valley and Wash   Mohave Co.   Smith Map, 1879; G. L. O., 1921.

In southwest part of county. Wash rises in T. 23 N., R. 19 W., northwest of Mineral. Flows south and southwest, enters Colorado river at Topock, A. T. & S. F. R. R. Named for Sacramento, Calif., by miners who came to Arizona with California regiments, 1863.

Sacramento Siding

See Griffith.

Saddle Canyon   Coconino Co.   Map, Kaibab N. F., 1926.

In T. 34 N., R. 4 E. Stream rises at Saddle mountain, flows northeast into Colorado river in sec. 5, T. 35 N., R. 5 E. So called After Saddle mountain, which lies between two ranges or ridges. Western people generally call a pass between two peaks or hills, a "saddle."

Saddle Mountain   Graham Co.   U. S. G. S. Map, 1923.

In T. 11 S., R. 21 E. Lower end Galiuro mountains. On Crook N. F. Descriptive name.

Saddle Mountain   Maricopa Co.   Map, Tonto N. F., 1927.

In T. 7 N., R. 8 E., west side Mazatzals. Near Sunflower mine. Descriptive name.

Saddle Mountain   Pinal Co.   G. L. O. Map, 1921.

Elevation 4,233 feet. In secs. 23, 24, T. 5 S., R. 16 E. Six miles east of Winkelman. Descriptive name. See Mount Turnbull.

Saddle Back Mountain   Maricopa Co.
                Scott Map, Maricopa Co., 1929; U. S. G. S., 1923.

In T. 1 N., R. 8 W. Desert hills west of Palo Verde hills, south side Parker branch, A. T. & S. F. R. R. Descriptive name, resembles a saddle.

Safford   Graham Co.   U. S. G. S. Map, 1923.

Elevation 2,914 feet. In T. 7 S., R. 26 E., south bank Gila river. According to McClintock, first settled by Americans who came here from Gila Bend, 1872. Joshua E. Bailey, one of them, named it for Governor Anson Pacely Killen Safford, then making a tour of the Territory.

Safford was county seat Graham county until 1881 when it was moved to Solomonville. Later when Greenlee county was created, it was returned to Safford. P. O. established March 5, 1875, Joshua E. Bailey, P. M.

Sage Peak   Cochise Co.

Elevation 7,500 feet. Coronado N. F. On top there has been erected a copper shield on which is engraved: "In memory of Ranger Harley H. Sage, who died in the service of his country November 13, 1913." Decision U.S.G.B.

Sahuaro Siding   Pima Co.   G. L. O. Map, 1921.

On Arizona Southern Ry. In T. 11 S., R. 8 E. Spelled Sahuaro by R. R. Company. Saguaro—decision U. S. G. B.

Sahuarita   Pima Co.   Smith Map, 1879, "Suarita"; G. L. O., 1921, "Sahuarito."

In T. 17 S., R. 14 E. Station, Tucson-Nogales branch, S. P. R. R. About 18 miles south Tucson on Santa Cruz river. "Established about 1911. So called because country around it is covered with Sahuaro or Giant Cactus." Paul Shoup.
Was an early-day stage station of same name. Hinton calls this place Columbus. He says "Roddick and Brown kept a good hotel and station here." P. O. established as Sahuarito (sic.) Sept. 4, 1884. Sahuarita—Sp. diminutive of saguaro. James K. Brown, P. M.

St. Clair Mountain and Spring   Yavapai Co.
                                        Map, Tonto N. F., 1927.

In T. 7 N., R. 6 E. "After William Saint Clair, cattleman and miner who lived at this spring with his family for many years." Letter, Joe H. Hand, Forest Ranger.

St. Cloud Mountains   Yavapai Co.   G. L. O. Map, 1909.

West side railroad at Hillside station, Ash Fork-Prescott branch, A. T. & S. F. R. R. Origin unknown.

St. David   Cochise Co.   G. L. O. Map, 1892-1921.

Settlement San Pedro river, originally a Mormon colony settled by four families of Merrills.
"Named after David W. Patton, Mormon apostle, killed by mob in Missouri." Letter, P. M., St. David.
This is now a spur station, E. P. & S. W. R. R., 5 miles from Benson. Artesian water was found here, 1888, at moderate depths, in T. 18 S., R. 21 E., about 6 miles southeast of Benson. P. O. established Sept. 28, 1881. Joseph McRae, P. M.

St. Joe Canyon   Coconino Co.   Map, Sitgreaves N. F., 1924.

Rises, St. Joe spring, 8 miles west of Wilford, Navajo Co. Flows northeast into Wildcat canyon, in T. 12 N., R. 15 E. See St. Joe spring for origin.

St. Joe Settlement   Pah Ute Co., Nevada
                            Smith Map, 1879; Eckhoff, 1880.

One of the Mormon settlements, 1865, on Muddy river in Pah Ute county, Nevada, then part of Arizona, but afterwards cut off and given to Nevada. See St. Thomas, Joseph City and Overton.

St. Joe Spring   Coconino Co.   G. L. O. Map, 1921; Sitgreaves N. F., 1924.

In sec. 8, T. 11½ N., R. 15 E. On St. Joe canyon. Located by Bishop Richard's boys, Will and Parley, from St. Joseph, who lived here 1883. About 1888, they sold their claim to Kerrens and Larson ("Hook" Larson), sheepmen, who ran sheep here for several years, and about 1906, sold it to George Scott.

St. Johns   Apache Co.   Reade Map, 1877; Smith, 1879; U. S. G. S., 1923.

In T. 13 N., R. 28 E. County seat, on Little Colorado river. "So called by Mexican settlers, who named it on Saint John's (San Juan's) day, June 24.

"Jose Seavedra and father, first settlers, arrived here in December, 1872, in a two-wheeled oxcart. They built first bridge across Little Colorado to cross a band of sheep. Road to Fort Apache from Zuni crossed here and they made good money allowing freighters to use the bridge. Seavedra filed on a homestead and took out a ditch in 1875." *St. John's Herald*, March, 1926.

"Wilford Woodruff selected a location March 29, 1880, for Mormon colonists about 1½ miles below present St. Johns. Erastus Snow, September 19, 1880, advised changing to higher ground adjoining the Mexican town on west and north, resulting in present townsite. P. O. named Salem was established, but owing to anti-Mormon feeling, was never opened." McClintock.

Sextus E. Johnson was later appointed P. M. April 5, 1880. Office established under name St. Johns.

There is a letter from Charley Banta dated April 21, 1921, in which he claims he gave the name "St. Johns," stating that he added the "s" to it to make it euphonious.

The fight between the Greer boys and Mexicans, in which Nathan C. Tenney and Jim Vaughn were killed, took place St. John's day, June 24, 1882. Tenney was killed while trying to stop the fight. Place said to have first been called "El Vadito," the little ford. See Colorado Bridge.

St. Johns Creek   Gila Co.   Map, Tonto N. F., 1926.

Dry Creek, about 4 miles south Payson. After William O. St. Johns, who settled on and patented a ranch in secs. 28-29, T. 10 N., R. 10 E.

"This ranch was a general stopping place on road from Globe to Payson. The old Ox Bow P. O. was at this ranch. St. Johns and his wife are buried in Payson cemetery." Letter, Fred Croxen.

St. John's Chapel or Mission   Pinal Co.   G. L. O. Map, 1912.

In sec. 5, T. 2 S., R. 2 E. About one mile from river near "Lower Gila crossing," some 5 miles south of Laveen.

"This is an Indian Mission school which had its inception in 1894 when a pioneer missionary named O'Connor gathered around him a few Indian children and started teaching them. There are now over three hundred children, boys and girls, Pimas, Papagos, Maricopas and Apaches. Franciscan Padres and Sisters of St. Francis are in charge." Place is also called Komatke, q.v. *Phoenix Republican.*

St. Joseph   Navajo Co.

P. O. by this name established October 30, 1879, Joseph H. Richards, P. M. Was the author's post office for his ranch at Chevelona Fork, 1883 to 1888. Railroad changed name to Joseph City about 1900 because of a St. Joseph elsewhere on its line. See also St. Joseph in Pah Ute county, Nevada.

St. Joseph   Pah Ute Co., Nevada

Town on Muddy river when Pah Ute was an Arizona county. Later added to Nevada. "This place was a stone fort on a high bluff such as this people built so often for protection against the Indians. There was a flour mill and cotton gin. Place was almost destroyed by fire in August, 1868." Old clipping. P. O. established August 26, 1867, William D. Karchner, P. M.

McClintock tells interestingly of it in his *"Mormon Settlement."*

St. Ludovic De Vacapa   Pima Co.

"In southwestern Arizona near Sonora line. It formed a ranchería at close of seventeenth century." Bancroft.

Coues spells it "Quitobac," a "small reed." He does not accept this meaning, however, although he gives no reason for not doing so.

Hornaday and Lumholtz call it Quitovaquito. "I made a halt of one day here at Quitovaquito, a small Indian settlement just within the U. S. boundary in order to procure, as a member of my party, a Papago Indian medicine man known as Cara Colorada, or Red Face, and also as Pancho. The place owes its Papago name, 'small springs,' to a number of diminutive springs with excellent water." Lumholtz. Bancroft also calls it San Luis de Bacapa. See Quitovac and Quitovaquito.

St. Michaels   Apache Co.   U. S. G. S. Map, 1923.

In T. 26 N., R. 31 E., 8 miles south of Fort Defiance, Navajo Ind. Res. Headquarters, Franciscan Brothers, Navajo school and mission. P. O. established July 29, 1902, John Walker, P. M. Until founding of mission this place was known as "Cienega Amarilla," "yellow swamp" or "meadow." Cienega was covered with what is called "salt grass" which turns yellow early in the fall. When the director of Indian Missions bought this place, 1896, he renamed it St. Michaels. See Cienega Amarilla.

St. Mathews Mountain   Yavapai Co.   Map, Prescott N. F., 1927.

In sec. 9, T. 16 N., R. 1 E. Near head of Munds draw, q.v. "I am told by one of the old timers that this name was given this mountain by 'Daddy' Perkins, well known cattleman who said a young woman climbed the peak once and left a card on top asking that it be named 'Saint Mathew,' so he began to call it by that name." Letter, Frank Grubb, Prescott.

St. Thomas   Pah Ute Co., Nevada   Smith Map, 1879; Eckhoff, 1880.

Originally in Arizona. An early 1865, Mormon settlement on Muddy river. Abandoned, 1871, according to Joseph Fish, "because the county of Pah Ute was cut off from Arizona and added to Nevada." See Joseph City. P. O. established July 23, 1866, James Leithead, P. M.

Salada

See Salt river.

Salah-Kai   Apache Co.   U. S. G. S. Map, 1923

Mesa, Navajo Ind. Res. near Navajo county line, lat. 36°, long. 110'. Meaning unknown.

Salsido

See Sauceda.

Salem

First Mormon settlement at St. Johns. See St. Johns.

Salero Hill   Santa Cruz Co.   Map, Coronado N. F., 1927.

Salero—"A salt cellar, salt mine." In northeast corner Baca Float Grant No. 3. "Here was located the Salero mine, one of Santa Rita Company's mines of which Prof. Wrightson was manager. Tradition says mine takes name from a padre who once fashioned a salt cellar out of a piece of silver ore to deck the bishop's table." Hinton.

"The Salero mine was where the padre in charge wishing to entertain his bishop in style and having no salt cellars ready ordered the Indians to dig out enough ore to make a solid silver basin."

Salero in Spanish means a salt mine, a salt pan. The writer has always had grave doubts about the salt cellar origin of this name, and believes it came originally from some nearby salt mine or deposit which suggested the name. P. O. established at mine August 13, 1884, Lizzie E. Durand, P. M.

Salinas River

See Salt river.·

Salome   Yuma Co.   G. L. O. Map, 1921.

In T. 5 N., R. 13 W., Parker branch A. T. & S. F. R. R., 55 miles west Wickenburg. Named for Mrs. Grace Salome Pratt, resident this section. Town made famous by Dick Wick Hall, who wrote much of his frog "that never learned to swim" and "Salome, where she danced." P. O. established April 14, 1905, Etta von Stauffer, P. M. Dick Wick Hall was once postmaster here.

Salome Creek   Gila Co.

Rises north of Roosevelt lake west slope Sierra Ancha. Flows southwest into lake. Stream originally named "Salome" after daughter of Herodias. The Spanish pronounced it "Sal-oh-may," with accent on last syllable.

This the early American settlers soon turned to "Sally May." As early as 1886 the name was commonly attributed to two daughters of an old (and mythical) settler, "Sally and May." Their existence is very unlikely. Bourke calls stream "Sal-u-may." On Roosevelt Quad and G.L.O. map, 1921, Sally May. On map, Tonto N. F., 1927, Salome.

Salome Peak   Yuma Co.   U. S. G. S. Map, 1923.

In T. 6 N., R. 14 W. South end Little Harcuvar mountains, 6 miles northwest of Salome, q.v.

Salmon Lake   Yavapai Co.   Map, Coconino N. F., 1928.

In sec. 18, T. 13 N., R. 8 E. Small lake at head of Meadow creek, about 25 miles east of Camp Verde, near Verde road. About 1880 a party was leaving Camp Verde for a turkey hunt in the mountains. Post butcher ·"Old Man" Williams, an awful spinner of wild yarns, told one of them "not to carry much grub for he had recently hidden a case of canned salmon in a tree near this lake which they could use." It was a fairy tale but accepted as truth. They spent several hours hunting the tree without success. Turkeys were scarce and they nearly starved. Lake and basin were always called Salmon for this affair.

Salt Banks

See Salt river.

Salt Creek   Coconino Co.   U. S. G. S. Map, 1923.

Rises in T. 16 N., R. 10 E., flows northeast, enters Clear creek in T. 18 N., R. 15 E., 8 miles south Winslow. There are several springs along this creek that are strongly impregnated with alkali which gave the name. See Jack's canyon.

Salt Creek   Gila Co.   Map, Coronado N. F., 1926.

Rises, San Carlos Ind. Res., northwest part of T. 1 S., R. 22 N., north slope Gila mountains. Flows west and south, enters San Carlos river in sec. 32, T. 2 S., R. 20 E. A large salt spring on this stream furnishes the name.

Salt Mountain   Gila Co.   Map, San Carlos Ind. Res., 1917.

In T. 2 S., R. 20 E. West side Salt creek. So called because of its location on Salt creek.

Salt River   Maricopa Co.   P. O. Route Map, 1929.

Town, north side Salt river near Lehi, east of Phoenix. P. O. established August 21, 1912, later moved to Scottsdale.

Salt River Bird Reservation   Gila Co.   Map, Tonto N. F., 1927.

Entire Roosevelt lake is set aside as a National Bird Preserve. All hunting on it strictly prohibited.

Salt River Indian Reservation   Maricopa Co.   G. L. O. Map, 1921.

On lower Verde and Salt rivers. Established by Executive Order June 14, 1879. Additional land added September 15, 1903, to include Camp McDowell Military Reservation. So called because originally it lay entirely along Salt river.

Salt River Mountains   Gila Co.   Map, Tonto N. F., 1927.

In T. 3 N., R. 14 E., south side Salt river at head Roosevelt lake. There is another range by this name near Phoenix.

Salt River Mountains   Maricopa Co.   G. L. O. Map, 1921.

In Ts. 2, 3, N., R. 1 W. Low range of hills at forks Gila and Salt rivers about 10 miles south of Phoenix. Pima name for these mountains is "Mo-hat-uk" (Greasy mountain). After a rain one notices shiny places on the sides of mountains as if they were greasy. It is the silica in wet rocks glistening in the sunshine.

"Mohatuk (Greasy mountain) is the extreme southern end of the Salt River mountains when seen from the Gila river side." Letter, Fr. Antonine, St. Johns Mission.

The Pimas explained this by the following myth: "Out of the primeval darkness after the flood came 'Elder Brother' as the Ruler, and 'Coyote' his subordinate. All the animals had been shut up in a dark cave. Coyote came to liberate them. Rabbit had died. How to dispose of his body was the problem. 'If we bury him Coyote will dig him up,' said one. 'If we put him in a tree Coyote will climb up and get him,' said another. Finally the Indians decided to burn Rabbit.

"Coyote was sent to the Sun to get some fire. Coyote looked back, saw smoke ascending, and returned. When he appeared the people formed a circle to shut him away from the burning body. Coyote beseeched them to let him see the body of his brother, 'even with only one eye.' He ran around in a circle seeking an opening and found a spot where two short men were standing. He jumped over their heads, bit out the heart of the burning rabbit and ran away with it.

"Coyote ran northward across the Gila where he ate the heart. As he did so the grease fell upon every stone of that mountain which accounts for its appearance and the name it now bears— 'Mo-hat-uk' (Greasy mountain)."

This is one of the many Piman myths or stories told Frank Russel of the Smithsonian Institution at Sacaton, Arizona in 1902, by several very old men and women. See Superstition mountains.

Salt River Draw   Gila Co.

In T. 8½ N., R. 16 E., flows south, enters Salt river in T. 5 N., R. 17 E. It is from this stream that the Salt river gets its saline quality and name. Military maps 1879 show a "salt works" located at junction of the two streams. In 1880, an Apache told the author that the Apaches had for ages secured quantities of salt from this spot. See also Salt river. G.L.O. map, 1921, shows "salt banks" at junction of the two streams which is undoubtedly the same as "salt works."

Salt River   Gila Co.

Formed in Gila county by junction White and Black rivers, in central part, Fort Apache Ind. Res., 20 miles west of Fort Apache, flows southwest, enters Gila about 12 miles southwest of Phoenix in southwest corner T. 1 N., R. 1 E.

Garces called it "Rio de la Asunción," or "Assumption." Fray Marcos called it "Rio Azul." So did Kino. "Its earliest name dates from 1539. Jaramillo, writing of the Coronado Expedition, called it 'Rio de las Balsas' or 'River of the Rafts, because it had to be crossed by such means." Kino map of 1700 shows it as "Rio Asunción." Also called the "Salada" or the "Salinas."

Water gets its saline qualities from several large salt springs near western boundary Fort Apache Ind. Res., east of Sombrero Butte. Stream also flows over large beds of salt—above them it is free from any such taint. Smith map, 1879 and Eckhoff, 1880 show name "salt works" on the river in Indian Reservation near mouth Canon creek.

On his old map, Kino, who was an Austrian, called the Salt "Rio Azul"—Blue river—or as he wrote it in German "Blau Fluss." He often put German names for places on his map. He wrote for example, "Azul, oder Blau Fluss."

Whipple called it the Salt in 1851, and writes of his surprise at its not being salt to the taste. McClintock thinks name "Asunción" undoubtedly comes from Friar Juan de la Asunción, whom Coues feels was actual discoverer of the Gila. See Salt River draw.

Salt River Peak   Gila Co.   Map, Crook N. F., 1926.

Elevation 3,360 feet. In sec. 3, T. 2 N., R. 14 E. West side Pinto creek.

Salt Springs Wash   Mohave Co.   U. S. G. S. Map, 1923.

In T. 28 N., R. 19 W. Rises north side Squaw peak, flows north into Colorado river at Virgin canyon. "The wash heads in some very salt or brackish springs, hence the name." Letter Forest Ranger.

Samaniego Hills   Pima Co.   G. L. O. Map, 1921.

At boundary Pinal and Pima counties, 15 miles northeast of Silver Bell. After Hon. M. G. Samaniego.

Samaniego Peak   Pima Co.   U. S. G. S. Map, 1923.

In T. 17 S., R. 11 E. In Sierrita mountains, west of town of Twin buttes. After M. G. Samaniego, well known businessman and politician of Tucson, 1875-1899.

Samaniego Ridge   Pima Co.   Map, Coronado N. F., 1927.

In T. 11 S., R. 15 E. Short ridge northwest of Mount Lemmon, near county line. After Hon. M. G. Samaniego.

George Roskruge placed this on his map of 1893 as Samaniego peak.

Sam Hill, Draw and Cabin   Gila Co.   Map, Tonto N. F., 1926.

In sec. 27, T. 9½ N., R. 10 E. "Sam Hill, an old prospector and pioneer lived in a cabin here for many years. Died here in his 84th year." Letter, Fred Croxen.

Sam Hughes Butte   Pima Co.

About 25 or 30 miles west of Tucson, north of Robles well. After Sam Hughes, prominent Tucson resident of the Eighties. See Hornaday's *Desert and Lava.*

Sample   Cochise Co.

Somewhere near Benson. "After Comer W. Sample, known as 'Red.' He was a rustler who was mixed up with the Bisbee massacre of December 8, 1883, and was hanged for his part in it." P. O. established July 26, 1886, Pablo Rebeil, P. M.

San Andres, Rio de

See Bill Williams River.

San Angeles de Quevavi

See Quebabi.

San Antonio River

See Verde.

San Bernardino   Cochise Co.   Smith Map, 1879; G. L. O., 1921.

In T. 24 S., R. 30 E. Old ranch headquarters on Mexican line. In early days occupied many times by troops following Apaches. Known best as Slaughter ranch after its owner, John Slaughter, famous cattleman and sheriff who lived here, 1884-1922.

"San Bernardino springs break out on the boundary line and flow south into Yaqui river of which San Bernardino river is the extreme head. These springs gave us an abundance of water for all our needs for the large command." Bourke, *An Apache Campaign.*

"San Bernardino ranch, purchased by John Slaughter, 1884, was originally a land grant of 1882 to Ignacio Pérez by government of Mexico. It covered 73,240 acres, mostly in Mexico. In days of Spain, Spanish soldiers stood at San Bernardino guarding the frontier. The mesa near the ranch house is still called 'Mesa de la Avansada' or Mesa of the Advance Guard." *Tombstone.*

Mormon battalion reached here December 3, 1846, guided by Leroux. Place had been abandoned by Mexicans sometime before because of Apache ravages. Ranch was enclosed by a high stone wall with two bastions. The military reported thousands of wild cattle grazing in this region. On San Pedro, troops were attacked by "wild bulls." Farish quotes extensively from Colonel Crooke's report on this "Battle with the Bulls."

Edward Pancoast in his *Diary of a Quaker 49r* gives an interesting account of this place as he found it September 19, 1846.

San Bernardino Land Grant   Cochise Co.   G. L. O. Map, 1921.

Mexican land grant lying partly in U. S. and partly in Mexico. Owned by John H. Slaughter. Grant was sold outright by Mexican government March 23, 1822, for $90, to Ignacio Pérez. He later on sold it to Slaughter, whose title was approved by U. S. Land Court for but 2,366 acres of the 8,688 acres claimed on the American side. See San Bernardino.

San Bernardino   Navajo Co.

Mission founded, 1629, at Hopi pueblo of Awatobi by Spanish, destroyed by Hopi, 1700. See Awatobi. See Coues, *On the Trail.*

San Caietano (sic)   Santa Cruz Co.

"This was a mission in Santa Cruz valley founded by Kino." Bolton. The nearby San Cayetano mountains, q.v., were undoubtedly named after this mission.

San Cayetano Mountains   Santa Cruz Co.   Elliott Map, 1866; U. S. G. S., 1923.

In Coronado N. F., in Baca Land Grant north of Calabasas. Cayetano, Spanish proper name, means "an islet in the sea." Undoubtedly named after San Caietano mission, which was near this range.

San Carlos (Saint Charles)

Origin of name San Carlos as used in Arizona is not absolutely certain.

"On January 20, 1767, fourteen priests embarked at San Blas, Mexico, on two ships, destined for 'Pimería Alta,' name then applied to that vast unknown region, covered broadly by northern Sonora in Mexico and southern Arizona in present United States area. One of these two ships was called the San Carlos." *Franciscans in Arizona.* One of these priests was the well known explorer-priest, Francisco Garces, who eventually reached California and southern Arizona.

"King Charles III, often called King Carlos III, in May, 1782, authorized the formation of Franciscan missions in the southwest into two independent custodies; one for Sonora; the other for the Indes. The new 'Custody' in Sonora was called the 'Custody of San Carlos.' This Custody was dissolved in August, 1791."

Garces, however, used the name at least ten years before this date. November 4, 1775, Garces writes: "This being the day of San Carlos and so of the King of Spain." And again, Nov. 28, 1775, speaking of the Gila river, Garces writes: "In its course it (the Gila) is joined by the Rio de Carlos." Coues—*Garces Diary.*

Garces in his wanderings through Arizona named many streams and other natural features and as he was in the region of the San Carlos river it is easy to believe he gave it that name. San Carlos river shows on Major Emory's map in his *Notes of a Military Reconnaissance* (1846-47). Emory's map of Arizona, compiled later, however, shows no such name. River shows on Rogers and Johnson maps of U. S., 1861, and generally on all subsequent maps.

"The expeditions to the new world were made on the order or command of Don Carlos II, and cost more than half a million (dollars)." See Bancroft's *North American States and Texas.* Also Bolton's *Spanish Explorations.*

Coues says: "January 20, 1768, Garces embarked at San Blas, Mexico. He was assigned to San Xavier del Bac (Arizona) and arrived there June 30, 1768. Carlos III was King of Spain from 1759 to 1788. He expelled the Jesuits which placed the Franciscans in power in America." Garces celebrated Carlos' birthday which was Nov. 4. Coues says further: "He, Garces, named the stream Nov. 27 and 30, 1775." From all this, it may well be assumed that the name San Carlos used in Arizona, was for Carlos III.

San Carlos, Town, Military Post and Post Office   Gila Co.

Located north side Gila river, near point where San Carlos river enters Gila.

"First post office established at San Carlos, Pinal Co., October 12, 1882, in what was then Gila county, located north side Gila river, Reuben Wood was appointed P. M., October 12, 1882." Letter from P. O. Department, May 2, 1928.

These points will all be covered with waters impounded by Coolidge dam, called "Lake San Carlos," q.v.

In 1931, P. O. at Rice was changed to San Carlos "to commemorate the old place." An unfortunate error, historically. The lake was sufficient to keep the name alive.

San Carlos Agency   Graham Co.

Established as headquarters for U. S. Indian Agent for San Carlos Apaches and other southern Apache tribes. Originally established on south bank of Gila, across river from Camp San Carlos, opposite mouth of San Carlos river.

San Carlos   Smith Map, 1879; G. L. O., 1892.

Post office established October 22, 1875, George H. Stevens, "Little Steve," P. M.

San Carlos, Camp   Gila Co.   Reade Map, 1877.

In T. 3 S., R. 19 E. North side San Carlos river about one mile from its junction with Gila. "Established as a military post and subpost of Fort Grant, May 29, 1873, by I troop, 5th U. S. Cavalry. Later F and M troops joined. Lieut. Jacob Almy of M troop was killed here May 29, 1873, by an Apache whose arrest was asked for by Indian Agent. Ceased to be a military post in July, 1900." Letter from War Department, May 15, 1928.

San Carlos Indian Reservation   Gila and Graham Cos.

Established by Executive Order, President Grant, December 14, 1872, out of White Mountain Ind. Res. Northern boundary formed by Black and Salt rivers. Established for the San Carlos, Warm Spring, and other southern Apache tribes.

"The southern part of former White Mountain Ind. Res. is now known as the San Carlos Ind. Res." Letter, Commissioner Indian Affairs, Oct. 30, 1928.

San Carlos Lake   Gila Co.

San Carlos Apache Ind. Res. Body of water impounded by Coolidge dam. Decision U.S.G.B. June 6, 1928.

San Carlos Mountains

See Mescal mountains.

San Carlos River   Graham Co.   Smith Map, 1879; Crook N. F., 1926.

In T. 1 N., R. 23 E. Rises south end Natanes Plateau; flows west and south into Gila river at town of San Carlos in sec. 4, T. 3 S., R. 19 E. See "San Carlos, the name."

San Cristobal Valley   Yuma Co.   U. S. G. S. Map, 1923.

In southeast part of Yuma county, east of Mohawk mountains. "The station on Southern Pacific is called 'Stoval,' q.v., a shortening of this name." Paul Shoup.

San Dionisio   Yuma Co.

Opposite site of Fort Yuma. Name given 1700 by Kino. On this site in 1854 was surveyed Colorado City, later Arizona City, later Yuma.

In September, 1700, Kino went down the Gila. "Crossing to the north side of the Gila he went down to its confluence with the Rio Colorado and the Yuma rancheria there on east side of latter river (Colorado). He named it San Dionisio, that being the ecclesiastical functionary on whose day he reached the spot. The name is printed 'Doonysio' on his map, 1701." Coues.

San Domingo, Rio   Cochise Co.

The present San Simon creek, also known to Spaniards as Rio Sauz: Sp., "willow," q.v.

San Fernando   Pima Co.   U. S. G. S. Map, 1923.

In T. 22 S., R. 8 E. Papago settlement at Mexican line. Headquarters for smugglers in early days. Named, 1889, by Arros brothers who lived here for several years. Just a name for the post office which was first called "La Osa," q.v. Headquarters for Col. Sturges' "La Osa" Cattle Co., about 1889-90. P. O. established as San Fernando, April 21, 1919. Reyes W. Pacheco, P. M.

San Francisco Mountains   Coconino Co.

Sp., "St. Francis." The plural is generally used in speaking of this group of peaks near Flagstaff. They lie principally in Ts. 22, 23 N., Rs. 6, 7 E. Three main peaks are: Agassiz, 12,300 feet; Fremont, 11,940 feet; Humphrey—highest in Arizona—, 12,655 feet. Mountains called "The High Place of Snow" by Hopi. Named, probably by Marcos de Niza, 1539, "The Kingdom of San Francisco."

The Hava Supais call the San Francisco mountains, "Hue-hass-a-patch." " 'Hue' in their language means mountain or big rock." G. Wharton James.

A recent review of the nomenclature of this region about Flagstaff has resulted in changing the decisions of the U. S. G. B. of some years ago. Mountains are now described approximately as follows:

"San Francisco Mountains. A region of volcanic peaks and craters in northern Arizona, located upon the area described by the U. S. G. B. as 'The Plateau of Arizona.' Bounded on the north by the Grand Canyon, on the east by the 'Desert of the Little Colorado,' on the south by the Mogollon escarpment, on the west by the Aubrey cliffs. It includes the Coconino Plateau, San Francisco Mountain Plateau, and the Mogollon Mesa."

The description might be more definite if it read; "On the east by the Little Colorado river, and Canyon Diablo."

On Dec. 6, 1933, the U. S. G. B. again reviewed their previous decisions and made the following on the single peak, this they designated as "San Francisco Mountain, an eroded volcano with serrated rim in Tps. 22, 23 N., R. 7 E., centering near lat. 35° 20' N., long. 111° 40' W. Known locally as the San Francisco Peaks, because of a number of prominent peaks on its rim. Name one of the oldest in the State dating probably back to 1540."

Coues says of these mountains: "When and by whom the San Francisco Mountains were first named and for which of the two eminent Saints of that name they were called, has escaped my observation so far. The name is a very old one. 'Sierra Napac' is what Garces called them." He overlooked de Niza's record of 1539, however.

Marcou, geologist with Whipple's party, says: "This cone is on left bank of Colorado Chiquito. It is unfortunate that this lofty and inspiring peak cannot be distinguished by a name which shall not lead to endless misapprehension of its position as being near the great city of the Pacific coast. If the Indian name for it can be learned it should be adopted." An amusing statement considering the distances involved. See Sierra Napac.

San Francisco River   Apache and Greenlee Cos.
Map, Apache N. F., Crook N. F.

Rising in T. 6 N., R. 30 E., south of Nutrioso village; flows southeast, enters New Mexico in T. 5 S., R. 31 E. Flows generally south, re-enters Arizona in Greenlee county in T. 2 S., R. 31 E. Enters Gila river about 6 miles south of Clifton in T. 5 S., R. 30 E.

Coues says: "This river was supposed to flow from the San Francisco mountains and so was given that name. As a branch of the Gila system it seems to have been mixed with the Verde. Garces called it the 'Rio de la Asunción.' "

Colonel Doniphan writes, Aug. 1, 1846: \"After 11 days from the headwaters of the Gila, in New Mexico, we came to the river San Francisco emptying into the Gila by its left bank." *Doniphan's Expedition*, 1846.

Whipple writes, 1853: "The Rio Verde was called the San Francisco by Leroux and it is thus designated by Captain Sitgreaves, who was then between San Francisco and Bill Williams mountains." He calls it "an error on the part of Leroux."

Name was transferred when the geography of region was more clearly established. G.L.O. map, 1866, has it "San Francisco or Verde river," showing a doubt even then.

San Francisco Wash   Coconino Co.   Map, Coconino N. F., 1928.

Rises east side Elden mountain; flows east into Canyon Diablo about 4 miles from Little Colorado river. Name derived from its source in San Francisco mountains.

San Ignacio del Babocomori Land Grant

See Babocomari.

San Ignacio de la Canoa Land Grant

See Canoa.

San José   Graham Co.   Smith Map, 1879; G. L. O., 1892-1921.

In T. 7 S., R. 27 E. Small hamlet south bank, Gila river, about 2 miles east of Solomonville. "Just a common Mexican name."

"In 1879, Mexicans here built a water wheel grist mill run by water from the irrigating ditch." P. O. established December 12, 1877, Julio Griego, P. M.

San José de Sonoita Land Grant

See Sonoita.

San Joseph de Cumars Mountains

See Estrella mountains.

San Juan   Cochise Co.

Station, E. P. & S. W. R. R. south of Pantano.

San Juan de las Boquillas Land Grant

See Boquillas.

San Luis Beltram de Bacapa

See St. Ludovic de Vacapa.

San Luis Mountains   Pima Co.   G. L. O. Map, 1921; Coronado N. F., 1927.

In T. 22 S., Rs. 9, 10 E. Short range at corner Santa Cruz county about 5 miles southwest of Arivaca. "Some Mexicans located a mine in these mountains which they called the San Luis from which the mountains were named."

San Marcelo

See Sonoita.

San Miguel   Pima Co.   Lumholtz Map, 1916; U. S. G. S., 1923.

Sp., "Saint Michael." In T. 21 S., R. 6 E. Indian village on Papago Ind. Res.

"A lately located Papago ranchería in a country of beautiful grassy plains or dunes. It is 10 miles north of boundary monument No. 143." Lumholtz. P. O. established June 15, 1917, Elizabeth T. Wolf, P. M.

San Miguel de Quebabi

See Quebabi.

San Pablo   Maricopa Co.

Mexican hamlet about a mile from original settlement of Tempe. Eventually swallowed up by Tempe as that town expanded. See San Pueblo.

"A new town, San Pablo, has been laid out near Haydens Ferry for which William Kirkland donated 70 acres of his land." *Arizona Sentinel*, May 3, 1873.

San Pablo de Quijouri or Quipuri   Cochise Co.

On San Pedro river near Fairbank. "On December 10, 1696, Kino started from Dolores and went to San Pablo de Quipuri, a place near the head of that branch of the Gila, now called the San Pedro, in the vicinity of the present Tombstone." Coues *Kino.*

San Pedro   Pima Co.

Station on San Pedro river which is possibly the Old Presidio of San Pedro on east side San Pedro river, known also as Fitz (sic) Jefferson's ranch. P. O. established April 22, 1872, Jacob Schaubliss, P. M. Presidio shows on Smith map, 1879, q.v.

San Pedro River   Cochise and Gila Cos.

One of two principal tributaries of Gila from south. "So called from a place of that name, 'Casas de San Pedro,' near its head in Sonora, Mexico, about lat. 31° 18', long 110°. Name does not appear on Kino's or Venando's maps. Called Quibivi or Hiburi river when Kino visited it, 1679." Coues, *Garces.*

Coues feels name San Pedro is "Post-Kinotic" and used long after Kino. River enters Arizona from Sonora near long. 110° flows north through Cochise and Pima counties, joins Gila near Dudleyville. Col. Graham, 1850, called it "Dirty River" (Rio Puerco). General St. George Cooke called it "José Pedro river." "Kino called it San Joseph de Terrenata." says Bolton.

Coues later calls it "Sobahipuris river." He says "Kino in 1699 called the San Pedro one of the four Evangelists, they being the Verde, Salt, Santa Cruz and San Pedro. Fray Marcos was on this river sometime in 1540 or thereabouts."

Hinton says, describing the road from Tucson to Camp Goodwin: "The banks of the San Pedro river are high and steep and about 10 feet apart." This width would hardly hold good today —1934.

Lieut. Col. Cooke was on the San Pedro, 1846. His report says "it carried a good stream of water and we caught fish in it 18 inches long."

San Pedro Valley   Cochise Co.

Valley proper extends north from a few miles above Tombstone to Cascabel. Artesian water is found at many places. Colton called this valley "Santa Ana de Hiburi" meaning doubtless "Quiburi."

First settled November 29, 1877, by **Philomen and Dudley** Thomas, Seth and Orin Merrill, and others. Friar Marcos de Niza passed down the valley, 1539, and Coronado's command, 1540. See also San Pedro river.

San Pueblo   Maricopa Co.

Name given "Mexican town" of Tempe. "A man named Kirkland who lived on Winchester Miller place organized an association known as San Pueblo Town Assn. The first house was built 1873 by a man named Sontag." Farish. Senator Carl Hayden, who was born and raised at Tempe, is doubtful whether this name, San Pueblo, is correct or was ever used.

"A short distance beyond (Tempe) was a community of Mexicans that had been named San Pablo." McClintock. See San Pablo.

San Rafael   Santa Cruz Co.   Smith Map, 1879; G. L. O., 1892-1921.

Mexican hamlet upper end of Cameron's San Rafael Grant.

San Rafael del Valle   Cochise Co.   Coronado N. F., 1927; G. L. O., 1908.

"San Rafael of the Valley." Short, narrow, Mexican Land Grant lying both sides San Pedro river south of Boquillas grant. Hereford is at its southern end. This tract of 20,034 acres was granted by Mexico, 1832. Title finally vested to Camou Brothers of Sonora, Mexico, by U. S. Land Court for 17,474 acres.

San Rafael de la Zanja Grant   Santa Cruz Co.

Sp., "San Rafael of the Ditch." Mexican Land Grant on border along Santa Cruz river. Made to Manuel Bustello, May, 1825. Owned by Cameron Brothers, Colin and Brewster, about 1880 to 1890 and used by them as a cattle ranch. Village of Lochiel on grant was their headquarters and named by Colin Cameron.

McClintock says: "It was made originally by Mexican government for 'four square leagues' of land in vicinity of Presidio of Santa Cruz. The Mexican surveyor obligingly laid it off 'four leagues square' which increased its acreage considerably. It was, however, only confirmed for 17,353 acres."

San Simon   Cochise Co.   Map, G. L. O., 1921.

Station S. P. R. R. in Cochise county. Valley about 50 miles long, in southeastern part of State. P. O. established March 16, 1881, Francis P. Austin, P. M.

San Simon boasts that it is the only town in Arizona that owns and operates a public bath house. An artesian well furnishes water and keys to bath house are distributed to all citizens. Name is very old, but its origin cannot be determined.

San Simon Head   Cochise Co.   G. L. O. Map, 1921.

In T. 16 S., R. 30 E., peak, eastern side Chiricahua mountains, in Coronado N. F. A prominent land mark from valley.

San Simon Peak   Cochise Co.   G. L. O. Map, 1921.

In T. 11 S., R. 31 E. On boundary between Cochise and Greenlee counties.

San Simon River and Valley   Cochise and Graham Cos.
                                                Smith Map, 1879.

Stream rising on western slope of Steins Peak range just over State line in New Mexico. Upper end is called "Rio Sauz." Its lower portion is often locally called the "Solomonville wash," as it enters the Gila near Solomonville. Also known as "Suauca," "Santo Domingo," and "Rio Suez." (Sp., willow.) Last name was used when the International boundary survey was made. See Santo Domingo.

San Xavier del Bac (Often written simply "Bac")
                Smith Map, 1879; Eckhoff, 1881; G. L. O., 1892.

In Santa Cruz valley, about 9 miles from Tucson. Became a mission about 1732 or perhaps as early as 1720. Founded by Jesuits for Papago Indians. In June, 1768, it came under Padre Garces who ministered it for eight or ten years.
Oldest mission in Arizona or California, according to Farish. Bancroft says, "About 1778 or 1780, mission was destroyed by Apaches." Present church is dated 1797, which Bancroft thinks was date of its completion. Bolton says, "San Xavier, April 28, 1700, Kino wrote in his diary 'we began the foundation of a very large and capacious church and house of San Xavier del Bac.'" Papagos called it "Where the river reappears in the sand." Lumholtz. Of San Xavier Poston wrote:

> "In San Xavier I love to linger,
> And muse on the march of Old Time's finger,
> For here with Christ in Holy union,
> It was I took my first communion."

"The next event of note to occur in the valley was the founding of the original mission of San Francisco Xavier del Bac. The fields at Bac were planted to grain, pastures stocked with horses, cattle, sheep and goats, and many of its thousand odd inhabitants were housed in adobe dwellings. Some time between 1701 and 1706, a church and a dwelling for the Padre were built at San Augustin de Oiaur.
"Upon the expulsion of the Jesuits from New Spain in 1767, Garces was ordered to San Xavier del Bac, reaching his new post June 30, 1768. Fr. Garces was a man of ample education, simple, and wonderfully sincere . . . . If Kino was the Christianizer of the valley of Santa Cruz, Garces was its civilizer." Donald Page, *Arizona Historical Review*, April, 1930. P. O. established as San Xavier, Aug. 7, 1915. Forman M. Grant, P. M.

Sanchez   Graham Co.   G. L. O. Map, 1909.

In Gila valley, near Solomonville.

"Lorenzo Sanchez settled here in Feb., 1889. He had a family of nine boys and three girls. About 1891 he got a school district established, pupils all being his own children. They named the place Sanchez in his honor." Letter, Mrs. Jennie Ringgold, Safford. P. O. established Aug. 19, 1901, Hignio Cortales, P. M.

Sanday (sic)   Yavapai Co.

Station A. T. & S. F. R. R. 7 miles north of Skull valley. "Origin unknown." A.G.W.

Sanders   Apache Co.

See Cheto.

Sand Dune Plateau, or San Dunes   Apache Co.
Mallory Map, 1876; Smith, 1879.

In extreme northeast corner of State, east of Calabasa mountains. Near here is a place marked "Diamond Fields," q.v., where the famous fake diamond fields were located.

Sand Tank Mountains   Maricopa Co.   G. L. O. Map, 1921.

In Ts. 6, 7, 8, 9 S., Rs. 1, 2, 3 W. Near Gila Bend, in southeast corner Maricopa county. The Sand Tanks near here were well known water holes from which mountains got their name.

Sandy   Mohave Co.

P. O. established by this name in Mohave county, Oct. 25, 1894, Mrs. Nellie C. Hunt, P. M. Not mapped but from post office records must have been somewhere on Big Sandy river after which it was probably named.

Sanenecheck   Navajo Co.   G. L. O. Map, 1921; U. S. G. S., 1923.

Elevation 6,680 feet. Peak, Navajo Ind. Res., north of Black mesa, near lat. 36° 30', long. 110° 35'. Decision U.S.G.B. Gregory shows it on his map as Sanenheck Rock about 15 miles southwest of Marsh pass. Father Haile writes that he does not know its meaning. Gregory, however, says it means "Thief Rock," in Navajo.

Sanford   Pima Co.   G. L. O. Map, 1892.

In T. 18 S., R. 17 E. Sometimes spelled Sandford. On Cienega creek about 4 miles south of Total Wreck mine.

"Denton G. Sanford of New York, came to Arizona, 1862. Located on the 'Cienega' 19 miles north of Camp Crittenden and 9 miles north of Fish ranch, q.v. This ranch is called Sanford on some old maps; on others, Empire. Sanford's daughter told me several years ago that her father named the ranch 'The Empire' after his native state." Letter, Mrs. George F. Kitt, Tucson.

Later Sanford located another ranch on Sonoita creek, Santa Cruz Co., q.v.

Sanford   Santa Cruz Co.

Ranch on Sonoita creek, eastern side Baca grant. On Benson-Nogales branch, S. P. R. R. There is a station on the ranch which the railroad calls Bloxton, about 17 miles northeast of Nogales.

"Sanford was a well known cattleman in this region as early as 1880. Then he sold his cattle and ran sheep, much to the disgust of his cattlemen neighbors. His cattle brand was D S on left hip." Cady, *Arizona's Yesterdays.* He tells of Sanford's activities in a very interesting way. The ranch is now known as the Circle Z Dude ranch. P. O. established Jan. 24, 1871, Larken W. Carr, P. M.

San Juan Capistrano
See Sacaton.

Santa Catalina Mountains   Pima Co.   G. L. O. Map, 1921; Coronado N. F., 1927.

Group of pine covered peaks and a favorite summer resort country. The early Spanish called it La Iglesia, "The Church," from its fancied resemblance to a great cathedral. In plain view from Tucson.

At the northern end of this range, Harold Bell Wright located his novel, *The Mine with the Iron Door*.

On some maps they are called "Santa Catarina."

Santa Catarina (sic)   Pima Co.

Santa Catalina. Some early geographers spelled this name wrong. The post office people seem also to have made the same error. So did Hinton. See Santa Catalina. P. O. established as Santa Catarina April 26, 1882, Louis Goodman, P. M.

Santa Cruz   Pinal Co.   Postal Route Map, 1929.

On Santa Cruz river close to S. P. R. R., about 50 miles west of Tucson. P. O. established January 11, 1910, Scott White, P. M.

Santa Cruz County

Created by Legislature March 15, 1899, out of Pima and Cochise counties. Nogales county seat. Name, of course, came from river.

Santa Cruz River   Santa Cruz and Pima Cos.   Smith Map, 1879.

Sp., "River of Holy Cross." Named by Kino. According to Bolton he also called it "Rio de Santa Maria." Rises in Sonora, Mexico, flows north and west past Tucson. Finally lost in desert near Maricopa station, S. P. R. R. It is mostly a dry wash, but a roaring torrent in rainy season. There is another river by this name in San Rafael grant, q.v.

Santa Cruz River   Santa Cruz Co.   G. L. O. Map, 1921.

Small stream rising northern part San Rafael grant, flows due south, enters Mexico at Lochiel. See also the larger Santa Cruz river to the west.

Santa Maria River   Yavapai and Mohave Cos.   G. L. O. Map, 1921; U. S. G. S., 1923.

Formed in T. 14 N., R. 7 W., by junction Kirkland creek and Connell gulch, flows southwest to form Bill Williams river at junction with Big Sandy river in Mohave county in T. 11 N., R. 12 W. On U.S.G.S. map, 1923, Connell gulch is called Cottonwood creek.

"Garces is not to be credited with the actual discovery of this stream for it had been located and named long before. Definite knowledge of it goes back to expedition of Juan de Onate, 1604-1605, who named it first, Rio de San Andrés, after St. Andrew, whose day is November 30, and very likely the actual date of discovery, as he started October 7, 1605. Name first appears upon Font's map and came into general use." Coues.

"Santa Maria, a name which the early Spanish map makers applied to the whole river." *Wheeler Report*. Careful search does not show its origin clearly. The writer's feeling is that it may possibly have been named after one of Espejo's party, Fray Juan de Santa Maria, a priest who was killed by natives in central New Mexico in June, 1851. See also Santa Cruz and Bill Williams rivers.

Santa Maria Mountains   Yavapai Co.   G. L. O. Map, 1921;
U. S. G. S., 1923.

Southeast corner Baca grant, extending southeast about 15 miles. On Prescott N. F., according to some maps, but not shown on the Forest Service maps. For probable origin see Santa Maria river.

Santa Maria Toll Road   Rand McNally Map, 1877.

One of several toll roads built in early years. According to Rand McNally's map, 1877, Santa Maria road ran from Kirkland to junction of Santa Maria and Bill Williams streams. See Wagon Roads.

Santa Rita

See Greaterville.

Santa Rita Mines

"Pumpelly reached here early in 1861 to investigate silver production." *Across America and Asia.*

Santa Rita Mountains   Santa Cruz and Pima Cos.
U. S. G. S. Map, 1923; Coronado N. F., 1927.

East side Santa Cruz river, north of Nogales. "The first sawmill ever erected in Arizona was put in Santa Ritas south of Tucson." Hamilton's *Arizona.*
Named for the well known female Catholic saint, but by whom is not known.

Santa Rita Range Reserve   Pima Co.   Map, Coronado N. F., 1927.

Area of about 50,000 acres set aside, 1906, by presidential proclamation for carrying on experiments in grazing cattle under southwestern range conditions. West side Santa Rita mountains, about 45 miles south of Tucson.

Santa Rosa, Valley, Wash and Indian Settlement   Pima Co.
Bryan Map, 1927; U. S. G. S., 1923.

In T. 15 S., R. 7 E., Papago Ind. Res. "At sunset we made camp in a very red desert at the very geographical center of the great Santa Rosa valley. Elevation 2,180 feet. Mostly the prospect was creosote bushes." Hornaday's *Desert and Lava.*
Lumholtz writes of this settlement: "It is in fact the largest summer rancheria of the Papagoes. Native name is Kuat-shi—'Big Peak.' Often called and written 'Kuarchi' or 'Archi,' meaning big peak or big mountain." See Kuarchi.

Santa Rosa Mountains   Pima Co.   Bryan Map, 1920;
U. S. G. S., 1923.

On Papago Ind. Res. near lat 32° 20′ long., 111° 50′. Lumholtz says, "Papago name is Kuarchi or Archi, meaning Big mountains."

Santa Teresa Mountains   Graham Co.   U. S. G. S. Map, 1923.

In Ts. 5, 6 S., R. 20 E. On Crook N. F. Origin unknown. See Tucson mountains.

Santa Domingo, Rio   Graham Co.   G. L. O. Map, 1866.

Stream by this name only on G.L.O. map, 1866. On Crook N. F., it shows as Goodwin wash. Rises, Santa Teresa mountains, flows northeasterly into Gila, at point where Camp Goodwin was located. See Goodwin.

Santan

See Nuggett.

Santan Mountain and Indian Village Pinal Co.
       G. L. O. Map, 1921; U. S. G. S., 1923.

Elevation 3,093 feet, in T. 3 S., R. 6 E. On Gila River Ind Res., north side Gila river. Village is in T. 3 S., R. 5 E. "A corruption of the original name, Santa Ana." Hodge.

"Some Indians of Quajote ranchería moved to the north bank of the Gila across from Sacaton. The Papagos called their new location Santa Ana, the name given by the early padres to the deserted ranchería at the foot of Santa Rosa mountain. It was soon shortened to Santan." Father Oblasser.

The history of the Pima "Calendar Sticks" speaks of Santan as early as 1857. That is, the Indian who translated the "Calendar Sticks" in 1910 used that name.

Santan and Casa Blanca, Pima Villages Pinal Co.

Whipple, 1854, does not mention Santan in his list of Pima villages. Neither do Ross Browne in 1864, Rustling, 1867, nor Russel, 1902, although the latter listed eighteen Pima towns. Russel's "Calendar Stick" story mentions Santan in 1857 and 1880, but the Indian translator was speaking in 1902 and might have confused dates.

George Santan was postmaster at Nugget, Gila county, 1881. Could he have been the source of the name?

Casa Blanca shows on the maps of 1870 and 1880. Ross Browne mentions it, 1863. Ammi White was agent here, 1864, for the Pimas and seems to have lived among them for several years before then. Could they have "Mexicanized" his name, White, into Blanca—White's House, e.g. Casa Blanca? The author is inclined to think so.

San Domingo River Graham Co.

See Rio Santa Domingo.

Sanup Plateau and Peak Mohave Co.
       Smith Map, 1879; U. S. G. S., 1923.

On north side Colorado river, north of Hualpai Ind. Res. Near lat. 35°, 50'. No explanation of this name discovered.

Under "Sannup" Hodge says: "A word said to have been used in Massachusetts as a designation for a married Indian man. Levett, in 1682, and Cotton Mather, 1686, both use the word in this sense." Hodge further says: "The word was not an Indian word but was one used by the whites to mean an Indian who was married." Word of course could have been used and understood by government men who surveyed the country in this region—Mohave—and who were often short of names for new points they mapped.

Sapphire Canyon Coconino Co. Map, Grand Canyon N. P., 1927.

In T. 32 N., R. 1 E. Small canyon in Grand Canyon. Heads at the rim and flows north into Colorado river in Granite gorge. So named by Powell for its coloring.

Sardinia Peak Pima Co. G. L. O. Map, 1921, "Sardine Mountain";
       Coronado N. F., 1927.

In T. 21 S., R. 12 E. "An old Mexican named Sarvinia, lived near this peak for many years. Old timers say it was called after him, but name became mixed up in time and anglicized." Letter, Forest Ranger Wingo.

Sasabe   Pima Co.
    Eckhoff, 1880, "Sassaby"; G. L. O., 1892-1921, "Sasabe."

In T. 28 S., R. 8 E. In Altar valley, principal port of entry into
U. S. from Altar district of Sonora. East side Pozo Verde mountains, about 40 miles northwest of Nogales. There is a town
on both sides of line. Papago word for this place is "Shas-
hoouk" or "Echo." Lumholtz says: "From best information obtainable, name is that of either an old Mexican or Papago
family." P. O. established Aug. 23, 1905. Teofilo E. Arros, P. M.

Sasabe Flat and Valley   Pima Co.   G. L. O. Map, 1892;
    U. S. G. S., 1923.

Village about 6 miles north of Mexican line, and present town
of Sasabe. Post office established as Sasabe Flat, Aug. 19, 1869,
Juan Elias, P. M. Name changed to Providence Wells by P. O.
Department, July 30, 1878, Yredalencia Aguirre, P. M. Providence Wells is not on any map. Sasabe Flat is a large open
valley in Ts. 20, 21 S., Rs. 8, 9 E., east side Baboquivari mountains. Named after border town.

Sasco   Pima Co.   U. S. G. S. Map, 1923.

In T. 10 S., R. 9 E. Station Arizona-Southern R. R., 8 miles
northeast of Silver Bell.
    "Initials Southern Arizona Smelting Company. Established
about 1910." Letter, Paul Shoup.
    P. O. established July 10, 1907. Charles C. Matthews, P. M.

Sauceda Mountains   Pima and Maricopa Cos.   G. L. O. Map, 1921.

Sp., "little willows." Northern side Papago Ind. Res. at lat.
32°, 30'. There is a nearby Indian village by this name. Often
spelled "Salceda", which is correct as both forms are in dictionaries. Name doubtless of Spanish origin, taken from word
"sauce," the botanical name for willow tree.

Saucida (sic)   Pima Co.   Lumholtz Map, 1916.

Papago rancheria, north side Papago reservation, about 25
miles south of Gila Bend. Seventeen miles east of Batamote
ranch. Lumholtz says: "This is one of the main Papago ran-
cherías. Papago word meaning 'where the willows grow.'" Lumholtz is wrong. This is clearly a Spanish word.

Sauls   Navajo Co.   U. S. G. S. Map, 1923.

Apache Ind. Res. At county line on Carrizo creek. An Indian
camp occupied by family of an Apache scout who was given
name of Saul by Lieut. Gatewood as early as 1882. When Lieut.
Gatewood was enlisting Apaches as scouts, it often became
necessary to give them American names, their own being too
long or not easily written or translated into English. The writer
helped him name several in 1880-81, at Fort Apache.

Sauz, Valle de   Cochise Co.

"From the Rio Mimbres to the Rio San Pedro is 152.5 miles.
Intermediate is the Valle de Sauz, 72 miles, where water is always found." Report, Sec'y War, 1855.
    Now called San Simon Valley. Is Rio de Sauz on Smith map,
1879; Eckhoff, 1880. Bartlett, 1852, called it El Cienega de Saux,
"willow cienega." See Sauceda.

Saw Buck Mountains   Graham Co.   U. S. G. S. Map, 1923.

In approximately T. 1 N., R. 26 E. South of Freeze-out creek, eastern part San Carlos Apache Ind. Res. "A descriptive name. Looks like an old pack saddle of the sawbuck variety." Letter J. W. Girdner.

Sawed Off Mountain   Greenlee Co.   Map, Crook N. F., 1920.

In sec. 30, T. 3 N., R. 30 E. Apache N. F. "Mr. Towles Casper named the mountain in 1883. Prominent point looking as if its tip had been sawed or cut off. Hence the name." Letter, Forest Ranger D. H. Suite.

Saw Mill Canyon   Pima Co.   G. L. O. Map, 1921.

On west side Santa Ritas about 5 miles north of Madera canyon. Flows northwest into Santa Cruz on Canoa grant. On Roskruge map, 1893, is called Dowdle canyon, after a nearby ranch owned by a man of this name.

Saw Mill Creek   Gila Co.   Map, San Carlos Ind. Res.

Stream rising at government saw mill northeast corner T. 3 N., R. 19 E. Flows north into Salt river about 6 miles east of Asbestos mines.

Sawtooth Mountain   Gila Co.   Map, Fort Apache Ind. Res., 1928.

In T. 6 N., R. 23 E., about 6 miles northwest of Fort Apache, 3 miles north of Kelly's butte. Descriptive name. A ragged looking mountain.

Sawtooth Mountains   Pinal Co.   U. S. G. S. Map, 1923.

In T. 9 S., R. 6 E., west side S. P. R. R. Descriptive name.

Sayers   Yavapai Co.

P. O. established November 17, 1908, George Sayers, P. M. Named for him. Exact location unknown.

Scanlon Ferry   Mohave Co.   G. L. O. Map, 1921; U. S. G. S., 1923.

In T. 21 S., R. 71 E. On Colorado river between Nevada and Arizona about 6 miles south of Greggs ferry. Fish who covers many small details that other historians have overlooked does not mention the man or his ferry.

Schell Gulch   Gila Co.   Map, Tonto N. F., 1926.

In sec. 3, T. 5 N., R. 13 E. Heads east Armer mountain. Flows due south into Roosevelt lake. "After an early settler by this name." Letter, Bud Armer.

Schnebly Hill   Yavapai Co.   Map, Coconino N. F., 1928.

"A very difficult hill on Oak creek for early teaming. So called after Elsworth Schnebly, first settler at Sedona." Letter, Ed Miller, Forest Supervisor, Flagstaff.

Schultz (sic)   Gila Co.   Globe Quad, 1892.

"East side Pinto creek near Bloody Tanks—name spelled Schultze by settler who located this ranch." P. O. established as Schultz, July 12, 1894, Lizzie Schneider, P. M.

Schultz Pass and Spring   Coconino Co.   Map, Coconino N. F., 1927.

Pass in secs. 14 and 15, T. 22 N., R. 7 E., north of Elden mountain. Spring at west end of pass. On map, Coconino N. F., spring is spelled Shultz while pass is spelled Schultz. On some other maps they are spelled Schults. Observatory peak west of Flagstaff was first named for him.

Both named after well known Flagstaff sheepman, whose application for a brand in Brand boards office at Phoenix signed his name C. H. Schultz.

Schultz Peak   Coconino Co.

"On San Francisco mountain in sec. 2, T. 22 N., R. 7 E., about 2 miles southwest of Fremont Peak, one of the San Francisco Peaks. Named locally for a pioneer sheepman." U. S. G. B., Dec., 1933.

Scott Mountain   Pinal Co.   Map, Crook N. F., 1926.

In sec. 6, T. 3 S., R. 14 E., about 3 miles northeast of Ray. Origin unknown.

Scottsdale   Maricopa Co.   G. L. O. Map, 1921.

Elevation 1,261 feet. In T. 2 N., R. 4 E. Village east of Phoenix. Established by and named after the Rev. Winfield Scott, Civil War veteran, later a chaplain in the regular army. Stationed at Angel Island, San Francisco, 1888. Located a farm here and as a little settlement grew up around him they called it Scottsdale.

Screwbean Spring   Mohave Co.   G. L. O. Map, 1921.

Sp., "tornillo." In T. 13 N., R. 19 W. In Chemehuevi valley 6 miles east Colorado river. "Screwbean," a desert tree which grows about the spring. Tornello is the Spanish word for a screw.

Seal Mountain   Yavapai Co.

Near Walnut Grove on Hassayampa. Said by Fish and one other historian to have been background for the first seal used in territory. Not found on any map.

There seem to have been at least four seals up to the present time. Apparently, Secretary McCormick brought with him either a seal ready for use or else a design from which one could be made. Probably the former. He describes this seal as follows: "A stalwart miner standing by his wheelbarrow with pick and shovel at his side. The auriferous hills behind him with the motto Ditat Deus (God enriches) below his figure."

These hills were popularly supposed to be the San Franciscos, which are absolutely non-mineral. Early residents declare it was a representation of Seal mountain near Walnut Grove. McClintock says this design without the wheelbarrow has been found on some early documents. Legislature, 1864, authorized a new seal, as follows:

"There shall be a view of the San Francisco mountains in the distance with a deer, columnar cactus and pine trees in the foreground."

There are two rather odd things about these seals. First, there is absolutely no mineral of any kind, certainly no gold, silver or copper in the San Francisco range. Second, there are no columnar cacti in the region.

By this act, the Secretary was authorized to use the "Former seal (evidently the McCormick affair) until the seal authorized in this Act is prepared."

Bancroft says: "This second seal was not put into use for the first time until published in the session Laws of 1883."
McClintock thinks the seal with the deer and pine trees, authorized in 1864, was used up to about 1890. There seem to be two of these seals with the deer, both dated 1863. One has the animal facing to the right with a single-bodied giant cactus (saguaro) at its nose. The other has the deer facing left with a branched saguaro in front of it.
With statehood, 1912, a new seal was adopted. It has so many details on its face that it is too crowded for good effect and is an artistic failure. The date, 1863, on all previous seals has also been eliminated. The motto, Ditat Deus, has been retained, about the only part of the early seals that has lived through the improvement (?) process.

Second Forest   Apache Co.   U. S. G. S. Map, 1923.

In T. 17 N., Rs. 24 and 25 E. One of the units of the Petrified Forest southeast of Holbrook. Originally these groups of trees were numbered from Holbrook, first, second, third, etc.

Second Mesa   Navajo Co.   U. S. G. S. Map, 1923.

In R. 17 E., T. 29 N. Hopi Ind. Res. The second mesa from south in group of Hopi mesas and villages.

Secret Mountain   Coconino Co.   Map, Coconino N. F., 1928.

In sec. 12, T. 18 N., R. 4 E. "W. W. Van Deren gave it this name. Certainly well named, for it lies between heads of Secret canyon and Low canyon. The narrow hogback is not over 50 feet wide and one could hunt for a week and not reach the top of mountain." Letter, Ed Miller.

Secret Pass, Secret Mine   Mohave Co.   G. L. O. Map, 1921.

In T. 21 N., R. 19 W. In Black mountains, 12 miles east of Colorado river. So named because it was hidden by mountains and found unexpectedly. It is a few miles north of Gold Road mine on old emigrant road of early days. Humphreys located and named it in the early Sixties.
"November 5, 1852, Camp No. 32. The pass was exceedingly rough and bordered by overhanging crags. We passed through unmolested and were cheered by the view of the Colorado winding far below through a broad valley. The barometer showed us to be about 3,200 feet above the river." Sitgreaves report.
P. O. established October 20, 1916. Ada Webster, P. M.

Secundo Well   Pima Co.   U. S. G. S. Map, 1923.

In T. 20 S., R. 9 E. Altar valley. "This well and a Papago ranchería was at northwest end Giju mountains, east side of Baboquivaris. About 15 miles northwest Cerro Colorado mine." Lumholtz. The Postmaster writes: "A Mexican named Secundo dug the well."

Sedona   Coconino Co.   Map, Coconino N. F., 1928.

In T. 17 N., R. 6 E. Settlement and Forest Ranger station on Oak creek. After Mrs. Carl Schnebly, wife of an early settler. Her given name was Sedona. P. O. established June 26, 1902. Theodore C. Schnebly, P. M.

Seepage Mountain   Yavapai Co.   Map, Prescott N. F., 1927.

In sec. 7, T. 16 N., R. 5 W.
"There is considerable seepage on south and east side of the mountain which gives it the name. Horse wash heads on its east side." Letter, Forest Supervisor Grubb.

Se-ga-toa Spring   Apache Co.   Gregory Map, 1916; U. S. G. S., 1923.

In T. 1 N., R. 9 W., Navajo Ind. Res. Navajo word meaning "water in the canyon." Near Tuye spring. Father Haile spells it Tseyi-to "Spring in the canyon."

Segi Mesas   Navajo Co.   Gregory Map, 1916; G. L. O., 1921.

On Navajo Ind. Res., near line of Colorado between Piute canyon and Moonlight creek. "The word Tseye or Tsegi in Navajo means 'canyon' or 'rocky places' A mesa trenched by canyons." Gregory. See Tsegi.

Sehili   Apache Co.   Gregory Map, 1916.

In T. 7 N., R. 6 W., on Defiance plateau—Navajo Ind. Res. Navajo, "Place where water disappears into a canyon." Haile. Settlement on Spruce brook near head of Canyon del Muerto.

Seligman   Yavapai Co.   G. L. O. Map. 1921.

Station, A. T. & S. F. R. R. Named for Jesse Seligman of Seligman Bros., New York bankers, connected with old Atlantic and Pacific R. R. First railroad to Prescott was built about 1888 from this point. Called Prescott and Arizona Central; T. S. Bullock, President.

Town then called Prescott Junction. Later Junction, q.v. When Ash Fork branch of A. T. & S. F. R. R. was built, this branch road was abandoned and rails removed. P. O. established April 18, 1895. Jacob W. Henderson, P. M.

Sells   Pima Co.   G. L. O. Map, 1921; Lumholtz, 1912.

In T. 17 S., R. 4 E., Indian village and agency Papago Ind. Res. West side Baboquivari range.

Originally called "Indian Oasis." Changed to Sells for Cato Sells, Commissioner Indian Affairs at Washington, 1917-1920 during his official term. It is about 20 miles from Mexican line.

The U.S.G.B. backed by strong local sentiment, protested vigorously against this change in an old established name. But without success. The P. O. and Indian Service would not reverse their action. Lumholtz locates it at extreme edge Artesia mountains. There is a U. S. Indian school here. P. O. established as Sells Dec. 14, 1918. Joseph Menager, P. M. He did not qualify and on April 26, 1919, William G. Power was appointed P. M.

Sembrich   Cochise Co.   Map, Coronado N. F., 1927.

In sec. 8, T. 23 S., R. 20 E. Old ranch on Ramsey canyon, east of Huachuca mountains, "Sembrich was an old time settler long since dead. One of first settlers in Huachucas, about 1879." Letter, Postmaster, Sunnyside, Arizona. P. O. established December 31, 1915, John W. Noel, P. M.

Senator   Yavapai Co.   G. L. O. Map, 1921.

Well known mine about 10 miles south of Prescott, north side Mount Union. Origin cannot be definitely determined.

"The Senator mine, to which a 10-stamp mill is attached, has on the dumps about $50,000 worth of ore which assays $85 per ton, gold." Hinton's *Hand Book*, 1878.

"Here the term 'Hassayamper' was first used by S. O. Fredericks, a hard rock miner from Nevada. He needed men at the Senator mine, men accustomed to the use of drills and hammers. Most local miners at that time were placer miners from California, who were working along the Hassayampa. Fredericks posted a notice 'Hard Rock miners wanted—No Hassayampers hired.'" Letter, Sharlot Hall.

P. O. established November 1, 1915. Mary Wells, P. M.

Seneca Howland, Mount

See Navajo mountain.

Sentinel   Yuma Co.   G. L. O. Map, 1921.

Station, S. P. R. R., 29 miles west of Gila Bend. Opened about 1881. After nearby Sentinel peak, well known land mark, q.v. P. O. established June 30, 1880. William H. Burke, P. M. See Burke.

Sentinel Butte   Pima Co.   Map, Coronado N. F., 1927.

Elevation 3,343 feet. In T. 15 S., R. 17 E., at upper end of Rincon valley. Southwest corner, Santa Rita division, Coronado N. F. "Stands at head of valley like a sentinel on guard." Letter, Forest Ranger.

Sentinel Peak   Cochise Co.

See Square Peak.

Sentinel Peak   Pima Co.   G. L. O. Map, 1915.

Mountain about 2 miles west of Tucson. Area purchased, 1931, by city for a park. Was a point in pioneer days on which look-outs were kept for hostile Apaches. University of Arizona students have placed a huge "A" at its crest, facing the city. Sometimes called "A" mountain, from the letter.

Donald Page, *Arizona Historical Review*, April, 1930, says: "The conical black hill that from time to time has been known as the Sierra de la Frente Negra; Picacho del Sentinela; Sentinel peak; Warners mountain; and finally 'A' mountain."

Sentinel Peak   Yuma Co.   G. L. O. Map, 1892-1921.

Elevation 689 feet. In T. 6 S., R. 8 W. Small but prominent peak. Nearby railroad station takes its name from this peak. "It stood out in the distance like a sentinel of the desert."

Separation Canyon and Rapids   Mohave Co.   U. S. G. S. Map, 1923.

On north side Colorado river, opposite Hualpai Ind. Res.

"So called by Major Powell because at this point above the rapids the Howlands and Dunn left the first party." Dellenbaugh.

Sereno   Coconino Co.   Map, Coronado N. F., 1927.

Station, main A. T. & S. F. R. R., 6 miles west of Williams. "Just a name." A.G.W.

Servoss   Cochise Co.   G. L. O. Map, 1921.

In T. 16 S., R. 24 E. Station, Cochise-Pearce branch, E. P. & S. W. R. R.

Rockfellow says: "Named for Walter E. Servoss of Rockfellow and Servoss, cattlemen. They owned the N Y ranch here. Their brand was N Y on left hip."

P. O. established December 15, 1915. Jeff D. Langford, P. M.

Set-silt-so Spring   Apache Co., Gregory Map, 1916; U. S. G. S., 1923.

In T. 12 N., R. 11 W. Navajo Ind. Res., on Chinlee creek. Gregory says it means "water dripping from rocks." U.S.G.S. map has it Set-sit-so.

Seven Cities of Cibola

See Seven Pueblos.

Seven Mile Canyon   Navajo Co.

Stream heading southeast corner of T. 5 N., R. 23 E. Runs north into east fork of White river, about 3 miles above Fort Apache. On Fort Apache Ind. Res.

So called because head of canyon was at Seven Mile hill on road to Fort Thomas, which was just that many miles from Apache. There is a spring at foot of the hill. Here a scout named Owens was killed by Apaches September 2, 1881. The day before this, three men with a four-horse team were ambushed and killed by the same Indians on top of hill.

The writer with G troop, 6th U. S. Cavalry, while scouting for hostiles September 10, 1881, found and buried these men where they fell.

Seven Mile Creek   Gila Co.   Map, Crook N. F., 1928.

Rises in eastern part T. 3 N., R. 15½ E., flows southeast into Fort Apache Ind. Res., enters San Carlos river in northeast corner T. 1 S., R., 18 E., about 2 miles above Rice school.

"It is almost exactly 7 miles in length."

Seven Mile Mountain   Gila Co.   Map, Crook N. F., 1926.

In T. 3 N., R. 17 E., east of Jackson butte, Fort Apache Ind. Res. "Mountain is about 7 miles from well known 'Seven Up' cow ranch. The boys named it for that reason." C. V. Christenson, P. M. Globe.

Seven Pueblos of Tusayan   Navajo Co.

Oraibi, meaning "Numerous eagle traps (?)."

Shipolovia, meaning "Houses strung out in a line," or "The place of peaches."

Mishongnovi, meaning "The hill of boulders." The Navajos call it "Tse-tso-kid," (Boulder hill).

Shongo-povi or Chimo-povi, one of the oldest of these pueblos, meaning "The place of the reeds."

Sichomovi, meaning "People of the middle houses."

Walpi, meaning "People of the kiva."

Hano, "The people of Hano are Tewans, whose ancestors moved from the Rio Grande to Tusayan during the great Pueblo revolt against Spanish authority in 1680." *Navajo Dictionary.*

Above are decisions of U.S.G.B.

Seymour   Maricopa Co.

After James Seymour who, 1879, bought the Vulture mine and built a mill on the Hassayampa about 11 miles below Vulture, 2 miles from Smith's mill.

Barney says "a town site was laid out here 1879 by Cusenberry and Seymour who then owned the Vulture mine. They erected a 20-stamp mill here. Company called Central Arizona Mining Company."

Arizona Gazetteer, 1881, lists this place as a "stage station and mill site" and says:

"Seymour was a New York man who bought the old Vulture mine after it was supposed to be all worked out and worthless. He discovered he had been taken in, but went to work to develop the mine. Spent $380,000 in erecting a 80-stamp mill and piping water 14 miles to the mine. Made all his money back and retired with a fortune."

P. O. established June 20, 1879. Isaac H. Levy, P. M.

Sezhini Butte   Apache Co.   G. L. O. Map, 1921.

In T. 5 N., R. 8 W. Navajo Ind. Res., north side Canyon de Chelly. Navajo Tsezhini "Black Rock." Haile.

S. H. Mountains   Yuma Co.   G. L. O. Map, 1921.

In Ts. 1, 2, 3, E., Rs. 14, 15, 16, W. Short range extending northwest to southeast. A rather vulgar origin. At a distance the peak resembles the edifice in the rear of most country dwellings. Early miners so called it for this resemblance.

Shannon Mountain   Greenlee Co.

On Chase creek about 7 miles above Clifton, where 1886, Charles M. Shannon and his partner, Bob Metcalf, discovered a valuable copper deposit afterwards owned and operated by the Shannon Mining Co.

Sharps Bar   Mohave Co.

Early gold mining camp at mouth of Black Canyon on Colorado river. After C. M. Sharp, early settler and sluice miner, in this region. A small mining camp, 1883-84.

Shato Spring, Stream and Plateau   Navajo Co.   G. L. O. Map, 1921.

On Navajo Ind. Res., near west line Navajo county, lat. 36° 25', long. 110° 35', west of Marsh pass. Navajo name "Sunny side to water"—that is, water on south side of a rock wall. "Sha-to"— "sunny side spring." Haile.

Sheep Creek   Maricopa Co.   Map, Tonto N. F., 1927.

In sec. 34, T. 8 N., R. 7, 8 E. East side Verde river. Rises at Sheep mountain, enters Verde in southwest corner T. 7 N., R. 7 E.

"This region was a well known sheep range and the early sheepmen gave these names to locate them." Joe Hand, Forest Ranger.

Sheep Dip Creek   Apache Co.   G. L. O. Map, 1921.

Rises in T. 6 N., R. 8 W., Navajo Ind. Res., flows northwest and joins Chinle creek in T. 8 N., R. 10 W.

Some years ago, government built and maintained a sheep dipping plant on this creek in which to dip scabby Navajo sheep.

Sheep Mountain   Yuma Co.   U. S. G. S. Map.

In T 10 S., R. 19 W. East side Gila mountains.

From best information obtainable was so called because of mountain sheep (big horns) on it and in the vicinity in early days.

Sheep Peak

See Growler peak.

Sheldon   Greenlee Co.   G. L. O. Map, 1921.

In T. 7 S., R. 31 E. Station, E. P. & S. W. R. R., near State line. Named for Governor Lionel Sheldon, Governor of New Mexico, 1883-84. P. O. established August 27, 1908, John F. Holder, P. M.

Sheldon Mountain   Maricopa Co. Scott Map, Maricopa Co., 1929.

Elevation 2,135 feet. In sec. 8, T. 2 N., R 6 E., Salt River Ind. Res. southern extremity McDowell mountains near lat. 33° 32'. Origin not known. Tall black lava peak standing out from range 3 miles southeast of Harold Baxter's desert home.

Sheridan Hills   Pima Co.   G. L. O. Map, 1921.

In T. 12 S., R. 2 E., Papago Ind. Res., about 12 miles north of Brownell. Called Cimmaron mountains on U.S.G.S. map, 1923. "Named in honor of General Phil. Sheridan." Letter, Col. J. Munsey, Sells, Ariz.

Sheridan Mountain   Yavapai Co.   Map, Prescott N. F., 1931.

Prescott N. F. "Tom Sheridan was an early settler in Williamson valley. Sold out and moved to this mountain, 1877, and engaged in horse raising." Letter, Frank Grubb, Prescott. In T. 16 N., R. 6 W. East of Cottonwood wash. S.E. of Baca grant.

Sherums Peak   Mohave Co.

See Sherum.

Shibell Ranch   Pima Co.   Smith Map, 1879; G. L. O., 1880.

About 21 miles northwest Tucson on old overland stage line, Maricopa to Tucson. After early pioneer, Charles Shibell. "Still nearer where the stages changed teams, at the base of the mountain, was the ranch of Charlie Shibell, the scene of as many encounters with Apaches as any other spot in the southwest." Bourke. See Mount Shibell.

Shibell, Mount   Santa Cruz Co.   Map, Coronado N. F., 1927.

On Baca grant No. 3; east side Santa Cruz river about 6 miles north of Calabasas. After Charlie Shibell.

Shim-o-pavy

See Chim-o-pavy.

Shinarump Cliffs   Mohave Co.   G. L. O. Map, 1921.

Eastern part Kaibab Ind. Res. West side, Kanab creek.

Shinumo Altar   Coconino Co.   G. L. O. Map, 1892-1921.

On Navajo Ind. Res. East side Colorado river, at Marble canyon, west of Echo cliffs. About 12 miles south of Roundy creek. Often called Mesa buttes. Dellenbaugh says, 1933: "I named it Shinumo Altar because from where I stood it looked like an altar. Name was not intended to be permanent but became so. Shinumo was for the Indians who had formerly occupied the country here. Was Pah Ute word for these so-called 'house building people.'"

"Around the camp fire the Major (Powell) told us something about the Shinumo, as he called them, who long ago inhabited these regions." *A Canyon Voyage.*

Just where Powell got this name "Shinumo" is hard to say. There is no such tribe listed in any reference book. Hodge is silent on the subject. They were possibly an early branch of the Hopi people. The word is said to be of Hopi origin and to mean "peace."

Shinumo Creek   Coconino Co.   Map, Grand Canyon N. P., 1917.

Rising, Shinumo Amphitheatre south of Kaibab N. F., flows southwest into Colorado river at Shinumo rapids in Granite gorge

Shipley   Mohave Co.

Station, A. T. & S. F. R. R., about 3 miles east of Peach springs. "This was just a blind siding put in to accommodate the welldrilling contractors, Shipley Brothers, who were drilling some wells in this vicinity." Letter, Division Superintendent, A. T. & S. F. R. R.

Shipolovi   Apache Co.   U. S. G. S. Tusayan Sheet, 1906.

Navajo name for this place is "Kinaz-ti, Row of Houses," or "Houses strung out in a line," which describes the place exactly. On Hopi Ind. Res. Decision U.S.G.B.

One of several Hopi pueblos located on Second or Middle mesa. Like Sichomovi, this is a modern pueblo of 18th century. G. W. James says it means "peach" or place of peaches. Bourke in *Hopi Snake Dance* says "peach orchard." There are peach orchards here producing large crops.

Shipp Mountain   Yavapai Co.   G. L. O. Map, 1921; Prescott N. F., 1927.

In sec. 6, T. 14 N., R. 7 W., west side and near head of Santa Maria river.

"Said to have been named for Jeff Shipp who started a cow ranch in lower Scott's basin, about 1880. His headquarters ranch was known as Cienega ranch on Santa Maria below Scott's basin. Afterwards sold out to Guy Schultz." Letter, Frank Grubb.

Shiva Temple   Coconino Co.

"Point in Grand Canyon named after one of the Hindu gods by Clarence Dutton," according to G. W. Jones.

Shivwits Plateau   Mohave Co.   Smith Map, 1879, "Sheavwitz"; U. S. G. S., 1923, "Shivwits."

In Great Bend of Colorado river, northwest Arizona. "Shinabits Spitz" or Coyote spring in Pah Ute. The "Shivwits mountain" or "Kaib," so called for Shivwits Indians. The high butte on this mountain was called Mount Dellenbaugh, by Major Powell, in honor of Frederick S. Dellenbaugh. The country around mountain is called "Para-shont," which in Shivwits means "plenty of water."

Shivwits—"A Paiute tribe formerly occupying a plateau in northwest Arizona bearing their name. There is a remnant of the tribe near St. George, Utah." Hodge.

Shiwits (sic.) Springs, "About these springs and in the deep gulches the Shiwits Indians live, cultivating little patches of corn, gathering seeds, eating the fruit and fleshy stalks of cactus plants, catching a rabbit or lizard now and then, dirty, squalid, but happy." Powell. Dellenbaugh writes that the Indians used the "vw" so as to sound like "b" which led some to spell the name "Shibits." Shivwits, decision U. S. G. B.

Shones Crossing   Navajo Co.   Map, Sitgreaves N. F., 1924.

In sec. 27, T. 12 N., R. 21 E., on Showlow creek. Stage line from Fort Apache crossed the Showlow here where John Shone, a discharged 6th Cavalry soldier from Fort Apache, located about 1879 and ran a bunch of cattle for many years. He had but one leg. The other was lost in a battle with Indians in Texas.

Shongopovi   Navajo Co.   U. S. G. S., 1906; Gregory, 1906.

In T. 28 N., R. 17 E., Hopi Ind. Res. Shongopavi; decision U.S.G.B.

Shongopavi—"A place of chumoa, a variety of grass or a reed." Hodge.

"This word has been changed through many years and now appears on post office records as Chimopovy. Original name means 'a tall jointed grass or reed.' One of the oldest Hopi pueblos." Letter, F. M. McBride. About 5 miles southeast of Walpi. See Chimopovy.

Short Creek   Mohave Co.   U. S. G. S. Map, 1923.

Stream and hamlet. Rises west side of Vermillion cliffs, flows northwest into Utah, in T. 41 N., R. 7 W. Mormon settlement just at Utah line. "The name explains itself—it is a very short stream." P. O. established June 26, 1914, Lydia M. Covington, P. M.

Showap

See Sowats.

Showlow   Navajo Co.

Mormon hamlet on creek of same name, about 35 miles north of Fort Apache. It was at first, about 1875, C. E. Cooley's home where he lived with his wife, "Mollie," daughter of old Chief Pedro of White Mountain Apache tribe. In 1881 Cooley sold half interest in his place to Henry Huning of Las Lunas, N. M., and they branched out in many ways. A first class saw mill was built, and the C. C. herd of cattle established and run for many years.

They enclosed some 100,000 acres of land with a barbed-wire fence which soon got them into trouble with the government and had to come down. They also had a large store and did a good business with settlers. About 1890 they fell out and ranch was sold to W. J. Flake for the Mormon church. Huning moved to Santa Barbara, California, where he died. Cooley moved back on to the Apache Reservation where he died, March 15, 1915.

Corydon E. Cooley, who was a government scout in Crook's campaigns, 1872 and 1873, located on what is now called Showlow creek about 1875. He and Marion Clark made the settlement together. They decided later there was room for but one location, so they agreed to play a game of Seven-Up to decide which of them should move. When the last hand was dealt Cooley needed but one point to win. Clark ran his cards over and said: "If you can show low you win." Cooley threw down his hand and said, "Showlow it is." Has been called Showlow ever since. Cooley told the author this story at Fort Apache in 1880.

Clark later moved up the creek near present town of Pinetop and located a ranch where he lived for many years.

P. O. established August 19, 1880. Corydon E. Cooley, P. M. The postoffice authorities insisted on spelling it Show Low. Changed to Showlow by Decision, U.S.G.B., 1933.

Showlow Creek   Navajo Co.   Map, Sitgreaves N. F., 1927.

Stream rising northeast corner, T. 8 N., R. 23 E., edge Fort Apache Ind. Res., about 2 miles southeast of Lakeside reservoir. Flows southwest, enters west side Silver creek about 3 miles above Taylor. .

For history see Showlow and Cooley ranch.

Shultz   Pinal Co.   G. L. O. Map, 1921.

In T. 8 S., R. 16 E. Mining camp in Black hills, west side of San Pedro river, about 4 miles southwest of Mammoth. Also known as Mammoth mine and Mohawk mine. "Named for Frank Shultz, who discovered Mammoth mine and had a store there about 1889." Letter, J. W. Lawson, P. M., Oracle.

P. O. established July 27, 1896. John B. Allen, P. M.

Shumway   Navajo Co.   G. L. O. Map, 1921; Sitgreaves N. F., 1926.

In sec. 25, T. 12 N., R. 21 E., 4 miles south of Taylor on Silver creek. Named for Charles Shumway, Mormon pioneer who settled here at an early date.

About 1886 or 1888, residents built a suspension bridge over the creek to connect the sections of the town which lay on both sides of stream. The author believes this was the first suspension bridge in Arizona.

P. O. established January 9, 1893. James Pearce, P. M.

Sibyl   Cochise Co.

Station, S. P. R. R., 9 miles east of Benson. Origin not known.

Sichomovi   Navajo Co.   U. S. G .S. Tusayan Sheet, 1906.

One of six or eight Hopi pueblos located on First or East mesa. This is a modern pueblo of the Eighteenth century. According to Hodge, word in Hopi means "Place of the Wild Currant Bush." Gregory says Navajo name for it is "Itt-hagi—half way house." James' *Painted Desert* says it means "a mound of flowers." Take your choice. Decision U.S.G.B.

Siddle Place   Gila Co.   Map, Tonto N. F., 1926.

In T. 11½ N., R. 10 E. Ranch, west side of East Verde about a mile and a half above Payson-Pine highway. After Henry Siddle, first settler on East Verde. "At one time in the Eighties Siddle sat on a hill above the ranch and watched the Apaches burn his cabin." Letter, Fred Croxen.

Sidney   Maricopa Co.   Breckenridge Map, Maricopa Co., 1891.

In T. 1 S., R. 3 W. Settlement in Buckeye valley, north side Gila river. Origin not known. See Buckeye.

Sieber Creek   Gila Co.   Smith Map, 1879; Eckhoff, 1880.

On Tonto N. F. Stream heading in Green valley. After Al Sieber, famous government scout. Flows south, enters east side Wild Rye at Gibson's ranch about 25 miles south of old Mazatzal City on East Fork of Verde.

"Al Sieber was a native of Germany, reared in Pennsylvania, enlisted in Civil War in a Minnesota regiment. Badly wounded at Gettysburg. After recovery, reenlisted in a Massachusetts regiment. Came to Arizona, 1868." McClintock.

For many years he was a government guide and scout under Crook and other army officers. His influence and control over Apaches was little short of marvelous. Was a tall, well-built, fine appearing man, always well dressed. He wore long, fancy, officer's boots on nearly all occasions. Absolutely unafraid and fearless. The author has seen him go into a camp of "tizwin" crazed Apaches at Fort Apache and kick and slap them about as if they were a lot of children. Not one of them resisted or showed any resentment or anger. In 1875 he was shot through the arm in a fight with Indians north of Phoenix, and again on June 1, 1887, he was shot through the leg in an attempt to disarm some Indian scouts at San Carlos. This permanently crippled him, although as the author recalls seeing him in 1880 or '81 he limped at that time from his Gettysburg wound. After the last wound in 1887, however, his condition was much worse and he got around with considerable difficulty. Spoke with a strong German accent. Accidentally killed by a rolling rock while overseeing a party of Apaches at work for Reclamation Service on a road near Roosevelt lake on February 19, 1907. Buried at Globe.

Sieber Point   Coconino Co.

In Grand Canyon N. P. near northeast corner of Park in lat. 36° and 18', long. 111° 57'. It is below Boundary ridge. Decision U.S.G.B.

Named for Al Sieber. Name suggested by the author. See Sieber creek.

Siebers Monument   Gila Co.

Erected by Territory of Arizona, 1907, to the memory of Al Sieber, a few miles north of Roosevelt dam and just below the road to Pine and Payson, where he was accidently killed. See Sieber creek.

Sierra Ancha   Gila Co.   Smith Map, 1879, et al.; G. L. O. Map, 1921.

Sp., "Wide Mountains." Range in Tonto N. F., about 30 miles northeast of Roosevelt lake, extending from T. 8 N., R. 11 E., southeasterly to include Baker mountain near south line of T. 6 N., R. 14 E.

When Roosevelt dam was built the Reclamation Service had a saw mill here and cut the timber used in construction work. No one can say how range came to be so called. Decision U.S.G.B.

Sierra Apache

See Apache mountain.

Sierra Azul (Blue Mountain)

Fabled mountain range said to lie in northwestern part of present Arizona. Much discussed by Spanish writers in latter part of fifteenth century. According to Posadas it was said to lie "one hundred leagues southwest of Santa Fe."

Torribio de Huerta, another Spaniard who investigated the story of huge deposits of quicksilver here in September, 1689, says: "Between Zuni and Moqui was located a place called Sierra Azul more than two hundred leagues long and full of silver."

Diego de Vargas was sent in 1691 to locate the alleged deposit said to be found in these mountains. He went there to investigate the story, brought back a quantity of the "Red ochre earth called amalgre by the Indians" which was sent to the city of Mexico for assay and investigation and was found not to contain a drop of the coveted mineral.

On both Spanish maps quoted the range is shown as adjacent to the Big Colorado river in northwestern Arizona and might well be taken for what we today know as the "Vermillion Cliffs." See "Legend of the Sierra Azul" by Jose Espinosa in New Mexico *Historical Review,* April, 1934.

Range shows as Sierra Azul on a French map of 1665 (W. L. Library, Congress, 225) and a Spanish map of 1757. (W. L. Library, Congress, 430).

Sierra Blanca Mountains   Pima Co.
                          Hornaday Map, U. S. G. S., 1923.

On Papago Ind. Res., near lat. 32° 20', long. 112° 20'.

"A bald ridge to the westward of Quijotoa." Hornaday, *Camp Fires.*

Sierra Bonita Ranch   Graham Co.   U. S. G. S. Map, 1923.

Sp., "pretty or beautiful mountains." In T. 10 S., R. 23 E.

The Grahams were often called Sierra Bonita. In 1872, Col. H. C. Hooker, who was an army beef contractor, discovered the spring at this point about 12 miles from Fort Grant at base of

Graham mountains. It shows on some old maps as "Sierra Bonita." Most modern maps, "Bonita."
He located it for his ranch headquarters. Here Augustin Thomas got the local color and story for his play, *Arizona*. P. O. established as Bonita, q.v. March 6, 1884. Edward Hooker, P. M.

Sierra Bonita Mountains   Graham Co.

"The Graham mountains were known by the Mexicans under this name." Bourke. See Graham.

Sierra Carlos   Gila Co.

See Mescal mountains.

Sierra de la Frente Negra   Pima Co.

See Sentinel peak.

Sierra del Calaveras   Pima Co.   G. L. O. Map, 1883.

On G.L.O. map, 1883, this shows as a range, south side of Arivaca grant about 6 miles north of boundary. Lies northwest of Oro Blanco. On later maps it shows as Gigas mountains. On G.L.O. map, 1883, there are two distinct ranges, the Gigas above the Arivaca grant, and the Calaveras below it. Grant seems to be in a valley between the two.
Origin of name Calaveras, cannot be learned.

Sierra de la Espuma   Pinal Co.

"Mountain of the foam." Given, of course, by the Spanish after hearing the Pima flood legend. Historical name for Superstition range east of Phoenix. So called because the end which faces the desert is a high, bold cliff, near the crest of which is a broad white stripe—a limestone formation—extending for several miles. This stripe the Pimas say is the "mark of the foam on the water of the flood which rose to that height." This was part of a Pima flood legend of an "Old Man" who controlled or worked with the forces of nature—rain, wind, clouds, etc. See Superstition. Not on any map under this name.

Sierra de San Ildefonso   Mohave Co.

"Garces called them so August 1, 1776. This of course is the Mohave range beginning above Needles." Coues. This Mohave range extends from the Needles about 40 miles southeast.

Sierra Estrella

See Estrella mountains.

Sierra Morena   Pima Co.   U. S. G. S. Map, 1923.

In T. 21 S., R. 5 E., on Papago Ind. Res., on Mexican line.
A very rocky hill. From the Spanish "morena," "a heap of stones, a moraine."
There was a Morena mine here as early as 1873. Hinton speaks of it. Did the mine get its name from the rocks or vice versa? No one can tell today.

Sierra Napac

"Sierra Napac, alluded to by Garces as 'these live in a Sierra they call Napac' is the San Francisco mountains. No doubt Napac is the scribe's error for Napao which Garces elsewhere uses for Navajo." Coues. This was Garces name for San Francisco mountains, q.v.

Sierra Panoche   Apache Co.
Elliott Map, 1884, "Pinta Hills"; U. S. G. S., 1923.

See Navajo mountains.

Sierra Pinta   Yuma Co.

Sp., "painted mountain." In extreme southeast corner of county east of Tule desert.

Sierra Prieta   Yavapai Co.   Map, Prescott N. F., 1927.

Sp., "dark mountain." Range immediately west of Prescott. See Black mesa.

Sierra Tonto   Yavapai Co.

"Nearly west is seen Picacho. A mesa to the southeast has been named Sierra Tonto." Whipple's *Report*. From his remarks Whipple was probably near Ash Fork at this time. This peak does not show on any map.

Sierrita Mountains   Pima Co.   G. L. O. Map, 1921; U. S. G. S., 1923.

Sp., "little mountains." In Ts. 17, 18 S., R. 11 E., west of Twin buttes.

Sierrita Prieta   Pinal Co.   G. L. O. Map, 1921. U. S. G. S., 1923, "Slate Mountain."

Sp., "little dark (or black) mountains."

In T. 10 S., R. 5 E. Papago Ind. Res. 8 miles southeast of Quijote. Papago name is "Schook toahk," or Black mountain.

Signal   Mohave Co.   G. L. O. Map, 1921.

In T. 13 N., R. 13 W. On Big Sandy river. Mining town, named for Signal mine. P. O. established October 15, 1877, Thomas E. Walker, P. M.

Signal   Mohave Co.

See Athos.

Signal Butte   Maricopa Co.   Scott Map, Maricopa Co., 1929.

Elevation 1,715 feet. In sec. 13, T. 1 N., R. 7 E. Desert peak near Roosevelt highway about 5 miles west of Youngsburg, and 12 miles east of Mesa.

The old time story goes for this peak; that it was used by Pimas to signal approach of their Apache enemies.

Signal Butte   Yuma Co.   G. L. O. Map, 1921; U. S. G. S., 1923.

In T. 7 S., R. 16 W., north side Gila river, near Norton.

Signal Mountain   Pinal Co.   Map, Crook N. F., 1927.

In T. 1 S., R. 14 E. East side Devil's canyon about 8 miles east of Silver King. See Signal Peak in Gila county.

"There is the usual story about this peak; that Apaches used it to signal by smoke from its top. Mebbe they did; mebbe they didn't. ¿Quién sabe?" Letter, Dan Williamson, Globe.

Signal Peak   Gila Co.   Map, Crook N. F., 1926.

In southwest corner of T. 1 S., R. 15 E., in Pinal range near head Ice House canyon.

"By two o'clock the following morning we reached a high mountain since called Signal Mountain, but were unable to reach the top in the darkness." Woolsey's *Report*, June, 1864.

There is another Signal mountain in sec. 13, T. 1 S., R. 12 E., northeast Silver King.

Woolsey later refers to "Signal mountain on north side of Salt river." He could refer to neither of these peaks which are both south of Salt river. It is impossible to locate this Signal mountain named by Woolsey.

Signal Peak and Mine   Mohave Co.   G. L. O. Map, 1921.

Anson Smith says: "This peak was named because the Indians used it as a point from which to make smoke and other signals in the old days."

Mine was on west bank of Big Sandy river in T. 13 N., R. 13 W. Was a well known producer of early days.

Signal Peak   Pinal Co.   Signal Peak Quad., 1924.

Elevation 2,277 feet. In sec. 29, T. 5 S., R. 7 E. South end Sacaton mountains Gila River Ind. Res.

Signal Peak   Yuma Co.   U. S. G. S. Map, 1923.

In T. 1 S., R. 18 W. West side Kofa mountains.

Silent   Yuma Co.   G. L. O. Map, 1892.

Mine and settlement about 10 miles north of Norton on Colorado river above Yuma. Was back from river about same distance. Probably named for Judge Silent, prominent attorney and mining man in this region in early days. See Springerville. See Pacific.

P. O. established November 8, 1880, Charles T. Norton, P. M., for whom town of Norton was named.

Shortly after office was opened under name Silent, it was changed to Pacific, q.v.

Silver Bell   Pima Co.   U. S. G. S. Map, 1923.

Mine and mountains in T. 11 S., R. 8 E., at end Arizona-Southern R. R. from Red Rock. Named for the mine.

P. O. established August 18, 1904, Roger W. Warren, P. M. Black, Territorial Commissioner of Immigration, calls it Silver Belle in his report, 1890.

Silver Butte   Gila Co.   U. S. G. S. Map, 1923.

Fort Apache Ind. Res., on north side Cedar creek, near lat. 33° 53′, long. 110° 10′. Origin unknown.

Silver Creek and Settlement   Navajo Co.
                U. S. G. S. Map, 1923; Sitgreaves N. F., 1924.

In T. 10 N., R. 24 E. Rising on boundary line, Fort Apache Ind. Res., at junction of Ortega draw and Brown wash, near Pineyon (sic), flowing northwest, entering Little Colorado about 4 miles south of Woodruff. So called by early settlers "because the stream was so clear and silvery."

Town called Silver was on the creek in Sec. 14, T. 11 N., R. 22 E. P. O. established October 27, 1905, Rafael Carillo, P. M.

Silver Creek   Cochise Co.   G. L. O. Map, 1921.

Small stream flowing southeast into Mexico. Rises at College peak in T. 23 S., R. 29 E.

According to an item in *Tombstone Epitaph*, General Crook, with some 300 Apache Indians camped here June 15, 1883. This was doubtless after Crook's capture of Geronimo's band while enroute with them to San Carlos.

Silver Mountain   Yavapai Co.   Map, Prescott N. F., 1927.

In sec. 7, T. 9 N., R. 1 W. "So called from rich silver deposit found here in early mining days." Letter, Harry Hartin, Prescott.

Silver Mountains   Yavapai Co.

On Hamilton's map, 1866, these show as "Bradshaw or Silver mountains." See Bradshaw.

Silver Peak   Yuma Co.   G. L. O. Map, 1921.

In T. 1 N., R. 12 W. Upper end, Little Horn mountains.

Silver King   Pinal Co.   Smith Map, 1879; G. L. O., 1921.

Very rich mine discovered by a soldier named Sullivan, 1872, who carried some specimens to Charles G. Mason at his ranch on Gila river.

"Sullivan would not tell where the mine was. He disappeared but in March, 1875, Mason and three companions discovered it. Sullivan turned up at the mine, 1882, a broken, poverty-stricken old man, who, after proving his story was employed by the company for the rest of his days." Farish.

According to McClintock: "It disbursed over $1,500,000 in dividends and was one of the few Arizona mines the stock of which was quoted regularly on San Francisco Stock Exchange. Ore was almost virgin silver and chunks of it could be pounded out flat like lead. Town is now a mere heap of adobes."

P. O. established December 21, 1877, S. B. Chapin, P. M. Hon. Perry Wildman of Tempe, member of Legislature of 1891, was postmaster here, June 19, 1882.

Silver Nuggett   Gila Co.

See Nuggett.

Silver Reef Mountains   Pinal Co.   G. L. O. Map, 1921.

In Ts. 8, 9 S., Rs. 4, 5 E., Papago Ind. Res.

It is about 20 miles due west of Picacho on S. P. R. R. "There is a so-called 'reef' here that carries some silver."

Silynarki   Pima Co.

Papago word meaning "hanging saddle." Papago Indian village in Santa Rosa valley. Papago Ind. Res.

See p. 311, "Santa Rosa Indians vs. A. B. Fall," for full information.

Simmons   Yavapai Co.   G. L. O. Map, 1909-1921.

In T. 17 N., R. 3 W. Southwest of Del Rio on Mint creek. Named after John A. Simmons, pioneer who settled here, 1880. First called "Crossroads."

P. O. established July 5, 1881, Stephen Breon, P. M. See Wilson.

Simmonsville   Pah Ute Co., Nevada.

Grist mill site on Muddy river above St. Joseph in region later turned over to Nevada. One of the early Muddy settlements. Nothing known of its origin.

Simpson Creek   Apache Co.   Gregory Map, 1916; U. S. G. S., 1923.

In T. 4 N., R. 6 E. Rises in Washington pass, New Mexico, on Navajo Ind. Res., flows west into Arizona, empties into Black lake. "Captain Simpson's expedition, 1849, was first party of white men to cross Chuska mountains by this route." Gregory. Creek named for Simpson.

Single Standard Gulch   Gila Co.

In upper Tonto Basin. After Single Standard mine. See Arrastra Gulch.

Sinking Ship Butte   Coconino Co.

Near south rim of canyon and lat. 35° 59', long. 111° 57' W. (Not Three Castles). The formation indicated as Three Castles is generally known as the Sinking Ship because of the dip or tilt of strata. Decision U.S.G.B.

Sinyala Canyon   Coconino Co.

On Grand Canyon N. P., one mile north of Mount Sinyala, near lat. 36° 19' N., long. 112° 42' W. Named for "Judge" Sinyala, Indian chief who lived on Havasupai reservation. Decision U.S.G.B.

Sinyala Mesa or Mountain   Coconino Co.
Map, Grand Canyon N. P., 1927.

Elevation 5,445 feet. Near lat. 36° 19', long. 112° 43'. Low tableland, left bank Colorado river, between Havasu creek and Sinyala canyon. Name suggested by Charles Sheldon for Havasupai chief. Decision U.S.G.B.

Sitgreaves Mountain   Coconino Co.   Map, Tusayan N. F., 1927.

After Capt. Lorenzo Sitgreaves, U. S. Top. Engr., who visited it 1852. In T. 23 N., R. 4 E. Fifteen miles west Mt. Humphrey. Sitgreaves was sent, 1851, to make cross country survey for wagon road via Zuni river in western New Mexico and eastern Arizona, thence down Little Colorado via San Francisco mountain region to Colorado river—his was first real survey of this region. Military escort commanded by Major H. L. Kendrick, for whom one of San Francisco peaks was named.

Sitgreaves National Forest   Navajo, Apache and Coconino Cos.

Created originally, 1898, by presidential proclamation, as Black Mesa Forest Reserve. In 1906, redesignated as Sitgreaves National Forest, after Captain Lorenzo Sitgreaves, Topographic Engineer, U. S. Army. Present area, 1933, 833,912 acres. Supervisor's office, Holbrook.

Sitgreaves Pass   Mohave Co.   G. L. O. Map, 1921, "Sitgreaves."

In T. 19 N., R. 20 W. In Ute or Black mountains, at town of Oatman. So called by Lieut. Ives because Sitgreaves' party passed through it. Coues, however, says "Sitgreaves did not cross by this pass as Ives states, but used the so-called Union pass. Beale named this pass (Sitgreaves) John Howells Pass for one of his men, October, 1857." Coues who locates this John Howells pass as east of Oatman, did such careful research work through here that his judgement is undoubtedly correct.

Sit Yat Ki   Navajo Co.

One of the Hopi towns about 4 miles northeast of Walpi on East Mesa. Hopi word meaning "yellow house," according to James in *Painted Desert*.

Shows on map Hopi Villages in Seventeenth Report, Bureau of Ethnology.

Six Mile Hill   Cochise Co.   G. L. O. Map, 1921.

In sec. 5, T. 1 S., R. 25 E. "This was called Six Mile hill before discovery of Pearce mine. The elder Pearce while hunting cattle rode to it where he idly picked up a bit of rock which contained free gold and led to discovery of mine. Hill is 6 miles from old Pearce ranch and about one mile from Pearce mine." Letter, L. F. Murphy, P. M., Pearce. See Pearce.

Sixtymile Creek   Coconino Co.

Enters Marble gorge on west side between Awatubi crest and Chuar butte, near lat. 36° 13'. About 60 miles below Lee Ferry. Decision U.S.G.B.

Skeleton Canyon   Cochise Co.   U. S. G. S. Map, 1923.

Coronado N. F., at southern end San Simon valley. Crosses line of New Mexico and Arizona into San Simon valley, in T. 21 S., R. 32 E.

"In this canyon, 1881 or 1882, Curly Bill, with other 'bad men,' waylaid a band of Mexican smugglers who were raiding the country. Some 14 or 15 were killed and their bodies left where they fell. For years these grisly relics made the ground white at the site of the massacre or battle. Some of the skulls picked up by cowboys became soap basins at San Simon valley ranches.

"Skeleton Canyon winds through the wildest part of the Peloncillo mountains from Animas valley in New Mexico to San Simon valley in Arizona." *Tombstone.*

Skeleton Mesa   Navajo Co.   G. L. O. Map, 1921.

On Navajo Ind. Res., head of Moonlight creek near State line. Postmaster at Kayenta writes: "Nobody can tell me the origin of this name."

Skeleton Ridge   Yavapai Co.   Map, Prescott N. F., 1926.

In T. 11 N., R. 6 E. Sharp ridge running southeast from Pine mountain to Squaw butte.

"This ridge derives its name from its shape. When seen from higher country it is a very narrow sharp ridge from which numerous ribs or ridges branch off, giving it appearance of a huge skeleton." Letter, Frank Grubb, Prescott.

Skinnersville

See Troy.

Skull Cave   Maricopa Co.   Map, Tonto N. F., 1926.

In T. 3 N., R. 10 E. For over half a century this cave has been known to all as "Apache Cave." Name changed by an outsider without regard to local sentiment or opinion. See Apache Cave —Apache Trail.

Skull Valley   Yavapai Co.   G. L. O. Map, 1921.

Elevation, 4,112 feet. In T. 13 N., R. 4 W. Station, Ash Fork-Phoenix branch A. T. & S. F. R. R., nearly due west of Prescott. "About 1865 there was a massacre by Indians, of many white men in this valley. The bones and skulls were thick all along the valley." Mike Burns in Farish's *History.*

According to General Thomas, U. S. A., name came from the massacre of emigrants who were killed together with many of their oxen, while enroute to Colorado river. The bodies were left unburied and the next white men over the route found the bones and skulls bleaching on the ground." McClintock.

Hinton says this place was first called "Ebles ranch." Fish says: "There was a fight here, 1864, between a bunch of soldiers under Lieut. Monteith and some Mohave and Tonto Apaches. They left without burying the dead Indians. Later on Major Willis sent a scouting party out which found and buried the dead whose bones and skulls were lying round everywhere. Major Willis then named it Skull valley." This is doubtless the true story of this name. P. O. established April 26, 1869, John C. Dunn, P. M.

Skunk Creek   Maricopa Co.   Scott Map, Maricopa Co.

Stream rising in T. 3 N., R. 1 E., New River mountains, near Marinette station, A. T. & S. F. R. R. north of Phoenix.

Sleeping Beauty Peak   Gila Co.   U. S. G. S. Globe Quad., 1902.

Elevation, 4,890 feet. Two miles northwest of Inspiration mine. "From the north the mountain, or peak, has considerable resemblance to the reclining figure of a woman." Letter, L. V. Christensen, Forest Ranger.

Slate Creek   Gila Co.   Map, Tonto N. F., 1926.

Dry creek, east side of Mazatzals, draining into Tonto creek in T. 7 N., R. 10 E. at Tonto ranger station. "So called because of dark slate formation here. Several cinnabar claims have been developed along this creek in recent years."

Slate Mountain   Coconino Co.   G. L. O. Map, 1921.

Elevation, 8,209 feet. In T. 24 N., R. 5 E., 6 miles due north of Kendrick peak. "A descriptive name. Formation and color is slate." Letter, G. W. Kimball, Williams.

Slate Mountain   Pinal Co.

See Sierrita Prieta.

Slaughter Mountain   Graham Co.   G. L. O. Map, 1921.

In Gila mountains, south side Ash Flat, about 25 miles due west Morenci. So named after Pete Slaughter, cattleman, who as early as 1885 grazed cattle on Apache reservation about here.

Slinkard Springs   Pinal Co.

"After Frank Slinkard, an outlaw who had his headquarters near here in late Nineties. With several others he is said to have robbed a Chinese merchant at Globe in 1899. Cannot locate it although referred to by several writers." Letter, Dan Williamson.

Small   Cochise Co.   G. L. O. Map, 1909.

In T. 22 S., R. 27 E. Station, E. P. & S. W. R. R. about 10 miles north of Douglas.

Smith Butte   Navajo Co.   G. L. O. Map, 1921.

In T. 19 N., R. 20 E., on Cottonwood wash, north of Joseph City. Named for "Bill A." Smith, cattleman, who about 1890 established a cow camp at Smith spring, also named after him, about 6 miles east of this butte.
"Known sometimes as Black Rock." Letter, Sena P. Hansen, P. M., Joseph City.

Smith Butte   Yavapai Co.   G. L. O. Map, 1892-1921;
                                                      Tusayan N. F., 1927.

In T. 21 N., R. 3 W., east side Black range, near head of Partridge creek.

Smith Canyon   Yavapai Co.   Map, Prescott N. F., 1927.

In Ts. 14, 15, 16 N., Rs. 5, 6 W. Rises southern side Seepage mountain; flows southwest into Cottonwood creek. "Named for John and William Smith, brothers, who ran the Dumb-bell brand cow outfit in Eighties. Their old ranch is located in sec. 5, T. 15 N., R. 5 W." Letter, Frank Grubb, Forest Supervisor.

Smith Spring   Navajo Co.   G. L. O. Map, 1921.
 In sec. 12, T. 20, R. 20 E. On Cottonwood wash east of Smith
butte, q.v. "This name has now given way to Black Rock spring
due to color of rock around it." Letter, Paul H. Roberts, Holbrook.

Smith Peak   Yuma Co.   G. L. O. Map, 1921.
 Elevation 4,957 feet. In T. 8 N., R. 11 W. At eastern end
Harcuvar mountains at Maricopa line. "Smith was an old timer,
who had a claim on this mountain which was known as Smith
peak." Letter, George A. Frissell, Aguila.

Smith's Mill   Maricopa Co.   G. L. O. Map, 1880-1892
 On Hassayampa river about 2 miles south of Seymour. Built
for reduction of Vulture ores by W. C. Smith, who later was a
banker in Tombstone. P. O. established June 27, 1874. Peter
Taylor, P. M.

Smithville   Graham Co.
 Now Pima. Settled, 1879-80. Named for Prophet Joseph
Smith of Mormon church. According to McClintock: "It was
settled by refugees from evicted settlement of Forestdale on
Apache Indian reservation. They moved down here and located." An evident error. The eviction took place in 1883. Town
was quite a place when the writer was there, 1881.

Smithville   Yavapai Co.
 Settlement on Camp Verde road, about 33 miles east of Prescott.
Listed as a "Stage and stopping station, 1881, Richard De Kuhn,
store and station keeper." *Arizona Gazetteer,* 1881.

Smoot Lake   Coconino Co.   Map, Tusayan N. F., 1927.
 In sec. 7, T. 24 N., R. 3 E. After an early stockman by this
name who had a summer ranch on lake.

Smurr   Maricopa Co.   G. L. O. Map, 1909.
 On main S. P. R. R., 10 miles west of Gila Bend, origin unknown.

Snake Gulch   Coconino Co.   Map, Kaibab N. F., 1926.
 Rises in sec. 1, T. 38 N., R. 1 W. Runs southeast into Kanab
creek in sec. 27, T. 38 N., R. 3 W. Long narrow canyon, west
side Kaibab forest.
 "It is an exceedingly crooked snake-like canyon, hence easily
got this name." Letter, Walter G. Mann, Kanab.

Snaketown   Pinal Co.   Gila Butte Quad.; U. S. G. S., 1914.
 In sec. 11, T. 3 S., R. 4 E. Pima Indian village about 7 miles
southwest of Santan. Pima word "Ska-kaik" meaning, "many
rattlesnakes."

Sniders Station   Yavapai Co.
 See Bumble Bee.

Snively Holes   Coconino Co.   Mallory Map, 1876.
 Short distance east of Bill Williams mountain, on one of the
early trails. Well known watering place. What are today called
"tanks" were designated as "holes" in those days. Jacob Snively
was early hunter, guide and prospector. Discovered gold placers
at Gila City, 1858. A Pennsylvanian who came to Arizona about
1857. Killed by Indians in White Picacho mountains, March 18,

1871. Jack Swilling went over there, 1878, and brought Snively's remains to Gillette, where they were buried. It was on this trip that Swilling was arrested for murder and died in Yuma penitentiary while awaiting his trial. Snively was private secretary to Gen. Sam Houston when latter was President of Texas. He also commanded troops in the Texan war for independence. Undoubtedly named for Jacob Snively.

Snowflake   Navajo Co.

In T. 13 N., R. 21 E. On Silver creek. "Sept. 27, 1878. At noon we drove across the creek where William Flake and party located. President Erastus Snow directed location of a townsite which was called Snowflake. S. G. Ladd, surveyor, was instructed to proceed to level the water ditch and survey the town plat and farm lands." *Little Colorado Stake History.*

Townsite was purchased from James Stinson by Mormon church, for 500 head of cattle. It was then called Stinson's Ranch. "Snowflake" was a "coined" word, or name, for the two Bishops, Snow and Flake. Shows as Snowflake City on Smith map, 1879. Snowflake was first county seat of Apache county. In 1879 court was held in Bishop Flake's house.

"I ran cattle on Silver creek for about five years and then sold my rights to William J. Flake for 500 head of cattle. The agreement was that when he paid me I was to leave the country and I left according to agreement." Letter, James Stinson, Kline, Colo., May 31, 1931.

P. O. established June 27, 1881, William D. Karchner, P. M. See Stinson valley.

Snowshed Peak   Cochise Co.   Map, Coronado N. F., 1927.

In T. 18 S., R. 30 E. at lower end Chiricahua mountains. About 2 miles southeast of Chiricahua peak. "The Snowshed is so called because the range resembles a vast shed or roof and is visible for miles. This peak and also Fly's peak and Chiricahua peak, are part of the Snowshed." Letter, J. C. Hancock, P. M., Paradise.

Snowstake Creek   Apache Co.   U. S. G. S. Map, 1923.

On Fort Apache Ind. Res. Rises east side Ord peak, flows northwest into White river east of Cooley. So called from snowstakes located here for snow-fall measurements.

Snowstorm Hill   Gila Co.

On Tonto N. F. In upper Tonto Basin. Hill about 2 miles west of Payson. After the Snowstorm mine, said to have been first mineral location in Upper Basin. On road from Payson to East Verde settlement.

"Old timers tell me it was so called because they found the mine during a terrible snow storm." Letter, Fred Croxen.

Snyder Hill   Pima Co.   U. S. G. S. Map, 1923.

In T. 15 S., R. 12 E. At south end Tucson mountains. Origin unknown.

Snyder Hole   Yavapai Co.

Not located. P. O. established by this name Feb. 21, 1881, S. M. Gray, P. M.

Sockdolager Rapids   Coconino Co.

Series of difficult rapids in Colorado river near lat. 36° 3′ N. long. 111° 57′ W. In Grand Canyon N. P. Decision, U.S.G.B. Origin unknown.

Socorro Peak　　Yuma Co.　　G. L. O. Map, 1921; U. S. G. S., 1923.

Sp., "succor, help." In T. 5 S., R. 11 W. At western end Harqua Hala mountains. Highest peak in these mountains and so called from the nearby Socorro mine. "Owners of this mine came here from Socorro, New Mexico." Letter, R. J. Quinn, Los Angeles.

Soldier Camp, Ranch, Hill and Wash　　Gila Co.
Map, Tonto N. F., 1926.

In secs. 23, 24, T. 9 N., R. 11 E. "Early ranch in Sierra Ancha range. Belongs now to the Ruth Wilbanks Cow outfit. So called because in Crook's army days this was a frequent camping ground for the soldiers."
Mountain is near the old camp. Wash rises west side Sierra Ancha range, flows northwest into Tonto creek, in sec. 9, T. 9 N., R. 11 E. "There is an old pre-historic fortification on the hill with walls 3 feet thick and 8 or 10 feet high. It has portholes through it covering all approaches." Letter, Fred Croxen.

Soldier Creek　　Gila Co.　　Map, Crook N. F., 1926.

Fort Apache Ind. Res. Rises south side Sombrero butte, flows southeast into Salt river. Origin unknown.

Soldier Lake　　Coconino Co.　　U. S. G. S. Map, 1923.

In sec. 6, T. 16 N., R. 11 E. Well known watering place about 4 miles southwest of Chaves pass. According to army reports, soldiers under Captain Charles King camped here after his big fight in October, 1874, with Apaches, in which he was severely wounded. See Sunset.

Soldiers Grave　　Pinal Co.

"That evening, May, 1864, I pushed on towards Tucson and next day reached what was known as Soldiers Grave, a road station established by Butterfield Stage Co. I rested my mule nearly all day."
This is the story by Charles B. Genung of his following a Mexican murderer. He eventually caught his man and saved the law all future trouble by "disposing of him according to local customs of the day."
Genung stopped here again on his way back to Prescott. He writes: "I watered my mule at Soldiers Grave and pushed on to Sacaton station, where I rested a few hours." Farish. Oddly enough, there is no such stage station on any list of stage stations nor on any list of watering places of those days.

Soldiers Hole　　Cochise Co.　　Smith Map, 1879; G. L. O., 1890.

In T. 20 S., R. 26 E., north side White river.
"Dave Estes, a Curly Bill man, told Earp he would find the mules at the McLowery ranch near Soldier Hole." *Tombstone.* Farish says: "It was an old station in 1879 on Butterfield stage line about 25 miles north of Mexican boundary. Was a well known watering place of early stage days."
There is also a Soldiers Hole at mouth of Bell canyon above old Camp Date creek in Yavapai county.

Solitaire Butte　　Mohave Co.　　G. L. O. Map, 1921.

Elevation, 6,000 feet, west of Hurricane ledge, north of Colorado river. See Poverty Knoll.

Solitude, Cape   Coconino Co.   U. S. G. S. Map, 1923;
Tusayan N. F., 1927.

In Grand Canyon, N. P. Huge promontory, south side Little
Colorado river at its junction with main river. On Marble canyon. "It stands solitary and alone."

Solomi Spring   Navajo Co.   Gregory Map, 1916.

In T. 29 N., R. 16 W. At west end Oraibi mesa. Hopi Ind. Res.
This doubtless should read Lo-lo-mi, Hopi word meaning "good."

Solomon   Graham Co.

Railroad station for Solomonville. The railroad people about
the time this station was established, seem to have had a bad
habit of shortening their station names "to save telegraphing,"
according to letters from railroad officials.

Solomonville   Graham Co.   G. L. O. Map, 1921.

Elevation 3,000 feet. In T. 7 S., R. 27 E. Named after I. E.
Solomon, who, 1876, opened a store at this point. R. R. Station
is Solomon. P. O. Guides and some maps have it Solomonsville.
In 1883, county seat was moved from Safford to this place, but
moved back again in 1915. According to a writer in the Globe
Silver Belt, William Kirkland, then mail carrier between Clifton
and this place, gave it the name Solomonville for his friend Solomon. P. O. established April 10, 1873, I. E. Solomon, P. M. See
Pueblo Viejo.

Sols Wash   Yavapai Co.

Rises Date Creek mountains, west of Congress, flows southeast
into Hassayampa, inside city limits of Wickenburg, about four
blocks from post office.
"I have been informed by old timers that the name originally
was 'Salt Wash,' from a salt spring at its head, but corrupted to
Sols Wash." Letter, B. A. Wilmoth.
The most satisfactory origin seems to be for a Yuma Indian,
Sol Francisco, who in 1856 secured release from captivity by
Indians of Olive Oatman. When he brought this girl to Yuma the
Whites loaded him with so many presents and honors that the
tribe elected him chief.
Shortly after this Sol Francisco was killed in fight near Mari-
copa Wells, between Yumas on one side and Pimas and Mari-
copas on the other. Dunn and other writers of this matter al-
ways speak of him as "El Sol Francisco" or simply as "Fran-
cisco."
The author has a copy of a letter written to Lieut. Mowry, then
U. S. Indian Agent for Arizona, from Commanding Officer at Fort
Yuma in September, 1857, which says:
"Our old friend Soll (sic) Francisco who acted as our agent in
rescuing Olive Oatman from the Mohaves a year ago, was killed."
He refers undoubtedly to Francisco's death in Maricopa Wells
fight.

Sombrero Butte   Pinal Co.   U. S. G. S., 1923.

Sp., "hat." In T. 9 S., R. 18 E. In Galiuro Mountains. Descriptive name; looks like a huge sombrero. There is another Sombrero butte in Gila county, q.v. P. O. established June 18, 1919,
Clara Johnson, P. M.

Sombrero Peak   Gila Co.   G. L. O. Map, 1921.

In T. 6 N., R. 15 E. Sp., "hat." Resembles a tall Mexican sombrero from a distance. Well known "turning point" on western boundary, Fort Apache Ind. Res.

This is the land mark named in the descriptions of the "Doc Thorn" diggings or mines for which much prospecting is done even today, 1933. In 1872, Gov. Safford, with a large party of prospectors, scoured this entire region east of Cherry creek looking for them without success.

Sombreretillo   Pima Co.

Sp., "very small hat." Town and mining camp in Quijotoas, in early Sixties. Hamilton's *Arizona* carries an advertisement of a stage line to this place from Tucson in 1884.

Somerton   Yuma Co.   G. L. O. Map, 1921.

In T. 25 S., R. 24 W. About 12 miles south of Yuma. Small farming community named about 1899 by Captain Yoakum, after his native town in Indiana.

P. O. established Dec. 23, 1899, Minnie E. Case, P. M.

Sonoita, Town and Creek   Santa Cruz Co.
G. L. O. Map, 1921; Coronado N. F., 1927.

In T. 20 S., R. 17 E. On Sonoita branch S. P. R. R. Creek rises east slope Santa Rita mountains, flows southwest into Santa Cruz river at Calabasas.

Hinton says: "The Aztec and Tubac mill sites, a ranch and a saw mill, are located here." It was 13 miles from Camp Crittenden by Hinton's mileage. See Sonoyta creek.

Sonoita Land Grant   Santa Cruz Co.   G. L. O. Map, 1923.

Known as San José de Sonoita, small Mexican land grant lying on both sides Sonoita river. Some 35 miles southeast of Tubac and 6 miles northeast of Calabasas. Sold to Leon Henores, May 15, 1825, for $105. U. S. Court of Land Claims approved title to Mateas Alsus, for 7,592 acres of the 12,147 claimed.

Sonora   Pinal Co.   G. L. O. Map, 1921.

Mining camp, in T. 3 S., R. 14 E., near Ray, on branch Arizona-Eastern R. R. On Amanda gulch. The usual name for any Mexican section of a southwestern town. P. O. established Jan. 29, 1912. Frank Abril, P. M.

Sonoyta, Mountains and Hamlet   Pima Co.
Smith Map, 1879, "Sonoyta"; G. L. O., 1921, "Sonoita."

On Papago Ind. Res. "The Papagos who lived here were known as 'Sand Papagoes.'" Hodge.

Papago settlement on line between U. S. and Mexico, near lat. 32°, long. 113°. Word in Papago is "Kavorston"—"at the foot of a rounded hill." Hodge however says it is "The place where corn will grow." The oasis was originally called Sonoita, Sonoitag, or Sonoidac. In Ortega's *Apostolicas Afanes*—the name is attributed to the Indians.

Coues says: "Kino visited it, 1699, and called it San Marcelo. It was then a Spanish mission. In 1751, name was changed to San Miguel, at the wish of Marquis de Villapuente, who at the time of his death endowed it."

Again Coues writes: "Sonoita, Sonoitac or Sonydag, was a rather notable place just over line of Arizona on a small water course. Sometimes called Rio Papago and Rio de Sonoita. Its history dates from Feb. 16, 1699, when it was a Papago rancheria visited by Kino and Manje. Kino visited it again, November 12, 1701. Father Henry Ruen was murdered here, 1751." *On the Trail of a Pioneer.* This should not be confused with the Sonoita northeast of Nogales.

Sonsela Buttes   Navajo Co.   G. L. O. Map, 1921.

Elevation 9,000 feet. In T. 4 N., R. 6 W. Very close to New Mexico line on Navajo Ind. Res. At head of Canyon de Chelly. Haile spells it "Sosela." Navajo word meaning "twin stars" or "two stars."

Sontag Creek   Gila Co.   Map, San Carlos Ind. Res., 1917.

San Carlos Ind. Res. Stream rising at "Dads Lookout," flowing southwest into Bear creek in T. 2 N., R. 19 E. Origin unknown.

Sopori Land Grant

See El Sopori.

Sopori Town and Creek   Pima Co.
Lumholtz Map, 1916; Coronado N. F., 1925.

In T. 22 S., R. 10 E. Stream rises near Oro Blanco, flows northeast into Santa Cruz above town of Amado. On Altar road. Probably a corruption of name the Spanish Padres gave the Papagos: "Sobai-puri."

Sorenson   Yavapai Co.

"Mining camp on Santa Maria river. P. O. established Dec. 24, 1903, Peter V. Sorensen, P. M. The place was named after him. It lasted only about 6 months." Letter, E. A. Putnam, Hillside.

South Butte   Pinal Co.   G. L. O. Map, 1921.

Elevation 2,815 feet. In sec. 11, T. 4 S., R. 11 E. About 10 miles southeast of Florence, south side Gila at "The Buttes." There are two buttes, one on each side of the river.

South Canyon   Coconino Co.   Map, Kaibab N. F., 1926.

Rises in sec. 14, T. 34 N., R. 3 E. Flows northeast into Red Rock canyon in sec. 20, T. 36 N., R. 5 E. There are two canyons here, heading close together and running in almost parallel lines, one north of the other, hence North and South canyons.

South Mountain   Pima Co.   U. S. G. S. Map, 1923.

Papago Ind. Res. at lat. 32°, long. 112° 10'. From its location.

Southerland Peak   Cochise Co.   Map, Coronado N. F., 1926.

In sec. 32, T. 23 S., R. 20 E. 3 miles south Forth Huachuca Mil. Res. "Named for old Jim Southerland, cattleman. Bought a ranch in Hayfield canyon on San Rafael grant, where he lived for several years. His death was from falling into a well he was digging on this place. Called the homeliest man in Arizona, of which he was quite proud. Known as 'Idaho Bill' because he came from that state." Letter, Robert A. Rodgers, Nogales.

Southern Pacific Mail Stage Line

"Kerhens (sic) and Mitchell claimed in 1878 that this line running from Yuma to Mesilla, New Mexico, was the longest stage line in the United States." Hinton. As U. S. Minister to Austria in 1909, he spelled his name Kerens.

Southwestern Experimental Station   Coconino Co.

See Fort Valley.

Sowap Canyon   U. S. G. S. Map, 1916; Kaibab Ind. Res., 1926.

See Sowats.

Sowats Canyon   Coconino Co.

Stream and canyon west side Kaibab plateau. Enters Jump Up canyon in T. 36 N., R. 5 W. "Name derived from a Piute word meaning the kind of tobacco which was used formerly by Piutes. It was not real tobacco, but a plant that satisfied their need for smoking. Word really is spelled 'Showap,' but seems to have been changed by White usage. Piutes don't know the word 'Sowats' at all." Letter, W. G. Mann, Kanab.

Spanish Ranch

See Chrystoval.

Spears Lake   Mohave Co.   G. L. O. Map, 1916.

Long narrow lake north of Doudville about 4 miles east of Colorado river, north side Mohave and Milltown R. R. "Named for Ben Spear, early Mineral Park storekeeper." Letter, O. D. M. Gaddis, Kingman.

Specter Terrace   Coconino Co.   Map, Grand Canyon N. P., 1927.

Near lat. 36° 19′, long. 112° 27′. Small spur with bench slopes extending northwest from Powell plateau, opposite Specter chasm. Decision U.S.G.B. At this point the Colorado flows northeast.

Spenazuma   Graham Co.

Mining camp in foothills, Santa Teresa mountains, on what is known as "San Carlos Strip."

Mining company organized, 1899, by Dr. Richard C. Flower, of New York. Mine was at Black Rock near Granite mountain. Name coined by Dr. Flower when asked by what name his mining company was to be called. "Any name that will cause them to spend their 'mazuma' was his reply. So it was called the Spenazuma." Letter from Flower, *Arizona Historical Review,* April, 1929.

Spencer Canyon   Mohave Co.   Smith Map, 1879; U. S. G. S., 1923.

In T. 27 N., R. 13 E. Hualpai Ind. Res., at lower end of Milkweed creek, near Colorado river. After Charlie Spencer, a squaw man, one of Crook's old scouts, 1872-73. Guide for Wheeler expedition, 1871. "Within sight of the 'Wickty-wizz,' Charlie Spencer still lived among his Hualpai kinsmen, not much the worse for the seven wounds he received while a scout." Bourke.

James, in *Painted Desert,* says: "When the Wallapai reserve was set aside, a man named Spencer was living on land included therein. He claimed two of their finest springs. He was soon murdered, whether by Whites or Indians I am unable to say." See Spencer creek.

Spencer Creek   Yavapai Co.   G. L. O. Map, 1892.

Rises near Gemini peaks, "The Twins" on some maps. Flows southwest into Sycamore creek. After Charlie Spencer who married a Hualpai squaw and settled in Spencer canyon, q.v.

"On March 23, 1868, Spencer, while carrying U. S. Mail from Camp Willow grove to Hardyville, was waylaid by the Hualpais and two men with him killed while he was severely wounded.

So close to camp that the shots were heard in the post. Men sent out, found Spencer lying wounded behind a pile of rocks, keeping the Indians at bay with his rifle." Letter, from Post Commander in Farish *Notes.*

Spine, The   Pinal Co.   Map, Crook N. F., 1926.

In southwest corner T. 3 S., R. 13 E. North side Gila, 6 miles west of Kelvin. "A narrow knife-like ridge."

Sponseller Lake   Apache Co.   Map, Apache N. F., 1926.

In sec. 7, T. 10 N., R. 24 E. Sitgreaves N. F. Floodwater lake, named after Joseph Sponseller, early sheepman who grazed sheep here, 1883. Few miles east of Sponseller mountain.

Sponseller Mountain   Navajo Co.   Map, Apache N. F., 1926.

In T. 10 N., R. 23 E. Sitgreaves N. F. Just west of Sponseller lake. After Joseph Sponseller.

Spotted Mountain   Gila Co.   U. S. G. S. Map, 1923.

Fort Apache Ind. Res. East side Salt river draw, near lat. 24°, long. 110° 35'. "Descriptive name. The mountain is 'spotted' due to bunches of timber scattered on its sides together with open places between them." Letter, Fred Croxen.

Spring Creek   Gila Co.   Map, Tonto N. F., 1927.

Rises north end Sierra Ancha range at Jerkey butte. Flows northwest into Tonto creek in sec. 36, T. 10 N., R. 12 E. So called because of many fine springs that form its headwaters.

Spring Lake   Navajo Co.   U. S. G. S. Map, 1923.

Near west boundary of county, Navajo Ind. Res. in Klethla valley, west side Black Mesa. Watering place, often dry. "It is called this because in the spring melting snows generally fill it."

Springerville   Apache Co.   G. L. O. Map, 1921.

Elevation 6,856 feet. "On Little Colorado river in Round valley. Settlement started, 1871, by William Milligan, Marion Clark, Anthony Long, and Joe McCollough." Farish *Notes.* After Henry Springer, pioneer merchant of Albuquerque who came here and opened a store before town was named. It was for a time, a "ward" of the Mormon church, called Omer Ward. See Round Valley. P. O. established Oct. 29, 1879. Charles Franklin Banta, P. M. Franklin later became A. F. Banta. He had been previously known as Charles Franklin. When appointed postmaster it is the author's recollection he decided to adopt officially the name Albert F. Banta.
"Springerville was declared by Judge Silent on July 9, 1880, the county seat of the new Apache county after a court count of votes cast in the election." Farish.

Spruce Brook   Apache Co.   U. S. G. S., 1923.

Navajo Ind. Res. Rises west side Chuska mountains near state line, flows southwest through Canyon del Muerto, joins Canyon de Chelly to form Chinle Creek.
There is a large body of spruce timber around head of this stream.

Spruce Mountain   Yavapai Co.   U. S. G. S. Map, 1923.

Prescott N. F., Sierra Prieta mountains, near Iron Springs west of Prescott.

"In early days there was a fine body of spruce on this mountain. Practically cleared out by miners and settlers in the Seventies."

Spud Rock   Pima Co.   Map, Coronado N. F., 1929.

Outstanding point of bare rock in plain view from Tucson at north end of Rincons, elevation 8,590 feet. About 24 miles east of Tucson. George F. Kitt of Tucson says: "Two Southern Pacific railroad engineers, William H. Barnett and Jim Miller, had a shack here and raised potatoes and cabbage on a little flat close to the rock. They called it Spud Rock for their major crop —spuds. Barnett fell from his horse one day coming down the trail and was killed."

Square Butte   Coconino Co.   G. L. O. Map, 1921.

On Navajo Ind. Res. at upper end of White mesa near head of Navajo creek. Descriptive name.

Square Peak   Cochise Co.   G. L. O. Map, 1921.

In T. 19 S., R. 30 E. Apparently same as Sentinel peak on Coronado N. F. map, 1927, q.v. Which was the original cannot be learned. Different maps locate them at apparently same spot.

Square Top Hills   Cochise Co.   G. L. O. Map, 1921.

Elevation main peak 5,492 feet. In Ts. 18, 19 S., R. 27 E. Two flat-top buttes. Prominent land marks at north end Swisshelm mountains. Descriptive name.

Squash Mountains   Navajo Co.

Northeast of Hopi villages. These appear on Smith map, 1879; Eckhoff, 1880; and Mallory, 1876, at head of Cottonwood wash, Navajo Ind. Res. They are probably the same as shown on later maps as Black mesa. Origin not known.

Squaw Butte   Gila Co.   Map, Crook N. F., 1926.

In T. 3 N., R. 14 E., east side Pinal creek.

Squaw Butte   Yavapai Co.   Map, Tonto N. F., 1927.

In sec. 18, T. 11 N., R. 6 E. At south end Skeleton ridge, about 2 miles west of Verde river. Just another "Squaw."

Squaw Creek   Greenlee Co.   G. L. O. Map, 1921; Crook N. F., 1926.

In T. 1 N., R. 30 E. Rises at Rose peak. Flows southeast into Blue river in sec. 35, T. 1 N., R. 30 E.

Squaw Creek   Yavapai Co.   Map, Tonto N. F., 1927.

Stream rising at C. P. Butte in T. 9 N., R. 5 E., flows southwest into Agua Fria river in T. 9 N., R. 2 E. Another Squaw creek.

Squaw Mountain   Cochise Co.   G. L. O. Map, 1921.

On west side S. P. R. R. in T. 20 S., R. 31 E., about 8 miles west of New Mexico line.

Squaw Mountain   Yavapai Co.   Map, Tonto N. F., 1927.

At northern end New River mountain, in sec. 36, T. 9 N., R. 3 E. Still another Squaw mountain.

Squaw Peak   Gila Co.   G. L. O. Map, 1921; Tonto N. F., 1927.

In sec. 31, T. 8 N., R. 14 E., lower end of Pleasant valley.

Squaw Peak   Maricopa Co.   U. S. G. S., 1923.

In T. 3 N., R. 3 E. In Phoenix mountains about 10 miles northeast of Phoenix close to Paradise valley. It is north of Camelback mountain. Named by Dr. O. A. Turney about 1910.

Squaw Peak   Navajo Co.   U. S. G. S. Map, 1923.

In T. 28 N., R. 19 E. In White Hills east side Detrital valley.

Squaw Peak   Yavapai Co.   G. L. O. Map, 1921.

In T. 13 N., R. 5 E. West side Verde river in Black Hills below Camp Verde. The writer was told, 1882, that Dudley Brooks named this peak. He was military telegraph operator at Camp Verde, 1878-81. Located a ranch near the peak when discharged and ran cattle there for several years.

Squaw Peak   Yavapai Co.   Map, Prescott N. F., 1927.

In sec. 34, T. 13 N., R. 5 W., about 4 miles west of Kirkland, west side Skull valley. Just another peak by this common name.

Squaw Peak   Yuma Co.   U. S. G. S. Map, 1923.

On southern side Kofa mountains, near long. 114°.

Squaw Peak   Yuma Co.   G. L. O. Map, 1921.

In Buckskin mountains, west of Swansea.

Squaw Tit Peak   Maricopa Co.   G. L. O. Map, 1921.

In T. 9 S., R. 2 W. Western side Sand Tank mountains, north of Papago Ind. Res. Descriptive name.

Stage Lines

The Southern Pacific Mail Stage Co. from Yuma to Mesilla, N. M. Kehrens (sic) and Mitchel, owners, claimed this was the longest stage line in U. S. in 1878, according to Hinton. It probably was at that time. Hinton spells it "Kehrens"; Kerens is correct. See Southern Pacific Mail Line.

Butterfield Stage Line, started semi-weekly in August, 1858. Cost Uncle Sam $600,000 a year to maintain.

San Antonio and San Diego semi-monthly stage line owned by I. C. Woods with James Burch as sub contractor. (J. Ross Browne.)

Standard   Navajo Co.   Post Route Map, 1929.

In T. 10 N., R. 20 E., about 3 miles south of Pinedale. "The Standard Lumber Co. built a saw mill here, 1922, Post Office named for them." Letter, Irene Halliday, P. M.

P. O. established October 17, 1924, Mrs. Agnes J. Cheshire, P. M.

Stanford Camp   Pinal Co.

Name given to old Fort Grant in 1862 for a California governor.

War Department report by Lieut. Col. J. R. West, 1st California volunteers, dated May 18, 1871, says: "Col. Carleton changed the name of this fort from Breckenridge and called it Fort Stanford in honor of Leland Stanford, Governor of California." See Camp Grant.

Stanley   Graham Co.   G. L. O. Map, 1921.

In sec. 28, T. 4 S., R. 19 E. Small settlement named after the nearby butte. P. O. established November 5, 1906, John Blake, **P. M.**

Stanley Butte   Graham Co.   U. S. G. S. Map, 1923.

In T. 5 S., R. 19 E. All old timers agree that this butte was named after Lieut. Stanley, stationed at Fort Grant in the Eighties. About 8 miles due south of San Carlos lake.

Stanton   Gila Co.

Arizona Gazetteer, 1881, lists this as "a stage station and post office in 1881 where the 10-stamp mill of the Mack Morris mine is located." Eighteen miles north of Globe.

Stanton   Yavapai Co.   G. L. O. Map, 1892.

On Date creek in Weaver mountains near Martinez canyon. Stage station on Prescott and Phoenix stage road. After Chas. B. Stanton who as early as 1866 kept a store and stage station here. He was charged with knowledge of the murder of Barney Martin and family. Was later assassinated, probably because of this knowledge.

P. O. established March 5, 1875, Charles P. Stanton, P. M.

Stanwix   Yuma Co.   Smith Map, 1879; U. S. G. S., 1923.

Stage station in Seventies on road from Yuma to Maricopa Wells, about 96 miles east of Yuma. Said to have been started by King Woolsey. Occupied by Confederate troops April, 1862, under Capt. Hunter. Confederates met the California column here April, 1862, and withdrew.

Also name of a station on S. P. R. R., 87 miles east of Yuma. Established about 1900.

About 1877 there was here an office on stage road of the military telegraph line that extended from San Diego across the Territory. William E. Guild, U. S. Signal Corps, was the operator. He was afterwards operator at Florence.

Careful search fails to disclose origin of this name, Stanwix. Poston in his book writes of being here in 1864.

He says:

"Here lived a fair Apache girl,
Of all her tribe the very pearl,
Who had abandoned her own race
To live here with a pale face."

History fails to record the name of the "pale face."

Star Mountain   Navajo Co.   G. L. O. Map, 1921;
                                               U. S. G. S. Map, 1923.

In T. 20 N., R. 19 E., on Hopi Ind. Res. northeast Egloffstein butte, 6 miles west of Stephens butte.

Star Well   Yuma Co.

"Well dug for water for North Star mine in nearby S. H. mountains." *Routes to the Desert.*

Stark   Cochise Co.   G. L. O. Map, 1909.

Station E. P. & S. W. R. R. about 5 miles north of Naco. "Station named after William Stark, who had a ranch here when the railroad was built." Letter, Robert A. Rodgers, Nogales.

P. O. established May 23, 1914, Solomon F. Pyle, P. M.

Starr Valley   Gila Co.   Map, Tonto N. F., 1927.

In southwest corner T. 10 N., R. 11 E. Valley on Box Canyon creek about 4 miles northeast of Payson, north side of Monument butte.

"A man named Starr located in this valley in 1877 and lived there for many years. Died and was buried there." Letter, Margaret Platt, Payson.

"Andrew M. Houston and his brother, Samuel, settled here in 1878 and named the valley after the old man they found living there. Starr was married to an Oregon Indian woman." Letter, Forest Ranger Fred Croxen.

State Well   Maricopa Co.   U. S. G. S. Map, 1923.

Water hole west of Gila Bend mountains, 8 miles east of county line.

Routes to the Desert says it was dug by men at work on the State highway at this point.

Steamboat Canyon   Apache Co.   G. L. O. Map, 1921.

Navajo Ind. Res. on west fork Pueblo Colorado wash, about 12 miles northwest of Ganado. "The erosion has formed a remarkable rock steamboat." Gregory.

Steamboat Mountain   Pinal Co.   Map, Crook N. F., 1926.

Peak on west side Dripping Springs mountains.

"So called because local cowboys thought it resembled a huge steamboat when seen from Gila river side." Letter, C. V. Christensen, Forest Ranger.

Steamboat Peak   Mohave Co.   G. L. O. Map, 1921.

In T. 12 N., R. 19 W., near Colorado river. Descriptive name.

Steamboat Wash   Pinal Co.   Map, Crook N. F., 1926.

In sec. 27, T. 4 S., R. 14 E. Rises Dripping Springs mountains, flows southwest into Gila river. Takes its name from the mountain.

Steam Pump   Pima Co.   Coronado N. F., 1927.

In T. 12 S., R. 14 E. Well known cattle watering place with a very deep well owned by George Pusch, of Tucson. Water is raised by a steam pump. Store and post office of early days.

Steeles Station   Cochise Co.   Hinton Map, 1877; G. L. O. Map, 1897.

In T. 13 S., R. 24 E., west side Sulphur Springs valley, south of Fort Grant. Fish says it was located at Croton springs, 1874.

Here was a ranch owned by Tom Steele. A stage station on Overland stage line, q.v. It was later called "Point of Mountain." When the railroad came along the nearby railroad station was called "Willcox" for General O. B. Willcox, commanding the Military District of Arizona. Point of Mountain was where a stage line started north to Fort Grant, Camp Thomas and Globe. Steele ran cattle around here in the Eighties, branded T S on left hip.

Stehr Lake   Yavapai Co.   Map, Coconino N. F., 1927.

In sec. 5, T. 11½ N., R. 7 E. Small lake west side Fossil creek. Lake named after Frederick W. Stehr, Treasurer, Arizona Power Co., which built the power plant on Fossil creek.

Stephen Butte   Navajo Co.   U. S. G. S. Map, 1923; Gregory, 1926.

In T. 26 N., R. 20 E., southeast corner Hopi Ind. Res., about 15 miles south of Keam canyon. After A. M. Stephen (Steve), early resident and government employee, who lived for many years at Keam canyon and died and is buried there.

Stephen A. Little, Camp   Santa Cruz Co.

Army post established 1910 when trouble with Mexico became serious. Was within city limits of Nogales. Named for a private soldier of regular army killed by a stray bullet from across the line during one of the many affairs between rival bands of Mexicans.

Stevens Ranch   Greenlee Co.   G. L. O. Map, 1912.

On Eagle creek near present "Double Circle" ranch, not far from mouth of Willow creek. Was owned by George Stevens or "Little Steve," a "squaw man" who had a ranch here in the Eighties. Claim has been made that Stevens was married to Cochise's daughter, but this is doubtful. Charley Hurrle, post interpreter at Fort Apache 1881-82, told the writer that she was one of the Warm Spring Apaches, probably a daughter of Victorio. Stevens always had a band of these Apaches hanging around his place. It was not far from here, 1880, that Captain Kramer and E Troop, 6th Cavalry, were ambushed by some of this band, several men wounded, and Sergeant Dan. Griffin killed. The troop was hurrying to Steven's aid called by a squaw who rode to Kramer's camp with the news that Stevens was in dire need of help. Soldiers always insisted it was a ruse by Victorio to get the troops there. See Little Giant.

Stewart Mountain   Maricopa Co.

G. L. O. Map, 1921; Tonto N. F., 1927.

Elevation 2,900 feet. In T. 3 N., R. 8 E. Mountain, south side Salt river. So called after nearby Stewart ranch, an old time cattle ranch. Stewart Mountain dam called for it.

"Jack Stewart ran cattle on the range and had a headquarters camp on Salt river near foot of this mountain from 1880 to about 1900." Letter, J. H. Sizer, Forest Service.

Stewart Mountain Dam   Maricopa Co.

Supplementary dam constructed by Salt River Valley Water Users Association as part of general reclamation project. This dam, some 35 miles from Phoenix, catches and holds water from dams above, much of which has already done service in turning the turbines of power plants at Roosevelt dam. See Stewart mountain.

Stewart Pocket   Gila Co.

Pocket or basin surrounded by granite hills, about 4 miles east of Payson. "Named after Ben Stewart, who settled in this pocket, which is really part of Starr valley. Ranch now owned by W. A. Packard and run as a fox farm." Letter, Forest Ranger Croxen.

Stiles Hill   Pinal Co.

See Poston butte.

Stiles Ranch   Navajo Co.   Gregory Map, 1916.

In T. 22 N., R. 19 E., on Cottonwood wash. Sometimes called Maddox, q.v. Was used as a cattle ranch for several years, 1890-96, by "Barney" (Barnett) Stiles, well known cattleman. Barney Stiles came to Holbrook as a cowboy with the Aztec Cattle Co. about 1887. A reliable man and a "top waddy."

Stinsons   Smith Map, 1879.

Ranch station on Silver creek on stage road, Camp Apache to Horse Head crossing on Little Colorado river, about 35 miles north of Camp Apache. Named after the owner, James Stinson, who located here, 1873; sold it to Mormon church in 1878.

"We arrived at Stinson's ranch after 25 miles, mostly malapais."
Vanished Arizona, 1874.
According to Farish, Dan Ming and a man named Evans were
partners with Stinson but drew out soon after. Later called
Snowflake, q.v.

Stinson Mountain   Yavapai Co.   Map, Prescott N. F., 1926.

In sec. 8, T. 16 N., R. 6 W., west side Cottonwood creek, southeast of Luis Maria Baca Grant. Yavapai county records show
that a man named Stinson took up a water right near this mountain in 1872. Mountain took its name from him. It is the author's
belief that this Stinson was the same James Stinson who later
located the Snowflake property. See Stinsons.

Stinson Valley   Navajo Co.

Named for James Stinson who first came to this valley in 1873.
Located cattle ranch on Silver creek, which afterwards became
Snowflake, q.v. Old timers always spoke of the site on which
Snowflake stands as "Stinson's valley." Crosby says: "Stinson
was first Probate Judge of Apache County."

Stinson Wash   Navajo Co.   Map, Sitgreaves N. F., 1924.

Dry wash rising in sec. 34, T. 11 N., R. 18 E., starts at reservation line, runs northeast into Cottonwood wash in sec. 9, T. 11
S., R. 19 E. After James Stinson, who 1873-78 had a ranch on
this wash. See Stinson Station and mountain. Also Snowflake.

Stockham   Pima Co.

Station S. P. R. R., 2 miles west of Tucson.
"After John Stockham, Jr., a prominent man in this vicinity."
Letter, Paul Shoup.

Stockton Creek   Graham Co.   Map, Crook N. F., 1926.

Rises southeast corner Pinaleno mountains, flows northeast,
enters Gila river about 2 miles east of Safford. See Stockton
pass.

Stockton Hill   Cochise Co.   Map, Coronado N. F., 1927.

Small hill about 7 miles east of Tombstone. See Stockton pass.

Stockton Hill   Mohave Co.   Smith Map, 1879; G. L. O., 1892.

In T. 22 N., R. 17 W. Named by members of California Column
for Stockton, California. The insane of the Territory, 1880-1890,
were sent to Stockton, California, for care, there being no local
asylum. "Because the first ore struck there was so rich that
everyone went crazy over it, they named it Stockton."
P. O. established as Stockton, December 5, 1889, William H.
Rogers, P. M.

Stockton Pass   Graham Co.   G. L. O. Map, 1892;
                                            Crook N. F., 1927.

In center of T. 25 E., R. 10 S. In Pinaleno mountains, Stockton
creek or wash. "After old man Stockton, well known cattleman
and character of early day days when Tombstone was booming,
who settled in this region in late Seventies. The old man had a
ranch on the creek. He was killed in a fight in Skeleton canyon
about 1881." *Tombstone.* Father of Ike, Bill and Phinn Clanton.
Also called Eagle pass.

Stoddard   Yavapai Co.   G. L. O. Map, 1921.

After Isaac T. Stoddard, Secretary of Arizona Territory, 1901-1907. He had a mine here which he called the Stoddard-Binghampton mine, after his native town Binghampton, N. Y. In T. 12 N., R. 2 E. On Big Bug creek near Mayer. P. O. established December 15, 1882. George W. Birdsall, P. M.

Stone Cabin   Pima Co.

P. O. established December 28, 1880, John P. Zimmerman, P. M. Not located.

Stone Cabin   Yuma Co.   G. L. O. Map, 1921.

In T. 1 S., R. 18 W. north end Castle Dome mountains.

"U. S. Troops built a stone cabin here on this site as a protection against Indians. It was as old when I came here thirty-seven years ago as it seems now. The walls are loopholed for rifle fire." Letter, Fred V. Kuehn, May 6, 1930.

Stone Ferry   Mohave Co.

On Colorado river, at mouth Virgin river.

"When the Mormons left southern Nevada, Daniel Boneli and his wife moved to a point 6 miles below the mouth of Virgin and there started a ferry still owned and operated (1921) by a son of the founder. This is the same ferry noted on government maps as Stones Ferry." McClintock, *Mormon Settlement.*

Just how this came to be called Stones Ferry cannot be learned. Eckhoff map, 1880, calls it "Stones." G.L.O. map, 1921, calls it "Stones Ferry."

Stoneman Grade   Pinal Co.

Well known grade, built by U. S. troops under General George Stoneman, later Governor of California, for whom grade was named. It began somewhere near the old mining camp of Pinal and went over the mountains to Globe. Malioton speaks of going over it in 1882. People of those days talked of "going over the Stoneman's grade," as we today talk about driving over the Apache Trail. It was a marvel of early road building.

Stoneman Lake   Coconino Co.   Smith Map, 1879.

In T. 16 N., R. 8 E., on Coconino N. F. Large crater-like depression 3 or 4 miles in circumference. Named after Gen. George Stoneman who, as a lieutenant, accompanied Col. St. George Cooke, with Mormon Battalion across the southwest to California, 1846.

It is evidently an old crater. "Said to have first been discovered by a Lieut. Owens of the U. S. Army while scouting for Apaches. He called it Owens lake. Far and away the most beautiful spot I ever saw in Arizona." *Vanished Arizona.*

P. O. established April 22, 1924, Phillip J. Morin, P. M.

Storm   Yavapai Co.

After original settler at this place, James P. Storm, for two years treasurer of Yavapai county.

P. O. established June 29, 1894, James P. Storm, P. M.

Storm Canyon   Gila Co.   Map, Crook N. F., 1926.

In T. 2 N., R. 15½ E. Heads at Apache peak, flows northwest into Salt river at Horse Bend.

"Three men, Jack Knighton, Bob Sloan and J. B. Henderson, out cattle hunting, were camped in this canyon in November, 1898. A heavy snow storm caught them. Their horses ran off, they had to foot it out and nearly froze to death." Letter, Roy Painter, Forest Ranger.

Stoval   Yuma Co.

In T. 7 S., R. 13 W. Station S. P. R. R. about 70 miles east of Yuma. "Located near the site of stage station on Gila river, known as Texas Hill. Railroad company adopted name for its station here in 1880. About 1882-83, a man from Los Angeles named Thornton started a colony of farmers here. Land was so fertile that he renamed the place Christvale. Railroad people however did not like it so cut it down to Crystoval." Letter, J. D. Carter, Phoenix.

"About 1911 this name was cut to Stoval to save telegraphing." Letter, Paul Shoup.

P. O. established Sept. 25, 1888, as Crystoval. Oscar F. Thornton, P. M. Re-established May 21, 1914, as Stoval, Melancton Walters, P. M. See Texas hill.

Stove Creek   Graham Co.   G. L. O. Map, 1921; U. S. G. S., 1923.

Small stream San Carlos Apache Ind. Res., enters Black river from south at approximately lat. 33° 30', long. 109° 50'. Origin unknown.

Strattons Camp   Pima Co.   Map, Coronado N. F., 1925.

In sec. 20, T. 11 S., R. 16 E. Summer camp and resort in Santa Catalinas foot of Marble peak. On road to Mount Lemmon from Oracle. So named after E. O. Stratton, early settler and cattleman of this region. Member Cattle Sanitary Board, 1897.

Strawberry   Gila Co.   U. S. G. S. Map, 1923.

In T. 12 N., R. 8 E. Settlement and valley in Tonto N. F. on Strawberry creek. Said to have been named by Isaac Lowthian, 1868. According to Mrs. Margaret Platt and others, early settlers found large quantities of wild strawberries along the creek. Hence the name.

P. O. established December 13, 1886, LaFayette P. Nash, P. M.

Strawberry Creek   Gila Co.   Map, Tonto N. F., 1927.

In T. 12 N., R. 8 E. Stream rising under the Rim, flows south-- west into Fossil creek in T. 11½ N., R. 8 E. See Strawberry valley.

Stray Horse   Greenlee Co.   Map, Crook N. F., 1927.

Elevation 7,600 feet. In Ts. 9, 10 S., R. 29 E. Creek, spring and divide north side Rose peak. "A stray horse appeared on this range in early days and remained there for several years until he died. Cattlemen thus began to call it by this name." Letter, Rex King, Safford.

Strickland Wash and Spring   Yavapai Co.

Map, Prescott N. F., 1927.

In T. 14 N., R. 3 W. Rises north side Little Granite peak, flows northwest into Chino valley near Simmons P. O.

"After George Arnold Strickland, local settler. He operated the Simmons stage station in the Seventies. Later went into sheep business and built a string of troughs to water sheep in wash at this spring." Letter, Frank Grubb, Prescott.

Stringtown   Maricopa Co.

Mormon settlement—now Alma. See Alma.

Sturdevant, Point   Coconino Co.

Grand Canyon N. P., about 2 miles west of suspension bridge across Colorado river. Named for Glen E. Sturdevant, park naturalist, drowned in river below this point, 1929. Decision U.S.G.B.

Sturges Ranch   Pima Co.

See La Osa.

S. U. Knolls   Apache Co.   Map, Apache N. F., 1926.

In T. 6 N., R. 28 E. Two well-known points or knolls in open prairie country on top of the mountain about 18 miles west of Springerville, where in the Eighties the S. U. Cattle Company, Stevens, Upshur and Burr, had a summer camp. Their brand was S. U.

Sub Agency   Graham Co.   Smith Map, 1879; Eckhoff, 1880.

Point on south side Gila river about 16 miles east of San Carlos. Established about 1878 as a sub agency about which were gathered the Chiricahua Apaches, who were never friendly with other Apaches excepting the Warm Springs, with whom they intermarried.

Sublime, Point   Coconino Co.   U. S. G. S. Map, 1923.

Elevation 7,465 feet. Grand Canyon N. P. at southern end Kaibab plateau, north side Colorado river. A bold headland from which there is a wonderful view of Canyon. Named by Clarence Dutton, 1880.

Sugar Loaf Mountain   Maricopa Co.   Map, Tonto N. F., 1927.

Elevation 2,880 feet. In sec. 15, T. 4 N., R. 8 E. East side Sycamore creek. Descriptive name. It is a smooth round mountain, known generally as "Sugar Loaf Mountain." About 15 miles east of Camp McDowell.

Sullivan   Yavapai Co.   G. L. O. Map, 1892.

In T. 21 N., R. 6 W., about 12 miles south of Seligman. Station on abandoned Prescott and Arizona railroad, "The Bullock Road" of 1887 from Seligman (then known as Prescott Junction) to Prescott. Headquarters for Hon. Jerry Sullivan's cattle ranch in upper Chino valley.

Sullivan Peak   Coconino Co.

Grand Canyon N. P. near west rim, southwest corner park, near lat. 36° 16′, long. 111° 59′. About one mile southwest of Point Imperial. Named for J. W. "Jerry" Sullivan, Arizona pioneer. Arrived Prescott December 2, 1868, born in Canada, 1844; stock raiser, banker and member Third State Legislature. Sullivan had a large cattle ranch in Chino valley south of Seligman. See Sullivan. Named by the author. Decision U.S.G.B.

Sullivan Springs   Yavapai Co.   Map, Prescott N. F., 1926.

East side Lane mountain in sec. 36, T. 10 N., R. 1 W.
"After a miner named Mathew Sullivan, who had a mining claim in this region and tried to build a wagon road from Lane mountain to Tip Top." Letter, Frank Grubb, Prescott.

Sulphur Hills   Cochise Co.   Smith Map, 1879; G. L. O., 1921.

In T. 17 S., Rs. 25, 26 E., in Sulphur Springs valley 6 miles northeast of Pearce.

Sulphur Springs Valley   Cochise Co.   G. L. O. Map, 1921.

Large fairly level plain in southeastern Cochise county, west of Dos Cabezas and Chiricahua mountains. About 20 miles wide and 50 to 60 miles long. Begins near Willcox and extends south to Douglas. Named for Sulphur springs, q.v. Known to early Spanish records as "Playas de las Pimas" or "The Beaches of the Pimas." Just who first called it Sulphur Springs valley has never been established. Shown on Hartley's map which is very old, as "Playas de las Pimas."

Sulphur Springs   Cochise Co.   Eckhoff Map, 1880;
                                          G. L. O., 1892-1921.

In sec. 6, T. 16 S., R. 25 E. John Rockfellow and other old timers say these two springs "were always favorite camping places, in spite of the water which was strongly impregnated with sulphur. Always good grass and an open range about them." Ten miles east of Dragoon pass, 6 miles due north Pearce.

When Gen. O. O. Howard established the Chiricahua Reservation, 1872, in Stronghold canyon, agency was located at the springs. See Stronghold.

Sultan   Yavapai Co.

"Name given post office after Sultan mine near it, on Santa Maria river." Letter, E. A. Putnam, Hillside.

P. O. established May 6, 1903, Harry La Montague, P. M.

Summer Haven   Pima Co.   Coronado N. F., 1929.

In T. 12 S., R. 16 E. Summer camp in Santa Catalinas east of Tucson. "Just a fanciful name."

P. O. established May 26, 1924, Frederick A. Kimball, P. M.

Summerland   Pinal Co.   G. L. O. Map, 1921.

In T. 6 S., R. 3 E., small settlement, 10 miles south of Maricopa, on Santa Rosa wash.

P. O. established May 6, 1914, Nixon W. Stanfield, P. M.

Sumner Butte   Coconino Co.

Grand Canyon N. P. On left bank Bright Angel creek, about one mile north of Colorado river near lat. 36° 7', long. 112° 5', and one mile southeast of Suspension bridge. Named for John C. Sumner, hunter and trapper with first Powell expedition through Grand Canyon, 1869. So named by Frank Bond. Decision U.S.G.B.

Sundown Ranch   Navajo Co.

See Aripine.

Sunflower Butte   Navajo Co.   Gregory Map, 1916; U. S. G. S., 1923.

In T. 22 N., R. 20 E., 20 miles north of Holbrook.

"Hundreds of sunflowers made of skin and wood by prehistoric Indians were excavated from caves here." *Report No. 65, U. S. Bureau Ethnology.*

Sunflower Valley   Maricopa Co.   Map, Tonto N. F., 1927.

In T. 7 N., R. 8 E., west slope Mazatzal mountains at head Sycamore creek. "In 1871 a military post was established here garrisoned by a few men as an outpost of Camp Reno." *Vincent Colyers Report.*

Colyer held an important conference with "Shelter Pau" and his Apache warriors and other Indians at this point, October 31 and November 1-2, 1871.

"Florance (sic) Packard once told me it had been so named by early settlers and army people for the large crop of Black Eyed Susans that grow all over the valley. Sunflower mine here was worked for quicksilver at one time." Forest Ranger Croxen.

Sunglow   Cochise Co.   G. L. O. Map, 1921.

In T. 18 S., R. 29 E. East slope Chiricahua range. "So called because it got the early glow of the sun in the morning." P. O. established December 2, 1922, Jeff Thompson, P. M.

Sunnyside   Cochise Co.   G. L. O. Map, 1921; Coronado N. F., 1927.

In sec. 15, T. 23 S., R. 19 E. Settlement in Huachuca mountains on Sunnyside canyon: "Established by a religious community in the Nineties. Their leader was Samuel Donnelly." P. O. established July 16, 1914, Lucy Langford, P. M.

Sunrise Springs   Apache Co.   U. S. G. S. Map, 1923.

In T. 4 S., R. 11 W., on Pueblo Colorado wash, Navajo Ind. Res. P. O. established April 12, 1912, Benjamin E. Harvey, P. M.

Sunset City   Navajo Co.   G. L. O. Map, 1892; McClintock Map.

Small Mormon settlement east side Little Colorado river, at mouth of Cottonwood wash which enters river here. It was about 3 miles east of present town of Winslow. Established, March, 1876, by party under Lot Smith, who so called it for Sunset Pass to southwest.

Smith was the Mormon Bishop in charge. They built a woolen mill here, depending on Navajo wool. Bishop Richards of St. Joseph once told the author they turned out some very good homespun cloth, etc., but said it was not a success for the Mormon women could equal if not beat it on their hand looms at home.

Mill building was quite large and of rough hewn cottonwood logs. Most of machinery was hand made, largely of wood and very crude. Bancroft speaks of a bridge across the river at this point, which was carried out by floods, 1881. In 1883, only the old mill and three or four houses were still standing. Mostly they were of hewn cottonwood logs. In the big floods of 1890, water stood 3 feet deep all over the old site clear back to Lee Ferry road to the northeast. That spring, the author's party moved a chuck wagon across on the railroad bridge which they planked over. The water was within a half-mile of Winslow. There is a small grave yard on top of a hill northeast of Sunset 2 miles from the rim on side of Cottonwood wash. Local people placed a marker there, May 30, 1933. Lot Smith lived here occasionally as late as 1886 and ran his herd of "Circle S" horses on adjoining range. In Sept., 1933, the author visited the old place. Not a sign of it remains. All buildings washed away by the river. Only the cemetery remains to mark the location. P. O. established July 5, 1876, Alfred Derrick, P. M.

In August, 1881, Capt. John G. Bourke returning from the Hopi snake dance spent Sunday here. He says: "The fort was a hollow square of cottonwood logs lined all around with small log rooms; they had neither doors nor windows on the outside. Two narrow openings or gates, one on each side, allowed entrance. It was a real fort about 150 feet square. At the time we found over 200 men, women, and children living in the fort." *On the Border.*

In 1933 the last vestige of the settlement was swept away by floods and nothing now remains except the old graveyard back in the hills about a mile.

Sunset Crater   Coconino Co.   U. S. G. S. Map, 1923;
                                                        Coconino N. F., 1928.

In sec. 24, T. 23 N., R. 8 E.   Volcanic cone which rises about 800 feet from a bed of lava and cinders.   So called because of its coloring, from the red cinders which give the peak a golden glow like a sunset.   East of San Francisco mountains, and about 12 miles northeast of Flagstaff.   Established as a National Monument, 1930.

Major Powell in his report says: "When seen from a distance in the setting sun the bright red cinders seem to be on fire. From this we gave it the name Sunset mountain."

Sunset Crossing   Navajo Co.   G. L. O. Map, 1892;
                                                        McClintock Map.

An early crossing of Little Colorado river.   Beale crossed here April 7, 1858, also Wheeler, 1870.   Here travel to points southwest could safely cross on a rock ledge that covered the river bed from bank to bank.   In flood time, of course, they had to wait for the water to fall.   Ford was about 6 miles east of present city of Winslow and 3 miles from settlement of Sunset.   So called because travelers from the east going to Prescott, Camp Verde and other places to southwest crossed the river here and went to the mountains through what was called Sunset pass, a break in the range about 20 miles south of Winslow.

Of this crossing, Mrs. Summerhayes says: "All the baggage and two ambulances were ferried over the waters of the Little Colorado.   They made a boat by stretching heavy sheets of canvas over the wagon box and then drawing it back and forth with long ropes." *Vanished Arizona.*

Hinton says: "Sunset Crossing is not passable at time of melting snows without the aid of rafts.   It is said to have been so called because the first soldiers that crossed it did so just at sunset."   In 1878 the Mormons from Sunset City built a rock dam here hoping it would withstand the floods.   It soon went out.

Sunset Pass   Coconino Co.   Map, Coronado N. F., 1927.

Bold mesa lying about 20 miles southwest of Winslow.   An offshoot of Mogollon range.   Jacks canyon or Salt creek, q.v., as it is sometimes called, divides the mesa, forming a pass.   The Mormons from Brigham City and Sunset had a lime kiln here, 1877.

It was here that Captain Charles King, Fifth U. S. Cavalry, and his command, had a fight with Apaches in October, 1874.   Captain King was badly wounded and was retired for disability in consequence.   His novel, *The Sunset Pass*, was based on this experience.

Sunset Peak   Greenlee Co.   Map, Crook N. F., 1926.

Elevation 6,983 feet.   In Ts. 3, 4 S., R. 30 E.   East side San Francisco river about 6 miles northeast of Clifton.

"It is the last peak in the range lit up by the setting sun. Was a signal station, 1886, during Miles' campaign against Apaches." J. W. Girdner, Forest Ranger.

Sunshine   Coconino Co.   G. L. O. Map, 1921.

In T. 12½ N., R. 20 E.   Station, A. T. & S. F. R. R.   "Originally called Sunset, but changed to Sunshine, 1902, because of another Sunset on the Santa Fe." A.G.W.   Named by S. J. Holsinger, for Meteor Crater operations about 12 miles south.

Supai (Indian Village)   Coconino Co.
Map, Tusayan N. F., 1927.

In T. 33 N., R. 4 W., in Supai or Havasu canyon. This is the main village of these people. They have fields of alfalfa, peach orchards, and do considerable farming.

John D. Lee, executed by United States Government for complicity in the Mountain Meadow massacre in southern Utah, hid away in this canyon in the Seventies. It was probably he who brought them alfalfa seed and peach trees. Several years ago a big flood came down the canyon and washed away some of their best lands.

Supai Canyon   Coconino Co.

See Cataract, also Hava Su canyon.

Supai   Coconino Co.   G. L. O. Map, 1921.

Station A. T. & S. F. R. R., five miles west Williams. After Havasupai Indians, q.v.

P. O. established September 5, 1896, Rufus C. Bauer, P. M.

Supai Indian Reservation   Yavapai Co.

Reservation for Supai or Havasupais. Withdrawn by President Hayes June 8, 1880. Was laid out along and including lower end and adjoining areas on both sides of Supai or Cataract canyon.

Superior   Pinal Co.   U. S. G. S. Map, 1923.

Elevation 2,730 feet. In T. 1 S., R. 12 E. After Superior, Michigan, where some of the Lake Superior and Arizona stockholders lived. Prosperous mining camp at northern end of branch road from Magma Junction. Magma Copper mine was first called Silver Queen.

Townsite laid out 1900 by George Lobb, called the "Father of Superior." Place first called Hastings after well-known clothing merchant of San Francisco, Cal., who operated the first mine here. Shows on old map of Pioneer Mining District of 1882 as Hastings, q. v.

Superstition Mountains   Pinal Co.

Elevation 5,030 feet. In T. 1 N., Rs. 9, 10 E. Huge uplift 40 miles east of Phoenix, about 6 miles south of and parallel with the Salt river. Name "Superstition" has been accounted for by stories told early settlers, especially the Spanish, by the Pimas, that these mountains or at least their front peak were "bad medicine." Indians said Apaches from its summit watched for wandering bands of Pimas or Maricopas and descended upon and killed them. "Their arrows could not fail them," so the Pimas said. Undoubtedly the valley Indians dreaded or revered these mountains as the case may be. These rough uninhabited mountains are a fine setting for legends of "lost" gold mines. The "Lost Dutchman" mine is one of these legendary affairs for which nothing historical exists. Romance, however, will live long after historical facts have faded away. On all maps. See Sierra de la Espuma.

Superstition Peak   Pinal Co.   Map, Tonto N. F., 1932.

An outstanding exceedingly rough broken peak, the highest in the range. In sec. 23, T. 1 N., R. 9 E. A bold crenellated upthrust of the Superstition range facing the desert to the south.

Can be seen from long distances, east, south and west. In Tonto National Forest. A general landmark all over the adjacent region. Elevation 5,057 feet. See Superstition mountains and Sierra de la Espuma for history.

Supply, Camp   Cochise Co.   G. L. O. Map, 1883.

Temporary military camp, San Bernardino creek, almost at Mexican line. Established about 1878. On some maps, called Camp Rucker, q.v. That post, however, was some 25 miles northwest of this camp. See Rucker.

Supply, Camp   Navajo Co.

Said to have been established by Kit Carson, 1863, on Little Colorado river, about a mile east of present Holbrook. Carson was then making his campaign against the Navajos. One of his men, Jack Conley "American Jack," once told me he was in charge of this camp for some time. Jack then lived at St. Johns. Drove St. Johns-Holbrook stage for several years.
See Walker's ranch in *Vanished Arizona*.

Surprise Canyon   Mohave Co.   U. S. G. S. Map, 1923.

In T. 29 N., R. 13 W. North side Colorado river, about 10 miles above mouth Kanab creek.
"We climbed up to see what they—Beaman and Riley—had named Surprise valley in January, 1872." Dellenbaugh.

Surprise Valley and Creek   Apache Co.   U.S.G.S. Map, 1921, 1923.

Dry wash rising in T. 17 N., R. 27 E., flowing southwest into north side Little Colorado river in T. 15 N., R. 25 E. There was once a small Mormon settlement here, about 10 miles northwest of Hunt.

Surprise Well   Maricopa Co.   G. L. O. Map, 1921; U. S. G. S., 1923.

On Centennial wash, north of Gila Bend mountains, about 12 miles west of Arlington settlement.
"Most wells in this part are from 100 to 300 feet deep. They found plenty of good water here at 40 feet, so they called it 'Surprise Well.'" Letter, H. C. Gable, Arlington.

Swansea   Yuma Co.   G. L. O. Map, 1921.

In T. 10 N., R. 15 W. About 10 miles south of Bill Williams Fork, on branch railroad out of Bouse. Named for the Welsh smelting city.
P. O. established March 25, 1909, Stella Siprell, P. M.

Sweetwater   Pinal Co.   Eckhoff Map, 1880; Map, Pima Ind. Res., 1900.

In sec. 11, T. 4 S., R. 5 E. On Pima and Maricopa Ind. Res., about 10 miles west of Sacaton.
Stage station on the Gila with a trading post and general store, about 5 miles northeast of Sacaton butte. See Tusonimo.

Swilling Butte   Coconino Co.

In Grand Canyon N. P., on west wall about 5 miles southeast of Point Imperial, near lat. 36° 14', long. 111° 55'. Named for J. W. Swilling, native of Georgia, who came to Arizona, 1859, died, 1878, at age of 47. Decision U.S.G.B. Named by Frank Bond. See Swilling Canal.

Swilling Canal   Maricopa Co.

"J. W. (Jack) Swilling was a member of Peeples party that found gold at Weaver, 1863. Came to Arizona, 1859. Lieutenant, Confederate Army, Civil War. In 1867 built first canal from Salt river above Phoenix, known later as the Town Ditch. Said to have given Phoenix its name on a suggestion from Darrel Duppa." Farish.

In his last years Swilling is said to have been given to excessive use of liquor and narcotics. An editorial in *Prescott Arizona Miner*, October 10, 1867, tells of his killing and scalping a "chileno" at Wickenburg, September 30, 1867, who had made some previous threats against Swilling. Swilling died August 12, 1878, in Yuma penitentiary while being held on a murder charge of which many believed him innocent. **See Snively Holes.** The D. A. R. erected a memorial fountain for him in Court House yard in Phoenix, 1930.

Swisshelm   Cochise Co.

Mining town. P. O. established September 12, 1907, Wilson R. Holland, P. M. Named for the nearby mountain range, q.v.

Swisshelm Mountains   Cochise Co.

About 25 miles east of Tombstone, east side Sulphur Springs valley, in Ts. 19, 20, 21 S., Rs. 27, 28 E.

This whole range from White River canyon south to Mexican boundary shows on Smith map, 1879, and Eckhoff, 1880, as Pedregosa mountains, q.v.

In 1878, Henry Hudson, John Swisshelm and J. W. Fleming, three prospectors in the Pedregosas renamed them Swisshelm mountains, for John Swisshelm. They also called a peak Fleming peak for one of the party. The record of its location in County Recorder's office in Tombstone, says: "About 40 miles south of Camp Bowie." Letter, Wm. Lutley, Tombstone. This would bring it at lower end of Swisshelm mountains. The Fleming peak of that day is undoubtedly the Swisshelm peak of G.L.O. map, 1921, q.v. The name was often misspelled "Swiss Helm."

Swisshelm Peak   Cochise Co.   G. L. O. Map, 1921.

Elevation 7,183 feet. In T. 20 S., R. 28 E. Named for John Swisshelm. See Swisshelm mountains.

Col. W. A. Glassford, chief signal officer for General Miles, here established one of the heliograph stations during his campaign against Geronimo, 1886. See Miles *Personal Recollections*.

Sycamore   Yavapai Co.   Map, Prescott N. F., 1927.

In sec. 9, T. 17 N., R. 2 E. Station, Drake-Clarksdale branch, A. T. & S. F. R. R., 59 miles southeast of Ash Fork. At mouth of Sycamore canyon, from which it takes its name.

Sycamore Canyon

See Bruce canyon.

Sycamore Creek   Coconino Co.   Prescott N. F., 1927.

Rises east slope Bill Williams mountain, flows southwest, enters Verde river in Sec. 8, T. 17 N., R. 3 E., in Yavapai county. Town and railroad station of Sycamore near its mouth.

Sycamore Creek   Gila Co.   Smith Map, 1879; Eckhoff, 1880.

Short stream, rises east slope Mazatzal mountains, flows east into Tonto creek, 25 miles north of Old Camp Reno.

"We arrived at a stream flowing easterly which we named Sycamore Creek." Woolsey's *Report* of June, 1864.

Sycamore Creek   Gila Co.

In eastern part of T. 4 N., R. 17 E. Rises near Corral mountain, Crook N. F., at reservation line, flows south into San Carlos river about 3 miles above Rice, in T. 1 S., R. 18 E. The usual Sycamore creek with many of these trees along its course. Many streams in central and northern Arizona carry fine specimens of Sycamore trees.

Sycamore Creek   Graham Co.   U. S. G. S. Map, 1923;
                                        Crook N. F., 1926.

In T. 4 N., R. 17 E. Stream in southwest corner San Carlos Apache Ind. Res., rises near west boundary of reservation on Natanes plateau, flows due south, enters San Carlos river about one mile above Rice.

Sycamore Creek   Maricopa Co.   G. L. O. Map, 1921.

Rises west slope Mazatzal mountains, flows southwest into Verde river at Camp McDowell.

Sandy wash carrying water occasionally. A Mexican named Jesus Otero had a cattle ranch on it about 1888.

Sycamore Creek   Mohave Co.   U. S. G. S. Map, 1923.

Rises west side Aquarius Cliffs, flows southwest into Big Sandy at Owen in T. 15 N., R. 13 W.

Sycamore Creek   Yavapai Co.   Map, Tonto N. F., 1927.

Rises, Midnight Mesa, flows southwest into Verde river at T. 8 N., R. 7 E. The well known Cavness ranch is on this stream. Sycamore trees line its banks.

Sycamore Creek   Yavapai Co.   U. S. G. S. Map, 1923.

In sec. 6, T. 14 N., R. 4 W. On Prescott N. F., northeast of Mount Josh, flows southwest into Santa Maria river in T. 14 N.

All the above Sycamore creeks are so called because of the trees of this name on their banks.

Sycamore Creek and Canyon   Yavapai Co.   U. S. G. S. Map, 1921.

Stream at lower end is a deep canyon. Rises eastern side Bill Williams mountain, flows southerly into Verde at Sycamore on Clarksdale branch railroad. Canyon has many large sycamore trees.

Sycamore Creek and Ranch   Yavapai Co.   G. L. O. Map, 1921;
                                                    Prescott N. F., 1927.

In sec. 6, T. 11 N., R. 4 E. An old ranch and Forest Ranger station on upper waters of creek, which rises north of Ranger station, flows southwest into Agua Fria, in sec. 2, T. 11 N., R. 3 E.

P. O. established as Sycamore, October 16, 1911, Ethelle Rosenberger, P. M.

Table Mountain   Greenlee Co.   Map, Crook N. F., 1926.

In T. 2 S., R. 28 E. On county line. "Top of these mountains is very flat, like a table top." Letter, J. W. Girdner, Forest Service.

Table Mountain   Mohave Co.   G. L. O. Map, 1921.

In T. 27 N., R. 18 W. Upper end Cerbat range, east of White Hills. Descriptive name.

Table Top Mountains and Peak   Pinal Co.   G. L. O. Map, 1920; U. S. G. S. Map, 1923.

In Ts. 6, 7, 8 S., Rs. 1, 2 E. Sometimes called Table rock or Table mountain. Table top, decision U.S.G.B. Thirty miles due west of Casa Grande. Descriptive name. Dr. Eugene Tripell, of Phoenix, worked some copper mines here, 1888.

Tachito Creek   Apache and Navajo Cos.
                    Gregory Map, 1916; G. L. O. Map, 1921.

Navajo Ind. Res. Rises at Yale point in Black Mesa. Flows southwest, joins First Mesa wash, in T. 31 N., R. 20 E. About 18 miles above Walpi, Gregory spells it Tah-chito.

Tachna   Yuma Co.

Station, S. P. R. R., about 45 miles east of Yuma, took the place of old stage station of Antelope Hill, q.v. "In the 17th century, a Greek padre named Tachnapolis found his way into Arizona from California and spent his last days with the Indians around here. They naturally shortened his name to Tachna or Tacha. As he grew older he always had a fire in his hut and a light at night. The Papagos called his place Tachna—'the bright spot' or 'bright light,' and the word has come to mean that in their language." Letter, Max B. Noah, Tachna. P. O. established as Tachna Jan. 9, 1888, Edwin Hayes, P. M. Closed and moved to Crystoval in July, 1898. On June 4, 1927, after nearly 35 years office was again established with Max B. Noah, P. M.

Tahuta Terrace   Coconino Co.

Grand Canyon N. P., near lat. 36° 23′, long. 112° 32′. Benchland area left (south) bank Colorado at northern end of Great Bend. "Named for Tahuta point just above, and after Tahuta Jones, a venerable Havasupai squaw." *U.S.G.S. Report.* Decision U.S.G.B.

Talahogan   Navajo Co.

"House at the water." Navajo word. Spring at Awatobi. Hodge thinks it should not have been given another name as it has always been known as Awatobi spring. Gregory placed it on his map, 1916, as Talahogan, a mistake historically.

"A recent settlement here by the Hopi has developed a spring with a good flow of water. It is a small oasis with fine fields and orchards irrigated from the springs." Letter, J. W. Hoover, U. S. Indian Agent. See Awatobi.

Talklai (sic)   Graham Co.

First name of post office at present Rice Indian School. On San Carlos Apache Ind. Res. P. O. established Dec. 19, 1900, James W. Balmer, P. M. Talkalai, as commonly spelled, was a half brother of Distalin, San Carlos Apache chief, and an Indian policeman under Agent J. P. Clum. On December 22, 1875, at San Carlos Agency, Distalin attacked Clum and several other agency officials intending to kill them all for some fancied wrong. Distalin was himself killed by two Indian police after a lively battle. One of the policemen was Distalin's half brother, Talkalai, who lived to be some 90 years old. Died at Miami, Arizona, March 4, 1930. Clum wrote a fine account of this affair for *Ari-*

zona Historical Review, April, 1930. In 1907, name of P. O. was changed to Rice in honor of Lieut. Sedgwick Rice, U. S. Indian Agent for several years at San Carlos. A good man but an unsatisfactory change in a geographical name. In June, 1931, Indian Service not content with having made one mistake, made a second by changing name Rice to San Carlos, a most unfortunate error. Old San Carlos town is buried under waters of the new lake which U.S.G.B. called Lake San Carlos. This should have been sufficient to keep the name San Carlos alive. See Rice.

Tamar Mountain   Apache Co.

See Wolf mountain.

Tam O'Shanter Peak   Gila Co.   Map, Crook N. F., 1926.

In sec. 15 T. 4 S., R. 15 E. Four miles northwest of Christmas, west side Dripping Springs valley. "Descriptive name, has a crest very like a Tam O'Shanter cap." Letter, Forest Ranger.

Tangle Creek   Yavapai Co.   Map, Tonto N. F., 1927.

Rises east side Hutch mesa, flows southeast, enters Verde river at southeast corner T. 9 N., R. 6 E. "From all local sources, this creek was called so for its very crooked course together with a tangle of underbrush along its banks."

Tank Mountains   Yuma Co.   U. S. G. S. Map, 1923.

In T. 3 S., R. 14 W. Southeast of Kofa range. "There are several good sized natural rock tanks in these mountains, which gave them the name."

Tank House Canyon   Gila Co.

See Rock House canyon.

Tanner Canyon and Trail   Coconino Co.
                    Map, Tusayan N. F., 1927; Grand Canyon N. P., 1927.

Trail down a side canyon entering Grand Canyon at Lipan point in T. 31 N., R. 5 E. Follows canyon to river, crosses it and goes out on north side near Saddle mountain. Was used in early days by prospectors and others crossing the canyon. In 1925, State tried to drive 5,000 deer across the canyon via this trail to the south side. Effort was a grand failure. Named after Seth B. Tanner, Mormon pioneer, who often used it while he lived at Tuba City.

Tanner Crossing   Coconino Co.   G. L. O. Map, 1921.

On Little Colorado, near Cameron bridge. Well known rock crossing or ford much used in early days when crossings of this river were dangerous on account of quicksand. After Seth Tanner of Tuba City.

Tanner Springs   Apache Co.   U. S. G. S. Map, 1923.

In northwest corner T. 21 N., R. 25 E. After Seth B. Tanner who settled here in early days and ran an Indian trading post. Edgar Smith of St. Johns afterwards claimed the springs which Navajos called "Kai-sani" "the willow mat." The section was on railroad land. Purchased by Reynolds Brothers of Texas, who made it headquarters for their Spur ranch, 1886 to 1900. Sheriff Glenn Reynolds killed near Globe by the Apache Kid was one of the brothers and ran the outfit for some years.

Tanque   Graham Co.   U. S. G. S. Map, 1923.

Sp., "a tank, water tank." In T. 9 S., R. 27 E. Station, Arizona Eastern R. R. in San Simon valley. "Just a railroad watering tank."

Tanque Verde Mountains   Pima Co.

Sp., "green tank." In T. 14 S., Rs. 16, 17 E. In Coronado N. F. at southern end Santa Catalina mountains, directly east of Tucson some 20 miles. Roskruge calls these mountains "Agua Verde range," on his map of 1893.

Tanque Verde Wash or Creek   Pima Co.   Map, Coronado N. F., 1927.

In T. 13 S., R. 18 E. Stream rising at crest of Santa Catalinas, flows northwest into Rillito about 2 miles east of old Fort Lowell. Roskruge calls it "Agua Verde."

Tapco   Yavapai Co.   Map, Santa Fe R. R.

Station Drake-Clarksdale R. R., 56 miles southeast of Ash Fork and 3 miles north of Clarksdale. "Name coined from first letter of each word of names 'The Arizona Power Co.'" Letter, B. W. Hugo.

Tapeats Creek   Coconino Co.   Map, Kaibab N. F., 1920; U. S. G. S., 1923.

Stream in Grand Canyon N. P., rising in sec. 36, T. 35 N., R. 1 E., west side Kaibab plateau flowing west into Colorado river. "We called it Tapeats creek because a Pai Ute Indian of that name and who claimed it, pointed it out to Major Powell." Dellenbaugh.

Tapeats Terrace   Coconino Co.

Grand Canyon N. P., near lat. 36° 23', long. 112° 26', A descending northwest extension from Powell, plateau with wide, low benches between Colorado river and Tapeats creek, q.v., for name.

Tartron   Maricopa Co.   U. S. G. S. Map, 1923.

In T. 6 S., R. 8 W. Station S. P. R. R., 25 miles southwest of Gila Bend. Established about 1890.

Taylor   Navajo Co.   G. L. O. Map, 1921.

In T. 12 N., R. 21 E. Settlement on Silver creek one mile south of Snowflake, named for John Taylor, President, Mormon church. Well known stopping place on early stage line, Holbrook to Fort Apache. Called Bagley, 1878. Then they tried to change to Walker but post office department would not approve because there was another Walker in Arizona. Name Taylor adopted 1881, P. O. established by that name March 28, 1881, Jesse N. Perkins, P. M. There was an earlier Taylor on Lower Colorado river near St. Joseph or Joseph City, q.v.

Taylor   Navajo Co.

Short-lived town on Little Colorado made by eight Mormon families from Beaver, Utah, under John Karchner. They located here in January, 1878, about 3 miles west of St. Joseph. They put in several dams on the river which soon went out. They gave it up at loss of fifth dam and in July, 1878, moved to Snowflake settlement. In 1885 there were several old foundations of their dams still to be seen along the river bank. Not to be confused with present Taylor on Silver creek.

Taylor Butte   Cochise Co.   G. L. O. Map, 1921.

In T. 22 S., R. 27 E. In Sulphur Springs valley about 12 miles above Douglas. "There is a stone quarry at this butte owned by a man named Taylor. There are two buttes, however, very much alike and commonly known as 'Twin Buttes,' q.v." Letter, A. O. Porter, Webb.

Taylor Pass   Graham Co.   Map, Crook N. F., 1926.

In T. 8 S., R. 22 E. Low east and west pass across Graham mountains. South of West peak, q.v. After John Taylor, local Mormon bishop.

Tea Kettle Mountain   Maricopa Co.   Scott Map, 1929.

In T. 9 S., R. 5 W. In desert about 24 miles south of Gila Bend and east of Midway station, Tucson-Cornelia R. R. So called for its resemblance to a huge tea kettle.

Teamsters Camp   Yuma Co.   Eckhoff Map, 1880.

Camping place on Yuma-Tucson road in old stage days, 86 miles east of Yuma. "Just east of the camp, the old road to the Ajo copper mines and on into Sonora led off to the south." Hinton. Poston writes in *Apache Land:*

"The teamsters camp we next approach
And meet an overland stage coach."

Teapot Mountain   Pinal Co.   U. S. G. S. Ray Quad., 1919.

About 2 miles northwest of Ray, near lat. 33°, 11', long. 111° 1'. So called from its name. Often called Tea Kettle mountain.

Tecolote   Pima Co.   G. L. O. Map, 1921.

Papago village in T. 19 S., R. 3 E. A name of pure Aztec derivation meaning "owl." On Papago Ind. Res.

Tees Too   Navajo Co.

In T. 24 N., R. 19 W. One of J. L. Hubbell's trading posts. About 12 miles south of south line Navajo Ind. Res. Called Cedar Springs P. O., 1910, with Charles Hubbell, P. M. "Name changed to Tees Too in Dec., 1930. The word in Navajo means 'cotton-wood trees.' 'Tees' is cottonwood tree and 'to' is water. Hence Cottonwood spring. It is about 5 miles north of Cedar springs. There are both cedars and cottonwoods here." Letter, J. W. Richards. See Cedar springs.

Telegraph Pass   Maricopa Co.   U. S. G. S. Florence Quad., 1914.

Elevation, 1,980 feet. In and through Salt River mountains, in T. 1 S., R. 3 E. Old military telegraph line from Maricopa Wells came to Phoenix through this pass. It was an air line between the two points.

Tempe   Maricopa Co.

On Salt river, 9 miles east of Phoenix. Hinton says:
"In 1870, Jack Swilling who a few years before had built the first irrigating canal in the valley at the present Phoenix, seeking new fields to conquer, went up the river and took out another canal near the black butte on the south side of the river.
"Darrel Duppa, who suggested the name of Phoenix, again came to the front with the name Tempe, because, as he explained 'its beautiful location reminded him of the lovely vale in Thessaly, celebrated by the classical poets.' And so it was christened by this somewhat exotic name.

"Just as the new name was finding its way into use, Charles T. Hayden, father of Senator Carl Hayden, happened along looking for a location.

" 'Don Carlos,' as he was called by old timers, was a trader and promoter, not a farmer. It looked like a good point for a store, so he opened one. Likewise he started a blacksmith and wagon shop; also a grist mill with water power from the canal. The river was often unfordable, and so Hayden operated a ferry with a long rope. Soon the place was known as 'Hayden's Ferry,' and so showed on many early maps. But the name 'Tempe' prevailed and the theme of a Greek poet found a place in the Arizona desert." Hinton.

Hinton always wrote this name "La Tempe," but as McClintock remarks, "the word is not Spanish and should be pronounced as spelled: Tempee."

McClintock and Farish both discuss at length these names and their interesting sponsors. P. O. established May 5, 1879, Andrew J. Post, P. M.

Tempe Butte   Maricopa Co.   Smith Map, 1879; Eckhoff, 1880; U. S. G. S., 1923.

Elevation 1,496 feet. On south bank Salt river at Tempe. Often called Hayden's Butte after C. T. Hayden.

Temple Bar   Mohave Co.   G. L. O. Map, 1921.

Early mining camp in Colorado river canyon, mouth of Virgin river. "Named from a rock formation which resembles an old temple. Camp was built on a sand bar thrown up in past ages. See *National Geographic Magazine*, May, 1924." Letter, Robert O. Gibson, St. Thomas, Nev.

Temple of Seti   Coconino Co.

High point in Grand Canyon. "So named by Thomas Moran." G. Wharton James. James fails to locate it definitely.

Temple Road   Mohave Co.

The builders of Mormon Temple at St. George, Utah, in early Seventies, secured all the timbers from the pine forest on Mount Trumbull. To reach the forest they built a wagon road from the top of Hurricane ledge, down its precipitous sides to the mountain. Old timers have often told the author of the roughness of this road. All hauling was done by ox teams. The St. George temple was first edifice of that character finished and put to use in Utah, antedating that at Salt Lake by some time. Up to about 1900, hundreds of young Mormon couples made the 350 mile trek by wagon from points on the Little Colorado and other settlements in northern Arizona, over the road down the Little Colorado, and Moencopi wash, across the Colorado on Lee Ferry, and up through Buckskin mountains and down the Hurricane ledge to St. George. Round trip took several months. It was taken to enable them to "go through the temple," as a preliminary to marriage. Generally they started in November and returned in the spring.

Tenneys Camp

See Woodruff.

Tenneys Gulch and Spring   Coconino Co.   Smith Map, 1879; G. L. O., 1892.

Spring near head of gulch rising western side Kaibab plateau. Flows west into Kanab wash. After Ammon Tenney, who was with Powell and party, 1870, when they traveled with Hamblin by Hopi villages to Fort Defiance. Tenney later settled at Taylor, Navajo county.

Terminus   Pinal Co.

Station, 1880, at end of track about 15 miles east of Maricopa station, S. P. R. R. P. O. established July 31, 1879, Charles Dane, P. M.

Teviston   Cochise Co.   Map, S. P. R. R.; G. L. O., 1892.

In T. 8 S., R. 28 E. Located and named, 1880, by Capt. Tevis, before arrival of railroad. In northeast corner of county. Railroad station of Bowie 24 miles east of Willcox is its present name. "Capt. Tevis, hotel man, watered his orchard from railroad well at Bowie." McFarland. According to P. O. records in Washington, Teviston was first called "Bean." P. O. established under that name Sept. 28, 1881, Harry A. Smith, P. M. Changed to Teviston, Dec. 27, 1881, William L. Martin, P. M. See Bowie.

Texas Hill   Yuma Co.   Hinton Map, 1878; U. S. G. S., 1923.

In T. 7 S., R. 14 W. Familiar stage station before railroad days; on Gila river near present railroad station of Stoval, or Crystoval, q.v. Of this place Poston writes: "Next Texas Hill looms on the plain." The writer ate dinner at this station in February, 1880. Shows as a mountain on north side of river on some early maps. But was always called Texas Hill.

Texas Pacific Land Grant

Grant of alternate sections, 40 miles wide, 20 on each side, proposed Texas-Pacific R. R. across southern Arizona. Vacated by Congress, 1884, because company failed to build line into Arizona in time to meet the requirements of government's grant. The Southern Pacific, which succeeded to the Texas-Pacific rights, tried to secure the land but U. S. Courts decided against them and it reverted to the government.

Thatcher   Graham Co.   G. L. O. Map, 1921.

In T. 7 S., R. 25 E. Mormon community on south bank Gila, on Arizona-Eastern R. R., 4 miles below Safford. Located about 1881. Named for Apostle Moses Thatcher of Mormon church. P. O. established March 10, 1888. Mrs. Elizabeth Layton, P. M.

Theatre Peak or Rock   Apache Co.   G. L. O. Map, 1921.

On Navajo Ind. Res., about 10 miles southwest of Chinle at head of Chinle valley.

Theba   Yuma Co.

Station, S. P. R. R., 10 miles west of Gila Bend. Origin unknown.

The Captains   Apache Co.   G. L. O. Map, 1921.

Two prominent buttes at forks of Canyon de Chelly and Monument canyon, Navajo Ind. Res. "These two points stand out in the valley like huge sentinels. The Mexicans named them Los Capitanos—The Captains."

The Needles

See Needles.

Theodore Roosevelt Indian School

See White river, Navajo county.

The Tonto Rim

See Black mesa.

The Table   Gila Co.   Map, Tonto N. F., 1926.

In sec. 34, T. 9½ N., R. 10 E., flat top mountain, east of Oxbow hill. "So called by Sam Hill, early prospector, who lived in a cabin near this mountain for many years." Letter, Fred Croxen.

The Tunnel   Gila Co.

Tonto N. F., near head of East Verde. In winter 1885-86 an outfit from Globe went in here and began a tunnel into the Rim part way up the cliff. Ostensibly it was for a railroad from Globe to Winslow. Work stopped after several months and was never resumed.

No one seemed to know who or what was back of the project. The author saw men getting a camp ready in Sept., 1885.

Forest Ranger Fred Croxen writes: "This tunnel was dug in winter of 1885-6. Is on sec. 2, T. 12 N., R. 10 E. Opening is some 16 feet wide and 20 high. Workmen left no trace of their identity. Ruins of a log cabin and rock foundations of two more at head of East Verde are all that is left of the camp. It is a mile southeast of General Springs forest fire lookout on Coconino N. F."

July, 1882, a band of Apaches fleeing from pursuing troops climbed the cliff here. Were overtaken and whipped in a fight a few miles back from the rim, July 17, 1882. See Big Dry Wash fight.

Thimble Mountain   Mohave Co.   G. L. O. Map, 1921.

In T. 19 N., R. 19 W. East side Ute mountains. Descriptive name. Looks like a huge thimble.

Thin Mountain   Pinal Co.   G. L. O. Map, 1921.

Elevation 1,750 feet. In T. 5 S., R. 7 E., Gila River Ind. Res. About 2 miles northeast of Sacaton peak. Descriptive name.

Thirteen Mile Rock   Yavapai Co.   Map, Coconino N. F., 1928.

In sec. 23, T. 13 N., R. 6 E. Prominent rock on Crook road, 13 miles east of Camp Verde, hence the name. So marked on military maps.

Thomas, Fort—Camp   Graham Co.   Smith Map, 1879;
                                              G. L. O., 1892.

Camp Thomas was established Aug. 12, 1876, on south bank Gila river, San Carlos Apache Ind. Res., 6 or 8 miles above old Camp Goodwin.

Because of its unhealthy location, camp was moved about 1878 up the Gila to Sec. 34, T. 4 S., R. 23 E. Called Camp Thomas for some years; changed to Fort Thomas, Feb. 28, 1883. Named for Gen. Thomas, U. S. A. Neither were more than camping places although important points from which troops scouted. When the railroad was built through here, station was first called Fort Thomas, but later changed to Geronimo. For a short time Fort Apache was called Camp Thomas.

Bandelier believed Fray Marcos crossed the Gila at Fort Thomas on his way to Cibola. Town just off military reservation from Fort Thomas was known as Maxey, q.v. Abandoned and troops removed April 10, 1890. P. O. established as Camp Thomas March 2, 1877, Frank Staples, P. M.

Thomas Peak   Apache Co.   Eckhoff Map, 1880; U. S. G. S., 1923.

Elevation, 11,470 feet. In T. 6 N., R. 26 E. Fort Apache Ind. Res. One of main peaks in White mountains east of Fort Apache. After Major General Thomas, U. S. A. Turning point on line between Ind. Res. and National Forest. Also called "Baldy" on some maps.

Thompson Arboretum   Pinal Co.   Map, Crook N. F., 1926.

On Phoenix-Superior highway, in Queen canyon about 3 miles west of Superior. Experimental station established by William Boyce Thompson, Yonkers N. Y., for plant research. Devoted especially to desert and southwestern plants, trees, etc.

Thompson Canyon   Coconino Co.   Map, Kaibab N. F., 1926.

In northern corner, T. 34 N., R. 3 E. "Rises in 'Little Park,' flows south into Bright Angel creek. Named for Thompson, one of partners in V. T. brand of cattle. His initial was part of the V. T. brand." Letter, Walter G. Mann. See V. T. Park.

Thompson Peak   Maricopa Co.   G. L. O. Map, 1921;
                                          Tonto N. F., 1927.

Elevation, 3,980 feet. In sec. 35, T. 4 N., R. 5 E. East side Paradise valley, one mile southeast of McDowell peak. Nobody knows for whom named.

Thompson Valley   Yavapai Co.   G. L. O. Map, 1921.

South of Skull valley on Kirkland creek. "This valley was really named for Lieut. Tompkins, U. S. Army, who, after the killing of Bell in Bells canyon in 1884, trailed the Indians to this valley. He found their almost warm camp, but they escaped into rough country nearby. Thompson moved here and lived in valley for years. His name gradually supplanted the officer's name." Letter, Mrs. Will Ritter.

Thorburn Mountain   Coconino Co.

"With the party (Beals), 1857, was Lieut. Thorburn, U. S. Navy, whose name was given to a mountain northwest of Sitgreaves." McClintock. See Red butte.

Thors Hammer   Coconino Co.

George Wharton James says: "I called it this because it is shaped like a hammer large enough to be the weapon of a god." James, however failed to locate it.

Thousand Cave Mountain   Apache Co.   G. L. O. Map, 1921.

In T. 13 N., R. 30 E. About 6 miles east of St. Johns. There are a number of caves here, discovered 1883, in which much pottery and other articles of prehistoric origin have been found.

Thousand Wells   Coconino Co.

"There is a place near the trail from mouth of Paria to Tusayan, where there is a collection of water pockets known as 'Thousand Wells.'" Powell.

Three Castles.

See Sinking Ship.

Three Mile Lake   Coconino Co.   Map, Tusayan N. F., 1927.

In sec. 9, T. 22 N., R. 2 E. Wet weather lake about 3 miles from Williams, on Grand Canyon R. R.

Three Sisters Buttes　　　Cochise Co.　　　　G. L. O. Map, 1921.

In T. 16 S., R. 25 E. Three buttes about 5 miles east of Servoss. J. A. Rockfellow writes: "Three small peaks so called by local people."

Three Sisters Buttes　　　Mohave Co.　　　　G. L. O. Map, 1921.

In T. 20 N., R. 10 W. Close to county line. "There are three buttes much alike and early comers gave them this name." Letter, O. D. M. Gaddis, Kingman.

Thumb Butte　　　Greenlee Co.　　　　U. S. G. S. Map, 1921.

In T. 7 S., R. 29 E. In Peloncillo mountains, on line between Greenlee and Graham counties. Descriptive name.

Thumb Butte　　　Santa Cruz Co.　　　　Roskruge Map, 1893; Coronado N. F., 1927.

In sec. 28, T. 23 S., R. 12 E. In Atascosa range, near head of Atascosa canyon. Small, rather outstanding butte, about 4 miles from boundary line.

Thumb Butte　　　Yavapai Co.　　　　Map, Prescott N. F., 1927.

In sec. 36, T. 12 N., R. 2 W. Prominent landmark west of Prescott. Hinton says: "Looking down on Prescott is a bold peak known as Thumb butte. Takes its name from a huge pile of rock which looks like a gigantic hand doubled close, with a large thumb slightly bent." Forest service has a fire lookout station here.

Thumb Butte　　　Yuma Co.　　　　U. S. G. S. Map, 1923.

In T. 5 S., R. 17 W.

Thunder River　　　Coconino Co.　　　　Map, Kaibab N. F., 1926.

Grand Canyon N. P. Rises north side Colorado, under Millet point, flows southwest into Colorado river in T. 34 N., R. 2 W. "Heads in two fine springs that flow out of a solid rock cliff. Named from the roar the water makes dashing over the rocks. It is 'white water' all the way to river." Letter, Walter G. Mann.

Tidwells Mill　　　Gila Co.　　　　Smith Map, 1879.

Mill for handling ore from Stonewall and other mines near McMillenville. "It was a custom mill built by Silas Tidwell for working ores from nearby mines. A very crude affair and not a success." Letter, Chas. M. Clark, Phoenix.

Timber Camp Mountain　　　Gila Co.　　　　Map, Crook N. F., 1921; U. S. G. S., 1923.

In T. 4 N., R. 17 E. Short range covered with a fair stand of yellow pine. About 8 miles northeast of McMillenville. In early days a saw mill was operated here, cutting timber for mines.

Tinaja Hills　　　Pima Co.　　　　G. L. O. Map 1921; U. S. G. S., 1923.

Sp., "a jug or earthen jar." In T. 18 S., R. 12 E. Four miles south of Twin buttes. Mexicans call a rock tank a "tinaja."

Tinajas Altas　　　Yuma Co.　　　　G. L. O. Map, 1921

Sp., "high tanks." Range in which several rain water tanks are located. In southern part of county, close to Mexican line at long. 114°. Named by de Anza, 1775. Papago name, Oovak, "where arrows were shot."

"These well known tinajas, eight in number, are in southern part of Gila range—Sierra de las Tinajas Altas—which stretches southeast from near Yuma. Other tanks are: Tinajas de la Cabeza Prieta (Tanks of the Black Head) and Agua Escondida (Hidden waters)." Lumholtz.

"The Spanish often liken a certain mountain shape to a water jar, 'tinaja.' Spelled in some dictionaries 'te' and in others 'ti.' Latter seems to be preferred."

Lieut. Michler, U. S. Engineer Corps, says, December 9, 1854: "There are eight of these tinajas, one above the other the highest two extremely difficult to reach." McClintock gives some interesting stories about the activities of the Boundary Survey in this vicinity. Tanks are noted on Kino's map.

Tin Town   Cochise Co.

Mexican suburb of Bisbee, occupied principally by Mexican miners and others working about the mines and smelter. Most of the shacks were built of flattened tin cans, hence the name.

Tipton, Mount   Mohave Co.   G. L. O. Map, 1921.

Elevation 7,364 feet. In T. 25 N., R. 18 W. In Cerbat range. So called by Ives for Lieut. Tipton, 3rd U. S. Artillery, one of his party, 1858.

Tip Top   Yavapai Co.   G. L. O. Map, 1921.

In T. 8 N., R. 1 E., Bradshaw mountains, on Rock creek. First claim here said to have been a "Tip top prospect," hence the name. P. O. established March 4, 1879, Winthrop A. Rowe, P. M.

Toapit   Pima Co.   U. S. G. S. Map, 1923.

In T. 11 S., R. 3 W. Indian village on Papago Ind. Res. Papago word meaning "white clay or white earth." Lumholtz.

Tobacco   Pima Co.

Arizona Sentinel, June 21, 1873, lists a number of new postoffices just established. Among them, Tobacco listed as being in Pima county, with A. Ryckmar, P. M. Cannot be located today.

Todds Basin   Mohave Co.

Four miles south of Mineral Park. "There was a mine called Todds mine here, 1882." Hinton.

Todilto Park   Apache Co.   1892 Army Maps.

Navajo word meaning "Sounding water." Valley in Chuska mountains. Father Haile says: "To-dil-do, a geyser or splashing water."

Todokozh Spring   Apache Co.   Gregory Map, 1916.

Navajo Ind. Res., northeast of Salahkai mesa, near lat. 36°, long. 110°. Navajo word meaning "Saline springs or water." Haile. Gregory says: "the water of this spring is 'sour' or 'sulphurous.'"

Tohadestoa Spring   Navajo Co.   Gregory Map, 1916.

Hopi Ind. Res. About 25 miles northeast Keam canyon, near Apache county line. Navajo word for "bubbling water," or "one hears the rush of water." Haile.

Tolani Lakes   Coconino Co.   G. L. O. Map, 1921.

Navajo Ind. Res., east side Corn creek, some 18 miles north of Leupp. "A group of lakes called Tolani by Navajos meaning 'many waters.' On road from Leupp to Oraibi." Gregory. Father Haile says: "Toth-lani, 'much water.'" P. O. established under name Tonolea, January 21, 1926. J. P. O'Farrell, P. M.

Tolchaco   Coconino Co.   G. L. O. Map, 1921.

On west bank Little Colorado, below mouth of San Francisco wash. Father Haile says: "Tolchiko, red water canyon." He also spells it Tolchaco. P. O. established March 31, 1903, as Tolchaco, Charles Robinson, P. M.

Tolfree   Cochise Co.

Tolfree once ran the hotel at head of Hance trail in Grand Canyon. Place named for him. P. O. established Aug. 13, 1894. Lyman H. Tolfree, P. M.

Tolladays Well   Yuma Co.   U. S. G. S. Map, 1923.

In T. 4 N., R. 12 W. About 6 miles northeast of Harquahala. Origin unknown.

Tolleson   Maricopa Co.   G. L. O. Map, 1921.

Elevation, 1,100 feet. In T. 1 N., R. 1 E. Station, Buckeye branch Arizona-Eastern R. R., 12 miles west of Phoenix. Named for W. G. Tolleson.

Tollgate, Camp   Mohave Co.

See Hualpais.

Toll Gate Ranch   Yavapai Co.   Eckhoff Map, 1880.

Station on road, Willow Grove to Prescott. About 40 miles northwest of Prescott at head of Williamson valley. Hinton lists it as having, "Plenty wood and water, road hilly." Nobody mentions any toll charges but there must have been some to account for name. Hinton speaks of "the new road to avoid the boggy part of road in winter time." It was probably here the toll charges were made.

Toll Roads

See Wagon Roads.

Toltec   Pinal Co.   G. L. O. Map, 1921.

In T. 7 S., R. 7 E. Station S. P. R. R. established 1881. "After the Toltec people, who preceded the Aztecs in Mexico." Letter, Agent S. P. R. R. P. O. established May 19, 1910, Charles Lazear, P. M.

Tompkins Valley

See Thompson valley.

Toms Creek   Coconino Co.   Map, Coconino N. F., 1928.

In T. 13 N., R. 9 E. Short stream runs northerly between "29 mile lake" and "29 mile butte," in West Clear creek. "So called after Tom Maitell, first settler on stream. He built his cabin just below where road crosses creek. Was often called 'Greasy Tom.' " Letter, W. J. Brown, Forest Ranger.

Tombstone   Cochise Co.

Elevation 4,536 feet. County seat, Cochise county, up to 1931, when it was removed to Bisbee. On branch E. P. & S. W. R. R. from Fairbank. In Mule mountains. Mine discovered, 1878, by Ed Schieffelin. Before leaving with his brother Al to prospect in Mule mountains he was advised not to go, for "all he would find would be his tombstone." So he named his mine "The Tombstone," which went for the camp later on. This origin is generally accepted.

However, listen to this: "Ed Schieffelin had no hand in the name. I was present at the meeting in May, 1878, when Tombstone was named. Schieffelin was not at the meeting. It was held at a place called 'Water Well' near where Schieffelin's monument now stands. Col. Whiteside, Lieut. Winchester, Murphy, McDowell, Reynolds, myself and a few others. Some one suggested 'Epitaph,' some 'Graveyard,' we finally adopted Tombstone because of the peculiar form of granite rocks here which stand out like tombstones in the moonlight." Max Marks in *Tucson Star*, 50th Anniversary Edition, 1927.

I fear Max came into this picture far too late to gain much credence for his story. At that, the rocks he mentions do resemble tombstones, in the dark—if one has sufficient imagination.

Tombstone was the original of Lewis' *Wolfville*. He speaks of the Bird Cage Theatre and other places which identify it. P. O. established Dec. 2, 1878, Richard Gird, P. M. John P. Clum, editor of *Epitaph*, became postmaster, June 4, 1880.

Tonolea

See Tolani.

Tonto   Gila Co.   G. L. O. Map, 1892.

In T. 7 N., R. 10 E. In Tonto N. F., on Tonto creek. Early day ranch at foot of "Jump off." Was post office for Cross Seven Cattle Co., also called Howells ranch. P. O. established Feb. 25, 1884. James B. Watkins, P. M.

Tonto Apaches

Sp., "fools." So called by early Spanish. "They are a mixture of several Apache and Yuman tribes, principally Coyoteros, Yavapai, Yuma, and Mohave. Were first placed on reservation at Camp Verde, 1873. Removed to San Carlos, 1875." Hodge.

Bancroft says: "Because of their notorious imbecility, the Spanish called them fools—stupid."

This seems hardly possible unless the Spanish themselves were very stupid or met first, some odd individuals of these peoples, who are by no means either fools or stupid.

Tonto Basin   Gila Co.   Map, Tonto N. F., 1927.

Generally described as an area bounded on north by Mogollon rim, on south by Salt river, on east by western boundary Fort Apache Ind. Res., and on west by crest of Mazatzal range. This area was known to the Spanish as "Apacheria" and shows under that name on many early maps. The "Mogollon Rim," on the north is an almost perpendicular cliff for many miles.

Tonto Basin   Gila Co.

P. O. on Tonto creek 25 miles north of Roosevelt at mouth of Reno creek where it enters Tonto creek. Originally known as "Packards Store." "Reno" Forest Ranger station located here.

Name first spelled in one word "Tontobasin." Complaint was made and post office department, very properly, changed it to two words, Tonto Basin. P. O. established May 8, 1929. Lillian L. Colcord, P. M.

Tonto Creek   Gila Co.   Map, Tonto N. F., 1927.

Rises "under the rim," below Promontory butte, flows southerly, enters western end Roosevelt lake in T. 5 N., R. 11 E.

"On June 8, 1864, we reached a stream which I called Tonto

creek, running south, about 30 miles long. The rock hereabouts changes to a bluish granite." Woolsey's report, June, 1864.

"Tonto creek drains a large part of the basin. Its head or source is in a huge spring in sec. 33, T. 12 N., R. 12 E., known as Tonto Spring." Letter, Fred. Croxen.

Tonto Mountain   Yavapai Co.   Map, Prescott N. F., 1927.

In sec. 23, T. 15 N., R. 4 W. Three miles east of Mt. Josh. After Tonto Apaches.

Tonto Mountain   Gila Co.   Map, Tonto N. F., 1927.

Peak at southeast corner T. 8 N., R. 8 E. In Mazatzal mountains.

Tonto National Forest   Gila Co.

This is an area first created by Presidential proclamation Oct. 3, 1905. A small area was taken from what was then known as the Black Mesa Forest Reserve, now Coconino N. F. At southern end, a small area was taken from the "Pinal Mountain Forest Reserve," now Crook N. F. Both areas were added to the Tonto. This made one large forest, all in the basin from the Rim down to Salt river. Area, 1932, 2,303,744 acres. The largest of all National Forests, excepting two in Alaska. Created to protect watershed of Roosevelt reservoir. Supervisors' headquarters were first at Globe, then moved to Roosevelt but finally to Phoenix March 5, 1923.

Tonto National Monument   Gila Co.   G. L. O. Map, 1921;
                                                       Tonto N. F., 1927.

In sec. 10, T. 3 N., R. 12 E. Set aside, 1907, as a National Monument to protect and preserve several fine pre-historic cliff dwellings in hills back of Livingston.

Tonto Spring

See Tonto creek.

Topaz Canyon   Coconino Co.   Map, Grand Canyon N. P., 1927.

In T. 31 N., R. 1 E. Heads at Canyon rim, flows north into Colorado river in Granite gorge. So named by Powell for its coloring.

Topeant or To-peat   Mohave Co.   Post Route Map, 1924.

Near Utah line, west of Cane springs. P. O. established as Topeat Jan. 26, 1921. Mattie W. Ruesch, P. M.

Tope Kobe Spring and Gorge   Coconino Co.
                                                 Map, Tusayan N. F., 1926.

In sec. 31, T. 33 N., R. 2 W. At head Lee canyon in Grand Canyon. Topo-coba, decision U. S. G. B. "Havasupai name meaning 'hill top spring' or 'spring at the top of a hill.'" James. According to James, it should be spelled "To-po-co-by-a." Spring is at top of a small hill.

Topock   Mohave Co.   U. S. G. S. Map, 1923.

Station, A. T. & S. F. R. R., on Colorado river at eastern end of bridge. Mohave word meaning "bridge." Was first called Acme. P. O. established March 6, 1906. Enos H. Morton, P. M.

Topawa   Pima Co.

In T. 18 S., R. 5 E. Village on Fresnal creek, Papago Ind. Res. "It is a Papago word meaning, 'a burned dog.'" Letter, Evelyn Bentley. "At a gathering of the Papagos, a dog was burned. So

the Indians named the temporal 'the place of the burned dog.' "
Also called "Beans," or "There are beans." This came from a red
bean with which the Indian boys played a game. Some Mexican
officials asked what the game was. The boys replied "mawi,"
which was the name of the game. So the Mexicans called it by
the name "Bean," or "where there are beans." Father Oblasser.
On G.L.O. map, 1921, spelled Topahun. Topowo, Lumholtz map,
1916.

Tordillo Mountains   Pinal Co.

See Picket Post.

Toreva   Navajo Co.

Trading post about 6 miles west of Polacca. On Hopi Ind. Res.
"Name Toreva is Hopi and means 'crooked' or 'twisted.' It is
applied to the spring at village because water comes from the
opening in a twisted or crooked manner." Letter, Ada C. Leh-
man, Toreva. P. O. established October 11, 1900, Frank S. Vor-
hies, P. M.

Tornado Peak and Mine   Gila Co.   Map, Crook N. F., 1926.

In T. 4 S., R. 15 E. Six miles north of Winkelman. Named
after Tornado Mining Co. A big gold strike was made here
March, 1927. "In early days a terrible tornado swept through
this section, which gave it its name as well as that of the mining company." Letter, O. E. Clendenner.

Tornado Valley   Mohave Co.

An error in name. See Toroweap. On G.L.O. map, 1921, as
Tornado.

Toroweap Valley   Mohave Co.

Large valley east of Trumbull division, Dixie N. F. At southern end Uinkaret plateau, draining into Colorado river. On
some maps as Tornado valley, evident error. Called Toroweap
on G.L.O. map, 1921; U.S.G.S., 1923. "At the foot of a sort of
valley the Uinkarets called Totoweap." Dellenbaugh.
   "Joe Lee, grandson of John D. Lee, who speaks the Pah Ute
tongue fluently, says word is Tonoweap, meaning 'greasewood.'
The suffix 'weap' in Pah Ute means canyon. Hence, Greasewood
canyon." Letter, M. R. Tillotson, Park Supt.
   "The word Toro-weap means a gully or wash, not a canyon
or deep gorge." W. R. Palmer, *Utah Historical Quarterly.* No
two authorities seem to agree on the prefix, "Toro." All of
them do agree that "weap" means a wash or valley. Greasewood canyon or valley is probably correct.

Torrance Well   Yuma Co.

In sec. 12, T. 7 N., R. 8 W. "Well dug by Clay Torrance. Water
hole on one of the desert roads." *Routes to the Desert.*

Tortilla Flat   Mohave Co.

"Immediately north of Virginia City is the Mexican settlement
of Tortilla Flat of which the leading industry is raising water-
melons, making adobes, and keeping 'bit' saloons." Hinton.
   Two bits was usual price for drinks. A "bit" saloon was considered low grade and not respectable. Virginia City is on some
old maps as New Virginia. See Virginia.

Tortilla Flat and Creek   Maricopa Co.

Sp., "pancakes." "So called for great masses of flat rocks like a giant platter stacked with tortillas." *Arizona Magazine,* March, 1916.

Creek rises about 6 or 8 miles from Salt river, just over line into Pinal county; flows northwest, enters Salt river at Mormon Flat. P. O. established Feb. 15, 1928, Mathis Johnson, P. M.

Tortilla Mountains   Pinal Co.   Smith Map, 1879; U. S. G. S., 1923.

Sp., "pancake." In Ts. 4, 5 S., Rs. 13, 14 E. Short range 4 miles southwest of Kelvin, south side of Gila river. A group distinct from Tortolitas or Tortolas near S. P. R. R. at Red Rock.

Tortilla Mountains   Pinal and Pima Cos.

See Tor-to-lita.

Tortolita Mountains   Pinal and Pima Cos.   G. L. O. Map, 1921; U. S. G. S., 1923.

In Ts. 10, 11 S., Rs. 12, 13 E. On east side S. P. R. R. near Red Rock, 20 miles northwest of Tucson. "From the summit of the Whetstone range . . . . to the northwest, are the Tortolita hills, near which Miller and Tappan were killed in ambush." Bourke.

According to Bourke, these men were members of a mining and exploring party enroute from Florence to Tucson, which was attacked by Indians. Tor-to-lita, Spanish word meaning "doves" or "little doves." According to early reports there were many doves in this vicinity.

Totabit   Pinal Co.   G. L. O. Map, 1921.

In T. 1 E., R. 10 S., in extreme southwest corner Pinal county. " 'To-ta-bitz,' Papago word meaning 'crooked.' Small village 10 miles from Cacate." Lumholtz.

Total Wreck   Pima Co.   G. L. O. Map, 1892.

In sec. 3, T. 18 S., R. 17 E. Early day mine about 9 miles south Pantano. Ed Vail says: "Mine received its name when John T. Dillon, who discovered it, came to my brother Walter in 1881 to get him to make out his recording papers. Walter asked him for a name. Dillon said: 'Well, the mineral formation is almost a total wreck,' alluding to the mixed formation. 'That's its name, Total Wreck,' said my brother." P. O. established Aug. 12, 1881, Nathan R. Vail, P. M.

Tourist   Coconino Co.   G. L. O. Map, 1909.

This is the old John Hance ranch east of Grand View. P. O. established under this name May 10, 1897, John Hance, P. M.

Tovar Mesa   Navajo Co.   G. L. O. Map, 1921.

In T. 25 N., Rs. 16, 17 E. At southwest corner Hopi Ind. Res., west of Egloffstein butte. For Pedro Tovar, one of Coronado's captains. The hotel at Grand Canyon is named for him. "Coronado sent Tovar to explore the country to the north of Zuni. He discovered the Hopis but did not locate the Grand Canyon. Cardenas was sent after Tovar's return and found it." Bancroft. See El Tovar.

Tower Butte   Coconino Co.   G. L. O. Map, 1921; U. S. G. S., 1923.

Navajo Ind. Res., north side of Navajo creek, in Rainbow plateau, near Colorado state line. Descriptive name.

Tower Mountain   Yavapai Co.

In sec. 4, T. 10 N., R. 10 W. Northwest of Crown King mine. "After George W. Tower, who mined here in 1873 and later owned what was known as the 'Potato Ranch.'" Letter, Frank Grubb, Prescott.

Tower of Babel   Coconino Co.   U. S. G. S. Map, 1923.

In T. 27 N., R. 9 W. Near Diamond creek, Hualpai Ind.. Res. Prominent butte on Diamond canyon.

Tower Creek   Yavapai Co.   Map, Prescott N. F., 1926.

In T. 10 N., R. 10 W. Rises north side Tower mountain from which it takes its name. Flows northwest into Blind Indian creek. See Tower mountain for origin.

Tres Alamos   Cochise Co.   Smith Map, 1879.

Sp., "three cottonwoods." Sometimes called "Dunbars." Bourke says it was owned by a man named Montgomery. On San Pedro river, 35 miles east of Tucson. Well known station on Butterfield stage line. When author was here in February, 1880, ranch house was under some huge cottonwoods. There was also a military telegraph station with a repairman to look after line. P. O. established Dec. 2, 1874, John Montgomery, P. M.

Tres Bellotas Canyon   Santa Cruz Co.   Map, Coronado N. F., 1927.

Sp., "three acorns." In southwest corner of county. Poston immortalized it in his *Apache Land*.

"The Oak, majestic, yields her quota
The fruit of which, we call Bellota."

Tres Cebollas   Cochise Co.

Sp., "three onions." Place originally so called. Is now the town of Bowie, q. v. Not found on any map under this name.

Trigo Mountains   Yuma Co.   U. S. G. S. Map, 1923.

Sp., "wheat." East bank of Colorado about 18 miles north of Yuma. According to local history, Yuma Indians at one time raised considerable wheat in river bottoms along here. Hence the name.

Triplets   Gila Co.   Map, San Carlos Indian Res., 1917.

Elevation 5,376 feet. In T. 1 S., R. 19 E. Three outstanding peaks on east side San Carlos river and north of old Camp San Carlos. About 2 miles east of Rice. Shows as Mount Triplett (sic) on one or two maps.

Tritle Peak   Coconino Co.

Grand Canyon N. P., near northeast corner of Park in lat. 36° 13', long. 111° 57'. On west canyon rim 4 miles south of Point Imperial. Named for F. A. Tritle, governor Arizona 1881-1885, mining expert, one of first owners of Jerome Copper mine. Decision U. S. G. B. Named by the author.

Tritle, Mount   Yavapai Co.   Map, Prescott N. F., 1927.

In southern part of T. 13 N., R. 2 W. Three miles west of Mount Union. So called for Gov. Tritle who was heavily interested in mines of this region.

Trout Creek   Mohave Co.   G. L. O. Map, 1892.

Formed by junction of Muddy and Francis creeks. Northwest of Baca Land Grant, flows southwest into Big Sandy, in T. 18 N.,

R. 13 W. "Trout creek is principal tributary of Big Sandy, rising near Aztec pass, in Juniper mountains. Flows southwest into Big Sandy. Creek abounds with excellent trout." Wheeler, 1871.

Trout Spring   Apache Co.   U. S. G. S. Map, 1923.

Navajo Ind. Res., 8 miles southwest of Chinle.

Troy   Pinal Co.   G. L. O. Map, 1921.

In T. 3 S., R. 14 E. Mining camp on Kane Springs canyon, near county line, about 8 miles northeast of Kelvin. Camp first called Skinnerville, afer a man named Skinner.

"After Troy-Manhattan Copper mine. Owners came from Troy, New York and New York City." Letter, Postmaster, Kelvin. P. O. established Aug. 5, 1901, Frank W. Hutchins, P. M.

Troy Mountain   Pinal Co.   Map, Crook N. F., 1926.

In sec. 21, T. 3 S., R. 14 E. At Troy mining camp near Florence. After mine and town.

Truit   Cochise Co.

In T. 21 S., R. 27 E. Ranch, Sulphur Springs valley east of S. P. R. R. Named for a cattleman and pioneer by this name who had a ranch here. Spelled Truitt, on G. L. O. map, 1909; Truit, which was correct, map Coronado N. F., 1927. P. O. established March 25, 1909, James H. Latimer, P. M.

Trumbull, Mount   Mohave Co.   G. L. O. Map, 1921;
                                             P. O. Route Map, 1929.

Elevation, 7,700 feet. In sec. 23, T. 35 N., R. 10 W. In Dixie N. F. in Uinkaret mountains. Powell named it for Senator Ly-man Trumbull of Connecticut. "The great mountain we call Mount Trumbull, in honor of the senator." Powell's Report, Sept. 20, 1869. According to Bolton, all timbers for Mormon Temple at St. George, Utah, were cut here and hauled over the so called "Temple road" to St. George. It is a dry farming region lying west of Mt. Trumbull Division, Kaibab N. F. See Temple road. P. O. established as Mt. Trumbull, April 6, 1920, Lillian B. Iverson, P. M.

Truxton   Mohave Co.   U. S. G. S. Map, 1921.

Station, A. T. & S. F. R. R., 12 miles west Peach springs. See Valentine.

Truxton Canyon and Spring   Mohave Co.   U. S. G. S. Map, 1923.

Spring named 1857, by Lieut. Edw. F. Beale, either for his grandfather, Commodore Thomas Truxton, or for one of his party by this same name. "At Truxton springs, the Indians stole a mule from us." Beale's Report, Apr. 26, 1858.

Canyon or wash rises in approximately T. 22 N., R. 13 E., east slope Peacock mountains. Flows into Red lake.

"Spring was called 'Peacock spring' by Lieut. Ives, for one of his men. Garces called it 'Arroyo de San Bernabé.'" Coues. George Beale, Lieut. Beale's brother, apparently with the party, called this canyon Engles canyon. He writes: "After breakfast our party was ordered to accompany the camel train to Truxton spring. We reached there after a short ride through Engles canyon in which the spring is located." This name has been dropped and canyon is now known as Truxton canyon or wash.

There seems to be considerable doubt as to some of Beale's place names along here. Coues, who went over the route personally says: "Truxton spring is one of the few place names we owe to Beale. Truxton was one of his men but whether spring we now call Truxton is the one originally named may be a question." See Peacock spring. Wheeler map, 1871, shows Truxton spring some 15 miles due south of Music mountain and almost straight east of Peacock spring. Wheeler camped here with his party Oct. 23, 1871, and says it was then garrisoned by C Troop, 3rd U. S. Cavalry.

Tsegi

See Canyon de Chelly.

Tuba Butte   Coconino Co.   G. L. O. Map, 1921.

On Hopi Ind. Res., about 10 miles northeast of Tuba City. After Tuba, Hopi chief. See Tuba City.

Tuba City   Coconino Co.   G. L. O. Map, 1921.

In T. 11 E., R. 32 N. Mormon colony, Navajo Ind. Res., located on Moenkopi creek. Prosperous little Navajo trading town, east side Little Colorado. After "Tuba," Hopi chief, who lived near the spring. In early days, 1871, Tuba often accompanied Jacob Hamblin as guide. Name Tuba is said to mean, in Hopi, "pine tree." Navajos call the place "tangled waters."

"Tuba is a veritable oasis—a patch of green in the midst of a forbidding desert. It has been the seat of an agricultural population long antedating the discovery of America. The Spanish padres found the ancestors of the Hopi cultivating corn and cotton in fields centuries old. There is a giant spring here." Gregory.

McClintock writes: "In 1879, John W. Young built a woolen mill here. It had 192 spindles. Yarn was first made in Jan., 1880. Abandoned principally because the Indians would not bring their wool to it; also due to lack of satisfactory laborers in the mill." Fish says this mill was at Moenkopi.

"June 20, 1892, Lot Smith was here shot and killed by Navajo Indians following a quarrel over grazing of Indian sheep. McClintock has some very interesting tales about Smith and his activities. Thomas W. Brookbank was first P. M., July 3, 1884.

Tubac   Santa Cruz Co.

Town on Santa Cruz river. Was a Presidio in 1752; a pueblo and mission, 1814-24. Lies in extreme northwest corner of Baca Land Grant No. 5.

Hodge says: "The word means 'adobe house' or 'round house ruins.' It is a settlement of Pima and Papago Indians on west bank of Santa Cruz about 45 miles south of Tucson." Coues says: "So called from the numerous ruined pueblos near it. The word means a house, or a ruined house."

"Most writers agree that 'Bac' was a word commonly used in conjunction with other names as 'San Xavier del Bac.' Tubac appears to have very little history back of 1752, nor does it appear on Kino's maps. In 1757, it contained 411 inhabitants; in 1848, about 250. In 1866, California Volunteers had a camp here called Camp Tubac."

Hinton says: "Tubac was headquarters for Santa Rita Mining Co., 1860-63." J. Ross Browne visited Tubac, 1853. He writes: "We found the old town of Tubac abandoned by its Mexican garrison. As the houses were good we occupied them during the ensuing winter, passing the time exploring the country. It had probably 150 silver mines within a radius of 16 miles. They have not been worked for 50 years." He returned, 1863, and wrote: "It is now a city of ruins and desolation."

Pumpelly, who visited it Oct., 1860, says: "A ride of 14 miles brought us to the old Spanish military post of Tubac. The ruins of the old village were occupied by a small mixed population of Mexicans and Americans, while nearly a hundred or more Papago Indians had raised a temporary camp of well-built reed lodges."

Cozzens was there 1858-59. He says: "The very elite of Arizona call Tubac their home. It had then some 800 people, one-sixth of whom were Germans who came from Germany to make homes in Arizona. A very attractive place with its peach orchards and pomegranates." There was also a small German colony near Tumacacori, q. v. The old records of Tubac, kept by Charles D. Poston, are now in County Recorder's office in Tucson. They include original certificates of Poston's appointment as alcalde, signed by the governor of New Mexico, Tubac then being a part of that territory. A weekly newspaper, *The Arizonian*, was started in Tubac, 1858, printed on a press brought by Wrightson brothers of the Santa Rita Co. to Mazatlan and hauled overland from there to Tubac. Was the first press brought into the territory and first newspaper printed there. Ed Cross was editor.

According to Bartlett, Mormons located a colony here, 1851, before the Gadsden Purchase, but did not remain long. He calls it "a God-forsaken place of dilapidated huts and buildings and an equally ruinous church." McClintock writes interestingly of this place.

Official records at Washington show many changes in Tubac post office. When opened, Tubac was in Doña Ana county, New Mexico. First P. O. established Feb. 21, 1859, Frederick Hulseman, P. M. Discontinued Oct. 24, 1860. Reestablished Jan. 2, 1861, Theodore Mohrucan, P. M. Discontinued again Feb. 14, 1863. Opened July 13, 1865 as in Pima county, Arizona, William E. Herrick, P. M. These changes were due of course to Civil War troubles.

Tubby Butte   Apache Co.   U. S. G. S. Map, 1923.

In T. 7 N., R. 6 W. High bluff in Chuska mountains, Navajo Ind. Res. Near New Mexico line. "The rock is highly impregnated with iron which colors waters of stream falling over the bluff. Navajos call the stream 'bish' (iron), 'dalnas' (falling down), literally 'iron falling down.' Origin of Tubby unknown." Letter, W. M. Stagg, Defiance.

Tuck-a-you Valley   Yavapai Co.   G. L. O. Map, 1921.

In Ts. 23, 24, 25 N., Rs. 8, 9 W. Open valley south of Hualpai Ind. Res., east of Yampai divide. South side A. T. & S. F. R. R.

Tuckers Pass   Coconino Co.

Beale named it after one of his party. "We started across the valley with the intention of going through Tuckers pass and joining train at Floyds peak which is about 12 miles distant." On July 11, 1859, Beale again writes: "I turned off the road and came into the valley at the head of which is Floyd's peak." This pass is not on any map, but Floyds peak is, which serves to locate it in a measure. See Floyds peak.

Tucket Canyon   Mohave Co.   G. L. O. Map, 1921.

North side Colorado river 10 miles east of Toroweap or Tornado valley. Near lat. 36° 30', long. 113°. Origin unknown.

Tucson   Pima Co.

Elevation 2,374 feet. On Santa Cruz river. County seat, Pima county. On S. P. R. R. Hodge and Coues both agree that name comes from the Piman "Sluyk-son," meaning a dark or brown spring. Originally it was probably a Papago word. Papagoes say "styuk" for black, and "zone" or "son" for foot or base of a hill; or near a spring. There was a Papago village in early days just across valley from Tucson at foot of what is today known as Sentinel peak, which they called by this name, Styuk-zone. See also Papago village of Little Tucson or Tucsonsito. Name has been variously spelled. Arricivita spelled it Tugson; Gen. Cooke spelled it Teuson, 1846; Emory, 1847, Tucson.

Franciscans in Arizona says: "Fr. Marcos visited Tucson, 1539. Kino, 1692; Garces saw it first, 1775. It was called Presidio of San José de Tucson." This work further says: "The Visita of San José de Tucson is situated 6 leagues north of San Xavier. A visita of Bac since 1763 it was still without either church or priest in 1772."

Kino located a settlement on his map which he called Tucsonimo. Bolton says, however: "this was a village on the Gila above Casa Grande which was called 'Encarnación' and said to have been some 26 leagues north of San Xavier."

Coues quotes Hodge as follows: "Its (Tucson's) settlement by Spaniards is reputed to date from 1560 but there is little doubt that it became a Spanish settlement not earlier than 1776. Before that time it was a Ranchería probably of mixed Pima, Papago, and Sobaipuri peoples. From 1763 it was regularly visited as San Juan de Tucson by the Missionary of San Xavier del Bac. In 1776, Presidio of Tubac was transferred there and name 'San Augustín de Tucson' applied. Its alleged great antiquity as a Spanish settlement is a fable.

"We have the first definite knowledge of Tucson as a 'Ranchería de Visita' of Bac mission, 1763. Tucson was doubtless second settlement by Europeans in United States with Santa Fe first by a few years, and St. Augustine, Florida, third. In 1848 population of Tucson was 760 persons, whites, Indians, and all."

Tucson was occupied by U. S. troops, 1856. August 16, 1856, a convention was held there to organize the Territory of Arizona as a political entity. Town was occupied by Confederate troops from Feb. to May, 1862. Tucson became capital Nov. 1, 1867, and held it until 1877.

Regarding the age of Tucson, Dr. Frank C. Lockwood writes: "Close study of Tucson's history indicates it was first viewed by European eyes in 1694. Shows first time on a map 1698 and was first established as a European town 1776."

Records U. S. Land Office show that in 1872 town bought two sections of government land for a town site paying $800 a section.

Donald Page in *Arizona Historical Review* gives an interesting account of first military occupation of Tucson, Dec. 1846. J. Ross Browne visited Tucson, 1864, as a government official. His account of what he saw is worth reading.

First P. O. established Dec. 4, 1856, Elias Brevort, P. M. Was then in Doña Ana county, New Mexico, and first post office established in what is now Arizona. See Revanton. Office closed temporarily Feb. 14, 1863, because of Civil War. Re-established July 13, 1865, with Mark Aldrich, P. M. First S. P. R. R. train reached Tucson Mar. 17, 1880. A post office called Tucson in Ross county, Ohio, 12 miles east of Chillicothe, was established May 10, 1896,

Zachariah Hines, P. M.   No one can tell us how this name was transplanted to Ohio.

Tucson Mountains   Pima Co.

In Ts. 13, 14 S., Rs. 11, 12 E.   West of Tucson.   Bourke calls them Santa Teresa mountains.   Coming down Cañada del Oro wash from old Fort Grant he writes: "Further along comes the Santa Teresa range just above Tucson."   Name does not show on any early maps.   There is a range by this name, Santa Teresa, in Graham county south of Mount Turnbull, q. v.

Smith map, 1879, Eckhoff, 1880, have it Sierra Tucson; G. L. O., 1892, Tucson Range; G. L. O., 1921, Tucson Mountains.

Tucson Wash   Pinal Co.   U. S. G. S. Winkelman Quad.

Rises near Oracle, flows northeast, enters San Pedro river above Mammoth.

Tucsonimo

See Tusonimo.

Tule   Apache Co.

First called El Tule.   There was a swampy place along river full of tules or cat-tails; hence the name.   About 15 miles south of St. Johns, on Little Colorado.   P. O. established Sept. 7, 1898, Severo Chavez, P. M.

Tule Desert and Well   Yuma Co.   G. L. O. Map, 1921; U. S. G. S., 1923.

Long open valley east Cabeza Prieta mountains extending into Mexico.   Almost due south of Mohawk station, S. P. R. R.   Well is at southern end Cabeza Prietas, 6 miles north of line.   Undoubtedly take their name from Tule mountains in Mexico, just over line.

Tule Lagoon   Yuma Co.   U. S. G. S. Map, 1923.

In T. 9 S., R. 24 W.   "An overflow lake 6 miles south of Yuma. At certain seasons it is full of tules."

Tule Wells   Cochise Co.   U. S. G. S. Map, 1923.

In T. 12 S., R. 31 E., in Peloncillo mountains, eastern side San Simon valley.

Tulleyville (sic)   Pima Co.

After P. R. Tully of Tully, Ochoa & Co.   Now Pantano, q. v. First called La Cienega.   P. O. established as Tully, June 21, 1880, John O'Dougherty, P. M.

Tully   Cochise Co.   R. R. Maps.

Station S. P. R. R., 11 miles east of Benson.   After senior member of early day firm Tully, Ochoa & Co., merchants, cattlemen, sheepmen, and bankers of Tucson.

Tully Peak   Pima Co.   Roskruge Map, 1893; Coronado N. F., 1929.

In T. 14 S., R. 16 E.   In Rincon mountains 6 miles west DeLong peak.   After P. R. Tully.   Named by George Roskruge.

Tumacacori de las Calabasas y Guebabi Grant   G. L. O. Map, 1879.

"This Grant was made, 1806, to Juan Laguna, governor of Tumacacori Indian Pueblo 'to replace title papers lost and destroyed.'   Land was abandoned temporarily.   In 1844, under an Act of Mexican Congress, was sold at auction for $500.   U. S.

Land Court rejected entire amount claimed, 73,246 acres." Mc-Clintock.

Claim lay on both sides Santa Cruz river above Nogales.

Tumacacori Mission and National Monument   Santa Cruz Co.
                                                   U. S. G. S. Map, 1923.

In T. 21 S., R. 13 E. On Santa Cruz river, about 12 miles northwest of Calabasas. Site of well-preserved mission church. First supposed to be on Garces N. F. In 1907, as Assistant U. S. Forester, the author recommended that it be made a National Monument. Subsequent survey showed it to be on private land. Owner was then given government land in exchange for that occupied by mission. Set aside as National Monument, Sept. 15, 1908.

"Papago 'Chu-uma Kakul.' The Spanish always turned the Papago 'ch' to T. For example: Papago 'Chuk-shon.' The Spanish made it Tucson, Tubac for 'Chuyac,' etc., etc. 'Chuuma' meaning a white stone; 'Kakuli' bending over; broadly tumacori 'Caleche Bluffs.'" Father Oblasser.

Mission erected latter part of 16th century. According to Kino it was sometimes called San José. Residence of a missionary as early as 1784, perhaps earlier.

Kino Memoirs say: "The Captain of the Cocomaricopas—had come from above the famous and great rancheria of San Matias del Tumogacori (Tutumagoydag)."

Farish claims it was a "Visita of Quebabi, but because of attacks by Apaches had become a complete ruin by 1770. Was rebuilt, 1791."

Was undoubtedly a Franciscan Mission for Papago Indians in 17th century. Lieut. Michler of Boundary Survey visited it, 1858. He writes: "I found two or three lone Germans living here. It stands in midst of rich fields." These Germans were doubtless some of those who came here with Brucknow and located near Tubac and silver mines in that region.

Tumacacori Mountains   Santa Cruz Co.   U. S. G. S. Map, 1923.

In Coronado N. F., southwest corner county, west side Santa Cruz river. So called after mission.

This range seems not to have been clearly defined. On U. S. G. S. map, 1923, it extends clear to Mexican line as Tucumcari (sic). On Coronado Forest map, 1927, upper end is Tumacacori, the lower Atasco. Two separate ranges. On Smith map, 1879, and Eckhoff, 1880, it is all Atascoso range. Smith locates Mount Wrightson at its southern end which is wrong. On G.L.O. map, 1892, the whole range is Santa Atascosos, while on G.L.O. map, 1912, upper end is Tumacacori—lower, Pajarito mountains. On same map for 1921, upper end is Tumacacori mountains, lower, Atascosa mountain. Atascosa Sp., "a barrier" or "obstruction."

Tucumcari is name of a mountain in southeastern New Mexico. How it was transferred over here is a geographic mystery.

Tungsten   Mohave Co.

See Athos.

Tunitcha Mountain   Apache Co.   G. L. O. Map, 1921.

Father Haile says: "Navajo word for 'much water,' or 'large water.'"

Peak in Chuska mountains. According to Gregory was so called by Simpson and earlier explorers.

Hodge says: "Tunicha, a tribe prominent in early history of lower Mississippi, because of their faithful service to them." (To whom?) Further on he writes: "Tunicha was mentioned as a Navajo settlement but actually intended to designate that part of tribe in and about Tunicha mountains in New Mexico." Just how the name got this far west is not at all clear.

Tunnel, The

See The Tunnel.

Turkey   Yavapai Co.   G. L. O. Map, 1924.

Mine and station at Turkey creek on Crown King branch R. R. from Prescott.

"Food was very low in camp and one of the miners killed a turkey."

P. O. established as Turkey Creek, Jan. 15, 1869, James A. Flannagan, P. M. Closed for several years; re-established March 21, 1903, Leverett P. Nellis, P. M. Closed, June, 1904. Later re-established as Cleator, q.v.

Turkey Creek   Coconino Co.   Map, Sitgreaves N. F., 1924.

Heads in Horseshoe lake, flows north into Willow creek, in sec. 29, T. 13 N., R. 13 E. There were many wild turkeys here in early days which gave the name. This is not the Turkey creek of Wheeler expedition however.

Turkey Creek   Yavapai Co.

Surgeon Woodhouse of Sitgreaves party, 1852, in his report says: "We saw numerous flocks of wild turkeys near the head of the Bill Williams river."

Two years later Wheeler camped here and named this stream. "Jan. 17, 1854. A large flock of turkeys was hunted in the grove and one killed. This suggested the name which was given to the stream. It was a clear and rapid stream flowing southeast." Wheeler Report.

Turkey Creek   Cochise Co.   Map, Coronado N. F., 1927.

Rises west side Chiricahua mountains, near Flys peak, flows west.

Letter in Pioneers Library, Tucson, signed R. E. Souers, says: "Turkey canyon was first settled by a man named Morris, (sic) who built and operated a saw mill here. When he first came he found wild turkeys very plentiful and so called it for that reason." This stream was undoubtedly first named after Philip Morse, a pioneer lumberman who built and operated the first saw mill in this region about 1872.

Stream is lost in Sulphur Springs valley near Pearce. Some times it is called Morse canyon.

"Where West Turkey canyon, sometimes known as Masie's canyon, opens out into Sulphur Springs valley, Coyote Smith's house stood in the open timber." *Tombstone.*

"Masie" was one of Geronimo's band, who, somewhere in Missouri, escaped from the train moving the tribe from Arizona to Fort Marion, Florida. Alone and with only his instincts to guide him, this Apache made his way back to Arizona without being seen by any one. On his arrival, he hid away in Turkey canyon, his old home, where he was not discovered for several months. His is a wonderful example of the "homing" instinct of his people. Read Frederick Remington's story about Masie, in *White Men and Red.*

"John Ringgold, called 'King of the Cowboys,' committed suicide in this canyon, July 18, 1882." Farish.

Turkey Creek   Navajo and Apache Cos.

Map, Fort Apache Ind. Res., 1927.

Rises about 12 miles east of Fort Apache, in T. 5 N., R. 25 E. Flows southwest, enters Black river near boundary of Gila and Navajo counties in T. 3 N., R. 22 E. So called from great flocks of wild turkeys found here in early days. G.L.O. map, 1927, shows a stockman's ranch in sec. 18, T. 4 N., R. 24 E. Here, Sept. 7, 1881, the writer with G Troop, 6th U. S. Cavalry, Capt. G. E. Overton, helped bury a man killed by Apaches a few days before while herding cattle for post butcher.

Here the Chiricahuas were held by Crook under Lieut. Britton Davis, 1885-86. From here they escaped to Mexico. Davis, who was severely censured for the escape, resigned from the army in consequence. See *The Truth About Geronimo.*

Turkey Mountain   Cochise Co.

See Chiricahua peak.

Turkey Mountain   Graham Co.   U. S. G. S. Map, 1923.

Southeast corner San Carlos Ind. Res., about 8 miles west of Morenci. "Wild turkeys were very plentiful on this mountain in early days." Letter, Forest Ranger Girdner.

Turkey Mountain   Greenlee Co.   Map, Crook N. F., 1926.

Elevation 6,736 feet. In sec. 1, T. 1 S., R. 29 E. So called because of wild turkeys found here in early days.

Turkey Springs   Navajo Co.   Map, Sitgreaves N. F., 1924.

In sec. 33, T. 11½ N., R. 16 E., 8 miles south of Walford, at head of one fork of Black canyon. About May, 1886, an old trapper named Woolf lived here. He found a wild turkey's nest full of eggs. The writer camped with the old fellow that night and we ate the whole nest full for breakfast. The springs had no name, so we agreed they should be called Turkey springs.

Turkey Tanks   Coconino Co.   G. L. O. Map, 1921;
Coconino N. F., 1928.

In sec. 35, T. 22 N., R. 9 E., on San Francisco wash. Well known water holes in days of wagon travel from Flagstaff to Colorado river points.

Turnbull, Mount   Graham Co.   Sitgreaves Map, 1851.

Elevation 7,700 feet. In T. 4 S., R. 20 E. On south boundary San Carlos Apache Ind. Res. Well known landmark. Emory mentions it Oct. 30, 1846: "Mount Turnbull terminating in a sharp cone has been in view down the valley for three days. Today at three o'clock P. M. we turned its base following the northern terminus of the same chain in which is Mount Graham."

November 7, 1847, Emory speaks of this mountain again. He says: "We called it also Saddle mountain because of its resemblance to a saddle. It is on the east side of San Pedro river and is an isolated peak of red sandstone."

Emory was then near junction San Pedro and Gila. He had with him as an assistant, Lieut. Charles N. Turnbull, U. S. Engineering Corps; and surely would have mentioned this if named for him. The origin of this name as that of nearby Mount Graham seems lost to history. In 1852 a Capt. Turnbull brought the first steamer, the "Uncle Sam," on a schooner to head of gulf of California where it was put together. This was six years after Emory saw and described it. No doubt named long before 1850. The interesting point about the name of this, and Mount Graham, is, that in 1846-47, they were both well within boundaries of Mexico and thus bore American names long before region was taken over by United States, which was not until the Treaty of Peace signed July 4, 1848. How did they receive their American names?

Hodge writes: "I am firmly of the opinion this was not named for Charles Nesbitt Turnbull but for his father, William Turnbull. The son at that time was a mere boy. The father was a distinguished U. S. Topographic Engineer who built the Aqueduct in 1832 to 1846, which brought Potomac river water to city of Washington."

Turner Ranch and Creek   Cochise Co.   Smith Map, 1879;
                                                Eckhoff, 1880.

East side Sulphur Springs valley, upper end Swisshelm mountains. "Named for Tom Turner, first sheriff, Santa Cruz county. Tom and his brother Al ran cattle here for many years." P. O. established Oct. 21, 1880, George Danforth, P. M.

Turner   Cochise Co.

"First name of Huachuca siding Benson branch S. P. R. R., where all freight for Fort Huachuca is unloaded. Called Turner after an old timer who was buried on one of the nearby hills. A granite monument was placed over his grave to mark the spot." Letter, Robert A. Rodgers, Forest Service.

Turquoise   Cochise Co.   G. L. O. Map, 1892.

"Lively silver camp, 1895, in district of that name, in Dragoon mountains, 16 miles east of Tombstone. They first found turquoise gems here, not so good as Tiffany's, but still very fair stones." Letter, Arthur J. Benedict. P. O. established Oct. 22, 1890, James D. Lowrey, P. M.

Turquoise Canyon   Coconino Co.   Map, Grand Canyon, N. P.

In T. 32 N., R. 1 W. On south wall, Grand Canyon. Flows north into Colorado river at Granite gorge. So named by Powell for its beautiful coloring. Decision U.S.G.B.

Turrett Butte or Peak   Gila Co.   Map, Tonto N. F., 1926.

In southwest corner T. 11 N., R. 4 E., west side Verde river, west of Bloody Basin.

"In 1872 some Apaches pursued by U. S. troops under Major George Randall, 23rd Infantry, took refuge on this butte, believing themselves safe from capture. Soldiers crawled up the face of mountain and waited until dawn to charge. Numbers of the Indians were so panic-stricken they jumped over the precipice and were dashed to death." Bourke.

"So called because from every side it resembles a huge black turret like that on a battle ship." Letter, Forest Ranger Joe Hand.

Turtle Back Mountain   Yuma Co.   G. L. O. Map, 1921.

About 16 miles northwest of Agua Caliente on Gila near county line. See Pass mountain.

Tusayan National Forest   Coconino Co.   G. L. O. Map, 1921.

On Coconino plateau south side Colorado river. Created 1898 as San Francisco Mountains Forest Reserve, West. Changed to

Coconino National Forest, 1908. Coconino Forest was divided July, 1910, and Tusayan National Forest created from western part. Tusayan covers 1,396,220 acres. Supervisors' headquarters, Williams, Arizona. After Tusayan Province of early Spanish discoverers.

Tusayan Province   Apache and Navajo Cos.

"Ta-sa-un," "Navajo word meaning 'a country of isolated buttes.' Spanish changed it to Tusayan." James. Name was applied broadly by Spanish to region about present Hopi villages. Dr. Fewkes thinks the Tusayan of Coronado's time was probably on or near Little Colorado river and that the Hopi had migrated northward between 1540 and 1583, when Espejo visited them in their present location. There is a fine map of Tusayan in *17th Report, U. S. Bureau Ethnology.* See "Seven Pueblos."

Tuscumbia Creek   Yavapai Co.   Map, Prescott N. F., 1927.

Small stream rising at Tuscumbia mountain; flows northeast into Turkey creek, in sec. 1, T. 11 N., R. 1 W. See Tuscumbia mountain.

Tuscumbia Mountain   Yavapai Co.   Map, Prescott N. F., 1926.

In sec. 21, T. 11 N., R. 1 W. "After Tuscumbia mine located by James Burd Wilson and James McLane. One came from Tennessee on the Tuscumbia river; the other from Alabama which had a Tuscumbia town. Hence the name." Letter, Forest Supervisor Grubb.

Tusonimo or Tusonimon   Pima Co.   Eckhoff Map, 1880; Pima Ind. Res., 1900.

"The ranchería, also called Encarnacion. 'Luz de terra incognito.'" Coues says further: "We went 4 leagues over the sterile plains to Tucsonimo or San Isabel, which was near Sweetwater on the Pima Ind. Res. on the Gila."

Capt. Manje, who went with Padre Kino, Nov. 1697, traveling west from Casa Grande, says: "On the 19th, having traversed four leagues we arrived at a town, Tusonimon, named from a great heap of horns of the wild or sylvan sheep which appears like a hill. They make the common subsistence of the inhabitants. From the highest of their houses there appears to be more than a hundred thousand horns in it."

Coues and Manje both spell this name Tucsonimo in one place and Tusonimon in another.

Tuthill, Camp   Coconino Co.

State military encampment located near Flagstaff. Legislature, 1928, appropriated funds for its building. Named after Dr. Alexander Mackenzie Tuthill of Phoenix, who became a Brigadier General in World War. He was for some years Chief Surgeon for Arizona Copper Co. at Bisbee.

Tuweap   Mohave Co.

P. O. established June 9, 1929, Mabel K. Hoffpanir, P. M. Ranch on north side Colorado river, east of Mount Trumbull. Origin unknown.

Tuye Spring   Apache Co.   G. L. O. Map, 1921.

In Chuska valley, Navajo Ind. Res., lat. 35° 50', long. 109° 50', in Steamboat canyon. "Navajo word meaning 'Echo of Thunder.'" Gregory. Father Haile says it is "Tuye" or "Tu-ye," "Dangerous Water." "A place that attracts lightning," hence "Thunder Water."

Tu-zigoot   Yavapai Co.

A pre-Columbian ruin dating about 1300 A. D. 2 miles east of Clarkdale on the east bank of the Verde river. It is near what was known in early days as Pecks lake which, from its peculiar shape, was called "Crooked Water" by the local Apache-Mohave Indians.

The archaeologists who excavated the ruin in 1933-34 gave it the Indian name and spelled it "Tu-zigoot." The author feels the word should have been spelled "To-zigoot." The word for water in both the Apache and Navajo languages is "To" generally spelled and pronounced as "Toe" by all authorities.

Under the direction of Dr. Byron Cummings of the University of Arizona and financed by the Yavapai County Chamber of Commerce the ruins of this great communal dwelling, have been carefully excavated; certain parts skilfully reconstructed and the whole made available to the public. It now constitutes one of the most interesting archaeological sites in the State. See Pecks lake.

Twenty-four Draw   Apache Co.   Map, Apache N. F., 1926.

Creek rising in sec. 6, T. 7 N., R. 27 E. At edge Fort Apache Ind. Res. Flows easterly into Little Colorado, of which it is one of the heads.

So called after well known Twenty-four Cattle Co., Smith, Carson and Tee. They started, in 1880, the first big range cattle outfit in this part of Arizona.

Twenty-nine Mile Butte   Coconino Co.   Map, Coconino N. F., 1928.

In sec. 29, T. 13 N., R. 9 E. East side Toms creek. Exactly 29 miles from Camp Verde on Crook road. So named for this reason.

Twenty-nine Mile Lake   Coconino Co.   Map, Coconino N. F., 1928.

Wet weather lake in sec. 36, T. 13 N., R. 9 E., north of Cinch Hook butte. After Twenty-nine Mile butte on nearby Crook road.

Twenty-seven Mile Lake   Coconino Co.   Map, Coconino N. F., 1927.

In sec. 23, T. 13 N., R. 9 E. Another of the numbered lakes along Crook road. It was just that many miles from Camp Verde.

Twin Buttes   Apache Co.   G. L. O. Map, 1921; U. S. G. S., 1923.

In T. 14 N., R. 27 E., two buttes on south bank Little Colorado river, opposite Hunt.

Twin Buttes   Cochise Co.

In T. 22 S., R. 27 E., Sulphur Springs valley, about 12 miles above Douglas. "Sometimes called Taylor buttes. A man named Taylor has a stone quarry at this butte, but common name for them is Twin buttes as there are two which look much alike." Letter, James Webb, Postmaster.

Twin Buttes   Navajo Co.   G. L. O. Map, 1921; U. S. G. S., 1923.

Elevation 5,685 feet. In T. 18 N., R. 23 E. Two prominent buttes about 4 miles south Carrizo station A. T. & S. F. R. R. Visible from Santa Fe trains and quite a landmark.

Twin Buttes Pima Co. U. S. G. S. Map, 1923.

In T. 18 S., R. 12 E. Two outstanding buttes; also town at end of short spur leaving Nogales branch, S. P. R. R., at Sahuarita (sic) station. P. O. established Dec. 29, 1906, Earl B. Rose, P. M.

Twin Buttes Pinal Co. G. L. O. Map, 1921.

In T. 4 S., R. 8 E. Gila River Ind. Res., about 3 miles north Gila river. Well known landmarks a few miles above Florence.

Twin Domes Pinal Co. Map, Crook N. F., 1926.

In sec. 23, T. 3 S., R. 13 E., west side Mineral creek and 2 miles west of Ray. "Two domes remarkably alike."

Twin Lakes Navajo Co. G. L. O. Map, 1921; Fort Apache Ind. Res., 1927.

In T. 10 N., R. 16 E. Two small crater lakes northwest corner Fort Apache Ind. Res. Close under the rim and convenient camping places, water always being sweet.

Twin Mesas Navajo Co. Gregory Map, 1916.

In T. 23 N., R. 22 E. Navajo Ind. Res. on lower Pueblo Colorado wash.

U. S. G. B. first called these "Zuni Mesas" but later changed to Twin because of Gregory's objection to forcing name Zuni upon this region. He felt it was out of place there. Two outstanding mesas close to each other.

Twin Springs Coconino Co.

See Andrews springs.

Two Bar Ridge Maricopa Co. G. L. O. Map, 1921; Tonto N. F., 1927.

In T. 3 N., R. 12 E. Long ridge east side Salt river below Roosevelt lake. So called from nearby Two Bar ranch, an early cattle ranch running the Two Bar brand.

Tyende Creek Navajo Co. Gregory Map, 1916; U. S. G. S., 1923.

Navajo Ind. Res. rises east of Marsh pass; flows northeast into Apache county; joins Chinle near northern boundary Arizona. "Navajo word meaning 'where they fell into a pit' or 'where animals mired.'" Gregory. There are many places in this region called "game pits," built by prehistoric or cliff dweller peoples. Game pits were deep holes dug by Indians into which deer, antelope and other animals would fall. Often they were in narrow defiles through which animals had to pass to escape from the Indians. They are found all over the Navajo country. The author once just escaped riding his horse into one.

According to Gregory: "Tyende is the chief western tributary of Chinle creek. Stream emerges from the many branched Laguna canyon at Marsh pass, rising near Keet Seel ruins, lat. 36° 50', long. 109° 40'. Flows southeast, turns northeast along eastern side Comb ridge, joining Chinle creek about 6 miles from Utah line. Total length about 62 miles."

Tyler

See Webb—see Kelton.

Tyson Wash Yuma Co. U. S. G. S. Map, 1923.

In T. 5 N., R. 22 W. East of Dome Rock mountains. Rises in Kofa mountains, runs northwest into Colorado river. See Tyson Wells.

Tyson Wells   Yuma Co.   Smith Map, 1879; Eckhoff, 1880.

Station on old stage road Ehrenberg to Prescott about 25 miles east of Ehrenberg. After Charley Tyson who lived here for a time. Known also as "Las Posas"—the wells. Tyson built a small stamp mill at Wickenburg, 1864.

"The ranch at Desert station was clean and attractive which was more than could be said of the place called Tyson Wells where we stopped the next night. It reeks of everything unclean, morally and physically." *Vanished Arizona.* P. O. established June 3, 1893, Michael Welz, P. M. See Quartzsite.

Uinkaret Plateau   Mohave Co.   G. L. O. Map, 1921.

North side Colorado river, west of Kaibab Ind. Res., northwest corner of State. "Piute word meaning 'pine mountain or where the pines grow.' Group of dead volcanoes with many black cinder cones. The Indian name Uin-ka-rets has been adopted by the people who live in sight of these highest peaks, so I have adopted that name." Powell.

Uncle Jim Point   Coconino Co.

Grand Canyon N. P. on north rim of canyon, near lat. 36° 13' N., long. 112° 2' W. (Not Natchi.) Named for Uncle Jim Owens, pioneer settler in this vicinity. Decision U. S. G. B.

Uncle Sam

"Name of first steamer to plough waters of Colorado river. Built, 1852. Commanded by Capt. Turnbull. Ran aground below Yuma, 1853, and was abandoned." McFarland's *History of Arizona.*

A careful study of available data shows that she came in sections around Cape Horn on sailing vessel "Capacity." Was put together at head of the gulf. Carrying a cargo of 35 tons and drawing 22 inches of water, she reached Yuma Dec. 29, 1852. McClintock says she was a side wheeler equipped with a 20-horse power locomotive engine. On June 22, 1854, she sank at her moorings at Pilot Knob about 5 miles below Yuma.

Uncle Sam Hill   Cochise Co.

Small peak about 4 miles southwest of Tombstone.

"Named for Uncle Sam mine which was worked in early days on side of the hill." Letter, James A. Lamb, Tombstone.

Union   Apache Co.

See Eagar and Round valley.

Union   Mohave Co.   G. L. O. Map, 1921.

Siding Chloride branch A. T. & S. F. R. R., 13 miles north of Kingman.

"This name was given this siding because the old wagon road to Union Pass from Kingman crossed track at this point. In early days wagon road from Hardyville to Prescott had its eastern outlet through Union Pass." Letter, O. D. M. Gaddis, Kingman.

Union, Mount   Yavapai Co.

Elevation 7,971 feet. Ten miles south of Prescott, near Senator mine, west of Big Bug mesa. Called "Union Peak" on some old maps. Very early name. Many gold mines and placers were located here in early Sixties. Peak named by a number of miners, Northerners in sentiment, who believed in the Union. See Mt. Davis.

Union Park

See Payson.

Union Pass Mohave Co. G. L. O. Map, 1921.

Elevation 3,680 feet. In Black range, T. 22 N., R. 19 W. "Union Pass is the one Beale's expedition used to cross the range Oct. 15, 16, 1857. Also one taken March 25, 1858, by Ives who calls it Sitgreaves Pass. Certainly Sitgreaves crossed the range by Union Pass Nov. 5, 1851, as shown correctly on Beale's map." Coues.

There is nothing definite to show who gave it this name. Beale called it "John Howells Pass" for one of his men. See Sitgreaves pass.

United Order; Mormon Institution.

See Orderville for history.

Unkakaniguts Coconino Co.

Ute word meaning, "people of the red lands." Powell applied this name to a small Pai Ute band formerly living in Long valley in southwest Utah. They lived along the Vermilion cliffs and this was their tribal name.

Updyke Tanks Coconino Co.

Named for George Updyke, pioneer, who blazed trail from Verde valley to Sunset crossing on Little Colorado. Now called Rattlesnake tanks, q.v.

Upset Rapids Coconino and Mohave Cos.

In Grand Canyon of Colorado river, 6 miles below Kanab creek. So named by U. S. G. S. because of an experience of Geological Survey party, 1923. Decision U. S. G. B.

Usery Mountain Maricopa Co. Map, Tonto N. F., 1927.

Elevation 2,970 feet. In southwest corner T. 2 N., R. 7 E., at Granite Reef dam, south side Salt river. "According to information given by M. A. Shill and Jack Frasier, was named for King Usery who had a ranch near this point about 1878 or 1880." Letter, J. H. Sizer, Forest Ranger.

Utah, Fort Maricopa Co.

Now Lehi, q.v.

Utahville Maricopa Co.

Mormon settlement of Lehi, q.v.

Ute Crossing

See Crossing of the Fathers.

Ute Mountains Mohave Co. G. L. O. Map, 1921.

Short range in Ts. 18, 19 N., Rs. 19, 20 W. Part of Black range directly east of Mohave City.

Ute Point Coconino Co.

See Moran Point.

Utting Yuma Co. G. L. O. Map, 1921.

Railroad siding, Parker branch A. T. & S. F. R. R., near Bouse. Named for Charles Utting, a Rough Rider, who lived at Phoenix.

Uturictuc

See Sacaton.

Vaca Hills   Pima Co.   U. S. G. S. Map, 1923.

Sp., "cow." Papago Ind. Res. near lat. 32° 20', long. 111° 40'.

Vadito, El   Apache Co.

Sp., "little crossing, little ford." From Vado, a ford. First name for place on Little Colorado river near what is now St. Johns, q.v. There was a good ford here.

Vado de los Padres

See Crossing of the Fathers.

Vah-Ki   Pinal Co.   U. S. G. S. Map, 1923.

In T. 3 S., R. 4 E. Pima Indian village, Gila River Ind. Res. Wright, *Long Ago Told*, spells it Vahah-kei-muh-lu, "a dragon fly." P. O. established June 13, 1916, Singleton I. Martin, P. M. See Casa Grande.

Vail   Pima Co.   Map, S. P. R. R., Sept., 1930; G. L. O., 1921.

Station S. P. R. R., 20 miles east of Tucson, between Empire and Rita stations. Established 1881. After Walter Vail of Vail and Gates, cattlemen of this region as early as 1880. Walter Vail had the distinction of recovering from the bite of a Gila monster he had captured on the round-up, May 10, 1890. Supposing the animal dead he tied it to his saddle. Feeling back as he rode to make sure it was there Vail put two fingers into the animal's mouth. The jaws closed like a vise. He rode several miles to camp where it was necessary to dissect the jaws to get the fingers loose. Vail suffered severely but recovered. A year later he was killed in a street car accident in Los Angeles.

There is another station by this name on adjacent E. P. & S. W. R. R. between Esmond and Pantano stations 20 miles east of Tucson. About 3 miles north of other Vail station.

Vail Lake   Coconino Co.

Coconino N. F. See Lambing lake.

Val de Chino   Yavapai Co.

Name Whipple gave to Chino valley, q.v.

Valentine State

See Arizona.

Valentine   Mohave Co.   G. L. O. Map, 1921; U. S. G. S., 1923.

In T. 23 N., R. 13 W. Station A. T. & S. F. R. R., Indian Agency. On a small outlying area of Hualpai Ind. Res. Named after Robert G. Valentine, U. S. Commissioner, Indian Affairs, 1908-10. Formerly called Truxton. P. O. established Feb. 24, 1910, Enos B. Atkinson, P. M.

Valeview   Santa Cruz Co.

P. O. established July 21, 1922, Clifford F. Peterson, P. M. This is all that is known of this place.

Valle   Coconino Co.   Map, Tusayan N. F., 1927.

Sp., "valley." In sec. 8, T. 26 N., R. 2 E. Small open valley along railroad.

Valle Redondo   Apache Co.

See Round valley.

Valley   Yavapai Co.   R. R. Maps.

Station, Ash Fork branch, A. T. & S. F. R. R., about 30 miles south of Ash Fork. "At head of Chino valley and so called for that reason." A.G.W.

Valley Heights   Maricopa Co.   U. S. G. S. Map, 1923.

In T. 3 N., R. 2 E. Small settlement on Arizona canal 5 miles northeast of Glendale. "It looks down over the valley." P. O. established May 13, 1914, Thomas J. Crowl, P. M.

Valshni Wash   Pima Co.   U. S. G. S. Map, 1923.

In T. 17 S., R. 1 E. Rises, western part Papago Ind. Res., near Copika mountains. Flows southeast into Mexico, west side of Baboquivari mountains. Also spelled Val-shima. Said to be a corruption of Papago word "Wah-shing" meaning "the Valley." Course of this wash is not clearly defined on maps.

Valverde   Yavapai Co.   G. L. O. Map, 1909.

Sp., "green valley." Three miles south of Humboldt on Agua Fria. About 1896 there was a large smelter here for handling ores from nearby mines. P. O. established Nov. 24, 1899, John L. Davis, P. M.

Vamori   Pima Co.   U. S. G. S. Map, 1923.

In T. 19 S., R. 4 E. Indian settlement, Papago Ind. Res. Papago word meaning "low place where water stays—a swamp." Evelyn Bentley.

Vanar   Cochise Co.   G. L. O. Map, 1921, "Vanar";
                                                U. S. G. S., 1923, "Vanor."

In T. 14 S., R. 22 E. Station, S. P. R. R., opened 1880. On State line. "Originally called Vanarian but later shortened to save telegraphing and make it easier to pronounce. Has no meaning that we know of." Paul Shoup. P. O. established April 3, 1915, Borden J. Rice, P. M.

Vaquero Mesa   Maricopa Co.   Map, Tonto N. F., 1927.

South side Salt river below Roosevelt dam. Senseless turning into Spanish of name Horse mesa, which this mesa has carried for 50 years or more. See Horse Mesa. See Apache Trail.

Vaseys Paradise   Coconino Co.

Section of Grand Canyon. "Powell so named it for Vasey, the botanist, a friend of his. It was only a lot of ferns, mosses, etc., but it was the first green spot we had seen since leaving the Paria." Dellenbaugh.

Vekol: Mine and Town   Pinal Co.   G. L. O. Map, 1892;
                                                U. S. G. S., 1923.

In T. 9 S., R. 2 E., Papago Ind. Res. Discovered by a Papago who showed it to John D. Walker. Farish says: "The owners took out over two million dollars." Papago word meaning "Grandmother." P. O. established Aug. 24, 1895, Byron B. De Nurr, P. M.

Vekol Mountains and Valley   Pinal Co.   G. L. O. Map, 1921.

Mountains on Papago Ind. Res., in T. 10 S., R. 3 E. After mine. Valley draining north along western line Pinal county into Santa Cruz wash, west side Table mountains. See Vekol mine.

Venezia   Yavapai Co.   U. S. G. S. Map, 1923; Prescott N. F., 1927.

In sec. 12, T. 12 N., R. 2 W. In Big Bug mountains, about 12 miles southeast of Prescott. "So called by F. Scopel, local settler, an Italian, for his native city, Venice." Letter, L. J. Putsch, Forest Ranger. P. O. established April 16, 1916, Don J. Tomlinson, P. M.

Ventano Canyon   Pima Co.   Map, Coronado N. F., 1927.

Heads west side of "The Window," in T. 12 S., R. 15 E., runs south into Rillito at Fort Lowell. Sp., "window," "an opening." See La Ventana.

Ventana Mesa   Apache Co.   G. L. O. Map, 1921.

Head of Chinle valley, Navajo Ind. Res. "Several natural windows or openings in the cliffs are found here." Gregory.

Vento Spring   Apache Co.   G. L. O. Map, 1921.

Sp., "an air hole—an opening or vent." Navajo Ind. Res., south of Pastora peak, west side Black Horse creek. "These cliffs are full of odd openings." Gregory.

Ventura   Yavapai Co.

Sp., "luck—fortune." Name of mine not far from Waggoner. P. O. established June 1, 1908, Forrest McKinley, P. M.

Verde   Yavapai Co.

Site of Jerome smelter. "Name changed to Clemenceau, Jan. 1, 1920, to avoid confusion with Camp Verde." See Clemenceau.

Verde, Fort or Camp   Yavapai Co.   U. S. G. S. Map, 1923.

In T. 14 N., R. 5 E. Established Jan., 1864, as Camp Lincoln. Changed to Camp Verde Nov. 23, 1868. Abandoned by G. O. No. 43, Headquarters Army, April 10, 1890. P. O. established here as Verde March 14, 1873, George W. Hance, P. M. One of oldest settlements on Verde river. The "Camp Sandy," of Capt. Charles King's historical novel, *The Colonel's Daughter.* Pauline Weaver died here, 1866. Remains now lie in yard at Governor's Mansion in Prescott.

Heitman says: "Established originally as Camp Lincoln by Capt. John S. Mason, 17th Infantry, commanding district. Was then about 5 miles south of present location."

Verde Hot Springs   Yavapai Co.   Map, Tonto N. F., 1927.

In T. 11½ N., R. 6 E. Prescott N. F., west side Verde river at Childs plant of Power Co. There are some hot springs here, used for medicinal purposes by Indians and whites for years.

Verde National Forest   Yavapai and Coconino Cos.

Lying both sides Verde river on western side Yavapai county. Established 1907, with supervisor's headquarters at Fort Verde. Combined with Prescott Forest, Feb., 1909.

Verde River   G. L. O. Map, 1921; U. S. G. S., 1923.

Sp., "green." Rises in T. 17 N., R. 2 W., west side Chino valley, north of Del Rio. "Breaks out of some large springs here which we consider as the actual head of Verde river." Letter, Frank Grubb, Prescott. Flows in a general easterly and southeasterly course entering Salt river near McDowell mountain in Maricopa county about 24 miles northeast of Phoenix. So called by early Spanish explorers from color of its waters.

"Oñate, 1604, called it alternately the San Antonio or Sacramento." *Franciscans in Arizona.*

Coues says: "For many years it was known wrongly as the San Francisco because it headed near those mountains in northern Arizona." By some early visitors called "Rio Alamos," or Cottonwood river, rather appropriate considering the number of these trees along its banks. However, Velarde, 1716, says: "The Verde is so called perhaps because it runs among greenish slopes or rocks." *New Mexico Historical Review*, April, 1931.

Coues says Garces gave it the name Verde.

Verde Road   Yavapai and Coconino Cos.

Pioneer military road Fort Verde to Fort Apache. Built, 1873, by troops under Gen. Crook to facilitate troop movements between Prescott, his headquarters, and Fort Apache. Extends along Tonto Basin rim, in places being about 3 feet from its edge. Soldiers marked nearly every mile on a pine tree or rock in huge Roman characters.

Also they named a string of wet weather lakes along it: Lake No. 1, Lake No. 2, etc. Not all of these show on any one map. When the author went over the road, 1885, trees were still plainly marked. It was also called "General Crook's" or "Crook's Road,".and is on Smith map, 1879, and Eckhoff, 1880, by that name. Cooley's ranch on Apache Ind. Res. at "Forks of the Road" was its eastern terminus.

"They decided to march the troops over Crook's Trail, I had never heard of it but ours was the first wagon train to pass over it." *Vanished Arizona*, 1874.

Verde Valley   Yavapai Co.

Fine agricultural area on Verde river in vicinity of old Camp Verde. "The first settlement was in 1865. Party from Prescott located near mouth of Clear creek. Two hundred acres were cleared first year. Barley threshed by hand sold at Whipple for $17 per 100." *Coconino Sun*, Dec. 5, 1905.

Vermejo, Rio   Apache Co.

Coronado called the Zuni by this name. See Zuni.

Vermilion Cliffs   Mohave Co.   U. S. G. S. Map, 1923.

East of Kaibab N. F. "We leave behind us a long line of cliffs many hundred feet high, composed of orange and vermillion sandstone. I have named them Vermillion Cliffs." Powell, Sept. 13, 1869. They form the eastern, southern and western sides of the Para Plateau.

Vernon   Apache Co.   U. S. G. S. Map, 1923.

In T. 10 N., R. 25 E. Settlement in southwestern part of county. "When B. H. Wilhelm and wife located here in 1890 they called their place the Vernon ranch, after W. T. Vernon, a friend of theirs. P. O. was named for it." Letter, Paul Roberts, Holbrook.

Vicksburg   Yuma Co.   G. L. O. Map, 1892-1921.

In T. 5 N., R. 14 W. Parker branch A. T. & S. F. R. R. Named for Vic Satterdahl, who started a store here in late Nineties. Satterdahlburg was too long, so his first name, "Vic," was used. P. O. established Nov. 15, 1906, Victor E. Setterdale (sic), P. M. This is as records at Washington spell this name.

View Point   Apache Co.   G. L. O. Map, 1921.

West side Lukachukai mountains. Navajo Ind. Res. "From this point there is a glorious view of surrounding region." Gregory.

Villa Buena   Maricopa Co.

Sp., "good house." In sec. 11, T. 1 N., R. 1 'E. Prehistoric ruin about 3 miles west of Laveen. Named by Dr. Turney, well known archaeologist.

Vinegar Creek   Mohave Co.

"Somewhere in this region is Vinegar creek, a 2-inch stream said to answer for vinegar." Hinton. He says it lay between Boulder and Burro creeks near Big Sandy river.

Vinegaron Well   Yuma Co.   U. S. G. S. Map, 1923.

Sp., "whip-tail scorpion." Has an odor of vinegar when alarmed. At head of Ranegas plain west of upper end Eagle Tail mountains, 12 miles west Maricopa county line.

Vinumkirk   Pima Co.   Lumholtz Map, 1916.

Papago word for "iron pipe." Papago Ind. Res. In Santa Rosa valley. Indian name for Quijotoa village. See Santa Rosa vs. A. B. Fall. "This name came from the iron pipe set in the ground by government surveyors to mark corners and elevation."

Virgin Canyon   Mohave Co.   U. S. G. S. Map, 1923.

In Colorado river on boundary between Nevada and Arizona. That part of river near mouth of Virgin. See Virgin river.

Virgin Mountains   Mohave Co.   U. S. G. S. Map, 1923.

In southeastern Nevada, extending across northwest corner of Arizona, east side Virgin river. Hinton map, 1877, calls them "Virginia mountains," an error, of course.

Virgin Peak   Yuma Co.   G. L. O. Map, 1921.

In T. 1 S., R. 13 W. North side Little Horn mountains, about 25 miles west of Maricopa county line.

Virgin River   Mohave Co.

"Rio de la Virgen" (sic). River of the Virgin. Undoubtedly given its name by early Spanish explorers. Indians call it Pahrush, which means "water that tastes salt."

Named Adams river by Jedediah Smith, 1826, for President Adams. Bolton says Escalante called it Pilar river, q.v. Rises in Kane county, Utah, flows southwest through northwest corner of Arizona into Nevada, joins Colorado river in Clark county, Nevada, at Boulder canyon in T. 20 S., R. 68 E.

Powell, 1867, spelled it Virgen. So did Ives, 1857. Powell doubtless got his spelling from Escalante who, 1776, named and spelled it Rio de la Virgen. Dellenbaugh in his first edition spells it both ways. Later, in his 1926 book, he has it Virgin.

Virginia City   Mohave Co.   Judge Map, 1911.

In T. 13 N., R. 13 W. Said to have been so named by first prospectors who came from Virginia City, Nevada. On Big Sandy near Signal, an early McCracken mill town. Smith map, 1879; Eckhoff, 1880, has it New Virginia.

"A few miles above the confluence of Big Sandy creek and Bill Williams river, are the twin towns of Virginia City and Signal. The basis of Virginia is the new McCracken 20-stamp mill, which is expected to crush daily 70 to 100 tons of ore. A population of 600 to 700 is claimed for the place." Hinton.

Hamilton says: "Owing to its almost perfect location Virginia is sure to build up rapidly."

Virginia City   Pima Co.   G. L. O. Map, 1892.

In T. 15 S., R. 2 E. Early settlement near Quijotoa mine. There is another Virginia in Mohave county. See Logan City; New Virginia, Brooklyn, and Quijotoa. Townsite laid out in fall of 1884, by W. J. Doherty and L. D. Chilson.

Vivian   Mohave Co.   Clason Map, 1908.

Station north end Mohave and Milltown R. R. about 4 miles from Goldroad. P. O. established March 1, 1904, James M. Knight, P. M.

Volunteer   Coconino Co.   U. S. G. S. Map, 1923; Coconino N. F., 1928.

In T. 21 N., R. 5 E. Mountain, spring and broad valley (Volunteer Prairie) south of Bellemont A. T. & S. F. R. R. Detachment, California Volunteer Regiment, which came to Arizona, 1863, camped here and named these features. Whipple's location of New Years spring, q.v., discovered Jan. 1, 1854, fits this spring very closely. Very likely it is the New Years spring found only on Smith map, 1879.

Vota   Cochise Co.

P. O. established April 31, 1881, Ira J. Richards, P. M. Originally in Pima county according to records in Washington.

V. T. Park

See DeMotte park.

Vulcans Throne   Coconino Co.   U. S. G. S. Map, 1923.

North side Colorado river in Toroweap valley about 6 miles southeast of Mount Emma. One of many fanciful names attached to places in canyon by members first U. S. Survey party which mapped it. They ran out of local names and fell back on Greek, Roman, and mythological names such as Wotans Throne, Zoroaster Temple, Krishna Temple, Holy Grail Peak, etc. There has been much criticism of them but after being on maps for over 50 years, the U.S.G.B. decided to retain them, which was doubtless wise.

"Capt. Dutton started this naming of features after Orientals with Vishnu Temple, Shiva Temple, etc. He did not like Indian names, thought them ugly. I had several arguments with him on the subject as I objected violently to Oriental and Egyptian nomenclature. I have continued to object ever since." Letter, Mr. Dellenbaugh, Feb. 14, 1933. The author agrees heartily with this eminent explorer and writer.

Vulture City   Maricopa Co.

Barney states that for a time this was name of town that grew up around Vulture mine. Pimas called the place "Pumpkin Patch" from the wild gourds which grew like pumpkins all over the flats in wet seasons and which they ate.

Vulture Mine, Mountains, and Peak   Maricopa Co.

G. L. O. Map, 1921; U. S. G. S., 1923.

In sec. 33, T. 6 N., R. 5 W., 8 miles west of the Hassayampa. Well known gold mine of early days. Almost directly west of

Morristown. So called by Henry Wickenburg, its discoverer, who, about 1863, while prospecting, saw buzzards hovering over the peak. Story seems to be well authenticated. Birds must, however, have been the common turkey buzzards, *Cathartes aura*, often called vultures. They are plentiful in this region.

Mountains are about 12 miles southwest of Wickenburg in T. 6 N., Rs. 5, 6 W., west of the Hassayampa.

Peak is a bald rough butte, due south of Wickenburg, at eastern end of Vulture mountains, about 6 miles west of Hassayampa river.

Wagathile Tank   Mohave Co.

Coues says: "This was called Black Tank, 1865. Was known thus as late as 1881, but now lettered on U.S.G.S. map as Wagathile tank. It was full of repulsive guajalotes."

Meaning or origin of name unknown unless it was Mohave name for ajolote (locally, Ariz.—guajalote), or water puppy.

Wagoner (sic)   Yavapai Co.   P. O. Guide, 1920; U. S. G. S., 1923.

In T. 10 N., R. 3 W. Named for Ed Waggoner, early settler. East of Weaver mountains, Prescott N. F. On Huss creek, at mouth of Blind Indian creek. Name spelled Waggoner by family, but post office authorities changed it. P. O. established as Wagoner June 6, 1893, Minerva A. Waggoner, P. M.

Wagon Roads

Early legislatures authorized building and operation of several wagon or toll roads. Tolls were rather high as viewed from today's costs. Santa Maria Wagon Road Co. was authorized to establish and operate a toll road from mouth of Bill Williams river to Prescott. Tolls were: "For two-horse wagons, horse, mule or oxen, four cents a mile; one-horse wagon, three and one-half cents a mile; horse and rider, two and one-half cents a mile. No charge for footmen." They were all authorized to dig wells and provide water for travellers, but could not charge persons for water for camp use, only for loose stock.

This Santa Maria route was probably used in those days more than any other highway in Arizona leading as it did from steamboat landings on the Colorado direct to Prescott and mines in that region. Favorite highway for army people and supplies for military purposes for northern end of Territory. On it were such well known camps as Oaks and Willows; Camp Tollgate; Willow Grove Springs; Camp Hualpai; Beales Spring; Truxton Camp, etc. It led directly northwest from Prescott, then followed closely present route of A. T. & S. F. R. R. down to Colorado river.

The Arizona Central Road Co. was from La Paz to Weaver and Prescott. Another was the Mohave and Prescott Toll Road Co. from Mohave to Prescott.

Prescott, Walnut Grove and Pima Road Co. was a north and south road running from Prescott to Pima villages with a toll charge of five cents a mile. There is, however, no record of any operation of the latter. The "Woolsey Trail" was another road to be operated north and south from Prescott without charge and as a "Country" (sic) road. See Woolsey Trail.

Wagon Tire Flat   Yavapai Co.   Map, Tusayan N. F., 1927.

In T. 19 N., R. 1 W., west side Rattlesnake wash. "For many years an old wagon tire lay against a tree on this flat. A memento of some pioneer's troubles."

Wahl Knoll   Apache Co.   Map, Apache N. F., 1926.

In sec. 22, T. 7 N., R. 28 E. Isolated knoll in "prairie" country on mountain west of Springerville. After John C. Wahl, early settler, farmer and stockman, who owned many cattle here in early Eighties. Wahl lived in Springerville.

Wa-Kota   Yavapai Co.

P. O. established Sept. 25, 1913, Louis G. Ochsenreiter, P. M. Origin and location unknown.

Walapai

See Hualpai.

Walcott Butte

In Grand Canyon. Named by G. Wharton James for Dr. Charles D. Walcott, Director, U. S. Geological Survey, later, Secretary, Smithsonian Institution, 1907-1917.

Walker Creek   Apache Co.   U. S. G. S. Map, 1923.

Navajo Ind. Res., rises west side Carrizo mountains, flows northwest into Chinle creek near Colorado state line.

"In the absence of a recognized name for this stream the liberty is taken of naming it Walker creek in honor of Capt. Walker of Macomb's Expedition, 1859. Capt. Walker crossed the stream at Ojo de Casa. Navajo, 'Hogan-Sa-a-ni'—Lone house in the desert." Gregory.

Walker   Navajo Co.

According to McClintock, this was first name for Taylor on Silver creek, q.v.

Walker   Yavapai Co.   U. S. G. S. Map, 1923.

In T. 13 N., R. 1 W. Mining district, and town on Lynx creek. Very old mining camp. From the best evidence obtainable it takes its name from Capt. Joseph R. Walker, scout, guide and commander of what was known as the Walker party. According to McClintock, he organized his party in California. After considerable wandering, they found themselves in northern Arizona, where they located and worked many mines. See Lynx creek. P. O. established Dec. 15, 1879, Wm. L. Lewis, P. M.

Walker Butte   Pinal Co.

Elevation 1,988 feet. In T. 4 S., R. 8 E. On Gila River Ind. Res. about 2 miles north of Gila river.

Undoubtedly named for Lieut. John D. Walker, who according to McClintock "lived for years among the Pimas and spoke their language fluently." Walker was a Lieut. of Co. C Regiment of Arizona men, organized 1864, to fight Apaches. Company C was composed entirely of Pima Indians.

In early days, Pimas called this peak "Cheene," q.v.; Smith map, 1879, "Cheene"; Sacaton Quad. 1907; G.L.O., 1921, "Walker Butte."

Walker Gulch   Yavapai Co.   Map, Prescott N. F., 1926.

In T. 13 N., R. 1 W. After Joe Walker (Joseph R.) leader of party that hunted for gold over northern Arizona. Gulch is one head of Lynx creek. Mining camp located about 18 miles south of Prescott, in Walker district.

Walker Lake   Coconino Co.

Walker lake, Coconino Co., in sec. 11, T. 23 N., R. 6 E., Coconino National Forest. Name appears on G.L.O. map of 1912. Decision U.S.G.B.

Walkers   Navajo Co.

Stage station between Snowflake (Stinsons) and Holbrook. Not on any map. In *Vanished Arizona*, Mrs. Summerhays writes: "Thirty miles the next day over a good road brought us to Walkers ranch on the site of old Camp Supply." This must have brought them to the Little Colorado river near Holbrook or Horsehead crossing, as it was then called. See Camp Supply.

Hinton writes: "Asa C. Walker was a pioneer of Arizona and New Mexico. Came from Iowa and located on the Little Colorado river near the junction with the Puerco in 1874. Ran cattle there for many years. Raised a large family and moved up to the White mountains about 1882." Undoubtedly named for him.

Walkers Pass   Yavapai Co.

Named for Capt. Joseph Walker, head of the Walker Expedition, 1863. This was a California prospecting party formed by Walker which looked for gold on Little Colorado river, 1860. He later took a party across mountains to Prescott. See McClintock. Had no connection with Walker filibustering party, 1853. Connor says: "There were two Walkers, father and son, Capt. John R. and John R., Jr."

Wallen, Camp   Pinal Co.   Smith Map, 1879;
G. L. O. Map, 1892, "Fort Wallen."

About 10 or 15 miles west of Tombstone on Babocomari creek, Babocomari Land Grant, in Mustang mountains. Military post, established March 9, 1864, and named for Col. H. D. Wallen, 14th Infantry, U. S. A., in command District of Arizona, 1860. Abandoned Oct. 31, 1869.

"The old quarters at Camp Wallen are now, 1873, occupied by the Messrs. McGarey, who have at least 7,000 sheep on the ranch. The military at Camp Huachuca have a garden at the old camp where they produce vegetables for the soldiers." Hinton's *Handbook*.

Wall's Well or Pozo de Federico, Rancheria   Pima Co.
Lumholtz Map, 1916.

In T. 15 S., R. 4 W. "In Papago, 'Kookatsh,' mountain crest. Sixteen miles east of Bate's well, at northern point of Sierra del Ajo." Letter, Frederick Wall, for whom named.

"Wall's Well, 2 miles east of Montezuma head, once seat of a serious mining industry, but now owned by the rabbits and ravens. Two huge boilers large enough to run a man-of-war is all that is left." Hornaday.

Walnut Canyon National Monument   Coconino Co.

In T. 21 N., R. 8 E. Group of ancient Indian habitations in cliffs along Walnut canyon, about 8 miles east of Flagstaff. Made a National Monument, Nov. 30, 1915. Lieut. Frederic Schwatka, U. S. A., and the writer, explored them, 1888. So called because in early days many large walnut trees were in the canyon.

Walnut Creek   Coconino Co.   U. S. G. S. Map, 1923.

In sec. 9, T. 20 W., R. 7 E. Rising in Clark's valley. Outlet of Lake Mary, enters San Francisco wash in T. 21 N., R. 8 E., about 8 miles east of Elden mesa. See Walnut Canyon National Monument.

Walnut Creek   Yavapai Co.   U. S. G. S. Map, 1923.

Rises east side Santa Maria mountains, flows northwest into Chino creek near Fritchie, in T. 18 N., R. 3 W.

"In early days this stream was lined with fine walnut trees. This is a regular stage station on Prescott-Mohave road, kept by Ed Scholey. There was a P. O. in 1880 with M. B. Cullenber, P. M." Hinton. Whipple, in 1853, called this Pueblo creek because of the numerous prehistoric ruins along the stream. See Aztec pass.

Walnut Grove   Apache Co.   U. S. G. S., St. Johns Sheet.

On Little Colorado river about 12 miles below Springerville. "There was a fine grove of walnut trees here." See Richville, Richey.

Walnut Grove   Yavapai Co.

On Hassayampa creek west of Crown King. So called from the grove of walnut trees. On Oct. 24, 1864, first Territorial Legislature attempted to move the capitol from Prescott to this point. February 22, 1890, a large dam, built by Lieut. (later Col. and Gov.) Brodie, burst, carrying death and destruction to those living below. Over 70 lives were lost and heavy damage suits ensued. Dam was built primarily for hydraulic mining. See La Paz and Aztlan. Lieut. Lyle of Wheeler's survey party visited this place, Oct. 15, 1871. He wrote: "At Walnut Grove is a settlement where we found well cultivated lands." P. O. established June 24, 1874, Miss Jane Oswald, P. M.

Walpi   Navajo Co.   U. S. G. S. Map, 1923.

In T. 28 N., R. 18 E. "Hopi word meaning 'notch in the cliff.' Regarded as the oldest Tusayan pueblo, its settlement dating from before middle of 16th century." Mindeleff.

"Name first applied to a place called by the Hopi, 'Kwetcaptutwi—ash heap terrace.' Located on First or East Mesa. From Wala, 'gap or notch,' and 'opi,' a location. The 'place of the notch,' descriptive name." Hodge. There is a decided "notch" or low place on crest of mesa between the two towns.

Wapatoe   Pima Co.

"The post office at Grant, Pima county, has been changed to Wapatoe and Richard Bush appointed post master." *Arizona Sentinel*, June 23, 1873. This was not Camp Grant nor any other military post and the name Grant does not appear on any map of Pima county.

"This name, 'Wapatoe,' was applied to a remnant of several tribes at mouth of Willamette river in Oregon by Lewis and Clark, 1805; is now used to designate a small remnant of Indians on Grande Ronde Reservation in Oregon." Hodge. How it wandered so far south is a mystery.

Ward Terrace   Coconino Co.   Gregory Map, 1916.

On Navajo Ind. Res. West side Moenkopi plateau, east side Little Colorado river. "Named for Lester E. Ward, whose work in the Painted Desert region marked the beginning of detailed stratigraphic studies for Navajo Reservation." Gregory.

Warm Spring Apaches

See Apache—Ojo Caliente.

Warners Hill   Pima Co.

See Sentinel Peak—Tucson.

Warren   Cochise Co.   G. L. O. Map, 1921.

Town, 4 miles below Bisbee, at mouth of canyon. When Bisbee began to get crowded people moved down here for homes. After George Warren, prospector.

"In 1877, George Warren, guiding some troops of regular cavalry in pursuit of Apaches through Mule pass, discovered outcroppings of copper ore on the side of what is now Queen mountain. Two years later Warren, with other prospectors, came from Tombstone and located several claims in which New York and California capitalists soon became interested." Letter, Wm. A. Greene.

Warrens Butte and Ranch   Pima Co.   G. L. O. Maps, 1892-1921.

In T. 17 S., R. 8 E. In Aravaipa or Altar valley. Origin unknown.

Washboard Creek   Navajo Co.   U. S. G. S. Map, 1923.

Dry wash heading in T. 16 N., R. 20 E., joining Little Colorado 5 miles north of Woodruff. So called because where it crossed the old stage road and military telegraph line to Apache, it was cut up with small arroyos, "like a washboard."

Washington   Santa Cruz Co.   G. L. O. Maps, 1892-1921.

In sec. 35, T. 23 S., R. 16 E. Early day mining camp in San Antonio canyon, east side Patagonia mountains, about 2 miles northeast of Mount Washington. "First mine here was called the Washington by its discoverer." P. O. established May 13, 1880, William B. Hopkins, P. M.

Washington, Mount   Santa Cruz Co.   Map, Coronado N. F., 1927.

About 2 miles from Mexican line at southern end Patagonia mountains. After nearby mine.

Wasson Peak   Pima Co.   G. L. O. Map, 1921.

In T. 13 S., R. 11 E., west side Tucson mountains, about 10 miles northwest of Tucson. Named for John Wasson of Tucson, early Surveyor-General and editor. There is also a Wasson peak in Yavapai county.

"One of the editors of the *Tucson Citizen* was Joe (John) Wasson, a very capable journalist with whom I was afterwards associated intimately in the Black Hills during the troubles with the Sioux and Cheyennes. He was a well informed man who had travelled much and seen life in all its phases." Bourke. His name was John but for some unknown reason nearly all early writers call him 'Joe.'"

Wasson Peak   Yavapai Co.   U. S. G. S. Bradshaw Quad., 1903.

In T. 10 N., R. 1 W., Prescott N. F. In Bradshaw mountains, about one mile southwest of Crown King. After John Wasson, editor, *Arizona Citizen*, Tucson, 1870; second Surveyor-General of Arizona, 1870-1882. See Wasson peak, Pima county.

Water Canyon   Apache Co.   Map, Apache N. F., 1926.

In sec. 19, T. 7 N., R. 29 E. Stream rises near Wahl Knolls, flows southerly into Little Colorado above Eagar. So called because first Mormon settlers secured most of their irrigating water from this stream.

Waterman Mountains   Pima Co.

In Ts. 12, 13 S., R. 9 E., southeast of Silver Bell. So called after mine here named for Governor Waterman of California, once secretary of California company which owned and developed several mines in this range. Hamilton visited these mines, 1884, and says: "They were in the Silver Bell district and very rich." See Abbie Waterman.

Waterman Wash   Maricopa Co.   G. L. O. Map, 1921; U. S. G. S., 1923.

Heads in T. 4 S., R. 1 W., southern end Maricopa mountains. Flows northwest, enters Gila river at eastern end, Buckeye hills, in T. 1 S., R. 3 W. Generally believed named after Waterman mountains to south. May, however, have been named after the old timer for whose wife Abbie Waterman peak was named, q. v.

Waters Ranger Station   Coconino Co.   Map, Sitgreaves N. F., 1927.

In sec. 35, T. 13 N., R. 13 E. Watering place of Waters Cattle Co., live stock outfit of St. Joseph, Mo., that ran a large herd of cattle on west side of Chevelon, 1883-1897. A Mr. Waters of St. Joseph was president, and E. R. Carr, a Presbyterian minister from that city, range manager for several years. Carr was a sincere Christian and whenever possible asked divine blessing before meals, even with the roundup wagon. Now a U. S. Forest Ranger Station.

Watervale   Cochise Co.

See Waterville.

Waterville   Cochise Co.   G. L. O. Map, 1892.

In T. 22 S., R. 19 E., 3 miles north of Tombstone. Also called Watervale. So named because of water seepage from wash at this point. Here it is said Schieffelin and Dick Gird did some of their first prospecting. Site of first store in Tombstone district.

Watson Peak   Yavapai Co.   Map, Prescott N. F., 1926.

In sec. 1, T. 9 N., R. 1 W. Peak immediately south of Lane mountain. After Henry Watson, who mined in this vicinity, 1882.

Wauba Yuma   Mohave Co.

Settlement, head of Bill Williams Fork in Mohave county. On map printed with Gov. McCormick's article on Arizona in *New York Tribune*, 1865. Mining district about 20 miles east of Hardyville in early Sixties.

"Wauba-Yuma was a Hualpai Indian chief killed at a freighter's camp near Beale's springs in Apr. 1866, by Sam Miller, who believed Indians under this chief had been killing white men. The chief came into Miller's camp and presented a paper which Bill Hardy had given him in a treaty of peace some time before. Miller did not look at the paper and shot the chief. This was the beginning of a long and costly Indian war. Miller later became a prominent citizen of Prescott." See McClintock's *History*.

Weaver   Yavapai Co.   Smith Map, 1879; Eckhoff, 1880.

Town located about 1863 by Pauline Weaver, for whom named. On Martinez creek in Bradshaw mountains, about 15 miles north of Wickenburg. Station on stage road, Prescott to Phoenix. Shows on some maps as Weaverville. See Octave, P. O. established May 26, 1899, Robert W. Warren, P. M.

Weaver Mountains   Yavapai Co.   Smith Map, 1879;
G. L. O., 1921.

Twenty miles north of Wickenburg. Named by Peeples after guide, Pauline Weaver, one of Arizona's first white settlers. His name is cut on the walls of Casa Grande, dated, 1833. Guided the Peeples' party through Territory, 1863. Died at Camp Verde, 1866. Remains removed to old Governor's Mansion in Prescott. about 1926.

Weaver Pass   Yuma Co.   G. L. O. Map, 1892; U. S. G. S., 1923.

In T. 1 N., R. 20 W. After Pauline Weaver. In Dome Rock mountains about 20 miles southeast Ehrenberg.

Weaver Peak   Yavapai Co.   G. L. O. Map, 1921.

In T. 11 N., R. 5 W., north end Weaver mountains, about 10 miles southwest from Kirkland. After Pauline Weaver. See Weaver mountains.

Weavers Needle   Gila Co.

See Needles mountain.

Weavers Needle   Pinal Co.

Elevation 4,535 feet. In T. 1 N., R. 9 E. On Tonto N. F. in Coronado mountains, east of Superstition mountains. There is some question whether this was named for Pauline Weaver, the scout, or merely because it is a sharp isolated peak. Everything indicates the scout as its origin. Weavers Needle decision U. S. G. B. Is "Weaver" on some maps; "Weavers," on others.

Webb   Cochise Co.   G. L. O. Map, 1921.

Stage station of early days. Originally located by and named for Robert M. Tyler. He applied for a post office, but authorities refused to call it Tyler, so Tyler named it for his father-in-law, J. D. Webb, which was acceptable. In Sulphur Springs valley on E. P. & S. W. R. R., 24 miles west of Douglas. P. O. established Nov. 19, 1909, Robert M. Tyler, P. M.

Webb Peak   Graham Co.   Map, Crook N. F., 1926.

In T. 8 S., R. 24 E. Near Graham mountain. Named after Wilfred T. Webb, prominent cattleman, farmer and politician of Gila valley for many years.

Webb Well   Maricopa Co.   U. S. G. S. Map, 1923.

Watering place, head of Arlington valley, east side Gila Bend mountains. After Sam Webb, well known citizen.

Webber Creek   Gila Co.   Smith Map, 1879; Tonto N. F., 1927.

In T. 11 N., R. 10 E. Stream rising under the Rim below Bakers butte, flows south entering west side East Fork of Verde, about 3 miles northeast of Payson.

"According to William Craig of Payson who settled on Webber creek in early Eighties, it was named for Webber, chief packer for an army outfit engaged in mapping Tonto Basin in 1879." Letter, Forest Ranger Croxen.

Webber Peak   Graham Co.   Map, Crook N. F., 1931.

In sec. 6, T. 16 S., R. 27 E., 10 miles due north of Solomonville. Originally known as Casimiro peak. Changed by decision U. S. G. B. "After John Webber, early settler in Gila valley. Nobody knows the name Casimiro. Commonly known all over the valley as Webber peak." Letter, Rex King.

Webster Mountain   Gila Co.   Map, Crook N. F., 1926.

In secs. 5, 6, T. 1 N., R. 14 E. Almost south of Barnes peak. After prominent stockman of this vicinity.

Webster   Pinal Co.   G. L. O. Map, 1909.

In T. 3 S., R. 8 E. Station, Arizona Eastern R. R., about 10 miles west of Florence.

Weldon   Pima Co.   G. L. O. Map, 1909.

In T. 16 S., R. 4 E. Settlement and station about 10 miles east of Quijotoa. P. O. established Sept. 17, 1904, J. Wight Giddings, P. M.

Wellton   Yuma Co.   U. S. G. S. Map, 1923.

Elevation 258 feet. Early station in Antelope valley, S. P. R. R., 38 miles east of Yuma. "The stage station of Adonde (Sp., where) was located 2 miles west. When the railroad came along they sunk some deep wells on a new site and, just for a name, called it Wellton." Letter, Supt. S. P. Co. P. O. established, Aug. 4, 1904, Benjamin M. Lee, P. M. Is close to Tacna.

Wellton Hills   Yuma Co.   U. S. G. S. Map, 1923.

In T. 10 S., R. 18 W., south of Wellton station, S. P. R. R. Named for nearby station, q. v.

Wenden   Yuma Co.   G. L. O. Map, 1921.

In T. 6 N., R. 12 W. Parker branch A. T. & S. F. R. R., 50 miles west of Wickenburg. See Wendendale.

Wendendale   Yuma Co.   G. L. O. Map, 1921.

Town first established 1905 under this name, Harry B. Hanna, P. M. P. O. authorities thought it was too long and on Aug. 7, 1907, name changed to Wenden. Otis E. Young, who named it for his home town in Ohio, was P. M. See Wenden.

Wepo Springs   Navajo Co.

In sec. 25, T. 29 N., R. 18 E. Hopi Ind. Res. Group of springs about 6 miles north of Walpi. Hopi word for "onion." Springs from which certain ceremonial races are run, especially at opening of snake ceremony. Hodge spells it Wih-po. Donaldson and Gregory spell it Wepo, which is decision U. S. G. B. See Onion. Not named but shown on Gregory map, 1916.

Wepo Wash   Navajo Co.   Gregory Map, 1916; G. L. O., 1921.

Rises northeast corner Hopi Ind. Res., flows southwest, joins Mesa wash in T. 28 N., R. 18 E., to form Polacca wash. Gregory says: "about 20 miles long."

Wertman

See Workman.

West·Cedar Creek   Navajo Co.   Map, Ft. Apache Ind. Res., 1928.

Rises in T. 8 N., R. 21 E., flows south into Middle Cedar creek in sec. 23, T. 7 N., R. 21 E. On Fort Apache Ind. Res.

West Cedar Mountain   Yavapai Co.   Map, Tonto N. F., 1927.

Cedar covered mountain in sec. 19, T. 9 N., R. 5 E., about 2 miles west of East Cedar mountain, and exactly on Tonto-Prescott N. F. boundary line.

West Chandler   Maricopa Co.

First called Kyrene, q.v.

West Chevelon   Coconino and Navajo Cos.   G. L. O. Map, 1921;
Sitgreaves N. F., 1927.

Stream rising near Promontory butte at Willow Creek Ranger
Station. In sec. 33, T. 12 N., R. 13 E., flows northeasterly east of
Waters Ranger Station. Enters main Chevelon at "Mormon
Crossing" near Marquette Ranger Station. Decision U.S.G.B.
See Chevelon for history.

West Clear Creek

See Clear creek.

West Fork of Black River   Apache Co.   Map, Apache N. F., 1926.

Stream heads east side Mount Thomas (Baldy) at edge of
Fort Apache Ind. Res. Rises within a mile or so of head of East
Fork of Little Colorado; flows southeast and joins East Fork of
Black river in sec. 11, T. 4½ N., R. 28 E., to form main Black
river.

West Fork Little Colorado River   Apache Co.
Map, Apache N. F., 1928.

Rises north side Mount Thomas (Baldy) on Fort Apache Ind.
Res. Flows northeast, joins East Fork to form Little Colorado,
in sec. 14, T. 7 N., R. 27 E.

West Peak   Graham Co.   Map, Crook N. F., 1926.

In sec. 18, T. 8 S., R. 23 E. In Graham mountains, 3 miles
northwest of Mount Graham, just south of Blue Jay peak. West
of Taylor pass. Named for its location on mountain. The Grahams are almost cut in two by Taylor pass.

West Point

See Logan.

West Poker Mountain   Apache Co.   Map, Ft. Apache Ind. Res.;
G. L. O., 1921.

On north side Black river at junction Black river and Willow
creek. About 6 miles west of Poker mountain, q.v.

Wet Beaver Creek   Coconino and Yavapai Cos.
Map, Prescott N. F., 1928.

In sec. 36, T. 15 N., R. 6 E. Rises near Apache Maid mountain
in Coconino N. F. at Montezuma Well. So called to distinguish
it from another branch of Beaver called Dry Beaver, which often
went dry.

Wetherell, Mrs.

See Azan-so-si.

Wheatfields   Apache Co.   U. S. G. S. Map, 1923; Gregory, 1926.

Creek rising Chuska mountains, New Mexico, in Navajo Ind.
Res. Flows southwest into Arizona, through Canyon de Chelly,
to join Chinle creek at Chinle.

Wheatfields   Gila Co.   Map, Crook N. F., 1926.

In sec. 7, T. 2 N., R. 15 E. Valley and settlement on Pinal creek
about 10 miles northwest of Globe. Fine open valley where
Apaches used to raise wheat. Woolsey and party looking for
Apaches, 1864, came through here and threshed out some wheat
for their own use. They then turned their horses into the fields.
Has since been called Wheatfields.

"The command moved down Tonto creek and up the Salt river and across to Pinal creek where a large field of wheat was discovered and destroyed." *Report*, Lieut. Col. G. B. Sanford, 3rd. U. S. Cavalry, April, 1870. P. O. established Oct. 20, 1880, E. F. Kellner, P. M.

Wheatfields   Navajo Co.   Gregory Map, 1926.

In T. 6 N., R. 6 W. Indian settlement and headquarters for a government irrigation project, 1909. West side Wheatfields creek, Navajo Ind. Res. Indian name is "To-des-i." "Navajos raise considerable wheat here." Letter, C. G. Newcomb, Crystal.

Wheeler Wash   Mohave Co.   G. L. O. Map, 1921.

Rises north of Hualpai peak north end Hualpai mountains; flows southeast, enters Big Sandy river in T. 19 N., R. 13 W. Wheeler passed through here, 1853, and it was doubtless named for him by some unknown later explorer.

Whetstone Mountains   Cochise and Pima Cos.

Smith Map, 1879; U. S. G. S., 1923.

In Ts. 18, 19 S., Rs. 18, 19 E., Coronado N. F., west side San Pedro valley. Scene of many Indian outrages and battles. "So called because there here exists a deposit or ledge of rock known as Novaculite or whetstone of the finest quality." Bourke.

Whipple   Yavapai Co.

Called Whipple Barracks; later, Fort Whipple; about 2 miles east of Prescott. After Brig. Gen. A. W. Whipple, killed at Chancellorsville, who served in Arizona as 2nd. Lieut. Topographical Engineers, in charge of boundary survey, 1850. Originally located Dec., 1863, at Postle's ranch in Chino valley, about 22 miles northeast of Prescott. Post established by Major E. B. Willis, 1st. California Infantry. Moved May, 1864, to Granite creek near Prescott.

"Fort Whipple was a ramshackle tumble-down palisade of unbarked pine logs, hewn from the adjacent slopes. Quarters for both officers and men were of logs with the exception of a one room shanty on the apex of the hill nearest the town, built of unseasoned, unpainted, pine planks, which served as Gen. Crook's headquarters." Bourke. See Camp Clark. P. O. established as Whipple Oct. 6, 1890, Julius Simons, P. M. Previous to that time the post office for the post was Prescott. Fort Myer, Va., near Washington, D. C., was first called Fort Whipple.

Whipple Barracks   Yavapai Co.

See Whipple.

Whipple Mountain   Mohave Co.

There is evidently some confusion between early explorers over this mountain. Ives says, in his report: "The Needles and a high peak of the mountain range which I have called Mount Whipple are the most conspicuous landmarks and designate the points where river enters and leaves the Chemehuevi valley."

Accepting this as definite, the mountain range would be the present Chemehuevi range with The Needles at its northern end and what we now call Grossman peak at lower end. Mount Whipple is not found on any modern map. See also Cygnus mountain which Marcou, the geologist, mentioned as having been named by him after Whipple.

Whipsau (sic) **Mine and Stream**   Yavapai Co.   Not mapped.

Stream rises upper end Wickenburg mountains near Constellation. Flows southeast into Castle creek near Hot springs. P. O. established June 22, 1900, John G. Spangler, P. M.

From Venice, California, July 5, 1930, Spangler writes: "Whipsau was a mining camp 35 miles north of Hot Springs Junction on Whipsau Gulch. Was headquarters for several mining companies, especially the Whipsau, owned by Col. Christy. Dr. J. M. Ford had a copper mine about 5 miles from camp. I had the honor of being first and last P. M. for camp. Also its store keeper, banker, mine auditor and peace maker. Tom Farish was Whipsau manager. Mrs. Spangler came to camp a bride of a few months as secretary to Mr. Farish."

The first mining timbers used were "whipsawed," hence the name.

Whiskey Creek   Apache Co.   U. S. G. S. Map, 1923.

In T. 5 N., R. 6 W. Navajo Ind. Res. Rises north side Sonsella buttes at State line. Joins Canyon de Chelly in T. 5 N., R. 7 W. No one can explain this name.

Whisper Mountain   Coconino Co.

Near Flagstaff—so named by its discoverer, Mr. Conrad, "because the slightest whisper of people talking there can be heard more than half a mile away. It is somewhere near Sunset mountain. Mr. Conrad, who discovered it, told of the mountain but unfortunately he died before we could definitely locate it." Letter, Forest Supervisor Miller.

White Cave Spring   Navajo Co.   Gregory Map, 1916; G. L. O., 1921.

In T. 31 N., R. 15 E. Hopi Ind. Res., west side Dinnebito wash, 9 miles southeast Blue canyon.

"A spring issues from a cave here of rather white or light colored rock."

White Cliff Creek   Mohave Co.

Stream rising near Fort Rock, flowing southwest into Big Sandy river at town of Cottonwood. Wheeler says: "The valley is covered with dense groves of cottonwood and broken into white cliffs of fantastic shapes. So we called the stream White Cliff creek." Called White Cliffs on Smith map, 1879; Eckhoff, 1880; G. L. O., 1892. Called Cottonwood on G. L. O. map, 1921, and Knight's creek on U. S. G. S., 1892.

A careful study shows all these as the same creek, entering Big Sandy in T. 20 N., R. 13 W., near settlement marked Cottonwood on later maps.

Wheeler's reference to "dense groves of cottonwoods" probably accounts for the change in name. It is also noted that hills at head of stream are called Cottonwood Cliffs on all maps, both early and modern. Coues says: "The Cottonwood Cliffs are simply the northward extension of the Aquarius range."

White Cone: Peak and Spring   Apache Co.

In T. 25 N., R. 21 E. Hopi Ind. Res., about 7 miles east of Egloffstein butte. "The peak is a remarkably light colored cone which gives it this name."

White Creek   Coconino Co.   U. S. G. S. Shinumo Quad., 1908.

North side Colorado river. Rises in Muav canyon, flows south into Shinumo creek, Grand Canyon N. P. Named for James White. See Whites butte.

White Hill   Coconino Co.   Map, Tusayan N. F., 1927.

In sec. 15, T. 25 N., R. 3 E. Solitary prairie hill. Is a chalky white limestone formation which gives it the name.

White Hills   Mohave Co.   G. L. O. Map, 1921; U. S. G. S., 1923.

In T. 27 N., R. 20 W. "Rich mines discovered here about 1887 by a Wallapai Indian named Jeff. Rock is light colored and at a distance hills are almost white." P. O. established Oct. 20, 1892, W. H. Taggart, P. M.

White Mesa   Coconino Co.   U. S. G. S. Map, 1923.

Eastern end Kaibito plateau near long. 111°. After James White. See Whites butte for origin.

White Mountain Indian Reservation

Official name is now Fort Apache Indian Reservation. See Apache Ind. Res.

White Mountains, or Sierra Blanca   Apache Co.

U. S. G. S. Map, 1923.

Group of peaks in eastern part Fort Apache Ind. Res., on line between reservation and Apache N. F. Highest peaks are Ord and Thomas, after two early army officers serving in Arizona. The White, Gila and Little Colorado rivers rise in this range. Kino map, 1701, and Sitgreaves, 1852, call them Mogollon mountains, q.v. Hartley map, 1865, calls them Sierra Blanco (sic).

In his message of 1871 the Governor of Arizona speaks of them as the White mountains. Kino also shows the Sierra Azul near there, doubtless from the Blue river. The Spanish would naturally give them a Spanish name so it is very likely that some Franciscan may have given the name, Sierra Blanca. Real origin is probably lost.

White Horse Hills   Coconino Co.

In sec. 26, T. 24 N., R. 6 E. "About 1885, a lone white horse located in these hills. Ranged here more than twenty years. The A 1 cowboys say she was a cream colored mare and gave birth to several cream-colored colts." Letter, George Hochderffer. Robinson calls these Marble hills but are best known by above name.

White Horse Pass   Pima Co.

In T. 8 S., R. 5 E. In Silver Reef mountains near Papago village of Chiu Chuschu, q. v. "So called because near the pass is a white rock formation resembling a horse's head with ears extended forward. Indians and Mexicans gave it this name." Letter, W. C. Straka, P. M.

White Horse Spring   Coconino Co.   Map, Coconino N. F., 1931.

Discovered, 1888, by Mrs. George Hochderffer. Known for several years as Marys spring after Mrs. Mary Baker Hochderffer (Mrs. George). Eventually best known as above after White Horse hills. Letter, George Hochderffer. In sec. 1, T. 23 N., R. 6 E. Northwest of Humphreys peak.

Whitehouse   Pima Co.   Map, Patagonia Quad., 1904.

In T. 19 S., R. 14 E. Coronado N. F., on Madero canyon, west side Santa Ritas. Favorite summer resort. At head of Madera canyon on Roskruge map, 1893.

White River   Cochise Co.

Pancoast mentions this stream in *A Quaker Forty-niner.* Commonly known as Whitewater, q. v.

White River   Gila and Navajo Cos.

Formed by junction at Fort Apache of North Fork and East Fork of White river. Flows southwest, enters Black river in sec. 28, T. 5 N., R. 20 E. As nearly as can be determined these creeks were called by this name because they came from the White mountains. This was explanation author received in 1880.

G.L.O. map, 1921, and. Fort Apache Ind. Res., "White River": Smith map, 1879, and G.L.O., 1892, "White Mountain Creek": Eckhoff, 1880, "White Mountain River."

White River   Navajo Co.   U. S. G. S. Map, 1923.

Headquarters U. S. Indian School, on north fork White river, about 3 miles north of Fort Apache. School now known as Theodore Roosevelt Indian School. Called White River Agency on map, Fort Apache Ind. Res., 1928. P. O. established Nov. 19, 1896, Effie W. Russell, P. M.

White Rock Springs   Mohave Co.

"We moved to Truxton's spring, then followed up through Engles pass by White Rock spring. We camped at the entrance to the pass." Beale Report. Cannot be located today.

Whites Butte   Coconino Co.

Grand Canyon N. P. On south canyon wall near lat. 36° 6', long. 112° 14', between Boucher and Hermit creeks. "Named for James White, surviving member of a prospecting party of three persons, Capt. C. Baker, James White, and Henry Strole, who undertook to go through the Grand Canyon. Baker was killed Aug. 24, 1867, by Indians in a canyon tributary to Grand river. White and Strole went down through the canyon on a raft of drift logs. Strole was washed from the raft while descending a rapid, Aug. 28, and drowned. White, after 14 days of incredible hardships, reached Callville." Decision U. S. G. B. Named by Frank Bond.

Whites Mill   Pinal Co.   Eckhoff Map, 1880.

Grist mill was built here by Ammi M. White, who in early days bought wheat from the Indians and turned out a very good grade of flour. Mill was on south side Gila river, west of Florence, near Pima villages.

"The old miller at Maricopa villages (Pima) was Ammi M. White. He had a trading post and mill prior to the Civil War. Captured and taken back to the Rio Grande by Capt. Hunter when the Confederates ambushed Capt. McCleave of the California Cavalry." McClintock.

J. Ross Browne says: "Ammi White had his trading station and mill near the Casa Blanca."

White sailed from San Francisco with Browne and Charles D. Poston for Arizona in December, 1863. Browne says White was U. S. Indian Agent to the Pimas. There is a fine description of the old man on page 29 of Browne's *Apache Country.* The author is very strongly inclined to credit the name, Casa Blanca, at this point to the natives' turning White's name into Spanish, i. e., "Casa Blanca"—"White's House." At least no one seems able to account for the name "Casa Blanca" q.v.

"The agent here, Old Ammi White,
    Gave us all a comfortable night.
A man of cultivated mind,
    He lives a recluse from mankind,
Contented here, in this Utopia,
    To spend his life with a Maricopa."—Poston, 1863.
White had a Maricopa woman for a wife.

Whites Well   Yuma Co.

In T. 9 S., R. 12 W. "This well was dug by Wesley White. They struck salt water at 110 feet." Letter, W. P. Johnson. U. S. G. S. map, 1923.

White Sage Wash   Coconino Co.   Map, Kaibab N. F., 1926.

Rises in T. 42 N., R. 4 W. Kane county, Utah. Flows into Johnson wash in Arizona, in sec. 15, T. 41 N., R. 1 W. "So called because it runs almost its entire length through a vast white sage flat."

White Spruce Mountain   Yavapai Co.   Map, Prescott N. F., 1927.

In sec. 6, T. 14 N., R. 3 W. East side Skull valley. In early days there was a dense growth of white spruce timber on this mountain.

White Tank Mountains   Maricopa Co.   Smith Map, 1879.

About 20 miles west of Peoria, directly north of Buckeye. Capt. Calderwood once told author this name was given these mountains for a man named White who dug a well and had a station on Prescott-Wickenburg stage road. Was on north side of mountains which soon began to be called "White's tank mountains." Mountains were not then named or at least do not show on any early map.

Whitewater   Cochise Co.

In T. 20 N., R. 26 E. Ranch and creek, lower end Sulphur Springs valley, some 22 miles east of Tombstone. Stream flows into Old Mexico at Douglas. "Received its name from the white deposit left on creek banks by the water which is strongly impregnated with alkali." Often called White river. Said to be actual headwaters of Yaqui river. Stream is marked "Under passage of White river," on both Smith map, 1879 and Eckhoff, 1880. Ranch shows on G. L. O. map, 1921 as about 20 miles east of Tombstone. Frequently used as camping place by U. S. troops while scouting for Indians in early Eighties. Crook made it his headquarters for some time. Shown on G. L. O. map, 1921, and map, Coronado N. F., 1927, as Whitewater draw. White river, on G. L. O. map, 1892.

Whitlock Cienega   Graham Co.   Smith Map, 1879,
    "Whitlock Cienega."

After Capt. Whitlock, U. S. A., who commanded U. S. troops in fight with Apaches near here. The early day name for what is now known as Whitlock's valley, q. v. On west side Peloncillo mountains. On some early maps called "Whitlocks camp."

Whitlock Hills   Graham Co.   U. S. G. S. Map, 1923.

Range of low hills east side upper end San Simon valley, northwest of Parks lake. See Whitlock cienega.

Whitlock Peak   Graham Co.   U. S. G. S. Map, 1923, "Peloncillo";
                                   G. L. O. Map, 1921; "Black Hills."
In Peloncillo or Black hills, on line of Graham and Greenlee
counties. After Capt. Whitlock. See Whitlock cienega.

Whitlock Valley   Graham Co.   U. S. G. S. Map, 1923.
Small valley about 15 or 20 miles long, lies between Whitlock
hills, on west and Peloncillo mountains on east. See Whitlock
cienega.

Whitlow Canyon   Pinal Co.   Florence Quad., 1900.
Heading east of Weavers Needle, runs south into Queen creek.
Named after an early cattleman, Whitlock, who lived near head
of creek where he ran a stage station, postoffice, and store.

Whitmore Pools   Coconino Co.   U. S. G. S. Map, 1923.
Named for Dr. James M. Whitmore, early settler, killed by Indians, 1866. He settled first at Pipe springs at south end of Kaibito plateau.

Whittum   Graham Co.   G. L. O. Map, 1897.
Located on upper Blue river. "So called after Nat. Whittum,
early day cattleman of this region, found dead in his cabin in
May, 1891. Everything indicated Apaches were the murderers."
P. O. established July 21, 1894, Isaac F. Castro, P. M. Later called
"Blue."

Wickenburg   Maricopa Co.
Elevation, 2,077 feet. On A. T. & S. F. R. R., on Hassayampa
creek in northwest part Maricopa county. After Henry Wickenburg, an Austrian, who discovered Vulture mine, 1863, about
15 miles from town. Came to Arizona, as a member of Weaver
party. Town is said to have been named by Gov. Goodwin, according to McClintock, who says: "His (Wickenburg's) death in
May, 1905, was by his own hand by a bullet through his head,
in his little adobe house on the Hassayampa, a short distance below the town he used to own." Fish says: "Wickenburg was so
named by James A. Moor, (he spells it this way) a friend of
Wickenburg who lived with him in 1864. Moor wrote several
letters to Governor Goodwin and always dated them Wickenburg." Barney also makes this same statement and says "the
town was platted by Bob Groom, 1868." See Vulture. P. O. established June 19, 1865, B. F. Howell, P. M.

Wickenburg Mountains   Yavapai and Maricopa Cos.
                                   U. S. G. S. Map, 1923.
East side A. T. & S. F. R. R., east of Wickenburg. After Henry
Wickenburg.

Wickieup   Mohave Co.   U. S. G. S. Map, 1923.
Town in T. 16 N., R. 14 W. "The Pah-Ute word for their huts.
There was quite a settlement of Pah Utes here once." Letter,
Postmaster, Wickieup.
"Wickieup—popular name for the brush shelter or mat cov-
ered houses of Pai Utes, Apaches and other tribes in Nevada,
Arizona and Utah. Origin is disputed but word is apparently
from the Sauk, Fox and Kickapoo, 'Wik-i-yap,' a lodge or dwel-
ling house." Hodge. Settlement on Big Sandy. P. O. established
April 22, 1922, William F. Buchanon, P. M.

Wickyty-wizz Canyon   Mohave Co.

Side canyon of Colorado river on Hualpai Ind. Res. where a squaw man named Spencer once lived. See Spencer.

Bourke says: "Capt. Thomas Byrne, 12th Infty., knew that if this small tribe—the Hualpais—went on the war path, it would take half a dozen regiments to dislodge them from the dizzy cliffs of the Music, Diamond and the Wickyty-wizz."

Wide Ruin Wash   Apache Co.   U. S. G. S. Map, 1923.

Heading in T. 24 N., R. 28 E., about 10 miles northeast of Wide Ruin, runs southwest, joins Pueblo Colorado wash to form Leroux wash in T. 21 N., R. 23 E. "Named for a pre-historic, ruined palace, 400 feet square, built across a narrow wash. It contains a rock walled well. Navajo name is 'kin-tquel,' a wide or large house." Gregory.

Wild Band Pools   Mohave Co.   Smith Map, 1879.

Southeast of Pipe springs, west side Kanab wash, near Hanging rock." Father Escalante visited and camped at these pools in 1776. So named later on because of bands of wild horses which watered here." Bolton.

Wildcat Canyon   Coconino and Navajo Cos.   U. S. G. S. Map, 1923.

Rises at Rim in Coconino county, running northeast into Navajo county, joins Chevelon Fork in T. 14 N., R. 15 E. So named by Robert (Bob) Casbeer, sheepman, whose herds were raided here one night by a wildcat which killed a large number of sheep. Previous to this, not named.

Wild Cat Peak   Coconino Co.   U. S. G. S. Map, 1923.

Elevation, 6,648 feet. On Navajo Ind. Res. near lat. 111°, at northwest corner Hopi Ind. Res. "The Navajos call it 'nic-dot-soe' or 'nish-duit-so'—'mountain lion.' " Gregory describes it as "On the Painted desert. An igneous needle east of Mormon ridge."

Wild Horse Canyon   Gila Co.   Map, San Carlos Ind. Res., 1917.

T. 1 S., R. 21 E. Stream rises south slope Gila mountains, flows southwest into Gila river, west of Calva station, on railroad, San Carlos Res. "For several years there was a band of wild horses running along this canyon. They were rounded up and shipped out or killed during the government's campaign to eradicate dourine among Indian ponies about 1910."

Wild Horse Lake   Navajo Co.   Map, Apache N. F., 1926.

In sec. 23, T. 10 N., R. 15½ E. Fort Apache Ind. Res. "D. B. (Red) Holcomb, who lived at Phoenix Park now called 'Hokum' Ranch, once built a trap corral here to capture wild horses." See Phoenix Park.

Wild Rye Creek   Gila Co.

When first settlers arrived here country was covered with luxurious growth of wild rye. Grows today in protected spots only. See Rye creek.

Wilford   Navajo Co.

On Black canyon, 6 miles south of Heber. Named for President Wilford Woodruff, of Mormon church. Settled by John Bushman and others from St. Joseph, 1882. Was quite a prosperous colony, 1883, the creek was running strong, a tannery was in full operation, many good sized comfortable log houses were built and the fields produced good crops. But when the wash went dry in 1885 and stayed that way for several years, all deserted it for Heber, where there was more water.

Wilgus   Cochise Co.   G. L. O. Map, 1892.

In T. 18 S., R. 28 E. West slope Chiricahuas, on Turkey creek. P. O. established as Wilgus Feb. 21, 1891, after William Wilgus Smith, P. M. Previous to that called Aztec, q.v. Smith was killed by Apaches about 1895.

Will-a-ha   Coconino Co.   G. L. O. Map, 1921.

In sec. 10, T. 27 N., R. 1 E. Station, Grand Canyon Branch R. R. Supai Indian word for "watering place" or "water hole." There was a large natural tank here that held water most of year. The author wintered his saddle horses here, 1888-89. It was then almost a virgin range; no stock of any kind, only a few antelope.

Willcox   Cochise Co.   U. S. G. S. Map, 1923.

Elevation, 4,164 feet. Named after General Orlando B. Willcox, commanding department Arizona, 1880-82. On S. P. R. R., 40 miles east of Benson, in Sulphur Springs valley. Before railroad to Globe was built, this was a lively shipping point for Fort Grant, San Carlos Agency, Globe, and other places north. The old "Point of Mountain" stage station was near Willcox. Here, previous to 1882, all passengers for Grant, Thomas, San Carlos, Globe and Fort Apache left overland stages and took a "buckboard" for rest of journey. Globe *Silver Belt*, December 14, 1889, says that the post office department recently issued an order to the effect that: "this name should be spelled with two l's thus 'Willcox.'"

Willcox Playa   Cochise Co.

Sp., playa—"a shore—a beach." In Ts. 14, 15 S., Rs. 24, 25 E. Large open area a few miles southwest of Willcox, an old lake bed covering about two townships. On G.L.O. map, 1921, is called Willcox Flat. On U.S.G.S. map, 1923, Willcox Playa. On Smith map, 1879, is simply "Playas."

Williams   Coconino Co.   G. L. O. Map, 1921.

Elevation, 6,748 feet. Important railroad, lumbering and livestock town, A. T. & S. F. R. R., 44 miles west of Flagstaff. Santa Fe has a branch to Grand Canyon from here. At foot of Bill Williams mountain, for which town was named. Charles T. Rogers, cattleman, who owned the 111 brand was first P. M., June 14, 1881. Rogers homesteaded land on which town was located.

Williams Fork   Mohave Co.

Settlement on Bill Williams Fork. This was an election precinct, 1870. "We cast 8 votes on Nov. 8, 1870." Letter, William Todd, in files, Arizona Pioneer Society, Tucson.

Williams Mountains   Mohave Co.   G. L. O. Map, 1921.

In Ts. 11, 12 N., R. 17 W. Short range about 12 miles east of Colorado river, on Mohave creek; near Bill Williams river. Named for river.

Williams River

See Bill Williams.

Williamson Valley   Yavapai Co.   G. L. O. Map, 1921.

East slope Santa Marias opening into Chino valley, west of Del Rio. Probably named after Lieut. Williamson of Ives party, 1858. P. O. called Williamson established Oct. 9, 1873, Mrs. Betsy Zimmerman, P. M. Called Wilson, 1875, q.v. Changed to Simmons on July 5, 1881.

Williamsport   Maricopa Co.

P. O. established Oct. 16, 1866, William Thompson, P. M. Not found on any map, but from notes in Post Office Dept., Washington, it must have been west of and not far from old Maricopa Wells station.

Willow Creek   Coconino Co.   U. S. G. S. Map, 1923; Sitgreaves N. F., 1924.

In sec. 32, T. 12 N., R. 13 E. Rises at Tonto Rim on northwest slope, Promontory butte, near Willow creek ranger station. Flows north into Leonard canyon. Upper end of canyon was a dense mass of willows, about 1885-86, which named it.

Willow Creek   Yavapai Co.   G. L. O. Map, 1912; Prescott N. F., 1927.

Stream rising near Thumb butte west of Prescott. Flows northeast, enters Granite creek about 3 miles above Prescott. Said to have been so named by J. D. Monihon, 1864.

Willow Grove, Camp   Yuma Co.   Smith Map, 1879

In T. 21 N., R. 12 W. Temporary soldier camp, 1866, on road between Mohave and Prescott. On White Cliff creek, about 12 or 14 miles southeast of Hackberry, south end Cottonwood cliffs. Heitman *List* says: "located 96 miles northeast of Fort Mohave. Established Aug. 23, 1867; abandoned September, 1869."

Willow Grove Springs   Mohave Co.   Smith Map, 1879; G. L. O. Map, 1921.

In T. 21 N., R. 11 W. In a pass through lower end Cottonwood cliffs. About 20 miles due west Cross mountain. "The small cluster of willow trees was most refreshing to our tired eyes. About 40 miles east of Beale springs." *Vanished Arizona.* This was probably the same as, or close to, Camp Willow Grove, q.v.

Willow Ranch   Yavapai Co.

The "Oaks and Willows" stage station, q.v. On Mohave-Prescott road. "The Imus Brothers owned the place and ran a store and station." *Arizona Gazetteer*, 1881. P. O. established Feb. 12, 1880, Edwin Imus, P. M.

Willow Springs   Coconino Co.   Gregory Map, 1916.

In T. 32 N., R. 9 E. On Navajo Ind. Res., in Painted Desert, 6 or 8 miles northeast of Moenkopi. Well known camping place on old road to Lee Ferry.

Willow Springs Canyon   Coconino Co.   Map, Sitgreaves N. F., 1924.

Heads close to Rim above Lake No. 1. Flows north into Chevelons Fork in sec. 33, T. 11½ N., R. 14 E. There were many willows in this canyon in early days, before cattle and sheep came in. Later on, elk did even more damage than the stock.

Wilmot   Pima Co.

Station S. P. R. R. about 7 miles east of Tucson. Origin not known.

Wilson, Mount   Mohave Co.   G. L. O. Map, 1892-1921.

East side Black canyon range, near lat. 36°, in extreme northwest corner of State. Origin unknown.

Wilson Mountain and Canyon   Yavapai Co.
Map, Coconino N. F., 1928.

Southwest corner T. 18 N., R. 6 E. "A man named Wilson was killed by a ·bear in this canyon and it was named from that event." Letter, Ed Miller, Flagstaff.

Wilson   Yavapai Co.   Eckhoff Map, 1880.

From P. O. records was in Williamson valley. P. O. established Jan. 24, 1875, William J. Simmons, P. M. First postoffice, 1873, called Williamson valley, which leads one to believe that Wilson was the present Simmons on Mint creek. See Williamson valley.

Winchester Mountains   Cochise Co.   U. S. G. S. Map, 1923;
Crook N. F., 1926.

In Ts. 11, 12, 13 S., Rs. 21, 22 E., northwest of Willcox. Josiah Winchester was a miner and prospector who hunted gold over southern Arizona. Doubtless these mountains were named for him, although there is no absolute proof. Possibly named for Lieut. Winchester, 5th U. S. Cavalry, who served in Arizona in early Seventies. Bourke often mentions him.

Winchester Peak   Yuma Co.   U. S. G. S. Map, 1923.

South end Granite Wash mountains, in T. 5 N., R. 14 W., 3 miles west of Salome. "Named for Josiah Winchester who owned the Desert mine about 1910." Letter, Mrs. John B. Martin, Salome.

Window, The   Pima Co.   Map, Coronado N. F., 1927.

In sec. 18, T. 12 S., R. 15 E. About 10 miles north of old Fort Lowell. At head of Ventano canyon. "The 'window' is an opening in rim rock or cliffs, high up on the Catalinas." Letter, Fred Winn, Tucson.

Window Mountain   Pima Co., G. L. O. Map, 1921; U. S. G. S., 1923.

In T. 12 S., R. 1 E. West of Papago Ind. Res. In Sheridan hills.

Windy Hill   Gila Co.

In sec. 24, T. 4 N., R. 12 E. Not Cerro de Temporal. High point projecting into south side Roosevelt lake, about 2 miles east of Roosevelt. Windy hill, decision U.S.G.B.

Wing Mountain   Coconino Co.   G. L. O. Map, 1921;
Tusayan N. F., 1927.

In sec. 20, T. 22 N., R. 6 E. Western end of Fort Valley. Mrs. G. A. Pearson of Flagstaff says: "Wing mountain is an old crater and at one time contained water. Interior shape resembles wing of a bird, hence the name." Letter, Forest Supervisor Dougherty.

George Hochderffer writes: "This was first known about 1884 as Mount Wainwright after Ellis Wainwright, St. Louis brewer, interested in the old A 1 Cattle company and for several years its general manager."

Winifred   Maricopa Co.   Scott Map, Maricopa Co., 1929.

Mining district 15 miles north of Phoenix, named for Winifred daughter of John Y. T. Smith of Phoenix, now Mrs. George W Buxton.

Winkelman   Pinal Co.   U. S. G. S. Map, 1923.

Elevation 2,021 feet. Station, Arizona Eastern R. R. at junction Gila and San Pedro rivers. After Pete Winkelman, early stockman. His ranch was about 8 miles northwest of this place in sec. 10, T. 5 S., R. 15 E.

Winona   Coconino Co.   G. L. O. Map, 1921.

In T. 21 N., R. 9 E. Fourteen miles east of Flagstaff. "First called Walnut but because of a duplication in names, changed to Winona, 1886. Winona was just another name." A.G.W. P. O. established June 19, 1924. Miss Myrtle Adams, P. M.

Winslow   Navajo Co.   G. L. O. Map, 1921.

Elevation 4,856 feet. Railroad division point A. T. & S. F. R. R., 2 miles west from Little Colorado river. "After Gen. Edward F. Winslow, president of St. Louis and San Francisco R. R., which owned one-half of the old Atlantic and Pacific railroad." A.G.W. The claim has been made by some old timers that place was named for an early inhabitant and prospector of vicinity named Tom Winslow. Mr. Wells should know however.

First settler said to have been "Doc" (F. C.) Demerest, hotel man who lived and did business for some time in a tent, in 1880. Shortly after this J. H. Breed, who for some years had a trading post and general store a few miles above at Sunset Crossing of Little Colorado, moved down and built the first stone building. P. O. established Jan. 10, 1882. U. L. Taylor, P. M.

Winters Well   Maricopa Co.   U. S. G. S. Map, 1923.

In T. 1 N., R. 6 W. North side Palo Verde hills. Noted watering place on desert. Cattle ranch belonging to E. H. Winters, who occupied the place for over 40 years, 1885-1925.

Wishbone Mountain   Apache Co.   Map, Sitgreaves N. F., 1926.

In sec. 7, T. 9 N., R. 25 E. "So called from its peculiar shape, like a huge wishbone." Letter, Paul Roberts, Holbrook.

Wittman   Maricopa Co.   Postal Map, 1929.

Station A. T. & S. F. R. R., 18 miles southeast of Wickenburg. First called Nadaburg, q.v. Changed to Wittman for man who financed rebuilding of Walnut Grove dam and irrigation plant.

Wittmore (sic) Springs   Coconino Co.   G. L. O. Map, 1892.

About 6 miles southwest of Mount Logan on north side Colorado river. An error in spelling. Dr. James A. Whitmore settled here about 1863. Named after him. Killed by Indians, January 8, 1866. He was a stockman and had several water holes around here. See Whitmore pools. See McClintock's *History*.

Wodo Butte   Coconino Co.

Near south rim Grand Canyon, 3 miles southeast of Supai village. So called by U.S.G.S. party, from name of an Indian family. Decision U.S.G.B.

Wolf Mountain   Apache Co.   Map, Apache N. F., 1926.

In sec. 6, T. 9 N., R. 25 E. On Sitgreaves N. F. "Called Tamar mountain by old timers. After Tamar Sheep company, which had a summer ranch near here. When forest service reconnaissance party worked here they did not know any name so called it 'Wolf,' just for a name." Letter, Paul H. Roberts, Holbrook.

Wolf Hole, Spring and Dry Lake   Mohave Co.   G. L. O. Map, 1921.

In approximately T. 39 N., R. 11 W. Under Hurricane ledge, north side of canyon. The Pah Ute Indians (Shivwits) called this spring "Shina-bitz-spits" or Coyote spring. Powell's party gave it this name, probably misunderstanding the word "Coyote" for wolf. See Shivwits plateau. P. O. established July 3, 1918, Dexter M. Parker, P. M.

Wolfley Dam

See Gila Bend canal.

Wolfley Hill   Pima Co.   G. L. O. Map, 1921.

In T. 21 S., R. 3 E., close to Mexican line. Named for Lewis Wolfley, 8th governor Arizona Territory.

Wood, Camp   Yavapai Co.   Map, Prescott N. F., 1927;
P. O. Route Map, 1929.

In T. 17 S., R. 6 W. Early day mail station and camping place east of Camp Wood mountain, near head Hide creek, about 15 miles west of Simmons. Origin unknown.

There is a local legend that this was an army post or sub-post, but if so, the name does not appear on any list of Arizona army posts or camps.

Wood Mountain and Canyon   Yavapai Co.
Map, Coconino N. F., 1927.

North end Chiricahua mountains, after Miles L. Wood, well known army contractor, who had a wood and hay camp here in early days. Came to Arizona, 1865, died El Centro, Cal., November 30, 1930.

Woods Canyon   Coconino Co.   Map, Sitgreaves N. F., 1924.

Stream and canyon rising at Carr lake near rim. Flows easterly into Willow Springs canyon in sec. 9, T. 11½ N., R. 14 E.

After J. X. (Jack) Woods, of Winslow, for many years popular passenger engineer on Atlantic and Pacific and A. T. & S. F. R. R. He owned a large number of sheep which grazed in this vicinity in the Eighties. When the Santa Fe started its fast passenger trains about 1890, Woods was one of the first engineers selected to run one of them. He retired about 1900. Died, Oakland, Cal., 1925.

Woods Canyon   Yavapai Co.   Map, Coconino N. F., 1928.

Heads in sec. 6, T. 12 N., R. 9 E. South of Mormon lake, runs southeast into Dry Beaver creek in sec. 24, T. 16 N., R. 6 E. There is another Woods canyon to the east in Coconino county. "So called after John Woods who, 1875, located and occupied a ranch on this canyon in sec. 11, T. 17 N., R. 7 E. He ran the 101 brand of cattle." Letter, Ed Miller, Flagstaff.

Woods Ranch   Pima Co.   G. L. O. Map, 1920.

In T. 16 S., R. 15 E. Eastern side Santa Rita range about 20 miles southeast of Tucson. Named for owner, John M. Wood. P. O. established under name Wood, July 2, 1881, John M. Wood, P. M.

Woodchute Mountain   Yavapai Co.   Map, Prescott N. F., 1927.

In T. 16 N., Rs. 1, 2 E. "Timbered mesa directly west of Jerome where wood for mines was cut in early years and sent down mountain side in a long chute that delivered it almost in the yards at mine. Hence the name."

Woodland   Navajo Co.   Map, Sitgreaves N. F., 1924.

In sec. 35, T. 9 N., R. 22 E. Mormon settlement at line, Apache Ind. Res. Name applied also to settlement at Lakeside for some time before name Lakeside was adopted.

Woodley   Pinal Co.   R. R. Maps.

Station, S.P.R.R., about 3 miles west of Ray Junction.

Woodruff   Navajo Co.   Smith Map, 1879; U. S. G. S., 1923.

In T. 16 N., R. 22 E. Town on Little Colorado, 12 miles southeast of Holbrook.

Settled by oné Luther Martin, 1870. Martin who was not a Mormon, later sold his land and water claims to the Mormons. Named for Wilford Woodruff of the Church. About 1893, after losing half a dozen dams in the river by floods, the Territory appropriated several thousand dollars of public funds to rebuild it. Otherwise the town was to be abandoned. P. O. established May 14, 1880, James Dean, P. M.

Woodruff Butte   Navajo Co.   U. S. G. S. Map, 1923.

Elevation 5,616 feet. Volcanic butte on Little Colorado near village of Woodruff. Sometimes called Black peak on maps.

Woody Mountain   Coconino Co.   Map, Coconino N. F., 1928.

Elevation, 8,054 feet. In sec. 3, T. 20 N., R. 6 E. About one and one-half miles southeast of Rogers lake. "A man named Woody located a ranch on this mountain, near a spring." Letter, E. G. Miller, Flagstaff.

Woolaroc   Greenlee Co.   Postal Route Map, 1930.

In T. 1 S., R. 28 E., at line of Apache Ind. Res. "Formerly called 'Double Circle' ranch. Named for famous airplane, 'Woolaroc.'" Letter, Willard L. Mabra, P. M. "The post office at Woolaroc, Arizona, was named in the following manner."

"The Assistant Postmaster General asked for a list of names suitable for the new office. Among them was 'Woolaroc,' suggested by Forest Ranger, W. Ellis Wiltbank, from the plane that won the Dole, 'Frisco to Hawaii' flight, very much in the press at the time, 1927." Letter, A. D. Molohon, Forest Ranger.

"The name 'Woolaroc' was that of the ship I flew to Honolulu in 1927. It is name of Frank Phillips' game preserve and estate in northern Oklahoma. Woolaroc means woods, lakes and rocks, which are all constituted on this preserve. We have built a stone museum where the 'Woolaroc' will be placed for posterity to see." Letter, Arthur C. Goebel.

P. O. established Oct. 12, 1927, Willard L. Mabra, P. M.

Woolfs Ranch or Crossing   Navajo Co.

McClintock says this was a name for "Reidheads" on Showlow creek, q.v. "Old man Woolf" was a hermit trapper and hunter who lived here in early days. He moved on down the Little Colorado, and about 1883 had a trapper's cabin below mouth of Canyon Diablo where he lived as late as 1884-85. He often camped at the author's ranch at Chevelons Fork. He "hated society and longed for solitude." See Reidheads.

Woolhouse Mountain   Navajo Co.   Map, Apache N. F., 1926.

In sec. 21, T. 10 N., R. 23 E. On Sitgreaves N. F. A prominent prairie mountain. "As early as 1884 Don Manuel Candelaria, of Concho, built a wool warehouse here where they sheared each spring. The wool was stored awaiting the coming of buyers who frequently could not reach the place because of bad roads or high waters." Letter, A. F. Potter, Los Angeles.

Woolsey Butte   Coconino Co.

' In Grand Canyon N. P. near lat. 36° 17', long. 111° 58'. About a mile northeast of Point Imperial. After King S. Woolsey, Arizona pioneer. Decision U.S.G.B.

Woolsey Lake   Apache Co.

In T. 7 N., R. 24 E. Lake about 2 miles southwest of McKay Peak, Fort Apache Ind. Res. Named for Theodore S. Woolsey, Jr., afterwards Major Woolsey, Forestry Regiment, 20th U. S. Engineers, in the World War. First Forest Supervisor, Black mesa, afterwards called Sitgreaves N. F. Named by G. M. Nyce.

Woolsey Peak   Maricopa Co.   U. S. G. S. Map, 1923.

In T. 3 S., R. 6 W. East side Gila Bend mountains. After King Woolsey, Arizona pioneer.

Woolsey Ranch   Maricopa Co.   Eckhoff Map, 1880.

Important early day ranch. Owned by King Woolsey. On north side of Gila, near Agua Caliente springs, which he also owned.

In southwest corner Maricopa county. Later Woolsey had a ranch on Agua Fria about 20 miles east of Prescott afterwards owned by Nathan Bowers. Woolsey thus seems to have owned two rather interesting places. Agua Fria, cold water; and Agua Caliente, hot water. Woolsey was Colonel of 1st Arizona Volunteers, member of first, second, seventh, eighth, and ninth Territorial Councils. President of the eighth and ninth Councils. Born in Alabama, came to Arizona, 1860. Bought this Agua Caliente ranch from a Mexican. Died at his farm near Phoenix, June 20, 1879, aged 47.

Woolsey Ranch   Yavapai Co.

This was the second of Woolsey's ranches. On head of Agua Fria, about 20 miles east of Prescott. Was known as the "Half Way" house. Woolsey later sold it to Nathan Bowers of Prescott who used it as headquarters for his cattle business. See Bowers.

Woolsey Tank   Maricopa Co.

Watering place east side Gila Bend mountains, near Woolsey peak. Is close to the "Perhaps mine." "Perhaps we will find gold—perhaps not." Named, of course, after peak.

Woolsey Trail

Third Act of First Territorial legislature, 1864, was "An act declaring certain routes as a country, (sic) road. Beginning at town of Prescott, thence continuing in a northeasterly direction, a distance of 25 miles to the Agua Frio (sic) ranch, thence in a southerly course to Big Bug creek, thence down said stream in a southeast course to Slate creek, thence south to Black canyon, or 'the new mines,' thence southerly to Bird springs, Casa Blanca, or the Pima villages; should be declared a country (sic) road free for all intents and purposes." Acts First Legislature, 1864.

Named for King Woolsey. This was in part what later became known as Black Canyon stage road.

ARIZONA PLACE NAMES 495

Workman (Wertman) Creek and Falls   Gila Co.

Stream rising in Sierra Ancha, on Baker mountain, flows northwest into Salome creek, in sec. 8, T. 6 N., R. 13 E. About 2 miles east of Greenback peak.

Former Forest Ranger, M. R. Stewart writes: "The man for whom this stream was named was Herbert Wertman. He lived about 4 miles below the falls in later Eighties. Falls are near head of Wertman creek and about 180 feet high."

Wertman was a packer in an army pack train at Fort Apache, 1880. He was over 6 feet tall, weighed about 140 pounds. Had long yellow hair which was always tied with a blue ribbon. Said he was born at Bald Knob, Michigan, which always brought a laugh. To the packers and soldiers, he was always "Bertie." The officers sometimes called him "Custer" after the noted general who also had long yellow hair. Altogether, Wertman was a most unusual character for those days.

Mount Wrightson (Old Baldy)   Santa Cruz Co.   Eckhoff Map, 1880; Coronado N. F., 1931.

Elevation, 9,432 feet. In sec. 18, T. 20 S., R. 14 E. East of Mount Hopkins in Santa Rita mountains, Coronado N. F. "After Mr. William Wrightson, Superintendent of Salero mine, who came to Arizona, 1858.

"Back from Tubac stands Mount Wrightson, after William Wrightson, manager of the Salero Mining Co., and Santa Rita mines. Formerly editor Cincinnati *Enquirer*. Killed by Apaches, 1861." Hinton.

A letter in files of Arizona Pioneer Historical Society at Tucson says he was editor, not of the *Enquirer*, but of a trade paper issued in Cincinnati.

"The Wrightson brothers have their name perpetuated in Mount Wrightson, one of the high peaks of southern Arizona. William, the elder, was killed by Apaches in the Sonoita valley as he and a man named Hopkins were surveying the Baca Float Grant." McClintock. The younger brother was also killed by Apaches near here a year or two later.

Pumpelly, writing as of 1860, says: "Four years later my successor, Mr. William Wrightson, was killed by Apaches within 500 yards of old Fort Buchanan."

Farish however gives 1864 as the date. Buchanan was near present town of Patagonia, close to mountain.

Elliott map, 1866, calls it Wright mountain, a mistake in spelling, of course. For over twenty years this name disappeared from the maps but was restored by a decision of U.S.G.B., in 1929. It was surely a crime to let such a commonplace name as "Baldy," replace that of a pioneer such as Wrightson was.

Wrightstown   Pima Co.   U. S. G. S. Map, 1923.

In T. 14 S., R. 15 E. On the Rillito, 12 miles east of Tucson. After Harold Bell Wright, author, who has a ranch home here. P. O. established Feb. 11, 1914. Frederick C. Wright, P. M.

Wrong Mountain   Pima Co.   Map, Coronado N. F., 1927.

Elevation 7,767 feet. In Rincon mountains, south of, and near Rincon peak. "Named by U.S.G.S. party about 1910 or 1912. They first took it to be Rincon peak, but later found they were wrong, and so called it Wrong mountain." Letter, J. S. Pomeroy, Forest Ranger.

Wupatki National Monument   Coconino Co.

In T. 25 N., Rs. 8, 9 E., 35 miles northeast of Flagstaff, on highway to Tuba City. West side Little Colorado river. Covers four Hopi ruins. Name means "great rain cloud ruins." Named by J. S. Clark of Flagstaff. The Hopi say the ruins were once occupied by the Snake clan people during their migration from the Grand Canyon where they came up from the Underground world. Later they migrated on east to the place where their descendants reside today. Created a National Monument Dec. 9, 1924.

Wynola (sic)   Pinal Co.   G. L. O. Map, 1921.

Station S. P. R. R. "Ten miles west of Red Rock. Established, 1881. Origin of name not known." Letter, Supt. S. P. R. R. On recent maps spelled Wymola.

Yaeger   Yavapai Co.   U. S. G. S. Map, 1923.

In T. 14 N., R. 1 E. Station, Middleton branch A. T. & S. F. R. R., 13 miles northeast of Prescott. After Louis Yaeger. See Yaeger canyon.

Yaeger Canyon   Coconino Co.   Map, Coconino N. F., 1928.

In T. 2 N., R. 11½ E. Heads at Rim near Bush spring. Few miles west of head of Leonard canyon. Flows north into East Clear creek near Chaves springs. After Louis Yaeger. See Yaeger canyon, Yavapai county.

Yaeger Canyon   Yavapai Co.   Map, Prescott N. F., 1927.

In sec. 7, T. 15 N., R. 2 E. About 2 miles southwest of Hickey mountain, flows southwest into Chino valley, in T. 14 N., R. 1 W. At lower end of this canyon Louis Yaeger, well-known young sheepman, brother of Harlow Yaeger, was murdered on May 9, 1911, by a drunken herder who was afterwards hanged. Stream and canyon named for Louis Yaeger.

Yale Point   Apache Co.   G. L. O. Map, 1921.

Elevation 8,050 feet. Navajo Ind. Res., at head Tachito wash. On Black mesa about 18 miles northwest of Chinle, near lat. 36°, long. 110°. Named by Gregory for Yale University.

Yampa Canyon   Coconino Co.

See Split Mountain canyon.

Yampai Station and Creek   Yavapai Co.   G. L. O. Map, 1921.

Station, A. T. & S. F. R. R., 14 miles east of Peach springs. After Yampai Divide at this point.

" 'Yampa,' a division of the Ute family about Green and Grand Rivers in Utah." Hodge.

Sitgreaves, 1851, speaks of the Yampai or Tonto Indians. He was then on west side of San Francisco mountains. He says: "I have called this stream Yampai creek." Sitgreaves' *Report*, 1851.

Stream cannot now be located.

Yampais (sic) **Springs**   Mohave Co.

On west slope Aquarius mountains, a few miles west of Cactus pass at foot of range. "We passed the Yampais springs and encamped on White Cliff creek 8 miles from the pass." Whipple Feb. 1, 1854.

Whipple named both the creek and spring.

Yarnell   Yavapai Co.   G. L. O. Map, 1923.

In T. 10 N., R. 5 W. Named for Yarnell family, early settlers. East side Weaver mountains, north of Peeples valley. Northeast Congress Junction.

"According to C. B. Hasford, Harrison Yarnell located and worked the Yarnell mine. He sold it about 1892. Died in Prescott, 1914." Letter, M. E. Pratt, Octave. P. O. established Oct. 18, 1892, Frank J. McKean, P. M.

Yava   Yavapai Co.   U. S. G. S. Map, 1923.

Mining camp on Kirkland creek, north of Hillside station, A. T. & S. F. R. R. "Short word for Yavapai. To save telegraphing." A.G.W. P. O. established May 8, 1916. Wm. W. Davis, P. M.

Yavapai County

After the Indian tribe. One of the four original counties created by First Territorial Legislature, 1864. Often called "The Mother of Counties."

Yavapai Indians

Hodge says: "They are a Yuman tribe popularly known as Apache-Mohave and Mohave-Apache. This tribe, before its removal to the Rio Verde agency in May, 1873, claimed as its range the Verde valley and the Black mesa from Salt river as far as Bill Williams mountain in western Arizona. Said to mean "The People of the Sun." This name also said to have been coined from an Indian and Spanish name: "Yava"—Indian, meaning "the hill"; and Spanish—"pais," country—"people of the hill country." The author heard this locally many years ago. Another authority gives it as "The people of the hills or of the east." This may well be for they were east of the Yumas, and in the mountains. Still another writer claims the word to be "Ya-mouth-pai-all," or "All mouth," i.e. "Talking people." The Hualpais called them "Nya-va-pi," East or Sun People, which would not be far wrong. None of these, however, seem quite convincing. The tribe is very likely the natives Sitgreaves met and called "Yampai." See his report.

Yellow Jacket Mountain   Pima Co.   Map, Coronado N. F., 1927.

In T. 22 S., R. 10 E. About 2 miles west of Oro Blanco. Named after Yellow Jacket mine nearby.

Yellow Medicine Butte   Maricopa Co.   U. S. G. S. Map, 1923.

In unsurveyed T. 2 S., R. 9 W. North end Gila Bend mountains. Meaning or origin unknown.

Yellow Medicine Tank and Wash   Yuma Co.

Well known watering place on Yellow Medicine wash from which it takes its name. Origin unknown. About 4 miles west of Fourth of July butte.

York   Greenlee Co.   G. L. O. Map, 1921.

In T. 6 S., R. 31 E. Station on Gila river. Named for George R. York, who, in early Eighties, owned a cattle ranch near this station. York and several others were killed here by Apaches in September, 1881. "York was buried at Ray. His widow was afterwards engaged to another man, who was himself killed by Apaches near this same ranch three days before the wedding day, in 1883." Letter in files of Arizona Pioneer Historical Society, Tucson. P. O. established at ranch Jan. 16, 1882. Miss Lou M. Butler, P. M.

Young   Gila Co.   Map, Tonto N. F., 1927.

Settlement on Cherry creek in Pleasant valley. So called after Wm. Young, early day cattleman, whose daughter was first P. M. here. Was in the very heart of the Pleasant Valley war of 1887. P. O. established June 25, 1890, Miss Ola Young, P. M.

Youngsberg   Pinal Co.   Scott Map, Maricopa Co., 1929.

In T. 1 N., R. 8 E. On Apache Trail to Roosevelt. Named for Hon. George U. Young, Secretary of Territory, 1909-10. It was post office for Goldfields mine owned mainly by Mr. Young. P. O. established June 8, 1920. Rollo Walling, P. M.

Yucca   Mohave Co.   G. L. O. Map, 1921.

In T. 17 N., R. 18 W. On Sacramento wash. Station A. T. & S. F. R. R., 23 miles west of Kingman. So called from many yuccas, *Yucca mohaviensis,* growing in this vicinity. P. O. established Aug. 28, 1905. Louis Janc, P. M.

Yule-ke-pai

See Apache-Yuma.

Yuma County

"In 1860, Mowry, elected first and second delegate to Congress, but not admitted, got out a map of Arizona, dividing it into four counties: Castle Dome, Ewell, Mesilla, and Doña Ana.

"The present Yuma county was called Castle Dome. Pima county was designated as Ewell. Mesilla county extended eastward clear to the Rio Grande in New Mexico. Doña Ana extended eastward to west boundary of Texas. The bill, known as the Gwin measure, creating this Arizona, never passed Congress." Farish.

When first territorial legislature met and organized for business, 1864. Yuma was one of the four counties named in the bill. So called for Yuma Indians.

Yuma Desert   Yuma Co.   G. L. O. Map, 1929.

Large fairly level region lying mostly south of Gila river, extending to Mexican line. Bounded on east by Gila river, and Tinajas mountains. Now part of Yuma Irrigation project.

Yuma, Fort   California

In Imperial county, California. McClintock says: "This post was established on Colorado river in September, 1849, as Camp Calhoun, by Lieut. Coutts, U. S. Dragoons, commanding military escort to Whipple Survey. Ferry was started soon after.

"Nov. 27, 1850, Capt. S. P. Heintzelman, 2nd U. S. Infantry, arrived from San Diego with three companies and changed name to Camp Independence. In March, 1851, name was changed to Camp Yuma. Post was abandoned for a time, but re-established in Feb., 1852, as Fort Yuma. Abandoned as a military post and turned over to the Interior Department, January, 1884." McClintock.

"Fort Yuma was delightful at this season—December, 1874. We crossed over one morning on the old rope ferry to Yuma City. There was no bridge then over the river." *Vanished Arizona.*

"Fort Yuma was originally located on both sides of river, half in Arizona and half in Southern California. By an Act of Congress, June 22, 1874, the part in Arizona was transferred to the interior department. Balance remained with War department until June 9, 1884, when by executive order it was also transferred to Interior department 'for Indian school purposes!' " Fish.

"In the office of the Indian school at Yuma is a blueprint of the fort from a drawing and data made in 1869. Written in one corner is this: 'Fort Yuma established as a camp, Nov. 27, 1850, to protect emigrants to southern California, by Brevet Major General Sam'l Heintzelman. Abandoned, Dec., 1851, afterwards permanently occupied as Fort Yuma Feb. 22, 1852.'" McClintock. See Fort Defiance, also Calhoun.

Yuma Indian Reservation   Yuma Co.   G. L. O. Map, 1921.

Small reservation set aside for the Yumas, 1863. Lies on both sides of river about equally in Arizona and California.

Yuma Indians

"Yah-may-o—'Son of the Captain.' Name applied to tribe through a misunderstanding of early Spanish missionaries. One of the chief divisions or tribes of Yuman family formerly residing on both sides of Colorado below junction with Gila. In 1910 there were about 650 under the Fort Yuma superintendent." Hodge. The Yumas are said to have been an unusually fine people, physically, when first Europeans saw them. Humboldt map, 1811, speaks of them as "Jumas."

Yuma Mountains   Yuma Co.   G. L. O. Map, 1921.

Small isolated group of hills on Yuma-Maricopa county line south of Harquahala mountains.

Yuma, the town   Yuma Co.

Elevation 137 feet. On Colorado river, southwest corner of State. Surveyed and survey filed at San Diego, 1854. California collected taxes on it for several years. Said to have been the only occupied place in 1854, in what is now Arizona. The author feels sure that Tubac antedated it by several years.

"While we were camped on the banks of the Colorado river, in July, 1854, we concluded to locate a town site on the strip of land opposite Fort Yuma. The actual survey showed 936 acres and this was quite large enough for a town site." Col. Poston, *Overland Monthly*, July, 1894.

Town first called Colorado City, also Arizona City, then Yuma City. On east side of river. An act of Territorial legislature, Feb. 2, 1873, reads as follows: "An Act, to change the name of Arizona City. Be it enacted, etc., that the name of Arizona City, the county seat of Yuma county, be, and is hereby, changed to Yuma, and shall be known as such from and after the passage of this act."

P. O. records at Washington show that John B. Dow was appointed P. M. at Colorado City March 17, 1858. It was then in Doña Ana county, New Mexico, and Dow's commission was issued that way.

These official records also show the post office was called Yuma before the passage of the legislative act in 1873 for the first post office was established under name Yuma, October 16, 1866, Francis Hutton, P. M.

"All authorities agree that it was called Colorado City at first. The big flood of 1862 practically wiped the village out and the rebuilt town was called Arizona City." McClintock.

In 1867, General J. F. Rusling wrote of this place:

"Directly opposite Fort Yuma, on eastern bank of Colorado, stands Arizona City, a straggling collection of adobe houses containing perhaps 200 inhabitants. Here, and at Fort Yuma, are located the government storehouses, shops, corrals, etc., as the grand depot for all the posts in Arizona. Hence considerable business centers here. But it is chiefly of a military nature and if the post and depot were removed, the city as such would speedily subside into its original sandhills. Being at junction of the Gila and Colorado, where the main route of travel crosses the latter, it is also the first place of any importance on the Colorado itself, and hence would seem to be well located for business, if Arizona had any business to speak of."

In 1874, the legislature authorized the Territorial Penitentiary Commissioners to purchase—"not less than 10 acres of land on which to locate the Territorial Penitentiary." This was first location of the Arizona Penal institution. Opened for business July 1, 1876. Writing of Yuma and its history, Donald Page, in *Arizona Historical Review*, April, 1930, says:

"Garces received his crown of martyrdom at the hands of the Yuma Indians, at the newly established mission of La Purisima Concepción, close to the site of Fort Yuma, on July 17, 1781, when the Spanish Padres, settlers, and soldiers at that place and at San Pedro y San Pablo de Bicuner, 8 leagues down the Colorado river, were all massacred.

"The padre's body was removed to San Pedro de Tubutama, where it was re-interred with all the honors due a fallen 'Soldier of the Cross.' And thus passed Tucson's founder." See Fort Yuma, also San Dionisio.

Yumtheska Mesa   Coconino Co.

Grand Canyon N. P. near lat. 36° 17′, long. 112° 45′. Small tableland area on left bank Havasu creek, just below "Yumtheska point." From name of a Havasupai family, suggested by members of Geological Survey party. Decision U.S.G.B.

Yunosi Point   Coconino Co.

In Grand Canyon N. P. On south rim of canyon, 5 miles below mouth of Havasu creek. So called on recommendation of U. S. Geological Survey for an Indian family by this name. Decision U.S.G.B.

Zellweger   Pinal Co.   G. L. O. Map, 1909.

Station, Arizona Eastern R. R., about 6 miles west of Kelvin Junction. South side Gila river.

"John Zellweger, Sr., had a cattle ranch in this vicinity many years ago and the station was named for him. Members of the family now live in Florence." Letter, Fred W. Lattin.

Zeniff   Navajo Co.   Post Route Map, 1929.

Located in T. 14 N., R. 18 E., near what was known in the Eighties as "Big Dry Lake," q.v. About 25 miles west of Snowflake, q.v. Zeniff is a character in the Book of Mormon. P. O. established Sept. 20, 1922. John A. Bowler, P. M.

Zenos   Maricopa Co.

Prophet of the Mormon Bible. "And all these things must surely come to pass, saith the prophet Zenos." This was the original name of Mesa. According to Hinton and others, the town was also called Hayden for a short time. The Mormon Co-op. store here was called the "Zenos Co-op." for many years after town name had been changed to Mesa. P. O. established under name Zenos, May 4, 1886, George Passey, P. M. Changed to Mesa, 1889.

Zilbetod Peak   Apache Co.   Gregory Map, 1916;
                                                       G. L. O. Map, 1921.

On Navajo Ind. Res. In Carrizo mountains, east of Pastora peak. On some maps, Carrizo mountains are called Pastora mountains. "Dzil," is Navajo for mountain; "be-tod," "it is bare," hence "Bare" or "Bald" mountain.

Zillesa Peak   Navajo Co.

In T. 31 N., R. 19 E. Hopi Ind. Res. Navajo word meaning "mountain surrounded by bare soil." Gregory.
Gregory map, 1916, says: "A long mesa." U.S.G.S. map, 1923, calls it a peak.

Zillnez   Navajo Co.   Gregory Map, 1916; G. L. O. Map, 1921.

On Navajo Ind. Res., headwaters of Tyende creek, north of Navajo National Monument. "Dzil," mountain; "nez," long. Haile.

Zil-tadin or **Dzil-tadin Mountain**   Maricopa Co.

Elevation 7,645 feet. In T. 3 N., R. 10 E. Ridge extending southeast from Four peaks, to breaks of Salt river. Locally called Pine ridge. "An Apache word, 'dzil,' meaning mountain, 'tadin,' a long mountain slope. Bourke, *Apache Campaign.*
This was one of some forty or more names attached to points along the Apache Trail by an enthusiast, whose sole idea seems to have been to "Spanishize" or "jazz up," the names along this highway. They were all approved by the U. S. G. B. in November, 1917, without sufficient consultation with local Arizona sentiment or authorities. They proved so objectionable to Arizonans that in 1932 the Board vacated most of them. Many of these places already had well known names which will stand until local sentiment calls for changes.
This name "Zil-tadin" was allowed to stand however because of early usage (see Bourke). Locally the Apache name is almost unknown. Neither name is found on any late maps.

Zil-tah-jini Peak   Navajo Co.   G. L. O. Map, 1923.

South side Black mesa, Navajo Ind. Res. About 6 miles east of Blue canyon. Faither Haile gives it as "Navajo—'Delth-na-zini,' 'standing cranes.' "

Zil-tusayan

See Fluted Rock.

Zonia   Yavapai Co.

P. O. established Feb. 9, 1900. John McCaffrey, P. M. Origin unknown.

Zuni River   Apache Co.   G. L. O. Map, 1921.

Rises in western New Mexico, enters Arizona in T. 17 N., R. 31 E. Flows southwest, enters Little Colorado river, 6 miles west of Hunt. From a Cochiti word "su-in-yi," meaning "people of the long nails." Frank Cushing. There is no known origin or reason for this name. Emory spells the name "Soones."
Stream named for Zuni Indians, whose village is on its banks in western New Mexico.

Zuni Point   Coconino Co.   U. S. G. S. Map, 1923.

In Grand Canyon N. P. South side Colorado river, near Grand View. At lat. 36° 1', long. 111° 55'. So named for Zuni people.

BIBLIOGRAPHY

Arizona Gazetteer. 1881.

Bancroft, H. H.—*Arizona and New Mexico.* 1889.

Bartlett, John R.—*Personal Narrative.* 1854.

Beale, Edward—*Journal of the Expedition of E. F. Beale and G. H. Heap from Missouri to California.* 1854-1858.

Bourke, John G.—*On the Border with Crook.* 1892. *An Apache Campaign.* 1883.

Bowles, Samuel—*Across the Continent.* 1865.

Browne, J. Ross—*Adventures in the Apache Country.* 1869.

Burns, Walter N.—*Tombstone.* 1928.

Cady, John H.—*Arizona's Yesterdays.*

Conklin, E.—*Picturesque Arizona.* 1877.

Cooke, Col. P. St. George—*Conquest of New Mexico and California.* 1878.

Coues, Dr. Elliott—*On the Trail of a Spanish Pioneer.* 1900.

Cozzens, Samuel—*The Marvellous Country.* 1874.

Cremony, John C.—*Life Among the Apaches.* 1877.

Davis, Britton—*The Truth About Geronimo.*

Dellenbaugh, F. S.—*Romance of the Colorado.* 1902. *A Canyon Voyage.* 1908.

DeLong, Sidney—*History of Arizona.* 1905.

Dunn, J. P.—*Massacres of the Mountains.* 1866.

Elliott, Wallace W. & Co.—*History of Arizona.* 1884.

Emory, Lieut. W. H.—*Notes of a Military Reconnaissance.* 1845.

Engelhardt, Z.—*Franciscans in Arizona.* 1899.

Farish, Thomas E.—*History of Arizona.* 1916.

Fish, Joseph—*Manuscript History of Arizona.* State Historian's Office.

Gannett, Henry—*Place Names in the U. S.*

Gregory, Herbert—*The Navajo Country.* U. S. Govt.

Haile, Father Berard—*Dictionary of the Navajo Language.* 1910.

Hamilton, Patrick—*History of Arizona.* 1884.

Hardy, R. W. H.—*Travels in Mexico.* 1829.

Heitman, Francis E.—*List of U. S. Army Posts.* War Dept.

Hinton, R. J.—*Handbook of Arizona.* 1878.

Hodge, F. W.—*Handbook of American Indians.* 1907.

Hornaday, W. T.—*Campfires in Desert and Lava.* 1908.

Ives, J. C.—*Report upon the Colorado River of the West.* U. S. Govt. 1857.

James, G. Wharton—*In and around the Grand Canyon.* 1911. *Indians of the Painted Desert.* 1903.

Lockwood, Frank C.—*Arizona Characters.*

Lumholtz, Carl—*New Trails in Mexico.* 1912.

McClintock, James H.—*History of Arizona.* 1916. *Mormon Settlement.* 1921.

McFarland Publishing Co.—*History of Arizona.* 1896.

Miles, Gen. N. A.—*Personal Recollections.* 1896.

Mowry, Sylvester—*Arizona and Sonora.* 1859.

Pattie, J. O.—*Personal Narrative.* 1833.

Poston, Charles D.—*Apache Land.* 1869.

Powell, J. W.—*Canyons of the Colorado.* 1859.

Pumpelly, Ralph—*Across America and Asia.* 1871.

Ransome, F. L.—*Geology of the Oatman District.* U. S. Govt.

Robinson, Will H.—*The Story of Arizona.* 1919.

Ross, C. P.—*Routes to the Desert.* U. S. Govt.

Russell, Frank—*Pima Myths.* 1903. U. S. Govt.

Simpson, Lieut. J. H.—*Expedition Into the Navajo Country.* 1850.

Sitgreaves, L.—*Expedition Down the Zuni and Colorado Rivers.* 1853.

Summerhayes, Martha—*Vanished Arizona.* 1873.

Taylor, Isaac—*Names and Their Histories.*

Twitchell, Ralph—*Leading Facts of New Mexico History.* 1911.

Visher, Wm. L.—*Pony Express.*

Wheeler, C. M.—*Report on U. S. Geographic Surveys.* 1878.

Wright, Harold Bell—*Long Ago Told.* 1929.

ABOUT THE AUTHOR

Will Croft Barnes (1858–1937) first came to Arizona as an enlisted caval-
ryman assigned to Fort Apache, where he earned the Medal of Honor for
gallantry in combat. He went on to become a rancher, state legislator, and
conservationist, assisting Gifford Pinchot in founding the U.S. Forest Service
and serving as its first assistant director. From 1905 to 1935, he traveled
constantly throughout Arizona, much of the time on horseback, gathering
the anecdotes and geographical information that would be published as
Arizona Place Names. Barnes was the author of *Western Grazing
Grounds and Forest Ranges* (1913), *The Story of the Range* (1925), and
Apaches and Longhorns (1941, reissued by the University of Arizona
Press in 1982).